LONDON
FOR CHILDREN
www.timeout.com

Time Out Guides Limited
Universal House
251 Tottenham Court Road
London W1T 7AB
Tel + 44 (0)20 7813 3000
Fax + 44 (0)20 7813 6001
Email guides@timeout.com
www.timeout.com

Editorial
Editor Ronnie Haydon
Deputy Editor Sam Le Quesne
Sub Editors Adam Barnes, Jan Fuscoe
Listings Editors Jill Emeny, Cathy Limb
Proofreader Simon Coppock
Indexer Jackie Brind

Editorial/Managing Director Peter Fiennes
Series Editor Sarah Guy
Deputy Series Editor Cath Phillips
Business Manager Gareth Garner
Guides Co-ordinator Holly Pick
Accountant Kemi Olufuwa

Design
Art Director Scott Moore
Art Editor Tracey Ridgewell
Senior Designer Oliver Knight
Designer Josephine Spencer
Digital Imaging Dan Conway
Advertising Designer Pete Ward

Picture Desk
Picture Editor Jael Marschner
Deputy Picture Editor Tracey Kerrigan
Picture Researcher Helen McFarland

Advertising
Sales Director/Sponsorship Mark Phillips
Sales Manager Alison Gray
Advertising Sales Ben Holt, Matthew Salandy, Jason Trotman
Copy Contoller Amy Nelson
Advertising Assistant Lucy Butler

Marketing
Marketing Director Mandy Martinez

Production
Production Director Mark Lamond

Time Out Group
Chairman Tony Elliott
Managing Director Mike Hardwick
Group Financial Director Richard Waterlow
Group Commercial Director Lesley Gill
Group General Manager Nichola Coulthard
Group Art Director John Oakey
Online Managing Director David Pepper
Group Production Director Steve Proctor
Group IT Director Simon Chappell
Group Circulation Director Jim Heinemann

Contributors
Introduction Ronnie Haydon. **The Story of London** Fiona Cumberpatch. **Festivals & Events** Sam Le Quesne. **Around Town** *Introduction* Ronnie Haydon; *South Bank & Bankside* Ronnie Haydon; *The City* James Mitchell (*Ghosts of the Old City* Sue Webster); *Holborn & Clerkenwell* Cyrus Shahrad; *Bloomsbury & Fitzrovia* Sue Webster; *Marylebone, West End* Kelley Knox; *Covent Garden & St Giles's* Cathy Limb; *Westminster* Cyrus Shahrad; *Kensington & Chelsea* Kathryn Miller; *North London* Jessica Eveleigh, Sue Webster; *East London* Simon Coppock; *South-east London* Ronnie Haydon; *South-west London* Ronnie Haydon; *West London* Pendle Harte; **Eating** Sam Le Quesne. **Shopping** Ronnie Haydon, Zoe Strimpel (*Let your mouse do the walking* Cathy Limb, *The best designers heaven knows* Kelley Knox, *Ideal homes* Jill Emeny. **Where to Stay** Natasha Polyviou. **Arts & Entertainment** Fiona Hook (*All singing, all dancing* Kelley Knox). **Parties** Jill Emeny. **Sport & Leisure** Andrew Shields. **Days Out** Ronnie Haydon (*City by the sea* Cyrus Shahrad). **Directory** Ronnie Haydon.

The Editor would like to thank Anna Beech at the Greater London Authority; Daisy Jaz Furrokh and Fox Furrokh; Jane, Bruce, John and Rick Jones; Finn Jordan; Teresa and Mary Trafford; Phoebe-Jane, Guy, Heather and Niall Weir and all contributors to previous editions of *Time Out London for Children*, whose work forms the basis for parts of this book.

Maps JS Graphics (john@jsgraphics.co.uk). **Walk maps** Tracey Ridgewell.

Illustrations Story of London by Jane Webster.

Cover Adrian Weinbrecht.
Openers pages 7, 275 Andrew Brackenbury; page 27 Jonathan Perugia; page 159 Alys Tomlinson; pages 213, 289 Heloise Bergman.
Photography pages 3, 21, 25, 49, 54, 60, 73, 111, 117, 120, 184, 191, 194, 200, 264 Heloise Bergman; pages 5, 40, 41, 46, 99, 104, 107, 113, 125, 132, 133, 154, 165, 224, 237, 267 Andrew Brackenbury; page 9 (c) Stapleton Collection/Corbis; pages 10, 12, 13 Mary Evans Picture Library; pages 14, 15 Getty Images; page 16 Rex Features; pages 17, 20 (c) Hulton-Deutsch Collection/Corbis; page 29 Barry Holmes; pages 30, 32, 37, 44, 45, 51, 53, 56, 64, 66, 77, 80, 83, 90, 93, 100, 101, 114, 148, 151, 152, 222, 248, 258, 268 Jonathan Perugia; page 35 Adrian Weinbrecht; page 75 Lukas Birk; pages 85, 125, 128, 129, 143, 145, 161, 169, 175, 178, 205, 219, 243, 247 Alys Tomlinson; page 136 Richard Lea-Hair/Historic Royal Palaces/newsteam.co.uk; page 164 Kevin Nicholson; page 197 Cathy Limb; page 261 Empics; page 279 Jael Marschner.
The following images were provided by the featured establishments/artists: pages 22, 35, 58, 68, 78, 108, 214, 226, 230, 242, 252, 254, 255, 257.

Repro by Icon Reproduction, Crowne House, 56-58 Southwark Street, London SE1 1UN.

Printed and bound by Cayfosa-Quebecor, Ctra. de Caldes km3, 08130 Sta. Perpetua de Mogoda, Barcelona, Spain.

ISBN 0 903446 200
Distribution by Seymour Ltd (020 7396 8000)
Distributed in USA by Publishers Group West

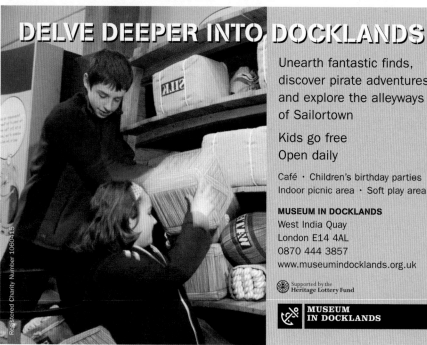
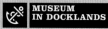

CONTENTS

INTRODUCTION

Children should get out more. The experts would have it that modern parents are bringing up a generation of sofa-bound lard-balls. If that's really true, we can't believe they can be doing so in London. This is the city that actively discourages the use of the family car by levying a congestion charge on drivers; it's where under-16s travel free on buses. London has a mayor who recently launched a detailed guide on developing play and leisure opportunities for all the capital's children and young people. Most importantly, London is the city whose free museums and galleries are the best in the world. Practically all of them have an education department, providing an events and activities programme for their youngest visitors. The biggest museums make provision for all age groups – just look at the Science Museum. From its adults-only Dana Centre for serious scientific discussion to its Basement Garden with puppets, puzzles and water play, its inclusivity is legendary. Why would any child prefer to play computer games when a free bus ride can take them to the treasures of the British Museum or the dinosaurs of the Natural History Museum. They're all free, they're all brilliant, and they all have parks nearby so the kids can race off the obesity gremlin. No, we reckon that in London, the kids will be all right. Just arm yourself with an *A-Z* and a Family Travelcard (which gives the kids free travel on all public transport at weekends) and follow the instructions in the various chapters of this guide.

TIME OUT LONDON FOR CHILDREN GUIDE

This is the fifth edition of the *Time Out London for Children Guide*, produced by the people behind the successful listings magazines and travel guide series. It is written by resident experts to provide you with all the information you'll need to explore the city, whether you're a local or a first-time visitor.

THE LOWDOWN ON THE LISTINGS

Addresses, phone numbers, websites, transport information, opening times, admission prices and credit card details are included in the listings.

Details of facilities, services and events were all checked and correct as we went to press. Before you go out of your way, however, we'd advise you to phone and check opening times, ticket prices and other particulars. While every effort has been made to ensure the accuracy of the information contained in this guide, the publishers cannot accept any responsibility for any errors it may contain.

FAMILY-FRIENDLY INFORMATION

Having visited all the places with our children, we've added essential information for families. Where we think it's important, we've stated whether a building can accommodate pushchairs ('buggy access'), or if there's a place to change a nappy ('nappy-changing facilities'). We've also listed the nearest picnic place.

Attractions are required to provide reasonable facilities for disabled visitors, although it's always best to check accessibility before setting out.

Disabled visitors requiring information about getting around the city can call GLAD (Greater London Action on Disability) on 7346 5808 or check the website www.glad.org.uk.

PRICES AND PAYMENT

We have noted where venues accept the following credit cards: American Express (AmEx), Diners Club (DC), MasterCard (MC) and Visa (V).

THE LIE OF THE LAND

Map references are included for each venue that falls on our street maps (starting on p310), but we recommend that you follow the example of the locals and invest in a standard A-Z map of the city.

PHONE NUMBERS

The area code for London is 020. All phone numbers given in this guide take this code unless otherwise stated, so add 020 if calling from outside London; otherwise, simply dial the number as written. The international dialling code for the UK is 44.

IN CONTEXT

THE VIEW FROM CITY HALL

Local politics? It's child's play.

On 4 August 2004 more than 15,000 children converged on Trafalgar Square for fun and games courtesy of the Mayor of London, Ken Livingstone. This annual National Playday event in central London – this year it's called Active8 (*see p23*) – is just one of a whole goody bag of policies and initiatives covered in the UK's first regional strategy to create a city responsive to the needs of under-18s (the snappily titled 'Making London Better for all Children and Young People'). With 1.61 million of them living here, the child population in London is actually growing, unlike in the rest of the country. The Children and Young People's Unit (CYPU) in the Mayor's Office was set up to make sure that children's voices are heard, and acted upon.

Deputy Mayor Nicky Gavron, who played a major role in developing the regional strategy programme, and Caroline Boswell, team leader of the CYPU, are all ears. They both know a thing or two about the challenges of bringing up children in this city. Gavron raised four children in London and is a grandmother of eight; Boswell lives in north London with her two, aged eight and 13. Both women, like many London parents, acknowledge the benefits of a London childhood, but see that children living in the capital have particular concerns.

'We did this survey of young Londoners aged 11 to 16,' explains Boswell. 'The majority of them were happy with the huge range of things to do here, but many have problems with affording them. More things to do free would be a priority.'

Nicky Gavron agrees. She's been campaigning to make London's places and spaces more accessible to children since the 1970s. Her interest in the importance of play dates back to her days as a young mother in north London, looking for affordable entertainment for her own children.

'Long before I became a councillor I was a community activist. I badgered Haringey council to open up schools during the holidays so that groups could use the facilities for holiday playschemes. That led to me setting up play associations across Haringey and other boroughs.'

A move to provide safe, traffic-free spaces (and to improve the existing play spaces in London) is another key aim of the strategy. Ample proof that such places are a magnet for young people can be found right outside the CYPU's offices at City Hall, where family groups regularly stroll along the South Bank. Both Boswell and Gavron love the convivial atmosphere.

'The area around here is such a great place to play in,' says Gavron. 'There's no traffic, and kids use it all the time. It's great to be a politician in this building, because you can look out from the meeting rooms and see kids skateboarding past. On sunny days the steps of the Scoop area, just outside the ground floor, are full of people. I'm also very keen to have a special park here, a grassy space at Potters Fields.'

The positive vibes coming out of City Hall are encouraging. With the Mayor (a new parent himself) expressing a desire to make a child-friendly city, combined with his recent promise to make all bus travel free for under-16s (scheduled to begin in August 2005), there's hope that life will improve for London's children. And not just for those who live around the trendy South Bank, but for all kids, throughout the capital.

'London children need improved services locally,' says Nicky Gavron, 'which is why we want to work on neighbourhood provision. We don't want to concentrate all tourism around the honeypot. There are loads of really good tourist attractions throughout the London boroughs'.

'We're projecting an increase in population equivalent to the size of Leeds,' Boswell explains. 'As child numbers in the city grow it's important that their needs are taken care of,' adds Gavron, 'but they don't have a loud voice, they don't have the vote. We want even the very young to have their say. I want children to know we're listening.'

One way that all London children can make themselves heard at City Hall is by visiting the new 'young Londoners' website, a platform for kids to get involved in making London better. Log on to www.london.gov.uk/young-london to see what you can do.

THE STORY OF LONDON

A lot can happen in 2,000 years.

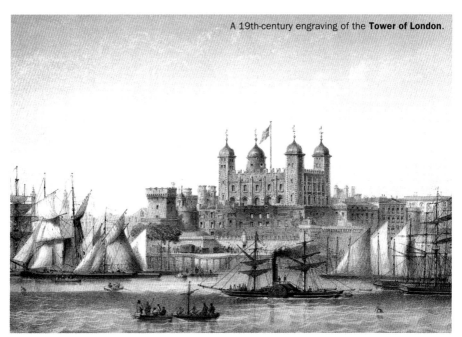

A 19th-century engraving of the **Tower of London**.

The story begins officially in AD 43 when Roman Emperor Claudius and his legions invaded. Not all historians are convinced, however, that it was the Romans who built the first settlement on the banks of the Thames. The Latin name Londinium could have any number of ancient origins. 'Llyn-don', for example, means town ('don') by the stream ('llyn'); 'lunnd' means marsh; 'Laindon', long hill; while the adjective 'londos' translates as fierce. Whoever was the first to stake their claim, we still have the Romans to thank for our ancient city wall (built in AD 200), remnants of which survive in the City of London today. The first bridge across the Thames, which crossed at roughly the point of the present-day London Bridge, was also a Roman achievement. It was built after the British outpost of the Empire was sacked by Boudicca, who led her armies against the soldiers who had seized her lands and raped her daughters. The settlement was almost destroyed, but the Romans rebuilt and surrounded their town with a defensive wall in an attempt to keep out rebellions. Another 200 years passed with the Romans in charge, but with the eventual decline of the Empire, the last troops were withdrawn in 410 and London was left to Angles and Saxons.

TRADING PLACES

Saxon settlers crossed the North Sea to set up homes and farms in eastern and southern England during the fifth and sixth centuries. They established a trading centre near the Roman city. Lundenwic, 'wic' meaning marketplace, stood about where Covent Garden is today. What is now Trafalgar Square was the site of farm buildings.

The **Great Plague** of 1665. *See p13*.

The Strand is so called because it used to be just that, a strand, or beach for grounding ships.

London's first bishop, Mellitus, was a missionary sent by the Pope. He converted the East Saxon King Sebert to Christianity and, in 604, founded a wooden cathedral, dedicated to St Paul, inside the old city walls. Although his people turned back to paganism after Sebert's death, later generations of Christians rebuilt St Paul's. In the ninth century another wave of invaders arrived: the Vikings. They crossed the North Sea to ransack London, forcing the king of the time, Alfred of Wessex, to reoccupy the old Roman town. As the Saxon city prospered, harassment from the Vikings continued until the 11th century when a Danish king – Cnut (Canute) took power from 1016 to 1040. During this time London replaced Winchester as the capital. Edward the Confessor, an English king, gained the throne in 1042 and set to building Westminster Abbey. He died a week after his abbey was consecrated in December 1065.

Edward's death was a pivotal moment in history. His cousin William, Duke of Normandy,

swore that his kinsman had promised him the crown. But Edward's brother-in-law Harold was a solid favourite with the English people. Their armies tried to settle the mattter at Hastings. On 14 October 1066 William defeated Harold and marched to London. He was crowned in the abbey on Christmas Day.

MARKET FORCES

William knew he had to keep things sweet with the wealthy merchants in the City of London, so he gave them independent trading rights in return for taxes. The charter stating these terms is kept at the Guildhall. But the king was still bothered by the possibly rebellious population, so he ordered strongholds to be built along the city wall. One of these is the White Tower, the tallest building in the Tower of London. The city became a hotbed of political struggle. Fighting for supremacy were three powerful bodies: the king and aristocracy; the Church; and the lord mayor and city guilds. In the early Middle Ages, the king made all the laws in the country, aided by lords and bishops. During the 14th and 15th centuries, the Palace of Westminster became the seat of law and government, and the king's meetings with the noblemen and clergy – called Parliaments – became increasingly important. As the number of advisors to the king grew, Parliament divided into two groups, the House of Lords (populated by nobles and members of the clergy chosen by the king) and the House of Commons (powerful people elected by rich merchants and landowners). Trade with Europe grew. Imports of spices, cloth, furs, precious metals and wine filled the wharves by London Bridge and people travelled from miles around to the markets, or 'cheaps', around Westcheap (now Cheapside). Foreign traders and craftsmen settled around the port of London. The population rocketed from about 18,000 in 1100 to more than 50,000 in the 1340s.

PESTILENCE

Overcrowding brought hygiene problems. The water supply, which came more or less directly from the Thames, was limited and polluted. In the east, Houndsditch gained its name because people threw dead dogs into the boundary ditch. At Smithfield meat market, meanwhile, butchers dumped animal guts willy-nilly. These filthy conditions became a breeding ground for the greatest catastrophe of the Middle Ages: the Black Death of 1348 and 1349. The plague came to London from Europe, carried by rats on ships. In this period about 30 per cent of the population died of the disease. The epidemic recurred in London on several occasions over the next three centuries, each time devastating the population.

With plague killing so many, London was left with a labour shortage, resulting in unrest among the overworked peasants. A poll tax – a charge of a shilling a head – was introduced, which prompted the poor to revolt. In 1381 thousands of them, led by Wat Tyler from Kent and Jack Straw from Essex, marched on London. In the rioting and looting that followed, the Savoy Palace on the Strand was destoyed, the Archbishop of Canterbury was murdered and hundreds of prisoners were set free. Eventually a 14-year-old King Richard II rode out to face the angry mob at Smithfield, but the Lord Mayor William Walworth, angered by Tyler's belligerence, stabbed the rebel leader to death. This stopped the rioting, and the ringleaders were hanged.

LONDON FACES Thomas Coram

The odds were stacked heavily enough against the poor in the teeming streets of 18th-century London, but if you were a single, pregnant woman, the outlook was uniquely grim. Though Paris and some other European cities had institutions for unwanted children, Barnardo's orphanages would not arrive in London for another century. Desperation sometimes drove women to leave their illegitimate babies on the workhouse steps, sell them to parish officers for a lump sum, or leave them to their fate by the roadside.

In Georgian times, around 1,000 babies were abandoned each year in London. It was the pitiful sight of these infants that motivated their unlikely saviour. Captain Thomas Coram was a childless tradesman who made money from shipbuilding businesses in the New World. After retiring to Rotherhithe, aged 54, and witnessing first-hand the plight of the destitute on his walks through the city, Coram wanted to set up a charitable organisation to establish a children's refuge.

It was a trailblazing idea. To achieve it, Coram needed signatures from influential people whose opinions might sway the monarch. Though wealthy, he lacked connections to high society. 'I could no more prevail with them than if I had asked them to pull down their breeches and present their backsides to the King and Queen,' he wrote in desperation.

In 1727, when George II came to the throne, Coram's persistence was rewarded. The Queen, Caroline, was moved by the foundlings' plight. Compassion became fashionable and other aristocratic women followed her lead. Coram was able to enlist his friend, the artist William Hogarth, to rouse extra support and finally, in 1739, the King signed a Royal Charter.

The first Foundling Hospital opened in temporary premises in Hatton Garden in 1741. On the first night, hundreds of women turned up, clutching babies in their arms. Only 30 boys could be taken in and the streets echoed with the wailing of heartbroken mothers. A permanent site, with more room for boys and girls to be given education and training, was founded in Bloomsbury.

Though conditions for the children were austere, the Hospital's reputation was illuminated by the glitterati who supported it. Hogarth designed the children's uniforms and persuaded fellow artists such as Joshua Reynolds to donate paintings to fill a permanent gallery. The composer George Frederic Handel gave a sell-out performance of the *Messiah* in the Chapel – the Live Aid of its day with Coram as the wild-haired Geldof figure.

But as London society flocked around the Hospital, Coram was squeezed out. His forthright views irritated the other governors, and he was sidelined from the cause that had used up his personal fortune and turned his hair grey. Although the founding father of charitable causes was to spend his last years in reduced circumstances, he remained justly proud of his vision: over the next two centuries Coram's Hospital would take in 27,000 children.

To find out more about Thomas Coram's legacy, *see p61.*

In Context

POWER STRUGGLES

The city blossomed under the Tudors and Stuarts. Buoyed up by trade from newly discovered lands, London became one of the largest cities in Europe. Henry VII left his mark on London by commissioning the building of the Henry VII Chapel in Westminster Abbey, where he and his queen are buried. His successor was, of course, the notorious wife collector (and dispatcher) Henry VIII. His first marriage to Catherine of Aragon failed to produce an heir, so the king, in 1527, decided (in defiance of the Catholic Church) that the union should be annulled. Demanding to be recognised as Supreme Head of the Church of England, Henry ordered the execution of anyone who refused to comply (including his chancellor Sir Thomas More). So England began its transition to Protestantism. The subsequent dissolution of its monasteries changed the face of London: the land sold off was given over to streets. Henry also founded the Royal Dockyards at Woolwich. The land he kept for hunting became the Royal Parks (Hyde, Regent's, Greenwich and Richmond). His daughter Queen Mary's five-year reign saw a brief Catholic revival. She was dubbed 'Bloody Mary' following her order to burn at the stake nearly 300 Protestants.

Mary's half-sister Elizabeth I oversaw a huge upsurge in commerce: the Royal Exchange was founded by Sir Thomas Gresham in 1566 and London became Europe's leading commercial centre. With Drake, Raleigh and Hawkins sailing to America and beyond, new trading enterprises were developed. By 1600 there were 200,000 people living in London, 12,000 of whom were beggars. Conditions were overcrowded and rat-infested, so plague was a constant threat.

London was a cultural centre, however, as well as a death trap. Two theatres, the Rose (1587) and the Globe (1599), were built on the south bank of the Thames, and the plays of William Shakespeare and Christopher Marlowe first performed. Earthier dramas took place on the street. At Bankside, people visited taverns and brothels, and engaged in bear-baiting and cockfighting.

London was a violent place. Elizabeth's successor, the Stuart James I, narrowly escaped being blown up. The Gunpowder Plot was instigated by a group of Catholics led by Guy Fawkes, who planned to protest at their persecution by dynamiting the Palace of Westminster from the cellar. Unfortunately for Fawkes, one of his co-conspirators warned his brother-in-law not to attend Parliament on 5 November – prompting a thorough search and the foiling of the scheme. Four plotters were killed while resisting arrest, while the remainder

Victorian London, as seen by Charles Dickens in *Oliver Twist.*

of the gang were dragged through the streets and executed, their heads displayed on spikes.

Although James I escaped death, his son Charles I wasn't so lucky. He stirred up trouble by threatening the City of London's tax-free status and sparked a civil war: Charles and his Royalists were the losers. The king was tried for treason and beheaded outside the Banqueting House in Whitehall in 1649. Once Oliver Cromwell's Puritans had declared Britain a Commonwealth, theatres and gambling dens were closed down.

The exiled Charles II was restored to the throne in 1660, and Londoners were relieved. But there was trouble ahead: the 1664-5 bubonic plague killed nearly 100,000 Londoners before a cold snap stopped it. At the height of the epidemic 10,000 people were dying each week. When plague was diagnosed in a house, the occupants were locked inside for 40 days, while watchmen outside ensured no one escaped. London reeked of death. The following year, an oven in Farriner's bakery in Pudding Lane started a fire that lasted three days and destroyed four-fifths of the City. Rumours of a Popish plot were everywhere, and Frenchman Robert Hubert was forced to confess to starting the fire. He was later hanged. Today Christopher Wren's Monument marks a spot near where the fire broke out. London was rebuilt in brick and stone. Christopher Wren, as well as completing his greatest work, the new St Paul's Cathedral, oversaw the rebuilding of 51 city churches.

In Context

A TALE OF TWO CITIES

With George, the great-grandson of James I, on the throne, the country had a German-speaking king. In Parliament, the Whig party, led by Sir Robert Walpole, was in power. Walpole was the first prime minister and was given 10 Downing Street as an official home. This address has been occupied by the serving prime minister ever since. At this time more crossings over the river were built. Westminster Bridge (built 1750) and Blackfriars Bridge (1763) joined London Bridge, which until then had been the only bridge to span the river. While the well-to-do enjoyed their Georgian homes, life for the poor was squalid. Living in slums, ruined by cheap and plentiful gin, it's little wonder people turned to street crime. Gangs emerged, who enjoyed near immunity from arrest. The infamous Gregory Gang, one of many that preyed on travellers, included notorious highwayman Dick Turpin.

The writer Henry Fielding and his brother John established a volunteer force of 'thief takers' in 1751 to help the parish constables and watchmen catch these criminals. This force, originally known as the Bow Street Runners, eventually became the Metropolitan Police (established 1829).

The rich had never had it so good when Victoria was crowned queen in 1837. Progress was impressive: five more bridges spanned the Thames and the city's first railway line (London Bridge to Greenwich) had been laid. Yet this city,

the administrative and financial capital of the British Empire, had a dark underbelly. Crammed into slums, the urban masses led a miserable – and malodorous – life, as Henry Mayhew (*see p17* **London faces**) documented. The summer of 1858 smelled particularly bad: the 'Great Stink' meant that politicians in the Houses of Parliament could not work with their windows open.

LONDON AT WAR

The new century started merrily enough with Edward VII taking the throne in 1901, but the gaiety wouldn't last. World War I saw the first bomb to be dropped on London. It came from a Zeppelin and landed near Guildhall. Terrifying nightly raids continued throughout the Great War, killing 650 people.

When it was finally over, those soldiers who had survived were promised 'homes for heroes' on their return. Yet few homes materialised and the nation's mood was bleak. Political change was set in motion. In 1924 David Lloyd George's Liberal Party was deposed in favour of a promised fresh start with the Labour Party, under Ramsay MacDonald. While the upper classes partied their way through the 'Roaring Twenties', the working classes were in the grip of mass unemployment. Dissatisfaction was expressed when all the workers downed tools to support the striking miners. The General Strike of 1926 lasted for nine days: the army distributed food and students

Londoners experience the Blitz in **World War II**.

drove buses. After the strike, unemployment continued to rise. The New York Stock Exchange crash of 1929 had a knock-on effect; the British economic situation was grim.

Nevertheless, the London County Council worked to improve conditions for its people. As the city's population grew (8.7 million in 1939), so did its sprawl. Suburbia expanded, and with it the tube lines. The main entertainment for people was the radio, until 1936, when the first television broadcast went out live from the British Broadcasting Corporation (BBC) at Alexandra Palace studios.

On 3 September 1939 Britain declared war on Germany. Londoners dug air-raid shelters and sent children and pregnant women to the countryside. In fact, the air raids did not begin until almost a year later. In September 1940 600 German bombers devastated east London and the docks. The raids continued for 57 nights in a row. Nearly 30,000 bombs were dropped on London alone; around 15,000 people were killed and 3.5 million houses destroyed or damaged. People sheltered in the tube stations – 79 of them became official shelters. They were safe unless the stations were hit. This happened at Marble Arch, Bank and Balham.

In 1944 a new type of bomb began flattening Londoners' homes – the fearsome V1 flying bomb, or doodlebug. These caused widespread destruction, as did their successor, the more powerful V2 rocket, 500 of which were dropped on east London. By the end of the war about a third of the city was in ruins.

In the General Election that took place soon after VE Day, Churchill was defeated by the Labour Party under Clement Attlee. The National Health Service was founded in 1948; public transport and communications were overhauled. But life in the city still seemed drab and austere. For Londoners facing a housing shortage there were ambitious initiatives. Some of the buildings whisked up – prefabricated bungalows – were supposed to be temporary, but many are still inhabited more than 60 years later. Many new high-rise estates were shoddy and many have since been pulled down.

It was not all doom for Londoners, though. The city hosted the Olympic Games in 1948 and, in 1951, the Festival of Britain, which celebrated all that was great about British technology and design. It took place on derelict land on the south bank of the river, which eventually became the site of the South Bank Centre arts complex. During the 1950s Britain enjoyed a gradual return to relative prosperity. Families were inspired to move to new towns away from the city, where air pollution was a problem. Clean Air Acts, the first in 1956 introduced as a result of the Great Smog four years earlier, finally ensured the reduction of noxious gas emissions. Inner London was also facing a labour shortage. Workers from the country's former colonies, particularly the West

Hey, hey, it's the Swinging Sixties: the **Beatles** bring colour to a drab world.

Indies, were recruited for London Transport and in the hospitals. Many immigrants faced an unfriendly reception from indigenous Londoners: matters came to a head in the Notting Hill race riots of 1958. Some parts of London were more tolerant; Soho, with its jazz joints and clubs, for one. The 1960s saw London – fashion capital of the world – swing.

To find out where the gigs were, people bought a weekly guide to London called *Time Out*; the first issue came out in August 1968. People from around the world flocked to Abbey Road, NW8, because of the Beatles album of the same name. Hyde Park was the place to be in the summer of '69 when the Rolling Stones played for half a million fans.

In the 1970s the lights went out, often literally, on London's glamour. Inflation, unemployment, strikes, IRA bombs and an increasingly fractured Labour government all contributed to an air of gloom. The punk explosion made a few sparks fly, but that was shortlived. Margaret Thatcher came to power in 1979, and the 1980s are regarded as her decade. Her Conservative government made sweeping changes, and stood up for 'market forces'. This was the era of the yuppie (Young Urban Professional), who cashed in on the Conservatives' monetarist policies and the arrival of the global economy. The gap between yuppies

and the less wealthy was only too apparent. It did not take long for the city's underdogs to snarl and riot, first in Brixton in 1981, and four years later in Tottenham.

One lasting legacy of the Thatcher era in London is the Docklands redevelopment. A scheme set up in 1981 to create a business centre in the docks to the east of the City, it was slow to take shape, but is now considered a success. Businesses and residents are continuing to move into buildings around the Isle of Dogs and the area exudes prosperity. But this is one prominent area of London with a split personality, because little of the wealth from the banks and businesses is filtering through to the community. In 1986 the Greater London Council, with its anti-Thatcher outlook, was abolished and County Hall was sold to a Japanese corporation. But history has a way of turning on you – the GLC's former leader, 'Red' Ken Livingstone, bided his time and, in 2000, was voted mayor with authority over all the city.

London in the early 1990s hit the buffers. A slump in house prices saw the reign of the yuppies come to an end. The last straw for beleaguered Londoners was the poll tax. Demonstrations led to riots in Trafalgar Square. It marked the loosening of Thatcher's grip, leading to her replacement by John Major in 1990. The recession continued. The numbers of rough sleepers rose in London as people lost their homes through unemployment and mortgage rate rises. The IRA stepped up its campaign against the mainland, bombing the City in 1992 (destroying the medieval church of St Ethelburga-the-Virgin) and Docklands in 1996. Many cheered up when Tony Blair's New Labour ousted the Tories in May 1997, but went into shock when, later that year, Princess Diana was killed. The gates of Kensington Palace were the focus for the nation's tears and bouquets.

DOME AND AWAY

Fireworks for the new millennium weren't confined to the celebratory kind. Labour continued with the Conservative-conceived Millennium Dome project. But the spectacular tent on the once-derelict Greenwich Peninsula failed to capture the zeitgeist and angry voices were raised about the massive sums of money swallowed up by the enterprise. After many false starts, the Dome is now finally being transformed into a

LONDON FACES Henry Mayhew

As Britain's Empire slowly expanded and industry boomed, London was nursing a dirty secret. Packed into slums, the urban poor were leading miserable lives, working long hours in bad conditions. Their health was blighted further by an elderly sewage system that meant city dwellers' waste flowed straight into the Thames, poisoning the water and provoking outbreaks of typhus and cholera.

'A strange incongruous chaos of wealth and want, of ambition and despair, of the brightest charity and the darkest crime,' wrote Henry Mayhew of his home city in 1849. The lawyer-turned-author, publisher and journalist is less well known than that other social commentator, Charles Dickens. In fact, Mayhew's densely detailed observations remained virtually forgotten until the 1950s.

Yet his exhaustive accounts of life on the street, pieced together from conversations with juvenile watercress sellers too tired to play, orphaned flower girls whose blooms masked the stink of their rooms, the boys whose livings depended on collecting dog droppings to sell to tanneries, and a weaver who confessed that he was glad his children were dead because he wouldn't have to worry about them anymore, are photographic in their detail.

It was a particularly devastating cholera epidemic in 1849, during which 13,000 people lost their lives in just three months, that motivated Mayhew to write. 'We saw drains and sewers emptying their filthy contents [into the river], we saw a whole tier of doorless privies in the open road... we heard bucket after bucket of filth splash into it... we were taken to a house where an infant lay dead of the cholera. We asked if they really did drink the water? The answer was they were obliged to...'

The *Morning Chronicle* published Mayhew's account of the impact of the cholera deaths and commissioned him to profile the poverty-stricken on a regular basis. Mayhew wrote at least two articles each week for over a year in this vein, before publishing his collected works as *London Labour and the London Poor* in 1851.

Feathers were ruffled: *The Economist* believed that publishing the material was 'unthinkingly

increasing the enormous funds already profusely destined to charitable purposes, adding to the number of virtual paupers and encouraging a reliance on public sympathy for help instead of self exertion.' But others, such as the Christian Socialist Charles Kingsley, welcomed the exposure of such uncomfortable truths.

Thankfully, improvements were made to ease the lot of Londoners. The drainage system was overhauled in 1860 when Joseph Bazalgette's drainage system was completed, and some slums were replaced by social housing introduced by philanthropists such as George Peabody.

It all smells sweeter now – sometimes, at least. But should we need a reminder of past horrors, just open Mayhew's pages and inhale.

In Context

Key Events

c66 BC Ludgate built by King Lud (legendary).
AD 43 The invasion of the Romans. Londinium is founded.
61 Boudicca sacks the city.
122 Emperor Hadrian visits Londinium.
200 A rebuilt Londinium is protected by a city wall.
410 The last Roman troops leave Britain.

over London; King Cnut reigns.
1042 King Edward builds Westminster Abbey.
1066 William, Duke of Normandy, defeats Harold.
1067 Work begins on the Tower of London.
1099 First recorded flood in London.
1123 St Bartholomew's Hospital founded.
1197 Henry Fitzailwyn becomes the first mayor of the London.
1240 First Parliament sits at Westminster.
1294 First recorded mention of Hammersmith.
1348-9 The Black Death ravages London.
1357 The first Sanitary Act passed in London.
1381 Wat Tyler leads the Peasants' Revolt.
1388 Tyburn, near Marble Arch, becomes the principal place of execution.
1397 Richard (Dick) Whittington becomes Lord Mayor.
1497 The first image of London published in a *Chronycle of Englonde*.
1513 Henry VIII founds Woolwich Royal Dockyard.
1534 Henry VIII breaks from the Catholic Church.
1554 300 Protestant martyrs burned at Smithfield.
1571 The first permanent gallows are set up at Tyburn.
1599 The Globe Theatre is built on Bankside.
1605 Guy Fawkes's Gunpowder Plot is discovered.
1635 London's first public postal service established.
1642 The Puritans defeat the Royalists at Turnham Green.
1649 Charles I is tried for treason and beheaded.
1664-5 The Great Plague kills thousands in the city.
1666 The Great Fire destroys London.
1675 Building starts on a new St Paul's.
1680 Downing Street built.
1686 The first May Fair takes place at Mayfair.

c600 Saxon London is built to the west.
604 The first St Paul's Cathedral is constructed.
841 First raid by the Vikings.
c871 The Danes occupy London.
886 King Alfred retakes London.
1013 The Danes take

1694 The Bank of England opens at Cheapside.
1711 St Paul's is completed.
1741 Thomas Coram founds his orphanage.
1750 Westminster Bridge is built.
1769 Blackfriars Bridge opens.
1784 The first balloon flight over London.
1803 The first railway (horse-drawn) opens.
1820 Regent's Canal opens.
1824 National Gallery founded.
1827 Regent's Park Zoo opens.
1829 Metropolitan Police founded.
1833 The London Fire Brigade is established.
1835 Madame Tussaud's opens.
1843 Trafalgar Square is laid out.
1851 The Great Exhibition takes place.
1858 The Great Stink permeates London.
1863 World's first underground railway opens.
1866 The Sanitation Act is passed.
1868 Last public execution in Newgate Prison.
1869 J Sainsbury grocery opens in Drury Lane.
1884 Greenwich Mean Time is established.
1888 Jack the Ripper preys on East End women.
1890 First electric underground railway opens.
1897 Motorised buses introduced.
1898 The first escalator is installed, in Harrods.
1909 Selfridges, the first department store, opens in London.
1915-18 Zeppelins bomb London.
1916 Horse-drawn buses disappear.
1940-4 The Blitz devastates much of London.
1948 Olympic Games held in London.
1951 The Festival of Britain takes place.
1952 The last of the city's 'pea-soupers'.
1953 Queen Elizabeth II is crowned.
1966 England win the World Cup at Wembley.
1975 Work begins on the Thames Barrier.
1982 The last of London's docks close.
1986 The Greater London Council is abolished.
1990 Poll Tax protestors riot.

1992 Canary Wharf Tower opens.
1997 A Labour government is elected; Britain mourns the death of Princess Diana.
2000 Ken Livingstone elected mayor.

In Context

2002 The Queen Mother dies, aged 101
2003 London's biggest ever public demonstration – against the war on Iraq.
2004 Ken Livingstone is re-elected.
2005 Labour is re-elected for a third term.

20,000-seat sports and entertainment complex. And London still has problems. Housing is both expensive and in short supply, leading some to campaign for a reintroduction of tower blocks. Transport is taking a long time to improve and, indeed, often seems to be getting much worse. Since the introduction of Ken Livingstone's £5 (soon to be £8) weekday congestion charge, traffic levels in central London have been significantly reduced, although controversy surrounds the proposed extension of the scheme. But the city continues to develop, as a number of inner-city regeneration schemes swing into action, and the tourists continue to come – with visitor numbers almost back to their pre-9/11 levels. If history shows anything, it is that London (and Londoners) can weather any storm. We're made of stern stuff.

LONDON FACES Isabella Beeton

Isabella Beeton claimed the crown of domestic goddess 150 years before Delia or Nigella put floury finger to mixing bowl. But while modern household saints slave over hot stoves in front of TV cameras to showcase their talents, Mrs Beeton and her mass-selling *Book of Household Management* was a triumph of marketing over culinary expertise. No pastry-rolling matron, Mrs B was a young, unconventional working mother of four, a journalist whose talent for research and editing informed her work more than any practical experience.

She was born in Cheapside in 1836 but, when her father became the manager of Epsom Race Course, their large family moved out of town. Isabella was given far more freedom than the usual middle-class Victorian child. After an unorthodox education in Germany, she married young entrepreneur Samuel Orchard Beeton in 1856. A maverick, and a firm believer in women's independence and equality, Sam was already a successful publisher of books and magazines.

His secret was the identification of a crucial gap in the market. With the growth of trade and industry in the Victorian era, the middle classes were expanding. Their core values of respectability, family and getting a good start in life chimed perfectly with Sam's entertaining yet improving titles such as *Beeton's Dictionary of Universal Information*, *Beeton's Book of Garden Management* and *The Englishwoman's Domestic Magazine*, which Isabella was soon editing.

She was only 21 when Sam set her to work on *Mrs Beeton's Book of Household Management*. As well as the 2,000 recipes, which were for the most part plain and frugal (and perfectly in tune with the Victorian mania for modesty), there were chapters on 'The Rearing and Management of Children', etiquette and everyday thriftiness – how to make gallons of soup to distribute to the poor, for example. Isabella did practise what she preached here, turning her house into a soup kitchen for the poorest children of Hatch End and Pinner during the cold winter of 1858.

Factual nuggets were interspersed with pearls of wisdom, some of them surprisingly forward-looking. 'To be a good housewife does not necessarily imply an abandonment of proper pleasures or amusing recreation,' wrote Isabella.

Go, girl! What's more, she juggled her life of work and family just like her 21st-century counterparts do today. 'If I had known beforehand that this book would have cost me the labour which it has, I should never have been courageous enough to commence it,' she confessed in the introduction to *Household Management*. But her stamina was rewarded when the book was published as one volume in 1861, and sold a massive 60,000 copies in the first year.

As the Beetons' business boomed, their private life was shattered by the loss of two babies in infancy. There was more tragedy to come. While delivering her fourth child, Isabella contracted puerperal fever, a fatal but common infection in new mothers at the time. She died aged just 28, a long way short of the matronly figure that her name never ceases to conjure up.

FESTIVALS & EVENTS

Inside, outside, on water and dry land, London's got it going on.

Chinese New Year Festival. *See p26.*

It's not only summertime that sees Londoners take to the streets with floats and banners. Parades take place for the **Mayor's Thames Festival** (*see p24*) in September, jumping dragons in the **Chinese New Year Festival** (*see p26*), which runs during the glum days of late January, and daft costumes galore when runners full of the joys of spring pound the streets in April's **London Marathon** (*see p26*). In autumn half-term come the fireworks – Guy Fawkes's plot is remembered on 5 November, and the Christmas holidays usher in festive lights and ice rinks. Circuses and fairs take over the parks all year round. To find out when child-friendly Zippo's Circus is coming to your part of town during its February to November tour of the capital, check www.zipposcircus.co.uk.

Every school holiday there's something to celebrate in London, so here are some dates for your diary. Check *Time Out* magazine every week for details of more festivals and events.

SUMMER

Coin Street Festival
Bernie Spain Gardens (next to Oxo Tower Wharf), SE1 9PH (7401 3610/www.coinstreet.org). Southwark tube/Waterloo tube/rail. **Date** June-Aug 2005. **Map** p318 N7.
Not one but a series of eight or so culturally themed weekday and weekend events celebrating different communities in the capital. Events take place on the South Bank and include music, dance and performance events for all ages with craft and refreshment stalls at each one. Celebrating Sanctuary is held during Refugee Week in June and Capital Age (call for details) is for the older community.

Beating Retreat
Horse Guards Parade, Whitehall, Westminster, SW1A 2AX (booking 7414 2271). Westminster tube/Charing Cross tube/rail. **Date** 1-2 June 2005. **Map** p317 K8.
This patriotic ceremony begins at 7pm, with the 'Retreat' beaten on drums by the Mounted Bands of the Household Cavalry and the Massed Bands of the Guards Division.

Derby Day
Epsom Downs Racecourse, Epsom Downs, Surrey KT18 5LQ (01372 470047/www.epsomderby.co.uk). Epsom rail, then 460 shuttle bus. **Date** 3-4 June 2005.
The most important flat race of the season has a carnival mood, but be prepared to pay for comfort or a good view. Oaks Day – the fillies version of the Derby – is on 3 June;

If there's one thing that Londoners do well, it's throw a party. The city's full programme of festivals and events reflects, and benefits from, the many varied interests and cultures of its visitors and residents; from bhangra to beluga, every walk of life gets to strut its stuff. The famous festivals, such as the **Notting Hill Carnival** (*see p23*), are famous Europe-wide and attract crowds accordingly. More enjoyable for young families are the gentler park-based events, such as the **Lambeth Country Show** (*see p23*), or, this year, the Greenwich-centric events that will form part of the Trafalgar Festival commemorating the 200th anniversary of the battle (*see p24* **Full Nelson**).

In Context

Time Out | London for Children **21**

4 June is the famous Derby Day. Stands and spectator enclosures at this prestigious flat race are open to all, from toffs in toppers in the grandstand, to families picnicking on the hill in the middle of the course.

Young Pavement Artists Competition

Colonnade Walk, 123 Buckingham Palace Road, SW1W 9SH (7732 1651). Victoria tube/rail. **Date** 4 June 2005. **Map** p316 H10.

To celebrate the 20th anniversary of what has now become a huge national event (there were some 20,000 entrants in 2004), the Woodland Trust is contributing trees to be planted by the schools entering this year's competition. Children aged four to 18 compete, and photographs of the best pieces are exhibited the following month. On the big day there is usually entertainment laid on, in the form of music, magicians, face painting, and mask- and puppet-making.

Trooping the Colour

Horse Guards Parade, Whitehall, Westminster, SW1A 2AX (7414 2271). Westminster tube/Charing Cross tube/rail. **Date** 11 June 2005. **Map** p317 K8.

Though the Queen was born on 21 April, this is her official birthday celebration. At 10.45am she makes the 15-minute journey from Buckingham Palace to Horse Guards Parade, then scurries back home to watch a midday Royal Air Force flypast and receive a formal gun salute from Green Park. After the ceremony, the Queen rides in a carriage back to Buckingham Palace at the head of her Guards, before taking the salute at the palace from the balcony, when the Royal Air Force flies past overhead and a 41-gun Royal Salute is fired in Green Park. At 1pm there's a 62-gun Royal Salute at the Tower.

London Garden Squares Weekend

Various venues across London (http//myweb. tiscali.co.uk/london.gardens/home.htm). **Date** 11-12 June 2005.

All those enchanting little private parks around the wealthy parts of town that tempt you but then lock you out are opened up for this event only. Maps are available to guide you to the gardens, which vary from Japanese-style retreats to secret 'children-only' play areas.

London Youth Games

Crystal Palace National Sports Centre, Ledrington Road, SE19 2BB (8778 0131/www.youthgames.org.uk). Crystal Palace rail. **Date** 11-30 June, 2-3 July 2005 (June dates vary, phone to confirm).

This mini-Olympics, now in its 28th year, sees 12,000 sporting hopefuls, all of them under 17, represent the 33 London boroughs in 26 different sports. The teams are selected locally, and activities include archery, fencing, canoeing, football, tennis, athletics and show jumping. Check the website for a programme. The Festival Village hosts DJs, street sports, graffiti art and dance demonstrations.

Royal National Theatre Summer Festival

South Bank, SE1 9PX (7452 3400/www.national theatre.org.uk). Waterloo tube/rail. **Date** 24 June-3 Sept 2005. **Map** p318 M7.

Watch This Space is a free outdoor summer festival of music and entertainment in Theatre Square, offering more than 100 world-class shows across its ten weeks.

Everyone goes a bit potty at the **Regent Street Festival**. *See p24.*

Performances takes place six days a week from Monday to Saturday, at lunchtimes, early evenings and late night Saturdays. It kicks off with a two day Spanish Fiesta, and goes on to showcase the best of street theatre, circus, cinema, art, dance and spectacle from all over the world. Special events for include a family day on 16 July.

City of London Festival

Venues across the City, EC2-EC4 (7377 0540/ www.colf.org). Bank, Barbican, Moorgate & St Paul's tube/Blackfriars, Cannon Street & Farringdon tube/rail. **Date** 27 June-13 July 2005.
Now in its 43rd year, the City of London Festival takes place in some of the finest buildings in the Square Mile including livery halls and churches. The programme is traditional classical music, such as concerts from the London Symphony Orchestra, as well as pieces from the worlds of jazz, dance, visual art, literature and theatre.

Wimbledon Lawn Tennis Championships

All England Lawn Tennis Club, PO Box 98, Church Road, Wimbledon, SW19 5AE (8944 1066/info 8946 2244). Southfields tube/Wimbledon tube/rail. **Date** 20 June-3 July 2005; 26 June-9 July 2006.
Wimbledon is the world's most prestigious tennis tournament and, when it's not raining, the best. Actually, even when it is raining. For Centre and Number One court seats, you'd have had to request an application form from the All England Lawn Tennis Club between August and the end of November. This form gives you access to the public ticket ballot; if you're one of the lucky ones, you'll be notified in late January. Otherwise you have to queue on the day of the match. Once in, you can wander the outside courts. In the afternoon, returned show-court tickets are available from the resale booth opposite Court One, so it may be worth hanging about to see stars in action.

Henley Royal Regatta

Henley Reach, Henley-on-Thames, Oxon RG9 2LY (01491 572153/www.hrr.co.uk). Henley-on-Thames rail. **Date** 29 June-3 July 2005.
First held in 1839, Henley is now a five-day affair. Boat races range from open events for men and women through club and student crews to junior boys.

Greenwich & Docklands International Festival (GDIF)

Various venues in Greenwich & Docklands (8305 1818/ www.festival.org). **Date** July 2005.
Greenwich & Docklands Festival has made a speciality of free outdoor spectacles and performances, ideal for families. Free theatrical, musical and site-specific events are held in the vicinity of Canary Wharf and across east London, combining community arts with grander projects.

Soho Festival

St Anne's Gardens & St Anne's Community Centre, Soho, W1D 6AE (74394303/ www.thesohosociety.org.uk). Tottenham Court Road tube. **Date** 10 July 2005. **Map** p315 K6.
Stalls of crafts, books and face-painting, plus music, displays by local artists, various competitions and a gusty alpine horn-blowing contest bring locals and guests together in aid of the Soho Society.

Lambeth Country Show

Brockwell Park, SE24 0NG (7926 9000). Brixton tube/rail, then 2, 3, 68, 196 bus/Herne Hill rail. **Date** mid July 2005.
This annual urban country show fills Brockwell Park with a mix of farmyard and domestic animal attractions (horse show, dog show, farm animals). Aside from meeting and greeting the beasts, kids can have fun on the bouncy castles and fairground rides, and there are also food and craft stalls, and a whole lot of music and dancing.

Summer in the Square

Trafalgar Square, Westminster, WC2 (7983 4100/ www.london.gov.uk). Embankment tube/Charing Cross tube/rail. **Date** July-Aug 2005. **Map** p317 K7.
An annual programme of free (and usually fun) live cultural performances for all ages, Summer in the Square is keenly supported by the Mayor of London.

BBC Sir Henry Wood Promenade Concerts

Royal Albert Hall, Kensington Gore, South Kensington, SW7 2AP (box office 7589 8212/www.bbc.co.uk/proms). Knightsbridge or South Kensington tube/9, 10, 52 bus. **Date** 15 July-10 Sept 2005. **Map** p313 D9.
This annual event brings together an eclectic range of mostly classical concerts over the course of two months. Most are televised, but there's nothing like seeing them in person. If you choose carefully you should able to find something in the grown-up Proms programme that the children will enjoy. Otherwise, call to ask about the dates of the popular Blue Peter Prom, or make a date (11 Sept 2005) with the CBBC Prom in the Park (in Hyde Park).

Active8

Hyde Park, W2 2UH (www.london./gov.uk). Hyde Park Corner, Knightsbridge, Lancaster Gate or Marble Arch tube. **Date** 3 Aug 2005. **Map** p311 E7.
What used to be known as Playday has moved to greener pastures (it first took place in Trafalgar Square). There's more room to manoeuvre here though, so expect a jolly day of family celebrations with a focus on the importance of play, with an under-fives zone, teens zone and body, mind and food zone among the attractions.

Fruitstock

Regent's Park, NW1 (8600 3939/www.fruitstock.com). Regent's Park tube. **Date** 6-7 Aug 2005 (subject to licence). **Map** p314 G3.
Although seemingly unlikely organisers, the Innocent fruit smoothies drink company's free summer bash has proved extremely popular in past years. This year, the third, will be pretty much the same: plenty of live music, a dance tent, posh food stalls, a farmers' market, activities for children and the chance to laze in the park on a rug with your pals.

Notting Hill Carnival

Notting Hill, W10, W11 (www.lnhc.org.uk). Ladbroke Grove, Notting Hill Gate & Westbourne Park tube. **Date** 28-29 Aug 2005.
Europe's biggest street party sees thousands of revellers show up each year to drink warm beer and wander about in posh Notting Hill. There is occasional live music and relentless and unavoidable sound systems (loaded on to

trucks, followed by unglamorous dancers in T-shirts). There's a glittering costume parade, but all too often you miss it because of the crowds.

The dinky nursery and playgroups carnival happens in Kensington Memorial Park two weeks before the parent event. This scaled-down festival has a children's steel band competition; mini-floats; children's, mother's and buggy competitions; and nursery fancy dress. Clubs cater for various age groups, from babies to 16-year-olds. Check the website for regular updates on all aspects of the carnival.

AUTUMN

Regent Street Festival
Regent Street, W1 (7287 9601/www.regentstreet online.com). Oxford Circus or Piccadilly Circus tube. **Date** 4 Sept 2005. **Map** p316 J7.
Celebrate central London with fairground attractions, theatre and a variety of live music supplied by the charitable organisation for emerging young talent City Showcase. The street is closed to traffic and taken over by thousands of visitors (in recent years, as many as 190,000). Expect a funfair, toy demos, a police exhibition area with dogs, horses and abseiling, and entertainers, storytelling, face-painters and magicians on Hamleys picnic 'lawn' directly outside the shop. Other stores also participate.

Trafalgar Great River Race
Thames, from Ham House, Richmond, Surrey, to Island Gardens, Greenwich, E14 (8398 9057/ www.greatriverrace.co.uk). **Date** 17 Sept 2005.
More than 260 'traditional' boats, from Chinese dragon boats to Viking longboats, vie in the UK traditional boat championship over a 22-mile (35km) course. This year's race commemorates Nelson's victory in 1805. The race begins at 2.30pm with the winners reaching the finish from

Full Nelson
....
A full two centuries have elapsed since Nelson, Hardy and the lads got the whole 'Britannia rules the waves' thing under way (has it really been that long...?). And in commemoration of this most patriotic of historical events, the National Maritime Museum in Greenwich (see p122) has set up the ambitious SeaBritain 2005 project (www.seabritain.com), a year-long, country-wide roster of events, exhibitions and activities.
The two main events in London will be the **Thames Nelson Flotilla** (16 Sept), a dramatic waterborne funeral procession from Greenwich to Whitehall, and **Nelson Night** (22 Oct), a musical celebration of all things nautical at the Royal Albert Hall (*see p23*).
  The Woodland Trust's **Tree for All** campaign (www.treeforall.org.uk) is also part of the Trafalgar Festival. Of specific interest to children (and, for that mattter, their parents) is the Trafalgar Woods project. The aim is to honour the fact that, as they put it, 'Britain's naval strength is founded on oak' by planting trees across the country. For information on planting near you, check out the website.

around 5.30pm. The best viewing point is riverside at Richmond Bridge, or along the South Bank, on the Millennium and Hungerford Bridges.

Mayor's Thames Festival
Between Westminster & Blackfriars Bridges (7928 8998/www.thamesfestival.org). Blackfriars or Waterloo tube/rail. **Date** 17-18 Sept 2005.
Always fun and occasionally spectacular, this waterfest runs from noon to 10pm all weekend and is highlighted by an atmospheric lantern procession and noisy firework finale on Sunday evening. But before the pyrotechnics kick off, there are riverside market stalls, various environmental activities and creative workshops, and a lively assortment of dance and music performances.

Horseman's Sunday
Church of St John's Hyde Park, Hyde Park Crescent, W2 2QD (7262 1732/www.stjohn-hydepark.com). Edgware Road or Lancaster Gate tube/Paddington tube/rail. **Map** p313 E6. **Date** 18 Sept 2005.
This ceremony dates back to 1969, when local riding stables fearing closure held an open-air service to protest. Starting at noon, a vicar rides out to bless and present rosettes to a procession of horses and riders, and delivers a short service with hymns and occasional guest speakers. While there's little interaction between onlookers and the horses, it's fun nonetheless to watch the equine pageant trip through Hyde Park.

City Harvest Festival
Capel Manor Gardens, Bullsmoor Lane, Enfield, Middx BN1 4RQ (8366 4442/www.capel.ac.uk). Turkey Street rail (Mon-Sat only)/217, 310 bus. **Date** 24 Sept 2005.
The urban farms we all love have a pleasant day out in the leafy acres of Enfield for this agricultural extravaganza. Events include a farm animal show and arena events, such as milking and shearing demonstrations, vegetable and plant sales, displays by craftspeople, food stalls, and all sorts of fun and games for children.

Children's Book Week
Book Trust, 45 East Hill, SW18 2QZ (8516 2977/ www.booktrust.org.uk). **Date** 1st week Oct 2005.
This annual event dedicated to children's literacy is run by the charitable Book Trust. The country-wide schedule of activities includes hands-on events and author visits. Libraries and schools will have details of local events, otherwise contact the Trust or visit their website.

Pearly Kings & Queens Harvest Festival
St Martin-in-the-Fields, Trafalgar Square, Westminster, WC2N 4JJ (7766 1100/www.pearly society.co.uk). Embankment tube/Charing Cross tube/ rail. **Date** 2 Oct 2005. **Map** p317 L7.
Pearly kings and queens – so-called because of the shiny white buttons sewn in elaborate designs on their dark suits – have their origins in the 'aristocracy' of London's early Victorian costermongers, who elected their own royalty to safeguard their interests. Now charity representatives, today's pearly monarchy gathers for this 3pm thanksgiving service in their traditional 'flash boy' outfits. The vicar also wears a pearly stole during attendance, and St Martin's is decorated with fruit and harvest baskets.

Punch & Judy Festival

Covent Garden Piazza, Covent Garden, WC2 (Paul Jackson 8393 8200/www.coventgardenmarket.co.uk). Covent Garden tube. **Date** 2 Oct 2005. **Map** p315 L6.
More domestic incidents involving the crocodile, a policeman and Mr Punch giving Judy a few slaps (and vice versa). Performances take place around the market building. This year the organisers are looking for young performers to have a go at staging a show (call for details) and to join the Punch and Judy Fellowship. Puppetry means prizes, and there's also puppet-related merchandise for sale.

The Baby Show

Olympia, Hammersmith Road, Kensington, W14 8UX (booking line 0870 122 1313/www.thebabyshow.co.uk). Kensington (Olympia) tube/rail. **Date** 21-23 Oct 2005.
If you have one, are expecting one or are even planning one, this is the place for you to find out all you will ever need to know about babies and buy an obscene amount of paraphernalia. Toddlers are also included in the remit of this three-day extravaganza. To try to list what's there would be an exercise in futility; for best results, consult the website and search for yourself.

Trafalgar Day Parade

Trafalgar Square, Westminster, WC2 (7928 8978/ www.trafalgar200.org). Charing Cross tube/rail. **Date** 23 Oct 2005.
Map p401 K7.
This year's commemoration of Nelson's victory at the Battle of Trafalgar (21 Oct 1805) will include a special service at St Paul's Cathedral in addition to the usual event in which more than 500 sea cadets parade with marching bands and musical performances. Events culminate in the laying of a wreath at the foot of Nelson's Column.

Christmas Lights & Tree

Covent Garden (7836 9136/www.coventgarden market.co.uk); Oxford Street (7976 1123/www.oxford street.co.uk); Regent Street (7152 5853/www.regent-street.co.uk); Bond Street (www.bondstreet association.com); Trafalgar Square (7983 4234/ www.london.gov.uk). **Date** Nov-Dec 2005.
Much of the childhood wonder still remains in the glittering lights on St Christopher's Place, Marylebone High Street, Bond Street and Kensington High Street. The giant fir tree in Trafalgar Square each year is a gift from the Norwegian people, in gratitude for Britain's role in liberating their country from the Nazis.

Bonfire Night

Date 5 Nov 2005.
Most public displays of pyrotechnics to commemorate the gunpowder plot are held on the weekend nearest 5 November; among the best in London are those at Battersea Park, Alexandra Palace and Crystal Palace. Alternatively, try to book a late ride on the relevant nights on the British Airways London Eye (*see p32*).

London to Brighton Veteran Car Run

From Serpentine Road, Hyde Park, W1 (01280 841062/www.lbvcr.com). Hyde Park Corner tube. **Date** 6 Nov 2005. **Map** p311 F8.
Get up at the crack of dawn to catch this parade of around 500 vintage motors, none of which exceeds 20mph on the

St Patrick's Day Parade & Festival. *See p26.*

way to Brighton, setting off from Hyde Park between 7.30am and 9am, aiming to reach Brighton before 4pm. Otherwise, join the crowds lining the rest of the route.

Lord Mayor's Show

Various streets in the City (7332 3456/www.lord mayorsshow.org). **Date** 12 Nov 2005.
Amid a procession of about 140 floats and more than 6,000 people, the newly elected Lord Mayor leaves Mansion House at 11am and travels through the City to the Royal Courts of Justice on the Strand, where he makes some vows before returning to Mansion House by 2.30pm. The event finishes with a firework display from a barge moored on the Thames between Waterloo and Blackfriars Bridges.

Discover Dogs

Earl's Court 2 (entrance on Lillie Road), SW5 9TA (7518 1012/www.the-kennel-club.org.uk). West Brompton tube. **Date** 12-13 Nov 2005. **Map** p312 A11.
This canine extravaganza continues to go from strength to strength (in 2004 some 22,000 dog lovers attended). It's far less formal than Crufts: you can meet more than 180 dogs, discuss pedigrees with breeders, and gather info on all matters of the mutt. The Good Citizen Dog Scheme offers discipline and agility courses, and you can also meet husky teams and watch police-dog agility demonstrations and Heelwork to Music displays.

State Opening of Parliament

House of Lords, Palace of Westminster, Westminster, SW1A 0PW (7219 4272/www.parliament.uk). Westminster tube. **Date** Nov 2006 (call for details & changes). **Map** p317 L9.
In a ceremony that has changed little since the 16th century, the Queen officially reopens Parliament after its summer recess. You can only see what goes on inside on telly, but if you join the throngs on the streets, you can watch Her Maj arrive and depart in her Irish or Australian State Coach, attended by the Household Cavalry.

In Context

WINTER

The London International Horse Show

Olympia, Hammersmith Road, Kensington, W14 8UX (01753 847900/www.olympiahorseshow.com). Kensington (Olympia) tube/rail. **Date** 13-19 Dec 2005.
This annual extravaganza for equestrian enthusiasts has dressage, showjumping and more frivolous events, such as the Shetland Pony Grand National, mounted police displays and dog agility contests. The FEI Dressage World Cup performances take place in the evening of the 13 and 14 December, with the Grand Prix on the Tuesday night and the Kur on the Wednesday night. Show jumping runs from 15-19 December; two performances take place each day at 1pm and 7pm. There are more than 100 trade stands, so you can even get in some Christmas shopping.

Frost Fair

Bankside Riverwalk, by Shakespeare's Globe, SE1 9DT (details from Tourism Unit, Southwark Council, 7525 1139). London Bridge tube/rail. **Date** mid Dec 2005.
This tradition started in the winter of 1564, when the Thames froze over and Londoners used the ice for their stalls and attractions. Sadly, no ice can be expected these days (although the ice slide outside Tate Modern was a blast last year), but the food and wine stalls, children's shows and musical attractions set up on Bankside make for a good week's entertainment in the run-up to Christmas.

Chinese New Year Festival

Around Gerrard Street, Chinatown, W1, Leicester Square, WC2 & Trafalgar Square, WC2 (7851 6686/ www.chinatownchinese.com). Leicester Square or Piccadilly Circus tube. **Date** 29 Jan 2006. **Map** p317 K7.
2006 is the Year of the Dog. Celebrations to mark it begin at 11am with a children's parade from Leicester Square gardens to Trafalgar Square, where the lion and dragon dance teams perform traditional dances. And there are, of course, firework displays (at lunchtime and at 5pm).

London International Mime Festival

Various venues across London (7637 5661/ www.mimefest.co.uk). **Date** 11-29 Jan 2006.
Surely the quietest festival the city has to offer, LIMF will invite 20 companies from the UK and abroad to perform a variety of shows for all ages. This year's highlight is the French outfit Compagnie 111, who will perform a slapstick show at the South Bank's Queen Elizabeth Hall. Free brochures available via phone or website.

National Storytelling Week

Various theatres, bookshops, libraries, schools & pubs around London (contact Del Reid 8866 4232/www.sfs. org.uk). **Date** 28 Jan-4 Feb 2006.
The sixth annual storytelling week sees venues across the country hosting events for tellers and listeners. The event is held by the Society for Storytelling, an organisation that aims to increase public awareness of the art, practice and value of oral storytelling and the narrative traditions of the peoples and cultures of the world. In 2005 more than 600 nationwide storytelling events and performances were organised, in theatres, bookshops, libraries, schools, museums and arts centres all over town, Details of the 2006 programme were unavailable as we went to press (check the website nearer the time), but there are usually storytelling events to suit all tastes and ages.

SPRING

Great Spitalfields Pancake Day Race

Dray Walk, Old Truman Brewery, 91 Brick Lane, E1 6QL (7375 0441/www.alternativearts.co.uk). Liverpool Street tube/rail. **Date** 28 Feb 2006. **Map** p319 S5.
The action starts at 12.30pm, with teams of four tossing pancakes as they run, all for a good cause, of course. Call in advance if you want to take part, or just show up if all you're after is seeing pancakes hit the pavement. Competitors should phone the organisers a few days in advance to avoid batter recriminations.

St Patrick's Day Parade & Festival

Trafalgar Square, Leicester Square & Covent Garden (7983 4100/www.london.gov.uk). **Date** 12 Mar 2006. **Map** p317 K7.
This fun, colourful and noisy parade departs from Hyde Park Corner at noon and continues to romp through the streets until 6pm.

London Marathon

Greenwich Park to the Mall via the Isle of Dogs, Victoria Embankment & St James's Park (7902 0200/ www.london-marathon.co.uk). Maze Hill rail & Charing Cross tube/rail. **Date** 23 Apr 2006.
One of the world's biggest metropolitan marathons, this event attracts 35,000 starters, many in outrageous costumes. Spectators are advised to arrive early; the front runners reach the 13-mile mark near the Tower of London at around 10am. If you think you're fit enough, runners' applications must be in by the October before the race.

London Harness Horse Parade

Battersea Park, Albert Bridge Road, Battersea, SW11 (01737 646132). Battersea Park or Queenstown Road rail/97, 137 bus. **Date** 17 Apr 2006. **Map** p313 F13.
On Easter Monday more than 300 working horses, donkeys and mules with various commercial and private carriages assemble at 9am for the main parade (noon-1pm).

Canalway Cavalcade

Little Venice, W9 (British Waterways London 7286 6101). Warwick Avenue tube. **Date** May bank hol weekend 2006.
The Inland Waterways see to it that this bank holiday boat rally transforms the pool of Little Venice with an assembly of more than 100 colourful narrowboats, all decked out in bunting and flowers. Events include craft, trade and food stalls; kids' activities; music; and boat trips. The beautiful lantern-light boat procession is a must-see – pray for fine weather. Phone to confirm dates.

May Fayre & Puppet Festival

St Paul's Church Garden, Bedford Street, Covent Garden, WC2E 9ED (7375 0441/www.alternative arts.co.uk). Covent Garden tube. **Date** 14 May 2006 (check website for details). **Map** p317 L7.
Celebrating the first recorded sighting of Mr Punch in England (by Pepys, in 1662), this free event offers puppetry galore from 10.30am to 5.30pm. A grand brass band procession around Covent Garden is followed by a service held in St Paul's (*see p76*), with Mr Punch in the pulpit. Then there are puppet shows, booths and stalls, as well as workshops for puppet-making and dressing up.

In Context

AROUND TOWN

Features

INTRODUCTION

Pace yourself, there's a lot to be done.

Rain or shine, for richer, for poorer, London provides ageless entertainment – fun for all the family, to coin a phrase. Take as an example a visit to **Somerset House** (*see p57*), where you get priceless artworks for sober study, workshops in the Learning Centre for that hands-on stuff and dancing fountains in the courtyard for toddlers who couldn't give a stuff about art but fancy stripping down to their pull-ups and capering in the water jets. Such diversity of appeal is present in dozens of the city's attractions – read about them in these Around Town pages. We list the picture-postcard sights as well as the best parks, museums, city farms and galleries off the beaten tourist track. We also suggest places to eat, walks to take, spaces to run wild in and activities to book up for. Always ring to check that a listed establishment is open before you visit.

USEFUL INFORMATION

If your sightseeing programme includes expensive places, such as **London Zoo** (*see p64*) and the **Tower of London** (*see p52*), a London Pass (0870 242 9988, www.londonpass.com) could well be of interest. This gives you pre-paid access to more than 50 attractions and costs from £27 daily per adult without travel, or £32 with travel. For children, the price is substantially cheaper: £18 without travel, £20 with.

The initials 'LP' included before the admission price in our listings means your London Pass grants free admission. 'EH' means English Heritage members, and their kids, get in free. 'NT' means National Trust members and their children get free admission.

Trips and tours

On the buses

Big Bus Company *48 Buckingham Palace Road, Westminster, SW1W 0RN (0800 169 1365/7233 9533/www.bigbustours.com).* **Departures** every 10-15 mins from Green Park, Victoria & Marble Arch. *Summer* 8.30am-6pm daily. *Winter* 8.30am-4.30pm daily. **Pick-up** Green Park (near the Ritz); Marble Arch (Speakers' Corner); Victoria (outside Thistle Victoria Hotel, 48 Buckingham Palace Road, SW1W 0RN). **Fares** £20 (£18 if booked online); £8 5-15s; free under-5s. Tickets valid for 24hrs, interchangeable between routes. **Credit** AmEx, DC, MC, V.
Open-top buses that offer two-hour tours, Big Bus also runs cruises and walking tours.

Original London Sightseeing Tour (*8877 1722/ www.theoriginaltour.com*). **Departures** *Summer* 9am-6pm daily. *Winter* 9am-5pm daily. **Pick-up** Grosvenor Gardens; Marble Arch (Speakers' Corner); Baker Street tube (forecourt); Coventry Street; Embankment tube; Trafalgar Square. **Fares** £16; £10 5-15s; free under-5s. £1 discount if booked online. **Credit** MC, V.
Kids Club tours include commentary and an activity pack.

Pedal power

London Bicycle Tour Company (*7928 6838/ www.londonbicycle.com*). **Fares** £3 per hr; £16 per 24hrs; £48 per week.
In addition to bicycles, rickshaws are also available.

London Pedicabs (*7093 3155/www.london pedicabs.com*). **Fares** from £3 per person (per mile). Rickshaws based around Covent Garden and Soho.

Take a walk

Cityside Walks (8449 4736, www.cityside walks.co.uk). **Tours** £5.50, £4 concessions.
Original London Walks (7624 3978/ www.walks.com). **Tours** £5.50 (£4.50 concessions).

TOP 5 Sights

For artistic souls
Start by exploring the art at **Tate Modern** (*see p41*), then the Activity Cart at the **Victoria & Albert Museum** (*see p89*).

For drama queens
Drama workshops at the **Theatre Museum** (*see p76*); Childsplay during performances at **Shakespeare's Globe** (*see p41*).

For enquiring minds
Palaeontology: the **Natural History Museum** (*see p88*). Technology: the **Science Museum** (*see p89*). Physiology: the **Hunterian Museum** (*see p55*). Zoology: **London Zoo** (*see p64*).

For tearaway toddlers
The shady tree-top encampment in the **Diana, Princess of Wales Memorial Playground** (*see p85*); the garden space rocket firing young imaginations at **Discover** (*see p110*).

For water babies
The fountains in the courtyard at **Somerset House** (*see p57*); the paddling pool in **Ravenscourt Park** (*see p154*).

View from above

Adventure Balloons *Winchfield Park, London Road, Hartley Wintney, Hants RG27 8HY (01252 844222/www.adventureballoons.co.uk).* **Flights** *London* May-Aug 5am Tue, Wed, Thur. **Fares** *London* £165 per person. **Credit** MC, V.
Balloon flights over London. Children have to be at least eight years old and they pay full price for a trip.

Cabair Helicopters *Elstree Aerodrome, Borehamwood, Herts WD6 3AW (8953 4411/ www.cabairhelicopters.com). Edgware tube/ Elstree rail.* **Flights** from 9.45am-4pm Sun (also occasional Sat). **Fares** £149. **Credit** MC, V.
Memorable 'helitours' over London. Over-sevens only.

Waterways

City Cruises *7740 0400/www.citycruises.com.*
The river's biggest pleasure cruise operator, whose fleet includes showboats and restaurant boats. City Cruises also organises sightseeing tours and sells Rail & River Rover tickets. *See also p292.*

London Duck Tours *55 York Road, SE1 7NJ (7928 3132/www.londonducktours.co.uk).* **Tours** Check website for departure details. **Fares** £17.50; £14 concessions, 13-15s; £12 under-12s; £53 family ticket (2+2). **Credit** AmEx, MC, V,
The City of Westminster organises these tours, which are conducted in a DUKW (an amphibious vehicle developed during World War II). Tours comprise a 75-minute road and river trip, and the bright yellow craft is great fun for kids. It never fails to produce squeals of delight as it drives into the water.

London Waterbus Company *7482 2660/ www.londonwaterbus.com.* **Tours** *1 Apr-30 Sept,* 10am, 11am, noon, 1.15pm, every hour 2-5pm daily. **Fares** *Single* £5.50; £3.70 3-15s. **Return** £7, £4.70 children. **No credit cards**.
Cruises along the Regent's Canal via Camden Lock, Regents Park and Little Venice. Check the website for good-value London Zoo admission via canal boat. All-day cruises are also available, when the focus is more on the industrial history and architecture of the areas that go floating by.

No fares please

From August 2005 children won't need a ticket to ride, because bus travel in London for the under-16s will be free. This means you can compile your own bus-based sightseeing trip, hopping on and off wherever you fancy. It's just a shame that you won't actually be able to 'hop' as bus passengers once did on the old Routemaster buses. That icon of the bus lane has been retired from service. There'll be no more inter-bus stop derring-do, such as rakish pole-hanging and running leaps on to the footplate for young Londoners. They'll have to think of other ways to dice with death. The only Routemasters you'll see after summer 2005 will be those pressed into service as tourist attractions.

Nonetheless, there's a shiny new fleet of red buses plying the bus lanes these days. The best for taking in top family attractions are, we reckon, numbers **RV1**, **12** and **52**. The single-decker, zero emission fuel-using RV1 to **Covent Garden** (*see p73*) goes from **Tower Bridge** (*see p52*), passing **City Hall** (*see p43*) and the building site destined to be the new Unicorn Theatre for Children. Once over the river, it takes a circuitous route to Tooley Street, opposite Hay's Galleria (for **HMS Belfast**, *see p39*), **London Dungeon** and **Winston Churchill's Britain at War Experience** (*for both, see p40*). It then trundles up Blackfriars Road to Upper Ground past the National Theatre and the **British Airways London Eye** (*see p32*).

The number 12 to Notting Hill Gate is a bendy bus, which can be picked up from Westminster Bridge near the **Houses of Parliament** (*see p79*) and **Westminster Abbey** (*see p82*). The bus circuits the Green before crawling up Whitehall on the way to **Trafalgar Square** (*see p80*). From here it's up Regent Street, passing **Hamley's** (*see p205*) – a giant among toyshops – then down Oxford Street to Marble Arch. When it goes past Hyde Park look out for Queensway tube as a stopping-off point to cross over to **Kensington Gardens** and the **Diana, Princess of Wales Memorial Playground** (*see p85*). Or stay on the bus for Notting Hill Gate, where you can pick up the number 52, a double-decker. This runs down to the eastern end of High Street Kensington to the southern end of **Kensington Gardens** (*see p87*). It passes the garish **Albert Memorial** (*see p87*) on the left, the **Royal Albert Hall** (*see p218*) and the northern end of Exhibition Road (stop here for the **Natural History Museum**, (*see p88*), and the **Science** and **Victoria & Albert** museums (*for both, see p89*). Kensington Road leads to Knightsbridge and **Harrod's** (*see p185*), terminating at Victoria Station, passing the Queen's back garden. If you want to see her front yard, sentries, tourists and all, alight at Hyde Park Corner and stretch your legs along Constitution Hill between Green Park and **Buckingham Palace** (*see p72*).

Around Town

SOUTH BANK & BANKSIDE

Riverside bling and hidden gems create a touristic treasure trove.

British Airways London Eye. See p32.

For centuries the marshy south side of the River Thames was the wrong side for gentlefolk. It was popular for all the wrong reasons (bear baiting and hard drinking being two of them). Even when its act was cleaned up, and the Festival of Britain was held here in 1951, the South Bank was still the Cinderella side of the Thames. It took the run-up to the Millennium party in the late 1990s, however, to really effect the transformation of the area from a shabby concrete muddle to the eminently strollable tourist attraction it is today. The British Airways London Eye, designed by architects Marks Barfield is a symbol of its success. The elegant **Millenium** and **Hungerford** footbridges, linking the area to the rest of the city, continue the theme. Add to these numerous art galleries, the faithfully reconstructed **Shakespeare's Globe**, the small, partly ancient **Southwark Cathedral** and various museums, and you can see why the South Bank and Bankside is now the arts and entertainment showpiece of the capital. More importantly still, its child appeal is legendary.

A useful starting point for the first-time visitor is the **Tourist Information Centre**, which remains in its temporary home in Vinopolis wine museum (1 Bank End, SE1 9BU), until at least February 2006. It's open 10am-6pm Tuesday to Saturday and can be contacted on 7357 9168. Parents fond of a tipple should note that the Vinopolis tasting tour is, for children, the least interesting Bankside attraction.

THE SOUTH BANK

The riverside stretch from Lambeth Bridge to Festival Pier provides culture on every level. At ground level, the **Museum of Garden History** is a little piece of paradise set slightly back from the river. It celebrates the original greenfingers, John Tradescant, who brought back exotic plants from tropical climes in the 16th century.

Pineapples were among his discoveries, which is why this fruit is set in stone on Lambeth Bridge.

From here it's a short riverside walk east under Westminster Bridge to London's major tourist zone. Top-flight entertainment comes courtesy of the **British Airways London Eye** – cash-strapped it may be, but it's still been voted the South Bank's top tourist attraction. Next door, the Jubilee Gardens and playground provide a useful distraction for children while they wait for their turn on the Eye. Plans to create a 'world-class park' from the Gardens within the next three years are part of an ongoing South Bank Centre revamp project. Almost opposite the London Eye, the grand County Hall – once the home of the Greater London Council – houses a mixed bag of cultural diversions. The **Saatchi** and **Dalí** galleries compete for attention, although the former has been divested of its shock value with the removal of its famous installations in favour of paintings. Underwater worlds are distilled into the tanks of the **London Aquarium**. Noisy **Namco Station** is its embarrassing lowbrow neighbour (the McDonald's here is always heaving with bad-

tempered families). Rise above them and eat out at Gabriel's Wharf, further east, or bring a picnic (*see p165* **Don't let them hamper you**).

Phase one of the transformation of the South Bank Centre is now over, with the renovation of the Queen Elizabeth Hall and the completion of a new building for arts and eats near Hungerford railway bridge. Phase two, however, is only just beginning. This will mean the closure of the Royal Festival Hall from the end of June 2005 for about 18 months for renovation work to improve 'audience comfort, acoustics and technical requirements in the auditorium'. The foyers and the brilliant Ballroom, scene of so many free arts events for children, will also be refurbished. The most exciting element of its transformation will be the creation of a new Education Centre, which will include a new technology suite, performance space and gamelan room, so that the South Bank education programme can be expanded. For more details, check www.rfh.org.uk.

It may be full steam ahead at the South Bank Centre, but the long-awaited transformation of the **National Film Theatre** (www.bfi.org.uk) into a

THE BEST Diversions on the South Bank

Design Museum
See p44.
Age 6-12. **Cost** free 6-11yrs; £4 12.
When 2-5pm Sat, Sun.
Children's creativity workshops take place at weekends. In June and July there's fun-palace building with Cedric Price; August is carnival; September is car design workshops; October is taken up with the Big Draw Event; November is Eileen Gray chair workshops, and December is Designing Christmas. Booking is essential, either by phone (7940 8782) or by email at education@designmuseum.org.

Florence Nightingale Museum
See p34.
Age from 5. **Cost** admission charge; workshops free. **When** weekends; daily during half term. Events may include craft work, such as making your own lamp, or poetry and performance sessions. Occasional actor-led performances include meeting nurses Nightingale and Seacole 'in person'. Trails and prizes are available; check the website for details.

HMS Belfast
See p39.
Age no age limit. **Cost** admission charge.
When Sat, Sun; during school holidays.
Themed handling sessions about life on board ship examine artefacts and equipment. Workshops during the school holidays cover art and crafts, medal-making and signalling

techniques, while Commonwealth Month (1-31 October 2005) offers art, craft, music and dance activities; check the website for details.

London Aquarium
See p34.
Age no age limit. **Cost** admission charge.
When different events daily.
Daily: see the rays being fed at 11.30am and learn about coral at 3.30pm.
Mon-Fri: divers feed the bottom dwellers (rays, skates, dogfish and congers) at noon.
Mon, Wed, Fri, Sun: learn about piranhas at 1pm, and about sharks at 2pm and 4pm.
Tue, Thur, Sat: see the sharks being fed at 2.30pm, and hear a talk at 4pm.

Tate Modern
See p41.
Age from 5. **Cost** free. **When** 11am–5pm Sun; occasionally during school holidays.
'Start': Kids explore the Landscape, Matter and Environment or Still Life galleries, using puzzles, toolboxes and art equipment to learn about and create their own art.
Age from 5. **Cost** free. **When** daily.
'Things to See and Do': Family trails available at the information desk get children sketching, writing and matching pictures to the art works.
Age 8-12. **Cost** £2. **When** daily.
'Children's Audio Tour': Narrated by Michael Rosen, this tour comprises two 30-minute discovery trails around the Tate's collection.

Florence Nightingale Museum.

National Film Centre on the South Bank may still take a while to get under way. Nonetheless, Movie Magic at weekends and during school holidays makes the NFT a great resource for children, whatever its future prospects.

The handsome **Oxo Tower Wharf**, with its deco tower that incorporates advertising for the famous stock-cube company, was saved from demolition in the 1970s by the Coin Street Community Builders, who are also responsible for the high-spirited Coin Street Festival every summer (*see p21*). **Gabriel's Wharf** with its pastel-coloured crafty shops and friendly cafés is another Coin Street enterprise.

BFI London IMAX Cinema

1 Charlie Chaplin Walk, SE1 8XR (0870 787 2525/ www.bfi.org.uk/imax). Waterloo tube/rail. **Open** 12.30-9.30pm Mon-Fri; 10.45am-9.45pm Sat, Sun. **Admission** £7.90; £4.95 4-15s; £6.50 concessions; add-on film £5.50 extra per adult or £3.95 extra per child; free under-4s. **Credit** AmEx, MC, V. **Map** p318 M8.
This drum-shaped IMAX cinema (it stands for 'image maximum', in case you've ever wondered), located at the hub of the roundabout at the southern end of Waterloo Bridge, contains the largest screen in the UK. The sheer size of the mechanics that make this system work is as impressive as the images you see on the screen: the projector is as big as a small house, while the visual and sound effects are enough to convince you that you're actually part of the action. The 480 seats are very steeply banked, so no one, not even a tot, has to look over anyone's head to see.

Check the website for details of new screenings at the IMAX, where old favourites *Into the Deep, T-Rex Back to the Cretaceous* and *Ghosts of the Abyss* are often joined by mega blockbusters, such as Tom Hanks in *The Polar Express*, which recently enjoyed huge success in its 3D format. Bear in mind that not all films screened are in 3D. *Buggy access. Café. Disabled access: lift, toilets. Nappy-changing facilities. Nearest picnic place: Jubilee Gardens.*

British Airways London Eye

Riverside Building (next to County Hall), Westminster Bridge Road, SE1 7PB (booking line 0870 500 0600/ customer services 0870 990 8883/www.ba-londoneye. com). Westminster tube/Waterloo tube/rail. **Open** Oct-Apr 9.30am-8pm daily. *May, June, Sept* 9.30am-9pm daily. *July, Aug* 9.30am-10pm daily. **Admission** £12.50; £10 concessions (not applicable weekends or in July or Aug); £6.50 5-15s; free under-5s. **Credit** AmEx, MC, V. **Map** p317 M8.
Hailed as the world's favourite tourist attraction in 2005, the Eye was originally intended to grace the South Bank for five years, but will be rotating over the Thames until at least 2025. It will probably become a permanent fixture; after all, they said the Eiffel Tower would stay up only for one year. The 450ft (137m) monster wheel, whose 32 glass capsules each hold 25 people, commands the best views over London. It attracts long queues on fine days, but the wait is rarely more than 30mins. Many people pre-book to get a 10% discount, taking a gamble with the weather. The views are brilliant, both by day and at night, when the out look is twinklier. The Eye gets festive with fairy lights at Christmas and yuletide-themed events for children. Hallowe'en specials, with trick or treat bags for those who dress up, go down a storm and the marketing department usually do something chocolatey for Easter. The nearby playground, partly funded by the Eye company, is a boon for those with young children. A guide to the landmarks, and photos of your trip, are on sale. The London Eye River Cruise Experience runs between March and October (call 0870 500 0600 for details).
Buggy access. Café. Disabled access: toilets. Nappy-changing facilities. Nearest picnic place: Jubilee Gardens. Shop.

Dalí Universe

County Hall (riverfront entrance), Riverside Building, Queen's Walk, SE1 7PB (7620 2720/www.dali universe.com). Westminster tube/Waterloo tube/rail. **Open** 10am-5.30pm daily. **Tours** phone for details. **Admission** (LP) *Oct-May* £8.50; £7 concessions; £5.50 8-16s; £3.50 4-7s; £23 family (2+2). *June-Sept* £9; £7.50 concessions; £5.50 8-16s; £3.50 4-7s; free under-4s; £24 family (2+2). **Credit** AmEx, DC, MC, V. **Map** p317 M8.
The main exhibition, curated by long-term Dalí friend Benjamin Levi, leaves you in no doubt as to the Spanish artist's eccentricity. The wall-mounted quotes by, and (silent) videos and photographs of, Dalí give an insight into his life. There are sculptures, watercolours (including his flamboyant tarot cards), rare etchings and lithographs. Many of the works seem like artistic comedy: melting clocks, long-legged elephants, crutches, lobsters, ants and stretched buttocks casting long shadows over dream-like sunny plains. The gallery also shows work by new artists. *Buggy access. Disabled access: lift, ramp, toilets. Nearest picnic place: Jubilee Gardens. Shop.*

Florence Nightingale Museum

St Thomas's Hospital, 2 Lambeth Palace Road, SE1 7EW (7620 0374/www.florence-nightingale.co.uk). Westminster tube/Waterloo tube/rail. **Open** 10am-5pm

YOU'LL FIND HIM AT LONDON AQUARIUM

Have fun finding the real clown fish, not to mention several different species of sharks, including the Sand Tiger pictured. London Aquarium is full of surprises with over 350 unique underwater species to discover.

Located in County Hall and right next to the London Eye, London Aquarium is only a short walk from Waterloo Station and just over Westminster Bridge from Big Ben and the Houses of Parliament.

So don't plan time out in London without visiting London's only aquarium!
Open every day from 10am to 6pm.

For further details call **020 7967 8000**
or log on to www.londonaquarium.co.uk

LONDON
AQUARIUM

Mon-Fri; 10am-4.30pm Sat, Sun (last entry 1hr before closing). **Admission** (LP) £5.80; £4.20 5-18s, concessions; free under-5s; £13 family (2+2). **Credit** AmEx, MC, V. **Map** p317 M9.

Florence's celebrity status on Key Stage 1 and 2 of the National Curriculum means that you often hear parents being instructed by six-year-olds on the finer points of the lamp lady's remarkable life. Any gaps in their formidable knowledge can be filled by the wealth of information provided in this enjoyably laid-out museum. Mementoes and tableaux depict the harshness of the field hospitals of Scutari, where Nurse Nightingale first came to public attention, but details of her privileged life before this, and the studious one thereafter, are just as interesting. A 20min film tells Florence's story, with Anna Massey giving her voice. Other displays include clothing, furniture, books, letters and portraits from her life in London and abroad.

This year, the museum celebrates the 200th anniversary of the birth of another Crimean war hero, Mary Seacole. A nurse of Jamaican and Scottish extraction, she was recently voted the greatest black Briton.

Trails for children aged 5-7 (I Spy Worksheet) and 7-10 (Find out about Flo!) are available at all times. *See also p31* **The best: Diversions on the South Bank**.
Buggy access. Disabled access: toilets. Nearest picnic place: benches by hospital entrance/Archbishop's Park. Shop. (In hospital: Café. Nappy-changing facilities. Restaurant.)

Hayward Gallery

Belvedere Road, SE1 8XX (7960 5226/box office 0870 169 1000/www.hayward.org.uk). Embankment tube/Waterloo tube/rail. **Open** *During exhibitions* 10am-6pm Mon, Thur, Sat, Sun; 10am-8pm Tue, Wed; 10am-9pm Fri. **Admission** £9; £4 concessions; £3 12-16s; free under-12s. Prices may vary, call to check. **Credit** AmEx, MC, V. **Map** p318 M8.

Inside the light, bright pavilion, designed by Daniel Graham, casual visitors can watch cartoons on touch screens or just wander around the visually confusing space created by curved, two-way mirrors. The neon tower on the gallery roof was commissioned by the Arts Council in 1970. Its yellow, red, green and blue tubes are controlled by changes in the direction and strength of the wind. For events that might be of interest to children in 2005, consult the gallery's website; in 2006, there will be an exhibition of art from the Pacific, called 'Oceania'.
Buggy access. Café. Disabled access: lift. Nappy-changing facilities. Nearest picnic place: Jubilee Gardens/riverside benches. Shop.

London Aquarium

County Hall (riverfront entrance), Riverside Building, Westminster Bridge Road, SE1 7PB (7967 8000/tours 7967 8007/www.londonaquarium.co.uk). Westminster tube/Waterloo tube/rail. **Open** 10am-6pm daily (last entry 5pm). Phone for late opening during holidays. Closed 25 Dec. **Tours** (groups of 10 or more) phone for details. **Admission** (LP) £8.75; £6.50 concessions, disabled; £5.25 3-14s; free under-3s; £25 family (2+2) (all prices £1 more during school holidays). **Credit** AmEx, MC, V. **Map** p317 M9.

Not all underwater life is here, but there are more than 350 species gliding around in the tanks. The one-million-litre Pacific tank is a source of fascination to children, where Brown sharks Rod and Jane, and Sandtiger sharks George, Zippy and Bungle, as well as Nurse and Zebra varieties,

glide about in deep, silvery contemplation. Don't miss feeding time (*see p31* **The best: Diversions on the South Bank**). The tropical tanks are aglow with several varieties of tetras, angelfish and that celebrity species, the clownfish. An interesting display about the tidal River Thames may get overlooked among the more exotic environments recreated in the Pacific, Atlantic, Mangrove, Rainforest and Coral tanks. The circular ray tank attracts large crowds of children keen to touch the flat fish as they skim along the surface. Conservation and breeding programmes are part of the Aquarium's brief, and visitors are directed towards the work of various campaigning organisations, including the Shark Trust, London Wildlife Trust, Seawatch Foundation and Marine Conservation Society. Children can pick up an activity sheet and trail as they go in, and the education department runs regular workshops and activities for children during school holidays – badge-making is always a popular one – check the website for details.
Buggy access. Café. Disabled access: lift, ramp, toilets. Nappy-changing facilities. Nearest picnic place: Jubilee Gardens. Shop.

London Fire Brigade Museum

94A Southwark Bridge Road, SE1 0EG (7587 2894/ www.london-fire.gov.uk). Borough tube/Southwark tube/rail/344 bus. **Tours** by appointment only 10.30am, 2pm Mon-Fri. Closed bank hols. **Admission** £3; £2 7-14s, concessions; free under-7s, school groups. **Credit** MC, V. **Map** p318 O9.

You have to plan ahead to visit this one – access is by pre-booked guide tour only. Tours last roughly an hour and present an entertaining, potted history of firefighting since the Great Fire in 1666. They take in the appliance bay, where pumps dating back to 1708 stand in tribute to blazes past. Small children are given colouring pencils and encouraged to draw any of the 20 fire engines, ranging from a horse-drawn, hand-pumped 1830s model to shiny red and brass vehicles from the early 20th century, and today's more streamlined heavyweights. Sadly, climbing on the vehicles is not allowed, but trying on uniforms is. Exhibits in the eight small rooms include equipment, mementoes and paintings, such as those executed by fire-men-artists recording their Blitz experiences. The museum also displays one of only three George Crosses to be awarded to firefighters.
Buggy access. Disabled access: toilets. Nappy-changing facilities. Nearest picnic place: Mint Street Park. Shop.

Museum of Garden History

Church of St Mary-at-Lambeth, Lambeth Palace Road, SE1 7LB (7401 8865/www.museumgardenhistory.org). Waterloo tube/rail then 507 bus/Lambeth North rail/C10, 77 bus. **Open** 10.30am-5pm daily. **Admission** free; suggested donation £3 (£2.50 concessions). **Credit** *Shop* (over £10) AmEx, MC, V. **Map** p317 L10.

The world's first museum dedicated to gardening is contained within the deconsecrated and refurbished church of St Mary's. The Tradescants, a pioneering family of gardeners and botanists, and Captain William Bligh, of *Bounty* fame, along with half a dozen Archbishops of Canterbury, are entombed in the graveyard. A replica of a 17th-century knot garden, arranged in geometric shapes to form the letter T, has been designed as a living memorial to the Tradescants. Look out for the Pedlar's Window, a stained-glass window illustrating a man and his dog. History has it that an early 16th-century pedlar came into an acre of

Around Town

London Aquarium.

land (now the site of County Hall) and donated it to the church on condition that an image of him be preserved in glass. The current window is the fourth, made in 1956 after its predecessor was destroyed in 1941.

Permanent exhibitions about ancient horticultural practices and tools are joined by a big annual one (from April 2005 until early 2006 it's 'A Company of Pleasures: Garden Renaissance at Hatfield House', which explores the world-famous gardens created by the Dowager Marchioness of Salisbury over 30 years). Free activities for children take place during the school holidays. Check the website for details of family events, and to find out more about the

 WALK Walk This Way

That the south bank of the Thames has become a favourite Sunday walk destination for families with young children and accompanying buggies, bikes, scooters and rollerskates has not been lost on the Cross River Partnership (CRP), the body responsible for the regeneration of the area. With funding from the London Development Agency, the CRP has commissioned the **South Bank Employers' Group** to research and publish a series of walking guides. Entitled *Walk This Way*, these cover Riverside London, the South Bank, Bermondsey and nearby areas easily accessed via the footbridges. The guide devised for young people throws in bite-sized

START
BANKSIDE

Shakespeare's Globe

CLINK ST

Clink Prison Museum

Golden Hinde

historical nuggets and interesting facts with the riverside walks.

It works on two levels: 'Above the Thames' takes you on the walks, across bridges and to tourist attractions; 'Below the Thames' is more of a factfile. It touches on (but doesn't lead you down) the sewers, London's lost rivers and the river's extensive wildlife.

Above the Thames three walking routes are suggested. There's a short stroll from the Houses of Parliament across Westminster Bridge then eastward to the National Theatre. The second walk takes you from Somerset House across Waterloo Bridge to Tate Modern.

Walk number three starts at **Shakespeare's Globe**, from where you keep the river on your left as you stroll under the foot of Southwark Bridge, where one wall is covered with an etching depicting the frost fairs in the days when the Thames was 'frozen o'er'. You walk as far as you can beside the river until you are diverted past Vinopolis the wine museum, down Clink Street, listening to the strains of monkish chanting emanating from the **Clink Prison Museum** on your right.

At the **Golden Hinde** you'll see the gardens of **Southwark Cathedral** just ahead. Turn left at the cathedral, taking the pavement studded with winking green and blue lights that goes under London Bridge (this is Montague Close). Keep walking until you emerge on Tooley Street, not far from the **London Dungeon**. From here follow the signs into **Hay's Galleria**. This is a rather odd touristy enclave, where there's a sparkly Christmas shop, stalls selling leather goods, London souvenirs, jewellery and accessories, an often deserted Café Rouge and various other coffee bars. The space is dominated by a ship-like sculpture by David Kemp, called *The Navigators*. A rather more substantial vessel looms outside on the river. Regain the Thames footpath to admire this floating wing of the Imperial War Museum, **HMS Belfast**. Carry on east until you reach Fiona Banner's shiny black

London Dungeon

London Bridge

HMS Belfast

Hay's Galleria

TOOLEY ST

THE QUEEN'S WALK

FINISH

sculptures (*Full Stop Slip Stream*, 2003) and City Hall, the unusually shaped glass-sided headquarters of Mayor Ken Livingstone, the London Assembly and the Greater London Authority. From autumn 2005, a much more exciting landmark for children, the brand new **Unicorn Theatre**, will be the main reason for walking this way.

Walking a few minutes more brings you to **Tower Bridge**. This is what a wealthy American developer allegedly thought he was buying when he invested in London Bridge, back in 1968, and had it shipped, stone by stone, to Arizona. We've still got Tower Bridge, and from the riverside walkway we can mount its steps to stroll over, pausing in the middle to admire its plainer concrete neighbour and river views, before setting off for the Tower of London, the main attraction of **The City** (*see p45*). *The Walk This Way series of guides can by ordered on 7202 6905/www.southbank london.com/walk_this_way/order_booklets.*

Clink Prison Museum. *See p39.*

museum's £40,000 grant from the Heritage Lottery Fund, which will be used to create a multimedia display highlighting the story of the borough of Lambeth. *Buggy access. Café. Disabled access: ramps, toilets. Nappy-changing facilities. Nearest picnic place: Archbishop's Park. Shop.*

Namco Station

County Hall (riverfront entrance), Westminster Bridge Road, SE1 7PB (7967 1066/www.namcoexperience. com). Westminster tube/Waterloo tube/rail. **Open** 10am-midnight daily. **Admission** (LP) free; games prices vary. **Map** p317 M9.
This is one of those dark, noisy hideaways beloved of kids with spare pocket money. There are more than 200 types of video games to waste your 'Nams' on (the unit of currency used to feed them). Bumper cars, Techno Bowling and pool tables lurk downstairs (as do over-18s, who inhabit a bar tuned to the sports channel). This pleasure dome shares its entrance with McDonald's: talk about teen paradise. *Bar. Buggy access. Disabled access: lift, toilets. Nappy-changing facilities. Nearest picnic place: Jubilee Gardens.*

Royal National Theatre

South Bank, SE1 9PX (info 7452 3400/box office 7452 3000/www.nationaltheatre.org.uk). Waterloo tube/rail. **Open** 10am-11pm Mon-Sat. *Box office* 10am-8pm Mon-Sat. Closed 24, 25 Dec, Good Friday. **Tickets** *Olivier & Lyttelton* £10-£38. *Cottesloe* £10-£27. *Standby* £10, £18. *Backstage tours* £5; £4 concessions, under-18s. **Credit** AmEx, DC, MC, V. **Map** p318 M8.
The outdoor space – Theatre Square – has done much to draw families' attention toward Sir Denys Lasdun's landmark concrete theatre complex. It's the home of the terrific Watch This Space season every summer (*see p22*). Indoors, too, the National is full of bright ideas to secure tomorrow's audiences. Around the ground-floor refresh-

ment area, free exhibitions and music events take place throughout the year. The NT runs a range of education and activity programmes, from half-term shows by visiting theatre companies to school-based initiatives (call 7452 3388 or visit the website for details).
Backstage tours (not suitable for under-sevens) occur three times a day, last an hour and may be booked at the information desk (£5, £4 under-18s). Tours take in the rehearsal rooms, workshops where costumes and props are made, dressing rooms and the stage, where the guide demonstrates some of the exciting items of stage machinery like the flying harnesses. *Café. Disabled access: lift, toilets. Nappy-changing facilities. Nearest picnic place: Bernie Spain Gardens. Restaurants. Shop.*

Saatchi Gallery

County Hall (riverfront & Belvedere Road entrances), SE1 7PB (7823 2363/www.saatchi-gallery.co.uk). Westminster tube/Waterloo tube/rail. **Open** 10am-8pm Mon-Thur, Sun; 10am-10pm Fri, Sat (last entry 45mins before closing). **Admission** £9; £6.75 concessions, 5-16s; £5.50 pre-booked groups; free under-5s; £26 family (2+2). **Credit** MC, V. **Map** p317 M9.
A great deal changed at the Saatchi during 2005. Marking the gallery's 20th anniversary (although it's only been in this location since 2002), the eponymous Charles Saatchi removed all the famous installations and replaced them with paintings. 'The Triumph of Painting', which will be exhibited in three stages throughout 2005 and 2006, will celebrate both established painters from the last 30 years or so and new young painters.
The Saatchi Gallery's education department works hard to encourage visits from school groups, and offers an incredibly cheap rate of entry to Lambeth schools. It also runs the Schools Art Prize, which, in 2005, will reflect the Triumph of Painting Series. Schools compete for a £15,000 prize, with a proportion of this money going directly to the

creator of the winning artwork (last year the winner was Louise Kerr of Northwood School, Middlesex). To get your school involved, contact the education department on 7823 1461. Entries should be in by 31 December 2005 and winners are announced on 1 February 2006. *Buggy access. Nearest picnic place: Jubilee Gardens. Shop.*

BANKSIDE

The riverside between London Bridge and Blackfriars Bridge, once the epicentre of bawdy Southwark, is still popular with tourists, who come these days for the history and culture. It's a far cry from the Bankside presided over by various Bishops of Winchester, who made money fining the women of easy virtue who used to ply their trade here. All that remains of the Palace of Winchester, home of successive bishops, is the rose window of the Great Hall on **Clink Street**.

The parish church during Shakespeare's time was St Saviour's, known since 1905 as **Southwark Cathedral**. It sits modestly away from the river, whereas the **Millennium Bridge** provides a pedestrian carriageway to the puffed-up competition across the water, namely St Paul's (*see p52*), from in front of **Tate Modern**. The wonkily ancient terrace of houses between Tate Modern and the Globe is owned by Southwark Cathedral. Sir Christopher Wren stayed in one of them during the building of St Paul's.

Borough Market, hard by Southwark Cathedral, is a top tourist attraction likely to become even more attractive to foodie visitors once the renovations are complete. This area south of the river had terrible associations for Charles Dickens, whose debtor father was imprisoned in Marshalsea prison, which once stood near Borough High Street, but was destroyed long ago.

Bramah Museum of Tea & Coffee

40 Southwark Street, SE1 1UN (7403 5650/ www.bramahmuseum.co.uk). London Bridge tube/ rail. **Open** 10am-6pm daily. **Admission** £4; £3.50 concessions; £10 family (2+4). **Credit** AmEx, MC, V. **Map** p317 P8.
Edward Bramah, who knows a thing or tea about brewing the perfect cuppa, runs this well-to-do museum. The displays and exhibitions constitute an informative tribute to the history of top hot beverages, with all sorts of forgotten tales about the tea trade's power to influence the course of history. Enjoy a lovely cup of tea at any time in the café (you don't have to visit the museum), plus scones, muffins and cakes if you're peckish.
Buggy access. Café. Disabled access: toilets. Nearest picnic place: Southwark Cathedral Gardens. Shop.

Clink Prison Museum

1 Clink Street, SE1 9DG (7403 0900/www.clink.co.uk). London Bridge tube/rail. **Open** *June-Sept* 10am-9pm daily. *Oct-May* 10am-6pm daily. **Tours** hourly when

available. **Admission** £5; £3.50 5-15s, concessions; free under-5s; £12 family (2+2). *Tours* £2. **Credit** MC, V. **Map** p318 P8.
A dangling cage containing a rotting corpse effigy announces the grisly presence of this prison exhibition. The original Clink (so called, it's said, because the inmates clanked their chains) was owned by the Bishops of Winchester from the 12th to the 18th centuries. Thieves, prostitutes and debtors served their sentences within its walls. It was demolished in 1780, but the foundation walls remain. Visitors walk past reconstructed cells with squeaking rats and raddled-looking speaking waxworks, and learn about hideously long incarcerations and torture methods. There's an opportunity for the kids to get hands on at the end, with execution blocks, fetters and foot crushers, thumb screws and chains, 70 per cent of which are original. There are plans afoot to revamp the Clink and improve its displays – check the website for details.
Buggy access. Nearest picnic place: Southwark Cathedral Gardens. Shop.

Golden Hinde

St Mary Overie Dock, Cathedral Street, SE1 9DE (0870 011 8700/www.goldenhinde.co.uk). Monument tube/London Bridge tube/rail. **Open** daily, times vary; phone for details. *Tours* phone for times. **Admission** £3.50; £3 concessions; £2.50 4-13s; free under-4s; £10 family (2+3). *Tours* (price includes entry) £4.50; £3.50 4-13s; free under-4s; £15 family (2+3). **Credit** MC, V. **Map** p319 P8.
Children love this handsome replica of Sir Francis Drake's 16th-century flagship. It was built in 1973 to commemorate the admiral-pirate's 400th birthday, after which it sailed to San Francisco. The main gun deck can't be more than 3ft (0.9m) high. The present 'crew' are actors who dress up and shout a lot. Weekends see the ship swarming with pirate children, as the birthday party service is as popular as ever. When it hasn't been taken over by cutlass-wielding youths, the five levels, recreated in minute detail, are fascinating to explore, but there can be no doubt that most of the ship's income comes from its child-friendliness. 'Living History' overnighters (April to September) are hugely popular with families and school groups, all of whom have to book ahead to live the Tudor life at sea. These take place on a Friday and cost £34 per child or adult, costumes and entertainment provided – bring a sleeping bag. The best time to visit is during the school holidays, when there are frequent storytelling sessions, and pirate and Peter Pan workshops (check the website for details). Pirate parties cost from £250 for 15 children and should be booked well ahead.
Nearest picnic place: Southwark Cathedral Gardens/ riverside benches. Shop.

HMS Belfast

Morgan's Lane, Tooley Street, SE1 2JH (7940 6300/ www.iwm.org.uk). Tower Hill tube/London Bridge tube/rail. **Open** *Mar-Oct* 10am-6pm daily. *Nov-Feb* 10am-5pm daily. Last entry 45mins before closing. **Admission** (LP) £8; £5 concessions; £3 disabled; free under-16s (must be accompanied by an adult). **Credit** MC, V. **Map** p319 R8.
This 11,500-ton World War II battlecruiser now enjoys a peaceful retirement on the Thames, her only distraction being the hordes of children that clamber over her decks at weekends and school holidays (*see also p31* **The best: Diversions on the South Bank**). Guided tours take in

Around Town

City Hall. See p43.

all nine decks, from the bridge to the boiler room, visiting the galley, sick bay, dentist, NAAFI canteen, mess deck and the permanent exhibition entitled 'HMS *Belfast* in War and Peace'. The guns that destroyed the German battleship *Scharnhorst* in 1943 and supported the D-Day landing a year later are, literally, a big attraction. There's usually a queue to climb into the port deck Bofors gun, which enthusiasts can swivel, elevate and aim.

The 'kip in a ship' experience is for groups of up to 50 children (schools and youth groups usually book these), who get to sleep in the original sailors' bunks for up to three days. Accompanying adults take the officers' cabins. Check the website for a full calendar of weekend and school holiday activities, including HMS *Belfast*'s role in the SeaBritain celebrations, and October's Commonwealth festivities. Although children's buggies can be left on the quarter deck, this attraction is most suited to over-fives. *Café. Disabled access; lift, toilets (check website for limitations). Nappy-changing facilities. Nearest picnic place: Potters Field. Shop.*

London Dungeon

28-34 Tooley Street, SE1 2SZ (7403 7221/www.the dungeons.com). London Bridge tube/rail. **Open** *Sept-June 9.30am-5.30pm daily. July, Aug 9.30am-7.30pm daily.* **Admission** £15.50; £12.25 OAPs, students; £10.95 5-15s; reductions for wheelchair users; free carers, under-5s. **Credit** AmEx, MC, V. **Map** p319 Q8. The Dungeon celebrates 30 gruesome years this year, and judging from the length of the weekend queues outside the Victorian railway arches that have always been its home, it'll be here for a while yet. This world of torture, death and disease is wreathed in dry-ice fog and echoes with blood-

curdling screeches. Costumed actors lurk, ready to jump out on you while you ogle horrors like the Great Plague exhibition: a medley of corpses, boils, projectile vomiting, worm-filled skulls and scuttling rats. Other hysterical revisions of horrible London history include the Great Fire and the 'Traitor Boat Ride to Hell', in which visitors play the part of condemned prisoners (death sentence guaranteed). Easter 2005 saw the unveiling of Britain's first horror mirror maze, the largest mirror labyrinth in the world. Designed by maze master Adrian Fisher, 'Labyrinth of the Lost' is a baffling network of catacombs, created by mirrors. It takes as its theme a mysterious ruined church found during archaeological excavations beneath All Hallows Church, Barking. Live actors and creepy special effects used to pump up the spook value include the 'Lady In Black', a former choirmistress at All Hallows whose ghost was reported on several occasions up to the 1930s.

Little horrors can also have a birthday party here. The price (from £16 per head for the basic package) doesn't seem quite so blood-curdling when you consider it includes a tour of the museum, an hour in the café's games centre, a themed photograph and a well-filled party bag. *Buggy access. Café. Disabled access; toilets. Nappy-changing facilities. Picnic place: Hay's Galleria. Shop.*

Old Operating Theatre, Museum & Herb Garret

9A St Thomas's Street, SE1 9RY (7188 2679/ www.thegarret.org.uk). London Bridge tube/rail. **Open** *10.30am-5pm daily (last entry 4.45pm).* Closed 15 Dec-5 Jan. **Admission** (LP) £4.75; £3.75 concessions; £2.75 6-16s; free under-6s; £12 family (2+4). **No credit cards. Map** p319 Q8.

Climb the spiral stairs in the ancient church of St Thomas to find a 300-year-old herb garret and Britain's only surviving 19th-century operating theatre. This was used between 1821 and 1862, before being boarded up and forgotten about until 1957. Displays of hideous instruments, bits of organs in formaldehyde and a scary child-size operating table are set out alongside bunches and jars of dried herbs in the atmospheric old room. Check the website for details of future school-holiday events, such as the slightly alarming 'Victorian Surgery' demonstration, and to find out if an application for funding to mend the roof has been successful. If it has, the place may close down for a few months, so do ring before visiting.
Nearest picnic place: Southwark Cathedral Gardens. Shop.

Shakespeare's Globe

21 New Globe Walk, Bankside, SE1 9DT (7401 9919/ tours 7902 1500/www.shakespeares-globe.org). Mansion House tube/London Bridge tube/rail. **Open** Box office (theatre bookings, May-Sept 2005) 10am-6pm daily. **Tours** 10am-5pm daily. From May-Sept, afternoon tours only visit the Rose Theatre, not the Globe. **Tickets** £5-£29. *Tours* £9; £7.50 concessions; £6.50 5-15s; free under-5s; £25 family (2+3). **Credit** AmEx, MC, V. **Map** p318 O7.
This reconstruction of the Bard's own theatre, built 100 yards from where the original stood, was the brainchild of actor Sam Wanamaker, who died before it was finished. Tours of the theatre take place all year round, but the historically authentic performances in the 'wooden O' (*Henry V*) run from May to September only. The remains of the Rose Theatre, where many of Shakespeare's early works were originally staged, lie around the corner in the basement of an office block (for details, check out the website: www.rosetheatre.org.uk).
Café. Disabled access: lift, toilet. Nappy-changing facilities. Restaurant. Shop.

Southwark Cathedral

London Bridge, SE1 9DA (7367 6700/tours 7367 6734/www.dswark.org/cathedral). London Bridge tube/rail. **Open** from 8am daily (closing times vary). *Restaurant* 10am-5pm daily. Closed 25 Dec, Good Friday, Easter Sunday. *Services* 8am, 8.15am, 12.30pm, 12.45pm, 5.30pm Mon-Fri; 9am, 9.15am, 4pm Sat; 8.45am, 9am, 11am, 3pm, 6.30pm Sun. **Admission** (LP) *Audio tour* £2.50; £2 OAPs; £1.25 under-16s, students. Donations appreciated. **Credit** MC, V. **Map** p319 P8.
The oldest Gothic building in London, this small but handsome cathedral was one of the few places south of the river that Charles Dickens had a kind word for. He, like us, found it inspirational, despite the fact it was hemmed in by buildings and the screeching railway.
Southwark Cathedral was known as St Saviour's church as far back as the 13th century. It fell into disrepair after the Reformation and parts of it were used as a bakery and a pigsty. In 1905 it was reclaimed as a cathedral. It now has an Education Centre, a shop and a refectory. As well as more recent memorials – including one for the 51 victims of the *Marchioness* riverboat tragedy – there are memorials to Shakespeare (whose brother Edmund is buried here), John Gower (arguably the first English poet) and John Harvard, benefactor of Harvard University. Children are drawn to the scary tomb in the chancel: it's topped by a stone carving of an emaciated body in a shroud. The windows contain images of Chaucer, who set

off on pilgrimage to Canterbury from a pub in Borough High Street, and John Bunyan, who preached locally. Centenary celebrations for 2005 are scheduled to include celebrity organ recitals and a big summer beanfeast with Borough Market next door.
Buggy access. Disabled access: lifts, ramps, toilets. Nappy-changing facilities. Nearest picnic place: gardens. Restaurant. Shop.

Tate Modern

Bankside, SE1 9TG (7887 8000/www.tate.org.uk). St Paul's tube/Blackfriars tube/rail. **Open** *Galleries* 10am-6pm Mon-Thur, Sun; 10am-10pm Fri, Sat. Last admission 45mins before closing. **Admission** free (charge for special exhibitions). **Map** p318 O7.
Visiting this former power station, with its awesome volumes of space, is an event in itself. The architects who converted it left relics of the building's industrial days – the original gantries and lifting gear in the vast Turbine Hall, where the Unilever Series of large-scale commissions are displayed, changing each year. The next in the series will be a new work by Rachel Whiteread (on display from 11 October to 26 March).
Activities for children (*see p31* **The best: Diversions on the South Bank**) are centred mostly on the Still Life/Object/Real Life galleries on Level 3. We particularly enjoy the Memento Mori room and Mark Dion's fabulous *Thames Dig* cabinet, full of everyday objects washed up on the shore below.
Buggy access. Café. Disabled access: lifts, toilets. Nappy-changing facilities. Nearest picnic place: grounds. Restaurant. Shops.

Tate Modern.

Winston Churchill's Britain at War Experience

64-66 Tooley Street, SE1 2TF (7403 3171/www. britainatwar.co.uk). London Bridge tube/rail. **Open** *Apr-Sept* 10am-5.30pm daily. *Oct-Mar* 10am-5pm daily. Last entry 30mins before closing. Closed 24-26 Dec. **Admission** £8.50; £5.50 concessions; £4.50 5-16s; free under-5s; £18 family (2+2). **Credit** AmEx, MC, V. **Map** p319 Q8.

This faded tribute to a London torn apart during the Blitz certainly evokes a feeling of wartime austerity. It hasn't changed in years, but nonetheless attracts a fair number of school trips and tourists. Displays and set pieces take in a BBC broadcasting room, a pub and even a burning street, with battered, pyjama-clad legs poking out of the rubble – the whole effect is chillingly staged to make you feel the action happened moments before. Occasional workshops and special displays take place during school holidays and, at any time, children can have a go at the Britain at War quiz sheets (there's a prize draw for entrants in the school holidays) or try on a variety of wartime hats and uniforms in the dressing-up corner near the 'Women at War' display and the Morrison and Andersen bomb shelters.

Buggy access. Disabled access: toilets. Nearest picnic place: Southwark Cathedral Gardens. Shop.

TOWER BRIDGE & BERMONDSEY

Walking from London Bridge to Tower Bridge takes you to the 13-acre riverside development known as More London, one of many business and leisure projects for architects Foster and Partners. The area's main landmark is **City Hall**, the rented home of the current London government. The ground floors are open to the public, and have changing exhibitions and a café. Outside, the Scoop is a performance space that seats several hundred people. Nearby, the building site that will become the new **Unicorn Theatre** (www.unicorn theatre.com), the first specially designed theatre for children in central London, is attracting regular celebrity sponsorship. The last million or so needed to finish the job is being raised this year: the theatre is scheduled to open in autumn 2005.

Just near Tower Bridge a noticeboard announces when the bridge will next open for tall ships to pass through (it does so about 500 times a year). Further east is the **Design Museum**. It's on Shad Thames, the main thoroughfare behind the wharves. Years ago dockworkers unloaded tea, coffee and spices to be stored in the warehouses now converted to smart apartments and offices.

Up past the Design Museum, across Jamaica Road and down Tanner Street, is historic Bermondsey Street, site of Zandra Rhodes's **Fashion & Textile Museum**. Nearby, St Saviour's Dock was a place of execution for pirates. Once this part of Bermondsey was all slimy tidal ditches surrounding a nasty

neighbourhood called Jacob's Island. Charles Dickens, appalled by conditions here, chose it as the place for Bill Sykes to meet his end in *Oliver Twist*. Bermondsey Square, further south, is all Starbucks and delis now, but the Friday antiques market (4am-2pm) has been around awhile. For decades Bermondsey was know as Biscuit Town, because of the preponderance of confectionery factories in this part of Southwark. Sadly for Jammy Dodger fans, the last biscuit factory, Peek Freans, closed down in 1989.

Design Museum

28 Shad Thames, SE1 2YD (7403 6933/ www.designmuseum.org). Tower Hill tube/London Bridge tube/rail/47, 100, 188 bus. **Open** 10am-5.45pm Mon-Thur, Sat, Sun; 10am-9pm Fri. **Admission** £6; £4 concessions; free under-12s. **Credit** AmEx, MC, V. **Map** p319 S9.

 LUNCH BOX

For recommended restaurants and cafés in the area, see reviews p160.

Amano Victor Wharf, Clink Street, SE1 9DG (7234 0000).
Auberge 35 Tooley Street, SE1 2PJ (7407 5267).
Azzuro 1 Sutton Walk, SE1 7ND (7620 1300).
Café Rouge Hay's Galleria, SE1 2HD (7378 0097).
Doggett's (pub) 1 Blackfriars Bridge, SE1 9UD (7633 9081).
EAT Oxo Tower Wharf, Bargehouse Street, SE1 9PH (7636 8309).
Festival Square Ground Floor, Royal Festival Hall, South Bank Centre, SE1 8XX (7928 2228).
Film Café Charlie Chaplin Walk, South Bank, SE1 8XR (7960 3118).
Founders' Arms (pub) 52 Hopton Street, SE1 9JH (7928 1899).
House of Crêpes 56 Upper Ground, SE1 9PP (7401 9816).
McDonald's St Thomas's Street, SE1 9RT (7378 6758; County Hall, Westminster Bridge Road, SE1 7PB (7928 1232).
Pizza Express 4 Borough High Street, SE1 9QQ (7407 2995); 24 New Globe Walk, SE1 9DS (7401 3977); The Cardamon Building, 31 Shad Thames, SE1 2YR (7403 8484); The White House, Belvedere Road, SE1 8YP (7928 4091).
Southwark Cathedral Refectory Southwark Cathedral, Montague Close, SE1 9DA (7407 5740).
Starbucks Winchester Wharf, Clink Street, SE1 9DG (7403 0951).
Studio Six 56 Upper Ground, SE1 9PP (7928 6243).
Tate Modern Restaurant 2nd Floor, Tate Modern, SE1 9TG (7401 5014).

Around Town

Millennium Bridge. *See p39.*

A suitably elegant building that mounts exhibitions devoted to design in all its forms. Outside the main building, the Design Museum Tank is a little outdoor gallery of constantly changing installations by leading contemporary designers; it also offers a taster of exhibitions within the museum. The main space has oft-changing temporary shows. Upcoming exhibitions include tributes to architect Cedric Price (1 July-9 Oct) and maverick designer Eileen Gray (24 Sept 2005-8 Jan 2006). The annual 'Designer of the Year' exhibition runs to June 2005.

Every child visiting the Design Museum is given a free Design Action Pack with observation and creativity exercises, including treasure trails of exhibits and a 'Spot the Building' game to identify the architectural landmarks visible from the riverfront terrace (among them the quirkier edifice, such as Foster's 'Gherkin' and Rogers' Lloyd's Building). The museum's acclaimed programme of children's creativity workshops – design-and-make sessions for those aged six to 12 – are now free for all except 12-year-olds, who pay £4 (*see p31* **The best: Diversions on the South Bank**).
Buggy access. Café. Disabled access: lift, toilets. Nappy-changing facilities. Nearest picnic place: Butler's Wharf riverside benches. Shop.

Fashion & Textile Museum

83 Bermondsey Street, SE1 3XF (7403 8664/ www.ftmlondon.org). London Bridge tube/rail. **Open** *June-Sept* 11am-5.45pm Tue-Sun. *Oct-May* 10am-4.45pm Tue-Sun. Last entry 30mins before closing. **Admission** £5; £3 concessions, 5-16s; free under-5s; £13 family (2+2). **Credit** MC, V. **Map** p319 Q8.

This pink and orange museum stands out like a beacon in grubby Bermondsey. It's the first exhibition space in the UK dedicated to the global fashion industry. The grand foyer, with its jewel-inlaid floor, leads to a long gallery and exhibition hall. The core collection comprises 3,000 garments donated by Zandra Rhodes, along with her archive collection of paper designs and sketchbooks, silk screens, finished textiles, completed garments and show videos. Until July 2005, there's a Zandra Rhodes retrospective, entitled 'A Lifelong Love Affair with Textiles'. A Biba exhibition is planned for November. Check the website for details of temporary exhibitions, related workshops, children's fashion-illustration courses and special courses for 14- to 17-year-olds.
Buggy access. Café. Disabled access: lift, toilet. Nearest picnic space: Bermondsey Playground/Leathermarket Gardens. Shop.

THE CITY

The city's historic business centre contains the ghosts of old Londinium.

The great dome of **St Paul's Cathedral**. *See p52*.

Tourists flock to the City of London, the 'Square Mile' of land formerly ringed by a Roman wall and the central reference point from which the West End and East End are defined. Today, the City is London's financial centre, and it is very much a serious place of business rather than entertainment; Londoners rarely visit unless they work in the area. For this reason, the Square Mile is vibrant and bustling during the week, yet something of a ghost town at weekends when an almost eerie calm descends on the pristine streets. Happily for the visitor, the weekend calm offers a more relaxed environment in which to take in the imposing architecture and historical sites. The

City may not be the capital's best place for children but, despite the grown-up atmosphere, there's a wide choice of attractions.

'The Square Mile' was once all of London. It is the oldest settled part of the metropolis and beneath the streets is an archaeological treasure-trove stretching back to the Stone Age. The remains of Roman Londinium's defences – impressively thick walls built by the Romans in AD 200 to keep out barbarians – can still be seen near Tower Hill and at London Wall. Look out for the **London Stone**, lodged in the side of the Chinese Overseas Bank in Cannon Street. It's thought to be the most historic relic in London, installed during the creation of the walled city.

Part of the City's charm is that the street layout has retained much of its medieval waywardness. Lanes that rambled past wooden shops and houses a thousand years ago now ramble and amble past skyscrapers. Tiny alleyways often lead to hidden surprises: a WWII bomb site transformed into a garden; an ancient church lit by candles; a row of picture-perfect Tudor houses.

In bad weather, the **Museum of London** is the best free family day out in the whole of London. In sunshine, at weekends and outside trading hours, it's possible to cycle with even quite young children around the City from one historic site to another, so sparse is the traffic.

Bank of England Museum

Entrance on Bartholomew Lane, EC2R 8AH (7601 5491/cinema bookings 7601 3985/www.bankofengland. co.uk/museum). Bank tube/DLR. **Open** 10am-5pm Mon-Fri. *Tours* by arrangement. Closed bank hols. **Admission** free; £1 audio guide. **Credit** *Shop* MC, V. **Map** p319 Q6.

The Bank's story, told here, also covers the evolution of the British economy. There's a recreation of an 18th-century banking hall (with bewigged and bestockinged mannequins); displays of old and modern notes and coins; early handwritten cheques; a million-pound note and ponderously impressive documents. Most exhibits are static, but there is an introductory film describing the Bank's origins, and an interactive foreign exchange dealing desk to test the skills of budding entrepreneurs. Dummies move and speak as you pass and a touch screen explains the origin of different features of British bank-notes. Children can fill out age-specific activity sheets (suitable for ages five to eight, nine to 12 and 13 to 16). There are quill and ink writing lessons on the last Tuesday of each month. Several events are planned to commemorate both

Around Town

Barbican Centre.

the 60th anniversary of the end of World War II and the bicentennial of the Battle of Trafalgar. Consult the Museum's website for details. Most popular of all is a perspex case with a hole into which visitors insert a hand to try to lift the gold bar encased within. Its value fluctuates daily (roughly £92,000 as we went to press), but its weight – 28lb (12.7kg) – is shocking to anyone who has ever fantasised about running off with a load of bullion.
Buggy access. Disabled: ramp, toilet. Nappy-changing facilities. Nearest picnic place: St Paul's Cathedral Garden. Shop.

Barbican Centre

Silk Street, EC2Y 8DS (7638 4141/box office 7638 8891/www.barbican.org.uk). Barbican tube/Moorgate tube/rail. **Open** *Box office* 10am-8pm Mon-Sat; noon-8pm Sun. **Admission** free; phone for details of ticket prices for events. **Credit** AmEx, MC, V. **Map** p318 P5.
This arts centre, which also contains 6,500 state of the art flats, is confusing to find your way around, with its labyrinthine walkways, stark tower blocks and windblown plazas. It may not be beautiful, but the range of cultural offerings is certainly big. There are also some pockets of pleasant calm: the fountains in the inner courtyard; the exotic plants and lazy koi carp in the conservatory (open to the public on Sunday afternoons); and the library, with its extensive children's section. You can still see remains of the Roman walls on which the Barbican (originally a fortified watch tower) was built. The building is undergoing a £12.5-million scheme to improve the foyers and entrances, scheduled for completion in spring 2006.
The Barbican Art Gallery, refurbished in 2004, hosts a number of exhibitions throughout the year. Check the website for details of family workshops.

The best child-related reasons to visit the Barbican are the Saturday morning Family Film Club (for families with children aged five to 11), the Family Concerts given by the resident London Symphony Orchestra and the imaginative series of activities throughout the holidays. To join the Family News mailing list and find out more about LSO and Barbican projects for children, call 7382 2333.
Bars. Buggy access. Cafés. Disabled access: lift, toilet. Nappy-changing facilities. Nearest picnic place: Barbican Lakeside Terrace. Restaurants. Shops.

Broadgate Arena

Broadgate Circle, EC2A 2BQ (7505 4068/ www.broadgateice.co.uk). Liverpool Street tube/rail. **Open** *Mid Oct-early Apr* noon-2.30pm, 3.30-5.30pm Mon-Thur; noon-2.30pm, 3.30-6pm, 7-9pm Fri; 11am-1pm, 2-4pm, 5-7pm Sat, Sun. *From early Apr* ring for details. **Admission** £8; £5 under-16s (incl skate hire). **No credit cards**. **Map** p319 Q5.
The smallest and least expensive of London's mushrooming selection of outdoor winter skating rinks is also open for longer than the others, until April. The rink has a circular form, enclosed by a sort of amphitheatre of offices and shops in Broadgate Circle. If you're prepared to support the kids in their first, clinging experience of the ice, skates available here range from child's size six; otherwise, why not consider skating lessons from Jacqueline Harbord. Or check out the live webcam views of the rink from the comfort of your own home. From April to October the rink is dismantled to make space for various corporate events, outdoor drama and music – call for details.
Buggy access. Cafés. Disabled access: lift, ramp, toilet. Nappy-changing facilities. Nearest picnic place: Finsbury Circus. Shops.

College of Arms

*Queen Victoria Street, EC4V 4BT (7248 2762/
www.college-of-arms.gov.uk). Mansion House tube/
Blackfriars tube/rail.* **Open** 10am-4pm Mon-Fri. Closed
bank hols. **Tours** by arrangement 6.30pm Mon-Fri;
prices vary. **Admission** free. **Map** p318 O7.
This beautiful 17th-century house with heraldic gates in
red, black and gold can be seen as you wander over the
Thames across the Millennium footbridge. The college
occasionally holds temporary exhibitions, but the main
business carried on here is the granting of arms by royal
heralds to modern knights and the tracing of family lin-
eages. You can get help with your own family tree by making an appointment, to which you should bring along as
much genealogical information as possible; a fee is charged
for the work according to how long it is expected to take.
Note that the College of Arms doesn't deal with information on clans – that's an entirely Scottish affair, we're told.
*Buggy access. Nearest picnic place: St Paul's Cathedral
Garden. Shop.*

Dr Johnson's House

*17 Gough Square, off Fleet Street, EC4A 3DE
(7353 3745/www.drjohnsonshouse.org). Chancery
Lane or Temple tube/Blackfriars tube/rail.* **Open**
May-Sept 11am-5.30pm Mon-Sat. *Oct-Apr* 11am-5pm
Mon-Sat. Closed 24-26 Dec, 1 Jan, bank hols. **Tours**
by arrangement; groups of 10 or more only.
Admission £4.50; £3.50 concessions; £1.50 under-18s;
free under-10s; £10 family (2+unlimited children).
Tours free. *Evening tours* by appointment only.
No credit cards. **Map** p318 N6.
Samuel Johnson didn't exactly explode on to the London
literary scene – quite the opposite. All but penniless, he
originally made the move from Lincolnshire to the capital
with the actor David Garrick – the two taking turns on the
one horse they could afford between them – and he was
only able to lodge in this Georgian townhouse (after several years of barely surviving in an Exeter Street attic)
with a £1,500 advance for his then prospective *Dictionary
of the English Language*. The house – where the first edition of the Dictionary was compiled – has been kept as a
testament to Dr Johnson's formidable life.
    The faithfully maintained Georgian interior contain
relics including a coffee cup belonging to his biographer
Boswell, a gout stool and a portrait of Francis Barber,
Johnson's Jamaican-born servant, secretary and close
friend. Make sure you read the information sheets quot-
ing Johnson's gossipy views and peruse the pictures of his
friends – a motley lot of Christians, tarts and 'decayed
tradesmen'. There are four replica Georgian costumes (two
for boys, two for girls) that kids can try on, as well as hats
and other period pieces.
Nearest picnic place: Lincoln's Inn Fields. Shop.

Guildhall

*Gresham Street, EC2P 2UJ (7606 3030/tours
7606 3030 ext 1463/www.corpoflondon.gov.uk).
St Paul's tube/Bank tube/DLR/Moorgate tube/rail.*
Open *May-Sept* 9.30am-5pm daily. *Oct-Apr*
9.30am-5pm Mon-Sat. Last entry 4.30pm. Closes for
functions; call ahead to check. **Tours** by arrangement;
groups of 10 or more only. **Admission** free.
Map p318 P6.
The Guildhall survived both the Great Fire of London and
the Blitz, making it one of the few structures in the City to
date to before 1666. Now it's the seat of local government;

the Court of Common Council meets at 1pm on various
Thursdays each month, in the 15th-century Great Hall
(visitors are welcome; phone for dates).
    You can also visit the Hall when it is not being used for
official business. It's a big, empty space with a vaulted ceiling and marble monuments, but there's little inside to
inspire children other than two wooden statues of Gog and
Magog on the West Gallery. These giants represent the
mythical conflict between Britons and Trojan invaders; the
result of this struggle was the founding of Albion's capital city, New Troy, on whose site London is said to stand.
On the north wall hangs a list of notable trials and grisly
executions. Visits to the Guildhall's enormous medieval
crypt are allowed only in the context of group tours.
    Of more immediate appeal is a room beyond the library
devoted to a collection of watches, clocks and marine
chronometers belonging to the Worshipful Company of
Clockmakers. This small museum contains a range of time-
pieces dating back to the 14th century, including important pieces by John Harrison and the watch Edmund
Hillary wore to the top of Everest. Many of the watches
and clocks are exquisite, and the museum does a good job
of explaining historical developments in the watchmaker's
art. The 700 exhibits include a silver skull watch said to
have belonged to Mary Queen of Scots (though more likely to be of 19th-century vintage), a 14th-century cast-iron
clock and tiny, highly detailed watch keys.
*Buggy access. Disabled access: lift, ramp, toilet. Nappy-
changing facilities. Nearest picnic place: grassy area
by London Wall. Shop.*

✕🍴 LUNCH BOX

*For recommended restaurants and cafés in the
area, see reviews pp161-162.*

Auberge 56 Mark Lane, EC3R 7NE
(7480 6789).
Barcelona Tapas 1A Bell Lane, E1 7LA
(7247 7014); 1 Beaufort House, St Botolph
Street, EC3A 7DT (7377 5111).
Browns 8 Old Jewry, EC2R 8DN (7606 6677).
Crypt Café St Paul's Cathedral, Ludgate Hill,
EC4M 8AD (7236 4128).
Chez Gerard 64 Bishopsgate, EC2N 4AJ
(7588 1200).
Gaucho Grill 1 Bell Inn Yard, EC3V 0BL
(7626 5180).
Just the Bridge 1 Paul's Walk, EC4V 3QQ
(7236 0000).
McDonald's 139-142 Cannon Street,
EC4N 5BP (7626 0027); 41 London Wall,
EC2M 5TE (7638 7787).
Pizza Express 125 London Wall,
EC2Y 5AS (7600 8880); 20-22 Leadenhall
Market, EC3V 1LR (7283 5113); 7 St Bride
Street, EC4A 4AS (7583 5126); 8 Russia Row,
EC2V 8BL (7796 0345).
S&M Café 48 Brushfield Street, E1 6AG
(7247 2252).
Tokyo City 46 Gresham Street, EC2V 7AY
(7726 0308).
Wagamama 1A Ropemaker Street, EC2V 0HR
(7588 2688).

Around Town

Guildhall Art Gallery

*Guildhall Yard, off Gresham Street, EC2P 2EJ
(7332 3700/www.guildhall-art-gallery.org.uk). Mansion
House or St Paul's tube/Bank tube/DLR/Moorgate
tube/rail/8, 25, 242 bus.* **Open** 10am-5pm Mon-Sat
(last entry 4.30pm); noon-4pm Sun (last entry 3.45pm).
Admission £2.50; £1 concessions; free under-16s.
Free to all after 3.30pm daily, all day Fri. **Credit**
(over £5) MC, V. **Map** p318 P6.

This high-class but under-frequented gallery allows families ample crowd-free opportunities to see famous artworks. Opened in 1999 (the original was destroyed by
bombing in 1941) the collection now seems biscuit-tin
conservative, but when the first gallery opened in the
19th century its daring exhibitions of work by the Pre-
Raphaelites earned it a certain glamorous notoriety. Start
in the basement and you'll see pieces by Dante Gabriel
Rossetti, Holman Hunt, Tissot and others, their lush photographic detail a treat for any visitor enthralled by frocks,
furs and peaches-and-cream complexions. A diptych by
Millais (*First and Second Sermon*) is just one of the paintings of children – this one illustrating the soporific effects
of church attendance. Amen to that. Of the 250 works on
display, highlights include a cluster of paintings of London
dating from the 17th century to the present: pubs in
Peckham, Chelsea pensioners and pre-war coppers all get
a showing. There are small tables and chairs scattered
around the museum, stocked with paper and colour pencils, so that children can sit and draw if the inspiration
takes them. The collection on show is only a small fraction
of the more than 4,000 works owned by the Guildhall.
Digital images of the rest of the collection are available to
view on computer terminals within the museum, but these
aren't always working.

Don't leave without popping down to the Roman
amphitheatre in the museum basement, discovered in 1988
after 2,000 years of neglect and excavated over several
years up to 1998. The remains are preserved in a protective environment and are open to the public. Sections of
stone wall are all that remain, but these have been given
the Hollywood treatment with atmospheric lighting and
eerie music. Unfortunately, the combination of draconian
'hands off' notices placed everywhere and the earnestly PC
tone of the information plaques detracts somewhat from
the impact of the genuinely interesting ruins.

School groups visit free and teachers receive a pack in
advance, detailing themes that accord with the National
Curriculum. A small shop at the entrance has a selection
of remarkably inexpensive prints and stationery.
*Buggy access. Disabled access: lift, toilet. Nappy-
changing facilities. Nearest picnic place: grassy area
by London Wall. Shop.*

The Monument

*Monument Street, EC3R 8AH (7626 2717/www.city
oflondon.gov.uk). Monument tube.* **Open** 10am-6pm
daily (last entry 5pm). **Admission** £2; £1 5-15s; free
under-5s. **No credit cards. Map** p319 Q7.

Most children are only too eager to scamper up the spiral
staircase, which numbers 311 steps, while you trudge after
them, breathlessly trying to explain the Monument's history. At 202ft (65m), the column marks the exact distance
to the bakery in Pudding Lane where the Great Fire of
London broke out in 1666. It was built by Sir Christopher
Wren and, despite the many skyscrapers being built nearby (the construction work and attendant cranes are best
appreciated from the caged viewing platform at the top),

Wesley's **Museum of Methodism**. *See p51.*

still stands out thanks to the golden urn of flames on top.
Children as young as two make it up the stairs independently, and two treats await them for their pains: the view
from the top and a certificate, given out at the bottom, to
commemorate their climbing feat.
Nearest picnic place: riverside by London Bridge.

Museum of London

*150 London Wall, EC2Y 5HN (0870 444 3852/
www.museumoflondon.org.uk). Barbican or St Paul's
tube/Moorgate tube/rail.* **Open** 10am-5.50pm Mon-Sat;
noon-5.50pm Sun (last admission 5.30pm). **Admission**
free. *Exhibitions* £5; £3 concessions. **Credit** *Shop*
AmEx, MC, V. **Map** p318 P5.

The Museum of London makes the city's history – from
prehistoric times to the present – dynamic and appealing
to visitors of all ages, and that's no mean feat. Flint arrow-
heads and fragments of pottery usually rate high on the
yawn scale, yet this museum's London Before London
gallery takes off with an evocative soundtrack, lyrical text
and clever mirror projections. The Great Fire installation,
an imaginative re-creation of the city in flames, has
delighted and frightened children for decades and is still
going strong. More recent times are covered in the World

City gallery, where black and white photographs of royalty and commoners are enlivened by audio accounts of their lives. Look out for the antique model aeroplanes hanging from the ceiling in this gallery; the Lord Mayor's red and gold state coach (still used annually in his Show) parked by the computer terminals. In good weather, the Barber Surgeons' Garden (partly enclosed by the ruined walls of the old Roman fort) is a lovely spot for a picnic; families can also eat packed lunches in the schools' room near the entrance.

A new wing will be opening in November 2005 and the existing Saxon, Medieval and Tudor galleries will be closed until the new Medieval London Gallery is unveiled. The exhibits will cover the end of Roman rule to the accession of Elizabeth I in 1558. Many of the archaeological finds will never have been seen before.

The museum also holds regular demonstrations and workshops in which kids can sample such aspects of old-London life as Roman parlour games and Victorian household chores. During weekends and school holidays there's no knowing who you might run into, or what you might end up doing. We've met Roman maidservants and Victorian shopkeepers here in the past.

Buggy access. Café. Disabled access; lift, toilet. Nappy-changing facilities. Nearest picnic place: Barber Surgeons' Garden. Shop.

Museum of Methodism & John Wesley's House

Wesley's Chapel, 49 City Road, EC1Y 1AU (7253 2262/www.wesleyschapel.org.uk). Moorgate or Old Street (exit 4) tube/rail. **Open** 10am-4pm Mon-Sat. Closed bank hols. **Tours** ad hoc arrangements on arrival; groups of 10 or more must phone ahead. **Admission** free; £2 donations requested. *Tours* free. **Credit** *Shop* MC, V. **Map** p319 Q4.

This lovely chapel, with its deep, gated courtyard ringed by Georgian buildings, is a haven from the thunderous traffic of City Road and known to Methodists worldwide as 'the Cathedral of World Methodism'. It was built by John Wesley in 1778 and his description of it – 'perfectly neat but not fine' – sums up the architecture. Museum displays in the crypt allude to Methodism's beginnings. Hogarthian prints portray the effects of poverty, alcoholism and moral degradation in 18th-century England.

 WALK Ghosts of the Old City

Even a child with no particular appetite for history and a positive distaste for walking can be lured on to a tour with talk of ghosts, ghouls and the shadowy possibility of seeing something spooky after dark.

This is not the primary aim of **London Walks'** guided tour, of course. Like other tours in the company's repertoire, the theme – along with the use of costumed actors – helps to bring architecture to life. An official tour of **St Paul's Cathedral** may leave you with a hazy idea of construction dates and the identity of various statues. But listening to 'Shaughan', a white-faced spectre in swirling black cape, talk about a certain ghost in the belltower, leaves you with a magpie collection of more intriguing facts. For example, the cathedral's architect, Sir Christopher Wren, was a Freemason and the golden fruits on each pinnacle of the roof are sculpted pineapples – the Masonic symbol of hospitality. And was there really a ghost that disappeared into the wall and reappeared higher up? There was certainly building work that uncovered a door behind the brick wall in that very place, and behind that door was a hitherto undiscovered staircase.

Shaughan's path around the City takes in many quaint alleyways, with names that recall their historical significance (Ave Maria Lane, Amen Court and The King's Wardrobe, for instance), but these are not as darkly terrifying as the walk's organisers might wish. The City and its monuments are remarkably well lit at night – a pleasing condition for young photographers. No, the dark aspects of the tour are all psychological. Many of them relate to the brutal goings-on at Newgate Prison. This jail stood on the site of what is now the Old Bailey (Central Criminal

Court, corner of Newgate Street and Old Bailey, EC4), and the execution of its inmates by hanging, evisceration and dismembering provides some of the grisliest tales of this tour.

At other moments Shaughan's theatrical talents lighten the mood with jokes, songs, poems and a healthy dose of scepticism. 'Scratching Fanny' was a charlatan who invented a knock-knock ghost to relieve the gullible of their coppers. But what of the poltergeist at the Viaduct Tavern (126 Newgate Street, EC1, 7600 1863), which invariably puts off walkers' dogs? (Too bad we had no canine company to test this assertion.) Most curious of all are the stories of apparitions floating between the floors of buildings. In the case of the 12th-century **St Bart's Hospital**, regular reports by patients and nursing staff of a pair of feet below the ceiling of one ward and a head and torso above the floor of the one above are attributed to the City's gradual sinking. This striking archaeological fact is best appreciated as you stand on the former graveyard of the church around the corner, where you are liable to stub your toe on the last few inches of the gravestones that still protrude above the grass. Do ghosts really occupy the same air space that they trod 800 years ago?

This is a walk that leaves you with a lot of questions – and it's no use pestering the erudite Shaughan, for after a cheerful pointer towards the one City pub that is open at weekends, he is off, cape billowing eerily behind him as he recedes into the night, promising more walks, as detailed on the leaflet.

For more guided, themed rambles around the capital, contact **London Walks** (7624 3978, www.walks.com).

Around Town

Tower of London. *See p52.*

John Wesley experienced a moment of grace that persuaded him to devote his life to serving God and helping the poor, and his rigorous and methodical programme of prayer, fasting and lifestyle led to him being dubbed a 'Methodist'. Artefacts on show in the preacher's house may be examined as part of the ad hoc tours given by stewards. These are naturally more lively than the museum and its missionary memorabilia; the house has been sympathetically restored and shows a kitchen with a range and no running water, and a bedroom with a tiny four-poster bed. In the study is a 'chamber horse' – if Wesley's foreign preaching tours did not offer enough equestrian exercise, this curious bouncing chair was supposed to simulate a good gallop.

Through the windows you can see Bunhill Fields, once set aside for victims of the Great Plague, but because it remained unconsecrated, became a dissenters' graveyard. Cross the road to wander through this secret garden, with its mossy graves tilted at odd angles and its memorials to nonconformists such as William Blake, Daniel Defoe and members of Oliver Cromwell's family.
Buggy access. Disabled access: lift, toilet. Nappy-changing facilities. Nearest picnic places: enclosed courtyard at entrance; Barber Surgeons' Garden; Bunhill Field Cemetery. Shop.

Postman's Park

Between King Edward Street & Aldersgate Street, EC1R 4JR (7374 4127/www.cityoflondon.gov.uk). St Paul's tube. **Open** 8am-dusk daily. **Admission** free. **Map** p318 O6.

Named for its proximity to a large sorting office (long since demolished), this green space is most famous for its Heroes' Wall, a canopy-covered expanse of ceramic plaques, inscribed in florid Victorian style, that pay tribute to ordinary people who died trying to save others. 'Frederick Alfred Croft, Inspector, aged 31,' begins one typical thumbnail drama. 'Saved a Lunatic Woman from Suicide at Woolwich Arsenal Station, But was Himself Run Over by the Train, Jan 11, 1878.' Many of the dead heroes were children who tried to rescue drowning companions; their fates offer gruesome morals for their modern peers.
Buggy access.

St Bartholomew's Hospital Museum

West Smithfield, EC1A 7BE (7601 8152). Barbican or St Paul's tube. **Open** 10am-4pm Tue-Fri. Closed for Christmas, Easter, bank hols. **Tours** 2pm Fri. **Admission** free. *Tours* £5; £4 concessions; accompanied children free. **No credit cards**. **Map** p318 O6.

One of London's medieval hospitals, St Bartholomew's reminds modern medical students that theirs is a fairly new science. St Bart's was built in 1123 by Rahere, a courtier of Henry I, after a near-death brush with malaria in Rome. The museum recalls the hospital's origins as a popular refuge for the chronically sick. Many sought miraculous cures, but more reliable remedies were rest, good diet and spiritual comfort. Leather 'lunatic restraints', a wooden head used by young would-be doctors to practise their head-drilling techniques (but also, apparently, as a football) and photographs documenting the slow progress of nurses from subordinate drudges to career women make mildly edifying exhibits. Don't miss the huge painting by William Hogarth, through the museum and up the stairs. Hogarth was born in Bartholomew's Close and offered his services free when he heard the hospital governors were about to commission a Venetian artist. His paintings of the Good Samaritan et al illustrate a fascinating range of skin and venereal diseases; quite a talking point.

Buggy access (ramp by arrangement). Café (in hospital). Nearest picnic place: hospital grounds. Shop.

St Paul's Cathedral

Ludgate Hill, EC4M 8AD (7236 4128/www.stpauls. co.uk). St Paul's tube. **Open** 8.30am-4pm Mon-Sat. *Galleries, crypt & ambulatory* 9.30am-4pm Mon-Sat. Closed for special services, sometimes at short notice. *Tours* 11am, 11.30am, 1.30pm, 2pm Mon-Sat. **Admission** (LP) *Cathedral, crypt & gallery* £8; £3.50 6-16s; £7 concessions; free under-6s; £19.50 family. *Tours* £2.50; £1 6-16s; £2 concessions; free under-6s. *Audio guide* £3.50; £3 concessions. **Credit** MC, V. **Map** p318 O6.

Looking a bit more dapper following the £5-million facelift of its main façade (part of an ongoing renovation project to mark the cathedral's 300th anniversary in 2008), this famous landmark is bound to impress children with its size and majesty, but its architectural details may well leave them underwhelmed. To prevent little eyes glazing over, you should try to book a tour, during which the practised arts of enthusiastic old retainers will bring the place alive with stories of royal christenings, marriages and deaths.

The architect of St Paul's, Sir Christopher Wren, is buried in the Crypt along with Nelson, Wellington and George Frampton, whose statue stretches out a hand containing a scaled-down replica of his Peter Pan sculpture from Kensington Gardens. Climbing up to the Whispering Gallery in the dome and testing the acoustics has to be the most thrilling part of any visit.

To experience St Paul's as a place of worship, try Choral Evensong at 5pm daily, for heavenly singing (the boys' choir sings on Mondays during term-time).

Buggy access. Café. Disabled access: ramps, lifts, toilet. Nappy-changing facilities. Nearest picnic space: garden. Restaurant. Shops.

St Swithin's Garden

Oxford Court, off Cannon Street, EC4N 5AD (no phone). Monument tube/Bank tube/DLR. **Open** 24hrs daily. **Admission** free. **Map** p319 Q7.

This small, carefully tended walled garden (down a small alley that leads behind an O₂ mobile phone shop) is the burial place of Catrin Glendwr and two of her children. Catrin was the daughter of Owain Glendwr, the Welsh hero whose uprising ended bloodily in 1413. A memorial sculpture is dedicated not only to her, but to the suffering of all women and children in war.

Buggy access.

Tower Bridge Exhibition

Tower Bridge, SE1 2UP (7403 3761/www.tower bridge.org.uk). Tower Hill tube/Tower Gateway DLR. **Open** *May-Sept* 10am-7pm daily (last entry 6pm). *Oct-Apr* 9.30am-6pm daily (last entry 5pm). **Admission** £5.50; £3 5-15s; £4.25 concessions; free under-5s; £14 family (2+2). **Credit** AmEx, MC, V. **Map** p319 R8.

Seeing inside London's most famous bridge is a quite a thrill for many visitors, depending on their age and

enthusiasm for engineering. A lift takes you up to the walk-ways over the river, but the view is partially obscured by the glass inserted into the original ironwork. A video acts out Victorian opposition to the bridge's construction, and period photographs show significant moments in its history, such as the sandy 'beach' created below the bridge in 1934 to entertain Londoners. Once at ground level again, the tour continues in the south tower, where smartly liveried engines slowly turn. Here there are talking animatronic coalmen and buttons to press – some of which start audio commentary on pumps and gaskets in eight different languages. More amusing is a wind-up seat demonstrating hydraulic power and a model that allows you to 'make the bridge go up'. This, after all, is what every visitor would like to see for real: it happens most often in summer (sometimes several times a day). To find out when the next opening will happen, call 7940 3984.

Buggy access. Disabled access: lift, toilet. Nappy-changing facilities. Nearest picnic place: Potters Field/ Tower of London Gardens. Shop.

Tower of London

Tower Hill, EC3N 4AB (info 0870 756 6060/ booking line 0870 756 7070/www.hrp.org.uk). Tower Hill tube/Tower Gateway DLR/Fenchurch Street rail. **Open** *Mar-Oct* 10am-6pm Mon, Sun; 9am-6pm Tue-Sat (last entry 5pm). *Nov-Feb* 10am-5pm Mon, Sun; 9am-5pm Tue-Sat (last entry 4pm). **Tours** *Beefeater tours* (outside only, weather permitting) every 30mins, all day. **Admission** (LP) £14.50; £11 concessions; £9.50 5-15s; free under-5s; £42 family (2+3). *Audio guide* £3. *Tours* free. **Credit** AmEx, MC, V. **Map** p319 R7.

There are so many elements to the Tower of London (which is made up of several towers – Bloody, Beauchamp, Bell and White to name but four) that the best, and most entertaining way, to make sense of it all is to follow a Beefeater. These Yeoman Warders, photogenic in their black and red finery, are genial hosts, and the tales they tell are fascinating: they're a mine of information about the history of the Tower, which has served as a fortress, a palace, a prison and a royal execution site over its 900-year existence. Stories of treason, torture and execution keep their audiences spellbound during the free 40min tour.

Hauntingly familiar, Traitor's Gate, the traditional river entrance to the Tower, was reserved for enemies of the state, and the chopping block on Tower Green, sends a shiver down the spine. The dazzling royal stash (Crown Jewels) are kept in the Jewel House, unsurprisingly, along with some vast pieces of silverware. There's a huge punch bowl that looks like it could serve as a child's bath.

It all gets conspiratorial at the top of the White Tower for the 'Gunpowder Plot Exhibition', which runs from July 2005 for one year. Audiovisual displays tell the Fawkes story and the Royal Armouries pile in with a display all about gunpowder's role through history. Weekends throughout July see costumed presenters re-enacting the Plot. Throughout August swordsmen are cutting and thrusting in a fully armed tournament, 1605-style, on the South Lawn. The tone turns medieval for the August Bank holiday (27-29 August 2005) when horsemen and fighters from the Royal Armouries show off their defensive skills. The Gunpowder Plot comes back to haunt the Tower in October half-term, when the entertainment is all conjecture: 'What would have happened if Guy Fawkes had succeeded?' Only one way to find out… get ye to the Tower.

Buggy access (Jewel House). Café. Nappy-changing facilities. Nearest picnic place: riverside benches; Trinity Square Memorial Gardens. Shops.

HOLBORN & CLERKENWELL

Studied calm with bursts of creativity.

One man's passion: **Sir John Soane's Museum**. *See p57.*

Charles Dickens is less than complimentary about Holborn's law institutions in *Bleak House*. He deems Temple Bar a 'leaden-headed old corporation', and dismisses the High Court of Chancery as that 'most pestilent of hoary sinners'. Pleasantries were never the old man's forte.

The 'pestilent' **High Court** – also known as the Royal Court of Justice – on the Strand, is a familiar sight, being a regular backdrop in television news reports. High-profile civil cases are heard here, and public entry is permitted only for children over 14. Across the Strand lie the labyrinthine **Inns of Court**; worth a wander, if only for the delightful views across the Embankment from the central **Inner Temple Gardens** (open 12.20-3pm Mon-Fri).

While the High Court is London's judicial heart, its veins and arteries run all over the area – from

the legal wig shops on Chancery Lane (bound to inspire a titter or two) to the various historic pubs that have refreshed lawyers for centuries, including the Old Nick (Sandland Street) and Ye Olde Cheshire Cheese (Wine Office Court); indeed, Dickens himself was occasionally known to blow the froth off a couple in the latter.

Another notable man of letters who haunted the area – the legendary diarist Samuel Pepys – is the subject of a permanent exhibition in the diminutive **Prince Henry's Room**. Across the road lies St Dunstan in the West (186A Fleet Street, EC4A 2HR, 7405 1929) where, according to his diaries, Pepys failed in his attempt to grope a lady during a sermon. St Dunstan's clock tower was the first in London to acquire a minute hand still ticking and two motorised giants still emerge on the hour and batter each other with cudgels, much to everyone's enjoyment. Other local churches of note include **St Mary le Strand** (free lunchtime recitals, Wed-Fri) and **St Clement Danes**, restored post-Blitz and now home to an RAF memorial. The architecturally contentious **'Roman' Baths** are nearby (Strand Lane, WC2R 2NA, 7447 6605). Reached via Surrey Street, down an atmospheric alley, the baths are now viewed through a window, unless you make an appointment to come during opening times (2-4pm Wed). Dickens was wont to take a cold plunge in them, and has David Copperfield do the same.

Your time might be more gainfully spent wandering around the three galleries at **Somerset House** – the **Courtauld Institute**, the **Gilbert Collection** and the **Hermitage Rooms** – all of them united by a range of children's activities and workshops, thanks to an excellent in-house Learning Centre.

Similarly accessible is the enigmatic **Sir John Soane's Museum**, one man's unusual catalogue of architecture throughout the ages, which is set beside secluded **Lincoln's Inn Fields**. On the other side is the Royal College of Surgeons' **Hunterian Museum**, re-opened in 2005 with the same wide-ranging collection of medical specimens, but now bolstered by a number of children's activities.

Finally, a stroll up Farringdon Road towards Clerkenwell provides yet another insight into the development of modern medicine: the **Museum & Library of the Order of St John** was once a 16th-century priory for the chivalric knights who were the basis for today's international St John Ambulance aid organisation. The original gatehouse remains, as does the crypt, which predates the 13th-century crypt of nearby **St Ethelreda's** on Ely Place. Elsewhere, Clerkenwell is comprised primarily of new media offices and the gastropubs that fuel them – although young magpies may like to marvel at the display windows of the various diamond merchants in Hatton Garden: they provide a stark contrast to the 'diamond in the rough' stallholders in nearby Leather Lane Market.

Courtauld Institute Gallery

Somerset House, Strand, WC2R 0RN (7848 2526/ education 7848 2526/www.courtauld.ac.uk/gallery). Covent Garden or Temple tube (closed Sun)/Charing Cross tube/rail. **Open** 10am-6pm daily (last entry 5.15pm). *Tours* phone for details. **Admission** £5; £4 concessions; free under-18s, students, registered unwaged. Free to all 10am-2pm Mon (not bank hols). *Annual ticket* £22. **Credit** MC, V. **Map** p317 M7.

Among the exhibitions at Somerset House (*see p57*), the Courtauld offers a fabulous permanent collection, and on a more manageable scale than the National Gallery. In residence is a huge corpus of Impressionist and

Inner Temple Gardens. *See p53*.

post-Impressionist paintings, a range of work by Renaissance artists (including Michelangelo and Leonardo) and some Rembrandt. There is also an East Wing dedicated to contemporary creations by current students at the Courtauld Institute of Art and regular blockbuster temporary exhibitions. While this might all seem light years away from poster paint and double-sided sticky tape, the Learning Centre at Somerset House brings exhibits to life across all three galleries (the Courtauld Institute, the Gilbert Collection and the Hermitage Rooms), with a range of regular Saturday workshops: those in summer 2005 see kids making jewellery based on priceless pieces in the Gilbert Collection (20 Aug) and creating patterned artwork inspired by the 'Circling the Square' exhibition of avant-garde Russian porcelain in the Hermitage Rooms (27 Aug). There are also Thursday Art Start workshops for artistically minded under-fives (7 July-25 Aug). Phone the Learning Centre (7420 9406) for more information.
Buggy access. Café. Lift. Nappy-changing facilities. Shop.

The Gilbert Collection

Somerset House, Strand, WC2R 1LA (7420 9400/ www.gilbert-collection.org.uk). Covent Garden or Temple tube (closed Sun)/Charing Cross tube/rail. **Open** 10am-6pm daily (last entry 5.15pm). *Tours* phone for details. **Admission** £5; £4 concessions; free under-18s, students, registered unwaged. *Annual ticket* £20. **Credit** AmEx, MC, V. **Map** p317 M7.

These extensive displays from the collection of the late, British-born real-estate magnate Sir Arthur Gilbert were given to the nation in 1996. The jewelled curios, gleaming silverware and ornate Italian mosaics are so resplendent that families would do well to don sunglasses before entering. Hands-on activities designed to open up the collection to little ones include the design and creation of everything from mock jewellery to elaborate fabric shields, while 'Exploring Precious Stones' sessions let you ogle crystals through high-powered microscopes. Workshops take place every Saturday (daily during school holidays) and are tailored to illuminate current temporary exhibitions. *Buggy access. Café. Lift. Nappy-changing facilities. Shop.*

The Hermitage Rooms

Somerset House, Strand, WC2R 1LA (information 7845 4630/www.hermitagerooms.co.uk). Covent Garden or Temple tube (closed Sun)/Charing Cross tube/rail. **Open** 10am-6pm daily (last entry 5.15pm). **Admission** £5; £4 concessions; free under-16s, students, registered unwaged. **Credit** MC, V. **Map** p317 M7.

A window into one of the world's greatest museums – St Petersburg's State Hermitage Museum – the Hermitage Rooms exhibit a selection of work from the Old Master, Impressionist and post-Impressionist collection of its Russian progenitor. A display of 'avant-garde porcelain from revolutionary Russia' runs until 30 September 2005. A range of regular weekend and holiday workshops for children are themed according to the current exhibition. *Buggy access. Café. Lift. Nappy-changing facilities. Shop.*

Hunterian Museum

The Royal College of Surgeons of England, 35-43 Lincoln's Inn Fields, WC2A 3PE (7869 6560/ www.rcseng.ac.uk). Holborn tube. **Open** 10am-5pm

WALK Above the law

It may be best known as the law-making and litigation capital of the UK, but there's more in the way of career opportunities in Holborn than funny-looking wigs and wooden hammers alone. Indeed, the area has the potential to inspire future architects, doctors and even writers – as this short and scenic walk will show.

Head down Kingsway from Holborn tube and take a left on to Remnant Street, which leads into **Lincoln's Inn Fields**, an oasis of studious serenity set back from the hustle and bustle of the main thoroughfare. The three fields originally belonged to the hospital of St John and St Giles, which leased them to the Inns of Court. Before the land was developed in the 17th century, the fields had bloody associations – in 1586 Anthony Babington and 13 fellow plotters were hung, drawn and quartered here after being found guilty of plotting to kill Elizabeth I.

Immediately on your left, at No.13 Lincoln's Inn Fields, is **Sir John Soane's Museum**, first port of call for those hoping to foster architectural aspirations in their offspring. Which is exactly what Sir John had in mind when, following his wife's death in 1815, he set about converting his home into a walk-in wonderland of architectural curiosities. Most remarkable is the lingering sense of his playful personality, which permeates not only the exhibits themselves (the juxtaposition of mirrors in the Library Dining Room that suggest a multitude of non-existent rooms, for example) but also the ideology behind them.

After failing to persuade his own sons to enter the architectural profession, Sir John left his museum to the public in the hope that he might convert other people's children to the cause – and who knows how many he's posthumously recruited?

Just opposite, on the south side of the square, the Royal College of Surgeons' **Hunterian Museum** reopened in February 2005 after a £3.2 million overhaul – and there's no better place to inspire a career in modern medicine. Be warned that the collection of specimens – many of them pickled in hundreds of jars, some of them dealing with a variety of gruesome diseases – offer a pretty unflinching montage of mortality.

Finally, turn right on to Chancery Lane, left on to Fleet Street and take a first left up Fetter Lane; in adjoining Gough Square is the house of writer Samuel Johnson, literary legend (and a different sort of doctor altogether). It was in this lovely Georgian building – now known simply as **Dr Johnson's House** *(see p47)* – that the great, hugely opinionated man of letters lived between 1747 and 1759, compiling the 41,000 entries for his pioneering *Dictionary of the English Language*. He's the one who wrote about people being tired of London and tired of life. It's probable that small children, by the time they get here, are simply tired of going on culturally stimulating walks around London. Treat them to a fizzy drink and a plate of fish and chips in the atmospheric and very friendly **Tipperary** pub (66 Fleet Street, EC4Y 1HT, 7583 6470), London's first Irish-themed pub, housed in one of the few buildings to survive the Great Fire and, most importantly for us, one of those City pubs that does allow children to come in too.

START Holborn

Sir John Soane's Museum

KINGSWAY

LINCOLN'S INN FIELDS

Lincoln's Inn Fields

NEW SQUARE

CHANCERY LANE

Hunterian Museum

Dr Johnson's House

FINISH

FETTER LANE

FLEET ST

Tipperary

Around Town

Tue-Sat. **Admission** free; donations appreciated.
Credit *Shop* MC, V. **Map** p318 M6.
Following a £3.2 million renovation and a grand reopening in February 2005, the Hunterian Museum in Lincoln's Inn Fields has gone from a labyrinthine collection of chaotically labelled artefacts to an open-minded museum with a broad educational agenda – and it's infinitely more family friendly as a result. Some of the pickled body parts may disturb the very young or squeamish, but the sheer volume of preserved specimen jars will elicit gasps of wonder from grossed-out children. There are amusing exhibits, too. Winston Churchill's false teeth, for example, specially designed so as not to impede that stirring lisp of his, or the skeleton of 'Irish Giant' Charles Byrne, who reached 7ft 7in (2.2m) in socks. Kids can also get a feel for the physician's lot by manipulating a number of model skeletons or trying on a unique skeletal body coat complete with accompanying major organs (not real ones, thankfully) and figuring out which slot in where. In the hands-on activity corners, picture-heavy medical books and carefully placed art and craft materials put everything in perspective. A programme of family workshops for kids aged eight and over was being developed as we went to press, as was a Young Zoologists' Club in association with UCL's Grant Museum, the Horniman in Dulwich (*see p133*) and the Natural History Museum (*see p88*): phone the Audience Development Officer on 7869 6561 for more information. *Buggy access. Lift. Nearest picnic place: Lincoln's Inn Fields. Shop.*

Museum & Library of the Order of St John
St John's Gate, St John's Lane, EC1M 4DA (7324 4070/www.sja.org.uk/history). Farringdon tube/rail/63, 55, 243 bus. **Open** 10am-5pm Mon-Fri; 10am-4pm Sat.

✕🍴 LUNCH BOX

For recommended restaurants and cafés in the area, see reviews p162.

Al's Bar 11-13 Exmouth Market, EC1R 4QD (7837 4821).
Bank Aldwych 1 Kingsway, WC2B 6XF (7379 9797).
Bierodrome 67 Kingsway, WC2B 6TD (7242 7469).
Fryer's Delight 19 Theobald's Road, WC1X 8SL (7405 4114).
Gallery Café basement of the Courtauld Institute Gallery, Somerset House, Strand, WC2R 1LA (7848 2526).
McDonald's 152-3 Fleet Street, EC4A 2DQ (7353 0543).
Pizza Express 99 High Holborn, WC1V 6LF (7831 5305).
Spaghetti House 20 Sicilian Avenue, WC1A 2QD (7405 5215).
Strada 8-10 Exmouth Market, EC1R 4YA (7278 0800).
Wagamama 109 Fleet Street, EC4A 2AB (7583 7889).
Yo! Sushi 95 Farringdon Road, EC1R 3BT (7841 0785).

Closed 24 Dec-2 Jan, bank hol weekends (phone to check). *Tours* 11am, 2.30pm Tue, Fri, Sat.
Admission free; suggested donations for tours £5, £3.50 concessions. **Credit** MC, V. **Map** p318 O4.
These days the Order of St John is usually associated with those nice folk who revive the swooners at sweaty stadium gigs, but it began with the crusaders in 11th-century Jerusalem. The Order has been chasing disease and pestilence ever since, and this museum gives an insight into the history not only of the knights, but also of the development of medicine. Exhibits are divided between a static collection of antiques (from holy relics to full suits of armour) and a brighter and more interactive room that showcases the Order's medical history. Here surgical models and tools of the trade (some of them satisfyingly gruesome) are displayed, as well as a primitive wooden ambulance (essentially a wheelbarrow). The museum is set beside St John's Gate, an evocative Tudor stone edifice and part of the original priory, and if you take the grand tour you'll see the extant 12th-century crypt. There's an annual roster of temporary exhibitions (most recently concerning the 500-year history of the priory itself), as well as year-round activity trails for younger groups. Meanwhile, those whose idea of 'activity' is actually joining up can become (depending on their age) Little Badgers or Cadets – membership is free (you only pay for the uniform) and the young lifesavers receive first-aid training, with exams at the end of it.
Buggy access (not tours). Shop.

Prince Henry's Room
17 Fleet Street, EC4Y 1AA (7936 4004). Temple tube (closed Sun)/11, 15, 172 bus. **Open** 11am-2pm Mon-Sat. Closed bank hol weekends. **Admission** free; donations appreciated. **Map** p318 N6.
This ornate, oak-panelled room is one of few in central London to have survived the Great Fire of 1666. The original Jacobean plaster ceiling is immaculately preserved, and is a popular subject for sketches by architecture students. Originally used by lawyers of Prince Henry, eldest son of King James I, the room was built in 1610 – the same year that the 14-year-old Henry became Prince of Wales. Four years later he died of typhoid, and it was his brother who succeeded to the throne as Charles I. The rest of the building – now an office – was once a tavern called the Prince's Arms, which happened to be a favoured haunt of the diarist Samuel Pepys. So it is that the cases in Prince Henry's Room actually display a range of Pepys memorabilia, including original portraits, newspaper clippings and – of course – extracts from his famous chronicle of 17th-century life. Kids already predisposed towards this portion of history will enjoy it, but don't expect the place to inflame younger imaginations.

St Clement Danes
Strand, WC2R 1DH (7242 8282). Temple tube (closed Sun)/1, 171, 172 bus. **Open** 9am-4pm Mon-Fri; 9am-3pm Sat, Sun. Closed bank hols. **Admission** free; donations appreciated. **Map** p318 M6.
No longer believed to be the church namechecked in the popular nursery rhyme 'Oranges and Lemons', St Clement's nonetheless does have bells – they ring in an annual ceremony that involves children from the local primary school choosing from a mountain of citrus fruits, as well as four times daily (9am, noon, 3pm, 6pm). They were silenced when the church, rebuilt by Christopher Wren (a fourth incarnation since it was founded in the

Somerset House.

Sir John Soane's Museum

*13 Lincoln's Inn Fields, WC2A 3BP (7405 2107/
education officer 7440 4247/www.soane.org).
Holborn tube.* **Open** 10am-5pm Tue-Sat; 10am-5pm,
6-9pm 1st Tue of mth. Closed bank hol weekends.
Tours 2.30pm Sat. **Admission** *free; donations
appreciated. Tours £3; free concessions, under-16s.*
Credit *Shop* AmEx, MC, V. **Map** p315 M5.
The son of a bricklayer, John Soane was only able to
indulge his passion for collecting artefacts after he
married into money. But it was a passion he then indulged
relentlessly and without prejudice. Far from confining
himself to relics of a specific period, he filled his home with
everything from an Ancient Egyptian sarcophagus to
paintings by his near contemporary, renowned satirist
William Hogarth. The latter's *Rake's Progress* is on
display in a room that also contains several of Soane's own
architectural plans, all nestled together in an elaborate and
utterly charming series of folding doors and walls. It is
such touches of ingenuity that elevate this museum from
a mere cabinet of (admittedly extraordinary) curiosities to
something altogether more beguiling. Regular free
Saturday workshops – mostly aimed at children aged
seven to 11 – cover a range of methods and materials (from
building toy theatres to designing and decorating mock
windows), but all tie neatly into a range of architectural
principles and practices (*see also p55* **Walk**). On the first
Tuesday of every month, you can visit in the evening when
the house is candlelit after dark.
Nearest picnic place: Lincoln's Inn Fields. Shop.

Somerset House

*Strand, WC2R 1LA (7845 4600/www.somerset-house.
org.uk). Covent Garden or Temple tube (closed Sun)/
Charing Cross tube/rail.* **Open** 10am-6pm daily
(last entry 5.15pm). *Courtyard & River Terrace*
Apr-Sept 10am-10pm daily. **Tours** phone for details.
Admission *Parts of South Building, Courtyard &
River Terrace free. Exhibitions vary; phone for details.*
Credit MC, V. **Map** p317 M7.
One small step into the vast courtyard of Somerset House
is one giant leap into the 18th century, with the elaborate
stone edifices that surround the courtyard shutting out all
but a whisper of traffic from the busy Strand. Erected on
the site of a long-demolished Tudor palace, this grand
exercise in neo-classical architecture – originally designed
to house public offices – is now home to three of the UK's
finest galleries: the Courtauld Institute Gallery, the Gilbert
Collection and the Hermitage Rooms (*see pp54-55*).
Somerset House is a family destination in and of itself, most
notably throughout December and January, when the
courtyard is transformed into a jolly ice rink, which, vast
crowds notwithstanding, is idyllic at Christmas time.
Equally inspired is the big square fountain in the
centre, which entertains everyone with waterjets that
dance in formation every hour. On hot summer days,
children love running down the brief corridors of water –
even more so when the corridors collapse and everyone
gets a bit of a soaking. The courtyard also provides a stage
for a programme of free family events during the summer
holidays, including puppet shows, storytelling and creative
workshops (the Family Free Time Festival runs from
24-27 July 2005). Throw in riverside views from the front
of the building and a couple of colourful cafés, and you'll
find your day has been pretty much planned for you.
*Buggy access. Cafés. Lift. Nappy-changing facilities.
Restaurant. Shops.*

ninth century), was gutted by air raids in 1941. After the
war, the Royal Air Force campaigned for its restoration,
and on 19 October 1958 St Clement's was reconsecrated
as the Central Church of the RAF. Spitfires may not get
young pulses racing as they did 60 years ago, but there is
a wealth of RAF memorabilia on display. The statue of
Arthur 'Bomber' Harris, the man behind the air force's
brutal raids on Dresden (so poignantly commemorated in
2005), arouses mixed feelings.
Buggy access.

St Ethelreda's

*14 Ely Place, EC1N 6RY (7405 1061). Chancery Lane
tube/Farringdon tube/rail.* **Open** 8.30am-7pm daily;
phone to check. **Admission** *free; donations
appreciated.* **Map** p318 N5.
Despite its postcode, Ely Place is, in fact, through a quirk
of legal history, under the jurisdiction of Cambridgeshire.
Much like the Vatican, it is even subject to its own laws
and precedents. Built by Bishop Luda of Ely in the 13th
century, it's the oldest Catholic church in Britain and serves
as London's only standing example of Gothic architecture
from that period. It survived the Great Fire of London
thanks to a change in the wind. These days the upper
church – rebuilt after damage caused by the Blitz – is used
for services. Ely Place is where David Copperfield meets
Agnes Wakefield in the Dickens novel. The strawberries
grown in the church gardens receive commendation in
Shakespeare's *Richard III*. In recognition of this, Ely Place
stages an annual Strawberrie Fayre festival, which takes
place on 26 June 2005, with plenty of traditional fun and
games and all proceeds going to charity.
Buggy access. Café (noon-2pm Mon-Fri).

Around Town

BLOOMSBURY & FITZROVIA

Coram's gifts to the children mean it's not purely academic round here.

British Museum.

Practically synonymous with the louche group of writers and artists who once colonised its townhouses, **Bloomsbury** might have lost some of its early 20th-century celebrity status. Nevertheless it's a fascinating place to visit, with a wealth of interesting architecture, unexpected green spaces and world-class museums.

Literature students can spend hours spotting blue plaques on the former residences of Virginia Woolf, WB Yeats, Edgar Allan Poe, Anthony Trollope and so on. The house where Charles Dickens spent part of his childhood is now a museum (*see p60*). Everyone is enthralled by the treasures of the **British Museum**, with children always keen to press their noses against the glass cabinets containing dead pharaohs, nicely painted up with gold hieroglyphs. On rainy days there's often a chance to practise copying those ancient pictorial squiggles at the less well-known **Petrie Museum of Egyptian Archaeology**.

The Petrie is one of half a dozen small venues of cultural interest in the area. Most appealing is probably the **Foundling Museum**, a memorial to London's abandoned children, which opened in 2004 and has been nominated for the prestigious Gulbenkian Prize for Museum of the Year. Its location is appealing as well: right next to the extensive inner city park, **Coram's Fields**, named after benefactor Thomas Coram.

Other names prominent in Bloomsbury and Fitzrovia are those left by the fourth Earl of Southampton, who built **Bloomsbury Square** around his house in the 1660s (none of this architecture remains), and the Russells – or Dukes of Bedford – who intermarried with the Southamptons and developed what has been a rural area dedicated to pig breeding into one of London's first planned suburbs. It was during the 18th and 19th centuries that the lovely Georgian squares and elegant terraces here were built in an easy-to-navigate grid style.

Amid so many delightful historic buildings, it would be easy to ignore the concrete Brunswick Centre, but this modernist development is home to the **Cartoon Art Trust Museum** and a plethora of handy, cheap eating venues.

Fitzrovia is less well defined than Bloomsbury. Its highlight, Fitzroy Square, is disappointingly paved over rather than verdant, although its main visitor attraction, **Pollock's Toy Museum**, is a hidden gem for adult collectors, and has weekly puppet shows and a great shop for younger visitors. The computer-game stores of **Tottenham Court Road** provide treats better suited to the 21st century.

More edifying is a tour of the university and medical buildings to the east of Tottenham Court

Road. Teenagers not done their homework yet? Entrance to these hallowed portals can only get more competitive. At their heart is **Senate House**, the towering monolith on Malet Street which housed the Ministry of Information in World War II and inspired George Orwell's Ministry of Truth in *1984* – its sheer height is awesome. Meanwhile, hordes of students thronging the streets seem happy enough in this peculiarly intellectual district, and if the burden of their studies gets too much, there are plenty of affordable bars and cafés in which to take refuge.

British Library
96 Euston Road, NW1 2DB (7412 7332/education 7412 7797/www.bl.uk). Euston or King's Cross tube/ rail. **Open** *9.30am-6pm Mon, Wed-Fri; 9.30am-8pm Tue; 9.30am-5pm Sat; 11am-5pm Sun, bank hols.* **Admission** *free; donations appreciated.* **Credit** *Shop* MC, V. **Map** p317 K3.

Once part of the British Museum but now housed in state-of-the-art premises close to King's Cross, the British Library has a staggering collection of 150 million items – growing all the time – spread over 388 miles (625km) of shelves in 1.2 million sq ft (112,000sq m) of space. Each year the library receives a copy of everything that is published in the UK and Ireland, including maps, newspapers, magazines, prints and drawings.

There is just one problem: the collection is strictly for reference and access is tricky. The only books you are likely to see as a casual visitor (especially one with minors in tow) are those housed in a six-storey, glass-walled tower at the centre of the building. This is the library of George III, known as the King's Library, and its impressive leather spines appear to be Bibles, medieval religious texts and other such august items.

Unsurprisingly, then, the British Library's most popular space is the John Ritblat Gallery. Here you can see the institution's treasures under glass: the Magna Carta or Great Charter of 1215, Leonardo da Vinci's notebook, the Lindisfarne Gospels of AD 721. Some of the illustrations are inspiring, their golden, illuminated letters twinkling in the subdued light. This is one of the frustrations associated with paper conservation, however: the whole of the British Library is necessarily gloomy. Children may enjoy extracts from the National Sound Archive – Kalahari Bushmen performing a healing dance, Bob Geldof at LiveAid or the quavery voice of Florence Nightingale through public headphones. Other items of interest include The Beatles' scribbled lyrics alongside recordings of their songs. The long wall flanking the library's ground floor café holds its philatelic collection – over 80,000 stamps from around the world on view in pull-out cases.

The major exhibition for 2005 (20 May-2 Oct) celebrates the 200th anniversary of the birth of Hans Christian Andersen. Designed by award-winning children's theatre company Theatre-rites, it will feature a range of activities for young visitors, including storytelling and puppets. During the summer holidays, the company will stage performances intent on immersing children (aged three to eight years) in Andersen's landscapes, stories and mythical characters. The Andersen exhibition is followed by a show about the Nobel Prize (2 Dec 2005-Mar 2006.)

During the summer months the Library stages a variety of musical and theatrical performances in its open-air piazza area – a haven from the thunderous thoroughfare that is the Euston Road. At other times there are regular free demonstrations of bookbinding, printing and calligraphy for children. During holidays, the Education Office organises workshops, activities and storytelling sessions for children aged five to 11 and their families. To join the Education Department's free mailing list, write to the address above, call 7412 7797 or check the website. (For dates and details of all events call 7412 7332.)
Buggy access. Café. Disabled access: lift, toilet. Nappy-changing facilities. Nearest picnic place: St James' Gardens. Restaurant. Shop.

British Museum
Great Russell Street, WC1B 3DG (7636 1555/recorded information 7323 8783/www.thebritishmuseum.ac.uk). Holborn, Russell Square or Tottenham Court Road tube. **Open** *Galleries 10am-5.30pm Mon-Wed, Sat, Sun; 10am-8.30pm Thur, Fri. Great Court 9am-6pm Mon-Wed, Sun; 9am-11pm Thur-Sat.* **Tours** *Highlights 10.30am, 1pm, 3pm daily; phone to check. EyeOpener frequently; phone to check.* **Admission** *(LP) free; donations appreciated. Temporary exhibitions prices vary; phone for details. Highlights tours £8; £5 under-11s, concessions. EyeOpener tours free.* **Credit** *Shop* AmEx, DC, MC, V. **Map** p317 K5.

Embodying the Enlightenment concept that all of the arts and sciences are connected, the world-famous collections in this 252-year-old giant are best appreciated in bite-sized chunks. The museum is well known for its Ancient Egyptian artefacts – the Rosetta Stone, the statues of the pharaohs and mummies in glass cases – and Ancient Greek treasures, including the Elgin Marbles. The Celts gallery contains the Lindow Man, killed in 300 BC and preserved in peat ever since.

The restored King's Library was built in the 1820s and its Grade I-listed interior is widely considered to be the finest neo-classical space in London. It now houses a splendid permanent exhibition, 'Enlightenment: Rethinking the World in the 18th Century', a 5,000-strong collection that examines that formative period of the museum's history. Temporary exhibitions planned for 2005 include 'Forgotten Empire: the world of Ancient Persia' (8 Sept 2005-10 Jan 2006), revealing the splendour of this vast empire (550 BC-330 BC) through the art and archaeological remains of its

TOP 5 | Events for kids

British Library
Be entertained by the Theatre-rites celebration of Andersen's tales. *See p59.*

British Museum
Join the Friends to sleepover with mummy. *See p59.*

Cartoon Art Trust Museum
Want to be the next Matt Groening? Check out the workshops here. *See p60.*

Petrie Museum of Egyptian Archaeology
Go all Indiana Jones. *See p63.*

Pollock's Toy Museum
Travel back in time with the special Saturday puppet shows. *See p63.*

Around Town

Pollock's Toy Museum. *See p63.*

rulers. The show will contain some of the finest pieces from the National Museum of Iran. 'Kabuki Heroes on the Osaka Stage (1780-1830)' may be appreciated by teenagers familiar with reality TV and pop idols

If the thought of making your own way round is all too overwhelming, the museum offers sampler tours of its top treasures (starting from the information desk) or EyeOpener tours, which concentrate on specific aspects of the collection, such as Africa, the Americas or Classical. They're not aimed specifically at children, but the volunteer guides are happy for families to dip in and out of them as they like. If you want to join one of the special family EyeOpeners, run twice daily during half-terms and irregularly through the school holidays, book at the information desk on arrival. Museum trails in the Reading Room help families navigate their way through the galleries in a more independent way.

Lasting childhood memories are sure to be the result of a museum sleepover, available only to Young Friends of the British Museum (membership costs £20). Membership also entitles kids to special activities aimed at all age groups, from handling sessions and behind-the-scenes visits with museum curators to lively discussion groups aimed at young teenagers ('Should the Elgin Marbles be returned to the Parthenon?' is a favourite topic). The treasures of the museum are also available for perusal in the souvenir guide (£6) or on the website.

Buggy access. Cafés. Disabled access: lift, toilet. Nappy-changing facilities. Nearest picnic place: Russell Square. Restaurant. Shops.

Cartoon Art Trust Museum

7 The Brunswick Centre, Bernard Street, WC1N 1AF (7278 7172/www.cartooncentre.com). Russell Square tube. **Open** 10am-5pm Tue-Sat. **Admission** free. **Credit** *Shop* MC, V. **Map** p317 L4.

This small, one-room museum, dedicated to collecting and preserving the best of British cartoons, caricatures, comics and animations, features a changing display of works from the Cartoon Art Trust's wide-ranging collection of humorous art. Heath Robinson, Steve Bell and Peter Brookes are among the artists represented in the space. Exhibitions rotate every two months or so, although the calendar for 2005/6 remains unfixed. Perhaps the best things, though, are the museum's workshops and events for young cartoonists (and their excitable guardians).

Children's cartoon workshops (£20/day) and animation workshops (£25/day) are run throughout the year. All the necessary materials are provided (young animators even get a video of their creations sent to them after the workshop) and the range of activities, usually based around popular characters and styles, such as *The Incredibles* or manga, are aimed at all abilities. Age ranges vary according to the workshops, but the free drop-in family-fun days offer something for everyone. The Cartoon Art Trust also runs the Young Cartoonist of the Year competition, awards for which are presented at the Cartoon Awards in October 2005. Note that the Cartoon Museum plans to move to larger premises during 2005; so call before visiting.

Buggy access. Nearest picnic place: Coram's Fields/Russell Square. Shop.

Charles Dickens Museum

48 Doughty Street, WC1N 2LX (7405 2127/ www.dickensmuseum.com). Russell Square tube. **Open** 10am-5pm Mon-Sat; 11am-5pm Sun. **Admission** £5; £4 concessions; £3 5-15s; free under-5s; £14 family (2+5). **Credit** AmEx, DC, MC, V. **Map** p317 M4.

Charles Dickens had a miserable childhood. His family was sent to Marshalsea Prison for debt and, at 12, Charles had to leave school and work in a shoe-polish factory. So, when his career took off after the publication of *The Pickwick Papers* in 1836, Dickens fled his poverty-stricken past and moved to this, the poshest house he could afford. Here he wrote *Oliver Twist* and *Nicholas Nickleby*, and entertained literary friends. The death of his 17-year-old sister-in-law Mary Hogarth, however, put an end to the Bloomsbury idyll. Soon after this event, Dickens moved from Doughty Street to a new home near Regent's Park. Strangely enough, Doughty Street, where he lived for just three years, is now the author's only surviving London residence; the opening of the Charles Dickens Museum on the premises

made certain that it would be full of memorabilia and arte-facts. Its passageways are decorated with paintings of Dickens characters, among them Little Nell, Uriah Heep and Little Dorrit. The rooms are full of Dickens's person-al effects: his lemon squeezer, a walking stick, his snuff box and more. Other displays include his personal letters, original manuscripts and the desk on which Dickens wrote *Oliver Twist*. In the basement there's a short film covering Dickens's life in London, and children's handling sessions, in which kids can write with the same type of quill pen used by the author, are held in the Library most Tuesdays and Wednesdays (11am-3pm, phone ahead).

Special events include readings by costumed actors from the 'Sparkler of Albion' company on Wednesday evenings (6.30pm; ticketed). Museum staff also plan to organise a new children's trail this year, using Dickens's best-known stories such as *Oliver Twist* and *A Christmas Carol*. *Buggy access. Disabled access: ramp. Nearest picnic place: Coram's Fields/Russell Square. Shop.*

Coram's Fields

93 Guilford Street, WC1N 1DN (7837 6138). Russell Square tube. **Open** *May-Aug* 9am-8pm daily. *Sept-Apr* 9am-dusk daily. **Admission** free. **Map** p317 L4.
A visit to the neighbourhood would be incomplete without a stroll through one of London's most famous parks. Established back in 1936, these seven acres (3ha) have become a city institution. Famous long before it became a park, the site dates back to 1747, the year retired sea cap-tain Thomas Coram established the Foundling Hospital for abandoned children (site of the new Foundling Museum, *see below*). After the orphanage was demolished in the 1920s, developers were poised to swoop but happily a cam-paign to turn the site into a children's park was successful.

Coram's Fields is the Elysian fields for children. There are lawns, sandpits, a paddling pool, an AstroTurf foot-ball pitch, a basketball court, a wooden climbing tower, swings, a helter-skelter chute, an assault-course pulley and a city farm, with sheep, goats, geese, ducks, rabbits, guinea pigs and an aviary. Occasionally during the summer, bands and circus performers entertain picnicking families.

Parents love the park because it's safe. It's permanently staffed, and no adults are allowed in the park unaccompa-nied by children. A range of sporting activities from foot-ball and basketball to aerobics and street dance, are all offered free (call the office for a list). Then there's t'ai chi, drama and other activities – some free, some not. A youth centre has free IT courses for 13- to 19-year-olds. The healthy-eating, vegetarian café is now open year round and, to make life easier for parents, there are toilets and shower rooms with disabled facilities, a nursery, a drop-in playgroup, and after-school and holiday play centres. *Buggy access. Café. Disabled access: toilet. Nappy-changing facilities.*

Foundling Museum

40 Brunswick Square, WC1N 1AZ (7841 3600/ www.foundlingmuseum.org.uk). Russell Square tube. **Open** 10am-6pm Tue-Sat; noon-6pm Sun. **Tours** by arrangement. **Admission** £5; £3 concessions; free under-16s. **Credit** AmEx, MC, V. **Map** p317 L4.
Two hundred and fifty years ago, 75 per cent of all chil-dren in London died before they were five years old. Ninety per cent of those raised in the workhouse met the same fate. A few people – notably the philanthropist Thomas Coram – worked to improve the situation. In 1739 Coram estab-lished a 'Hospital for the Maintenance and Education of Exposed and Deserted Children', taking in abandoned infants and caring for them until they were old enough to be apprenticed. The Foundling Museum, which stands in a beautifully restored building adjacent to the original site of the Hospital, tells the story of those children and the adults who campaigned for them. Most prominent of these were William Hogarth, whose support and gifts of paint-ings caused the Foundling Hospital to become established as Britain's first public art gallery, and George Frideric Handel, another foundling governor now honoured with an important collection of his manuscripts and ephemera on the top floor of the museum. More touching, however, is the array of humble keepsakes left with the foundlings – tin hearts, buttons, a piece of shell engraved with the child's name and date of birth, or a scrap of poetry: 'Go

WALK Leafy spaces and concrete jungles

From Russell Square tube station walk down Bernard Street with the **Brunswick Centre** on your left. This shrine to concrete, which does at least have sunny balconies facing Coram's Fields, is also home to the Renoir art cinema, the **Cartoon Art Trust Museum** and many cheap, studenty eating places.

Across Grenville Street, however, the prospect is undeniably more attractive. On Brunswick Square, the award-winning **Foundling Museum** is a worthwhile diversion, and you could spend the whole day in **Coram's Fields** and forget about the rest of the walk altogether.

If you can resist the park, walk down Lansdowne Terrace, then cross over Guilford Street on the south side to **Lamb's Conduit Street**, a quiet and largely pedestrianised enclave full of quirky retailers like Persephone Books (publishers of rare or forgotten fiction in beautiful editions). The Italian restaurant at the north end, Ciao Bella (see p63 **Lunch box**), does huge plates of pasta. The Lamb Bookshop, in the middle of the street, is full of literary bargains that make excellent children's birthday presents.

Wandering westwards along **Great Ormond Street** will give you the opportunity to count your blessings, as you pass the children's hospital famously still benefiting from the royalties accruing to JM Barrie's *Peter Pan*. Medical buildings predominate in this district. Other specialist hospitals provide architectural grandeur on Queen Square, a quiet backwater where public gardens make for a pleasant resting place. Get the kids to spot the cat – a discreet statue in one corner commemorating a local resident. If there is mutiny in the ranks at this stage, at one end of the square, behind the Mary Ward Centre and October Gallery, you'll find a convenient little playground known as the **Old Gloucester Street Gardens**.

From Queen Square you can fiddle through **Cosmo Place**, an alley notable for its china shop (Cosmo China, No.11 – personalised gifts for christenings and weddings are a speciality). This leads you to **Southampton Row**, a busy thoroughfare best avoided unless you feel like splashing out on some handmade paper for future craft activities at Falkiner Fine Papers (No.76).

Russell Square, slightly to the north and quite near the starting point, is a good place to cross. It has been greatly improved by formal landscaping, and the glass-fronted café allows views over the lawns. In summer, the ground-level fountains are the perfect thing for cooling hot feet.

Turn off Montague Place and head through the back door of the **British Museum**, where the ancient world is your oyster. The Great Court offers yet another opportunity to drink coffee (not to mention a chance to practise racing skids on its polished marble floors). Leaving via the porticoed main entrance takes you to the bookish shopping quarter of Coptic Street and Museum Street. It's hard to interest even studious youngsters in these old prints and first editions, but they may be amused by **Playin' Games** (No.33), a toy and games shop on Museum Street. Otherwise stay on Great Russell Street and peer into the historic paint shop, **L Cornelissen & Son** (No.105), which supplies film companies. At the end of the street is **Tottenham Court Road**. Alas, the manor house it is named after is long gone and the flashy plethora of computer-game shops, fast-food outlets and another concrete eyesore in your line of vision (Centrepoint) may send you scuttling to the tube – if you can drag the children away.

Renoir

Coram's Fields

HUNTER ST

LANSDOWNE TERRACE

START

BERNARD STREET

GRENVILLE ST

Russell Square

Foundling Museum

LAMB'S CONDUIT ST

Great Ormond Street Hospital

GREAT ORMOND ST

Russell Square Gardens

RUSSELL SQUARE

SOUTHAMPTON ROW

MONTAGUE PL

British Museum

GREAT RUSSELL STREET

MUSEUM ST

Playin' Games

FINISH — Tottenham Court Road

gentle babe.../And all thy life be happiness and love.' School holidays see a number of artistic events for children with their carers – painting self-portraits or maybe 'improving' the Foundling Museum's lamb, designed by William Hogarth. Sunday 12 June 2005 is the museum's first birthday and a free family day is planned. Call ahead or check the website for details of other regular events. *Buggy access. Café. Disabled access: lift. Nappy-changing facilities. Nearest picnic place: Brunswick Square; Coram's Fields. Shop.*

Foundling Museum. *See p61*.

Petrie Museum of Egyptian Archaeology

University College London, Malet Place, WC1E 6BT (7679 2884/www.petrie.ucl.ac.uk). Goodge Street or Warren Street tube/29, 73, 134 bus. **Open** 1-5pm Tue-Fri; 10am-1pm Sat. Closed 24 Dec-2 Jan, Easter hols. **Admission** free; donations appreciated. **Map** p317 K4.
If the British Museum has all the big Ancient Egyptian showstoppers, the Petrie Museum of Archaeology contains the pieces that made up the minutiae of Egyptian life: make-up pots, grooming accessories, jewellery and, most famously, the world's oldest piece of clothing (a dress that was worn by a teenager in 2800 BC). Some of the collection might be rather heavy going for young children, but there are items that might just take their fancy: for instance, a collection of ancient toys, a rat trap and the coiffured head of a mummy, with eyelashes and -brows still intact. The dim surroundings give the place a wonderfully spooky, tomb-like atmosphere – pick up a free torch from reception and explore the dusty aisles like a true adventurer. In the summer holidays there are family backpacks with themed trails through the museum, and hicroglyphic writing workshops and playschemes, all based around the contents of the collections. Activities such as 'Animals in Egypt' let children handle animal specimens, including giant snake skins. Other events crop up regularly; call ahead to see what's on, or encourage your kids' teachers to visit the website and order packs aimed at 7- to 11-year-olds, to be used in conjunction with a museum visit.
Buggy access. Disabled access: lift, toilet. Nearest picnic place: Gordon Square. Shop.

Pollock's Toy Museum

1 Scala Street (entrance on Whitfield Street), W1T 2HL (7636 3452/www.pollockstoymuseum.com). Goodge Street tube. **Open** 10am-5pm Mon-Sat. **Admission** £3 adults; £1.50 3-16s; free under-3s. **Credit** MC, V.

This intimate, privately run museum takes its name from Benjamin Pollock, who was the last of the Victorian toy theatre printers. Its somewhat ramshackle home is formed of two old houses joined together on the corner of Whitfield Street, and anyone may enter the ground-floor shop, where a pleasing range of said toy theatres, plus other quaintly old-fashioned toys, are on sale. A tour of the upper floors, with their tiny rooms and proudly creaking floorboards, reveals the battered treasures of nurseries that have been carefully and lovingly gathered together from all over the world. Ancient teddy bears, curiously lifelike wax and china dolls, tin cars and planes, and American novelty money boxes that eat up coins are some of the curiosities on show. The nostalgia value of old board games, clockwork trains and Robertson's gollies can hardly be overestimated for adults. For young children, however, the displays can seem hopelessly static and irrelevant. What they enjoy most are the shop and the regular free puppet shows, which tend to be held on Saturdays throughout the year (check the website or phone for dates). Typically performed with beautiful exemplars of the puppet-maker's art and staged with a crackling soundtrack of suitably wistful music (and, of course, a great deal of atmospheric tra-la), these little gems bring the Toy Museum to life. A unique and beguiling experience.
Nappy-changing facilities. Shop.

✖🍴 LUNCH BOX

For recommended restaurants and cafés in the area, see reviews pp162-164.

Apostrophe 216 Tottenham Court Road, W1T 7PT (7436 6688).
Busaba Eathai 22 Store Street, WC1E 7DF (7299 7900).
Ciao Bella 86-90 Lamb's Conduit Street, WC1N 3LZ (7242 4119).
Cigala 54 Lamb's Conduit Street, WC1N 3LW (7405 1717).
Coram's Fields Café Coram's Fields WC1N 1DN (7837 6138).
Court Café British Museum, Great Russell Street, WC1B 3DG (7636 1555).
Fryer's Delight 19 Theobald's Road, WC1X 8SL (7405 4114).
Goodfellas 50 Lamb's Conduit Street, WC1N 3LH (7405 7088).
Lino's Café 21A Store Street, WC1E 7DH (7636 9133).
Navarru's 67 Charlotte Street, W1T 4PH (7637 7713).
Pizza Express 30 Coptic Street, WC1A 1NS (7636 3232).
Sheng's Tea House 68 Millman Street, WC1N 3EF (7405 3697).
Spaghetti House 20 Sicilian Avenue, WC1A 2QD (7405 5215).
Wagamama 4A Streatham Street, WC1A 1JB (7323 9223).
Wagamama 14A Irving Street, WC2H 7AF (7839 2323).
Yo! Sushi myhotcl, 11-13 Bayley Street, WC1B 3HD (7636 0076).

MARYLEBONE

Home to waxwork celebs, giddy debs and very few plebs.

Around Town

Always an affluent area, Marylebone seemed a bit staid until the tail end of the last century. Wedged between the pedestrian crush of **Oxford Street** shoppers and the traffic jams of **Marylebone Road** it made little effort to capitalise on its prime position next to the West End. A concerted effort by the landowners, Howard de Walden, began the slow journey to fashionability in the 1990s – regenerating the area by cherry-picking a mix of cool independent shops, restaurants and tasteful chain stores to lure in the consumers. The arrival of the grand dame of pop, Madonna, sealed the star appeal of this rediscovered quarter. Marylebone is now back on the map as one of London's desirable upmarket villages, which is how it started off 250 years ago.

The name comes from St Mary (the parish church) on the stream (bourne), the stream being the Tyburn river which now runs underground but re-emerges briefly into the lake at **Regent's Park**. Marylebone's development was typical of the way London has expanded over the last 300 years. Rich families would buy up large plots of land around the city then lease them to developers who built on them. The freeholder would receive ground rent, which in total added up to more money than they could extract from renting the land for agricultural use. Also, on expiry of the leases (typically 60 years), the land with the buildings reverted back to them so they won on all fronts. A major part of Marylebone was bought by the Duke of Newcastle in the early 1800s; Howard de Walden Estate is run by his descendants.

But Marylebone has more than history and shopping to recommend it. **Madame Tussauds**, much to the bemusement of Londoners, is the most popular paid-for attraction in the capital. **Regent's Park** has the largest outdoor sports area in central London, and a boating lake and playgrounds. Within the grounds is **London Zoo**, with as many squealing youngsters as mammals on a sunny summer's day. Grand Hereford House is testament to Marylebone's glory days; it now houses the **Wallace Collection**, which inspires a family-friendly workshop programme. Collections of less reliable quality can be found at **Alfie's Antique Market** off Edgware Road, the largest of its kind in the country.

Taking the air in **Regents Park**. See p66.

London Central Mosque

146 Park Road, NW8 7RG (7724 3363/www.iccuk.org). Baker Street tube/13, 82, 133 bus. **Open** 9.30am-6pm daily. **Admission** free.

The complex is much bigger than the dome and minaret imply. Offices around a large courtyard accommodate London's most important Islamic Cultural Centre; inside the reception are a bookshop and an information booth.

Men and boys enter the prayer hall via doors on the ground floor; women and girls pass through the 'toilets & *wudhu*' (washing facilities) to head upstairs to a screened-off balcony. Inside the dome is a huge chandelier encircled by Arabic tiles. Visitors must remove their shoes; women should wear a headscarf for entry.

Buggy access. Café. Disabled access: ramp, toilet. Nappy-changing facilities. Nearest picnic place: Regent's Park. Shop.

London Zoo

Regent's Park, NW1 4RY (7722 3333/www. londonzoo.co.uk/www.zsl.org). Baker Street or Camden Town tube, then 274 or C2 bus. **Open** *Mar-late Oct* 10am-5.30pm daily. *Oct-Feb* 10am-4pm daily. Check website for any changes. **Admission** £14; £12 concessions; £10.75 3-15s; free under-3s; £45 family ticket (2+2 or 1+3). **Credit** AmEx, MC, V. **Map** p314 G2.

This world-famous zoo is owned and run by ZSL (the Zoological Society of London), a worldwide conservation, scientific and educational charity. Conservation goals are clearly stated around the zoo and informative talks given, often pointing out harmful practices that threaten wildlife.

Check the website before a visit for the daily timetable of events so you don't miss anything important. You can pick up a route map from the entrance or follow the green line route painted on the pathways to save yourself going round in circles. With over 850 species in its 36 acres, it's best not to try to see everything in one go. Special events are always laid on for the school holidays and a trail can also be picked up on entry. This leads to the activity centre where children can make brass rubbings and mobiles. The daily Animals in Action show is particularly popular with young visitors (*see p66* **Heads up!**).

As far as the animals are concerned, there have been a few changes regarding habitat. New attractions for 2005 include the Komodo dragon house, a brand-new squirrel monkey walk-through forest and an African bird walk – all so much more innovative than the old-fashioned aviaries and enclosures one usually associates with zoos. Even the old favourites are going through changes: the famous Lubetkin penguin pool had been taken over by porcupines when we last visited. Apparently, this is because the zoo's current colony of penguins hail from South Africa and prefer an enclosure that mimics their native coastland. The iconic building's listed status means that any changes that need to be made must be done so after much consultation, so porcupines, who clearly aren't that prickly about building design, are making themselves at home until the Lubetkin pool's future is decided.

The B.U.G.S! biodiversity centre does a grand job of demonstrating the complexity of our world, housing fish, insects, invertebrates, birds, spiders, mammals and reptiles within its walls. It's very information-intensive but a little light relief in the form of the children's zoo is just a short walk away. Here the tame llamas and sheep get the fight hugged out of them by delighted children in the touch paddocks. The adjoining Petcare centre houses some unusual choices – cages of rats, snakes and spiders. Not so much hugging goes on there. Then there are the larger mammals, the reptile house, the aquarium and a surreal moonlit world to see. Don't miss the meerkats and otters.

In the summer kids will be tempted by the bouncy castle (£1 a ride) and merry-go-round (£1 for 5mins) but we prefer to fritter away our pocket money in the shop. *Buggy access. Café. Disabled access: ramps, toilet. Nappy-changing facilities. Nearest picnic space: zoo grounds. Restaurant. Shop.*

Madame Tussauds/The London Planetarium

Marylebone Road, NW1 5LR (0870 400 3000/www. madame-tussauds.co.uk). Baker Street tube/13, 27, 74, 113, 159 bus. **Open** 9.30am-6pm daily (last entry 5.30pm). Times vary during holiday periods. **Admission** *9.30am-5pm Mon-Fri, 9.30am-3pm Sat, Sun* £19.99; £16.99 concessions; £15.99 5-15s. *3-5pm Sat, Sun* £15.99; £12.99 concessions; £11.99 5-15s. *5-5.30pm daily* £11; £9 concessions; £6 5-15s. Internet booking only for family tickets. **Credit** AmEx, MC, V. **Map** p314 G4.

Madame Tussauds hit the headlines during the run-up to Christmas 2004 when its VIP room was turned into 'a celebrity stable', with Posh, Becks and Kylie contributing to a waxen nativity scene. There's nothing particularly shocking in there these days, unless you count the fact that the latest Madonna effigy appears to be developing jowls. Barely any adult Londoners go to Madame Tussauds willingly, but the kids we've accompanied here love it, and so do the tourists. No one can resist comparing their height with the biggest stars, who turn out in fact to be rather little – hard guy Sylvester Stallone is a mediocre 5ft 7in (1.7m). Beyoncé, mid bootie shake, proves an irresistible invitation for some 'hands on' shots, as does La Lopez, but girls get their own back with Brad Pitt's bottom. You have to pay if you want a photo with the A-lists.

The chamber of horrors, all serial killers and brutality has the guillotine that removed Marie Antoinette's head. Madame Tussauds' namesake (immortalised in wax in the main gallery) lived in Louis XIV's France during the French revolution and made casts of guillotined heads. The Chamber Live is a section of the chamber reserved for 'live serial killers' (actors, presumably). Children enjoy the final themed ride in a London taxi on a whistlestop tour of significant events in London's history.

The newly refurbished **Planetarium** is the site for 'Warriors', a short stage show of a heroic fight beneath the stunning digital screen that is the real star. The same dazzling digital effects are used for 'Journey to Infinity', a short tour through our solar system and beyond.

The route to the exit naturally leads to the shop, which has all the pap a child could want, as well as a booth where you can print out your own digital snaps for 29p each. No buggies are allowed but a £5 deposit secures the use of a baby carrier – first come, first served.

Café. Disabled access: lift, toilet. Nappy-changing facilities. Nearest picnic place: Regent's Park. Shop.

LUNCH BOX

For recommended restaurants and cafés in the area, *see reviews pp164-166*.

Boathouse Café Hanover Gate, Outer Circle, Regent's Park, NW1 4RL (7724 4069).
Caffè Caldesi 118 Marylebone Lane, W1U 2QF (7935 1144).
Carluccio's Caffè St Christopher's Place, W1U 1AY (7935 5927); 8 Market Place, W1W 8AG (7636 2228).
Eat & Two Veg 50 Marylebone High Street, W1U 5HN (7258 8595).
Golden Hind 73 Marylebone Lane, W1U 2PN (7486 3644).
Honest Sausage Broadwalk, Off Chester Road, Regent's Park, NW1 4NU (7224 3872).
La Galette 56 Paddington Street, W1U 4HY (7935 1554).
La Spighetta 43 Blandford Street, W1U 7HF (7486 7340).
Oasis Café London Zoo, Regent's Park, NW1 4RY (7722 3333).
Pâtisserie Valerie at Sagne 105 Marylebone High Street, W1U 4RS (7935 6240).
Paul 115 Marylebone High Street, W1U 4SB (7224 5615).
Queen Mary's Garden Café Inner Circle, Regent's Park, NW1 4NU (7935 5729).
Tootsies Grill 35 James Street, W1M 5HX (7486 1611).

Around Town

Regent's Park

*The Store Yard, Inner Circle, Regent's Park, NW1 4NR
(7486 7905/www.royalparks.gov.uk). Baker Street,
Great Portland Street, Camden Town or Regent's Park
tube.* **Open** 5am-30mins before dusk daily. **Admission**
free. **Map** p314 G3.
Like all the Royal Parks, Regent's Park was once woodland and meadows; it was used by Henry VIII for hunting.
Landscaped in 1811 by the architect John Nash, crown
architect and friend of the Prince Regent, it wasn't until
1845, during the reign of Queen Victoria, that the great
unwashed were even allowed into the park, and this was
only for two days a week.
All over the park, the planting schemes in the flowerbeds
are of breathtaking intricacy and colour. Sporty types
appreciate the park as the biggest outdoor sports facility
in central London, with tennis and netball courts, an athletics track, and football and hockey pitches. A brand new
sports pavilion is also planned – Active England have
given £2m towards the project, which together with
£100,000 from the London Marathon Charitable Trust,

Heads up !

There's so much to do on a trip to the zoo, as the
song tells us, but however packed your London
Zoo schedule might be don't miss the daily
Animals in Action show in the auditorium (it
usually takes place at noon; check the daily
events link on the website for details). The action
unfolds in a small open-air theatre, which quickly
packs out on busy days. Thankfully, the raked
seating means little ones can see from the back.
When everyone's settled, animals appear on cue,
flying over the backdrop or dashing in from the
wings. Mac the hawk is one of the stars,
demonstrating his precise navigational skills as
he swoops low, just inches over audience
members' heads. Cue choruses of oohs! and
aahhs! as the airborne hunter dips and dives. His
handler informs the audience that Mac's
threatening presence is enough to keep the area
free of urban pigeons, who can be seen pecking
in their gormless way all over the safer areas of
the zoological gardens. Once Mac has left the
building, however, the fat grey scavengers are
back on the stage, looking for leftovers. A certain
amount of anthropomorphism on the part of the
handlers and presenters adds to the

entertainment value. Each animal is given a
human personality to help children better
understand their behavioural habits in the wild. A
chorus line of perky meerkats are presented as
easygoing and sociable creatures who always look
after their mates (hence the two-legged stance).
Another star performer is a parrot with an
exhibitionist streak – a born performer with what
appears to be perfect comic timing. It's all very
light-hearted, but the conservation and animal
welfare message is carefully driven home
alongside the entertainment. All the animals in
the show, we're reliably informed, have been
hand-reared. Some are abandoned pets brought
to the zoo by various animal charities, others may
have been rejected at birth.

Be warned, however, that some unfortunate
audience members may leave with more than they
bargained for. When the auditorium is packed,
latecomers find one bench ominously empty. They
soon find out why much later, after they've made
themselves comfortable. Regular attendees know
that the bench in question is under a rope where
the avian performers perch. And when a bird
perches, it invariably poos.

means the park is on the way to becoming sports central in London. Arts enthusiasts, meanwhile, pray for a dry summer to fully appreciate the magic of the park's Open Air Theatre, which nestles attractively within a woodland setting, with sound effects supplied by the rustling of the leaves in the breeze (and rain pounding on the boards, if you're unlucky). The alfresco performance season runs from May to September. The programme for 2005 includes *Twelfth Night*, *The Wind in the Willows* and *HMS Pinafore*. Free lunchtime and evening concerts on the bandstand by the boating lake are also planned.

For children, there are four well-maintained playgrounds, each with a sandpit and toilets; one is close to the London Central Mosque, whose golden dome can be seen from all over the park (*see p64*) and the boating lake; there's another by Marylebone Road, north of Portland Place; the third is by the Camden Town entrance; and the last lies at the foot of Primrose Hill. The shallow boating lake is one of the nicest places to spend a summer's afternoon, with rowing boats available for hire by the hour (£6 for adults, £4 for children), but there is also a small, circular lake for kids who want to mess about in pedalos. These cost £3 for 20mins and the youngsters must pass a height test to use them (they have to be big enough to reach the pedals).

The Regent's Park Wildlife Watch Group runs free activities for six-to-ten year-olds on the third Sunday of every month from 2pm to 4pm; for more details, call 7935 7430. *Buggy access. Cafés. Disabled access: toilets. Nappy-changing facilities.*

St James's Spanish Place

22 George Street, W1U 3QY (7935 0943/www.spanishplace.hemscott.net). Baker Street or Bond Street tube. **Open** 6.30am-7pm daily. *Services* 7.15am, 12.30pm, 6pm Mon-Fri; 10am, 6pm Sat; 8.30am, 9.30am (Old Rite), 10.30am (Sung Latin), noon, 4pm, 7pm Sun. **Admission** free. **Map** p314 G5.

Locals sometimes call this Gothic edifice 'the Spanish church', although its associations with that country officially ceased in 1827. The Spanish Embassy was established in this area after the restoration of Charles II, first on Ormond Street and then at Hartford house, Manchester Square, where the Wallace Collection (*see below*) is now housed. The first St James's was built in 1791, just after the repeal of laws banning Catholic worship; the present church opened opposite the original in 1890. A lot of continental Catholics live nearby, so it's well attended at Mass. There's a palpable sense of peace, with the interior always bathed in a soft golden light, thanks to the ornate gilt decorations and many votive candles. The basement accommodates a Montessori nursery, and family events are held here; check the noticeboards for details. *Disabled access: toilet (currently under construction). Nearest picnic place: Regent's Park. Shop.*

Sherlock Holmes Museum

221B Baker Street, NW1 6XE (7935 8866/www.sherlock-holmes.co.uk). Baker Street tube/74, 139, 189 bus. **Open** 9.30am-6pm daily (last entry 5.30pm). **Admission** £6; £4 6-16s; free under-6s. **Credit** AmEx, MC, V. **Map** p311 F4.

When the famous books were written No.221 was a fictional address: Baker Street didn't extend that far. Now, however, it does and the office development on the site regularly receives letters addressed to Holmes. The commercial museum is really one for the fans (if you know about the famous detective but haven't read the books the

significance of many of the exhibits will elude you). Purists, however, will delight in the care with which fictional detail has been faithfully reproduced. If you're not up on Victorian criminals you'll probably think the photos above Holmes's fireplace are of his relatives. The house is set up as if the master detective and sidekick are in situ, complete with an affable 'Mr Watson' who cheerily urges you to take photos. A children's quiz (ask at the desk) explains some of the Victorian exhibits. The two uppermost floors are devoted to a display of waxwork figures in murderous or cadaverous poses, enacting dramatic scenes from the books; slightly peculiar, but children seem to like them. The museum shop is stuffed with Sherlock paraphernalia and books: deerstalker hats are universally popular. *Nearest picnic place: Regent's Park. Shop.*

Wallace Collection

Hertford House, Manchester Square, W1U 3BN (7935 0687/www.wallacecollection.org). Bond Street tube/2, 10, 12, 30, 74, 113 bus. **Open** 10am-5pm Mon-Sat; noon-5pm Sun. Closed 24-26 Dec, 1 Jan, Good Friday, 1 May. **Admission** free. **Credit** *Shop* MC, V. **Map** p314 G5.

This opulent mansion house is crammed with fabulous Louis XIV and XV furniture, many world-famous paintings and objets d'art, as well as gilded clocks, mirrors, snuff boxes and porcelain. It also houses one of the finest collections of armour in the UK. Five generations of the Hertford family made their personal contributions but the largest part of the collection was amassed by the Fourth Marquess of Hertford, a great Francophile who had bought it for safekeeping from the ravages of the French Revolution. It was inherited by his illegitimate son, Richard Wallace and bequeathed to the nation by Wallace's widow in 1897 with the proviso that it be kept in its entirety. The mansion has been expertly adapted for public viewing and the visitors' facilities include a lecture theatre and a dedicated education room for schools. Café Bagatelle in the central courtyard is far posher than your average museum catering, but it's a splendid place for a light lunch and they do have a kids' menu (mains around £4.50) and high chairs.

Admission is free but there is a fee to view the temporary exhibitions: these always have workshops to complement the theme. Even those with a scant knowledge of art history are likely to recognise some of the prize paintings in the main collections – Frans Hals's *Laughing Cavalier* and Fragonard's *The Swing* have graced many a postcard. For the first Sunday of every month there is 'The Little Draw,' a miniature version of the annual Big Draw event that takes place nationally in galleries every October. From 1.30-4.30pm families can pick up art materials and a drawing board and get sketching with help from the gallery's in-house artist. The regular armour workshops have a hands-on approach, helping children discover how heavy the armour and weapons are, letting them handle items like 3,000-year-old bronze swords and oriental daggers decorated with jade and gold, and have a go at making their own warrior gear. Free general guided tours of the Collection are usually given on weekdays at 1pm, Wednesdays and Saturdays at 11:30pm, and Sundays at 3pm; these are sometimes replaced by specialist gallery talks covering aspects of the Collection in more detail, check the website for daily events.

All educational events have strictly limited numbers, so it's best to book well in advance. *Buggy access. Disabled access: lift, toilet. Nappy-changing facilities. Nearest picnic place: grounds. Restaurant. Shop.*

Around Town

WEST END

Glitz and glamour, cash and crowds.

Handel House Museum.

MAYFAIR

The most expensive property on the Monopoly board, Mayfair (named after a rowdy fair that took place round here in, er, May) is bigwig country. Generally it's the area between **Oxford Street**, **Regent Street**, **Piccadilly** and **Park Lane**, which was developed into a posh new neighbourhood by the Grosvenor and Berkeley families in the 1700s. They built a series of squares surrounded by elegant houses. The three biggest squares – Hanover, Berkeley and Grosvenor – are ringed by offices and embassies these days.

Crowded **Oxford Street** constitutes the area's more downmarket border. It attracts 20 million visitors a year with its mix of high-street chains and department stores. If you're not shopping it's best to avoid the area. **Regent Street** was developed by the Crown Estate, which wanted a piece of Oxford Street's financial success for itself. Nash designed the road in 1813, plotting the route as a social dividing line that separated the smart mansions to the west from the slums in the east. To achieve this he had to put the curve in at the

end. Shops were designed with large balconies to attract the spending public in all weathers. Today **Hamleys** toy shop (*see p209*) is the main draw for kids. On Regent Street's **Family Day** (4 Sept 2005) this normally congested thoroughfare is closed to traffic for a Victorian fairground.

For first-time visitors a stop-off at tacky **Piccadilly Circus** is a must. On the southern side of the garish, neon-lit Circus is the statue of the Angel of Christian Charity (generally known as **Eros**) – cups used to hang from chains for passers-by to get a drink from the fountain. To the east is the **Trocadero**; this once plush theatre is now a garish entertainment arcade loved by kids and detested by parents in equal measure.

Faraday Museum/Royal Institute
21 Albemarle Street, W1S 4BS (7409 2992/www. rigb.org). Green Park tube. **Open** 9am-5pm Mon-Fri. Closed bank hols. **Tours** by arrangement. **Admission** £1; 50p concessions. *Tours* £5. **No credit cards.** **Map** p316 J7.
Science is boring? The Royal Institute is here to prove otherwise. As well as celebrating the great historical discoveries made within its hallowed halls the Institute sets its sights firmly on the future with a state-of-the-art lab for PhD students. For schools and families there are regular lectures on everything from climate change to muscles and joints. The latter is illustrated with videos on breakdancing. The talks are for a range of ages, from five to over-16, all are linked to the National Curriculum. Look for the FF (Family Friendly) symbol next to events. Workshops include 'The Magic Word is Science' (2 July 2005), which demonstrates some magic tricks then explains the method behind them. Within the Institute is a small museum devoted to Faraday, famous for his discovery of electro magnetic induction. He carried out his most important work while at the Institute and his original lab is on display. It's most relevant to the over-sevens, who will have touched on electricity in science lessons.

The museum will be closed for redevelopment from January to December 2006 when it will be transformed into a modern interactive exhibition space every bit as lively as the centre's events. Faraday's laboratory will be moved to the modern lab upstairs.
Buggy access. Disabled access: toilet. Lift. Nearest picnic place: Berkeley Square/Green Park.

Handel House Museum
25 Brook Street (entrance at rear), W1K 4HB (7495 1685/www.handelhouse.org). Bond Street tube. **Open** 10am-6pm Tue, Wed, Fri, Sat; 10am-8pm Thur; noon-6pm Sun. **Admission** £5; £4.50 concessions; £2 6-16s; free under-6s. **Credit** MC, V. **Map** p316 H6.

Once the home of composer George Frideric Handel this museum has endeared itself to families for providing an imaginative introduction to classical music. Though the focus is on baroque, workshops explore its inspirations and influences and are not averse to throwing modern styles into the mix. One event saw musicians fusing the works of one Jimi Hendrix with baroque – not quite as far-fetched as it sounds, Hendrix occupied the top two rooms at No.23 so the curators like to commemorate his musical legacy as well.

Enthusiastic volunteers liven up a visit for children, telling Handel-based anecdotes and identifying the portraits on the walls. The building's upper rooms house some original letters and first edition printed scores but most of the action takes place in the music room. Pride of place goes to a replica of Handel's harpsichord – performances take place regularly. One of the main achievements of the museum has been to bring live music back into the house. Saturday afternoons are a drop-in for kids – with a Handel

 WALK From palatial pomp to people's church

Timing isn't essential for this walk, but it will definitely make it more memorable. Start off at around 11.30am at the Horse Guards end of **St James's Park** (see p71) and take a leisurely stroll the length of the lake, passing Duck Island. At the end you will come to **Buckingham Palace** at around 11.45am to catch the end of the **Changing of the Guard** (arrive at 11.30am if you want to see the whole bagpipes-and-brass shebang). The best viewpoint is from the Victoria memorial, facing the main gates

Charles II, used to walk through the park picking flowers and distributing them to the ladies-in-waiting. This infuriated his queen, Catherine of Braganza, who had all the beds removed. There are still only wild flowers in Green Park to this day. When you reach the northern boundary turn right on to Piccadilly. You will pass the gleaming Ritz hotel, with its uniformed doormen. It would be fab to stop off here for refreshments, but a cheaper place to rest your legs is across the road at the **Royal Academy**. Walk through to the lift at the back and take it to the top floor – the Sackler Wing. At the end of the corridor the priceless marble sculpture by Michelangelo has its own viewing seat. Back outside, opposite the RA, is **Fortnum & Mason**, a department store that was

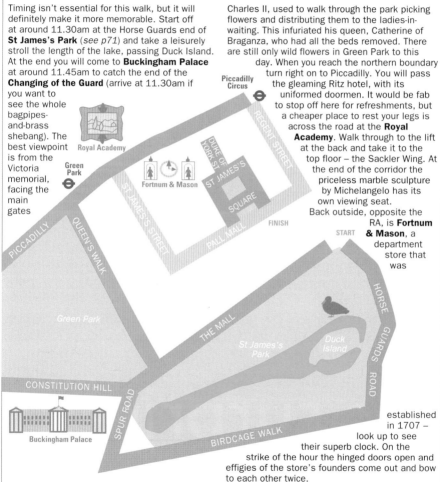

established in 1707 – look up to see their superb clock. On the strike of the hour the hinged doors open and effigies of the store's founders come out and bow to each other twice.

A few yards further up Piccadilly is pretty **St James's Church**, which, from Tuesday to Saturday, has a market in its courtyard. For sunny days there's a handy picnic spot in **St James's Square**. Turn right down the alley directly after the church then left down Duke of York Street.

of the Palace, as this is where all the troops exit. From here cut through to Piccadilly by walking up **Green Park**, to your right. The direction to Piccadilly is signposted. There are no flowerbeds in this park – one tale attributes this to a jealous royal. Apparently our 17th-century monarch, King

Around Town

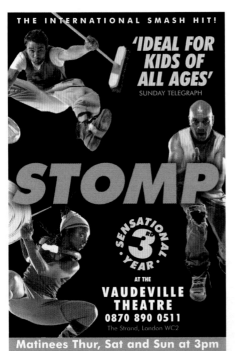

activity bag for them to get stuck into – and workshops are held monthly on everything from world music (for tots) to instrument workshops for those who have learnt the basics at school. Occasional special events include storytelling based on Handel's operas with music accompaniment, plus dressing up in 18th-century clothes. Call or check out the website for precise dates and times. *Buggy access. Disabled access: toilet. Lift. Nearest picnic place: Hanover Square. Shop.*

Trocadero

Coventry Street, W1D 7DH (7439 1791/www.troc.co.uk). Piccadilly Circus tube. **Open** 10am-midnight Mon-Thur, Sun; 10am-1am Fri, Sat. **Admission** free; individual attractions vary. **Credit** varies. **Map** p317 K7.

The Trocadero is an electronic nirvana for kids. Be warned, however, that the pulsating music, flashing lights and mayhem can induce filthy temper tantrums in normally equable parents threatened with arcade-induced penury.

There's plenty to do for older children with bottomless pockets. The full-sized dodgems on the upper storey, along with tenpin bowling, are mainly populated by young teens. In the arcades dance fans can bop on glowing squares to a sequence dictated on a screen, would-be musos learn to drum and others to navigate a plane and even a spaceship – be prepared to be spun around 360° for this. More boisterous kids can test their strength on a punchball or get thrown off the bucking bronco. The racing car berths are packed with goggle-eyed youngsters. The photo sticker booths and temporary tattoo stands are popular money grabbers. Until November 2005 'Titanic: The World Class Collection' is an award-winning exhibition on the first floor (admission £9; children £5). Check the website for school-holiday promotional events. In addition to all this is a multi-screen cinema and many sweet, ice-cream and accessory concessions (now there's a surprise). Parents may gaze longingly at the relative calm of the sports bar, but under 18s are not allowed in.

Buggy access. Cafés. Disabled access: toilet. Lift. Nappy-changing facilities. Nearest picnic place: Leicester Square/Trafalgar Square. Restaurants. Shops.

✕🍴 LUNCH BOX

For recommended restaurants and cafés in the area, see reviews pp166-168.

Chocolate Society 34 Shepherd Market, W1J 7QN (7495 0302).
McDonald's (there are seven along Oxford Street from Tottenham Court Road to Marble Arch).
Miso 66 Haymarket, SW1Y 4RF (7930 4800).
Pâtisserie Valerie 44 Old Compton Street, W1D 4TY (7437 3466).
Pizza Express 29 Wardour Street, W1D 6PS (7437 7215); 10 Dean Street, W1D 5RW (7437 9595); 20 Greek Street, W1D 4DU (7734 7430).
Satsuma 56 Wardour Street, W1D 4JG (7437 8338).
Sofra 18 Shepherd Street, W1Y 7HU (7493 3320).
Spiga 84-86 Wardour Street, W1D 0TA (7734 3444)
Zoomslide Café The Photographers' Gallery, 5 Great Newport Street, WC2H 7HY (7831 1772).

LEICESTER SQUARE TO PICCADILLY

From Piccadilly Circus you can beat a path with the hordes of tourists to **Leicester Square**, the site of London's film premières. The square has its own small walk of fame featuring stars' handprints. Northwards is **Chinatown**, where the Chinese community established itself in the 1950s. Bordered by kitsch gates and accessorised with oriental-style phone boxes it has the whiff of a theme park about it. Plans are afoot to modernise this pocket of the West End with a brand new shopping centre. Still further north, across Shaftesbury Avenue, is **Soho**, centre of gay London and home to the film industry and the remnants of the sex industry. It's not really a destination for children but there are a few reasonably priced restaurants.

Away from the Circus, you can catch glimpses of Piccadilly's glossy past in the smart Victorian shopping arcades, designed to protect shoppers from mud and manure. One is the **Burlington Arcade**. According to old laws it is illegal to sing, whistle or hurry in the arcade and there are beadles wearing top hats on duty to ensure nobody does. So mind you just saunter through, humming under your breath. Just next door to the arcade is the **Royal Academy of Arts**.

To the south are two royal parks, **Green Park**, whose plainness appeals mainly to joggers, and the rather more interesting **St James's Park**. A lake, playground and excellent restaurant, Inn The Park (*see p172*), mean you'll be jostling for buggy space at weekends. Between the two parks, the country's poshest resident keeps a eye on her capital from **Buckingham Palace**.

Apsley House: The Wellington Museum

149 Piccadilly, Hyde Park Corner, W1J 7NT (7499 5676/www.english-heritage.org.uk). Hyde Park Corner tube. **Open** *Apr-Oct* 10am-5pm Tue-Sun. *Nov-Mar* 10am-4pm Tue-Sun. Also opens Mon bank hols all year. **Tours** by arrangement. **Admission** £4.95 (includes audio guide if available); £3.70 concessions; £2.50 under-16s. *Tours* phone for details. **Credit** MC, V. **Map** p316 G8.

Arthur Wellesley, better known as the first Duke of Wellington, hero of Waterloo in 1815, bought Apsley House on his return from the campaign. The house was commonly known as No.1 London for being the first house one saw after entering the city at the Knightsbridge toll gates.

The rooms at Apsley are so magnificently proportioned, a giant could walk around comfortably inside. The extensive wall space is covered with paintings by masters such as Velázquez, Caravaggio and Rubens. The collection includes many pieces from the Spanish Royal Collection that Wellington recovered from Joseph Bonaparte. In the basement are casts of the death masks of both Wellington and Napoleon as well as an impressive medal collection.

Schoolchildren getting to grips with British battle chronology are frequent visitors in term-time. The audio

Around Town

guide can be heavy going but a new children's trail in the form of a Wellington Boot helps leaven things. Waterloo week (14-19 June 2005) is always celebrated in style, and this year Apsley House will be teaming up with the National Army museum for a whole range of battle-based activities and crafts.

Buggy access. Lift. Nearest picnic place: Hyde Park. Shop.

Buckingham Palace & Royal Mews

SW1A 1AA (7766 7300/www.royal.gov.uk). Green Park or St James's Park tube/Victoria tube/rail. **Open** *State Rooms* early Aug-late Sept 9.30am-6pm daily (last entry 4.15pm). *Royal Mews* Mar-July, Oct 11am-4pm Mon-Thur, Sat, Sun (last entry 3.15pm); Aug-Sept 10am-5pm daily (last entry 4.15pm). *Queen's Gallery* 10am-4.30pm daily. Closed Fri in Mar & July, during Ascot & state occasions. **Admission** (LP) £13.50; £11.50 concessions; £7 5-16s; free under-5s; £34 family (2+2). *Royal Mews* £6; £5 concessions; £3.50 5-16s; free under-5s; £15.50 family (2+2). *Queen's Gallery* £7.50; £6 OAPs, students; £4 5-16s; free under-5s; £19 family (2+3). **Credit** AmEx, MC, V. **Map** p316 H9.

Every summer when her majesty leaves for her Scottish holiday the 19 state rooms are opened to the public. Buckingham House was acquired by George III in 1762 but it wasn't until Queen Victoria moved in, in 1837, that it became the official royal residence. Not amused by the lack of space – too few bedrooms and nurseries – Victoria had Marble Arch moved to make way for more building.

On display is part of the royal art collection, including paintings by Rembrandt, Rubens, Vermeer and Canaletto. This year has a special exhibition celebrating our *entente cordiale* with France during World War II. A collection of gifts from the president include dolls clothed by some of Paris's most famous couturiers of the time. The palace has an education department and activity room for schools and families, an audio trail and a trail for the rambling gardens.

The Queen's Gallery was built in place of Queen Victoria's private chapel, which was bombed in 1940. It is now an exhibition space designed to show off pieces from all parts of Liz's art collection. Two small cabinet rooms house the fabulous diamond and pearl diadem, as modelled by the queen on postage stamps, as well as the largest cut diamond in the world, the Cullinan 1.

Exhibitions for 2005 are 'Enchanting the Eye: Dutch Paintings of the Golden Age' and 'Treasures from the Royal Collection'. A family workshop and kids' trail complements each. Save time to explore the E-Gallery, where easy-to-use touch screens let you select objects from the collection, magnify them and even take them apart.

A popular part of a royal visit for young ones is the stables in the Royal Mews. Here, depending on how you time your visit, kids can see the horses being fed, mucked out and exercised. On show is the gold state coach, last used in 2002 for the Queen's Golden Jubilee.

Buggy access (baby slings supplied in State Rooms, Royal Mews). Disabled access: lift, toilet (Buckingham Palace). Nappy-changing facilities (Buckingham Palace). Nearest picnic place: Green Park. Shop.

Royal Academy of Arts

Burlington House, Piccadilly, W1J 0BD (7300 8000/ www.royalacademy.org.uk). Green Park or Piccadilly Circus tube. **Open** *Temporary exhibitions* 10am-6pm Mon-Thur, Sat, Sun; 10am-10pm Fri. *John Madejski Fine Rooms* 1-4.30pm Tue-Fri; 10am-6pm Sat, Sun. Opening times can vary for exhibitions. **Admission**
Fine Rooms free. *Exhibitions* vary; free under-8s. **Credit** AmEx, DC, MC, V. **Map** p316 J7.

The Academy opened in 1768 as the nation's first art school and it still runs art courses for post-graduates. It moved to its present address in 1867, and is known for headline-grabbing exhibitions such as 'Aztecs' and 'Matisse, His Art and His Textiles'. Just as popular is the egalitarian summer exhibition (7 June-15 Aug 2005) to which anyone can submit their work. The diversity of the pieces on display makes it a stimulating visit for all ages – inspired children can pick up an art tray and create their own masterpiece. The family workshop for this year's event sees members of the Royal Philharmonic Orchestra composing music inspired by the art on show. Also on view are the refurbished John Madejski Fine Rooms, which are used to showcase a selection of the Academy's own collection. Up on the 4th floor is the priceless Michelangelo sculpture, next to the Sackler Wing of Galleries.

Buggy access. Café. Disabled: ramp, toilets. Lift. Nappy-changing facilities. Nearest picnic place: Green Park/St James's Square. Restaurant. Shop.

St James's Church Piccadilly

197 Piccadilly, W1J 9LL (7734 4511/www.st-james-piccadilly.org). Piccadilly Circus tube. **Open** 8am-6.30pm daily (phone for details of evening events). **Admission** free. **Map** p316 J7.

St James's is an oasis of colour and charm. This is especially true of its churchyard garden, which harbours a vibrant market offering antiques (Tue) or arts and crafts (Wed-Sat). The entire scene is shrouded in low trees, with weather-beaten statues, a glass-fronted Caffè Nero (with heated terrace) and even an old tin caravan (used as a Samaritans-style listening centre). Inside St James's is as vibrant as out: it has a well-founded reputation for indiscriminate openness.

Sir Christopher Wren began the church in 1676 (it's believed to be one of his favourite works). Haydn, Handel and Mendelssohn were all resident organists. William Blake was baptised here, but he died a pauper and was buried with other dissenters in Bunhill Fields.

Buggy access. Café. Disabled: ramp. Nearest picnic place: St James's Square/church gardens.

Wellington Arch

Hyde Park Corner, W1J 7JZ (7930 2726/www.english-heritage.org.uk). Hyde Park Corner tube. **Open** *Apr-Oct* 10am-5pm Wed-Sun. *Nov-Mar* 10am-4pm Wed-Sun. **Admission** £3; £2.30 concessions; £1.50 5-16s; free under-5s. **Credit** MC, V. **Map** p316 G8.

Neighbouring Wellington Arch is well worth bolting on to a visit to Apsley House (*see p71*). A photo gallery of equivalent celebratory arches all over the world, from Paris to China, provides a global perspective on 'Arch' art. For many cultures this symbolic structure represents the gateway to a city, and has been used to commemorate military victories right back to Roman times. Our Wellington Arch is a combination of both, situated as it was at the western entrance to London. As well as relating the history of the Arch there is also a great display on how important figures have been commemorated through the ages, encouraging children to think about who they might commemorate and how. If there are eight or so people visiting, the Arch's curator may gather everyone together for an impromptu tour, picking out all the famous sights.

Buggy access. Lift. Nearest picnic place: Hyde Park. Shop.

COVENT GARDEN & ST GILES'S

Showy museums and secret gardens await in London's tourist honeypot.

Phoenix Garden. *See p75.*

Once the land around **Covent Garden** belonged to the Convent of St Peter at Westminster, but it lost its religion with the dissolution of the monasteries and was handed over by the Crown to John Russell, the first Earl of Bedford. In the 1630s, the earl commissioned master architect Inigo Jones to design a series of Palladian arcades based on classical Italian piazzas. The resulting tall terraces opening on to a central courtyard proved popular with wealthy tenants, until the fruit and vegetable market expanded on to their patch. This forced the well-to-do to move further west over the course of the next century, in search of more fragrant lodgings, and the market came to dominate the main square. Covent Garden soon became a hangout for less fussy artists, literary and theatrical folk.

It was only in 1973 – when the vegetable market moved south to Vauxhall – that the piazza was reclaimed by the shops, cafés, bars and licensed street artists that today make it one of London's biggest tourist attractions. Performers book weeks in advance to act in front of the portico of **St Paul's**, but on any given day you'll find mime artists and musicians scattered about the square. Every summer there are open-air operatics courtesy of the **Royal Opera House**. The area's oldest theatre is the **Theatre Royal Drury Lane** (Catherine Street, WC2B 5JF, 7494 5000); its largest is the **Coliseum** (St Martin's Lane, WC2N 4ES, 7632 8300), home to English National Opera. For an interactive look at the area's theatrical history, visit the **Theatre Museum**. **London's Transport Museum**, whose collection of old buses and trains is a big hit with children, undergoes major refurbishment from August 2005, but promises new galleries and exhibits when it reopens in November 2006. The rest of Covent Garden, especially around Neal Street, is dominated by pricey boutiques, although more affordable fashion can be found in the **Thomas Neal Centre** and around the alternative enclave of **Neal's Yard**. A lively clutter of veggie cafés, New Age crystal shops, herbalists and skate-wear emporiums, the Yard is a testament to the sit-ins and demonstrations that saved the area from corporate redevelopment in the 1970s, and it remains blissfully, colourfully unaltered. Up the road, meanwhile, **St Giles's** is less renowned as a tourist attraction and its reputation is seedier than that of Covent Garden. Reviled by Charles Dickens and immortalised in Hogarth's *Gin Lane*, this area was rife with crime and prostitution until the Irish slums were levelled in 1847 to make way for New Oxford Street. Only the church of **St Giles-in-the-Fields** (60 St Giles High Street, WC2H 8LG, 7240 2532) remained. Named after the patron saint of outcasts, the church originated as the chapel of a leper colony, founded in 1011; the first victims of the plague of 1665 were discovered in this dirty neighbourhood. Nowadays, the churchyard gardens provide a

Around Town

family-friendly spot offering lunchtime classical recitals on Fridays at 1pm. **Phoenix Garden** provides sanctuary from the surrounding chaos. Otherwise, a rich musical heritage (still manifest in its guitar and music shops) makes **Denmark Street** – once known as 'Tin Pan Alley' – rock.

At the end of the street, **Charing Cross Road** is famous for bookshops – Foyles, Blackwell's, Borders – but there are independents selling remaindered stock. Heading towards **Leicester Square** (*see p71*), more specialist bookshops and a comic shops can be found around Cecil Court.

 WALK Round and round the garden

Start at **Centrepoint**, the lofty 1980s office tower that looms over Tottenham Court Road tube station, at the meeting of New Oxford Street and St Giles High Street. Turn your back on the undiscerning crowds tramping purposefully down Oxford Street and head east. Walk down St Giles High Street, the route in bygone days of criminals (and carts carrying their coffins) on their way to the Tyburn gallows in Marble Arch from Newgate (now Old Bailey). This was where they'd have their last drink (a drugged brew known as the St Giles Bowl), and where their corpses were returned to be interred.

In the garden of **St Giles-in-the-Fields** church you can see – on the side wall of the Angel pub backing on to the churchyard – a faded, peeling advertisement for a 'Continental Garage' which was 'Ouvert Jour/Nuit'. The garden itself is a lovely spot for a runaround; there are plenty of benches and a play area with slide, swings and a basketball hoop. This playground backs on to Stacey Street, and the entrance of **Phoenix Garden**. If the gate is locked, double back and walk down the short alley to the right of the church, leading past the **Phoenix Theatre**'s stage door and down Phoenix Street to the garden. Opposite the park entrance on Stacey Street, cross Shaftesbury Avenue and walk up Mercer Street; this leads to **Seven Dials** roundabout. Named after both the number of sundials mounted on the central monument (the seventh formed by the pillar itself) and the number of streets leading off it, these streets were among the worst slums in Dickensian London, described as being 'lost in the unwholesome vapour which hangs over the house-tops'. Now the area couldn't be more fashionable, it fairly buzzes with trendier-than-thou boutiques, expensive coffee shops and hair salons. On **Earlham Street** to the right you'll find a small street market flogging everything from flowers to T-shirts. Walk down Monmouth Street to the left, and duck through a covered alleyway

into **Neal's Yard** half-way down on the left. This lively, colourful collection of veggie cafés and New Age shops is almost like stepping back in time to the hippie era; it also makes a great place to stop and refuel. The **World Food Café** (*see p172*) and **Neal's Yard Dairy** (*see p165*) dish up healthy food and have dining areas with lovely views over the yard (the stairs might make them difficult to reach if you have a buggy).

Exiting the yard and turning left along Shorts Gardens brings you to **Neal Street**, a narrow thoroughfare that is filled with yet more pricey shoe shops and boutiques. At the top, turn left into Long Acre (high-street chains like Gap and Hennes suddenly seem like old friends after all the cutting-edge boutiques). Two streets along is Bow Street where you'll find the **Magistrates Court**. This is where London's first police force, the Bow Street Runners, was established in 1749 by the novelist Henry Fielding to combat crime and prostitution in an area then notorious for its bawdy houses. At the end of Bow Street turn right into Russell Street for the **Theatre Museum**, and up into the Piazza. Circumnavigating the Piazza clockwise, **London's Transport Museum** is on the left, with the covered **Jubilee Market** further up, and, turning right, **St Paul's** church and **Covent Garden Market**. Finally, on the corner, is the **Royal Opera House**, where you can take the escalator up to the Amphitheatre Bar and through to the terrace with views of the costume-making department and a covered loggia that overlooks **Covent Garden Piazza**. Here you can treat the family to one of the excellent, if posh and pricey (like everything associated with the ROH), sandwich platters and let this most colourful part of central London entertain you.

Tottenham Court Road

Centre Point

START

ST GILES HIGH ST

Phoenix Garden

NEW COMP ST

SHAFTESBURY AVENUE

NEAL STREET

SHORTS GARDENS

EARLHAM ST

Seven Dials

MONMOUTH STREET

LONG ACRE

BOW STREET

Neal Street

Bow Street Magistrates Court

FINISH

Royal Opera House

Around Town

Travelling in style in **Covent Garden Piazza**. *See p73.*

London's Transport Museum

Covent Garden Piazza, WC2E 7BB (7379 6344/ www.ltmuseum.co.uk). Covent Garden tube. **Open** 10am-6pm Mon-Thur, Sat, Sun; 10am-6pm Fri. **Admission** £5.95; £4.50 concessions; free under-16s when accompanied by an adult. **Credit** MC, V. **Map** p317 L7.

LTM close in August 2005 for an £18m refurbishment, so if you're thinking of visiting during the summer holidays, do ring first. When it reopens in November 2006, it will tell the story of urban transport and its impact on London and Londoners since 1800. Environmental conditions had previously prevented three-quarters of the collections from being shown; adaptations to the glazed roof promise to improve display areas and allow the first exhibiting of works such as Harry Beck's first sketches of his famous diagrammatic Tube map and original posters by surrealist Man Ray. New galleries featuring listening posts and interactive displays are planned, and families will still be able to follow trails and climb aboard many vehicles. In the meantime, these renovations don't entirely eliminate LTM's public presence: events are planned at their depot in Acton Town, so check the website for details of activities and online exhibitions. There's a great gift shop, too – children love the vehicular toys and souvenirs bearing the famous tube station roundel, and there are racks of nostalgic advertising posters, prints and postcards. *Buggy storage. Disabled access: lift, ramp, toilets. Nappy-changing facilities. Shop.*

Phoenix Garden

21 Stacey Street (entrance on St Giles Passage), WC2H 8DG (7379 3187). Tottenham Court Road tube. **Open** dawn-dusk daily. **Admission** free; donations appreciated. **Map** p315 K6.

Appropriately named, this Phoenix rose from the site of a car park, proving that all is not lost in the war against urban decay. Finding the garden's scrabble of crooked pathways, trellises and fragmented statues is a delightful surprise and once you know it's there (tucked away behind the Odeon cinema on Shaftesbury Avenue – rather handily, its entrance is right next to the playground in the garden of St Giles-in-the-Fields) it will become a favourite sanctuary from bustling multitudes. It also makes for a great picnic spot in good weather: gather ingredients from Neal's Yard (*see p165*) and enjoy the simple pleasure of sitting on a sunny bench and throwing sandwich crumbs to Cockney sparrows (the brown-feathered variety) – an increasingly rare sight in central London these days. The garden's planting is designed to encourage wildlife (so you'll find plenty of nesting birds, fluttering butterflies and creepy crawlies) and children will love the nature sanctuary, including a frog pond, in the recently extended back area of the garden. Staff rely on volunteers, so give what you can. Once a new kitchen is installed, tea and coffee will be available from the shed and there are often plants on sale; do buy some. Seasoned gardeners can offer hands-on assistance; call for details of how you can help. *Buggy access. Kiosk.*

Royal Opera House

Bow Street, WC2E 9DD (7240 1200/box office 7304 4000/www.royaloperahouse.org). Covent Garden tube. **Open** *Box office* 10am-8pm Mon-Sat. **Tours** 10.30am, 12.30pm, 2.30pm Mon-Sat (times may vary, book in advance). **Tickets** *Tours* £8; £7 under-18s, concessions. **Credit** AmEx, DC, MC, V. **Map** p317 L6.

Opera isn't renowned for appealing to the shorter attention span, and is usually considered too 'civilised' for the stereotypical modern kid. But the ROH is anything but stuffy:

its great glass ceilings make it a bright and airy space; regular free recital tasters are given (1-2pm Mon, pick up a ticket from the box office from 10am on the day), and the upstairs café offers terraced seating with fantastic views. Families hoping to take in a show can attend pre-performance workshops explaining the nuances of this highly stylised medium, but there are several annual productions that are less likely to go over younger heads (such as the recent *La Fille Mal Gardée*). Previous hits have included *Wind in the Willows* and *Clockwork*, based on Philip Pullman's short story. Children's commissions for 2005 include *Timecode*, an 'up-close theatrical encounter' with dance and music for the over-sevens about how we all use our time. Child-friendly Christmas shows are also planned for the 2005/6 festive season. Guided tours (£8; no under-eights) allow curious kids a unique glimpse into working dressing rooms and rehearsal halls. Over-16s keen to rack up some invaluable hands-on stage experience and admin skills should apply to the ROH's education department, which runs an unpaid work experience scheme.
Buggy access. Disabled access: lift, toilets. Nappy-changing facilities. Nearest picnic place: Covent Garden Piazza/St Paul's churchyard. Restaurants. Shop.

St Paul's Covent Garden

Bedford Street, WC2E 9ED (7836 5221/www.actors church.org). Covent Garden tube. **Open** 9am-4.30pm Mon-Fri; 9am-12.30pm Sun. *Services* 1.10pm Wed; 11am Sun. *Choral evensong* 4pm 2nd Sun of mth. Closed 1 Jan, bank hols. **Admission** free; donations appreciated. **Map** p317 L6.
Dominating the west side of the Piazza, St Paul's is the last extant section of Inigo Jones's original Palladian square s, and its peaceful interior offers respite from the carnival of tourists outside. It's far from emotionally detached from the theatrical heritage of its surroundings, though: the consecrated 'Actors Church' has walls adorned with

✕ LUNCH BOX

For recommended restaurants and cafés in the area, see reviews pp168-172.

Café Pasta 2-4 Garrick Street, WC2E 9BH (7497 2779).
Christopher's 18 Wellington Street, WC2E 7DD (7240 4222).
Great American Bagel Factory 18 Endell Street, WC2H 9BD (7497 1115).
Pizza Express 9 Bow Street, WC2E 7AH (7240 3443); 147 Strand, WC2R 1JA (7836 7716).
Pizza Paradiso 31 Catherine Street, WC2B 5JS (7836 3609).
Spaghetti House 24 Cranbourn Street, WC2H 7AB (7836 8168).
Strada 6 Great Queen Street, WC2B 5DH (7405 6293).
12 Bar Club 22-23 Denmark Place, WC2H 8NL (7916 6989).
Wagamama 1 Tavistock Street, WC2E 7PG (7836 3330).
West Cornwall Pasty Company 1 The Market, WC2E 8RA (7836 8336).

plaques commemorating the legends of screen and stage, including Charlie Chaplin, Noel Coward and Vivien Leigh. The church has served as a backdrop for several cameos in the history of theatre: on 9 May 1662 Samuel Pepys described being 'mighty pleased' after witnessing the first recorded Punch and Judy show here, an event marked by the annual May Fayre & Puppet Festival (held on the second Sunday in May; *see p26*), and George Bernard Shaw set the opening to *Pygmalion* under the ornate portico. That same portico is most notable today as a performance site for street entertainers. Well worth a watch, these appearance slots are booked up weeks in advance, and wannabes are strictly auditioned by the Covent Garden Market Committee before receiving permission to perform. Other dates for the diary include the Midsummer Fayre (10 July 2005), a joint fundraising venture organised with the Royal Theatrical Fund. Think village fête transported to WC2; in the garden you'll find tea tents, stalls manned by RTF actors, a big band, games and raffles, and a celebrity tent for autograph-hunters. At 11am on the first Sunday of each month Junior Church meets; under-10s can try storytelling, drama and art activities, then rejoin their parents after the service. The church also hosts regular concerts, and productions from the Mountview Academy of Theatre Arts; at Christmas over 30 carol services are held.
Buggy access. Disabled access: ramp. Nearest picnic place: churchyard.

Theatre Museum

Russell Street, WC2E 7PR (7943 4700/group bookings 7943 4806/www.theatremuseum.org). Covent Garden tube. **Open** 10am-6pm Tue-Sun. Closed bank hols. **Tours** noon daily. Call for school hols tour times. **Admission** free. **Credit** *Shop* AmEx, MC, V. **Map** p317 L6.
Britain's national museum of performing arts celebrates the history of live entertainment with testaments to bygone heroes and the shows that cast them into the public eye. There's also an excellent programme of children's activities. The maze-like basement galleries (reached via a corridor decorated with actors' handprints and signatures) will probably appeal more to older children with the patience for glass-encased curios; however, the regular make-up demonstrations (observe or be a model) and costume workshops are engaging for all visitors. On Saturdays, 3- to 14-year-olds can get stuck into Stage Truck's range of creative activities (1.30-5pm; also Thur in school holidays); storytelling sessions inspired by museum exhibits are also fun – volunteers assist with special effects and 'act out' to create atmosphere for the stories. These are held from 1.30-2pm on the first Saturday of the month, plus Wednesdays and Fridays during school holidays. The Kids Theatre Club, a joint venture with the Society of London Theatres based on West End shows, is a drama workshop for 8- to 12-year-olds to play games and try out performing with theatre professionals. Times are 10am-noon on Saturdays (£5 charge); booking is essential. Since May 2004, the '2D>3D' exhibition has examined how contemporary theatre designers develop creative concepts from 2D sketches into 3D models and, finally, full-sized realisation – host pieces include a sofa-sized spider designed for a touring production of *The Hobbit*. Check the website for details of exhibitions ('Brits on Broadway' runs 22 June 2005-30 Oct 2006) and drama birthday parties at the museum (£200, maximum 15 children, aged 5-12 years).
Buggy access. Disabled access: ramp, toilets. Nappy-changing facilities. Nearest picnic place: Covent Garden Piazza/St Paul's churchyard. Shop.

WESTMINSTER

Claiming the lion's share of London's historical greatness.

Churchill Museum & Cabinet War Rooms. See p78.

From the Prime Minister in Parliament to noble Nelson on his column, and from the glorious dead in Westminster Abbey to the Old Masters in the National Gallery, more Great Britons have become the stuff of legend in or around Westminster than anywhere else in London.

Nor is it just the people: architecturally, Westminster claims some of the capital's most instantly recognisable landmarks, and no amount of backpack-wielding snappers, open-top tour buses or tacky plastic merchandising can detract from the sheer excitement a monument like the **Houses of Parliament** inspires in kids and adults alike. Aesthetically, if not geographically, this is the very centre of London.

Royal Westminster may exude an air of 'look but don't touch', but it's only keeping up appearances, and the truth of it is that this is a simply great place for families to get involved. Sure, children may be able to do little but gawp at Charles Barry's neo-Gothic Palace of Westminster, but they can always nip over the road to the oft-neglected **Jewel Tower** – a rare fragment of the original medieval palace – where a permanent exhibition is dedicated to the development of Parliament. True, there's little they can do

with the steely eyed Horse Guards stationed on **Whitehall** but try (and fail) to stare them out, but they can always pop into the nearby **Guards' Museum** for a more in-depth look at these most dashing of royal recruits – even dress up like one if they want. And while the equally inscrutable Ministry of Defence has little time to entertain children, the excellent **Cabinet War Rooms** (this year boasting a brand new **Churchill Museum**) certainly does.

Nowhere in Westminster, however, is more likely to instil a sense of the area's attachment to nobility than **Westminster Abbey**: the list of those buried here reads like a 'Who's Who' of British history (Chaucer, Darwin, Newton – not to mention virtually every royal to have died in the last 500 years). Those who'd rather pass on the entry fee can loiter at their leisure in **Westminster Cathedral** – the viewing gallery at the top of the 273-foot (83-metre) Campanile Bell Tower is a must – or take in a free lunchtime concert at the more central **St Martin-in-the-Fields**.

There's a Brass Rubbing Centre in the latter – just one example of the area's dedication to fostering children's interest in the creative arts. Others can be found in the comprehensive

Tate Britain. *See p82.*

programme of children's workshops at the world-class trio of the **Tate Britain**, the **National Gallery** and the **National Portrait Gallery**, between them hosting so many masterpieces that you could spend an entire day in each.

There are numerous secluded spaces to chill and recharge the batteries among the hubbub. Not least of these is **St James's Park**. The less well-known Victoria Tower Gardens (off Millbank) boasts a riverside setting next to Parliament, as well as a small playground. For the full Westminster experience, however, it has to be sandwiches in the fully reinvigorated public arts forum that is **Trafalgar Square** (*see p80* **Pigeon English**); just don't tell Ken you fed crumbs to the pigeons, or you'll never be invited back.

Banqueting House

Whitehall, SW1A 2ER (7930 4179/www.hrp.org.uk). Westminster tube/Charing Cross tube/rail. **Open** 10am-5pm Mon-Sat (last entry 4.30pm). Sometimes closes at short notice; phone to check. Closed bank hols. **Admission** (LP) £4; £3 concessions; £2.60 5-15s; free under-5s. **Credit** MC, V. **Map** p317 L8.

Designed by Inigo Jones for James I, the Hall was intended to be used for state and ceremonial occasions. Sure enough, its opening in 1622 was marked by a traditional Twelfth Night masque. But such jollities were a distant memory when, in 1649, James's son Charles I was found guilty of treason by Cromwell's revolutionary forces and beheaded outside. These rich historical associations pull in today's tourists (the Sealed Knot Civil War re-enactment society even plays out the execution one Sunday each January), although Jones's architecture is magnificent on its own: from the extravagant main hall to the cryptic undercroft (conceived as a drinking den for James I). Rubens' original ceilings are still in place, despite extensive fire damage in 1698 and removal for their own safety during World War II. Audio guides (included in the ticket price) bring the scene to life for children. The Hall is also a venue for regular Monday lunchtime classical concerts throughout the

year. These are primarily aimed at adults, but there's a lighter Christmas concert in December (call or check the website for the precise date).

Buggy access. Cloakroom for buggy storage. Disabled access: toilets. Nappy-changing facilities. Nearest picnic place: St James's Park. Shop.

Churchill Museum & Cabinet War Rooms

Clive Steps, King Charles Street, SW1A 2AQ (7930 6961/www.iwm.org.uk). St James's Park or Westminster tube/3, 12, 24, 53, 159 bus. **Open** 10am-6pm daily (last entry 5pm). **Admission** £10; £8 concessions; £5 unemployed; £4-£5 disabled & carers; free under-16s (prices incl audio guides). **Credit** MC, V. **Map** p317 K9.

Churchill's secret underground HQ in World War II, the Cabinet War Rooms resembles a time capsule, sealed against the intervening years. From these halls – a subterranean maze of tunnels and secret rooms – Britain's military minds steered the war effort. The rooms have been maintained as a testament to those dark hours. The same maps chart progress on the same walls; the same steel beams – hurriedly put up to reinforce the building against bombs – still line the low ceilings. It's an atmospheric and effective installation guaranteed to bring the period to life for kids, who can take advantage of a number of activities including paper trails (downloadable from the website) and audio tours, with an expanded programme of family workshops in the school holidays. Summer 2005, for example, sees the Family History Project (25-29 July, 22-26 Aug) giving young ones the means and the tools to trace their family lineage; there are also talks on life in wartime Britain – some of them from actors dressed in period costume – and various online resources in the cutting-edge Clore Educational Centre. New for 2005 is the expansive and authoritative Churchill Museum (*see* **A man in full**).

Buggy access. Café. Disabled access: lift, toilet. Nappy-changing facilities. Nearest picnic place: St James's Park. Shop.

Guards' Museum

Wellington Barracks, Birdcage Walk, SW1E 6HQ (7414 3428/www.armymuseums.org.uk). St James's Park tube. **Open** 10am-4pm daily (last entry 3.30pm). Closed 19 Dec 2005-1 Apr 2006. *Tours* by arrangement; phone for details. **Admission** (LP) £2; £1 concessions; free under-16s. **Credit** *Shop* MC, V. **Map** p316 J9.

Children will get the most out of this little museum as a follow-up to seeing the Changing of the Guard at nearby Buckingham Palace (*see p72*). Otherwise its static displays may seem a little dusty. Most interesting for kids is a room set up to resemble a tent in the Crimean War. There's also a display of the first Gulf War, including helmets, a tin of Iraqi boot polish and, unsettlingly, Allied instructions for the treatment of prisoners of war ('do not chat or show any other sign of kindness to POW'). It's not all gung-ho, however: other notable items at the museum include Florence Nightingale's cup, and military tunics worn by a 16-year-old Queen Elizabeth. If the museum is quiet enough, staff happily let kids try on the 'one-size-fits-all' bearskin hats and regimental tunics they keep hidden behind the counter. There's also a range of military miniatures behind glass at the Guards Toy Soldier Centre and Shop – though mostly out of pocket-money range.

Buggy access. Disabled access: lift. Nearest picnic place: St James's Park. Shop.

A man in full

It's been some years since war has produced a really endearing personality – let's be honest, Iraq has hardly been a publicity exercise for the likes of Bush or Blair – which only adds to the legacy of Churchill as the unflappable and eminently quotable wartime Prime Minister. So iconic is the image of Churchill – an elegant if quite literally 'well-rounded' figure, cigar in hand – that kids who see him giving speeches on the big screen at the new Churchill Museum often ask the name of the actor playing him.

Which is exactly why the Museum – located in the subterranean **Cabinet War Rooms** (*see p78*) – opened in February 2005; on one level to commemorate the 40th anniversary of Churchill's death, but on a more permanent basis to flesh out his incredibly complex character for generations to come. And in keeping with the colourful nature of its subject, there's plenty in the museum to keep little ones amused. The centrepiece of the display is an enormous digital Lifeline (essentially a flat-screen monitor the length and breadth of a banquet hall table) in which is stored, chronologically, literally thousands of Churchill-related documents and images, many of them brought to life with pyrotechnic animations (a soaring V2 rocket, the sonic devastation of the atomic bomb), all accessed by an ingenious point-and-click system.

All this may be a bit overwhelming for younger kids, but there's thankfully an abundance of more touchy-feely things for little fingers to get to grips with – from the virtual palette that allows them to recreate Churchill's oil paintings on a digital screen, to the wooden mock-up of his family home in Chatsworth, Kent, complete with sights, sounds and smells (from an adjustable view of his wife Clementine's bedroom to the scent of her perfume or his cigar). There's even an interactive fish pond.

The Museum isn't afraid to promote the idea that Churchill was an occasionally ridiculous character: from his purple one-piece 'romper' suits and personalised dining table with a section cut out for his stomach, to his unconventional breakfast menus (melon, omelette or ham and eggs, followed by a cutlet or leg of chicken, marmalade and coffee), there's plenty here to laugh at.

Ultimately, after assimilating all the biographical footnotes (including the fact that he was a terrible student; escaped from an African POW camp; and arrested women's lib protesters by the lorryload) and artefacts (well-loved toy soldiers, one Nobel Peace Prize and, of course, a half-chewed cigar), kids are often left with a mental image quite different from the one they arrived with. Yet the image remains strangely familiar, with its protruding belly, V-sign and all.

Houses of Parliament

Parliament Square, SW1A 0AA (Commons info 7219 4272/Lords info 7219 3107/tours 0870 906 3773/ www.parliament.uk). Westminster tube. **Open** (when in session) *House of Commons Visitors' Gallery* 2.30-10.30pm Mon; 11.30am-7.30pm Tue-Thur; 9.30am-3pm Fri. Closed bank hols. *House of Lords Visitors' Gallery* from 2.30pm Mon-Wed; from 11am Thur, Fri. *Tours* summer recess only; phone for details. **Admission** *Visitors' Gallery* free. *Tours* £7; £5 concessions, 5-16s; free under-5s, disabled; £22 family (2+2). **Credit** *Tours* MC, V. **Map** p317 L9.

Generations of political activists have made this neo-Gothic building the focus of their protests. Brian Haw is one such. He left his Worcestershire home in June 2001 to begin a vigil in Parliament Square to campaign against sanctions (and later war) in Iraq. Across the road, Parliament looks on unmoved. The Palace of Westminster became a permanent home for Parliament in 1532, when Henry VIII relocated to Whitehall. These days the only parts of the original palace still standing are Westminster Hall, where the Queen Mother's body lay in state before her funeral in 2002, and the Jewel Tower (*see below*); the rest was destroyed by fire in 1834. The building we see today was rebuilt by Charles Barry and Augustus Pugin. Children are usually satisfied by the mere proximity of the big old bell known as Big Ben. The various stories behind its name certainly make for more interesting listening than sessions of the Commons or Lords, which are open daily to families with children old enough to sign their name. The wait can stretch into hours. Prime Minister's Questions (every Wednesday) tends to be oversubscribed: it is easiest to get inside the Commons between 6pm and 10.30pm on Mondays, after 1.30pm on Tuesdays, Wednesdays and Thursdays, and at 9am on Fridays (phone to check opening times in advance). If possible, book tickets with your local MP, who can also arrange a tour of the building. *Buggy access. Café. Disabled access: lifts, toilets. Nearest picnic place: Victoria Tower Gardens. Shop.*

Jewel Tower

Abingdon Street, SW1P 3JY (7222 2219/www. english-heritage.org.uk). Westminster tube. **Open** *Apr-Oct* 10am-5pm daily. *Nov-Mar* 10am-4pm daily. Last entry 30mins before closing. **Admission** (EH/LP) £2.60; £2 concessions; £1.30 5-16s; free under-5s. Call to check prices for special events. **Credit** MC, V. **Map** p317 L9.

One of the two parts of medieval Westminster Palace still standing, the fragmentary Jewel Tower or 'King's Privy Wardrobe' originally marked the south-western corner of the palace grounds. The tower was built in 1365 to house the private treasures of Edward III. A moat (now filled) was channelled from the Thames – primarily to protect the royal loot, although it had the added advantage of bringing fresh fish to the kitchen door. Since being built the tower has served as both a repository for Parliamentary records and a Board of Trade testing centre for weights and measures, but these days English Heritage keeps it open to the public – winding staircases, unrestored ribbed vault and all. A 'Parliament Past and Present' exhibition looks at the development of today's parliamentary structure, but younger kids will probably be more interested in the ancient sword on display in the on-site shop. It dates back to around AD 800 and looks like something on loan from Middle Earth. *Nearest picnic place: surrounding green. Shop.*

Around Town

Pigeon English

Ken Livingstone's *fatwa* against the Trafalgar Square pigeons is taking effect. Since he outlawed the area's long-serving seed seller and banned all feeding of the already bloated birds in 2001, the number of wings in Trafalgar Square has steadily declined. Good news for Nelson – the droppings are said to be eroding his chiselled jawline – but a shame for young ones who'll never know the hysterical pleasure of having a fat pigeon sit on their head and peck seed from their tender scalp.

Getting rid of the pigeons was only part of the plan. In giving Londoners 'a public space to be proud of', the Greater London Authority has over the last couple of years installed new paving, lighting and street furniture, opened an alfresco Café in the Square and public toilets, and – most mercifully – pedestrianised the north road that had for years effectively turned the square into a giant, smog-choked roundabout.

The transformation of this most famous of London landmarks is spectacular, but it goes further than looks alone – indeed, a reinvigorated programme of cultural happenings has given the square a new lease of life. While still the undisputed hub of political activism in London (several anti-war marches have culminated here in recent years, and Nelson Mandela addressed a debt-relief rally in February 2005), the range of annual events is now as creative as it is cathartic. Since its reopening in August 2003, Trafalgar Square has seen a huge range of events tied into various world cultures, including Brazilian samba, Caribbean steel bands and Malaysian performance art, with many of them aimed specifically at families. Forthcoming attractions include a Children's Art Day in July, packed with hands-on activities, and a series of events as part of the **Summer in the Square** festival, with giant puppet shows, dance and music (visit www.london.gov.uk for more information, or phone 7983 4100).

It's not all a big song and dance. Since the refurbishment, Trafalgar Square has become a public centre for contemporary art installations – some of them more static than others. The celebrated Fourth Plinth project, for example, sees a panel of judges select one piece of contemporary sculpture every other year to occupy the traditionally empty plinth on the north-west corner of the square (the others are fairly starchy bronze busts of George IV, Sir Charles Napier and Sir Henry Havelock, but insufficient funds prevented a commissioned equestrian statue from ever taking its pride of place on the fourth plinth). The current winner (Marc Quinn's gentle *Alison Lapper Pregnant*) will be replaced by German artist Thomas Schütte's refractive Perspex colourscape, *Hotel for the Birds*, in summer 2006.

Less self-explanatory art projects have also been drawn to the square; in October 2004, Doug Fisher set tongues wagging (and jaws chomping) when he unceremoniously piled 30,000 bananas in front of the National Gallery. Perhaps most maverick of all, however, was Bristolian graffiti artist and anonymous celebrity Banksy who, after 11 September 2001, scrawled 'Bury the dead, not the truth' on the pedestal of Nelson's Column, inadvertently fusing the square's subversive political past and its more creative public present.

The authorities got rid of it pretty sharpish. Which is great news for the kids, because – ironically enough – war will be the last thing on their minds as they clamber gleefully over the lions guarding the 170-foot (52-metre) testament to Britain's most celebrated military commander. Nelson's turf is finally becoming the family forum it was always destined to be; from where he's standing, the future must look pretty sweet.

National Gallery

Trafalgar Square, WC2N 5DN (information line 7747 2885/www.nationalgallery.org.uk). Charing Cross tube/rail/24, 29, 176 bus. **Open** 10am-6pm Mon, Tue, Thur-Sun; 10am-9pm Wed. *Tours* 11.30am, 2.30pm Mon, Tue, Thur, Fri, Sun; 11.30am, 2.30pm, 6pm, 6.30pm Wed; 11.30am, 12.30pm, 2.30pm, 3.30pm Sat. **Admission** (LP) free. *Temporary exhibitions* prices vary. *Tours* free. **Credit** *Shop* MC, V. **Map** p317 K7.

A national treasure, with one of the finest collections of classic Western European paintings in the world (including Van Gogh's *Sunflowers* and Da Vinci's *The Virgin of the Rocks*), and it makes certain that its younger guests have a lot of fun discovering them. There are listening posts offering headphone commentaries on more than 1,000 pieces from the collection, while a Micro Gallery allows children to personalise and print out their own themed tours from a number of computer terminals in the more modern Sainsbury Wing. There are also child-oriented audio tours and paper trails ('Monster Hunt', for example). Best of all, though, are the laid-back children's workshops, including the 'Magic Carpet' storytelling sessions, aimed at under-fives and run on weekdays during school holidays, and the 'Second Weekend' workshops, which fall (naturally) on the second weekend of every month and are led by a contemporary artist, focusing each time on a different painting from the galleries. All materials are provided, and the sessions take place at 11.30am on Saturdays and Sundays (repeated at 2.30pm). The remaining three weekends of the month bring an array of staff talks, starting at 11.30am, which are constructed around paintings chosen to appeal to all ages. Forthcoming exhibitions include work by George Stubbs (until 25 Sept 2005) and Peter Paul Rubens (26 Oct 2005 to 15 Jan 2006).
Buggy access. Café. Disabled access: lift, toilets. Lifts. Nappy-changing facilities. Nearest picnic place: Leicester Square/Trafalgar Square. Restaurant. Shop.

National Portrait Gallery

2 St Martin's Place, WC2H 0HE (7306 0055/ tours 7312 2483/www.npg.org.uk). Leicester Square tube/Charing Cross tube/rail/24, 29, 176 bus. **Open** 10am-6pm Mon-Wed, Sat, Sun; 10am-9pm Thur, Fri. Closed Good Friday. *Tours* times vary, call or check website for details. **Admission** free. *Temporary exhibitions* prices vary. *Audio guide* free (suggested donation £3). *Tours* free. **Credit** AmEx, MC, V. **Map** p317 K7.

What makes the NPG so unique is its philosophy: the collections are concerned with history, not art, gathering together a pantheon of those who have contributed to creating British society. Thus a short wander around its halls will turn up faces as far removed as William Shakespeare and Benny Hill, captured in a variety of media (paintings, photographs, sculptures) by artists ranging from medieval illuminators to celebrity snappers like Mario Testino. The permanent collection is organised by period – the restored Regency galleries were reopened in 2003 – and there are regular temporary exhibitions, including (until Sept 2005) a child-friendly 'Family Faces' exhibition in the Studio gallery, with hands-on activities and a big box of dressing-up clothes to put younger visitors in the picture. To help families make head or tail of more adult-orientated exhibitions, the gallery provides free family rucksacks on a first-come, first-served basis. The rucksacks correspond to one of three galleries – Tudor, Victorian and 20th Century – and each is stuffed with activities (for three- to 12-year-

olds) from jigsaws and dressing-up items to paper trails. There are also regular holiday workshops tying into the various exhibitions; recently these were inspired by a display of photographs of the Mexican artist Frida Kahlo, and saw little ones decorating Mexican masks and plates, and making skeletal Day of the Dead puppets.
Buggy access. Café. Disabled access (Orange Street entrance): lifts, ramps, toilets. Nappy-changing facilities. Nearest picnic place: Leicester Square/Trafalgar Square. Restaurant. Shops.

St James's Park

SW1A 2JB (7930 1793/www.royalparks.org.uk). St James's Park tube/3, 11, 12, 24, 53, 211 bus. **Open** 5am-midnight daily. **Map** p317 K8.

As a Royal Park, St James's isn't exactly maintained with little ones in mind, but it's still a delightful spot for families to escape the crowds. Its immaculately manicured gardens may be no-go zones for bicycles, in-line skates and other wheeled instruments, but there's a good children's playground and plenty of space for an impromptu picnic. In 2004 the Inn The Park (*see p172*) restaurant opened its doors to people of all ages. Best of all, however, is the range of feathered friends – gulls, swans, geese, pelicans – wandering over from their breeding grounds on Duck Island. You can watch the pelicans being fed between 2pm and 3pm each day, and the park is bordered by Buckingham Palace (*see p72*), the Cabinet War Rooms (*see p78*) and the Guards' Museum (*see p78*).
Buggy access. Disabled access: toilet. Kiosk. Nappy-changing facilities. Restaurant.

St Martin-in-the-Fields

Trafalgar Square, WC2N 4JJ (7766 1100/Brass Rubbing Centre 7930 9306/www.stmartin-in-the-fields.org). Leicester Square tube/Charing Cross tube/rail. **Open** *Church* 8am-6.30pm daily. *Brass Rubbing Centre* 10am-6pm Mon-Sat; noon-6pm Sun. *Evening concerts* Thur-Sat & alternate Tue 7.30pm. **Admission** free. *Brass Rubbing* (LP) £2.90-£15 (special rates for groups & families). *Evening concerts* prices vary. **Credit** MC, V. **Map** p317 L7.

Believe it or not, St Martin offers more than just a glorious porch for confused tourists to park on while checking their maps. For a start, the interior of the church is an unusually bright and cheering sanctuary of sculptures, paintings and potted plants, all presided over by an intricately carved baroque ceiling. It makes an inspired refuge from the mass of tourists outside, never more so than during one of the free lunchtime choral recitals or ticketed evening concerts (1pm and 7.30pm respectively; check the website for details). What makes St Martin such fun for children, though, is its fantastic 18th-century crypt, home not only to hearty self-service fodder at the excellent Café in the Crypt (*see p172*), but also to London's only Brass Rubbing Centre. Here kids can create their own lasting memento of medieval London, with knights and dragons among the images available. Rubbings – which take about an hour to complete – are supervised, and all materials provided. Backed by a lottery grant of almost £15 million, two years of major renovations are finally underway to bring the beleaguered church and crypt up to date – under the patronage of Prince Charles, no less, who calls St Martin 'one of the vital parts of our national heritage'.
Buggy access. Café. Disabled access: ramp to church, toilet. Nearest picnic place: Leicester Square/Trafalgar Square. Shop.

🍴 LUNCH BOX

For recommended restaurants and cafés in the area, see reviews pp172-173.

Café in the Crypt St Martin-in-the-Fields, WC2N 4JJ (7839 4342).

Cathedral Kitchen Westminster Cathedral, Victoria Street, SW1P 1QW (7798 9055).

Gallery Café National Gallery, Trafalgar Square, WC2N 5DN (7747 2885).

Inn The Park St James's Park, SW1A 2BJ (7451 9999).

Jenny Lo's Tea House 14 Eccleston Street, SW1W 9LT (7259 0399).

Laughing Halibut 38 Strutton Ground, SW1P 2HR (7799 2844).

McDonald's 155 Victoria Street, SW1E 5NA (7828 6911).

Pizza Express 85 Victoria Street, SW1H 0HW (7222 5270).

Ponti's Café 127 Victoria Street, SW1E 6RD (7828 7242).

The Portrait Restaurant National Portrait Gallery, St Martin's Place, WC2H 0HE (7312 2490).

Texas Embassy Cantina 1 Cockspur Street, SW1Y 5DL (7925 0077).

West Cornwall Pasty Company 5 Strutton Ground, SW1P 2HY (7233 3777).

Tate Britain

Millbank, SW1P 4RG (7887 8008/www.tate.org.uk). Pimlico tube/C10, 77A, 88 bus. **Open** 10am-5.50pm daily. **Tours** 11am, noon, 2pm, 3pm Mon-Fri; noon, 3pm Sat, Sun. **Admission** (LP) free. *Temporary exhibitions* prices vary. *Tours* free. **Credit** MC, V. **Map** p317 L7.

'Old' Tate's collection of British fine art from 1500 to the present day includes a permanent collection that unites artists from Blake to Bacon in a grand riverside setting. This allows neighbouring galleries to focus on themes as diverse as 18th-century seascapes and visions of religious apocalypse, while still leaving several large halls free for staging regular temporary shows. Best of all is the Tate's ongoing effort to help younger audiences engage with and enjoy the art on display. For example, the Art Space (1-5pm Sat, Sun) serves as a handsome cross between a crèche and a chill-out room, replete with creative toys and games for when the never-ending halls are getting a little much for younger attention spans. Equally charming is the time-honoured Art Trolley, wheeled out every Saturday and Sunday (11am-5pm), and packed with a wide range of make-and-do activities, while 'Tate Tales', on the first Sunday of each month, sees resident storytellers spinning yarns about individual works. There's also a range of events for schools and a number of themed workshops during half-term and holiday breaks, as well as various activity bags, audio tours and paper trails waiting behind the information desk for little explorers.

Buggy access. Café. Disabled access: ramps, toilets. Lift. Nappy-changing facilities. Nearest picnic place: lawns (either side of gallery)/Riverside Gardens (by Vauxhall Bridge). Restaurant. Shop.

Westminster Abbey

20 Dean's Yard, SW1P 3PA (7222 5152/tours 7654 4900/www.westminster-abbey.org). St James's Park or Westminster tube/11, 12, 24, 88, 159, 211 bus. **Open** *Chapter House, Nave & Royal Chapels* 9.30am-3.45pm Mon, Tue, Thur, Fri; 9.30am-7pm Wed; 9.30am-1.45pm Sat. *Abbey Museum* 10.30am-4pm Mon-Sat. *Cloisters* 8am-6pm Mon-Sat. *College Garden* Apr-Sept 10am-6pm Tue-Thur; Oct-Mar 10am-4pm Tue-Thur. Last entry 1hr before closing. **Tours** phone for details. **Admission** £8; £6 11-15s, concessions; free under-11s with paying adult; £18 family (2+2). *Chapter House* free. *Abbey Museum* (EH/LP) free (audio guide £3). **Credit** MC, V. **Map** p317 K9.

The location for every coronation since 1066, and a final resting place for many crowned heads (and bodies), Westminster Abbey has had a nave-ful of British royals. The abbey was consecrated in 1065, eight days before the death of Edward the Confessor. His body remains entombed in the abbey, although where exactly is unknown: it was removed from his elaborate shrine and reburied at an unmarked location during the Reformation. Elizabeth I is also interred here, as is Mary Queen of Scots. Poets' Corner is home to the graves of Dryden, Samuel Johnson, Browning and Tennyson, while several 20th-century martyrs (including Martin Luther King Jr) have been immortalised in 15th-century niches above the west door. Indeed, from the extraordinary nave – the highest roof in Britain at 101ft (31m) – to the seemingly endless sea of stained glass, Westminster Abbey is an inspired and inspiring place for all ages.

Buggy access. Café. Disabled access: toilets. Nearest picnic place: college gardens (10am-6pm Tue-Thur)/ St James's Park. Shop.

Westminster Cathedral

Victoria Street, SW1P 1QW (7798 9055/tours 7798 9064/www.westminstercathedral.org.uk). St James's Park tube/Victoria tube/rail/11, 24, 211, 507 bus. **Open** 7am-7pm Mon-Fri, Sun; 8am-7pm Sat. *Campanile* Apr-Nov 9.30am-12.30pm, 1-5pm daily; Dec-Mar 9.30am-12.30pm, 1-5pm Thur-Sun. **Tours** by arrangement; phone for details. **Admission** free; donations appreciated. *Campanile* £3; £1.50 concessions; £7 family (2+2). *Audio guide* £2.50; £1.50 concessions. **No credit cards. Map** p316 J10.

London's Catholic cathedral has relative newcomer status among Westminster's other religious edifices: the elaborate neo-Byzantine exterior (inspired by the Hagia Sophia in Istanbul) was completed at the beginning of the 20th century. Although the cavernous interior sparkles with coloured mosaics and marbled stone pillars – not to mention a cross the size of a semi-detached house hovering eerily above the altar – the high ceiling remains an ominous and unpainted black, casting a strange shadow over the many characters below who are crouched in prayer, crossing themselves with holy water or chatting quietly to the priest. Tourists are welcome (although they're respectfully asked not to break the reverie; the shop sells a neat little workbook that leads kids on an activity trail around the building, and the Cathedral Kitchen is on hand to provide half-time refreshments. If you have a head for heights, the 273ft (83m) Campanile Bell Tower is topped by a four-sided gallery with spectacular views across London; there's a lift all the way to the top. Consult the cathedral's excellent website for details of choral and music recitals.

Buggy access. Café. Disabled access: ramp. Shop.

KENSINGTON & CHELSEA

Marvellous museums, posh parks and an all-embracing celebrity presence.

Diana, Princess of Wales Memorial Fountain.

The Royal Borough of Kensington and Chelsea is home to three of London's most popular learned institutions, a grand royal palace and a pair of plush parks. Such a wealth of attractions for families, in fact, that come rain or shine you will find plenty to do. The **Natural History Museum** most famously houses the dinosaurs, the **Science Museum** shows how science touches all aspects of life, and beautiful treasures are the mainstay of the **Victoria & Albert Museum**. But it's not all about learning in the Royal Borough. **Hyde Park** and **Kensington Gardens** are fine public spaces, with a brace of tributes to the People's Princess. The **Diana, Princess of Wales Memorial Playground** is a top attraction for kids, and the **Diana, Princess of Wales Memorial Fountain** is *some* paddling pool (actually, it's toe-dangling

only, and looking somewhat diminished by its new tarmac border). Then there's the oldest boating lake in the capital, the **Serpentine**, and **Kensington Palace**, birthplace of Queen Victoria in 1819 and home to the late Princesses Diana and Margaret.

Chelsea's famous **Sloane Square** is presided over by the world-renowned Royal Court Theatre and marks the start of its high street, modish **King's Road**. The **National Army Museum** and the Chelsea Royal Hospital, site of the Chelsea Flower Show, are a short walk away.

Baden-Powell House

65-67 Queen's Gate, SW7 5JS (7584 7031/ www.scoutbase.org.uk). South Kensington tube. **Open** 7am-10pm daily. Closed 22 Dec-3 Jan. **Admission** free. **Credit** MC, V. **Map** p313 D10.
Opened in 1961 (refurbished in 1997), Robert Baden-Powell's memorial hostel provides accommodation for about 300,000 people from 30 different countries each year, with family rooms for visitors with children. There's an exhibition on the ground floor about the Chief Scout's life. *Buggy access. Café. Disabled access: toilet. Nappy-changing facilities. Nearest picnic place: Natural History Museum gardens. Shop.*

Chelsea Physic Garden

66 Royal Hospital Road (entrance on Swan Walk), SW3 4HS (7352 5646/www.chelseaphysicgarden.co.uk). Sloane Square tube/11, 19, 239 bus. **Open** *Apr-Oct* noon-5pm Wed; 2-6pm Sun. **Tours** times vary, call to check. **Admission** £5; £3 5-16s, concessions (not incl OAPs); free under-5s. *Tours* free. **Credit** *Shop* AmEx, MC, V. **Map** p313 F12.
The garden was set up in 1673, but the key phase of development was under Sir Hans Sloane in the 18th century. Its beds contain healing herbs and rare trees, dye plants and medicinal vegetables; plants are also sold. Public opening hours are restricted – because it is primarily a centre for research and education. That said, the education department organises activity days with interesting botanical themes over Easter and summer holidays. Activity days should be pre-booked, are suitable for seven- to 11-year-olds, cost £5 per child per day and will take place on the following days in 2005: 26, 27 July; 2-3, 9-11, 16-17 August. The annual Summer Fair (11am-6pm, 26 June 2005) makes a fun family day out. Educational visits and teacher-training days can also be arranged. *Buggy access. Café. Disabled access: ramp, toilet. Nappy-changing facilities. Shop.*

WALK On the trail of Princess Diana

You can barely take a step in **Kensington Gardens** without happening upon some memorial or other to the late Diana Spencer, whose ambition to be the 'Queen of all (our) hearts' would appear to have been fulfilled. Walk this way to explore all the parkland tributes to the late Princess of Wales. At a leisurely pace, this should take you around two hours and, as all the paths are asphalt, it's fine for pushing a buggy. Enter at the Black Lion Gate, so you can begin with playtime in the **Diana, Princess of Wales Memorial Playground**. Once you've managed to drag the children away from this wonderland, follow the Broad Walk towards handsome **Kensington Palace**, where many royals have lived in the past, and where Princess Diana herself also had apartments. You can walk up to the grand front door for a closer look without having to pay the entrance fee, but if you decide to go in for a visit allow at least an hour to see it all. From the Broad Walk, take the path just to the north of the Round Pond and join the **Diana, Princess of Wales Memorial Walk** – it's marked by brass domes, one foot (30cm) in diameter, set into the path. (The Memorial Walk actually follows a circular route that starts and finishes at Hyde Park Corner and measures a little over seven miles (11km) in length, but for this walk follow only the Kensington Gardens section). Walk towards the imposing statue of horse and rider, 'Physical Energy', by George Frederick Watts. This spot has great views: there's Kensington Palace and the Round Pond to the west, south-eastwards sits the **Serpentine Gallery**, while to the south glistens Queen Victoria's monument to Prince Albert. It didn't always shine, having been blackened in World War I to prevent it being targeted by Zeppelins; it was also damaged during World War II.

Back on the walk, you'll pass George Frampton's small statue of **Peter Pan**, which has stood next to the Long Water since 1912. The formal Italian Gardens, a little further on, were built in 1862 and incorporate pretty fountains, although eagle-eyed infants will be far more interested in the small playground just up the slope. There are children's toilets near here if needed. Once you have coaxed everyone back to the Memorial Walk, follow the path around the Long Water towards the main road. At the top of the hill turn right, cross the road and walk towards the Serpentine Bridge, where you can finish off by dangling your feet in the **Diana, Princess of Wales Memorial Fountain**. Mind how you go; we don't want any nasty accidents. Look out for the trees laden with impassioned tributes to the dead princess; some of the poetry is quite hysterical.

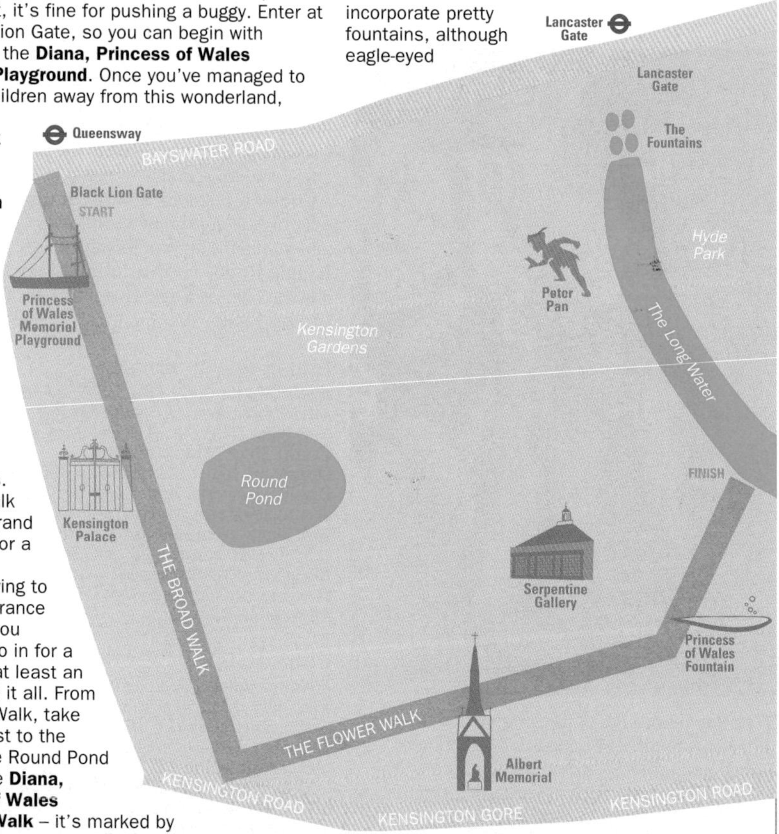

Lancaster Gate

Lancaster Gate

Queensway

BAYSWATER ROAD

The Fountains

Black Lion Gate
START

Hyde Park

Princess of Wales Memorial Playground

Kensington Gardens

Peter Pan

The Long Water

Round Pond

FINISH

Kensington Palace

THE BROAD WALK

Serpentine Gallery

Princess of Wales Fountain

THE FLOWER WALK

Albert Memorial

KENSINGTON ROAD

KENSINGTON GORE

KENSINGTON ROAD

Diana, Princess of Wales Memorial Playground

Near Black Lion Gate, Broad Walk, Kensington Gardens, W8 2UH (7298 2117/recorded info 7298 2141/www.royalparks.gov.uk). Bayswater or Queensway tube/12, 148, 390 bus. **Open** *Summer* 10am-8pm daily. *Winter* 10am-4pm (or 1hr before dusk, if earlier) daily. **Admission** free. All adults & children over 12 must be accompanied by a child. **Map** p310 C7.

This commemorative play area is a wonderland for youngsters. The focal point is a pirate ship in a sea of fine, white sand. Children enjoy scaling the rigging to the crow's nest and adore the ship's wheel, cabins, pulleys and ropes. During the summer months the mermaids' fountain and rocky outcrops are fab for water play. Beyond these shipshape glories lies the tepee camp: a trio of wigwams, each large enough to hold a sizeable tribe. The tree-house encampment has walkways, ladders, slides and 'tree phones'. The area's connection with Peter Pan's creator JM Barrie is remembered in images from the story etched into the glass in the Home Under the Ground (which also houses the toilets and playground office). Many of the playground's attractions appeal to the senses: scented shrubs, whispering willows and bamboo are planted throughout, footfall chimes and touchy-feely sculpture engage young visitors. Much of the equipment has been designed for use by children with special needs, including those in wheelchairs. There's plenty of seating for parents and the newly refurbished café has a children's menu. During the school summer holidays there's a programme of free entertainment, such as visits by clowns or storytelling sessions (11am, 1pm, 3pm Mon-Fri).

Unaccompanied adults aren't allowed in, but they can view the gardens between 9.30am and 10am daily.
Buggy access. Café. Disabled access: toilet. Kiosk. Nappy-changing facilities. Nearest picnic place: Kensington Gardens.

Hyde Park

W2 2UH (7298 2100/www.royalparks.gov.uk). Hyde Park Corner, Knightsbridge, Lancaster Gate or Marble Arch tube/2, 8, 10, 12, 23, 38, 73, 94 bus. **Open** 5am-midnight daily. **Map** p311 E7.

Hyde Park is the largest of London's Royal Parks (1.5 miles/2.5km long and about a mile/1.5km wide) and was the first to be opened to the public. Year round the park's perimeter is popular with both in-line and roller-skaters, as well as with bike- and horse-riders (there are riding schools near Rotten Row, part of the wide riding track around Hyde Park). If you're cycling, stick to the designated tracks; only children under ten are allowed to cycle on the footpaths. At the west side of the park is the Serpentine, London's oldest boating lake, which has its complement of ducks, coots, swans and tufty-headed grebes. You can rent rowing boats and pedalos from March to October. The Serpentine also has its own swimming club, whose members are so keen that they've been known to break the winter ice to indulge in their daily dip.

The park's new water feature, the Diana, Princess of Wales Memorial Fountain, is on a gentle slope near the Serpentine bridge and was opened by the Queen in July 2004. The circular structure, which was designed by American architect Kathryn Gustafson, is a Cornish granite channel filled with running water. The fountain was beset with problems in its inaugural summer: slippery stones, leaf-clogged pumps, algae and muddy banks resulted in its closure on several occasions. Work to help

Waterplay at the **Science Museum**. *See p89.*

Around Town

Big savings
with the 'extended' Family Railcard

60% off kids' fares   ## Adults save 1/3

Family size savings are waiting for you with a Family Railcard. Kids get 60% off and adults save 1/3 on most rail fares throughout Britain. It costs just £20 for a whole year and up to 4 adults and 4 children can travel on one card – they don't even have to be related.

Pick up a leaflet at any staffed train station or
call 08457 48 49 50 for the telesales number of your local Train Company.

National Rail   www.family-railcard.co.uk   Family Railcard

prevent such problems happening again took place in early 2005 and the fountain reopened to the public in May.

At the park's eastern end, near Marble Arch, is Speakers' Corner, the world's oldest platform for public speaking. The right to free speech is exercised here every Sunday. Talking of exercise, you can watch the Household Cavalry emerge smartly from their barracks on South Carriage Drive at 10.30am every morning (9.30am on Sundays). They ride across the park to Horse Guards Parade, prior to the Changing of the Guard.

Buggy access. Cafés. Disabled access: toilets.

Kensington Gardens

W8 2UH (7298 2117/www.royalparks.gov.uk). Bayswater, High Street Kensington, Lancaster Gate or Queensway tube/9, 12, 28, 49, 148 bus. **Open** 6am-midnight daily. **Map** p310 C7.

These gardens cover 260 acres (105ha) and meet Hyde Park at the Serpentine. The best element, as far as children are concerned, is undoubtedly the Diana, Princess of Wales Memorial Playground (*see p85*), but the Serpentine Gallery (*see p89*) should not be overlooked. No one could ignore the overblown Albert Memorial, complete with a thrice-life-size statue of Prince Albert, picked out in gold and seated under a 180ft/55m-high canopy and spire (for guided tours ring 7495 0916). Children like the Round Pond, with its eels and sticklebacks, ducks and geese. By Long Water there's a bronze statue of Peter Pan, built by Sir George Frampton in 1912 to honour Pan's creator, JM Barrie. There's usually a Peter Pan-themed fun day to mark the birthday of the boy who never grew up, it's planned for 23 July 2005, check the website for more details. Kensington Gardens is also home to what surely must be the poshest park café in the capital: the Orangery, a grand glass-fronted building designed by Sir John Vanburgh in 1704. It's open daily throughout the year for morning coffee, light lunches and afternoon tea, and has a children's menu and high chairs.

Buggy access. Cafés. Disabled access: toilet.

Kensington Palace

W8 4PX (7937 9561/booking line 0870 751 5180/ www.hrp.org.uk). Bayswater, High Street Kensington or Queensway tube/9, 10, 49, 52, 70 bus. **Open** Mar-Oct 10am-6pm daily. Nov-Feb 10am-5pm daily. Last entry 1hr before closing. Closed 24-26 Dec. **Admission** (LP) incl audio guide £11; £7.15-15s; £8.30 concessions; free under-5s; £32 family (2+3). **Credit** MC, V. **Map** p310 B8.

William III and his wife Mary came to live in this Jacobean mansion in 1689 when Kensington was a country village. The couple moved from Whitehall Palace to escape the smoggy air, which played havoc with William's asthma, having commissioned Sir Christopher Wren to turn the existing house into a palace. Since then many royals have called it home. Queen Victoria, born and baptised here, enjoyed living in Kensington so much that she awarded the borough its 'Royal' status. The Duke and Duchess of Kent have apartments in the palace. The palace is open for tours of the State Apartments, the King's Gallery and, the most popular part, the Royal Ceremonial Dress Collection, which includes worn by Princess Diana. Until September (although the date may be extended) there's a display of dresses from the Queen's wardrobe 1945-72, including the gown she wore to meet Marilyn Monroe in 1956.

Buggy access. Disabled access: toilet. Nappy-changing facilities. Nearest picnic place: grounds. Restaurant. Shop.

National Army Museum

Royal Hospital Road, SW3 4HT (7730 0717/ www.national-army-museum.ac.uk). Sloane Square tube/11, 137, 239 bus. **Open** 10am-5.30pm daily. Closed bank hols. **Admission** free. **Credit** *Shop* AmEx, MC, V. **Map** p313 F12.

No prizes for guessing what's on offer here: the whole history of the British Army marching past in ceremonial uniform. Prime exhibits include 'The Road to Waterloo', a version of the famous battle starring 75,000 toy soldiers; the skeleton of Napoleon's beloved mount, Marengo; and Florence Nightingale's lamp. Children love the deliciously bizarre exhibits like the frostbitten fingers of Major 'Bronco' Lane, conqueror of Mount Everest. The 'Redcoats' gallery starts at Agincourt in 1415 and ends with the red-coats in the American War of Independence; 'The Nation in Arms' covers both World Wars, with reconstructions of a trench in the 'World at War 1914-1946' exhibition, and a D-Day landing craft. There's more military hardware to get hands on with up in 'The Modern Army' exhibition; a Challenger tank simulator pulls in junior punters.

✕ LUNCH BOX

For recommended restaurants and cafés in the area, see reviews pp173-174.

ASK 222 Kensington High Street, W8 7RG (7937 5540).
Benihana 77 King's Road, Chelsea, SW3 4NX (7376 7799).
Café Crêperie 2 Exhibition Road, SW7 2HF (7589 8947).
Carluccio's Caffè 1 Old Brompton Road, SW7 3HZ (7581 8101).
Ed's Easy Diner 362 King's Road, Chelsea, SW3 5UZ (7352 1956).
Gelateria Valerie 9 Duke of York Square, Chelsea, SW3 4LY (7730 7978).
Giraffe 7 Kensington High Street, W8 5NP (7938 1221).
Great Escape Café National Army Museum, Royal Hospital Road, SW3 4HT (7730 0717).
Green Fields Café 13 Exhibition Road, SW7 2HE (7584 1396).
Manicomio 85 Duke of York Square, Chelsea, SW3 4LY (7730 3366).
Najma 17 & 19 Bute Street, SW7 3EY (7584 4434).
The Orangery Kensington Palace, Kensington Gardens, W8 2UH (7376 0239).
Oratory 234 Brompton Road, SW3 2BB (7584 3493).
Pâtisserie Valerie 215 Brompton Road, SW3 2EJ (7823 9971); 27 Kensington Church Street, W8 4LL (7937 9574).
Pâtisserie Valerie's Left Wing Café 81 Duke of York Square, SW3 4LY (7730 7094).
Pizza Express The Pheasantry, 152 King's Road, SW3 4UT (7351 5031).
Pizza Organic 20 Old Brompton Road, SW7 3DL (7589 9613).
Wagamama 26A Kensington High Street, W8 4PF (7376 1717).

Around Town

In the Special Events gallery, there's a free exhibition called 'The British Army and the Crimean War' (until 31 Oct 2005) and soldiers from the past are brought to life by actors on TV screens and children can try on replica uniforms, try to solve a 3D puzzle or learn semaphore. The museum puts on themed weekend events, usually involving costumed interpreters activities (*see below* **Hands on**). Forthcoming topics will include 'Camouflage in the Modern Army' (6-7 Aug), 'Animals in War' (3-4 Sept) and 'Christmas in World War II' (10-11 Dec). The museum is also involved in living history events at other locations. Examples are: 'Waterloo Wargame', to be held at Apsley House (18-19 June 2005) in association with English Heritage, and a large-scale commemorative event for VE-VJ Day in St James's Park (23-24 July 2005). The Great Escape Café sells children's lunches (around £4) that include a sandwich, fruit juice and a piece of fruit.

Buggy access. Café. Disabled access: lift, ramps, toilet. Nappy-changing facilities. Nearest picnic place: benches outside museum/Chelsea Hospital grounds. Shop.

Natural History Museum

Cromwell Road, SW7 5BD (information 7942 5725/ switchboard 7942 5000/www.nhm.ac.uk). South Kensington tube. **Open** 10am-5.50pm Mon-Sat; 11am-5.50pm Sun. Closed 24-26 Dec. **Tours** 11am-4pm daily, every 30mins(depending on guide availability). **Admission** free; charges apply for special exhibitions. *Tours* free. **Credit** *Shop* MC, V. **Map** p313 D10.

You couldn't see all 70 million plants, animals, fossils, rocks and minerals held in this giant museum in a month of Sundays. Keep little ones interested by selecting a few areas to focus on. Young folk zoom in on the dinosaurs but there's much more to wonder at (see *below* **Hands on**).

From the front entrance on the Cromwell Road visitors enter the spectacular main hall of the Life Galleries, with its huge cast of a Diplodocus skeleton. If you turn left, you'll find yourself first in the Dinosaur gallery, with its animatronic Tyrannosaurus rex, and then in the Human Biology section (gallery 22), with its many interactive exhibits.

From here, make your way to the blue whale (three buses long) via the stuffed mammals. Creepy Crawlies (gallery 33) has a colony of leafcutter ants and some robotic arthropods. To mug up on the earth's different environments and biological diversity, Ecology (gallery 32) is the place. Spare some time for the Bird gallery (gallery 40); there's a stuffed dodo there, and an egg from the elephant bird.

The Earth Galleries can be accessed from Exhibition Road via an escalator that passes through a giant suspended globe. There are fewer interactive elements, but the earthquake simulation is always a winner. You'll find it and the volcanoes upstairs, while downstairs exhibits trace the history of our planet from the Big Bang to the present.

The Darwin Centre, whose first stage of development was completed in 2002, houses about 22 million specimens, with 450,000 stored in jars of alcohol – there's a mummified finger and whole monkeys in tanks. There are 14 free tours daily, each lasting half an hour, which allow punters (children must be at least ten years old) to encounter the scientists who work here; book your place on arrival at the museum. The second, final phase will store the insect and plant collections and is due for completion in 2008.

From 9 July 2005 to 26 February 2006 'Diamonds' examines the precious stone from its formation in the depths of the Earth to its place in the 21st century's culture of bling. The annual Wildlife Photographer of the Year show runs from October 2005 to spring 2006. At Family Learning Weekend (20-21 Aug) three-year-olds and over can discover all things natural history in activities from pond-dipping to animation workshops. Outside, the Wildlife Garden (open Apr-Oct) provides a variety of British habitats for mammals, amphibians, insects and birds. Until October 2005 you can see a site-specific installation created by environmental artist Diane Maclean. A popular mini-beast safari is among the regular tours (£1.50), which take place between April and July; check the website.

Buggy access. Cafés. Disabled access (Exhibition Road entrance): lift, toilet. Nappy-changing facilities. Nearest picnic place: indoor eating area/museum grounds. Restaurant. Shops.

Hands on art, science, history

The heavyweight museums monopolising this chapter have imaginative ways of keeping your children engaged, especially when school's out.

The giant **Natural History Museum** (*see above*) organises a variety of school holiday events and weekend workshops; check the website or ring 7942 5000 or 5011 to hunt them down. Explorer Backpacks, available from the cloakroom in the Earth Galleries (free, deposit required) contain drawing materials and clues to help under-sevens find items in the museum. Take inquisitive seven- to 14-year-olds to the Investigate gallery, a hands-on area with hundreds of specimens that can be handled, measured and drawn.

The **Science Museum** (*see right*) has several free play areas packed with interactive exhibits and the museum puts on educational events and workshops every half-term and during school holidays – they can't be booked in advance, so turn up early on the day. To get advance details of these events, sign up for the email newsletter on the museum's website.

The **Victoria & Albert Museum** (*see right*) is full of ideas for filling rainy Sunday mornings and half-term holidays. Facilities for children include activity backpacks (available 10.30am-4.30pm Sat), which contain stories, games and objects linked to the collections. On Sundays (10.30am-5pm) children aged three to 12 flock to the Activity Cart, filled with art materials and worthy distractions. Family trails that keep children occupied for around 45 minutes are available daily. A wide range of well-organised activities is laid on in school holidays – T-shirt printing was a memorable one that we enjoyed last October half-term – and at half-term; for details, see the website or call 7942 2211.

The **National Army Museum** (*see p87*) provides trails to guide families round the museum. There are also arts and crafts workshops alongside their themed weekend events, when children, under the watchful eye of costumed interpreters, might take part in a hobbyhorse cavalry, make trench art or try their hand at archaeology.

Oratory Catholic Church

Thurloe Place, Brompton Road, SW7 2RP (7808 0900). South Kensington tube/14, 74 bus. **Open** 6.30am-8pm daily. *Services* 7am, 10am, 12.30pm, 6pm Mon-Sat; 7am, 8am, 9am, 10am, 11am, 12.30pm, 4.30pm, 7pm Sun. **Admission** free; donations appreciated. **Map** p313 E10.

Also known as the Brompton Oratory, this is the second largest Catholic church in the city (Westminster Cathedral occupies top slot). Full of marble and mosaics, it's designed to strike awe into mortal hearts. Many of the internal decorations are much older than the building itself: Mazzuoli's late 17th-century statues of the apostles, for example, once stood in Siena Cathedral. If the kids are less than inspired, point out that the church was used by Russian spies as a dead letter box during the Cold War. The Oratory's Junior Choir sings Mass at 10am each Sunday, and Schola, the boys' choir of the London Oratory School in Fulham, performs Mass on term-time Saturday evenings.
Buggy access. Disabled access: ramp. Shop.

Science Museum

Exhibition Road, SW7 2DD (7942 4454/ booking & information line 0870 870 4868/www.sciencemuseum.org.uk). South Kensington tube. **Open** 10am-5.45pm daily. **Admission** free; charges apply for special exhibitions. **Credit** *IMAX cinema, shops* AmEx, MC, V. **Map** p313 D9.

Children go a bundle on learning through play (*see left* **Hands on**) at one of the museum's six play zones, each of which has been created with an age range or development stage in mind. Under sixes dig 'The Garden' area in the basement, where they can discover the principles of science in the three different zones: Water, Construction, and Sound and Light. On the ground floor in the Wellcome Wing, the 'Pattern Pod' introduces under-eights to patterns and repetition in the natural world. The 'Launch Pad' is museum's largest interactive gallery, with plenty to push, pull, look at and listen to. Several times a day a 20min exploration of the concept of structure – in the form of a bubble show – takes place in the science show area.

Elsewhere, the museum's vast collection includes landmark inventions such as Stephenson's Rocket, Arkwright's spinning machine, Whittle's turbojet engine and the Apollo 10 command module. You might encounter historical characters in the galleries – Albert Einstein, Amy Johnson or perhaps Thomas Crapper. These are played by actors, who help visitors get to grips with inventions and theories (ring 0870 870 4868 for a schedule of their appearances). The Wellcome Wing embodies the notion of learning while having fun. There's also a five-storey IMAX cinema (tickets are £7.50-£9 for adults, £6-£7.50 for under-16s).

In January 2005, the museum began a ten-year-long project to revamp its galleries. The first one to be redeveloped was the Energy Hall on the ground floor, home to the magnificent machines of the Industrial Revolution. Next door, the interactive Energy gallery explores how we power modern life in the 21st century – and beyond.

'Science Night' sleepovers are held once a month (eight-to 11-year-olds, in groups of five or more), with an evening of activities that might include creating slime or balloon-powered buggies to take home. You have to book as much as two months ahead (24hr information line 7942 4747).
Buggy access. Cafés. Disabled access: lift, toilet. Nappy-changing facilities. Nearest picnic place: Hyde Park (outdoor); museum basement & 1st floor (indoor). Restaurant. Shop.

Serpentine Gallery

Kensington Gardens (nr Albert Memorial), W2 3XA (7402 6075/www.serpentinegallery.org). Lancaster Gate or South Kensington tube. **Open** 10am-6pm daily. **Admission** free; donations appreciated. **Credit** AmEx, MC, V. **Map** p311 D8.

It may be housed in a 1930s tearoom, but this lovely, light gallery is a coolly cutting-edge space for contemporary art. The gallery's family programme includes artist-led workshops and trails relating to the current exhibitions. Additional events are held each summer, and include 'Art in the Open' day on (noon-5pm, 20 Aug 2005) when Kensington Gardens is used as a site for artistic events and activities. Upcoming highlights at the gallery include contemporary works by Rirkrit Tiravanija (late June-Aug2005), and large-scale installations by Russian husband and wife, Ilya and Emilia Kabakov (mid Oct-Dec 2005). The 2005 summer pavilion will be designed by Portuguese duo Álvaro Siza and Eduardo Souto de Moura.
Buggy access. Disabled access: toilets. Nappy-changing facilities. Nearest picnic place: Hyde Park/Kensington Gardens. Shop.

Victoria & Albert Museum

Cromwell Road, SW7 2RL (7942 2000/www.vam.ac.uk). South Kensington tube. **Open** 10am-5.45pm Mon, Tue, Thur-Sun; 10am-10pm Wed & last Fri of mth. *Tours* daily; phone for details. **Admission** free; charges apply for special exhibitions. **Credit** *Shop* AmEx, MC, V. **Map** p313 E10.

The V&A dazzles. In the Grand Entrance hangs Dale Chihuly's breathtaking green and blue glass chandelier, a taster to the many other beautiful objects in the collections of costume, jewellery, textiles, metalwork, glass, furniture, photographs, drawings, paintings, sculpture and architecture from cultures across the world.

Home-grown treasures – including the Great Bed of Ware – are housed in the British Galleries, where you'll find a range of interactive exhibits for children (*see also left* **Hands on**). In the Victorian Discovery Area, for example, there are corsets and crinolines to try on; you can also try your hand at building a model Crystal Palace or a chair. The 18th-Century Discovery Area has children making domestic objects, and there is tapestry to weave and armour to be tried out in the Tudor and Stuart Discovery Area. The Architecture gallery and study centre opened in autumn 2004. It's a little cramped, particularly if you're pushing a buggy, but is nevertheless informative. You can view videos, models, plans and descriptions of various architectural styles. The V&A's Photography gallery presents work from the museum's famous collection.

The museum is undergoing an extensive ten-year refurbishment, so a number of galleries will temporarily close or relocate; call the booking office on 7942 2211 to check if a particular gallery will be open when you visit. The Kim Wilkie-designed Garden is due to reopen on 24 July 2005; the Morris, Gamble and Poynter rooms will close at the end of July 2005 while they are converted into a restaurant; the Jewellery galleries will be closed until 2008.

Upcoming shows include: 'Style and Splendour – Queen Maud of Norway's Wardrobe' 1896-1938 (until 8 Jan 2006; Touch Me (9 June-21 Aug 2005), an interactive contemporary design display and 'Modernism' (spring 2006).
Buggy access. Café. Disabled access: lift, ramps, toilets. Nappy-changing facilities. Nearest picnic place: Pirelli Gardens, museum garden & basement picnic room. Restaurant. Shop.

Around Town

NORTH LONDON

Wild woodland walks and upmarket 'hoods, all within a few square miles.

On top of the world:
Primrose Hill. *See p91.*

CAMDEN TOWN

Camden has had a long association with seediness – a prerequisite to being one of London's most fashionable addresses – and it still retains seedy undertones, particularly near the market, where many modern teenagers want to explore. Cheap lodging houses dominated the area around the time when the **Regent's Canal** was laid out in 1816, and it was rough in Victorian times too, according to Charles Dickens, who grew up in Bayham Street (south-east of the tube station).

In later decades, Irish and Greek immigrants laid down roots here, and by the 1960s Camden had earned itself a raffish, bohemian character. Before long, arty types began to move into the tall spacious houses set out in elegant crescents; these days, Camden has a middle-class flavour.

Inevitably, teenagers will want to visit **Camden Lock** – despite all assurances that it is no longer the alternative, craft-oriented market of its 1980s heyday, young people are still irresistibly drawn – so brace yourself for junky jewellery, leather, outlandish footwear, weird furniture and louche

fashion. The MTV studios on Hawley Crescent, NW1, are a draw for star-spotters. When it all gets too much, smart visitors leave the Camden crowds (be warned: the tube is exit-only at busy times) to take refuge in Primrose Hill (*see p91*).

One way to escape the frantic atmosphere is on the **canal**, where narrowboats offer a passenger service to Little Venice, a trip that could combine a visit to the excellent Puppet Theatre Barge (opposite 35 Blomfield Road, W9 2PF, 7249 6876, www.puppetbarge.com). Boats heading west pass through **London Zoo** (*see p64*), and some allow you to break your journey there. The 45-minute one-way trip passes elegant terraces with gardens backing on to the canal, willow-fringed towpaths and converted warehouses.

Jewish Museum, Camden

Raymond Burton House, 129-131 Albert Street, NW1 7NB (7284 1997/www.jewishmuseum.org.uk). Camden Town tube. **Open** 10am-4pm Mon-Thur; 10am-5pm Sun. Closed public hols, inc Christmas Day, Jewish festivals. **Admission** (LP) £3.50; £2.50 OAPs; £1.50 5-16s, concessions; free under-5s; £8 family (2+2). **Credit** MC, V.

The history of the Jewish population of Britain, from medieval times up to the present day, is brought to life in this museum. Although it's undoubtedly of interest to students of history and world religions, it's neither too dry nor too academic for the young. Monthly activities for children (pre-booking essential) educate in a fun way with puppet shows, storytelling and family workshops. Permanent exhibits that draw crowds of youngsters include a sparkling, jewelled breastplate depicting the 12 tribes, a silver scroll case in the shape of a fish and a coconut-shell kiddush cup. Temporary exhibitions can be fascinating: 2005-6 will explore the experiences of immigrants from around the world settling in Britain; the moving story of the rescue of 10,000 children from Nazi Europe on the Kindertransport; and the fascinating life of Albert Einstein. *Buggy access. Disabled access: lift, toilets. Nearest picnic place: Regent's Park. Shop.*

AROUND CAMDEN

The borough of Camden stretches south to Holborn (*see p53*), where the library (32-38 Theobald's Road, WC1X 8PA, 7974 6342) houses Camden's Local Studies and Archives Centre. No appointments are necessary and it's a lot more fun than the internet.

East of Camden Town, there are two other as yet little-known destinations. The **Camley Street Natural Park** is tucked away in the industrial hinterland of King's Cross and, just across York Way, you'll find the **London Canal Museum**, which has all the history of the local waterways. King's Cross Station has become an unlikely tourist attraction in the wake of Harry Potter fever. Camera-wielding families come for the newly installed sign: 'Platform 9¾'. Children pose here, adopting a leaping stance as if they were about to enter the magical void famously used by the rookie wizard.

To the west of Camden Town, **Primrose Hill** has long been a chi-chi outpost of villagey smartness, but in recent years its reputation has been enhanced by the numerous celebs who have opted to live – and bring up their kids – here. Separated from its brasher neighbour only by a railway footbridge, the high street (Regent's Park Road) is café heaven. Just off the main drag is Manna (4 Erskine Road, NW3 3AJ, 7722 8028), a spacious vegetarian place where the cooking is good enough for kids not to notice they're being asked to eat healthy stuff. As well as attractive cafés, restaurants, pubs and shops alongside the park, Primrose Hill has some of the prettiest houses in north London, making it well worth an ogle, especially en route to nearby **Regent's Park** (*see p66*). Primrose Hill itself is a smallish park, with a nice play area that is secure for small children and a big sandpit. The hill is ideal for flying kites and offers views over London Zoo

and Regent's Park. As at many parks, there's a good local firework display on the weekend closest to Bonfire Night, but it can get horribly crowded, which means either a long walk for little legs or a long wait if you are able to dig in early. If you're planning to eat afterwards, book well in advance, as nearby restaurants get packed out.

Back over the railway footbridge in **Chalk Farm** is the Roundhouse (7424 9991, www.roundhouse.org.uk). Currently undergoing redevelopment into an exciting performance space, it will reopen in late 2005 as a centre for the arts, including music, theatre, dance, circus and digital media, as well as an outreach programme for children.

Camley Street Natural Park
12 Camley Street, NW1 0PW (7833 2311/www.wild london.org.uk). King's Cross tube/rail. **Open** May-Sept 9am-5pm Mon-Thur; 11am-5pm Sat, Sun. *Oct-Apr* 9am-5pm Mon-Thur; 10am-4pm Sat, Sun. Closed 20 Dec-1 Jan. **Admission** free. **Map** p315 L2.
The London Wildlife Trust's flagship reserve is tiny by national standards, yet manages to combine woods, ponds, marshes and flower meadows. The visitors' centre is a rustic cabin stuffed with bird, bat and spider studies, arty insect sculptures and a wealth of information on urban flora and fauna. *See also p97* **Running wild**.
Buggy access. Disabled access: toilets. Nappy-changing facilities.

London Canal Museum
12-13 New Wharf Road, N1 9RT (7713 0836/ www.canalmuseum.org.uk). King's Cross tube/rail. **Open** 10am-4.30pm Tue-Sun, bank hol Mon. Last entry 3.45pm. **Admission** (LP) £3; £2 concessions; £1.50 8-15s; free under-8s. **Credit** MC, V. **Map** p315 M2.
Welcoming to families, this small shrine to life on Britain's canals is perfect for youngsters of all ages. Apart from panels of text relating the historic importance of the waterways, there is a real narrowboat to explore, complete with recorded domestic dialogue; a children's corner with canal-themed books and lots of pictures of Rosie and Jim to colour in; a life-size 'horse' in its stable; and videos intimating just how hard (and grimy) life afloat used to be. An important personal element is available in the form of a touch-screen display introducing visitors to the life and times of one Carlo Gatti. Gatti, sometime owner of the warehouse at 12 New Wharf Road, was an Italian-Swiss immigrant who rose from humble chestnut seller to wealthy ice-cream manufacturer, simply by importing ice blocks from the frozen lakes of Norway. The ice was stored in two deep, circular ice wells below the warehouse – throw in pennies to appreciate the drop. The displays relating to the commercial history of ice-cream are also fascinating. The shop has some lovely, inexpensive artefacts with curious child appeal, from enamelware painted with 'castles and roses' to lace-and-ribbon plates. Regular craft sessions in the school holidays often involve recreating such items. Check out the 'what's on' section of the museum's website for information on temporary exhibitions and activites. *Buggy access. Disabled access: lift, toilets. Nappy-changing facilities. Nearest picnic place: museum terrace/canal towpath. Shop.*

ST JOHN'S WOOD

Not really north London except by virtue of its postcode, this upmarket residential area just west of Regent's Park is pleasant to stroll around and boasts the lovely grounds of **St John's Wood Church** (Lord's Roundabout, NW8 7NE, 7586 3864, www.stjohnswoodchurch.org), with its picnic tables, wildlife walk, meadow ground and play area. It's a great stopping-off point before or after visiting **Lord's Cricket Ground**. Among the pricey clothes shops on St John's Wood High Street is the useful children's shoe shop Instep (No.45, NW8 7NJ, 7722 7634) and a branch of Maison Blanc (No.37, NW8 7NJ, 7586 1982, www.maisonblanc.co.uk) for delicious cakes.

Further north is **Abbey Road**, home of the recording studios and immortalised on the cover of the Beatles album of the same name. Tourists can often be seen risking life and limb on the zebra crossing to re-enact said cover. Have a giggle at their expense before sauntering to check out Oscar's Den (7328 6683,www.oscarsden.com) at No.127. This is one of the best party shops in town; it can provide everything from balloons to celebrity lookalikes.

Lord's Cricket Ground & MCC Museum

St John's Wood Road, NW8 8QN (7432 1033/ www.lords.org). St John's Wood tube/13, 46, 82, 113, 274 bus. **Open** *Oct-Mar* noon, 2pm daily. *Apr-Sept* 10am, noon, 2pm daily. Closed 25, 26 Dec, 1 Jan, all major matches & preparation days; phone to check. **Admission** £8; £6 concessions; £5 5-15s; free under-5s; £22 family (2+2). **Credit** MC, V.
Best known as the home of the celebrated Ashes urn, the Marylebone Cricket Club Museum is the world's oldest sporting museum. It includes, among myriad paintings, photos and battered bats, eccentricities such as a reconstruction of the shot that killed a passing sparrow in 1936, together with the stuffed bird and the ball. The guided tour takes visitors into the Mound Stand (so-called because it's built on a burial mound from the Great Plague), the pavilion and the recently refurbished visitors' dressing room, and the historic Long Room. Other displays include memorabilia and cricket kit used by some of the greatest players of all time – among them such luminaries as Victor Trumper, Don Bradman and WG Grace. A useful range of cricket kit and equipment for both children and adults is available for purchase.
Buggy access. Disabled access: toilets. Lifts. Nappy-changing facilities. Nearest picnic place: St John's churchyard playground. Shop.

HAMPSTEAD & AROUND

Like Highgate (*see p95*), Hampstead sits on a hill and was a place rich people went to live to escape the stench and disease of London in former times. It still has a villagey atmosphere, mainly due to its narrow streets and graceful, period architecture. There is almost nowhere to park, so families often make a beeline for the heath car park on East Heath Road. From here, it's a 20-minute dawdle up to the village, perhaps pausing at the playground opposite **2 Willow Road** (7435 6166). This modernist house was built by Ernö Goldfinger in 1939 and is now open on a tour-only basis, so there's no chance of dragging under-11s round it. But you get a very good view of many rooms while pushing a swing, and it's consoling to think that James Bond's creator, Ian Fleming, hated the architect so much he named a villain after him. Up in the village itself are legions of cafés (though none, perhaps, so atmospheric as Louis Pâtisserie at 32 Heath Street; 7435 9908) and the pedestrian-only lanes make for peaceful shopping.

Hampstead has many famous sons – witness **Keats House** and the **Freud Museum** (20 Maresfield Gardens, NW3 5SX, 7435 2002, www.freud.org.uk), home to a famous couch but only likely to be of interest to students of psychoanalysis. **Burgh House** (New End Square, NW3 1LT, 7431 0144, www.burghhouse.org.uk), a Queen Anne house containing a small museum about the area's history, has a charming café and garden away from the weekend crowds. The natural pleasures of **Hampstead Heath** – running wild, cycling, gathering conkers and climbing trees – are, obviously, the major attraction of the area. A good combination might be a walk through the Vale of Health (spot the blue plaque for DH Lawrence) to the top of Hampstead, then down the hill to the village for refreshment (there are several well-known chain restaurants here). Several of the pubs between heath and village have been made over into sophisticated eateries and are no longer a good bet for fish and chips, but walking south on the heath to **South End Green** and the car park will bring you to Polly's (55 South End Road, NW3 2QB, 7794 8144), a nice place for tea. Alternatively, move on to the 'heath extension', or **Golders Hill**, where the Italian-oriented park café (*see p175*), smooth, winding paths, a lovely playground, fallow deer and an aviary full of many pretty, exotic birds await.

Camden Arts Centre

Corner of Arkwright Road and Finchley Road, NW3 6DG (7472 5500/www.camdenartscentre.org). Finchley Road tube/Finchley Road & Frognal rail. **Open** 10am-6pm Tue, Thur-Sun; 10am-9pm Wed. Closed bank hols. **Admission** free. **Credit** *Shop* MC, V.
Following a snazzy £4m refurbishment programme, this intriguing venue dedicated to the visual arts reopened at the beginning of 2004. Its three new galleries host exhibitions by international and British artists, a state-of-the-art

Lazy days at **Kenwood House**. *See p95.*

ceramics studio and a busy programme of courses for both adults and children. Typically, half-terms feature two-day courses in, say, clay and mixed media for £40 (£24 concessions). Four different term-time courses cater for young people of different age groups – call for details and inspiration. More casually, drop into the charming café (*see p174*) – recently refurbished to the tune of £4 million – overlooking replanted gardens.
Buggy access. Café. Disabled access: toilets. Lifts. Nappy-changing facilities. Shop.

Fenton House

3 Hampstead Grove, NW3 6RT (7435 3471/ information 01494 755563/box office 01494 755572/ www.nationaltrust.org.uk). Hampstead tube/Hampstead Heath rail. **Open** *Mar* 2-5pm Sat, Sun. *Apr-Oct* 2-5pm Wed-Fri; 11am-5pm Sat, Sun, bank hols. Last entry 4.30pm. *Tours* phone for times. **Admission** (NT) £4.80; £2.40 5-15s; free under-5s; £12 family.
No credit cards.
Another of Hampstead's covetable period dwellings, Fenton House is enjoyed by adults for its William and Mary architecture, its award-winning garden and its quirky Benton Fletcher collection of early keyboard instruments. Children enjoy it in a different way: a summer stroll through the orchard, vegetable garden and lawns is always agreeable, and the harpsichords, clavichords, virginals and spinets will probably be like no instrument they have ever seen before. There is also a porcelain collection that includes a 'curious grotesque teapot' and several poodles. Apple Day in October is celebrated in the orchard, and older children may well be fascinated by the fortnightly summer concerts utilising instruments in the collection.
Baby slings for hire. Buggy access. Disabled access: ramp. Nappy-changing facilities.

Hampstead Heath

NW5 1QR (8348 9908). Kentish Town tube/Gospel Oak or Hampstead Heath rail/214, C2, C11 bus. **Open** dawn-dusk daily.
This undulating swathe of grass, woods and lakes seems so vast (almost 800 acres/320 hectares) that it's possible to imagine yourself in several different places all on the same day. Toil up Parliament Hill to fly a kite, watch other (often highly skilled) kite flyers, or simply rest awhile, gazing down over the city for miles and miles. Stay at the bottom of the hill to play tennis, bowls, *boules*; to feed the ducks on the first lake or admire the model boats (occasionally noisy) on the second.
The heath is maintained by the Corporation of London; in recent years, the various ponds, which are fed by an underground stream thought to be the old River Fleet, have been cleaned up. Bathing is segregated, and since the Ladies Bathing Pond is located in a secluded enclosure, entry is barred to all males and to girls under eight. Consequently, family bathing is probably best undertaken in the lido close to Gospel Oak station. The playground on that side of the heath is excellent, not least because it has free access to a shallow paddling pool during the summer months (note that costumes must be worn even by the tiniest children). Less well known is the adventure playground behind the athletics track, where leaping, bouncing and climbing from challenging, timber-framed playframes is the order of the day.
Though a beautiful place in winter, it is during the warmer months that the heath comes into its own as a source of entertainment for children. Clowns, bouncy castles, magicians, storytellers and puppeteers perform free of charge in different locations each week (pick up a leaflet from the Parliament Hill information office). There are also tennis courses, learn-to-fish days, bat walks and themed

WALK Up the hill and down

Easily accessible for buggies, this walk up Primrose Hill to Regent's Canal will take you the best part of a pleasurable afternoon.

Starting at Chalk Farm tube, turn right out of the station and take a left up Bridge Approach. As you walk over the wide, graffiti-lined bridge and approach Primrose Hill, the houses become whiter, cleaner and grander. Cross over Gloucester Avenue (the Pembroke pub on your left) and on to **Regent's Park Road**, Primrose Hill's café-lined high street. Just before you reach the full slew of shops and brasseries, take a right into Berkeley Road, opposite **Trojka** (101 Regent's Park Road, NW1 8UR, 7483 3765), a lovely Russian tearoom.

Follow the curve of Berkeley Road round to the right until you emerge into **Chalcott Square**, where the exteriors of the houses are painted in bright pinks, blues, yellows, greens and purples. A blue plaque beside the door of No.3 reveals that the poet Sylvia Plath lived there between 1960 and '61. Chalcott Square's small playground offers an early interlude before you make your way up Sharpleshall Street, then left back on to Regent's Park Road and towards the hilly expanse of Primrose Hill.

Entering by the gate on Primrose Hill Road take the path up the hill to the right. The London skyline is revealed to your left, with London Zoo's pyramidal Snowdon Aviary prominent in the foreground. Where the path forks, veer left and continue upwards and onwards until you reach the summit of **Primrose Hill**. The viewing point offers the capital's iconic sights laid out in a dramatic panorama from east to west. An embossed silver map of the skyline will help children identify the 'Gherkin' (Swiss Re Tower), the BT Tower, the London Eye and many more.

Once you've finished gawping, briefly turn back the way you came, but this time take the path down to your right. At the bottom of the hill, where the path meets a cluster of trees, cross over the junction and follow the path ahead. Then take the second path to your right and follow it up until you reach a large playground, with a mini adventure playground, sandpit and attended toilets. There are plenty of picnic benches.

Turning left out of the playground, exit Primrose Hill Park and cross over Prince Albert Road at the zebra crossing. Ahead you will see a sign for the main entrance to London Zoo, which would lead you to a bridge running over the Regent's Canal. Ignore it, however, and instead take the path to your right that zig-zags down to the canalside.

Turn left at the bottom of the path to begin your walk along the canal. Stroll as briskly or as slowly as the chief pace-setter insists, stopping to peer through the cages of the Snowdon Aviary on your left and the compounds of **London Zoo** (see p64) on your right. Eventually, the canal will swoop round to the left, taking you beneath a wide bridge and along one of its most enchanting stretches between here and Camden Town. Kids will no doubt be just as envious as you are of the immaculate gardens (some with tree houses) that roll down to the water's edge, where little boats bob beside wooden jetties.

Having passed under a sixth bridge, turn left up the walkway that leads to Gloucester Avenue – look out for the silver plaques of frogs and other water-loving wildlife mounted high on the brick wall on your left.

Immediately to your right you will be confronted with the glass window of **Melrose & Morgan** delicatessen (No.42, NW1 8JD, 7722 0011), filled with loaves of organic bread and crates of similarly pure apple juice.

Now on the final stretch of your walk, follow Gloucester Avenue until you meet the Pembroke and once again cross the railway bridge. On the other side, this time, turn right on to the tail end of Regent's Park Road following its last few yards until it meets **Chalk Farm Road**. Directly opposite, you will spy your journey's glorious end, the renowned ice-cream parlour, **Marine Ices** (see p175).

Chalk Farm

ADELAIDE ROAD

START

CHALK FARM RD

FINISH

Marine Ices

REGENT'S PARK ROAD

BERKELEY ROAD

CHALCOTT SQ

GLOUCESTER AVENUE

SYLVIA PLATH LIVED HERE

3 Chalcott Square

Melrose & Morgan

REGENT'S PARK ROAD

Primrose Hill

PRINCE ALBERT ROAD

Regent's Canal

London Zoo

nature trails. More accessible these days is a children's 'secret garden' and wildlife pond, near the tennis courts; call at the information centre to gain entry. *See also p97* **Running wild.**
Buggy access. Cafés. Disabled access: toilets. Nappy-changing facilities.

Keats House

Keats Grove, NW3 2RR (7435 2062/www.cityof london.gov.uk/keats). Belsize Park or Hampstead tube/Hampstead Heath rail/24, 46, 168 bus. **Open** 1-5pm Tue-Sun, bank hol Mon. **Tours** 3pm Sat, Sun. **Admission** £3.50; £1.75 concessions; free under-16s. Weekend tours incl in admission price. **Credit** MC, V.
You need to be a real fan of Keats's poetry and the Romantics in general to appreciate the resonances in this house. It is, admittedly, on one of Hampstead's most beautiful streets, the white stucco Regency architecture set off by clouds of blossom in spring. Kindly attendants from the Corporation of London can provide line drawings of the house for children to colour in while their parents tour august rooms once belonging to Keats's friend, Charles Brown. A chaise longue is set up in the position where Keats spent his days gazing out of the window after becoming ill in the 1820s, and the house is full of handsome pieces of antique furniture, portraits of the poet and his friends, and photocopied sheets of the poems. There's also a (new) tree in the garden near the spot where Keats is said to have sat writing 'Ode to a Nightingale'. During July and August 2005 there will be 'teddy bears' picnics' at the house for children; call for details of other events.
Buggy access (ground floor only). Nearest picnic place: house gardens. Shop.

Kentish Town City Farm

1 Cressfield Close, off Grafton Road, NW5 4BN (7916 5421). Chalk Farm or Kentish Town tube/ Gospel Oak rail. **Open** 9am-5.30pm daily. Closed 25 Dec. **Admission** free; donations appreciated.
Completely hidden from view down a side road with a high, blank gate, this is a slice of the countryside in London. It's an absolute delight in almost any season, for it stretches way beyond the farmyard, where Aylesbury ducks bathe noisily, goats head-butt each other at the trough and a large white pig teeters about, like a fat old lady on stilettos. Horses, cows, chickens, cats and rabbits are other inhabitants, all of which seem to be busy reproducing. Several gardens (for locals, including Bangladeshi women growing coriander, mooli and curry plants; for pensioners in typical allotment style; and for visitors, featuring carnivorous plants and other curiosities), orchards and enclosures for sheep line the railway line.
A pond with a dipping platform is full of frogs, and a riding school is the scene of weekend pony rides (1.30pm Sat, Sun, weather permitting, £1). The railway arch forms an impromptu proscenium for children's drama, while a classroom is used for a plethora of inventive craft and play sessions. The after-school pottery club, cookery club and other classes are kept fairly quiet; most things here are free and very popular with locals. An energetic education officer, however, welcomes school visits from all boroughs and anyone can come to the May Day celebrations, Easter egg hunt, Apple Day (October) and so on.
Buggy access. Disabled access: ramp, toilet. Nappy-changing facilities. Nearest picnic place: on the farm.

Kenwood House/Iveagh Bequest

Hampstead Lane, NW3 7JR (8348 1286/www.english-heritage.org.uk). Hampstead tube/Golders Green tube, then 210 bus. **Open** *Apr-Oct* 11am-5pm daily. *Nov-Mar* 11am-4pm daily. **Tours** by appointment only. **Admission** (EH) free; donations appreciated. *Tours* £3; £2 concessions; £1.50 under-16s. **Credit** MC, V.
Strike out across the verdant plains and wooded hillsides of Hampstead Heath from almost any direction and a path will lead you, willy-nilly, to Kenwood House. Hot chocolate and cream teas in winter or classy lemonade and ice-creams in summer persuade small feet that the trek is worthwhile, as the Brew House café (*see p174*), set in the old kitchens, is the best, if a little pricey, catering venue for miles around. The house itself is a white stucco mansion, built in the classical style for the Earl of Mansfield by Robert Adam in 1767-9 and bequeathed to the nation in 1927. It houses the Iveagh Bequest, an impressive collection of paintings that includes works by Reynolds, Turner and Van Dyck, as well as a Rembrandt self-portrait tucked into a darkened corner of the Dining Room and a rare Vermeer (*The Guitar Player*). Hogarth, Guardi and a couple of classic flirtatious Bouchers round out the collection. There's also a vast library. Of special interest to children are the annual Easter egg hunt, St George's Day 'dragon trails', kite-making workshops and spooky Hallowe'en storytelling days.
Volunteer group Heath Hands also has its office here – it plans family events throughout the year, mostly to do with improving the look of the heath and the estate gardens; call for details or pick up a leaflet at the visitors' centre in the Kenwood House Estate Office. Left to their own devices, most youngsters will find ample amusement in the vicinity: running through the Ivy Arch, hiding in the vast rhododendron bushes or rolling down the grass slopes in front of the house.
Buggy access. Café. Disabled access: ramps, toilets. Nappy-changing facilities. Shop.

HIGHGATE & ARCHWAY

Like Hampstead (*see p92*), Highgate is a pretty, hilly village bursting with rummage-worthy shops, child-friendly pubs – and wealthy residents who greatly treasure the sylvan backdrop. One of the main reasons to bring children here is **Highgate Wood**, one of the rare bits of surviving original woodland in the capital, which has a delightful setting, a well-designed play area and a pleasant café. Waterlow Park, containing **Lauderdale House**, is also gorgeous.

Next door, **Highgate Cemetery** (Swains Lane, N6 6PJ, 8340 1834, www.highgate-cemetery.org) is on the visiting list of many a tourist, much to the annoyance of the Friends of Highgate Cemetery, who prefer to play down the visitor pull of their historic patch. Kids are, in fact, discouraged from visiting the place unless they're coming to see the grave of a relative, but if you long to pay respects to Karl Marx, Mary Ann Evans (aka George Eliot), Max Wall or any of the other admired figures who now repose in the Eastern Cemetery, you can bring children to enjoy the peace and beauty of this delightful boneyard, as long as they're well behaved. The Western Cemetery is out of bounds to casual visitors (adults and kids aged eight and over can pay £3 for a guided tour, which brings the departed to life and affords a chance to see the eerie catacombs).

A little further down the hill from the tube station is Shepherd's Close, from where you can access the Parkland Walk (which runs to Finsbury Park). Hornsey Lane, on the other side of Highgate Hill, leads you to the **Archway**, a Victorian viaduct spanning what is now the A1 and offering views of the City and the East End. Jackson's Lane arts centre (269A Archway Road, N6 5AA, box office 8341 4421, www.jacksonslane.org.uk) puts on shows for children most Saturdays, and a popular, large-scale panto at Christmas.

Highgate Wood/Queen's Wood

Muswell Hill Road, N10 3JN (8444 6129/www. cityoflondon.gov.uk/openspaces). Highgate tube/ 43, 134, 263 bus. **Open** 7.30am-dusk daily.
These 70 acres (28ha) are some of the last remaining ancient woodlands in London, and are full of gently swaying oaks and hornbeams. The wood has been lovingly tended by the Corporation of London and its trusty team of woodsmen (and women) since 1886, when the Lord Mayor declared the wood 'an open space for ever'. Carpeted with bluebells and wild flowers in spring and dappled with sunlight filtered by the trees, this corner of London really doesn't feel like London at all.

The wood is carefully managed: trees are coppiced in the traditional way, areas are fenced off to encourage new growth, boxes are provided for owls, bats and hedgehogs to live in, and everything that moves is chronicled. The bird population has increased dramatically in recent years, both in types and numbers. You can pick up leaflets about the wildlife in the visitors' information hut beside the café, or join one of the bird identification walks or nature trails. The award-winning children's playground has been carefully planned to allow wheelchair-users and their more mobile friends to play together. The bridge and tower structure is accessible to buggies and wheelchairs, the swings are designed to be used by children who need more support, and there are Braille noticeboards. For sporty types, there's a football and cricket field (in front of the café), and exercise equipment has recently been installed among the trees. *See also p97* **Running wild**.
Buggy access. Café. Disabled access: toilet. Nappy-changing facilities.

Lauderdale House

Highgate Hill, Waterlow Park, N6 5HG (8348 8716/ restaurant 8341 4807/www.lauderdale.org.uk). Archway tube/143, 210, 271, W5 bus. **Open** 11am-4pm Tue-Fri; 1.30-5pm Sat; noon-5pm Sun; phone to check weekend openings. *Restaurant* 10am-dusk Tue-Sun. Closed 24 Dec-mid Jan. **Admission** free. **No credit cards.**
The pretty, 16th-century Lauderdale House, once home of Nell Gwynne, is the centrepiece of Highgate's secluded park. A favoured venue for wedding receptions and other bashes, it's sometimes closed to the public. Saturdays, however, are sacrosanct, because that's when children come for their morning shows, usually aimed at the threes to eights. Ring for details of craft fairs, musical events, exhibitions by local artists and other events held in the arts centre. In the summer, weather permitting, the parkland surrounding the house hosts open-air shows. Whatever's on, it's lovely to sit on the terrace of the café and admire the view over a coffee and ice-cream or an Italian meal; book ahead if you fancy having Sunday lunch here. Fans of the house and park may join a free mailing list to be advised of upcoming events.

Beautiful Waterlow Park, in which the house is set, has several lakes, a toddlers' playground and grassy slopes that are great for picnicking. The Grade II-listed park, donated by Sir Sidney Waterlow as 'a garden for the gardenless', was awarded £1.2m of Heritage Lottery money for improvement in 2003. Most of the restoration work is now complete, including the 17th-century terrace garden and the conversion of the depot building into workshops, an activities room and toilets.
Buggy access (ground floor only). Café/restaurant. Disabled access: toilets (ground floor). Nearest picnic place: Waterlow Park.

ISLINGTON

'Merry' Islington was first famous as an idyllic village – Henry VIII owned houses for hunting in the area – but today is known as one of London's premier urban residential areas, a buzzy district characterised by its mix of graceful, listed Victorian and Georgian houses, trendy bars and shops, and flourishing arts centres. On a Friday night the streets are thronging with the after-work crowd, but there's also plenty here for those not yet of drinking age.

Islington has 11 theatres and is home to the Anna Scher Theatre School, where many *EastEnders* cast members learned their trade – would-be Walfordites can expect a five-year wait to join. The **Little Angel Theatre** (14 Dagmar Passage, N1 2DN, 7226 1787, www.littleangel theatre.com) is a celebrated, purpose-built puppet theatre. Every June the area hosts a two-week festival of music, theatre and art, and there are regular exhibitions at the Business Design Centre. Wednesdays and Saturdays see antiques markets in pedestrianised **Camden Passage**; many stalls have items of interest for older children, including classic toys.

Playground-loving kids rate **Highbury Fields**, where the equipment is challenging but extremely crowded on sunny days. Footie fans of the Gunner variety may like to tour **Arsenal Football Club** before it relocates for the 2006/7 season. Due north of Arsenal, the other big park in the area is **Finsbury Park**, for which the borough of Islington shares responsibility with the boroughs of Haringey and Hackney. It's a great sprawling green space that, until recently, had become very shabby and run down. Fortunately, there's help at hand in the shape of the Finsbury Park Partnership, set up to bid for a slice of the government's Single Regeneration Budget in 1999. The Finsbury Park area, which includes the huge railway and tube station, housing estates and commercial districts, was awarded £25m. The park's regeneration is supposed to be complete by the time the project ends in 2006. There's no

shortage of sporting facilities, notably the **Michael Sobell Leisure Centre** (Hornsey Road, N7 7NY, 7609 2166, www.aquaterra.org) with its climbing walls, trampolining, table tennis, squash and badminton, and mini ice rink. A star attraction for the under-threes is the Sobell Safari, an indoor playground on four floors, with tunnels, slides and ball ponds. Nearby, on Green Lanes, the

 # RUNNING WILD

It's wild up north. You don't have to hike far to get back to nature. **Highgate Woods**' supervised children's playground and its fairytale café, set in the middle of a cricket field like some latter-day gingerbread house, are both well known. But the Woods are also home to some 70 different species of birds, alongside the foxes, grey squirrels, five species of bat, 180 species of moth, 12 species of butterfly and 80 species of spider. Anyone interested in observing some of this wildlife should check out the wealth of activities put on by the Corporation of London, both in Highgate Wood and on Hampstead Heath. Guided walks aim to identify birds and their song, uncover beetles, or spy on bats or moths. Some events involve displays by birds of prey, an informative entertainment that also takes place occasionally on **Hampstead Heath** – dates and times can be found at www.cityoflondon.gov.uk/openspaces.

Part of the heath has been designated a Site of Special Scientific Interest by English Nature; this includes the area to the right of the tennis courts on **Parliament Hill Fields**, which is known locally as 'the secret garden'. This garden has traditionally featured in the annual summer open days, when pond-dipping is allowed. Sadly, events on the heath may be drastically curtailed in 2005 and 2006 due to well-publicised budgetary deficits at the Corporation of London, a financial calamity also affecting the future of the swimming ponds, where adults and children over eight can experience the rare thrill of bobbing about with ducks and fish. Check the website and local press for more news of these and other facilities important to nature lovers, including the restocking of the upgraded aviaries at **Golders Hill Heath** extension.

Meanwhile, lesser-known green spaces provide hidden treats. **Gillespie Park** (191 Drayton Park, N5) has a range of beautiful wildlife habitats, including woodland, meadow, wetland and ponds, and is the site of an **Ecology Centre** where helpful staff advise children how to get frogs into their gardens, attract birds and butterflies, and so on. Nature-themed workshops run in the holidays, too.

Barnsbury Wood (Crescent Street, N1, 7354 5162) is a truly magical place, tucked away behind private gardens, and only open on Tuesday afternoons (2-4pm) and some weekends

in summer for organised picnics (check the wildlife diaries in Islington libraries for dates). It's also the setting for an annual play by the Wadham Players (8527 4690), happening on 17 July in 2005.

Equally elusive are the **Railway Fields**, a 'Green Flag' award-winning green space with its entrance on Green Lanes, N22, where highly decorative iron gates, featuring foxes, birds and mice, seem nearly always shut. Behind these gates, however, is an enchanting mixture of woodland, scrub, meadow, a pond and marshland. A Swiss chalet-style hut is used for school visits. Formerly a railway goods yard, the Fields are acclaimed for their wildflowers and attendant butterflies. To gain entry, try calling the conservation officer who is often on site in the afternoons supervising school visits (8348 6005). Another useful contact is the Haringey parks customer careline (8489 5662, www.haringey.gov.uk).

In Stoke Newington, **Clissold Park**, with its café, playground, tennis courts, ponds, outdoor paddling pool and animal enclosures, is deservedly popular. But if the crowds get a bit too much on sunny days, try **Abney Park Cemetery**. While still plainly a burial ground, its decaying monuments – draped urns, angels, Celtic crosses, saints and shepherds – add Romantic interest to a local nature reserve where trees and plants are now in the ascendency. Although owned by Hackney Council, the park is run by a trust with a very active volunteer programme; adults can drop in to help with gardening and restoration work, while children are treated to workshops where they might make shadow puppets of woodland creatures or kites in the shape of butterflies, birds and bats.

Closer to central London, **Camley Street Natural Park** is a true oasis amid the dusty horror of ongoing heavy engineering works preparing for the Channel Tunnel link. Hazel, rowan and silver birch trees offer shelter to tiny wrens; the canal flowing past has coots, mallard and moorhens. Children are delighted with the grasshoppers, dragonflies and blue butterflies in summer. Pond-dipping is a regular part of educational and holiday activities for kids; this is especially exciting in summer when newts are in abundance. Camley Street is used by the London Wildlife Trust for its wildlife watch club; for information on how to join, visit www.wildlondon.org.uk.

Around Town

Castle Climbing Centre (07776 176007, www.geckos.co.uk) is one of London's top climbing venues. You'll find it in a Grade II-listed Victorian folly (previously a water tower) modelled on Stirling Castle. Within the grounds, in a separate building, is another ball pond.

Those who crave the scent of the countryside can commune with pigs at **Freightliners City Farm** or learn about green activities at the **Islington Ecology Centre**. Rural flavours – in a form that trendy urban types can stomach (think ruby chard) – can be sampled every Sunday from 10am to 2pm at the Islington Farmers' Market (Essex Road, opposite Islington Green, N1, 7704 9659). Look out for happily picnicking families sampling their farmers' market goodies on the green. They're sensible: most eateries on Upper Street are expensive. The Turkish restaurants are great value, however, and very friendly, with the three branches of the very popular Gallipoli (No.102, N1 1QN, 7359 0630; Gallipoli Again, No.120, N1 1QP, 7359 1578; Gallipoli Bazaar, No.107, N1 1QP, 7226 5333) also serving hearty English breakfasts. The S&M Café (*see p176*) is another affordable option, as is Giraffe (29-31 Essex Road, N1 2SA, 7359 5999; *see also p164*).

Chapel Market (on the street of the same name) is a gloriously downmarket bargain bin of fruit and vegetables, linen, partyware, toys and not always durables, presided over by rowdy costers. It's still thriving, despite competition from the **N1 Shopping Centre** that links Liverpool Road with Upper Street. The centre is home to branches of reliable childrenswear chains, restaurants like Wagamama and Yo Sushi!, and an eight-screen cinema.

Arsenal Football Club

Arsenal Stadium, Avenell Road, N5 1BU (7704 4000/box office 7704 4040/tours 7704 4504/ www.arsenal.com). Arsenal tube/Finsbury Park tube/ rail. **Open** *Museum* 10am-4pm Fri. Phone to check other days. *Gunners shop* 9.30am-5pm Mon-Fri, before & after all 1st-team home games. *World of Sport shop* 9.30am-6pm Mon-Sat. **Tours** 11am, noon, 1pm, 2pm, 3pm Mon-Fri. **Admission** *Museum* £4; £2 under-16s; £10 family. *Tour & museum* £8; £4 concessions, under-16s; £20 family. **Credit** *Shop* MC, V.

The bulldozers have dug in and work has begun on Arsenal's controversial new stadium at Ashburton Grove, but until it opens in 2006/7, Highbury is still, as it proudly claims at its entrance, 'the home of football'. So, if north London youngsters incline towards the red rather than the white, there is still time to visit this historic football ground. Tour guests may check out the pitch, changing rooms, trophy room, boardroom, press room and museum, which has memorabilia, information about the club's early days and a Gunner-tastic video. The shops stock replica kit (in all sizes) and souvenirs.

Nearest picnic place: Gillespie Park. Shops.

Freightliners City Farm

Paradise Park, Sheringham Road, off Liverpool Road, N7 8PF (7609 0467/www.freightlinersfarm.org.uk). Caledonian Road or Holloway Road tube/Highbury & Islington tube/rail. **Open** *Summer* 10am-4.45pm Tue-Sun. *Winter* 10am-4pm Tue-Sun. Closed 25 Dec-1 Jan. **Admission** free; donations appreciated.

A stone's throw from Pentonville Prison, this city farm (next to the playground in Paradise Park) is a bucolic hint that all could be different in the world if only Nature were a universal inspiration. Forget run-of-the-mill establishments with their token livestock, Freightliners positively teems with life: there are rabbits, cows, goats, cats, geese, pigs, as well as all kinds of poultry. The animals, many of them rare breeds, are impressive. Giant Flemish rabbits are the biggest you will see anywhere; guineafowl run amok in other animals' pens; exotic cockerels with feathered feet squawk alarmingly in your path; bees fly lazily around their hives. You can buy hen and duck eggs of all hues, plus own-grown veg and plants when in season. Playschemes run in summer and are justifiably popular. And, at any time of year, there is an overwhelming scent of straw and manure – bliss.

Buggy access. Café. Disabled access: toilets. Nappy-changing facilities. Nearest picnic place: farm picnic area. Shop (reopens Sept 2005).

Highbury Fields

Highbury Crescent, N5 1RR (7527 4971). Highbury & Islington tube/rail/19, 30, 43, 271 bus. **Open** *Park* 24hrs. *Playground* dawn-dusk daily.

Islington's largest outdoor space repays careful exploration. Hidden behind Highbury Pool and a series of high bushes is an unusual playground that combines old-fashioned thrills (such as a circular train demanding passenger propulsion, Flintstone-style, and a long, alarmingly steep slide) with more recent additions, like the flying fox and giant, web-like climbing frames. The outdoor tennis courts have been refurbished and are used by the excellent Islington Tennis Centre. A stroll across Highbury Fields can take you from busy Upper Street past imposing period terraces to Highbury Barn, a trendy enclave boasting several excellent food shops, restaurants and cafés.

Buggy access. Café.

Islington Ecology Centre

191 Drayton Park, N5 1PH (7354 5162/ www.islington.gov.uk). Arsenal tube. **Open** *Park* 8am-dusk Mon-Fri; 9am-dusk Sat; 10am-dusk Sun. Closed Arsenal FC home matches. *Centre drop-in sessions* 10am-noon Tue; 2-4pm Thur; for other times phone to check. **Admission** free; donations appreciated.

This imaginative redevelopment of former railway land led to the founding of Islington's largest nature reserve: Gillespie Park. It has woodland, meadows, wetland and ponds, and the Ecology Centre is its educational heart. Staff are endlessly enthusiastic and helpful on the subject of all natural things in the borough. An events diary is published biannually with events suitable for families, from moth evenings to junk modelling. See *p97* **Running wild**.

Buggy access.

The Islington Museum

Islington Town Hall, Upper Street, N1 2UD (7527 2837). Highbury & Islington tube/rail. **Open** 11am-5pm Wed-Sat; 2-4pm Sun. **Admission** free.

Abney Park Cemetery & Nature Reserve. *See p100.*

Around Town

The Islington Museum is housed in the former Assembly Hall, next to Islington Town Hall. It has two galleries: one houses a permanent collection illustrating, in an undeniably pedestrian way, the history of Islington from prehistoric times to World War II. The other has temporary exhibitions of work by local artists and community groups and on local history themes – these tend to be more fun.
Buggy access. Disabled access. Shop.

STOKE NEWINGTON

North-east of Islington, Stoke Newington and, to a certain extent, its more rough-and-ready neighbour Dalston, become more fashionable every year. 'Stokey', has the edge when it comes to family-friendliness. It's still a pleasantly bohemian, unpolished sort of area, with good independent shops and numerous places to eat and drink. The heart of the area is Stoke Newington Church Street, which hosts north London's best street festival every June. Stoke Newington is blessed with two fine green spaces: **Clissold Park**, where local families congregate, and the rambling old cemetery of **Abney Park**.

Dalston has the biggest street market for miles around, full of Afro-Caribbean, Greek and Turkish wares and unfeasibly cheap tracksuits.

Abney Park Cemetery & Nature Reserve

Stoke Newington High Street, N16 0LN (7275 7557/ www.abney-park.org.uk). Stoke Newington rail/73, 106, *149, 243, 276, 349 bus.* **Open** dawn-dusk daily.
Visitors' centre 9.30am-5pm Mon-Fri. **Admission** free.
A romantically decayed Victorian cemetery, Abney Park is a hub of conservation activity. An environmental classroom at the Stoke Newington High Street entrance is the scene of many free workshops for children and adults. The visitors' centre doubles as a shop for guides to green London and other such environmentally aware literature.
See also p97 **Running wild**.
Buggy access. Disabled access: toilet (visitors' centre). Shop.

Clissold Park

Stoke Newington Church Street, N16 5HJ (7923 3660). Stoke Newington rail/73, 149, 329, 476 bus. **Open** *Park 7.30am-dusk daily.* **Admission** free.
There is no tube station in Stoke Newington, but it is possible for energetic families to cycle to Clissold Park from Finsbury Park, utilising the parkland trails and the mercifully wide pavements along Green Lanes. The whole trip should take no more than 30mins – perhaps terminating at Clissold Park's café. The latter is set in a handsome, listed Georgian building (extensive renovations were, as we went to press, still in progress).

There is lots to discover on a pleasant amble around Clissold Park: enclosures of fallow deer, an aviary full of interesting, exotic birds, several ponds supporting various waterfowl, an outdoor stage for children to cavort on whenever it is not in use by bands, and tennis courts that carers could use while kids are in the adjoining playground. The courts are home to the Hackney wing of the City Tennis Centre (7254 4235); ring for details of its programme – family tennis evenings, junior clubs and tournaments, and coaching are all available. The bowling green here appears run-down to the point of dereliction, but the playground is lovely, with modern equipment and lots of shady picnic tables.

Clissold Park: such a deer place.

Buggy access (in park, steps at café). Café. Disabled access: toilets (in front of café). Nappy-changing facilities (on request).

CROUCH END & MUSWELL HILL

These pleasantly unspoilt areas, close enough to Highgate for smartness and close enough to Finsbury Park for street cred, have become the settlement of choice for north Londoners looking for more space to breathe. Architecturally, they are blessed with a wealth of Victorian and Edwardian housing (check out the scenery, pre-1890s building boom, at the Bruce Castle Museum – *see p103*), which in the past has not been expensive due to the lack of transport links. This, together with decent primary schools, has made these areas popular with young families, and many of the shops and cafés reflect that trend.

The area's best-known attraction has to be **Alexandra Park & Palace**, but there are plenty of other green spaces. Priory Park in Middle Lane is great for cycling, rollerskating and football, and has a paddling pool, formal gardens and tennis courts; its Rainbow Café is a shining example of what other park cafés could be like. Stationers Park, between Denton Road and Mayfield Road, has a good adventure playground, a pre-school children's play area and (free) tennis courts. Park Road Pools has both indoor and outdoor swimming pools, though the latter gets packed out on summer weekends. Hidden tracts of greenery off Park Road allow ample space for the North Middlesex Sports Club, plus various other tennis and cricket clubs; these are the scenes of various sport-related holiday playschemes and of after-school coaching.

There are so many family-oriented restaurants in Crouch End that you'd stumble into one if you were blindfolded and spun round three times. Pizza Bella (4-6 Park Road, N8 8DD, 8342 8541) is a popular birthday party venue, with saintly waiters to pick up the pieces, and Banners (*see p174*) is another great favourite.

Alexandra Park & Palace

Alexandra Palace Way, N22 7AY (park 8444 7696/ information 8365 2121/boating 8889 9089/www. alexandrapalace.com). Wood Green tube/ Alexandra Palace rail/W3, 144 bus. **Open** *Park* 24hrs daily. *Palace times vary depending on exhibitions.* **Admission** free.

The Ally Pally (as it is affectionately known) has had some bad luck. It burnt down twice – once in 1863, just weeks after opening, and once in 1980 – only to rise like a phoenix on each occasion as a grandiloquent place of public entertainment. The only trouble is that, on closer inspection, the buildings are still in dire need of repair. Such is the projected cost that progress towards a refurbishment programme is exceedingly slow and no plans can be announced until 2006. Outside, however, things are looking up. The children's playground reopens in summer 2005 after a thorough facelift as part of the park's £3.6m refurbishment project. All in all, the palace on the hill and its environs have much to offer. Chief interest for children is the ice-skating rink, along with (in summer) the boating lake and pitch-and-putt course. Walking around the park affords breathtaking views of London, and there's plenty of space for picnics. In bad weather, try the café in the garden centre. Firework Night in November is the best night of the year, with lots of room for spectators and pyrotechnics that can be seen for miles around.

Buggy access. Disabled access: lift, ramps, toilets. Nappy-changing facilities (ice rink). Nearest picnic place: picnic area by boating lake.

FINCHLEY

Finchley is one of those London outposts that have been waiting to 'come up' for several years now, but haven't yet managed it. Not that it isn't thoroughly affluent and well served by public transport (it has three tube stations). It just hasn't got the desirable status of other smart north London villages. Its saving graces are its cosmopolitan background (it has large Jewish and Japanese communities), its air of general prosperity and its peaceful, tree-lined streets.

A short way south of Finchley Central tube station – the heart of what was once a village and is now a rather dowdy cluster of small shops and cheap Turkish and Chinese restaurants – is **Avenue House** and its beautifully landscaped gardens, which were given to the nation in 1918. A five-minute walk north from the station gets you to Victoria Park, just off Ballards Lane between Finchley Central and North Finchley; here you'll find a bowling green, playground and tennis courts; in July it also provides a venue for the Finchley Carnival.

For indoor entertainment, the **Great North Leisure Park** (Leisure Way, High Road, N12) – better known among the locals as Warner Village – is an ugly but useful US-style entertainment complex. The cinema, Finchley Warner Village (08712 240240), has a Saturday morning kids' club. There's also an extremely popular swimming pool – a good spot for children's parties – kitted out with a vigorous wave machine and swirling currents for (as all the signs say) 'rough and tumble fun'. Non-swimmers should wear armbands. The Hollywood Bowl bowling alley (Leisure Way, High Road, N12 0QZ, 8446 6667, www.hollywoodbowl.co.uk) has a bar and burger restaurant; adjacent to it is an amusement arcade.

It doesn't have to be fast food when it comes to eating out in Finchley, though. The area is well set up with excellent eating places. The coolest place to be seen with your kids is probably Rani (7 Long Lane, N3 2PR, 8349 4386), a brightly coloured Gujarati/East African vegetarian restaurant that does children's menus. Fish

and chip lovers are blessed with the renowned Two Brothers Fish Restaurant (297-303 Regent's Park Road, N3 1DP, 8346 0469).

In East Finchley, the Phoenix Cinema (52 High Road, N2 9PJ, 8883 2233, www.phoenixcinema. co.uk) has children's films on Saturdays. The Old Manor House, on East End Road, has been transformed into a cultural centre, which includes ritual baths, a school and the absorbing **Jewish Museum, Finchley**.

If you and your offspring decide to get away from it all, try the **Dollis Valley Green Walk**, which forms part of the London Loop that encircles the city and links green spaces from Moat Mount, near Mill Hill in the north, to Hampstead Garden Suburb in the south. Setting off with a map is advisable, as the way isn't very well signposted; for more details visit www.londonwalking.com.

Avenue House

17-19 East End Road, N3 3QE (8346 7812/ www.avenuehouse.org.uk). Finchley Central tube/ 82, 125 bus. **Open** *Ink Museum* 2-4pm Tue-Thur. **Admission** free; donations appreciated.
The Ink Museum, situated in one room of this lovely building, commemorates former Avenue House owner 'Inky' Stephens and his father Henry, inventor in 1837 of the blue-black ink that is used to this day on birth and marriage certificates. (Stephens' ink factory was once on the site of the Islington Ecology Centre, *see p98*.) The rest of Avenue House is open to view only on certain days of the year – phone for details – but some of the rooms can be hired out and it's undoubtedly a grand venue for children's parties. Otherwise, the grounds are open free of charge from 7am until dusk, and offer a pleasantly situated playground and buggy-accessible tree trail.
Buggy access. Café (Mar-Sept). Disabled access: toilet. Nappy-changing facilities. Nearest picnic place: Avenue House grounds. Shop.

Jewish Museum, Finchley

Sternberg Centre, 80 East End Road, N3 2SY (8349 1143/www.jewishmuseum.org.uk). Finchley Central tube/143 bus. **Open** 10.30am-5pm Mon-Thur; 10.30am-4.30pm Sun. Closed bank hols, Jewish hols, Sun in Aug. **Admission** (LP) £2; £1 concessions, 12-16s; free under-12s. **No credit cards.**
This more northerly branch of the informative Jewish Museum (*see p90*) focuses on Jewish social history. There's a reconstructed sewing workshop on the ground floor, which gives an idea of sweatshop life in the 19th century, and a display on the evolution of an East End family bagel business. Upstairs an exhibition traces the life of Leon Greenman, a British Jew who survived Auschwitz. The Holocaust Exhibition may be considered too upsetting for young children, but staff leave it to the discretion of parents; the images are more likely to be understood by people of at least secondary school age. This branch also has a 12,000-strong photographic archive, augmented by 2,000 oral history tapes.
Buggy access. Café (lunchtimes Mon-Thur). Nearest picnic place: museum garden/Avenue House gardens. Shop.

FURTHER NORTH

Jump on a bus going up the dreary A10 towards Tottenham and you eventually pass White Hart Lane, the home of **Tottenham Hotspur Football Club**, a tour of which is much easier to get into than a match. Just down from here is **Bruce Castle**, an island of stateliness in run-down surroundings.

Further west, the North Circular (an escape route or a vehicle trap, depending on traffic) leads to **Brent Cross Shopping Centre** with its large range of chains and a handy crèche, thence to IKEA, purveyor of affordable flatpacks. It's not just the home furnishings that attract people here: take the Edgware Road if you have a yen for Japanese goods. **Oriental City** (399 Edgware Road, NW9 0JJ, 8200 0009) is a mall with several good places to eat, including a big self-service buffet. The shops are fascinating, with wind-dried ducks, odd-looking veg and oriental toiletries, though it's the amusement arcade that children love – and it's a lot less seedy than its counterparts in central London.

Set sail in a westerly direction from Brent Cross to the peace and quiet of the **Welsh Harp Reservoir** (Cool Oak Lane, NW9 3BG, 8205 1240). This huge open space is not only a beauty spot, but has been recognised as a Site of Special Scientific Interest. The informative environmental centre is a good starting point for nature trips. The leafy waterside areas provide space for games pitches, tennis courts, playgrounds and picnics.

Further north, in Hendon, the extensively revamped **Royal Air Force Museum Hendon** is a lavish tribute to the history of flying machines and the magnificent men who piloted them.

Bruce Castle Museum

Lordship Lane, N17 8NU (8808 8772/www.haringey.gov.uk). Wood Green tube, then 123 or 243 bus/Seven Sisters tube/rail, then 123 or 243 bus/Bruce Grove rail. **Open** 1-5pm Wed-Sun. **Admission** free.
This local museum, set in an unexpectedly beautiful 16th-century manor house and holding the entire collections of the borough of Haringey, is a lively place much appreciated for its weekend and holiday children's activities. Sunday afternoons (2-4pm) always see some craft session or other in progress; this means adults can peruse the photographs of local streets in Victorian times undisturbed (Muswell Hill as a muddy cart track; quaint shopfronts on North London high streets; rolling green pastures now filled with housing). The building itself was owned by successive generations of the Coleraine family and is said to be haunted by one of them still. More concrete is the lasting influence of Rowland Hill, a progressive schoolmaster on this site and subsequently a postal reformer: his ideas led to the formation of the Penny Post. He is featured in a room devoted to local inventors, which has plenty of buttons to push and pull. Other displays, geared towards the war years, are popular with grandparents. The museum's archives may be visited by appointment; if you live in Haringey, there's every chance your own street will be featured in a historic photo that may be copied to take home. Outside, the 20 acres (8ha) of grounds make for good picnicking; there's a playground and a collection of antique postboxes.
Buggy access. Car park (in Church Lane, free). Disabled access: lift, toilet. Nappy-changing facilities. Shop.

Royal Air Force Museum Hendon

Grahame Park Way, NW9 5LL (8205 2266/www.rafmuseum.org). Colindale tube/Mill Hill Broadway rail/303 bus. **Open** 10am-6pm daily. Closed 24-26 Dec, 1 Jan. *Tours* daily; times vary, phone for details. **Admission** free. *Tours* free. **Credit** MC, V.
The newly renovated RAF Museum makes a brilliant day out. The big exhibits – Camel, Tempest, Gypsy Moth, Mosquito, Harrier and so on – are parked at ground level or hung in dogfight poses from the rafters of the ultra-modern Milestones of Flight building. As you take a break in the café, helicopter blades jut out above your head, while a little further on miniature parachutists go up and down in a tube or drop off a wire into the hands of kids eager to learn about the laws of gravity. More interactive games are available in the Aeronauts gallery, many in the guise of pilot aptitude tests. This gallery is really one giant playground: who could resist guiding a beach ball through hoops on a stream of hot air, or trying out the controls in a Jet Provost cockpit? Only the flight simulator (over-eights only) carries an extra charge; everything else is gloriously free, so although a comprehensive tour is exhausting, you can come as often as you like. More low-key than the Milestones of Flight gallery are the atmospheric and dimly lit Battle of Britain building, and the restored Grahame-White Aircraft Factory, with its pleasing architecture and beautiful biplanes, all string-and-canvas wings and polished wooden propellers.

Activities for children and adults take place all year: workshops include hot-air balloon making, rocket science, and Search and Rescue role-playing. The workshops are always very popular, so book ahead. Quizzes, Pulsar Battlezone interactive laser games, face-painting, aircraft displays and giant garden games are also on the cards. The fun-packed Summer Festival Weekend at the end of August is a must.
Buggy access. Café. Disabled access: ramps, toilets. Lift. Nappy-changing facilities. Nearest picnic place: on-site picnic area. Restaurant. Shop.

Tottenham Hotspur Football Club

Bill Nicholson Way, 748 High Road, N17 0AP (8365 5000/ticket office 0870 420 5000/www.spurs.co.uk). White Hart Lane rail. **Open** *Tours* 11am Mon-Sat. **Admission** *Tours* £8 adults; £5 under-16s, OAPs. **Credit** (only in advance) MC, V.
Tours of the pitchside, the tunnel, changing rooms, boardrooms and press rooms take place regularly, but the Saturday ones tend to be booked up well in advance. Note that they cannot take place on a match day, nor the day before; indeed their regularity depends on a minimum number of customers, so don't turn up on spec. Tours last about an hour to an hour and a half, depending on how chatty the punters are. Finish in the megastore, where you can blow £50 on a shirt or 50p on a souvenir pencil.
Buggy access. Disabled access: toilet. Shop.

EAST LONDON

Where grime meets green.

One crafty kid at the **Geffrye Museum**.

SPITALFIELDS & AROUND

When adults discuss Spitalfields and Whitechapel, the terms 'multiculturalism' and 'gentrification' never seem very far away; where children are concerned, 'Brick Lane' and 'all-you-can-eat buffet' are probably nearer the mark. Nonetheless, the influx of affluent new residents to the area has made for increasingly inviting attractions for all the family, and the ease of access to Spitalfields from the rest of the city makes it a good starting point for an adventure in East London.

If you head north from Aldgate East tube station, you pass Tubby Isaacs' stall (purveyor of whelks and jellied eels since 1919) at the foot of Goulston Street on your way to Petticoat Lane Market (usually just a handful of stalls, but hectic on Sunday afternoons). On parallel Old Castle Street, the **Women's Library** (7320 2222, www.thewomenslibrary.ac.uk), a former wash house, holds free exhibitions (9.30am-5.30pm Mon-Wed, Fri; 9.30am-8pm Thur; 10am-4pm Sat),

workshops and family activities (11am-1pm, 2-4pm Thur, 22 July-19 Aug 2005), as well as the best collection relating to women's history in the country. The Wash House Café will sustain those too cautious to give Tubby's crab sticks a go.

A little further north is the terrific **Spitalfields Market**, which is easily reached by heading east from Liverpool Street station – heading along Brushfield Street you'll get a great view of Nicholas Hawksmoor's awesome, Grade I-listed **Christ Church** (7247 7202; 11am-4pm Tue, 1-4pm Sun). Built in 1714, the church reopened in 2004 after two years and £10m of restoration. Be warned: the market gets busy on a Sunday, so it can be difficult to negotiate with kids.

North of the market and church, Folgate Street has **Dennis Severs' House**. Branching off elegant Fournier Street (which runs alongside the church towards Brick Lane), you'll find the minor jewel that is **19 Princelet Street**. **Brick Lane** itself is firmly established on the tourist – and cultural, given the raft of books about the place – maps. The focal point of an immigrant community of Indians, Pakistanis and Bangladeshis from the 1950s to the 1970s, Brick Lane is at the heart of an area that boasts more than 50 curry houses. Your main problem is keeping the restaurant touts at bay long enough for you to read the samey menus; Sweet & Spicy (No.40, E1 6RF, 7247 1081) and Aladin (No.132, E1 6RU, 7247 8210) are both decent options. Brick Lane Beigel Bake (No.159, E1 6SB, 7729 0616) harks back to an earlier period of Jewish immigration.

On Whitechapel Road the **Whitechapel Bell Foundry** (Nos.32-34, E1 1DY, 7247 2599, www.whitechapelbellfoundry.co.uk) runs tours (10am, 2pm Sat), for over-14s. Pop into the foyer to see the huge frame of Big Ben surrounding the door. The **Royal London Hospital Museum** has more macabre attractions.

A tidy step north from Spitalfields, you'll find yourself in Shoreditch and Hoxton. The trendy artists and advertising types who flocked here in the 1990s didn't bring a whole heap of family entertainment with them, but the **Geffrye Museum** is a gem; if that's not reason enough to visit, Faulkner's chip shop (see p177) and Sông Quê (see p179) might be.

Dennis Severs' House

18 Folgate Street, E1 6BX (7247 4013/www.dennis severshouse.co.uk). Liverpool Street tube/rail. **Open** 2-5pm 1st & 3rd Sun of mth; noon-2pm Mon (following 1st & 3rd Sun of mth); Mon evenings (times vary). **Admission** £8 Sun; £5 noon-2pm Mon; £12 Mon evenings. No under-10s. **Credit** MC, V. **Map** p319 R5.
Only Sir John Soane's Museum (*see p57*) can rival Dennis Severs' House for atmosphere, especially on candlelit evenings. Bought in the late 1970s by Dennis Severs (who died in 1999), the building is now what its founder called a 'still-life drama'. Each of the ten rooms stages a period in the life of the house, making it appear as though the various occupants from 1724 to 1914 might pop back at any moment: the hearth crackles, the wine glasses stand half-drunk, the smell of cooking lingers. Severs wouldn't let children in the place, feeling they couldn't muster the level of imaginative engagement his house demanded, but staff now welcome 'young adults'. Still, a reverential hush is the required mode of behaviour – no giggling when you see the chamber pot is full of wee.
Nearest picnic place: Broadgate Circus (Liverpool Street station).

Geffrye Museum

136 Kingsland Road, E2 8EA (7739 9893/www. geffrye-museum.org.uk). Liverpool Street tube/rail, then 149, 242 bus/Old Street tube/rail, then 243 bus. **Open** 10am-5pm Tue-Sat; noon-5pm Sun, bank hol Mon. Closed Good Fri, 24-26 Dec, 1 Jan. **Admission** free; donations appreciated. *Almshouse* £2; £1 concessions; free under-16s. Under-8s must be accompanied by an adult.
The Geffrye is gorgeous inside and out. It was built as almshouses in 1715, one of which has been restored to its 18th-century glory (check the website for public openings). In 1914 the place was converted into a furniture and interior design museum. Now rooms represent different periods in history from the Elizabethan era to the present day. You can't actually enter them – all are open on the third side, so you can see everything without having to worry about precious objects slipping from grubby little fingers – but there are period chairs in several anterooms that can be rigorously tested for comfort; on weekend afternoons there's an art trolley and a Quiz Desk. The second, newer half of the museum has rooms from the 1930s to the 1990s, and temporary arts and crafts exhibitions downstairs. The walled Herb Garden is open from April to October each year, but the airy restaurant that overlooks it is a pleasure year round (and serves children's portions). An imaginative and extremely popular programme of school holiday and weekend events for children reflects the changing exhibitions. Upcoming Saturday Specials include the fascinating-sounding Food Furniture (4 June 2005), the Big Draw (1 Oct 2005) and Christmas Crafts (3 Dec 2005). The ever-popular summer holiday activities (26 July-19 Aug) will, in 2005, get kids discovering the plants and insects that live in the gardens, as well as making insect sculptures, miniature gardens, soaps and lotions. Summer Sundays combine live music, storytelling and a craft activity, along with stalls selling unusual plants. Coinciding with the 'West Indian Front Room: Three Generations of Change in the Black British Home' exhibition (18 Oct 2005-19 Feb 2006), October half-term activities will include African and Caribbean storytelling, and the chance to build a room in a box and make pottery and batik (10.30am12.30pm, 2-4pm 25-28 Oct 2005). Make a date in your diary to visit at Christmas, when the museum's 12 period rooms are evocatively decorated in appropriately themed festive style and there' are various jolly activities for over-excited children to take part in. Phone or check the website for more details.
Buggy access. Disabled access: lift, toilet. Nappy-changing facilities. Nearest picnic place: museum grounds. Restaurant. Shop.

19 Princelet Street

Spitalfields, E1 6QH (7247 5352/www.19princeletstreet.org.uk). Aldgate East tube/Liverpool Street tube/rail. **Open** check website or phone for occasional open days. Group tours by appointment. **Admission** free; donations appreciated. **Map** p319 S5.
This Grade II*-listed building makes an unusual museum. First, it's the only museum in Europe dedicated to immigration and cultural diversity. Second, the opening hours are infrequent, to say the least (just 20 days in 2004), in order that the fabric of the fragile building be preserved until trustees raise the £3m required to open on a more permanent basis. No.19 was first home to Huguenot silk weavers – you can still see a big bobbin hanging above the door – then to Irish dockers. In 1869 Eastern European Jews converted the house into a synagogue and, in the 20th century, it hosted English lessons for Bangladeshi women. When families arrive these days, the adults are given a description of the house's history to peruse while they queue, and children get a quiz sheet to guide them round. On the ground floor and in the basement, the main exhibition, 'Suitcases and Sanctuary', was made by artists in collaboration with local schoolchildren. The kids have written diary entries in the role of Huguenots fleeing persecution, acted out the plight of Irish families escaping the potato famine, and designed posters that might attract West Indian migrants; explainers are on hand to tell you about the house or their own experiences of the working synagogue. Upstairs temporary exhibitions make the most of the atmospheric coloured skylights. Check the website or phone for details of opening dates and special events.

Royal London Hospital Archives & Museum

St Philip's Church, Newark Street, E1 2AA (7480 4823/www.brlcf.org.uk). Whitechapel tube. **Open** 10am-4.30pm Mon-Fri. Closed 24 Dec-2 Jan, bank hols & adjacent days. **Admission** free.
Founded in 1740 by a 22-year-old surgeon called John Harrison, the Royal London Hospital was once the biggest general hospital in the UK. This single-room museum covers its growth from voluntary institution to pioneering 21st-century hospital. The 1934 X-ray control unit could have been created by a mad inventor from a sci-fi B-movie, but the museum is mostly a serious-minded affair. The development of nursing and childcare is traced through displays on Florence Nightingale and war heroine Edith Cavell, there's a replica of the hat former patient Joseph Merrick (the 'Elephant Man') wore to conceal his swollen head, and a video screen showing quaint period films about the hospital. The case on forensics tucked into a corner is disturbing: there's a grisly drawing of what Jack the Ripper did to Catherine Eddowes (not very far away, either), and a photo of the notorious 'From Hell' letter.
Buggy access. Café (in hospital). Disabled access: lift, ramp, toilet. Nappy-changing facilities (in hospital). Shop.

Around Town

Spitalfields City Farm

Weaver Street, off Pedley Street, E1 5HJ (7247 8762/ www.spitalfieldscityfarm.org). Whitechapel tube. **Open** *Summer* 10am-4.30pm Tue-Sun. *Winter* 10am-4pm Tue-Sun. Closed 25 Dec-1 Jan. **Admission** free; donations appreciated.

This community farm was established in 1978 after local allotments were lost to property developers. Gradually reorganising some of its land to make way for the East London line extension, the farm currently has geese honking about, a daily goat-milking demo, mice and rabbits for stroking, and a full complement of cows, pigs and sheep. Poultry, gardeners and all the livestock produce free-range eggs, seasonal vegetables and manure (in that order). Keen eight to 13 year-olds can join the Young Farmers Club, which runs a play scheme on Saturdays; there's also a parent and toddler group for under-fives (Tue, Sun). Visitors can often enjoy donkey rides (£1), and special annual events include a sheep-shearing day, the Spitalfields Show in September and Apple Day in October. *Buggy access. Disabled access: toilets. Nappy-changing facilities. Nearest picnic place: Allen Gardens. Shop.*

Whitechapel Art Gallery

80-82 Whitechapel High Street, E1 7QX (7522 7888/ www.whitechapel.org). Aldgate East tube/15, 25, 254 bus. **Open** 11am-6pm Tue, Wed, Fri-Sun; 11am-9pm Thur. Closed 24-26 Dec, 1 Jan. **Tours** 2.30pm Sun; call to check dates. **Admission** free (1 paying show a year). **Map** p319 S6.

The Whitechapel has a strong educational and community programme for children: when the gallery was founded in 1901, Reverend Canon Barnett insisted on it. So while continuing its proud history of bringing excellent modern art to the East End (the gallery helped revive the fortunes of such then-neglected figures as George Stubbs and, amazingly, JMW Turner, as well as being the first place to exhibit Hockney and Gilbert & George), the Whitechapel has ensured local schools benefit from a progressive programme of artist residencies, sometimes resulting in collaborative exhibitions. There are also exhibition-specific workshops. A £3.26m grant from the Heritage Lottery Fund will enable the gallery to expand into the building next door, which used to be the public library. Due to open in autumn 2007, the extension will allow for major increases in the space available to the galleries and for school/community events, as well as adding a restaurant to the swish gallery café. *Buggy access. Café. Disabled access: lift, toilet. Nappy-changing facilities. Nearest picnic place: Altab Ali Park Shop.*

BETHNAL GREEN TO HACKNEY

East of the Spitalfields cluster old-style East End characters begin to reassert themselves: you'll find plenty along Bethnal Green Road and in the lovely little caff E Pellicci (No.332, 7739 4873) – little is the word; don't even think about buggies. If you can get everyone up and out early enough, Columbia Road Flower Market (between Gosset Road and the Royal Oak pub, 8am-2pm Sun) makes a lovely morning excursion; getting a bagel to go from Jones Dairy Café (*see p179*) fends off hunger pangs. But the real draw is the mighty **Museum of Childhood at Bethnal Green** – at least until the end of October 2005, when it closes for an ambitious refurbishment programme. Just next door, York Hall has a decent swimming pool (Old Ford Road, E2 9PJ, 8980 2243).

Hackney has been the subject of plans for improved transport links for well over a decade, and, if London's Olympic bid is successful in July 2005, there should be little to prevent the East London Line finally arriving here. In any case, with under-16s getting free bus travel from September 2005, there's never been a better time to lose the train habit and hop on a northbound bus.

The centre of Hackney is Town Hall Square on Mare Street, where you'll find the beautiful old **Hackney Empire** (www.hackneyempire.co.uk). Finally reopened in January 2004 after painfully slow refurbishment, the handsome new Empire was just one part of Hackney's plan to create a 'cultural quarter'. Central to this scheme were Hackney Museum, housed in the Central Library, and a large-scale local music venue, Ocean, just across the road. The latter went into receivership in 2004, but the museum is going strong.

For somewhere with such a definitively urban reputation, Hackney has a surprising number of green spaces – surprising, that is, until you learn that as late as the 19th century it was almost entirely rural. Adjoining the brilliant **Hackney City Farm**, **Haggerston Park** (Audrey Street, off Goldsmith Row, E2 8QH, 7739 6288) has pretty gardens beside a large pond, as well as places for ball games and BMX riding, and a spanking new, wood-built playground. Head north up Goldsmith's Row, cross Regent's Canal and you're on **Broadway Market**. The chi-chi shops and restaurants along this strip include Little Georgia (No.2, 7249 9070, www.littlegeorgia.co.uk), chic but friendly gastropub the Cat & Mutton (No.76, 7254 5599, www.catandmutton.co.uk) and Holistic Health (64 Broadway Market, E8 4QJ, 7275 8434), specialists in holistic therapies for tots. The area's sleek incomers buy their organic fruit and vegetables at the bustling Saturday **farmers' market** (www.broadway-market.co.uk), which has a dedicated Brat Park Corner. There's a play area with hopscotch, chess and draughts marked out on the ground, storytelling and face-painting for under-sevens (12.30pm), and the Broadway Knitters Club plan to meet here monthly, supplying special giant needles so that children can have a bash. **London Fields** (Westside, E8) is right at the top of the market.

Further east, across the River Lee Navigation, lie 300 acres (120 hectares) of **Hackney Marshes**, a great place to take the air. It's fine kite-flying

Around Town

Hackney City Farm. *See p108.*

The **Museum of Childhood at Bethnal Green** has been celebrating playtime for well over a century.

country and provides a muddy home for English Sunday League, American and Gaelic football, rugby and cricket. North up the river you'll find the very pretty **Springfield Park**, which looks east past the narrow boats of Springfield Marina and out over breezy Walthamstow Marshes. Refreshments are available at **Springfield Park Café** (8806 0444, www.sparkcafe.co.uk), in the White Lodge at the top of the park's steep hill, which is notably child-oriented.

Clowns International Gallery & Museum

All Saints Centre, Haggerston Road, E8 4HT (office hours only 0870 128 4336/www.clownsinter national.co.uk). Dalston Kingsland or London Fields rail, then 38, 149, 236, 243 bus. **Open** noon-5pm 1st Fri of mth; other times by appointment. **Admission** free; donations appreciated.
Run by volunteers, this single-room gallery is the work of the world's oldest-established organisation for clowns. It traces the history of clowning from 16th-century *commedia dell'arte* to clown doctoring in present-day hospitals. The displays of props, costumes and photos include a comedy car suspended from the roof and a case full of painted eggs, each showing a real clown's particular make-up. For details of the Clown Social or other events, check the website; the 'find a clown' section also allows you to find local member clowns and junior clowns. To arrange a workshop or school event at the gallery, phone Mattie Faint on the listed number.
Buggy access. Disabled access: toilet. Nearest picnic place: Stonebridge Common (opposite). Shop.

Hackney City Farm

1A Goldsmiths Row, E2 8QA (7729 6381/www. hackneycityfarm.co.uk). Cambridge Heath Road rail, then 26, 48, 55 bus. **Open** 10am-4.30pm Tue-Sun & bank hol Mon. Closed 25, 26 Dec, 1 Jan. **Admission** free; donations appreciated.
This former brewery is now a cobbled farmyard with variously exotic chickens, turkeys and ducks pecking around it. Pigs, geese, sheep and cattle grumble away in the various pens, and, if you visit in spring, there's a good chance you'll get to bottle-feed the lambs (phone in advance to check). On Wednesdays children have regular pottery sessions (2-4pm), while the farm's organic vegetables box scheme runs from 5.30pm; there's also drop-in pottery on a Sunday (2-4.30pm). 'Music and Movement' sessions take place on a Thursday (2.5 to 4 year-olds; 1.15-2pm, 2.15-3pm) and Friday (under 2.5 year-olds; 11.15am-noon). There are also popular summer play schemes and cycle workshops (and dedicated bike racks in the courtyard), as well as occasional storytelling and circus skills events. Revive yourself in the fabulous organic café, Frizzante (*see p179*), stock up on fresh honey and eggs from the shop – a new deli opened here in February 2005 – or relax in the tranquil farm garden, complete with a female scarecrow with yellow straw bunches. The meeting room is available for children's parties.
Buggy access. Café. Disabled access: ramp, toilet. Nappy-changing facilities. Nearest picnic place: farm gardens. Shop.

Hackney Museum

Technology & Learning Centre, 1 Reading Lane, off Mare Street, E8 1GQ (8356 3500/www.hackney. gov.uk/hackneymuseum). Hackney Central rail. **Open**

9.30am-5.30pm Tue, Wed, Fri; 9.30am-8pm Thur; 10am-5pm Sat. Closed bank hols. **Admission** free.
Hackney Museum's resources and hands-on activities were financed to the tune of £400,000 by the Heritage Lottery Fund, with the museum designed to help visitors explore the 1,000 years of Hackney's history. There's a full-size model of an Anglo Saxon log boat to load up and clamber on board (the original is sunk into the floor beside it), and you can time yourself making matchboxes to see whether you would have survived working in a Victorian factory (in the 1860s you earned tuppence for 144 boxes, so the simple answer is that you wouldn't). Touch screens let you trace family history or take a virtual tour of a Victorian house. There are also free Explorer Pads, full of activities, available at the entrance. Phone or check the website for details of exhibitions and the changing programme of drop-in events (family workshops are usually on the first Saturday of the month).
Buggy access. Café (Fab Food, next door). Disabled access: toilets. Nappy-changing facilities. Nearest picnic place: benches in square/London Fields. Shop.

Museum of Childhood at Bethnal Green

Cambridge Heath Road, E2 9PA (8983 5200/recorded info 8980 2415/www.museumofchildhood.org.uk). Bethnal Green tube/rail. **Open** 10am-5.50pm Mon-Thur, Sat, Sun. Closed 24-26 Dec, 1 Jan. **Admission** free.
Under-8s must be accompanied by an adult.
The Museum of Childhood was established in 1872, as part of the V&A (*see p89*). It is now the UK's biggest collection of toys and childhood paraphernalia, containing some 6,000 games and toys. You can enjoy neat cabinets that display board games, early electronic toys, puppets from all over the world and children's clothes from various periods. The several huge dolls' houses on the first floor draw a lingering crowd to eye the carefully constructed miniature furniture or admire the porcelain dolls and their tiny accessories. The 'Good Times' play area, with its dressing-up box, popular sand box and pier-end wonky mirrors sitting happily alongside interactive computer stations, was part of the last round of refurbishments completed in 2003.
The next stage, financed by a £3.5m grant from the Heritage Lottery Fund, will see a brand-new entrance hall, more space for community projects, and refurbished displays in the mezzanine galleries. The museum will be closed for some of the work – provisionally 12 months from 31 Oct 2005 – although the project is not due to be completed until Jan 2007. Until then, we're all going to make the most of this most endearing of museums by visiting the summer exhibition exploring the history of world sport. It will keep the children entertained with penalty shoot-outs, basketball trials against the clock, and tests of their suppleness and the speed of their reflexes. So all couch potatoes should start training now. Apart from the exhibition, there are the regular events during the week, such as object handling for schools (11am-2pm) and puppetry or arts and crafts for under-fives (2-3pm); at weekends staff run Art Smarts (arts and crafts; 11am-2pm), Ants in my Pants (dance and movement; 2-3pm) and a soft play area for under-fives (40min, £1.80). Story Hour is from 3pm daily. It's also worth joining the free kids' club: it gives a 10% discount in the lovely little shop and free soft-play sessions for pre-schoolers.
Buggy access. Café. Disabled: ramps, lift, toilet. Nappy-changing facilities. Nearest picnic place: tables in front of museum. Shop.

Sutton House

2 & 4 Homerton High Street, E9 6JQ (8986 2264/ www.nationaltrust.org.uk). Bethnal Green tube, then 106 bus/Hackney Central rail. **Open** 1-5pm Fri, Sat; 11.30am-5pm Sun, bank hol Mon. *Gallery* 11.30am-5pm Wed-Sun. Closed *Gallery* 19 Dec-18 Jan. *Historic Rooms* 19 Dec-20 Jan. **Admission** (NT) £2.50; 50p 5-16s; free under-5s; £5.50 family (2+2). *Tours* free after entry, phone for details. **Credit** MC, V.
This is the oldest brick house in east London, built around 1535 for Henry VIII's secretary of state Sir Ralph Sadleir. In the late 1980s it was a community centre, but a grand National Trust restoration project saved the building's original interiors, including the decorated oak-panel rooms. As well as Jacobean paintings and Georgian and Victorian interiors, there's some squatters' graffiti – and don't forget to look in on the 16th-century *garderobe*. On Fridays in August 'Art in the Courtyard' lays on free craft activities for kids (£2.50 for adults). Seasonal events usually include May's popular Spring Fete and the perennially successful Christmas Craft Fair on 3-4 Dec (both £2 adults, children free), as well as the Hallowe'en House Tour (over-8s only), Victorian Christmas Carols (16 Dec), led by costumed actors, and Christmas Carols (17 Dec), with a brass band; all cost £6 for adults, £3.50 children. For details of the regular classical concerts, see the Sutton House Music Society website (www.shms.org.uk). Snacks, cakes and drinks are served in the cosy Brick Place Café.
Café. Disabled access: toilet. Nappy-changing facilities. Nearest picnic place: St John's churchyard. Shop.

MILE END TO WEST HAM

The nondescript council estates that gather around the arterial Mile End Road would encourage few people come here, but Mile End has two impressive parks: **Victoria Park** is the older statesman, while **Mile End Park** is an ambitious newcomer with the additional attraction of the **Ragged School Museum**. Towards town, you'll also find **Stepping Stones Farm**, with Stepney Green's bijou playground practically next door.
Further east in Bow you'll find industrial heritage that predates the Victoriana – grain was being unloaded from boats for grinding at **Three Mills** as early as the 11th century – and then the new-look Stratford. The focal point for ambitious regeneration plans that will take in the whole of east London – not to mention that 2012 Olympic bid – the place is steadily improving, with Gerry Raffles Square providing both a cinema and the **Theatre Royal Stratford East** (8534 0310). Head to the other side of the bus station to find Stratford's only die-cast children's attraction: **Discover**. **West Ham Park** provides breathing space; there's a museum at **West Ham United Football Club** for football fans; and the food and fashion stalls at **Queen's Market** (Tue, Thur-Sat) give Green Street a bit of zing. As do curries at Mobeen (No.224, E7 8LE, 8470 2419) and Vijay's Chawalla (Nos.268-270, E7 8LF, 8470 3535).

Discover

1 Bridge Terrace, E15 4BG (8536 5563/ www.discover.org.uk). Stratford tube/rail/DLR. **Open** *Term-time* 10am-5pm Tue-Sun. *School hols* 10am-5pm daily. **Admission** *Garden* free. *Story Trail* £3.50; £2.50 concessions; free under-2s. **Credit** MC, V.

A baby space monster called Hootah welcomes under-nines and their carers to this interactive play centre. Hootah has visited from the faraway planet Squiggly Diggly, which has run out of stories, on a mission to collect new stories to take back home. The journey starts with the Lollipopter, which takes the kids through a whole series of story settings. Children, with a little help from their adults and some beaming humanoids called Story Builders, take a dream ticket and write or draw the place they want to visit. Further in, there are opportunities to fly on a magic carpet, cross a rickety-rackety bridge across the sparkly river, get lost in curtains of plastic worms, hide in secret caves, dress up, and make puppets out of wooden spoons at the well-equipped art tables. Visitors can buy a special Story Book Bag (£1), in which to keep all the stories and treasures they make along the way. In addition, kids can head outside into the Discover Garden (free), which has a space rocket to climb in, slides and chunky wooden climbing frames, living willow tunnels for hide and seek, a wet-play area for fine weather, and picnic benches. There's a refreshment area for coffee, cold drinks and snacks. Regular weekend drop-in activities include 'Stories in a Bag', during which children and a Story Builder create a tale using a random selection of objects, while bookable events for half-terms and holidays may include mask making and home-made puppet shows. Discover also does parties for a gratifyingly low price of £6.50 per head.
Buggy access. Disabled access: ramp, toilet. Nappy-changing facilities. Nearest picnic place: ground-floor area. Shop.

Mile End Park

Locksley Street, E14 7EJ (7364 4147/children's park 7093 2253). Mile End tube. **Open** 24hrs daily. **Admission** free.

Mile End Park is for many the quintessential modern urban park. The south end of the park has a great playground (funded by HSBC to the tune of £2m), with rope slide, scrambling wall, complicated climbing frame, swings and see-saw, as well as a dedicated area for under-fives. The Play Park is now enhanced by a refreshments kiosk and toilet, and the Play Pavilion hosts 'stay and play' sessions (12.30-3pm Mon-Fri). A little to the north, the go-kart track provides thrills and spills for older children, and an Adventure Park should be open by summer 2005. There's a fully staffed drop-in centre for 11 to 17 year-olds, along with a dark green youth shelter for teenagerly hanging out – the solar-powered lighting is indicative of the park's commitment to meeting environmental concerns. Placid strolls can be taken past the pretty fountain in the Terraced Gardens and over the Green Bridge spanning Mile End Road, complete with trees growing above the passing traffic. Regent's Canal runs up the western side of the park, with bird life, cyclists and local fishermen in more-or-less

 RUNNING WILD

Everything from German hairy snails to peregrine falcons have been spotted in East London. Surprised? Don't be. East London has two natural attractions that are the envy of the city. The first, **Epping Forest**, is a huge expanse of ancient woodland. Information on organised events such as bat walks (24 July; 11, 15 Sept 2005) is available from the Information Centre (*see p119*). **Wanstead Park** (*see p118*), an historic southern part of the forest, hosts an annual spring bluebell walk under the auspices of the the park's WREN Conservation Group (www.wrengroup.fsnet.co.uk); if anyone can help you find a rare digger wasp or a water scorpion, WREN can.

Second, **Lee Valley Regional Park** (*see p118*) is a series of wetland habitats created out of gravel pits and reservoirs. There are 32 species of mammal here (including water voles, Apr-Sept), as well as 21 kinds of dragonfly (May-Sept). Waymarked walks, some providing easy buggy access, take you to see orchids, grasshoppers and water lilies. The birdwatching is excellent: winter brings 10,000 migrant waterbirds from chillier climes (the Lee Valley Birdwatching Fair takes place for a couple of days each February) and summer is the time to enjoy the kingfishers.

Cemeteries are always a good bet for signs of wildlife – most of the humans in them are in no position to disturb it. At **Tower Hamlets Cemetery Park** (entrances on Southern Grove & Cantrell Road, E3; www.towerhamletscemetery.org; 8am-1hr before dusk daily) children aged 8 to 14 can enjoy Wildlife Watch group Bow Beasties - turn up on the third Sunday of the month at 10.30am. There are also bat, butterfly, spring bulb and dawn chorus walks; information is available from the Soanes Centre (8252 6644). **Mudchute Farm & Park** (*see p114*) offers a pleasant 31 acres (13ha) in which to wander, more than half the total open public space on the Isle of Dogs. For more information on walks, conservation projects or arts and crafts events in either of these reserves, contact the Local Nature Reserves Officer Kenneth Greenway (7515 5901); both reserves have numbered nature trails. Further east, **East Ham Nature Reserve** (see p116) has nearly nine acres (4ha) of overgrown Norman churchyard - the largest in London - to run around in. The several nature trails here are all rather haphazardly marked, and hardly designed for buggies, but even the longest is walkable in half an hour and the air of neglect helps the kids feel like genuine explorers.

Finally, the regular and developing programme of environmentally friendly events at **Mile End Park** (*see p110*) includes wild flower (19 June 2005), butterfly (9 July), bat (26 Aug) and dragon and damsel fly (27 Aug) walks, as well as pond dipping (30 July, 20 Aug). And don't miss the annual Spider Safari, which should be tracking down the park's resident tree-dwelling jumping spiders some time in May.

happy coexistence. North of Mile End Road, thrill-seekers will find Mile End Climbing Wall (Haverfield Road, E3 5BE, 8980 0289) and nature lovers are able to potter around tranquil ponds at the centre of the Arts Park and Ecological Park (pumped using power from a 30ft/9m tall wind turbine). The park also has praiseworthy educational and community development aims, bringing sculptures into the park and holding temporary exhibitions (there's a children's art expo planned for the summer). On 12 June 2005, the Mile End Town & Country Show will offer a plethora of attractions, ranging from donkey cart rides and square dancing to weaving demonstrations, falconry displays and the opportunity to make your own boat... and, worryingly, to then test it on the eco-ponds.

Buggy access. Café. Disabled access: toilets. Nearest picnic place: ground-floor area.

Ragged School Museum

46-50 Copperfield Road, E3 4RR (8980 6405/www.raggedschoolmuseum.org.uk). Mile End tube. **Open** 10am-5pm Wed, Thur; 2-5pm 1st Sun of mth. Closed 24 Dec-1 Jan. *Tours* by arrangement; phone for details. **Admission** free.

Ragged schools were charitable organisations that provided a basic education for orphaned, poor and down-and-out children, and it was Dr Barnardo who, in 1877, converted these particular canalside warehouses into what became the largest of London's ragged schools. A typically sparse Victorian classroom has been recreated on the first floor, while the second floor has a replica Edwardian kitchen, with a fine array of outmoded domestic appliances (a meat safe and some carpet beaters, for example). School groups come from all over London to be given old-fashioned names such as Walter and Agatha, and endure the tender mercies of a hatchet-faced 'schoolmistress' (a museum actress), before being introduced to the exquisite torture of scrubbing clothes on a washboard or cranking a mangle. The permanent local history exhibition on the ground floor, 'Tower Hamlets: A Journey through Time', will be of more interest to adults than children, but it's enlivened with objects to handle and things to sniff. In the basement you'll find the Towpath Café. Family workshops on the first Sunday of each month give members of the public access to the re-enactments, while school holidays offer structured, themed activities for kids: under-sixes can enjoy arts and crafts activities, storytelling and sometimes music sessions; trails and workshops entertain the six-12s.

Buggy access (ground floor only). Disabled access: toilet. Nappy-changing facilities. Nearest picnic place: Mile End Park. Shop.

Three Mills Island

Lea Rivers Trust, Three Mill Lane, E3 3DU (River Lee Tidal Mill Trust 8980 4626/schools programmes 8981 0040/www.leariverstrust.co.uk). Bromley-by-Bow tube. **Open** *House Mill* May-Nov 2-5pm Sun. Phone to check other times. *Funday Sundays* Mar-Dec 11am-5pm 1st Sun of mth. **Admission** *Mill* tour £2; free under-16s. **No credit cards.**

The House Mill, built in 1776, is the oldest and largest tidal mill left standing in Britain. It was used to grind the grain for gin distilling. Taken over in 1989 as part of a big restoration project by the Tidal Mills Trust, it now has a visitors' centre that provides a history of the area, maps for walkers, a little souvenir shop and a café (open Mon-Fri and when the House Mill is open). Outside, Riverside Green and Three Mills Green are pleasant for picnicking

The Clock Mill, **Three Mills Island.**

and strolling (*see p115* **Walk**). The first Sunday of the month is Funday Sunday (usually Mar-Dec; phone to confirm), during which children are able to take part in a variety of workshops, often with some species of an environmental theme. The Christmas Fayre (5 Dec) usually attracts huge numbers of people.

Buggy access. Café. Disabled access: lift, toilet (in Tesco if House Mill is closed). Nearest picnic place: Riverside Green/Three Mills Green.

Stepping Stones Farm

Stepney Way (junction with Stepney High Street), E1 3DG (7790 8204). Stepney Green tube. **Open** *Apr-mid Oct* 9.30am-6pm Tue-Sun, bank hols. *Mid Oct-Mar* 9.30am-dusk Tue-Sun, bank hols. **Admission** free; donations appreciated.

This 4.5-acre (2ha) community farm has been run by hard-working volunteers since 1979. The livestock is constantly changing, but expect to find cows, sheep, goats, pigs and donkeys, as well as poultry, rabbits, guinea pigs and some ferrets. Young ones can let rip in the improved play area, where a sandpit and toy tractors await; keen gardeners can buy manure of varying pungency; and conscientious greens bring kitchen waste to the community composting bins. There's also a wildlife pond and picnic area, and the activities room is stocked with arts

Around Town

and crafts materials. Annual events include an Easter egg hunt, 'Christmas on the Farm' and, always popular in the area, summer weekend activities; ring for details. *Buggy access. Café. Disabled access: toilet. Nappy-changing facilities. Shop.*

Victoria Park

Old Ford Road, E3 5DS (8985 1957). Mile End tube/Cambridge Heath or Hackney Wick rail/8, 26, 30, 55, 253, 277, S2 bus. **Open** 6am-dusk daily. Closed 25 Dec.
Victoria Park was opened in 1845 after demands for more public space were met by an extraordinarily generous £100,000 in donations. With its wide carriageways, smart lamp-posts and wrought-iron gates, the park was conceived as the Regent's Park of the East End, and at 240 acres (97ha) it is the largest area of formal parkland this side of town. Poverty-stricken locals made good use of the park's two lakes as baths, but somehow there are still fish in the Western Lake (you can help deplete the stock by getting a free fishing licence); Britain's oldest Model Boat Club convenes around the other lake, near Crown Gate East, every second Sunday. There are fallow deer in an enclosure on the east side of the park, and tennis courts, a bowling green and football, hockey and cricket pitches. After a morning in one of the two playgrounds, stop off for refreshments at the Lakeside Pavilion Café (which reopened, with new toilets nearby, in May 2004) and watch the geese, swans and ducks play under the fountain. Two very different musical interludes are planned for the summer. A giant screen will provide a live relay of the Royal Opera's *La Bohème* on 30 June 2005, while a Fusion East showcase day for the artistic talents of local youth on 22 July 2005 will be followed by a weekend of live music. *Buggy access. Café. Disabled access: toilets. Nappy-changing facilities.*

West Ham Park

Upton Lane, E7 9PU (8472 3584/www.cityoflondon. gov.uk/openspaces/westhampark). Stratford tube/ rail/104, 238 bus. **Open** 7.30am-30mins before dusk daily.
Run by the Corporation of London, West Ham Park is neat and civilised, with pretty ornamental gardens and lovely trees. The playground, which has a full-time attendant, has some impressive climbing apparatus, a wooden prairie locomotive to clamber on and a Wendy house corner. There are 12 tennis courts (the annual tennis clinic is held in June), three cricket nets (Essex CCC run free training for under-16s in July), two football pitches, a running track and a rounders area. The pre-war paddling pool (late May-Aug) is another attraction. From late July to August there are children's events on Monday and Friday afternoons; a bouncy castle arrives each Wednesday; and there are occasional Sunday concerts. For refreshments (hot and cold) an ice-cream van lingers tantalisingly close to the playground (from noon daily, Easter to Oct).
Buggy access. Disabled access: toilet. Nappy-changing facilities.

West Ham United Football Club

Boleyn Ground, Green Street, E13 9AZ (8548 2748/ www.whufc.com). Upton Park tube. **Open** *Museum/ shop* 9.30am-5pm Mon-Sat. Closed 25 Dec. **Admission** *Museum* £6; £4 concessions, 5-16s; free under-5s; £15 family (2+2). *Tours* £10; £5 concessions, 5-16s; free under-5s. **Credit** MC, V.

As we went to press, West Ham United's latest attempt to return to the Premiership wasn't looking entirely blessed, but their fan base remains broad and committed. The club's museum cost a cool £4m and tells the story of the club from its origins in 1895 as the Thames Iron Works FC through glory days under Ron Greenwood to the more troublesome present. Those who aren't fans of the claret and blue will make a bee-line for the Champions Collection: it includes the World Cup winners' medals of Sir Geoff Hurst, Bobby Moore and Martin Peters. Book in advance if you're visiting on a match day.
Bars. Buggy access. Disabled access: toilet. Shop.

DOCKLANDS

In the decade since the 1990s recession, Docklands has become a rather chipper destination. More than just the modern alternative to a City address for financiers, this part of London has plenty of entertainment options, even for visitors whose suits are still in the wardrobe – though the thicket of towerblocks now crowding iconic Canary Wharf Tower proves the bankers are still here in numbers. The best way to get around Docklands is on the **Docklands Light Railway** (DLR; 7363 9700). With various extensions over the years, the DLR now reaches from Bank in the City to Beckton in the east, from Lewisham south of Thames to Stratford in the north. The real beauty of the network is that much of it runs on raised tracks, making a journey a sightseeing pleasure. Pick quiet times (weekdays after 10am and before 5pm) and the kids can sit in the front windows of the train and pretend to drive.

To take things a step more touristy, snap up a Rail & River Rover ticket (£9 adult, £4.50 children, under-fives free, £25 family), which combines travel on the Docklands Light Railway with City Cruises sightseeing boats. Disembark at Tower Pier to check out the marina of St Katharine Docks, with its flash yachts and Thames barges. Then stroll the ten minutes past **Tower Bridge** and the **Tower of London** (for both, *see p52*) to the DLR station at Tower Gateway. Alternatively, stay on board until you reach Greenwich Pier (for Greenwich's numerous attractions, *see p121*), then take the DLR back under the river for sightseeing on the Isle of Dogs. If you want to dock at Canary Wharf itself, there's a separate fast commuter service.

The westernmost point to fall under the Docklands banner is **Wapping**. Until well into the 19th century, convicted pirates were brought at low tide to Execution Dock (at Wapping New Stairs), hanged and left in chains until three tides had washed over them. A rather new-looking noose dangles from the 16th-century Prospect of Whitby pub (57 Wapping Wall, E1W 3SH, 7481 1095), with its splendid riverside courtyard, and a

Smiles all round at **West Ham Park**.

couple of pirate ships (sadly, you can't board either) reside in dry docks by the ornamental canal at the usually deserted Tobacco Docks would-be mall. Food options here include Pizza Express (78 Wapping Lane, E1W 2RT, 7481 8436) or, nearer St Katharine Docks, Smollensky's (Hermitage Wharf, 22 Wapping High Street, E1W 1NJ, 7680 1818). Between Wapping and the Isle of Dogs is **Limehouse**, so-called because medieval lime kilns once stood here. A century ago this was a bustling commercial port; now it's a marina with posh yachts and jolly narrow boats, surrounded by luxury flats. The impressively lofty white church north-east of the basin, **St Anne's Limehouse**, was designed by Hawksmoor between 1712 and 1724; the kids will probably manage to raise a little interest for the man-sized pyramid in the north-west corner of the churchyard. More importantly, the basin is a good starting point for canal walks: head north up Regent's Canal for Mile End Park (*see p110*), or take a longer walk north-east on Limehouse Cut to Three Mills Island (*see p111*).

The **Isle of Dogs**, however, is the pre-eminent destination for visitors – not something many people would have said during the docks' long years of post-war decline, nor during the divisive redevelopments of the 1980s. You can explore all the area's history, as well as such arcane areas of debate as whether the Isle of Dogs is an island and

what dogs have to do with it (answers: not really, not much), at the excellent **Museum in Docklands**. The museum is across the bouncing bridge (it's supported on floats) from Cabot Square, which looks up at that famous tower. The impact of Cesar Pelli's 800-foot-high (244-metre) monster edifice, actually called **One Canada Square**, may have been diminished by the duller buildings that now surround it, but it's still a stunner. Tables outside Carluccio's Caffè (Nash Court, E14 5AJ, 7719 1749) provide a good vantage point if you're peckish. The kids might enjoy finding artworks along Canary Wharf's public sculpture trail (click the 'Lifestyle' link at www.canarywharf.com or phone 7418 2000 for a map): they include bits of floor or wall or light, more impressive pieces like Pierre Vivant's *Traffic Light Tree*, and oddities like Constance de Jong's *Speaking of the River* – riverside benches with concealed loudspeakers in the arms, triggered when people sit down. The fountain in Cabot Square is lovely and there are benches, but the Japanese Garden beside the Jubilee Line tube station is the best place to picnic. There are useful chain shops in the mall (Gap Kids, HMV), as well as a Waitrose for the sandwich makings. Or you could treat yourself to posh dim sum at Royal China (*see p179*) down by the river.

A southbound DLR ride from Canary Wharf takes you to **Mudchute**, once just a dump of silt

Museum in Docklands.

Around Town

dug out of Millwall Dock. In the 1970s locals fought off property developers to ensure the place was preserved as an unlikely park and natural habitat, with lovely **Mudchute City Farm** the principal result. There's also an uninspiring playground by the station and lots of flat green grass for running about on. You can walk to **Island Gardens** (cross the main road from the eponymous station) with its unbeatable view of Greenwich over the Thames. There's also the spookily drippy and echoing Victorian foot tunnel under the river; the attendant-operated lifts (7am-7pm Mon-Sat, 10am-5.30pm Sun) are large enough for a fleet of buggies, but it's quite a long walk through to the **Cutty Sark** (*see p122*).

Mudchute City Farm

Pier Street, Isle of Dogs, E14 3HP (7515 5901/ www.mudchute.org). Crossharbour/Island Gardens DLR. **Open** 9am-4pm daily. Closed 25 Dec-1 Jan. **Admission** free; donations appreciated.
Ducks, chickens, goats, pigs and llamas, plus rare breeds of sheep, pigs and cattle all live on what is the largest city farm in London. Depending on the time of year, you can help the farmers bottle-feed lambs or watch them shear sheep or milk the goats (contact education officer Denise Lara for details). Local kids can join the pony club or Young Farmers Club, and everyone, wherever they live, can enjoy summer arts and crafts workshops and play schemes. There's a small aviary and petting corner for cuddling

guinea pigs and bunnies, a volunteer-run café (usually open mid morning to early afternoon) and, during school hols, a shop for souvenirs and riding accessories. A new 64-place nursery opened in 2004 (10am-5pm Wed-Sun), along with a garden centre specialising in plants for urban gardens. *Buggy access. Café. Disabled access: toilet. Nappy-changing facilities. Shop.*

Museum in Docklands

No.1 Warehouse, West India Quay, Hertsmere Road, E14 4AL (0870 444 3857/recorded info 0870 444 3856/www.museumindocklands.org.uk). Canary Wharf tube/West India Quay DLR. **Open** 10am-6pm daily. Closed 24-26 Dec, 1 Jan. **Admission** (annual ticket, allows for multiple visits) £5; £3 concessions; free under-16s. **Credit** MC, V.
This £15m museum, which shares its collection with the Museum of London (*see p49*), is housed in a Grade I-listed Georgian warehouse. Spread over five floors, the museum has displays that range from a 4,000-year-old timber figure found in Dagenham to a discussion of the economic effects of containerisation. First, Tony Robinson enthusiastically narrates the city's Roman history on a series of touch screens. Then you pass models of London Bridge, narwhal tusks, a dangling gibbet cage and a reconstructed quay. The next floor has a sickly sweet-smelling rum warehouse and the sickly smelling Sailortown – a reconstruction of a mid 19th-century Wapping slum. The Docklands at War gallery is as moving as it is vivid. Sections covering more recent history are unlikely to grab young 'uns, but they will like the Mudlarks Gallery. There, under-12s can build Canary Wharf tower, play at stevedores balancing cargo in the hull

WALK Water ways

A walk along the rivers of **Three Mills Island** combines, in a surprisingly compact space, industrial heritage and natural calm. There's bad news, though: to get there, you have to go left from Bromley-by-Bow tube station and thold your nose as you go hrough an unthreatening but wee-stinky underpass, with steep stairs at both ends. Head left down the hill alongside the grimly busy A102 and you'll fetch up in front of Tesco – where bus-savvy visitors can simply hop off an F2 from Stratford.

Turn right and breathe a sigh of relief when you see the mills. To the right, the **Clock Mill** is instantly recognisable by its pair of white-tipped black conical roofs, its clocktower bell chiming the hours. Go straight over the little bridge that spans the Lea Navigation Canal. To the right of the cobbled courtyard is **Bow Creek**; to the left stands the **House Mill** with its café.

Turn right through the kissing gate between the Clock Mill and the film studio. The path curves left, with the wall on your right low enough for the kids to safely admire muddy Bow Creek or the tribe of gasometers on the far side of Channelsea River. Completing an almost full semi-circle, you'll find yourselves at a bridge – a good spot for Pooh Sticks.

For a longer walk, taking you all the way to Joseph Bazalgette's **Abbey Mills Pumping Station**, cross the bridge. Otherwise, keep to the path for **Three Mills Green**. You'll get a good view of the pumping station – albeit through trees – from the steep hillock in the corner of the green.

Those heading to Abbey Mills should turn right immediately after the bridge. Follow the path that lazily curves alongside a twisty creek through head-high foliage. When you reach benches and gravel-filled planters, walk up beside a huge spiral of piping, reminiscent of a giant ammonite. You're right beside Bazalgette's bizarrely Byzantine masterwork, the most impressive part of the engineer's successful battle against the Great Stink of 1858. Its red, brown and black brickwork is classic industrial Victoriana, made strange by

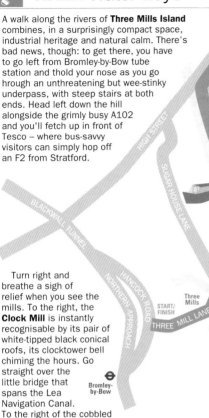

Abbey Mills Pumping Station

fitments and a cupola that are a florid mix of green and magenta. Sadly, you're able to view it only through the fence or – reasonably tall or liftable people only – from the Greenway.

The Greenway is the broad path running along the north side of the pumping station. Head left to where it joins the main road and go left along the High Street. Turn left again on to the towpath by Three Mills Wall River, over another little bridge and find the lazier parts of the family on Three Mills Green. Here, a big pair of hands, clasped at each wrist, commemorate a ghastly well accident – and offer a cautionary tale about the perils of selflessly courageous rescue attempts.

The towpath takes you back to the courtyard past charming painted narrowboats with their hanging baskets and planters. Pop into the café for own-made cakes or 5p lollipops, then either retrace your steps homewards or sit awhile under the weeping willows on the strip of land between the Lea Navigation Canal and Bow Creek.

One last thing: be warned that estuarine rivers have low tides as well as high, so Bow Creek becomes pungent mudflats for part of each day. Low tide is great for watching the swans, ducks and coots dabbling around, but if twinkly water prettiness is your preference, check tide times at http://easytide.ukho.gov.uk/EasyTide before you set off.

Around Town

of a clipper, try on a deep-sea diver's helmet or dig around in the archaeological detritus of the Foreshore Discovery Box; under-fives have their own soft-play area. Events run by the museum include dramatic narratives from costumed actors playing, for example, a Lascar (Indian) sailor or an Irish pub landlady, and holiday and half-term drop-in craft and handling events; check the website for details or to join the mailing list. The Thames Gallery, an easy-to-miss mezzanine below the second floor, will reopen as a resource area and library in late 2005. In addition to the research room, there will be an open area where computers provide photographs and digitised archive material, help visitors with family history research, and give access to the National Maritime Museum's Port Cities website, with its compelling Time Pirates Adventure game.

Buggy access. Café. Disabled access: lift, toilet. Nappy-changing facilities. Nearest picnic place: quayside benches, refectory. Restaurant. Shop.

EAST OF DOCKLANDS

The DLR splits after Westferry station: one branch goes south via Island Gardens station to Lewisham in South-east London (*see p124*), the other east via Poplar to Beckton. A new spur of the network is due to open in December 2005, which excites us no end. Why? Because it will run directly from Canning Town via London City Airport and the marvellous **Thames Barrier Park**. Until then, active families determined to see this unusual modern park have to face a half-hour walk from Custom House DLR. The walk over the pointy footbridge high above Royal Victoria Dock is enjoyable enough (there are lifts at each end, though they're not always working), but you'll have to negotiate North Woolwich Road at the other end – there are wide pavements, at least.

Over Connaught Bridge on the north side of Royal Albert Docks is the **London Regatta Centre** (Dockside Road, E16 2QD, 7511 2211). Sit and watch rowers puff and pant or follow the planes landing at London City Airport from the Regatta Centre's restaurant and bar. A footbridge over Royal Albert Way takes you into **Beckton District Park** (Stansfeld Road, E6 5LT, 8430 2000 ext 23639), which has a wild-flower meadow and woodland walk, plus a good-sized lake at its northern end. The Millennium Tree Trail takes you past 50 trees from five different continents. There are play areas, cricket and football facilities, a trim trail and a summer snack kiosk.

To the south, **North Woolwich Old Station Museum** is next to the North Woolwich Silverlink station. The tidy **Royal Victoria Gardens** are next door. There's a foot tunnel to the south bank for some **Firepower** (*see p127*), but the good old, free Woolwich ferry (8921 5786), which takes pedestrians and cars across the river every 10 minutes daily, is always fun.

Eastbound, **Beckton** is the last DLR stop. The 'Beckton Alp' no longer functions as a dry ski slope, but lovers of the outdoors are well served by **Docklands Equestrian Centre** (2 Claps Gate Lane, E6 7JF, 7511 3917), the little **East Ham Nature Reserve** and **Newham City Farm**. Otherwise, Beckton is mainly new builds and retail parks.

East Ham Nature Reserve

Norman Road, E6 4HN (8470 4525). East Ham tube/Beckton DLR. **Open** *Nov-Feb* 10am-5pm Tue-Fri; 1-4pm Sat, Sun. *Mar-Oct* 10am-5pm Mon-Fri; 2-5pm Sat, Sun. Closed bank hols. **Admission** free.
The East Ham Nature Reserve combines a little museum with the largest churchyard in London, with beguilingly shaggy nature trails (*see p110 Running wild*). The museum comprises two rooms: one contains an 1893 schoolroom to terrify the kids, a wartime kitchen to terrify the mums and a real incendiary bomb that will help nobody relax; the other has a case of stuffed birds and mammals, all looking a bit weary, plus a case each of beetles and butterflies.
Buggy access. Disabled access: toilet. Nearest picnic place: grounds.

Newham City Farm

Stansfeld Road, E16 3RD (7474 4960/recorded info 7476 1170). Royal Albert DLR/262, 300, 376 bus. **Open** *Summer* 10am-5pm Tue-Sun, bank hols. *Winter* 10am-4pm Tue-Sun. Closed 25 Dec, 1 Jan. **Admission** free; donations appreciated.
Having taken on extra staff in the last year, Newham City Farm is now open six days a week. The farmyard animals (a shire horse, cows, Kune Kune pigs, sheep, goats, poultry) take centre stage, but there are also littler chaps to pet (rabbits, guinea pigs, a ferret) and an exotic finch house, as well as a kookaburra and a buzzard. The farm's school programme is well established, and there are plans to appoint paid staff to the visitor centre to improve the facilities for more casual visitors. There are ample picnic areas and, depending on volunteer availability, refreshments sold on site. Fun days (usually in summer) offer the likes of sheep-shearing demonstrations, rides on a shire-horse-drawn cart and felt making, as well as a Friends stall selling pot plants and jigsaws. The young volunteer scheme gets kids involved at weekends and during the holidays.
Buggy access. Café. Disabled access: toilets. Nearest picnic place: grounds.

North Woolwich Old Station Museum

Pier Road, E16 2JJ (7474 7244). North Woolwich rail/101, 473, 474 bus. **Open** *Jan-Nov* 1-5pm Sat, Sun. *School holidays* 1-5pm daily. *Miniature railway* Apr-Oct 1st & 2nd Sun of mth. **Admission** free. **Rides** £1.
The Old Station Museum contains carefully preserved old engines, timetables, signs and other relics from the age of steam travel. There's a preserved ticket office and plenty of models and info, but the children will probably want to head out to the back and poke around Coffee Pot (a Victorian commuter train from the 1890s) and Pickett (from the 1940s). They can climb all over Dudley the Diesel, who will sometimes even be able to take them for a spin (just along the platform and back). There's outside play equipment and, indoors, a Brio layout and a computer running a Thomas the Tank Engine program and the

Hornby Virtual Railway. The museum's small shop sells souvenirs and snacks. During school holidays, drop-in Wednesday afternoon arts and crafts sessions keep fledgling railway buffs amused. Staff permitting, there are weekend soft-play sessions (1.30-2.30pm).
Buggy access. Disabled access. Nappy-changing facilities. Shop.

Thames Barrier Park
Barrier Point Road, off North Woolwich Road, E16 2HP (7511 4111/www.thamesbarrierpark.org.uk). Canning Town tube/DLR, then 474 bus. **Open** dawn-dusk daily. **Admission** free.
Right on the river by the space-age Thames Barrier (the Barrier's visitor centre is actually on the south side; *see p128*), this crisp, modern park centres on a concrete and granite channel the width of a small motorway. Called the Green Dock, it is filled with fragrant honeysuckle and wavy yew hedges, giving it excellent hide-and-seek-ability – with the two pedestrian bridges overhead adding a whole extra dimension to the game. At the riverfront there's a 'Pavilion of Remembrance', commemorating those who lost their lives in the Blitz. The flat lawns are beautifully manicured, perfect for picnics and games. There's a playground packed with apparatus; a basketball hoop and five-a-side court for sporty folk; and plenty of ducks, geese, swans and oyster catchers picking around the gleaming mudflats. The tea pavilion is now open (10am-4pm Mon-Fri). While work continues on the new DLR station (due to be completed in late 2005), the park entrance and temporary car park are on the north-east corner, and the lovely fountains are out of action. But look on the bright side: lack of transport means you'll have the place pretty much to yourselves. Enjoy it while it lasts.
Buggy access. Café. Disabled access: toilet. Free parking. Nappy-changing facilities.

WALTHAMSTOW & WANSTEAD
Walthamstow has a split personality. Five minutes' walk east of Walthamstow Central (the last stop north on the Victoria line) you'll find yourself in quaint and charming **Walthamstow Village**. Around St Mary's Church there's a village ambience and some grisly history: Vinegar Alley was once a trench full of the stuff, intended to prevent pestilence spreading from the mass graves of Black Death victims in the churchyard. The half-timbered Ancient House opposite pre-dates the Plague, although the current incarnation is a painstaking 1934 restoration designed to look authentically saggy. Pamphlets recounting such historical gems are available at the **Vestry House Museum**. Orford Road boasts the Village Kitchen (No.41, E17 9NJ, 8509 2144) for reasonably priced lunches (Fri-Sun), otherwise the Village pub (No.31, 8521 9982) has a patio.

The rest of Walthamstow is as busy as the Village is quiet, especially the famous street market. Comprising 450 stalls, it runs the length of Walthamstow High Street and lays reasonable claim to being Europe's longest daily street market. **Lloyd Park**, on Forest Road, lies to the

Docklands viewed from across the water.

north, with the **William Morris Gallery** at the southern entrance, near a scented garden for the visually impaired, an aviary of budgies and cockatiels, and a lake with strangely black water. At the far end of the park is a play area and skate park. Across the North Circular Road the art deco façade of Walthamstow Stadium (Chingford Road, E4 8SJ, 8498 3311) is worth a look; this greyhound track runs family race days, and its restaurant, the Stowaway Grill does dogs' dinners in a good way.

The **Walthamstow Marshes** are at the end of Coppermill Lane (you might prefer to cycle or drive there: it's a good 15-minute walk from St James Street rail station). Ideal for picnics and walks by the River Lee, the marshes are where doughty Sir Edwin Alliot Verdon Roe made the first all-British powered flight on 23 July 1909 in his triplane 'Yellow Terror'. He flew a tremendous 900 feet (not quite 300 metres). The marshes employ a pleasingly low-tech method of horticultural maintenance: a herd of cows is let loose in July to munch the grass until it's all gone, usually by January the following year.

East of Walthamstow, **Wanstead** is another urban village – as local homeowners are proud to point out. There's another St Mary's church, Grade I listed and dating to 1790, but the attraction for visitors, especially those with kids, is Wanstead's greenery: **Wanstead Flats** and especially **Wanstead Park**.

Wanstead Park

Warren Road, E11 (8508 0028). Wanstead tube. **Open** dawn-dusk daily. **Admission** free.
Nowadays, Wanstead Park is managed by the Corporation of London as part of Epping Forest. Heavily wooded, the park also has several beautiful water features (the Ornamental Water and the three ponds – Perch, Heronry and Shoulder of Mutton). At the fenced-off end of the Ornamental Water is a ruined grotto, built in the early 1760s with a boathouse below and domed, shell-encrusted chamber above; it's now all tumble-down Romantic. The other important ruin in the park is the Temple, once a fancy summerhouse, which has the park toilets to one side. Both structures (the grotto and Temple, not the toilets) are Grade II listed, but the children will get far more excited by the ball-throwing and kite-flying possibilities on the extensive grassy area between the Temple and the tea stall. The Wren Conservation and Wildlife Group (*see p110* **Running wild**) are a good point of contact for nature lovers. There is an annual programme of activities in the park, including family walks (book on the listed number) and all manner of drop-in arts and craft sessions.
Buggy access. Café. Disabled access. Free parking.

Vestry House Museum

Vestry Road, E17 6HZ (8509 1917/www.lbwf.gov.uk). Walthamstow Central tube/rail. **Open** 10am-1pm, 2-5.30pm Mon-Fri; 10am-1pm, 2-5pm Sat. Closed 25, 26 Dec, 1 Jan, bank hols. *Tours* groups only, by prior arrangement. **Admission** free.

On our most recent visit we were delighted to see a resplendent pair of shiny fireman's helmets, one silver and one gold, in the entrance to the Vestry House. It is in such details that the charm of this museum lies. You'll also find a reconstructed police cell (the building was a prison from 1840 to 1870) manned by dodgy manikins; displays of toys and games; a milk cart and bakery cart; and a range of domestic goods. In the clothes section the pre-war bathing suit is a hoot, the 1957 bikini a horror. A Lottery-funded refurbishment in 2002 relandscaped the lovely, walled back garden, using plants that 18th-century workhouse inmates are known to have nurtured here, and created a gallery for the Bremer car. Built by local engineer Frederick Bremer in 1892-4, this was one of the first cars built in Britain – certainly the first in London. The tiny shop is surprisingly well stocked. As we went to press, the Vestry House's programme of children's activities was at a halt until permanent curatorial staff could be appointed.
Buggy access (downstairs only). Disabled access: toilets (downstairs only). Nappy-changing facilities. Nearest picnic place: museum garden. Shop.

William Morris Gallery

Lloyd Park, Forest Road, E17 4PP (8527 3782/ www.lbwf.gov.uk/wmg). Blackhorse Road tube, then 123 bus. **Open** 10am-1pm, 2-5pm Tue-Sat; 1st Sun of mth. Closed 25, 26 Dec, 1 Jan, bank hols. *Tours* phone for details. **Admission** free.
This was the childhood home of the famous designer and socialist, born in Walthamstow in 1834. The gallery seems rather muted, with the lighting kept low to protect exhibits, although the family quiz trail encourages younger children to examine the beautiful designs – some of which (a giant roc molesting a tiny ship, or animal tiles of a dodo and an aardvark-headed dragon eating its own tail) are plenty lively. Objects cover everything from Morris's medieval-style helmet and sword (too slender to impress bloodthirsty lads, forsooth) to complex woven hangings and even the great man's cup and saucer, dutifully kept by Edward and Georgina Burne-Jones for Morris's regular Sunday visit (their own cups were deemed too small). Upstairs, past the rather imposing drawing of the Archangel Raphael, you'll find mainly artworks of middling interest, plus some more furniture. A dedicated education co-ordinator is due to be appointed in 2005, so check the website for details of an new programme of activities.
Buggy access. Disabled access: ramp (ground floor). Nearest picnic place: Lloyd Park. Shop.

LEE VALLEY REGIONAL PARK

Starting east of Hackney (*see p106*) and heading north-east all the way into Hertfordshire, Lee Valley Regional Park is a network of lakes, waterways, parks and countryside areas that covers a vast area on either side of the River Lee. There's plenty to do, though a gentle guided walk is a good way to set about it. The park's ideal for picnics, walking or fishing; it's well signposted and open year round. It's a nature lover's paradise (*see p110* **Running wild**), but other attractions include the **Lee Valley Riding Centre** (Lea Bridge Road, E10 7QL, 8556 2629) and **Lee Valley Cycle Circuit** (Quarter Mile Lane, E10

5PD, 8534 6085), next to the M11 extension. The **Lee Valley Boat Centre** (Old Nazeing Road, Broxbourne, Herts EN10 6LX, 01992 462085) is the place to hire a boat by the hour or to book a narrowboat holiday.

The small town of **Waltham Abbey** is a good point of access. It has plenty of cafés and shops and an Augustinian abbey to visit: founded in 1060 by King Harold, it is also reputed to be where he was buried. Once one of the largest in the country, the abbey had its own farm, fishponds and brewery; only the gateway, a few walls and a stone bridge remain, but the gardens contain a variety of public artworks and there's a 'Sensory Trail' highlighting the natural history of the area. The **Royal Gunpowder Mills** and **Epping Forest** are but a ten-minute drive from the town.

Lee Valley Park Farms

Stubbins Hall Lane, Crooked Mile, Waltham Abbey, Essex EN9 2EG (01992 702200/www.leevalleypark. org.uk). Broxbourne or Waltham Cross rail. **Open** 10am-4.30pm Mon-Fri; 10am-5.30pm or dusk if earlier Sat, Sun. **Admission** £4.10; £3.60 concessions; £3.10 3-16s; £16.50 family (2+3). **Credit** MC, V.
Hayes Hill Farm is a rare breeds centre, with a 'Tudor Barn' for sheltered picnics, a restored gypsy caravan and an adventure play area. Visitors can watch the milking of cows (from 2.30pm daily) at the nearby commercial farm Holyfield – and talk to the farmer via an intercom. Livestock includes sheep, goats, cows, llamas and even water buffalo. There's also the Pet Centre where you'll meet all sorts of little furry and scaly things. There are guided tours for school parties and tractor trailer rides (1.45pm weekends, school holidays, Apr-Oct, weather permitting), as well as special events, no doubt involving pumpkins and pine trees, for Hallowe'en and Christmas.
Buggy access. Café. Disabled access: toilets. Nappy-changing facilities. Shop.

Royal Gunpowder Mills

Beaulieu Drive, Waltham Abbey, Essex EN9 1JY (01992 707370/www.royalgunpowdermills.com). Waltham Cross rail, then 213, 250, 251 bus. **Open** Apr-9 Oct 2005 11am-5pm Sat, Sun (last entry 3pm), bank hols; 11am-5pm daily for school groups.
Admission £5.50; £4.70 concessions; £3 5-16s; free under-5s; £17 family (2+3). **Credit** MC, V.
The Royal Gunpowder Mills were involved in the making of explosives for more than 300 years. Gunpowder production began here in the 1660s; later, the manufacture of guncotton, nitro-glycerine, cordite paste and the highly explosive tetryl was undertaken; and after World War II the mills were a research centre for non-nuclear explosives and propellants. Few of the more than 20 historic buildings on the 175-acre site have been renovated, in a deliberate attempt to convey their long and complex past. The visitors' centre runs an introductory film, as well as having an informative, hands-on exhibition that concentrates on the human story behind gunpowder. You can explore the extremely dangerous process of nitroglycerine manufacture, try on workers' boots and use their tools, or put cannon balls into a chute. A 'guided land train' (actually a tractor and trailer) takes visitors on a woodland tour

(£1.50; £1 children). The educational programme offers Victorian Life, Home Front and (seasonally) Victorian Christmas sessions, as well as Explorer Programmes that cover everything from investigations of the natural surroundings to the making of air-powered paper rockets. This year is the 400th anniversary of the Gunpowder Plot: there's an illustrated talk and costumed re-enactment of Catesby's last stand (10-11 Sept), followed by the Guy Fawkes Experience (24-25 Sept). The costumed re-enactments are popular and usually involve some kind of live firing. New acquisitions include two locomotives, the Woolwich and the Carnegie, which are being cleaned up and having steps installed – let the scrambling commence! *Buggy access. Café. Disabled access: lift, ramps, toilets. Nappy-changing facilities. Nearest picnic place: on site. Shop.*

EPPING FOREST

The biggest public space in London, **Epping Forest** (www.cityoflondon.gov.uk/openspaces) is a gift for walkers, riders and cyclists, not to mention wildlife fans (*see p110* **Running wild**). It measures 12 miles long and 22 miles across (19 by 35 kilometres) and was saved from development by the Corporation of London in 1878. Commoners still have grazing rights and, each summer, English Longhorn cattle can be seen chewing the cud. The forest contains Iron Age earthworks and two listed buildings – the Temple in Wanstead Park (*see p118*) and the fully restored, 16th-century **Queen Elizabeth's Hunting Lodge** (Rangers Road, E4 7QH, 8529 6681; under-16s must be accompanied by adults) on the Chingford side of the forest. The latter has a quiz trail, opportunities for dressing up as a Tudor and, in the kitchen area, you can smell food made from four-century-old recipes. If you're coming to the forest by public transport, Chingford railway station gives access to the Hunting Lodge and some lovely strolls. Loughton and Theydon Bois (Central Line) are the forest's nearest tube stops, though it's a two-mile (three-kilometre) uphill walk from both – a struggle for some adults, let alone small children. The best advice is to get a map and plan your route in advance – or use the car. At High Beech car park there's a small tea hut as well as the **Epping Forest Information Centre** (High Beech, Loughton, Essex IG10 4AF, 8508 0028, www.eppingforest.co.uk, May-Sept 10am-5pm Mon-Sat, 11am-5pm Sun; Oct-Apr 11am-3pm Mon-Fri, 10am-4pm Sat, 11am-4pm Sun), with a children's area, disabled toilet and shop. For a real back-to-nature feeling, between May and September you can pitch your tent at the **Debden House campsite** (Debden Green, Loughton, Essex IG10 2NZ, 8508 3008; £5/night, £3/night children) and listen to the owls hoot.

SOUTH-EAST LONDON

Stay riverside for maritime history, go inland for the land the Tube forgot.

Stroll on! **Greenwich Park** stretches all the way up the hill. *See p122.*

ROTHERHITHE

The Pilgrim Fathers set sail from here in the *Mayflower* in 1620. Rotherhithe was known as a shipbuilding village then, and it still flaunts its salty seadog associations. There are wharves, warehouses and ancient seafarers' pubs. One of them, the Angel, on Bermondsey Wall East, has a smugglers' trapdoor from its less salubrious days.

The seamen's church of **St Mary's Rotherhithe** (St Marychurch Street, SE16 4JE, 7231 2465) was built by local sailors in 1715. Unless you come for a service you'll have to glimpse its treasures, including a communion table made from timber from the Battle of Trafalgar gunship *Temeraire*, through a vandal-proof glass partition. Nearby, the **Brunel Engine House & Tunnel Exhibition** celebrates the world's first underwater tunnel. Every year, the area around St Mary's Churchyard and the Engine House hosts the Rotherhithe Festival (3 July 2005).

The Norwegian Church and Seaman's Mission lie at the mouth of another tunnel, the Rotherhithe car one. There are several Scandinavian churches around here; relics of Rotherhithe's historical links with Nordic sailors, which dates right back to the Vikings. Across Jamaica Road, **Southwark Park** is London's oldest municipal park.

Crossing Lower Road from Southwark Park brings you to Canada Water, the Surrey Quays Shopping Centre and attendant leisure activities: a cinema, Arbuckles burger restaurant (Mast Leisure Park, Surrey Quays Road, SE16 2XU, 7232 1901), the biggest sports store in Europe (Decathlon, *see p202*) and a Hollywood Bowl. You'll also find the **Surrey Docks Watersports Centre** (Greenland Dock, Rope Street, SE16 7SX, 7237 4009), which runs sailing and canoeing courses during school holidays.

Brunel Engine House & Tunnel Exhibition

Brunel Engine House, Railway Avenue, SE16 4LF (7231 3840/www.brunelenginehouse.org.uk). Rotherhithe tube. **Open** *1-5pm Thur-Sun.* **Admission** *£2; £1 concessions, 5-16s; free under-5s; £5 family (2+2).* **No credit cards.**
The Victorians called the world's first underwater tunnel, 'the Eighth Wonder of the World' and it's story is told in this museum in the original engine house. The Thames Tunnel was designed by Marc Isambard Brunel with the help of his more famous son, Isambard Kingdom. The main thrust of the exhibition is the construction of the tunnel, completed in 1843 and now used for the East London tube line. It also provides a general Victorian history lesson: the museum welcomes school groups and has information packs for Key Stages 2 and 4. Details of a plan to create a new museum in the original shaft as a tribute to the Brunels can be seen inside.
Thanks to a Heritage Lottery Fund grant, there are plans in this particular pipeline to revamp the exhibition, making it more accessible to children. In fact kids get quite a lot out of this place as it is. As well as the annual playscheme and tunnel 'Fancy Fair' (1-14 Aug 2005), the organisation's giant Brunel puppet has a starring role in the Thames Festival (17, 18 Sept 2005). The new exhibition and children's facilities open on 10 November 2005. 'National Science Week' (March 2006) sees appropriate children's events, as do celebrations for the anniversary of the tunnel opening', which take place on 25 March 2005.
Buggy access/storage. Nearest picnic place: museum gardens & riverbank. Shop.

Southwark Park

Gomm Road, SE16 2UA (park rangers 7232 2091/art gallery 7237 1230). Canada Water tube. **Open** *Park 8am-1hr before dusk daily. Gallery (during exhibitions) noon-6pm Wed-Sun in summer, 11am-4pm Wed-Sun in winter; phone ahead to check.* **Admission** *free.*
Southwark Park was restored to its original Victorian grandeur with the help of a lottery grant. The loveliest bit is the boating lake (fully operational in summer), where kids can feed the ducks and swans, but the whole place is pleasing. There's a wildlife garden, an ornate old-fashioned bandstand, tennis courts, a bright playground, playing fields and an information centre. You'll also find a curious little gallery smack in the middle of the park. Its shows include the annual 'Open Exhibition' (23 Nov-11 Dec 2005), which always features children's work. The Bermondsey Festival parade ends here to kick off a summer extravaganza known as 'The Event' (9 July 2005).
Buggy access. Café (opens summer 2005). Disabled access: toilet. Nappy-changing facilities (in gallery).

Surrey Docks Farm

Rotherhithe Street, SE16 5EY (7231 1010). Canada Water tube then 225, 381 bus. **Open** *10am-5pm Tue-Thur, 10am-1pm, 2-5pm Sat, Sun, school hols. Closed Fri.* **Admission** *free (except for school parties & playschemes); donations appreciated.*
This riverside organic farm was opened in the early 1970s in an attempt to bring a bit of nature to a depressed neighbourhood. Currently its residents include a herd of milking goats, sheep, cows, pigs, poultry, donkeys and bees (if you're lucky, there'll be fab local honey for sale in the shop). There's a classroom, a dairy and a forge where a blacksmith holds evening classes. The duck pond and a herb and vegetable garden offer further bucolic delights. Children enjoy clambering over the animal sculptures on the riverbank, just outside the farm. There's a summer playscheme run here, but it gets booked up way ahead. *See also p123* **Top 10 Adventures.**
Buggy access. Café. Disabled access: ramps, toilets. Nearest picnic place: riverside. Shop.

DEPTFORD & GREENWICH

Lewisham borough's trendy riverside bit is Deptford – an area whose star is in the ascendent thanks, in part, to the presence of the intriguing, iridescent **Laban** dance centre (Creekside, Deptford, SE8 3DZ (8691 8600/www.laban.org)). Visitors are allowed into the reception area, café and grounds, but if you want a closer look you have to book yourself on a £5 tour.

Smart apartment blocks boasting river views continue to stack up Thameside, but you only need to walk inland to rambunctious old Deptford High Street to see that this traditionally working-class neighbourhood is little changed. Take time to admire **St Nicholas's Church** on Deptford Green; known as the sailors' church, it dates to 1697 and has timber-shivering skulls and crossbones carved on the gate piers. The **Albany Theatre** (Douglas Way, Deptford SE8, 8692 4446/www.thealbany.org.uk) is a great community resource, which runs family shows on Sundays.

Set sail easterly from Deptford for historic maritime **Greenwich**, a UNESCO World Heritage Site. Henry VIII loved this part of the world so much that he built a palace here. Since his time, Greenwich has been in and out of fashion: William and Mary chose not to live in the palace, turning it into the seamen's hospital now known as the **Old Royal Naval College**. For a good overview of Greenwich delights, visit the Tourist Information Centre in the Greenwich Gateway Visitor Centre.

Fancy arriving by boat? Thames Cruises (7930 3373, www.thamescruises.com), Catamaran Cruises (7987 1185) or City Cruises (7930 9033, www.citycruises.com) all float by Greenwich Pier, just by the weathered old tea clipper, the **Cutty Sark**. Not far fom here is **Greenwich Market**, open at weekends. From the riverside it's a ten-minute walk up the steep slopes of gorgeous Greenwich Park to the **Royal Observatory & Planetarium**. For those who find this an uphill struggle, a shuttle bus runs from Greenwich Pier to the **National Maritime Museum** and up to the top of the hill every 15 minutes or so. Tickets last all day and cost £1.50 for adults, 50p for children and nothing for under-fives. The Docklands Light Railway (DLR) offers the Rail & River Rover (7363 9700, www.dlr.co.uk), a family pass that is also valid on some cruise boats.

From Greenwich the Thames Path (*see p126* **Domeward Bound**) can take you to the Greenwich Peninsula, on which the **Millennium Dome** rots gently. That structure is to become a sport and leisure complex at the heart of a brand new town (and possibly an Olympian venue). It has also been reported that an exhibition of the treasures of Tutankhamen will take place in the Dome in about two years' time. Further ambitions for the surrounding area include a grand piazza with water jets, video screens and a 180-foot (nearly 60-metre) illuminated spire. Pie in the sky? We'll see, but until this wonderland materialises, the Peninsula is home to a yacht club, a Holiday Inn, a UCI cinema multiplex and the **Greenwich Peninsula Ecology Park** (*see below*).

Cutty Sark

King William Walk, SE10 9HT (8858 3445/www.cutty sark.org.uk). Cutty Sark DLR/Greenwich DLR/rail. **Open** 10am-5pm daily (last entry 4.30pm). *Tours* Mon-Fri; depending on availability. **Admission** (LP) £4.50; £3.25 concessions; £3.20 5-16s; free under-5s; £12 family (2+3). *Tours* free. **Credit** MC, V.
Launched in 1869 from Dumbarton on the Clyde, the *Cutty Sark* took tea to China and later wool to Australia. Now a museum, the lower hold contains a large collection of handsome figureheads from merchant ships.

The world's only Grade I-listed ship and last surviving tea clipper, built by Hercules Linton in 1869, the *Cutty Sark* is in a parlous state after doing sterling service as a tourist attraction. It's calculated that it will cost about £25m to save her. In January 2005 the Heritage Lottery Fund granted £11.75m toward the project (see the website for latest developments). The plan is that during the repair process the ship will be encased in a transparent inflatable envelope, so visitors can see the restoration work in progress. There are also plans for a new learning centre and catering facilities once the essential repairs have been effected. Work on the restoration is due to begin in October 2006.
See also p123 **Top 10 Adventures**.
Buggy storage. Nearest picnic place: Cutty Sark Gardens. Shop.

Fan Museum

12 Crooms Hill, SE10 8ER (8305 1441/www.fan-museum.org). Cutty Sark DLR/Greenwich DLR/rail. **Open** 11am-5pm Tue-Sat; noon-5pm Sun. Closed 25 Dec,1 Jan, Easter. **Admission** £3.50; £2.50 concessions; free under-7s. Free OAPs, disabled 2-5pm Tue. **Credit** MC, V.

Give this place a whirl if the children are interested in pretty things, fashion and design, but realistically it is one for the over-tens. A pair of restored Georgian townhouses is home to more than 3,000 fans, although only a fraction of the collection is on display, with fans retired periodically to give them a rest. There are fantastically ornate and very old fans here from all over the world and every period since the 11th century. Alongside the permanent exhibitions, changing displays include, for 2005, a display to mark the bicentenary of the Battle of Trafalgar. The Orangery is a beautiful, all hand-painted murals and exquisite furnishing: take tea there with your little finger cocked on Tuesdays and Sunday afternoons. Check the website for exhibition dates and details of fan-making workshops.
Buggy access. Disabled access: lift, toilet. Nearest picnic place: Greenwich Park. Shop.

Greenwich Park

Blackheath Gate, Charlton Way, SE10 8QY (visitors centre 8293 0703/www.royalparks.org.uk). Cutty Sark DLR/Greenwich DLR/rail/Maze Hill rail/1, 53, 177, 180, 188, 286 bus/riverboat to Greenwich Pier. **Open** 6am-dusk daily.
The oldest Royal Park, Greenwich dates from 1433. Its grassy hills are made for roly-polying down, its shady avenues of trees perfect for squirrel chasing, and the views over the river and Docklands from the Wolfe monument are inspiring. The playground is at the bottom of the hill, near the National Maritime Museum and the boating lake, and is well equipped for all ages (although worryingly shade-free on hot days). The trees are magnificent. One of the sweet chestnuts here is 400 years old, and the famous Queen Elizabeth oak is thought to date from the 12th century. Henry VIII and Anne Boleyn danced round it, and for a time its hollow trunk was used as a lock-up for criminals. A storm brought down the long-dead husk in 1991, but next to its preserved remains stands an adolescent tree planted by Prince Philip for the Queen's Golden Jubilee.

Just outside the top gates, across Charlton Way, a group of donkeys stand saddled and resigned – rides for children along Duke Humphrey Road cost about £1. Free fun for under-tens is provided by the Royal Parks' summer entertainments programme and includes alfresco theatricals, plus circus skill and craft workshops (25 July-19 Aug 2005; 7298 2078 or check the website for details).
Buggy access. Cafés. Disabled access: toilets. Nappy-changing facilities.

Greenwich Peninsula Ecology Park

Thames Pulh, John Harrison Way, SE10 0QZ (8293 1904/www.urbanecology.org.uk). North Greenwich tube/108, 161, 422, 472, 486 bus. **Open** 10am-5pm Wed-Sun. **Admission** free.
A pond-dipping, bird-watching haven run by the Trust for Urban Ecology for English Partnerships. The park is reserved for schools on Mondays and Tuesdays. The rest of the week, it's all yours. *See also p131* **Running wild**.
Buggy access. Disabled access: toilets. Nappy-changing facilities. Nearest picnic place: southern park.

National Maritime Museum

Romney Road, SE10 9NF (8858 4422/information 8312 6565/tours 8312 6608/www.nmm.ac.uk). Cutty Sark DLR/Greenwich DLR/rail. **Open** July-Aug 10am-6pm daily. Sept-June 10am-5pm daily. *Tours* phone for details. **Admission** free; donations appreciated. **Credit** *Shop* MC, V.

This most elegant museum charts the nation's seafaring history. Of the permanent galleries, 'Planet Ocean' is all about the mysteries of the sea, and visitors can have a go at making waves and explore tides; 'Explorers' is devoted to pioneers of sea travel; 'Passengers' is a paean to glamourous old ocean liners; and 'Maritime London' tells the capital's nautical history through old prints and model ships. Upstairs, 'Seapower' covers naval battles from Gallipoli to the Falklands, and the 'Art of the Sea' is the world's largest maritime art collection.

Continuing up, Level 3 has the 'All Hands' gallery: all hands-on and interactive, and based on the lives of seafarers. Children can play with a variety of exhibits, including Morse code machines, ships' wheels and a cargo-handling model. 'Shipmates', an activity room off the gallery, is used for children's craft sessions. As usual, you can't leave without a sojourn in the gift shop; here it runs the vaguely nautical gamut from dolphin-shaped water pistols for 50p to models of HMS *Victory* for £85.

'Nelson and Napoleon' is the big exhibition of 2005 (7 July-13 Nov), marking the 200th anniversary of the Battle of Trafalgar. Summer 2005 sees the opening of a new permanent gallery entitled 'Your Ocean', which describes how all life is dependent on the sea.

The Neptune Planetarium is a temporary planetarium, in use while the Royal Observatory's 'Time and Space' project is being developed for spring 2007. This will provide an immersive whole-dome cinema experience, including some live shows presented by an astronomer.

Costumed actors and storytellers entertain the kids with crafts and stories during school holidays and at weekends, *see right* **Top 10 Adventures**.
Buggy access. Café. Disabled access: lifts, ramps, toilets. Nappy-changing facilities. Nearest picnic place: Greenwich Park. Restaurant. Shop.

Old Royal Naval College

King William Walk, SE10 9LW (8269 4747/tours 8269 4791/www.greenwichfoundation.org.uk). Cutty Sark DLR/Greenwich DLR/rail. **Open** 10am-5pm daily (last entry 4.15pm). *Tours* by arrangement. **Admission** free. **Credit** *Shop* MC, V.

The majestic Old Royal Naval College was built by Sir Christopher Wren in 1696. The buildings were originally a hospital, then a naval college and are now part of the University of Greenwich. The public are allowed into the rococo chapel and Painted Hall; the amazing painted tribute to William and Mary took beleaguered artist Sir James Thornhill 19 years to complete. In 1806 the body of Lord Nelson was laid in state here while thousands came to pay their respects. In the chapel there are free organ recitals on the first Sunday of each month.

The Greenwich Gateway Visitor Centre, in the Pepys Building, has an exhibition on 2,000 years of Greenwich history, the story of the Royal Hospital for Seamen and information on other Greenwich attractions.

At weekends and during school holidays, the College runs events and re-enactments (*see* **Top 10 Adventures**). Handlers from Raphael Falconry let fly on 9 and 10 July 2005 and Samuel Pepys drops in for a chat during August. On 1 and 2 October 2005 there's a commemoration of the Battle of Trafalgar with costumed 19th-century sailors demonstrating life on board. From December 2005 until January 2006 the ice rink comes back to the College. See the website for more details.
Buggy access. Café. Disabled access: toilet. Nappy-changing facilities. Nearest picnic place: Naval College grounds. Restaurant. Shop.

TOP 10 Adventures

Goat whispering in Surrey Docks Farm
They'll only listen if you buy a bag of goat food, then those ravenous ruminants will follow you to the ends of the earth. Watch out for muggers. Last time we were there a particularly giddy goat nicked our Kit-Kat. *See p121.*

A sailor's life for all on board the *Cutty Sark*
Drop-in storytelling workshops explore the seafaring life. Skills demonstrations run by crafts people and sailors are also programmed, and Nannie's Nook offers games, dressing-up and stories at weekends and during school holidays. See *p122.*

Yo ho ahoy! at the National Maritime Museum
The always child-friendly Maritime Museum runs a 'Crow's Nest Adventure' (interactive tours for ages two to six years); craft sessions and sailor-themed sing-songs. All kinds of workshops and performances take place on Family Sundays (last Sun every month). *See p122.*

Fire and ice at the Old Royal Naval College
After a summer of historical role-playing, starting with costumed horseplay from King Charles II's musket men in June and ending with Nelson's crew in October, all is serene when the ice rink appears for the winter. *See p123.*

Welcome to the Queen's House of fun
The last Sunday of every month in the Queen's House is a family day, when children can get crafty, play games, dance about and generally have a right royal knees-up. *See p124.*

Young guns go for it at Firepower
The Command Post's paintball range gives you ten balls to splatter at targets for £1.50 and the Rolling Rock's 12ft (3.7m) climbing wall has a moving surface: try getting to the top (£1.50 says you can't). *See p127.*

Blitz kids at the Imperial War Museum
The 'Children's War' exhibition is all about evacuees, air raid precautions, rationing, school and work, entertainment and VE day celebrations. Hear about it direct from those who lived through it as children. *See p129.*

Burn rubber in Burgess Park
Aged eight to 16? Book a party at the little kart track in the park, and if you love it, take out a year's membership for £40. Beginners are welcome and tuition is available. *See p130.*

Crash, bang, wallop at the Horniman
There's always something noisy going on at the 'Hands On Base' here. Musical instruments from around the world are up for grabs at family sessions on Saturday afternoons and during school holidays. Or open a Discovery Box for toys, puppets, masks and more. *See p132.*

Go bananas in Dulwich Park
Those crazy guys at London Recumbents can hire you a 'banana bike', tandems, trikes or bog-standard machines. They'll teach you how to ride them, too. *See p132.*

Around Town

Queen's House

Romney Road, SE10 9NF (8312 6565/www.nmm.ac. uk). Cutty Sark DLR/Greenwich DLR/rail. **Open** 10am-5pm daily (last entry 4.30pm). *Tours* noon, 2.30pm. **Admission** free; occasional charge for temporary exhibitions. *Tours* free. **Credit** (over £5) MC, V.
Designed in 1616 by Inigo Jones for James I's wife, Anne of Denmark, Queen's House so pleased its royal resident that she dubbed it the 'house of delights'. The house is now home to the National Maritime Museum's impressive art collection, which includes portraits of famous maritime figures and works by Hogarth and Gainsborough. More importantly, it's also home to a ghost, famously captured on film by a couple of Canadian visitors in 1966 but spotted as recently as 2002 by a gallery assistant. Family Sundays (last Sunday of every month) see party games, performances, dancing, and art and craft activities; no need to book, but ring before coming to check what's on. *See also p123* **Top 10 Adventures**.
A colonnade connects the building to the National Maritime Museum (*see above*). An exhibition of maritime photography mounted by the National Trust and Magnum entitled 'The Coast Exposed' runs until January 2006. *Buggy access. Disabled access: lift, ramps, toilets. Nappy-changing facilities. Nearest picnic place: Greenwich Park.*

Ranger's House

Chesterfield Walk, SE10 8QX (8853 0035/www. english-heritage.org.uk). Blackheath rail or Greenwich DLR/rail/53 bus. **Open** Mar-late Sept 10am-5pm Wed-Sun & bank hols. *Oct-Dec* group bookings only. Closed Jan-Mar 2006. **Admission** (EH) £5.30; £4 concessions; £2.70 5-16s; free under-5s. **Credit** MC, V.
This red-brick villa – formerly the official residence of the Greenwich Park Ranger and, prior to that, a 'grace and favour' home to minor royals – was built in 1720. It now contains the collection of treasure amassed by millionaire diamond magnate Julius Wernher, who died in 1912. His priceless collection of 19th-century art, including jewellery, bronzes, tapestries, furniture, porcelain and paintings, is one of the most unusual in the world. Displayed in 12 elegant rooms, this glittering spectacle shows what Britain's richest man liked to spend his dosh on – enamelled skulls, miniature coffins and jewel-encrusted reptiles are just some of the unusual items that caught Wernher's eye. *Buggy storage. Disabled access: lifts, toilets. Nearest picnic place: Greenwich Park. Shop.*

Royal Observatory & Planetarium

Greenwich Park, SE10 9NF (8312 6565/www.rog. nmm.ac.uk). Cutty Sark DLR/Greenwich DLR/rail. **Open** 10am-5pm daily (last entry 4.30pm). *Tours* phone for details. **Admission** free. *Tours* free. **Credit** MC, V.
Built for Charles II by Wren in 1675, this observatory now examines the life of John Flamsteed, the Royal Astronomer, who was assigned the weighty task of mapping the heavens. A series of set-piece rooms evoke the Flamsteed household. Elsewhere, there are cases and cases of clocks and watches, from hourglasses to a mind-bogglingly accurate atomic clock. The dome houses the largest refracting telescope in the country – and eighth largest in the world. In the courtyard is the Prime Meridian Line – star of a billion snaps of happy tourists with a foot in each hemisphere. You can pay £1 to receive a certificate marking your visit. Visitors are occasionally treated to a talk about the Royal Astronomer by a performer in 17th-century costume.

The planetarium in the South Building at the Royal Observatory closed on 31 October. A state-of-the-art planetarium is being built as part of the 'Time and Space Project' – a redevelopment of the 330 year-old observatory, partly financed by the Heritage lottery Fund, which will by 2007 open up one-third of the site previously closed to visitors. *Buggy access (courtyard only). Nappy-changing facilities. Nearest picnic place: Greenwich Park. Shop.*

BLACKHEATH & LEWISHAM

Windswept **Blackheath** (the name probably comes from 'Bleak Heath'), kite-flying central, is home to many sports clubs: the Royal Blackheath Golf Club (established 1745), the Blackheath Hockey Club (1861) and the Blackheath Football Club (1862), which actually plays rugby union. Nearby Blackheath village has some excellent shops and cafés, but the traffic can be depressing. **Blackheath Halls** (23 Lee Road, SE3 9RQ, 8318 9758, www.blackheathhalls.com) programmes plenty of children's activities: theatre productions, dance workshops, films, a young bands programme, a youth jazz orchestra and an all-ages community orchestra. On Sundays there's a farmers' market in Blackheath station car park.

South-west of Blackheath lies rough old **Lewisham**, currently bracing itself for a much need town-centre regeneration programme. If you keep walking down the fancifully named Lewisham Promenade you'll end up in Catford, with its landmark black-and-white cat over an ugly shopping centre, the beautiful old art deco **Broadway Theatre** and trees lit up by blue light bulbs. Lewisham borough has many parks. **Mountsfield Park** (Stainton Road, SE6) hosts People's Day (16 July 2005), an annual summer festival (call 8318 3986 for details). Also in the area is Sydenham Wells Park (Wells Park Road, SE26) and **Manor House & Gardens**.

Age Exchange Reminiscence Centre

11 Blackheath Village, SE3 9LA (8318 9105/www.age-exchange.org.uk). Blackheath rail. **Open** 10am-5pm Mon-Sat. **Admission** free. Groups must book in advance, for a small charge. **Credit** MC, V.
A registered charity that aims to improve the quality of life for older people by emphasising the value of memories, Age Exchange have created a wonderfully nostalgic museum experience. A mock up of a grocer's shop from about 60 years ago has drawers to open up enabling you to explore the comestibles of old. An old-fashioned sweetie shop has classics like rhubarb and custard and rosy apples, and a sitting room circa 1940s, with nostalgic toys, a stove, old-style furnishings and crockery. There's also a little café and theatre space at the back. The centre's programme of exhibitions are based around older people's memories – check the website for dates of future attractions. *Buggy access. Café. Disabled access: toilets. Nearest picnic place: centre gardens. Shop.*

Around Town

On board the **Cutty Sark**. *See p122*.

WALK Domeward bound

Following the river seaward from historic maritime Greenwich takes you very quickly from the elegance and opulence of Henry's playground, through a gritty industrial landscape of endless building projects to that millennium-madness tent, the Dome, which was reported to have cost a whopping £28.7 million to keep empty for the past five years – but it's destined to become a leisure complex one day.

Start at the **Cutty Sark Gardens**. Pass Greenwich Pier, on your left, and keep the Old Royal Naval College to your right. Listen for the sound of string quartets in rehearsal as you pass the building inhabited by Trinity School of Music.

Duck down the little road at the **Trafalgar Tavern**. It's called Crane Street and takes you past the Trinity Hospital Almshouses, adjacent to an old disused power station with vast chimneys. Next up is the **Cutty Sark Tavern**, a handy child-friendly pub that looks out over the river at Iron Wharf. Keep walking bravely east as the path becomes a bit deserted and scary, passing through archways of buddleia and goat willow as nature reclaims land faster than the developers do. For a while you can see the Dome in front of you, as you pass the grain refinery. There's a viewing jetty with benches, and the yellow spokes of the Dome can be seen behind old shells of industrial buildings. Sit and watch the cormorants airing their wing feathers on rusting hulks of old boats and gaze out over the wide, brown river to the Isle of Dogs.

From here follow signs to North Greenwich station, a riverside route (an alternative is to cross the peninsula on an inland path to the Thames Barrier). If you choose the Dome, the path takes you to a freshly planted border of trees and shrubs which fails to

detract from the vast piles of ballast and the noises off from lorries, bulldozers, diggers – all evidence that the much-vaunted regeneration of this barren land is in full swing. The **Dome** itself peeps coyly from behind tall blue fences. Is it a

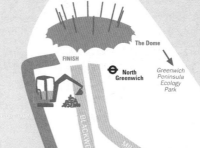

trump card in London's Olympic bid, or has this millennium folly put the kibosh on the

dream? Time will tell, after we've gone to press. Go through an unmanned barrier to Millennium Way, and the bus and tube stations. At least handsome North Greenwich station was hailed as a millennium triumph. Take a look if you take the tube home, or continue across acres of deserted car parking that wasn't filled even when the Dome was open. Your destination? The **Greenwich Peninsula Ecology Park** (*see* *p122*), a much more interesting millennium venture.

Manor House & Gardens

*Old Road, SE13 5SY (8318 1358/www.lewisham.gov.
uk). Hither Green rail.* **Open** *Café & park* 9am-dusk
daily. *House & library* 9.30am-5pm Mon, Sat; 9.30am-
7pm Tue, Thur. **Admission** free.
This 1772 manor house, once the home of George Baring
the illustrious banker, is now one of the grandest local
libraries in London; the children's section is particularly
sweet (there's a parent-and-toddler session there on
Tuesday mornings). In the garden is an ancient ice house,
which opens to the public occasionally. The park outside,
with its central lake, raised platform for wildfowl feeding
and unchallenging play area, is all the better for the child-
friendly park café, Pistachio's, and its menu of simple, own-
made hot meals, ice-cream, drinks and snacks.
Buggy access. Café. Disabled access: toilets.

CHARLTON & WOOLWICH

A pleasant cyclepath runs from Blackheath to the
once well-to-do area of **Charlton**, which still
retains villagey charm around the church and
remnants of the green. Until 1872 the area was the
focus of the rowdy Charlton Horn Fair
(recompense from King John for seducing a local
miller's wife). Today, **Charlton House** is the
main attraction. Its once grand terrace looks out
over a grim looking Charlton Park. **Maryon
Wilson Park**, across the road, is more pleasant.
It has a small farm (organised tours only; 1.30pm
Wed during term time; 1.30pm Mon, Wed, Fri in
school hols; call 8319 4253 for details). The
northernmost bit of Maryon Park leads to
Woolwich Church Street and the river, spanned by
London's lifeline, the **Thames Barrier**.

The riverscape at **Woolwich** looks bleak, when
you consider that it's on the wrong side of the
Thames Barrier to be protected from a surge
tide. Its former role as anchorage for the hellish
Victorian prison ships (described by Charles
Dickens in *Great Expectations*) didn't do
Woolwich many favours, either.

The last prison ships were removed 150 years
ago, but vessels to take note of nowadays are the
splendid, free **Woolwich ferry** (8921 5786).
These diesel-driven boats replaced a paddle
steamer that had been in use until 1889. They take
pedestrians and cars across the river every 10
minutes daily. If you take the ferry to the north
shore, you disembark right by the North
Woolwich Old Station Museum (*see p116*) and
Royal Victoria Gardens. Just by the ferry terminal
on the south bank is the **Waterfront Leisure
Centre** (Woolwich High Street, SE18 6DL, 8317
5000), with its 'wild and wet' pools and an indoor
playground for children aged up to nine. The town
centre has a market and loads of cheap eating
places, not least Britain's first McDonald's (it
opened on Woolwich High Street in 1974).

Long ago, the Woolwich Arsenal was a source of
real pride in the area. Established in Tudor times
as the country's main source of munitions, by
World War I, the Arsenal stretched 32 miles (51
kilometres) along the river, had its own internal
railway system and employed 72,000 people.
Much of the land was sold off during the 1960s,
but thankfully the main section, with its beautiful
cluster of Georgian buildings, has been preserved.
The grounds are now open to the public, as is
Firepower, the artillery museum. South of here,
the Royal Artillery Barracks is famous for having
the longest Georgian façade in the country. For
more on the Arsenal, visit the **Greenwich
Heritage Centre** (Artillery Square, Royal
Arsenal, SE18 4DX, 8854 2452; open 9am-5pm
Tue-Sat). The centre has a large collection of
historical sources – books, maps, drawings and
manuscripts – and an archaeological archive
and natural history specimens. There are also
fascinating historical displays concerning the
Arsenal and Greenwich borough.

Charlton House

*Charlton Road, SE7 8RE (8856 3951/www.greenwich.
gov.uk). Charlton rail/53, 54, 380, 422 bus.* **Open**
Library 2-7pm Mon, Thur; 10am-12.30pm, 1.30-5.30pm
Tue, Fri; 10am-12.30pm, 1.30-5pm Sat. *Toy library*
10.30am-12.30pm, 1.30-3.30pm Mon, Tue, Fri.
Admission free.
From the outside, this Jacobean manor house looks like the
grandest of stately homes – which, once upon a time, it
was. Built in 1612, it housed the tutor of Henry, eldest son
of James I. These days it's a community centre and library,
but glimpses of its glorious past can be seen in the creaky
oak staircase, marble fireplaces and ornate plaster ceilings.
The library has a good children's section (children's
activities take place 10.30am Mon), and is a rather
delightful home to the Charlton Toy Library (8319 0055).
Outside, the venerable mulberry tree, dating back to 1608,
receives many visitors each year.
*Buggy access. Café. Disabled access: ramps, toilets.
Lifts. Nappy-changing facilities. Nearest picnic area:
Charlton House grounds.*

Firepower

*Royal Arsenal, SE18 6ST (8855 7755/www.firepower.
org.uk). Woolwich Arsenal rail.* **Open** *Nov-Mar*
10.30am-5pm Fri-Sun (last entry 3pm). *Apr-Oct*
10.30am-5pm Wed-Sun (last entry 4pm). **Admission**
(LP) £5; £4.50 concessions; £2.50 5-16s; free under-5s;
£12 family (2+2 or 1+3). **Credit** MC, V.
The Royal Artillery Museum occupies some fine buildings
in the heritage corner of the historic Royal Arsenal.
Exhibits trace the evolution of artillery from primitive
catapults to nuclear warheads. By way of introduction to
the Gunners and their history, there's an affecting
seven-minute film in the Breech cinema, then visitors are
bombarded on all sides by a multimedia presentation called
'Fields of Fire', which covers various 20th-century wars
and can be rather alarming for tinies. Other galleries in this
building include the Gunnery Hall (full of howitzers and

Around Town

Wacky races in **Burgess Park**. *See p130.*

tanks), the Real Weapon gallery (which shows you how guns work) and the medal gallery.

Phase Two, opened by Dame Vera Lynn on 31 March 2004, includes a huge collection of trophy guns and the Cold War gallery, which focuses on the 'monster bits' (ginormous tanks and guns used in military conflict from 1945 to the present). Each piece is in its own bay, surrounded by vast iconic photographs to give it its place in history. Of most interest to children, however, is the first-floor Command Post (*see p123* **Top 10 Adventures**).

Special events take place throughout the year. There are various armoury displays and demonstrations, gun salutes for royal occasions, musical nights and, brilliantly, 'camouflage' party packages for little birthday soldiers (call 8312 7111 for details).

Buggy access. Café. Disabled access: ramps, toilets. Lift. Nappy-changing facilities. Nearest picnic place: riverside. Shop.

Thames Barrier Information & Learning Centre

1 Unity Way, SE18 5NJ (8305 4188/www. environment-agency.gov.uk). North Greenwich tube/Charlton rail/riverboats to & from Greenwich Pier (8305 0300) & Westminster Pier (7930 3373)/177, 180 bus. **Open** *Apr-late Sept* 10.30am-4.30pm daily. *End Sept-Mar* 11am-3.30pm daily. Closed 24 Dec-2 Jan. **Admission** *Exhibition* £1.50; £1 concessions; 75p 5-16s; free under-5s. **Credit** MC, V.

The key player in London's flood defence system looks like a cross between the Sydney Opera House and row of giant metallic shark's fins spanning the 1,700ft (520m) Woolwich Reach. The Barrier is the world's largest adjustable dam and was built in 1982 at a cost of £535m; since then it has saved London from flooding at least 67 times. The small but interesting Learning Centre explains how it all works and has a map that shows which parts of London would be submerged if it stopped working. Outside, a new garden and playground area is planned. Time your visit to see the barrier in action: every September there's a full-scale testing, with a partial test closure once a month (ring for

dates). The Barrier celebrated its 21st birthday in May 2005 with another full-scale test in front of admiring crowds, wearing party hats, perhaps. The best way to see the barrier is by boat: Campion Cruises (8305 0300) runs trips from Greenwich (Mar-Oct only).
Café. Shop.

KENNINGTON & THE ELEPHANT

Kennington Park, once the main place of execution for the county of Surrey, is the remains of a common where, during the 18th and 19th centuries, John Wesley and other preachers addressed the crowds. During the 19th century it was also used for games of cricket, until the **Oval Cricket Ground** was built. There were no gibbets or preachers there when Charlie Chaplin was growing up nearby, but he still found it a profoundly miserable place. The adventure playground and playroom named after him (Bolton Cresent, SE5, 7735 1819) have made it slightly cheerier but the many squats and run-down housing that lie behind them – earmarked for regeneration – are a pretty depressing sight.

North of Kennington Park Road the **Imperial War Museum** fills a building formerly used as a lunatic asylum, beyond which lies London's roundabout of shame, the **Elephant & Castle.** Comprising a stained, red 1960s mall with uninspiring shops and coffee bars, all marooned in a whirl of traffic, its days are numbered. The Elephant and Castle Regeneration group (www.elephantandcastle.org.uk) with the London Development Agency plan to demolish the shopping centre and rebuild a pleasant town centre by 2012. Hurrah.

Brit Oval

Kennington Oval, SE11 5SS (ticket office 7582 7764/ 6660/tours 7820 5750/www.surreycricket.com). Oval tube. **Open** Ticket office 9.30am-4pm Mon-Fri. *Tours* by arrangement; phone for details. **Admission** varies; depending on match. **Credit** MC, V.

London's most famous skewed circle is also a landmark venue in the history of national and international cricket. The brand new £24-million LCS stand, completed in time for the 1st Test in May 2005, has added new terraces, a community education centre and a swanky aerofoil roof.

Membership for under-18s is £10 per year, including free entry to all games (the last domestic match of 2005 is 25 September). The Oval continues to work with local children, offering Outreach coaching for 250 London schools, as well as school tours, educational workshops and young people's tournaments (including a girls-only series). The club is developing a second community venue for young cricketers at Kennington Park.

Buggy access. Café. Disabled access: ramps, toilets. Nappy-changing facilities. Shops.

Imperial War Museum

Lambeth Road, SE1 6HZ (7416 5000/www.iwm.org. uk). Lambeth North tube/Elephant & Castle tube/rail. **Open** 10am 6pm daily. **Admission** free; donations appreciated. *Exhibition* prices vary. *Audio guides* £2.50-£3. **Credit** MC, V.

The IWM isn't for everyone: housed in an old lunatic asylum, the extensive collections of 'important' military weapons tend to send kids diving through halls and dodging imaginary machine-gun fire, which may rile some parents. Much more interesting – if no less disturbing – are the excellent WWI and II galleries, displaying poetry by Wilfred Owen, Siegfried Sassoon and their contemporaries, as well as a reconstructed Somme trench and a look at life on the Home Front. Between the two galleries there's a countdown clock-face, whose minute hand ticks off the number of people killed in war. On 31 December 1999 the figure reached was 100m. When we visited it stood at 103,807,575. And counting.

Spring 2005 saw the opening of the new 'Children's War' exhibition, exploringthe conflict of 1939-45 through the eyes of children, which features a revamped 1940's house and interactive exhibits, such as secret boxes full of wartime treasures and artefacts, and dressing-up clothes to try on. It runs until 2008, *see also p123* **Top 10 Adventures**; The 'Secret War' exhibition takes aspiring (James) Bonds on a whirlwind tour of British espionage. There's also a 200-seat cinema that shows a range of drama and documentary footage of conflicts through history. The Holocaust Exhibition, on the third floor, traces the history of anti-Semitism and the rise of Hitler. Shocking images of brutality and suffering make it unsuitable for children under 14, but it's the vast collection of salvaged shoes, clothes, spectacles and other mementoes, as well as testimonials from survivors, that break the heart. On the fourth floor, 'Crimes against Humanity' covering genocide and ethnic violence in our time, leaves you in no doubt about the pointlessness of war (over-16s only).

Various temporary exhibitions operate throughout the year, and there is a rolling educational programme offering audio guides, workshops and talks by costumed actors. Other exhibitions for 2005 include, until 31 July, 'Great Escapes' – some of the audacious escape attempts made by Allied prisoners of war in World War II and 'Lawrence of Arabia' (autumn 2005) – marking the 70th anniversary of the death of TE Lawrence.

Buggy access. Café Disabled access: lifts, ramps, toilets. Lifts. Nappy-changing facilities. Nearest picnic place: Geraldine Mary Harmsworth Park. Shops.

CAMBERWELL & PECKHAM

Once a picturesque farming village, rural enough to support a new species of butterfly, the Camberwell Beauty, identified in 1748, these days **Camberwell Green** is decidedly less verdant. It has a small children's playground, although health-conscious families may question the benefits of breathing in the fumes from one of

London's most congested crossroads. Far better to retreat to the sanctuary of nearby **Burgess Park** or prettier **Ruskin Park**, near the top of Denmark Hill (the latter is one of the few London parks that still dares to fill up its large, shallow paddling pool for hot tots during the summer). The proliferation of lively bars and cafés on Camberwell Church Street suggests some kind of gentrification continues apace.

Peckham is another place that's made some positive changes of late – although cynics might suggest it couldn't have got any worse. When Will Alsop's terribly modern **Peckham Library** won the RIBA award for Britain's best new building in 2000, it was the first bit of good press the area had received since early reviews of *Only Fools and Horses*. Next door to the library, the Peckham Pulse health club (7525 4999, www.fusion-lifestyle.com) is helping things along nicely: it boasts excellent child and baby facilities, including health clinics and a resident homeopath, as well as a useful (if not over healthful) café. There are also after-school activities from community forums like New Peckham Varieties (7708 5401), which runs performance workshops with the Magic Eye Theatre.

Astoundingly, central Peckham earned itself a place in the top ten best high streets in London in a recent survey. We find its depressing numbers of bargain emporia, grubby market stalls and downmarket chains less than appealing, but it takes all sorts. Further up Peckham Rye Common is where William Blake claimed to have encountered his first angel as a child. Its inner circle, containing the playgrounds and pond, is closed until July 2005 for a Heritage Lottery Fund-financed regeneration. Overgrown **Nunhead Cemetery**, to the east, is a less cultivated but equally tranquil retreat.

Burgess Park

Albany Road, SE5 0RJ (park rangers 7525 1066/ www.southwark.gov.uk). Elephant & Castle tube/rail then 12, 42, 63, 68, 171, 343 bus. **Open** *24hrs daily.* **Admission** *free.*
At first glance Burgess Park looks flat, featureless, and unlikely to win any prizes for beauty but community-wise it's a godsend. Planned in 1943, the construction involved demolishing terraced housing and many residents being uprooted and relocated to the notorious Aylesbury Estate, that much publicised symbol of stalled urban regeneration. In an area in dire need of community initiatives, Burgess Park has attractions for all ages. For young tearaways, there's a busy little kart track (7525 1101; *see also p123* **Top 10 Adventures**), an adventure playground, an indoor games room and an award-winning BMX track. Then there is Chumleigh Gardens, home to Southwark Rangers, which has a café and features various garden styles: English country, a fragrant Mediterranean, a meditative Islamic, and a flamboyant Caribbean.

Recent efforts have resulted in the creation of the Heart Garden – a fruit and vegetable patch planted, tended and harvested by those with long-term illnesses – while, on Wednesdays and Thursdays throughout the year, the Peckham Sure Start programme organises creative outdoor games and activities for families with young children (phone for more information).
Buggy access. Café. Disabled access: toilets.

Livesey Museum for Children

682 Old Kent Road, SE15 1JF (7639 5604/www.livesey museum.org.uk). Elephant & Castle tube/rail, then 53 bus. **Open** *10am-5pm Tue-Sat (last entry 4.30pm). Closed bank hols.* **Admission** *free.*
The first library in Camberwell (opened in 1890), the Livesey was converted into a museum and reopened in 1974 by Poet Laureate, Sir John Betjeman. Since then, it has developed into an interactive children's museum, showing temporary hands-on exhibitions for children under 12, their families, carers and teachers. There's an agreeable little courtyard area, with olde-worlde items (old milk churns, an ancient pillar box) salvaged from the museum's days as a bastion of local history. The Education Room is full of curiosities for little ones to explore. The 'Energy' exhibition (until 27 Aug 2005) looks at all aspects of fuel and power, with interactive displays on forces, sustainability and nutrition. The museum closes for a few months over the summer holidays to bulldoze the last exhibition (the months vary each year), reopening in November 2005 with 'Myths and Legends'.
Buggy access. Nappy-changing facilities. Nearest picnic place: museum courtyard.

Nunhead Cemetery

Limesford Road or Linden Grove (entrances), SE15 3LP (information 7732 9535). Nunhead rail. **Open** *Summer 8.30am-7pm daily. Winter 8.30am-4pm daily.* **Tours** *2pm last Sun of mth.* **Admission** *free; donations to FONC appreciated.*
A Heritage Lottery Fund grant has helped rebuild the chapel in the centre of this atmospheric Victorian cemetery, and the paths that cross it are all nicely resurfaced. Volunteers continue to work on the land around the broken statues and stone monuments that have been upturned over time by roots of trees and ivy, although the plot clearance is carried out with a view to keeping Nunhead's overgrown charm. The tree-filled cemetery is a nature reserve for various species of insect, bird and butterfly, and from its highest points offers some fine views of the city – framed by tangled branches and fragmentary angels. There are guided tours on the last Sunday of each month, meeting at the Linden Grove gates at 2pm.
Buggy access.

Peckham Library

122 Peckham Hill Street, SE15 5JR (7525 0200). Peckham Rye or Queen's Road rail/12, 36, 63, 171 bus. **Open** *9am-8pm Mon, Tue, Thur, Fri; 10am-8pm Wed; 10am-5pm Sat; noon-4pm Sun.* **Admission** *free.*
Family activities that take place inside Will Alsop's award-winning design include creative baby and toddler sessions every Tuesday morning (10.30am), with storytelling, songs and crafts on the cards, and the Sure Start reading group for under-fives the same afternoon (1.30pm). At both, kids are encouraged to make use of the wide selection of children's books in the bright pink children's library on the fourth floor. Mondays and Fridays ring in the ominous

Homework Club (4-7pm), there are craft sessions on Tuesdays after school, and meetings of the Teenage Reading Group (TRG) on the second Tuesday and Family Reading Group (FRG) on the last Thursday of each month, with an extended programme of holiday workshops to make those precious summer days whizz by even faster. The square outside hosts a farmers' market on Sundays (9.30am-1.30pm; phone 7525 0856 for information). *Buggy access. Disabled access: toilets. Lift. Nappy-changing facilities.*

South London Gallery
65 Peckham Road, SE5 8UH (7703 6120/www.south londongallery.org). Peckham Rye rail/12, 36, 171, 345 bus. **Open** noon-6pm Tue-Sun. Closed 25, 26 Dec, bank hols. **Admission** free.
It is rumoured that Peckham will become the next Hoxton and this excellent gallery goes some way towards supporting such claims. Work on display tends towards the cutting edge: artists including Tracey Emin and Bill Viola have exhibited here in the past, and the gallery has a forward-thinking approach and futuristic atmosphere. Which is only appropriate: founded in 1868 as the South London

Working Men's College, its original principal was biologist TH Huxley, grandfather of Aldous Huxley, the author of *Brave New World* and advocate of hallucinogenic experiences. Check the website for details of their comprehensive new education programme.
Buggy access. Disabled access: lift, ramp, toilets. Nappy-changing facilities. Nearest picnic place: gallery garden (during summer).

DULWICH & HERNE HILL
The peaceful streets and leafy parks of Dulwich make this prosperous area one of the safest places for kids to blossom in the capital. It's also home to a huge number of family restaurants, cafés and quaint little boozers. Dulwich Village is the centre of attention: peppered around delightful **Dulwich Park** are the grand buildings of Dulwich College, site of the Edward Alleyn Theatre and its public drama school. **Dulwich Picture Gallery** is lovely, and each May the village comes to life for

---

RUNNING WILD

South-east London's rakish charms extend to strange little pockets of wilderness in the most unexpected places (not to mention great flocks of ring-necked parakeets squawking around many of the parks). Take Rotherhithe, whose green spaces include **Lavender Pond and Nature Park** (Lavender Road, SE16 5DZ), one of the oldest urban nature reserves in England. It was created from an old dock inlet in 1981 and now supports newts, frogs, dragonflies, herons and tufted ducks. The refurbished **Pumphouse** (7231 2976) here is used as a river museum for school groups. Other ecology parks, tirelessly promoted by the Trust for Urban Ecology and its volunteers, include **Russia Dock Woodland** and **Stave Hill Ecological Park**, both havens for wildlife.

Take a walk on Deptford's **Creekside** (Creekside Centre, 14 Creekside, SE8 4SA, 8692 9922, http://home.btconnect.com/creekside) for regular weekend activities for families (check the website for details and to sign up for the mailing list). You might even see a kingfisher flash by.

The **Greenwich Peninsula** gives children plenty of riverside space to run around. It's the scene of frenzied building activity to make this once derelict part of the riverscape a brand new town and potential offshoot of Olympics 2012 action. Its local wildlife centre – the **Greenwich Peninsula Ecology Park** (*see p122*) – was a lot less bother to establish. A wetland area with woodland, marsh, meadow, lakes and streams, it has only been around for five years or so, but already it supports frogs, toads, dragonflies, many bird species and hosts a wide variety of children's entertainment. Children are plied with various quizzes and trails to follow as they explore, as well as regular activities involving pondlife, mud

and gumboots. The centre's Open Day takes place every year (19 June 2005) and the Frog Day is usually the first weekend in March. The summer play event takes bugs as its theme and runs from the end of July to early September.

Peckham and Dulwich do rural idyll surprisingly well. As well as the recently regenerated Peckham Rye Common (a place 'where angels dance', according to William Blake), there are ancient woodlands. **Dulwich** and **Sydenham Hill** woods (8699 5698) form the largest remaining tracts of the old Great North Wood that once stretched from Deptford to Selhurst. More than 200 species of trees and flowering plants – including wild garlic, early dog violet and bugle – support fungi, rare insects, birds and elusive woodland mammals. The London Wildlife Trust has managed the wood since 1982 and, not far away, has established its own **Centre for Wildlife Gardening** (*see p133*). Local families fill their gardens with the native woodland and pond plants raised here, giving a donation to the LWT as payment. The area is teeming with wildlife: bees, birds, butterflies and bugs buzz, flit and flutter to their heart's content in the wildlife meadow. For children, there's a play area and a sandpit, while the visitors' centre holds tanks of fish and stick insects. Every March families descend on the centre for Frog Day. Eight- to ten-year-olds can cement their relationship with Mother Nature by joining the Wildlife Watch club (£10 per year) and attending activities like pond-dipping or bat-walking. Conservation activities are open to all and take place throughout the year. To join, contact the centre or London Wildlife Trust (Ground floor, Skyline House, 200 Union Street, SE1 0LW, 7261 0447, www.wildlondon.org.uk).

Around Town

the annual Dulwich Festival (8299 1011, www.dulwichfestival.co.uk), which positively bristles with children's activities. Sydenham Hill Wood – across the South Circular from Dulwich Park – is also worth a visit, if only to scout out the bird life. The area's most amazing wildlife collection is at the **Horniman Museum** in nearby Forest Hill, the idyllic grounds of which also offer great views across the city.

East Dulwich isn't quite so picturesque, but it does have an excellent selection of child-friendly shops and cafés on Lordship Lane – the Goose Green end of which is home to a good children's playground. Nearby, the **London Wildlife Trust Centre for Wildlife Gardening** has turned a bus depot into a gardening mecca.

The shops, pubs and restaurants of Half Moon Lane in **Herne Hill** are popular with young families. Children round here have the choice of two parks, Southwark's splendid, Victorian Dulwich Park or Lambeth's rather grittier, hillier **Brockwell Park** (*see p137*).

Dulwich Park

College Road, SE21 7BQ (park ranger 8693 5737/ www.southwark.gov.uk). North Dulwich or West Dulwich rail. **Open** 8am-dusk daily.
The park was formally landscaped in 1890, but had served as a scenic retreat long before that. Queen Mary was a regular visitor (one of the park's four gates is named after her). Visitors today are treated to the Pavilion Café (*see p180*),

a much-loved playground complete with 'spider's web' climbing frame, boat hire on the lake (£5.25 for 30mins), novelty bike hire from London Recumbents (8299 6636, www.londonrecumbents.com; *see also p123* **Top 10 Adventures**) and a number of sculpted gardens (including the original American Garden, home to one of London's largest collections of rhododendrons and azaleas, as well as herons, cormorants and the occasional kingfisher). Extensive improvements include a new boating house for the 2006 season and a comprehensive programme of children's activities in the refurbished cricket pavilion, which should be up and running next year. *Buggy access. Café. Disabled access: ramps, toilets. Nappy-changing facilities (café).*

Dulwich Picture Gallery

Gallery Road, SE21 7AD (8693 5254/www.dulwich picturegallery.org.uk). North Dulwich or West Dulwich rail/P4 bus. **Open** 10am-5pm Tue-Fri; 11am-5pm Sat, Sun, bank hol Mon. Closed 24-26 Dec, 1 Jan, Good Friday. **Tours** 3pm Sat, Sun. **Admission** £4; £3 concessions; free under-16s. *Tours* free. **Credit** MC, V.
Widely held to be the first purpose-built art gallery in the country, this neo-classical building – designed by John Soane in 1811 – also remains one of its best. Despite being anything but enormous, the gallery houses an outstanding collection of work by European Old Masters and offers a fine introduction to the baroque era through pieces by such as Rembrandt, Rubens, Poussin and – batting for the home team – the great Thomas Gainsborough.

Popular Thursday after-school classes for seven to tens run during term. Prices vary, but average £40-£50 per term, while the Saturday Art School for 11- to 14-year-olds costs roughly £55 for five weeks, and involves more advanced classes such as printmaking, figure drawing and sculpture. Younger children (from age six) can get creative

Chilling in the **Horniman Museum** gardens.

at individual half-day holiday workshops (week-long courses run throughout the summer) tied into seasonal themes like Nativity or Easter Egg-making, while family group activities on the first Sunday of every month allow parents to join the fun (2-3.30pm, free with entry ticket).

Exhibitions for 2005 include an exhibition of the early work of Graham Sutherland (15 June-25 Sept 2005) and a Beatrix Potter retrospective (12 Oct 2005-22 Jan 2006). *Buggy access. Café. Disabled access: ramps, toilets. Nappy-changing facilities. Nearest picnic place: gallery gardens. Shop.*

Horniman Museum

100 London Road, SE23 3PQ (8699 1872/www. horniman.ac.uk). Forest Hill rail/122, 176, 185, 312, P4 bus. **Open** 10.30am-5.30pm daily. **Admission** free; donations appreciated. **Credit** *Shop* MC, V.
Travelling tea trader Frederick J Horniman assembled a great number of curiosities, first in his home at Forest Hill and later in this jolly art nouveau museum, which was left to the people of London in 1901. The recently smartened up Natural History gallery has spooky skeletons, pickled animals, stuffed birds and insect models are in old-fashioned glass cases, all presided over by a large, rather threadbare, overstuffed walrus on a centre plinth.

In 2005 the focus is on African Worlds, making the Horniman Britain's first permanent gallery to spotlight African cultural history and artistic expression. Here, the world's second largest continent is presented through the eyes of artists, diviners, anthropologists, elders and those forced into exile. Treasures include a 3,500-year-old mummy and the majestic Nigerian Igbo Ijele – a 20ft (6m) ceremonial mask, the only one of its kind in Britain.

The Centenary Gallery celebrates a century of collecting, with its puppets, more masks, models and icons. In the Music Room, the walls are hung with hundreds of instruments of every type, with touch screens on tables for you to hear their sound and a 'Hands On' room for visitors to bash away at world instruments, such as Thai croaking toads and a bodhrán from Ireland. There's also an aquarium, cases of exotic reptiles and an observation beehive in the Environment Room. The gardens, with their animal enclosure and elegant conservatory, are lovely, and the spacious café a welcome pit stop.

Under-fivess storytelling takes place every Friday and family storytelling is every Saturday. The Aquarium, in need of modernisation, has been awarded a much needed grant for it 'Funding Nemo' campaign. Feeding time in the Aquarium is every Wednesday (noon-12.30pm). School holidays and Saturdays see art and craft workshops and 'Hands On Base' activities throughout the year. Check the website for details or sign up for the mailing list. *See also p123* **Top ten adventures**.
Buggy access/storage. Café. Disabled access: lift, ramps, toilets. Nappy-changing facilities. Nearest picnic place: Horniman Gardens. Shop.

London Wildlife Trust Centre for Wildlife Gardening

28 Marsden Road, SE15 4EE (7252 9186/www.wild london.org.uk). East Dulwich rail. **Open** 10.30am-4.30pm Tue-Thur, Sun. **Admission** free.
The London Wildlife Trust has for more than 20 years been reclaiming derelict land for nature reserves, and this fantastic centre – created on a disused bus depot – is one of their best, with areas of woodland, marshland, a herb garden, a pond area and a nursery for plants and trees. *See also p131* **Running wild**.
Buggy access. Disabled access: toilets. Nappy-changing facilities. Nearest picnic place: wildlife garden. Shop.

CRYSTAL PALACE

Sir Joseph Paxton's incredible glass structure, which housed the era-defining Great Exhibition of 1851, was moved here from Hyde Park. The new Crystal Palace at Sydenham was opened by Queen Victoria on 10 June, 1854 and became a massively popular theme park. In 1911, the year of King George V's coronation, the Crystal Palace was home to the Festival of Empire. Three-quarter size models of the parliament buildings of Empire and Commonwealth countries were erected in the grounds. The Palace and surrounding parkland continued to pack in the punters until 1936, when the building was destroyed by fire. These days the crumbling remains – ivy-tangled stone staircases to nowhere, sculpted lions covered with graffiti and giant plaster dinosaurs – lend the park the air of a lost civilisation. All this might change, however, if a plan to build a whole new Crystal Palace goes ahead, but we won't know for certain for a year or so. The aesthetically uninspired National Sports Centre, in the south-eastern corner of the park, continues to be a premier venue for national athletics (as well as the occasional rock concert). The **Crystal Palace Museum** expounds the rise and fall of Paxton's greenhouse.

Around Town

Crystal Palace Museum

Anerley Hill, SE19 2BA (8676 0700). Crystal Palace rail. **Open** 11am-5pm Sun, bank hol Mon. **Admission** free.

To find out more about the majestic exhibition that gave this area its name, pop into this friendly museum, housed in the old engineering school where John Logie Baird invented the television. The limited opening hours are down to the fact that the museum is run entirely by dedicated volunteers, but school groups are welcome on weekdays provided teachers book a few weeks ahead. The 'exhibition of an exhibition' includes some enchanting Victorian artefacts from the original Hyde Park production, as well as video and audio presentations about the great glass building and the monumental show it housed. A small Logie Baird display marks the birth of home entertainment; from June 1934 the Baird Television Company had four studios at Crystal Palace.

Nearest picnic place: Crystal Palace Park. Shop.

Crystal Palace Park

Thicket Road, SE20 8DT (8778 9496/www.bromley. gov.uk). Crystal Palace rail/2, 3, 63, 122, 157, 227 bus. **Open** 7.30am-dusk daily. **Admission** free.

When parkland in Sydenham was selected as the landing site for the elaborate glass building that had housed Prince Albert's Great Exhibition in 1851, Crystal Palace Park was born. It stood grandly amongst exquisitely landscaped gardens, near an amusement park and ponds overlooked by life-size model dinosaurs. Then a fire in 1936 destroyed the Palace, so only the park was left. Its lake, those famous Victorian reptiles and a long-defunct fairground and zoo, continued to amuse London families for the next 70 years or so, but the various elements of the park suffered wear and tear. A refurbishment programme has been going on for years. The London Development Agency is going to take up the Crystal Park challenge in 2006 – consultations with locals and visitors about the makeover started in September 2004. Meanwhile, the 'monsters' (the remains of a Victorian prehistoric theme park created by Benjamin Waterhouse-Hawkins), restored in 2003, sit menacingly around the freshly landscaped tidal lake, the hornbeam maze has been replanted and we're all waiting for the little farm to be rebuilt. The Crystal Palace Park Museum (*see above*) is close to where the original palace once stood. The National Sports Centre, although shockingly ugly and in need of cosmetic attention, nonetheless has a busy programme of events for all ages and abilities and one of the few Olympic-sized (50m/160ft) pools in London.

Buggy access. Café. Disabled access: toilets. Nappy-changing facilities.

FURTHER SOUTH-EAST

The outlying suburbs have their moments. Bexleyheath, in particular, has some grand old houses and spectacular parkland. The **Red House** (13 Red House Lane, Bexleyheath, Kent DA6 8JF, 01494 755 588) was home to William Morris, the founding father of the Arts & Crafts Movement, who lived here for five years until 1864. Now owned by the National Trust, the Red House contains original furnishings, stained glass and paintings, but is more of interest to students of art and design than to small children.

Between Bexleyheath and Welling, huge Danson Park (attributed to the great landscape gardener 'Capability' Brown) contains the 18th-century Palladian villa, Danson Mansion (8304 9130; open 11am-5pm Wed, Thur, Sun, closed winter from 30 Oct), restored by Bexley Heritage Trust. The park itself (Park Ranger Service, 8304 2631) hosts an annual summer fair (2-3 July 2005) and its huge sailing lake is home to an annual canoe polo tournament (19-21 August 2005) that attracts competitors from ten nations. Danson Park's woodland garden has the 200-year-old Charter Oak, named one of the 'Great Trees of London'. More award-winning gardens, this time containing a stunning Tudor mansion, can be enjoyed at **Hall Place**, just up the road in Bexley.

The area around Eltham and Bexley is dotted with meadows and woodlands. **Oxleas Wood** (across the Shooters Hill Road from Falconwood rail station, in Welling, Kent) is an 8,000-year-old piece of woodland, dating back to the Ice Age. The wood was to be uprooted back in the mid 1990s – until a campaign stopped the bulldozers. Its paths link up with the Green Chain Walk (8921 5028, www.greenchain.com), a 40-mile (64-kilometre) network starting near the Thames Barrier (*see p128*) and ending at Crystal Palace. The Oxleas Wood path starts at Erith and takes in the remains of 12th-century **Lesnes Abbey**, a fine picnic place with toilets, an information centre and views of the towerblocks to the north.

Organic **Woodlands Farm** is open to the public and can be found just off Shooters Hill (the name of this area of Kent as well as the road that leads to it from near Blackheath). Across the A20, the village of **Chislehurst** has its very own Druids' caves to tempt day trippers underground.

Further west, beyond Beckenham and Bromley, Croydon would prefer to be known as a city in its own right, but despite a couple of applications for city status it remains one of London's busier southern suburbs. Croydon is notable for its tram system, the huge Whitgift Centre for shopping and the wonderful **Croydon Clocktower** arts centre. The Warehouse Theatre Company (62 Dingwall Road, Croydon, Surrey CR0 2NF, 8681 1257, www.warehousetheatre.co.uk) offers drama workshops during the holidays and children's productions on Saturdays.

Chislehurst Caves

Chislehurst, Old Hill, Kent BR7 5NB (8467 3264/ www.chislehurstcaves.co.uk). Chislehurst rail. **Open** 9am-5pm Wed-Sun. *Tours* phone for details. **Admission** £4; £2 children, OAPs.

The spooky caves at Chislehurst were carved out of the hillside by Druids digging for chalk and flint (they also came here to make grisly human sacrifices). In due course the Romans were to extract chalk from here and, more recently, the caves were used as a World War I ammunition dump and, in the 1930s, a mushroom farm. But the caves only became famous during World War II, when they were Britain's largest bomb shelter.

The 45min tour covers less than a mile (2km). It's not strenuous, but it isn't for the claustrophobic – the damp gloominess is likely to give very small children the heebie-jeebies, especially when your guide extinguishes the lights to show you how dark it is. If you fancied it, you could even have a birthday party in the café here.
Café. Nappy-changing facilities. Shop.

Croydon Clocktower

Katharine Street, Croydon, Surrey CR9 1ET (box office 8253 1030/tourist information 8253 1009/ www.croydon.gov.uk/clocktower). East Croydon or West Croydon rail/George Street tram. **Open** *Clocktower & library* 9am-7pm Mon; 9am-6pm Tue, Wed, Fri; 9.30am-6pm Thur; 9am-5pm Sat. *Clocktower Café* 9.30am-5.30pm Mon-Sat. Closed bank hols. *Tourist Information Centre* 9am-6pm Mon-Wed, Fri; 9am-5pm Sat. *Museum & galleries* Closed until spring 2006. **Admission** free.
Croydon Clocktower, built in 1896, is a splendid Victorian building – a stark contrast to all the surrounding office blocks. Its brilliant little museum is currently closed for refurbishment until spring 2006, so many of the events, workshops and activities relating to local history will this year take place in the Clocktower Court, the library, Croydon's Whitgift shopping centre or other local venues (check the website for details). The David Lean cinema has a kids' club (11am Sat). The Clocktower also provides a Saturday crèche. Braithwaite Hall, the centre's theatre, hosts weekend and holiday theatre productions for children every month. To find out what's on, pick up a brochure or check the website. The library hosts story, music and art sessions and runs a homework help club.
Buggy access. Café. Disabled access: lifts, ramps, toilets. Nappy-changing facilities. Nearest picnic place: Queen's Gardens.

Eltham Palace

Court Yard, off Court Road, SE9 5QE (8294 2548/ www.english-heritage.org.uk). Eltham rail. **Open** *Apr-Oct* 10am-5pm Mon-Wed, Sun. *Nov-Mar* 10am-4pm Mon-Wed, Sun. Closed 22 Dec-31 Jan. **Admission** (EH) *House & grounds* (incl audio tour) £7.30; £5.50 concessions; £3.70 5-16s; free under-5s; £18.30 family. *Grounds only* £4.60; £3.50 concessions; £2.30 5-16s; free under-5s. **Credit** MC, V.
A magnificent royal residence from the 13th century through to Henry VIII's heyday, Eltham Palace fell out of favour in the latter part of Henry's reign. After parliament took possession of the place, then sold it on, it fell into ruin. Its Great Hall, the most substantial surviving medieval hall outside the Palace of Westminster, was used as a barn for many years. It was not until 1931 that the Palace came back into fashion again, thanks to the substantial wealth of Stephen Courtauld, a patron of the arts, who, with his society wife Virginia, was looking for a country seat close to town. The Courtaulds commissioned a thoroughly modern house to stand among the relics of the old palace. The Great Hall with its stained glass and intricate hammer beam roof – pressed into service for glamorous society parties, as well as concerts and banquets plus a 15th-century stone bridge over the moat and various medieval ruins, are all that's left of the royal

original. Visitors don blue plastic shoe protectors to tour the rooms of the Courtauld home. The interior is all polished veneer and chunky marble, with mod cons such as concealed lighting, underfloor heating and a room-to-room vacuuming system. Even the Courtauld's beloved pet ring-tailed lemur, Mah-Jongg, lived the life of Riley in his specially designed lodgings. The extensive grounds are beautifully restored and the traditional tearoom and shop have a distinctly 1930s flavour.

Quiz sheets and trails for children to follow through the house and grounds are available free. The palace and gardens are used for open-air performances of Shakespeare during the summer, an Art Deco Fair (15 May & 11 Sept 2005) and a carol concert (14 Dec 2005). Check the website for details.
Buggy storage. Café. Disabled access: lift, toilets. Nappy-changing facilities. Nearest picnic place: palace grounds. Shop.

Hall Place & Gardens

Bourne Road, Bexley, Kent DA5 1PQ (01322 526 574/ www.hallplaceandgardens.com). Bexley rail/B15, 132, 229, 492 bus. **Open** *Apr-Oct* 10am-5pm Mon-Sat; 11am-5pm Sun, bank hols. *Nov-Mar* 10am-4pm Tue-Sat. **Admission** free. **Credit** *Shop* MC, V.
This enchanting Tudor mansion, on the banks of the River Cray, was built nearly 500 years ago for the Lord Mayor of London, Sir John Champneys. Its fine panelled Great Hall, with minstrels' gallery, is a favourite venue for music societies and chamber groups, and the 160 acres (65ha) of gardens, with their topiary, herb garden, model allotments and sub-tropical plant houses, have won several Green Flag awards. A new environmental education garden in the walled nursery has a pond-dipping area, (to catch 'mini beasts'), a small meadow and a Tudor knot garden. In the Austen gallery there's a hands-on Science Project exhibition about lasers and lights (5 Aug-2 Sept), and regular art and photography exhibitions take place in the Chapel and Dashwood galleries. Half-term art and craft activities cater for children aged from three years, and the Easter and summer holidays see egg trails, garden festivals and open-air theatre productions, while Christmas is celebrated with merry workshops, craft fairs and carols.
Buggy access. Café. Disabled access: lifts, ramps, toilets. Garden centre. Nappy-changing facilities. Shop.

Woodlands Farm

331 Shooters Hill, Welling, Kent DA16 3RP (8319 8900/www.thewoodlandsfarmtrust.org). Falconwood rail/89, 486 bus. **Open** 9.30am-4.30pm daily.
Admission free; donations appreciated.
Spread out over 89 acres (36ha) on the border of Greenwich and Bexley, Woodlands Farm is a reminder of the rural way of life once enjoyed in this area. In 1995 the farm was nearly bulldozed to make way for a proposed East London crossing. Fortunately the Farm Trust, with the help of Lottery money, came to the rescue. It bought the derelict farmhouse and surrounding field, and turned them into a thriving organic enterprise. There are some noisy geese, hens, a flock of sheep, a cow and some Shetland ponies. A core staff keeps the place ticking over, but volunteers are welcome to don their gumboots and help out. The farm hosts educational group visits, giving lessons on farm-animal care, conservation, composting, and the history of farming. The newly planted orchard with apples, plums and pears– echoing the Kent of yore – is growing on well.
Buggy access. Nearest picnic place: farm grounds. Shop.

Around Town

SOUTH-WEST LONDON

Where commons, parks, gardens and nature trails abound.

Two many cooks at **Hampton Court Palace**. *See p147.*

VAUXHALL & STOCKWELL

It was all Chinese pavilions, orchestras, fountains and lamplit lovers' walks back in the 18th century when Vauxhall's Pleasure Gardens were in fashion. These days the gateway to the city's prosperous south-western neighbourhoods is distinguished by lanes of roaring traffic. Spring Park is a bleak expanse of green by the main road and railway arches, but when crossing it in an easterly direction, an unmistakable rural odour hits the nostrils. Could that be horse manure you smell? Was that a sheep bleating? Yes and yes. **Vauxhall City Farm** is the best reason for coming here. Vauxhall Park (South Lambeth Road, at the junction with Fentiman Road, SW8) has tennis courts, a bowling green, a play area, a One O'Clock Club and a fenced ball-game area. Another green space is Bonnington Square's

Pleasure Garden, a bosky, bohemian enclave that started life as a play area during the 1970s. It lay neglected for years until local residents created a secret garden with rustic seating and scented plants. Vauxhall Bridge spans the river alongside 'Spy Central', the MI6 building, which was once the target of a missile attack from the Real IRA.

The best places for children to play in around **Stockwell** rely on volunteers to run the activities and events. Slade Gardens Adventure Playground (Lorn Road, SW9) is Lambeth's biggest and best playground, with an aerial runway and giant swing, a nature garden and play areas. Over on Stockwell's west side, Larkhall Park (on Larkhall Rise) is a well-maintained local authority park, but the best resource for children is outside its boundaries: **Oasis Children's Venture** (7720 4276) is an initiative run by local people and manages three projects in the area: there's a cycle centre and adventure playground, plus a kart track and a nature garden. There are plans to redevelop the site to create a new cycle track. The recently resurfaced Stockwell Bowl Skatepark, at the start of Stockwell Road as you leave Brixton, is open access and is very popular with local baggy-trousered boarders.

Vauxhall City Farm

24 St Oswald's Place (entrance on Tyers Street), SE11 5JE (7582 4204). Vauxhall tube/rail/2, 36, 44, 77 bus. **Open** 10.30am-4pm Wed-Sun. Closed 1 wk in late summer, phone to check. **Admission** free; donations appreciated.

Livestock have been reared in the grassy paddocks and roomy loose boxes on this little farm since 1977, and a keen team of staff and volunteers care for the poultry, pigs, sheep, cows, donkeys and horses. Exciting developments in the last year have been a famous victory at the Capel Manor Show, where farms are judged on the quality of their stock and the knowledge of their volunteer staff. Vauxhall scored highly in both categories. Some fancy duck breeds also won prizes at a poultry show. Vauxhall City Farm is always busy: its premises are used by education, refugee and gardening groups; it also runs Sunday art classes, offers subsidised riding lessons for local children, and has a popular after-school club and summer playscheme.

Buggy access. Disabled access: toilet. Nappy-changing facilities.

BRIXTON

The marshy wastelands of Brixton were good farming land until 1816, when Vauxhall Bridge improved access to central London. From then on the area developed rapidly as a suburb. One of Brixton's main thoroughfares, Electric Avenue (immortalised in the song by Eddy Grant), is so named because it was one of the first shopping streets in London to be lit by electricity. Now the capital of liberal Lambeth, and south London's busiest area, Brixton is best known for its nightlife, but families visiting in daylight hours can have fun exploring nearby **Brockwell Park** or the terrific **Brixton Market**, which is bursting with everything from exotic fish to cheap electrical goods. It's hard to believe that during its heyday – between 1900 and 1915 – the sedate suburb of Brixton boasted a greyhound track and nine cinemas. The **Ritzy** cinema (Coldharbour Lane, SW2 1JG, 0870 755 0062, www.ritzycinema.co.uk) is now the only one, but it hosts a cracking Kids Club every Saturday morning.

Brockwell Park

Dulwich Road, SE24 0PA (7926 0105). Herne Hill rail. **Open** 7am-dusk daily.

A successful Heritage Lottery Fund bid will ensure this park receives a much-needed refurbishment. Up on the hill, the impressive Victorian house containing the First Come

First Served Café (8671 5217) is overdue a paint and plaster job, and the once-enchanting walled garden could do with some replanting. Despite its shabby bits, however, Brockwell Park, with its lovely, sandy playground for tinies, and larger, more challenging facilities for older kids, is a great refuge from the chaos of Brixton, just 10mins walk away. There are football, BMX and basketball facilities, but its biggest claim to fame is the ever-cash-strapped lido – an outdoor pool that more than makes up for the cold water with its elegant 1930s architecture, exotic greenery and a good programme of children's activities in summer (check www.brockwelllido.com for summer 2005 openings). Another highlight is the annual Lambeth Country Show (16-17 July 2005) which manages to defy the surrounding urban sprawl by charming kids silly with live music, animal displays, food stalls and more.

Buggy access. Café. Disabled access: toilets. Nappy-changing facilities.

STREATHAM

Today's seemingly infinite **Streatham High Road**, often a traffic-clogged nightmare (and voted by listeners to Radio 4's *Today* programme as 'Britain's street of shame'), has its roots in Streatham's Anglo-Saxon name (it means 'the dwellings by the street'). The street really dominates now, although back in the 18th century this neighbourhood was a pleasant rural resting point between London and Croydon. Until World War I, and despite the installation of major railway routes, gracious family homes surrounded by woodland and fields imbued Streatham with gentility. Following the war enormous areas of housing swallowed up the countryside and the area became increasingly urban. Today the area has attractions for the young: Streatham Megabowl, the Streatham Ice Arena and Playscape Pro Racing (for all, *see chapter* **Sport & Leisure**) are all big players in the birthday treat stakes.

Another point in Streatham's favour is its designation as a conservation area, with green sites like the hidden treasure of the formal garden, known as the Rookery, on **Streatham Common** providing excellent landmarks for children and families. Cicero's Café (2 Rookery Road, SW4 9DD, 7498 0770) pulls in the crowds, although it's only open at weekends during the winter. Sat snugly on the tip of the common, the café is all warm-coloured walls, flowers and fairy lights, while the outside tables are popular with toddlers who can play with scattered toys in the gated yard.

BATTERSEA

A small farming settlement with its roots in the Saxon age, Battersea was famous for its market gardens until the 19th century. The coming of the

Around Town

railways blotted out the rural peace. At its centre, Clapham Junction became the world's busiest railway junction. Interestingly, the area is now as yuppified as everywhere else in Wandsworth, but stakes its claim to individuality with gems like the Battersea Arts Centre (Lavender Hill, SW11 5TN, 7223 2223, www.bac.org.uk). **Battersea Park**, which contains **Battersea Children's Zoo** and an adventure playground, is another source of pride. Not far from the south-western edge of the park, the child-friendly Latchmere Leisure Centre (Burns Road, SW11 2DY, 7207 8004, www.kinetika.org) has two leisure pools and a wave machine. Its junior activities, run by the Fun House Club, include arts and crafts, a bouncy castle and competitions in school holidays. There's a Playzone soft-play area too.

A landmark reminder of Battersea's industrial past, Sir Giles Gilbert Scott's **Battersea Power Station** (1933) has been closed for the last two decades. The building is slated to be restored as a leisure and business complex, but not much seems to be going on there at the present time. The area's other major kids' attraction lies between Battersea Park and the power station: **Battersea Dogs' Home**.

Battersea Children's Zoo

Battersea Park, SW11 4NJ (01298 814099/ www.batterseazoo.co.uk). Sloane Square tube, then 19, 137 bus/Battersea Park or Queenstown Road rail/156, 345 bus. **Open** 10am-5pm daily. **Admission** £4.95; £3.75 3-15s; free under-3s; £15.50 family (2+2). **Credit** MC, V. **Map** p313 F13.
Under new ownership since summer 2004, the Children's Zoo has now reopened after extensive improvements. These include some brand new enclosures, such as the Barleymow Farm (offering a farmyard experience for kids), the vast Lemur Land and the Mouse House (a cute little compartmentalised unit housing the cuddlier members of the rodent family, including chipmunks and harvest mice). Most of the animals have been rehoused (including the emus, the Vietnamese pot-bellied pig and the pygmy goats) and the meerkat enclosure has been craftily redesigned so that kids can go down a tunnel and pop out on a level with the creatures. The Lemon Tree Café offers some decent refreshment, and an all-new outdoor play area provides ample opportunity to work up a thirst and an appetite. You can also book birthday parties here (call for details).
Buggy access. Café. Disabled access. Nappy-changing facilities. Shop.

Battersea Dogs' Home

4 Battersea Park Road, SW8 4AA (7622 3626/ www.dogshome.org). Vauxhall tube/rail, then 44 bus/Battersea Park or Queenstown Road rail/344 bus. **Open** *Viewings* 10.30am-4.15pm Mon-Wed, Fri; 10.30am-3.15pm Sat, Sun, bank hols. Closed 25, 26 Dec, 1 Jan, Good Friday. **Admission** £1; 50p 5-16s, concessions; free under-5s. **Credit** *Shop* MC, V.
It's hardly a tourist attraction, but this world-famous home for canines lost and found does welcome casual visitors as

well as those who are willing to give a dog or cat a good home. Be warned that rescuing an animal is a complicated business. You have to make several visits and convince the staff that your circumstances match the animal you're paying to adopt. In fact, it can be particularly tricky to rescue a dog from Battersea if you have children, as many of the animals are not suited to family life.

It's an interesting place to look round, however. It has a souvenir and pet-accessory shop, a café and a wall of brass plaques commemorating long-gone canines and their owners. The centre also offers Behaviour Hotline talks in your home. Sessions include how to choose the right puppy (or kitten), teaching your pet new tricks and dealing with bad behaviour. Phone for further details, or download fact-sheets on adopting a pet from the website.
Buggy access. Café. Disabled access: lift, ramp, toilet. Nearest picnic place: Battersea Park. Shop.

Battersea Park

SW11 4NJ (8871 7530/boating lake 7262 1330/ www.wandsworth.gov.uk). Sloane Square tube, then 19, 137 bus/Battersea Park or Queenstown Road rail. **Open** 8am-dusk daily. **Map** p313 F13.
The jewel of Wandsworth, Battersea's 200 acres (83ha) were formally opened in 1858. The park's high Victorian style has recently been rescued by a major programme of work, which has restored many of the lakes, fountains and carriageways , the riverside promenade, and the pleasure gardens that were laid out for the 1951 Festival of Britain. The Restoration Project work was officially opened by the Duke of Edinburgh on 4 June 2004.

The lake , with its islands and heronry, attract huge numbers of migratory waterfowl and the wilder parts of the park, such as the small nature reserves managed by the London Wildlife Trust, support large numbers of butterflies, including the rare White-letter Hairstreak.

Battersea Park is well equipped for active fun. The Battersea Park Millennium Arena (8871 7537) has an eight-lane running track, 19 floodlit tennis courts, a netball court, an all-weather sports pitch and a state-of-the-art fitness centre with sauna. Tennis coaching is available to anyone over the age of eight, and the children's summer tennis camp takes place over two weeks in August every year. You can take a rowing boat out from the boating house on to the Victorian lake (£6/hr, £2.50/hr children; May-Sept). Nearby, London Recumbents (7498 6543; Sat, Sun, bank holidays, school holidays) offers bikes, tandems, trikes or banana bikes for hire. The south-west corner of the park has a large One O'Clock Club, toddlers' playground, play equipment for under-eights and adventure playground – one of London's biggest – for children aged eight to 15 (8871 7539).

The Italian-styled Gondola al Parco café (7978 1655) has tables overlooking the boating lake, but the loveliest landmark is the lofty Peace Pagoda, donated in 1985 by Japanese monks and nuns to commemorate Hiroshima Day. It stands serenely opposite the Children's Zoo, in the centre of the park's northern edge.
Buggy access. Café. Disabled access: toilets. Nappy-changing facilities.

CLAPHAM & WANDSWORTH

The open grassy areas, tree-lined paths and little woods of **Clapham Common** are a reminder of the area's 17th-century reputation for clean air.

Wealthy folk would flock here to escape plague-ridden central London. The criminal fraternity knew that and so highwaymen made use of this patch. Most famous was cunning Robert Forrester, who found that wearing ladies' nighties helped him in his mission to rob passing stagecoaches.

Nowadays the daylight robbery is all down to the price of houses. If they can afford them, young families aspire to settle in this desirable area. The heart of the neighbourhood lies around Clapham Common. Abbeville village, south-east of the tube station, is full of smart shops, cafés and restaurants; Clapham Old Town, north-east of the common along the Pavement, is another upscale area, with traditional pubs and shops.

The area around Wandsworth and Clapham Common is generally considered one of the most desirable places in London to bring up a family and is known as 'Nappy Valley'. Accordingly, breezy **Wandsworth Common** adds to its ornamental areas, sports pitches, tennis courts, bowling areas and lake (you need membership for seasonal fishing) more child-focused activities like the **Environment Centre** and **Lady Allen Adventure Playground**. Shopping in the Nappy Valley is terrific, thanks to **Northcote Road**, with its market and singular range of shops. On Wandsworth borough's westerly reaches, across the railway tracks from the common, it's all a bit more rough and ready. Here lies distant King George's Park, the **Kimber BMX/Adventure Playground** and the Wandle Recreation Centre (Mapleton Road, SW18 4DN, 8871 1149, www.kinetika.org), a sports centre with football pitches and an indoor play centre on the banks of the Wandle river.

These are slightly off the beaten track, but they they're worth travelling to if you're in charge of any two-wheel tearaways or a team of dedicated footie players. The River Wandle, which flows out of ponds at Carshalton and Beddington in Surrey, bisects the meadowland around **Morden Hall Park** (see p140) and flows towards Wandsworth. The Wandle Trail footpath runs alongside the river, passing through grim industrial landscape and newly regenerated wildlife havens. Towards Earlsfield, down Magdalen Road, lurks **It's a Kid's Thing** (279 Magdalen Road, SW18 3NZ, 8739 0909, www.itsakidsthing.info), one of those indoor adventure playgrounds that induce over-excitement in children and headaches in adults.

Environment Centre

Wandsworth Common, Dorlcote Road, SW18 3RT (8871 3863/www.theenvironmentcentre.org). Wandsworth Common rail. **Open** *11am-2pm Sat, Sun, occasional Tue, Fri; days vary, check website for details.* **Admission** *free.*

London Wildcare, a registered charity, have taken over the splendid wooden cabin and wildlife garden here on Wandsworth Common. Activities take place at weekends and during school holidays. *See also p142* **Running wild**. *Buggy access. Disabled access: toilets.*

Kimber BMX/Adventure Playground

King George's Park, Kimber Road, SW18 4NN (8870 2168). Earlsfield rail, then 44 or 270 bus. **Open** *Term-time 3.30-7pm Tue-Fri; 11am-6pm Sat. Holidays 11am-6pm Mon-Sat.* **Admission** *free.*

Kimber has all the usual variously challenging platforms, ropes, tyres and ladders, big swings, little swings and monkey bars, plus the added attractions of a basketball court and a small BMX track. If you don't have your own bike to skid around on, you can usually hire one at the playground (though do phone ahead to check availability). For showery days there's also an indoor games room with table tennis, as well as kitchens and arts and crafts rooms. The five ramps of the skateboard park are open to anyone who brings their own protective clothing. *Buggy access. Disabled access: ramp, toilet. Shop.*

Lady Allen Adventure Playground

Chivalry Road, SW11 1HT (7228 0278/www.kids-online.org.uk). Clapham Junction rail. **Open** *Term-time 10am-6pm Tue-Fri; 10am-4pm Sat. School holidays 10am-4pm Mon-Fri.* **Admission** *£1 donation per non-disabled child.*

On the north-west corner of Wandsworth Common, this well-designed playground lets children with special needs and disabilities swing, slide, climb ropes, dangle off monkey bars and generally muck about with their mates in a very safe, well-supervised environment. Children with disabilities can use this wonderful playground during all opening hours; non-disabled children are also admitted, but only at certain times (phone for details). *Buggy access. Disabled access: ramps, toilets. Nappy-changing facilities. Nearest picnic place: inside & outside seating.*

Wandsworth Museum

The Courthouse, 11 Garratt Lane, SW18 4AQ (8871 7074/www.wandsworth.gov.uk). Clapham Junction rail, then 39, 77A, 156, 170, 337 bus/ Wandsworth Town rail/28, 37, 44, 220, 270 bus. **Open** *10am-5pm Tue-Fri; 2-5pm Sat, Sun. Closed bank hols.* **Admission** *free.* **Credit** *Shop* MC, V.

This tiny space offers temporary exhibitions throughout the year, as well as giving a history of Wandsworth from prehistoric times to the present day. Displays include an Ice Age fossilised skull of a woolly rhino (found during the construction of Battersea Power Station), a model of Wandle Mills, a World War II shelter and a Southfields chemist's shop. The downstairs museum area exhibits such treasures as an Iron Age sword and scabbard unearthed on the Thames foreshore at Wandsworth, cooking and farming tools from Wandsworth's Roman period, and swords, scabbards and sundry weaponry from the medieval villages of Batricesage (Battersea), Baelgeham (Balham), Puttenhythe (Putney), Totinge (Tooting) and Waendelesorde (Wandsworth). Interactive exhibits let children make a brass rubbing of a Putney knight or get their hands on an ancient flint hand-axe or a Roman helmet.

A favourite term-time trip for local schools and school-holiday venue for families, the museum offers activities geared towards both the under-sixes and children aged six

Around Town

and above. Some are connected with the exhibitions, others link in with nationwide events, such as Black History Month (Oct) and the Big Draw (15 Oct 2005). Activities take place upstairs in the Education Centre – they're popular, so book in advance.
Buggy access. Disabled access: toilet. Nappy-changing facilities. Nearest picnic place: King George's Park/ Old Burial Ground. Shop.

TOOTING

Its high street has been a thoroughfare since Roman times, once serving as the main road from Londinium to Regnum (Chichester), and Tooting itself has gone on to become an airy suburban residence for city workers. However, it has always retained an aura of detachment – perhaps because of its position between two large commons: Wandsworth and Tooting Bec.

Described in the early 19th century as a 'very pretty district of hills and woods and tiny streams', picturesque Tooting became infamous in 1849 for its Infant Pauper Asylum, where a cholera epidemic killed 118 children out of the 1,500 forced to live there in overcrowded and insanitary conditions. Charles Dickens wrote about the tragedy in 'A Walk in a Workhouse'.

These days there is little evidence of poverty in the smart residential roads around **Tooting Common** (Tooting Bec Road, SW17). This is a lovely, wide open space with woods, tennis courts, ponds, football pitches and an athletics track. The common also offers the bracing joys of **Tooting Bec Lido** (8871 7198), as well as the best under-eights playground for miles. Tooting is also home to a well-established Asian community, with October/November seeing the annual Diwali 'Festival of Light' celebrated with a street party and lights strung along Tooting High Street and Upper Tooting Road. This means there are some brilliant restaurants for South Asian food. Their proprietors may stop short of kiddie menus and balloons, but babies and children are welcome.

WIMBLEDON

One of the first south London villages given a railway link – back in 1838 – Wimbledon is world famous for one, sporting reason. Tennis fans of all ages can have fun at the **Wimbledon Lawn Tennis Museum**, opened by the Duke of Kent as part of the centenary celebrations of the Lawn Tennis Championships, which started life here in 1877. Otherwise, there's the wonderful **Wimbledon Common** (*see p141* **Walk**), with its nature trails, horse rides, cycle paths, golf courses and sports grounds. Not to mention a Womble or two.

Wimbledon's shopping centre, just near the rail and tube station, is clean, bright and family-friendly. Special activities for children are often organised for the school holidays, and there's a crèche for parents wanting to shop in peace. From the shopping centre, the main street (Wimbledon Broadway) carries you past the **New Wimbledon Theatre** (The Broadway, SW19 1QG, 0870 060 6646), whose studio theatre regularly programmes children's productions. Further down towards South Wimbledon tube station is the jaunty **Polka Theatre for Children**, which has its own attractive café and small playground. It's a lovely place to pop into even if you're not seeing a show, although we wouldn't want you to miss its consistently good productions for young people. Not far from the theatre, just off Merton High Street, Tiger's Eye (42 Station Road, SW19 2LP, 8543 1655) is a vast barn of an indoor playcentre for children up to the age of ten.

Venture further south from Wimbledon, or alternatively follow the Northern Line to the bitter end, and you will be rewarded with the fabulous **Morden Hall Park**, a former deer park on the River Wandle.

Deen City Farm
39 Windsor Avenue, SW19 2RR (8543 5300/ www.deencityfarm.co.uk). Colliers Wood tube, then 200 bus. **Open** 10am-4.30pm Tue-Sun. **Admission** free; donations welcome.
Familiar pigs, goats, rabbits and poultry join rare breeds, which include Jacob sheep, a British White cow and recent additions Kimby and Milo – two alpacas. A tidy-sized community farm, Deen City works as an educational resource for all ages, with volunteer schemes for those who fancy getting their hands dirty. Children's activities include Young Farmer days for eight to 13s who can learn to feed, groom and clean out the animals during the school holidays. The riding school has facilities for the disabled and runs Own a Pony Days (bookings on 8543 5858, but be advised to book well ahead, as their diary is pretty full). *Buggy access. Café. Disabled access: toilet. Nappy-changing facilities. Shop.*

Morden Hall Park
Morden Hall Road, Morden SM4 5JD (8545 6850/ www.nationaltrust.org.uk). Morden tube. **Open** 8am-6pm daily. **Admission** free. **Credit** *Shop* AmEx, MC, V.
This is National Trust-owned parkland of uncommon beauty. The Morden Hall of the title is run as a private restaurant, so public access is limited to the extensive meadows, woodland and a network of waterways (the River Wandle flows past here). Between May and September the rose garden is a delight, but the park gives south Londoners an accessible, reviving dose of country-side all year round. The Snuff Mill Environmental Centre, housed in one of several historic buildings in the park, has been closed for building works, but it should be open on occasional weekends for a Wildlife Watch group from summer 2005 (phone 8545 6852 for details). Craftspeople,

WALK Wombling free

This walk covers the lakes, bogs and woodlands that give Wimbledon its 'leafy' connotations. The only Wombles you're likely to see, it must be admitted, are the cuddly toys in the **Wimbledon Windmill Museum** shop, but who's to say that while you're keeping your eyes peeled for the multitude of wildlife that inhabits Wimbledon Common, a Womble might not hove into view?

Start at Wimbledon station. Turn right up Wimbledon Hill Road towards the high street. If you're embarking on this walk between 2.30-5pm on a Saturday or Sunday, you might want to make a small diversion to the Wimbledon Society's free **Museum of Local History** (22 Ridgeway, SW19 4QN, 8296 9914). This can be found a little way down Ridgeway, on the right. It charts the 3,000-year history of the area,

from Neanderthal beginnings through to its development into the famously 'leafy' suburb full of smart houses. After the history lesson, walk back to the main road (Wimbledon High Street) and continue on your way towards the common. Turn left on to Southside Common. Pass the green and an ancient natural pond known as Rushmere, before turning right to an area known as the Crooked Billet. The ancient pub here – **Hand in Hand** (6 Crooked Billet, SW19 4RQ, 8946 5720) – dates back to the 17th century and is rumoured to have its own ghost. Babies and children are welcome in certain parts of this well-to-do hostelry, and can choose from their own menu should the family decide to return here for lunch.

From Crooked Billet proceed along Westside to Hanford Row, beside which a footpath leads to opulent **Cannizaro House**, a huge mansion once occupied by the First Lord of the Admiralty under William Pitt. Both Pitt and George III stayed here. The house is now a hotel, but the gardens are open to the public. Look out for the aviary as you stroll along the paths towards Camp Road. This is the road that leads you out of Cannizaro Park to **Wimbledon Common**. Between the two golf clubs (Royal Wimbledon and Wimbledon Common) lies **Caesar's Camp**. This area was once an Iron Age fort, so it in fact predates Caesar by about 500 years. Evidence of the ancient earthworks remain.

From here you can choose a short walk north along one of the many paths criss-crossing the common. Alternatively, keeping to the top of the hill and following Windmill Road toward Putney Heath makes this a brief walk, along drier paths unmashed by horses' hooves. Plunging further west from Caesar's Camp takes you along one of the many horse rides. These are well used and are often churned up following wet weather (Wimbledon Common rangers do their rounds on horseback).

This longer walk circumvents Wimbledon Common Golf Course, past the War Memorial and Memorial Gardens, along the stag ride. Keep Putney Vale Cemetery to your left before choosing one of the many wooded paths on the nature trail to **Queen's Mere**, a large, peaceful lake with ducks and geese to feed. Climbing upward from here brings you to the car park and the walk's end point, the **Wimbledon Windmill Museum**, whose shop sells Womble postcards.

Around Town

furniture restorers and artists occupy many of the old estate buildings, and the Riverside Café is a beautiful place from which to admire the surrounds, while having tea. *Buggy access. Café. Disabled access: toilets. Nappy-changing facilities. Shop.*

Wimbledon Lawn Tennis Museum

Centre Court, All England Lawn Tennis Club, Church Road, SW19 5AE (8946 6131/www.wimbledon.org/ museum). Southfields tube/39, 93, 200, 493 bus. **Open** 10.30am-5pm daily. *During championships* spectators only. **Admission** £6; £5 concessions; £3.75 5-16s; free under-5s. **Credit** AmEx, MC, V.

This museum, which opened in 1977, celebrates the glorious game by offering memorabilia from famous players, views of Centre Court and an education programme. The eclectic collection of artefacts here has grown to include memorabilia such as Victorian flannels, racket presses and tea sets, trophies from former champions, even 'I love Wimbledon' T-shirts and stickers. There are also videos of matches, an art gallery and an area displaying the changing styles of women's tennis gear since the game first began. You can take a tour of the whole jolly complex, including Court 1, the players' boards and the hallowed Centre Court, where the finals are played.

School groups are particularly well catered for, with the museum's Education Unit running classroom activities and workshops for children up to the age of 11, as well as presiding over a developing programme for secondary school or college-based visitors. Family activities happen throughout the year. Hallowe'en sees a Ghostly Children's Tour (11.30am-1pm 28 Oct 2005), a light-hearted tour of the grounds with spooky tales of Championship ghosts. Various historical workshops acquaint visitors with famous faces from Wimbledon's past, among them Maud

 # RUNNING WILD

You can hardly take a walk in Lambeth, Wandsworth, Richmond or Merton without squelching into a protected wetland habitat and disturbing an urban frog or two. There are nature reserves all over the place, from the mean streets of Stockwell to the deer-trodden savannah of Richmond Park.

One of the most child-oriented places to go wild is the **Environment Room**, based in a wooden cabin on Wandsworth Common. Volunteers and staff from the charity London Wildcare host weekend and school-holiday craft activities, talks, walks and workshops here, and events are advertised on the website, usually a month in advance. As London Wildcare also runs a wildlife hospital in Wallington (visit www.london wildlifehospital.org for open days), wildlife sessions for families often take on a 'show and tell' quality, when staff bring in rescued baby hedgehogs, fox cubs, frogs or slow worms to meet the visitors.

Adult twitchers training their binoculars on the various habitats of the **WWT Wetland Centre** might not care for flocks of fidgety children in their hides, so they know by now to confine their visits to term-time to enjoy the peace. In any case, the weekend and school-holiday activities for children are well organised enough to prevent stress, either in the resident feathered population or the migratory Barboured one. The centre's 'edutainers' oversee activities like pond dipping, craft activities or season-specific high jinks, such as an Easter egg watch (starring real ducklings) and even winter pantos (a recent example being *Duck Whittington*). Summer evening bat-spotting walks (specific Thursdays in May, July, August and September; check the website for details) are hugely popular, so must be booked ahead. These go on till 11pm, so are only suited to accompanied children aged from eight years.

East Sheen Common, backing on to Richmond Park, is a small nature trail through 13 areas of woodlands, ponds and streams marked with

orange posts. A wildlife-watching leaflet, available from the resident ranger (8876 2382), tells you about the animals and insects that live around here. You'll be lucky if you see the badgers (they have an active nightlife), but visit in spring and you should hear frogs croaking and woodpeckers tapping. Summer brings butterflies to the meadow flowers and woodland floor; autumn provides berries for the birds. Contact the ranger for details of kids' activities and guided walks.

South of Wimbledon Common, **Fishpond Wood & Beverley Meads** nature trail (entrance near Beverley Meads car park at the end of Barham Road, SW20) is also open at all times. It leads through the five-acre (2ha) site, passing oak avenues and coppiced hazel woodland that has a profusion of bluebells in springtime. Seasonal ponds have plenty of amphibians and dragonflies. The final section of the trail follows a footpath on to Wimbledon Common.

Way out on the westerly reaches of Twickenham, **Crane Park Island** (entrance on Ellerman Avenue, TW1, 8755 2339) is one of the London Wildlife Trust's staffed reserves. It used to be the old Hounslow Gunpowder Mills, but is now a peaceful haven surrounded by the River Crane, where woodland, scrub and reedbeds provide a home for the increasingly scarce water vole. Work is now in progress to turn the tower, an imposing relic of the old mills, into a nature study centre.

If all this seems a little too wild, be assured that you can keep the natural world at a safe distance at the **Royal Botanic Gardens** at Kew, where a new observatory, made from Welsh oak, gives a 360-degree view of the gardens' Wildlife Zone. The observatory's hollow woven walls have been filled with soil to allow plant camouflage – each of the six windows cut into it looks out over a different habitat. There's pond and wetland, deciduous woodland and beetle banks out there, and you don't even have to get your gumboots wet to study them.

Watson, the first Ladies Champion back in 1884. William Renshaw, seven times Wimbledon Champion in the 1880s, can give tips on improving your game, and William Coleman, Head Groundsman in the 1920s, tells of the mysteries of the Centre Court grass, the pony roller and horse boots. Visit the website for dates and times for 2005.

Note that the Museum will be closed from November 2005 to Easter 2006. There will be a visitor centre, together with a café, replacing the existing museum; tours will depart every hour, at a discounted rate.

Buggy access. Café. Disabled access: lift, toilet. Nappy-changing facilities. Shop.

Wimbledon Windmill Museum

Windmill Road, Wimbledon Common, SW19 5NR (8947 2825/www.wimbledonwindmillmuseum.org.uk). Wimbledon tube/rail. **Open** *Apr-Oct* 2-5pm Sat; 11am-5pm Sun & bank hols; school groups by appointment only. **Admission** £1; 50p children, concessions. **No credit cards.**

John Betjemen wrote a verse tribute – 'Old Surrey Working Woman' – to this Wimbledon landmark as part of the Wimbledon Windmill Restoration Appeal. The old dear, built in 1817, is still working, but only on high days and holidays. It's believed to be the only remaining example of a hollow post flour mill in this country, and its restored interior is full of display cases containing working models of many other types of windmill, each with a button to push to watch the sails go round. Other hands-on exhibits feature various pieces of grain-grinding equipment, including pestles and mortars and hand querns (grinding stones). Such items are put to good use during occasional children's workshops. Dioramas, tool and machinery displays, videos, sieving and weighing exhibitions, and a small Robert Baden-Powell exhibition (the founder of the scout movement wrote *Scouting for Boys* here in 1908) make up the rest of the museum. Run and maintained by the Wimbledon Windmill Museum Trust, the museum relies on volunteers and the work of Norman Plastow, FRIBA, who made all the models inside.

Buggy access (ground floor). Café. Car park. Shop.

PUTNEY & BARNES

Peaceful riverside **Putney** was a fishing and farming community until it became popular with Tudor celebrity commuters such as Thomas Cromwell. These days it's familiar to millions as the starting point of the annual Varsity Boat Race. The river takes on a semi-rural aspect at Putney Bridge – looking back down the Thames you'll catch glimpses of London's skyline, but upstream the Putney treeline is pretty well all that the eye can see. Back from the river, the busy high street is all you'd expect of this affluent area. Putney has more than its fair share of smart clothes and toyshops for children, and the Putney Exchange Shopping Centre is consumer heaven. Opposite the centre, above Halfords, the first of several promised new children's 'edutainment' centres opened in April. **Eddie Catz** (68-70 High Street, SW15 1SF, 0845 201 1268, www.eddiecatz.com)

Plain sailing at **Wimbledon Windmill Museum**.

is one of those indoor playcentres with all the ball ponds and playframes you'd expect, as well as a 'hands-on Discovery Zone' that houses a travelling exhibition where kids learn through play, as well as getting hot and sweaty.

For a bit of the great outdoors, there are a few options. **Putney Heath** is the eastern edge of the huge piece of common land (three times the size of Hampstead Heath, *see p93*) that eventually peters out where Wimbledon Common joins Richmond Park, but it has no areas set aside for children's play. Infinitely tamer – but with more activities geared to the younger ones – are **King George's Park** and **Leaders Gardens** at the end of Asilone Road. This dainty little riverside park is a delight for all family members, with two play areas and tennis courts.

The Boat Race between Oxford and Cambridge Universities traditionally finishes in Mortlake, and illustrious former inhabitants of these parts include former prime minister Earl Grey, writer Henry Fielding and composer Gustav Holst. Hints of a more reckless kind of fame can be found near **Barnes Common**, in the form of Marc Bolan's flower-bedecked memorial. The Mini he was travelling in hit a sycamore tree here on 16 September 1977, killing the young rock star. Of most interest to visiting families, however, is the **WWT Wetland Centre**, one of the area's up-and-coming stars.

WWT Wetland Centre

*Queen Elizabeth's Walk, SW13 9WT (8409 4400/
www.wwt.org.uk). Hammersmith tube, then 33, 72,
209 (alight at Red Lion pub) or 283 (Duck Bus direct
to Centre) bus.* **Open** *Summer* 9.30am-6pm daily.
Winter 9.30am-5pm daily. Last entry 1hr before closing.
Closed 25 Dec. *Tours* 11am, 2pm daily. *Feeding tours*
noon, 3.30pm daily. **Admission** £6.75; £5.50
concessions; £4 4-16s; free under-4s; £17.50 family
(2+2). *Tours* free. *Feeding tours* free. **Credit** MC, V.
It may have opened just five years ago, but already this
105-acre (42ha) reserve is generally considered the best
urban site in Europe for watching nature. One of nine
Wetland visitor centres, the London site, a mere four miles
(6.5km) from the West End, supports a range of rare or
threatened wildlife. There are at least 150 species of bird,
such as the Hawaiian Goose, White-headed Duck,
Red-breasted Goose and Blue Duck. The site has 27,000
trees and 300,000 aquatic plants, and in summer, 300 varieties of butterfly flutter by. The centre is divided into a
permanent section, where the exotic and endangered waterfowl are given appropriate (notwithstanding the English
weather) habitats to play in, and open water lakes,
reedbeds and mudflats that attract scores of insects, with
flocks of migratory birds not far behind them.

If the weather's atrocious, it's possible to view parts
of the reserve from indoors through CCTV cameras, but
it's best to get outside with the binoculars (which can be
rented here) and head for one of the three strategically
placed hides. Young children might find it hard to keep
quiet within the hides, and they won't be popular if they
scare away fellow birdwatchers within and wild birds
without – so they're probably best off sticking to the
permanent habitats (watch out for the prehistoric-looking
Magpie Geese) or joining one of the centre's impressively
informed guides for a tour. The visitors' centre has various bird identification displays, and the Water's Edge café
combines pretty good grub with an outdoor terrace.
There's a popular programme of weekend and school-
holiday activities for children; check the website or phone
for details. *See also p142* **Running wild**.
*Buggy access. Café. Car park. Disabled access: lifts,
toilet. Nappy-changing facilities. Shop.*

RICHMOND & KEW

Richmond, once known as Shene, was the seat
of kings during the 12th century, when Henry I
lived at Sheen Palace on the south-west corner of
what is now Richmond Green. Edward III had a
riverside palace here in the mid 1300s and Henry
VII built Richmond Palace in 1501. Elizabeth I
spent her last few summers there, before dying
in Richmond in 1603. All that remains of the
palace now is the gateway on Richmond Green,
a picturesque spot once famous for jousting
tournaments. There are few royal connections
these days (though many famous folk live
hereabouts), but this most royal of boroughs
still retains enough attractions to make it a
pleasure park for little princes and princesses,
especially those who enjoy outdoor pursuits.
Further west, **Kew** is famed for its majestic
Botanic Gardens and its royal, bucolic air.

East Sheen Common Nature Trail

*East Sheen Common, Fife Road, SW14 7EW (Ranger
8876 2382/Borough Ecology Officer 8831 6125).
Hammersmith tube, then 33 bus/Mortlake rail, then
15min walk.* **Open** dawn-dusk daily. **Admission** free.
The common, owned by the National Trust and managed
by the London Borough of Richmond, is a short circular
walk, taking in woodland glades, ponds and streams. *See
also p142* **Running wild**.

Museum of Richmond

*Old Town Hall, Whittaker Avenue, Richmond, Surrey
TW9 1TP (8332 1141/www.museumofrichmond.com).
Richmond tube/rail.* **Open** 11am-5pm Tue-Sat. Closed
25, 26 Dec, 1 Jan. **Admission** free.
With so many royal connections, it's only fitting that
Richmond should have a museum that loyally parades its
regal history, detailing the lives of silver-spooned former
residents from the 12th-century Henry I to Elizabeth I four
centuries later. There are permanent and temporary
displays, and the programme of children's activities
includes workshops for pre-schoolers. Harry the Herald's
Saturday Club, for five- to 11-year-olds, takes place on the
third Saturday of every month (10-11.15am, £5 per child).
An under-fives club, Mini-Heralds, takes place on the third
Wednesday of every month (2-2.40pm, £1 per child). Free
trails and drop-in activities change with the museum's
various exhibitions, so consult the website for details.
*Buggy access. Disabled access: lift, toilets. Nearest picnic
place: Richmond Green/riverside. Shop.*

National Archives

*Kew, Richmond, Surrey TW9 4DU (8876 3444/
www.pro.gov.uk/education). Kew Gardens tube, then
10min walk/65, 391 bus, then 5min walk.* **Open** 9am-
5pm Mon, Wed, Fri; 10am-7pm Tue; 9am-7pm Thur;
9.30am-5pm Sat. **Tours** 11am, 2pm Sat (booking
necessary). **Admission** free. *Tours* free.
The erstwhile Public Record Office is now known as the
National Archives. Devoted to keeping the records of 1,000
years of central government and the law courts, the
Archives have, unsurprisingly, a fascinating Education
and Visitor Centre. More surprising is its accessibility to
families and children. The museum spans British history
from the Domesday Book to the Festival of Britain, with
an engaging online 'Secrets and Spies' exhibition detailing
the history of British espionage. The millions of historical
documents go back as far as the Norman Conquest, some
relating to the lives of everyday people. The summer 2005
exhibition, 'Captains, Pirates and Castaways', runs until
19 November. School-holiday family events will involve
dressing up, storytelling and craft sessions based around
the three main themes of the exhibition: 'Britain and the
sea'; 'Heroes and reputations'; 'Pirates and castaways'.
Captain Bligh's will and Nelson's diary will be among the
many artefacts on display. Check the website for details or
call the interpretation department on 8392 5202.
*Buggy access. Café. Disabled access: lifts, toilet.
Nappy-changing facilities. Nearest picnic place:
National Archives grounds. Shop.*

Richmond Park

*Holly Lodge, Richmond, Surrey TW10 5HS (8948
3209/www.royalparks.gov.uk).* **Open** *Summer*
7am-30mins before dusk. *Winter* 7.30am-30mins
before dusk. **Admission** free.

What's new at Kew?

It's all very well wandering the verdant acres of the **Royal Botanic Gardens** at Kew, but most small children would rather be climbing inside a giant flower. That's what would-be botanists have a chance to do at the new **Climbers & Creepers** play zone, which opened in the gardens in spring 2005. Designed for children aged from three to nine, this new facility has indoor and outdoor play areas with more than 20 different activities. While they climb, bounce, slide and dig, the children are absorbing bite-sized facts about the role of plants in the environment.

When they climb into the flower in the indoor area, for example, they're discovering the bee's role in pollination. Pushing through the blackberry tangle prompts giant ripe fruits to light up and speak, while sliding into the pitcher plant model gives the lowdown on these and other carnivorous plant species. Digging in a pit filled with granular rubber material may unearth some fossilised plants, but it's usually full of dribbling toddlers. Real live insects add to the excitement: in one corner a wall of worker bees get busy in their see-through beehive; in the other, a large butterfly enclosure demonstrates their relationship with flowers; and, at floor level, an army of leafcutter ants stream along a clear plastic runway to their undergound nest. Children lie on their stomachs and watch in wonder as the arthropods march by.

Activities in the Grow Zone, such as cutting, sticking and colouring-in, take place at weekends and during school holidays, and there is a separate learning area for school groups (teachers may rest assured that Climbers & Creepers ticks boxes in KS1 and KS2 of the National Curriculum) as well as special events.

Buzz outdoors for Air Play, where things get more physical. It's an adventure playground with climbing frames, look-out posts, things to dangle from, whizz round and jump off. There are hammocks and water jets for wet play and little shelters for hiding in. A gently undulating safety surface ensures that all your little climbers and creepers enjoy happy landings.

Climbers & Creepers

www.kew.org/climbersandcreepers. **Open** *Summer* 11am-5.30pm daily. *Winter* 11am-3.30pm. **Admission** free (accompanying adults pay admission fee; for full listings, *see p146*).

Extensive Richmond Park, eight miles (13km) across at its widest point, is the biggest city park in Europe and rivalled only by Epping Forest (see p119) as the nearest London gets to wild countryside. Picturesque herds of red and fallow deer roam freely, a source of much fascination to children, but do bear in mind that these seemingly shy and gentle wild animals can be fierce in autumn during the rutting season. The whole family needs to pay heed to the signs that warn you not to get too close.

A great way to see the park is by bike: a well-kept cycle path rings the perimeter. If it's too much hassle to bring your own, it's possible to hire them from Richmond Park Cycle Hire (07050 209249) at Roehampton Gate. Adult bikes with tag-alongs (for the over-fives) and child-seats are available, as are children's bikes for those who have already learnt how to ride without stabilisers.

Tucked away in the middle of the park is Isabella Plantation, a secluded and tranquil woodland garden. It's primarily home to acid-loving plants such as camellias, azaleas and rhododendrons, and is best seen in all its fabulous flowering glory in early summer or in late September, when it blazes with autumn colour. Criss-crossed with streams and ponds, stepping stones and wooden bridges, it makes fun walking for children. There are also plenty of benches and grassy glades where you can picnic.

While you're here, take a moment to stroll to King Henry VIII's Mound. Follow the twisting path up this leafy hillock and, from the top, you'll have a spectacular view right across London. On a clear day, the London Eye and St Paul's Cathedral can easily be made out. Alternatively, you could stroll along Terrace Walk, a famous Victorian promenade that stretches all the way from the philosopher Bertrand Russell's childhood home, Pembroke Lodge (now a café and a great lunch spot for the picnic-less), and beyond the park to Richmond Hill, continuing the wonderful views of west London and beyond.

Like all the Royal Parks, Richmond hosts a programme of summer events for families, which is usually publicised at the gate lodge or on the website.
Café

Royal Botanic Gardens (Kew Gardens)

Richmond, Surrey TW9 3AB (8332 5655/ information 8940 1171/www.kew.org.uk). Kew Gardens tube/rail/Kew Bridge rail/riverboat to Kew Pier. **Open** *Late Mar-Aug* 9.30am-6.30pm Mon-Fri; 9.30am-7.30pm Sat, Sun, bank hols. *Sept, Oct* 9.30am-6pm daily. *Late Oct-early Feb* 9.30am-4.15pm daily. *Early Feb-late Mar* 9.30am-5.30pm daily. **Admission** (LP) £10; £7 concessions, late entry; free under-17s. **Credit** AmEx, DC, MC, V.

There is a huge amount of ground to cover at Kew, and small children will soon protest if you attempt to see everything in one visit. Once they've clocked Climbers & Creepers (see p145 **What's new at Kew?**), most won't want to go any further anyway. The 300 acres (120ha) of gardens are split into 47 areas, so it's a good idea to arm yourself with the map provided at the ticket office to plan your route. Little legs might prefer to ride the Kew Explorer people mover, which plies a circular route around the gardens (£3.50; £1 concessions, under-17s).

The monuments, gardens, buildings and landscapes are divided into eight zones. Most visitors start at the Entrance Zone, which has the Broad Walk, Nash conservatory and the Orangery restaurant. This leads to the Pagoda Vista Zone, with the glorious Japanese Gateway taking you to the serene gardens of Peace, Activity and Harmony. Perhaps most popular of all is the Palm House Zone. The

famous glass-constructed building (designed by Decimus Burton and Richard Taylor in 1848) has spectacular and enormous exotic plants from Africa, Asia and America, and a series of spiral staircases that allows you to view them all from a gallery. The Palm House has its resident record-breakers in the form of the oldest pot plant in the world and the tallest palm under glass. It's just one of the sites chosen to display works from Dale Chihuly as part of the exhibition *Gardens of Glass*, which runs until January 2006 (see website for details).

Kew boasts three glasshouses and will soon have a fourth; this new £800,000 effort, designed by Wilkinson Eyre Architects to keep alpine plants cool, will open next year. The Syon Vista Zone, with – obviously enough – views of Syon House across the Thames, is dominated by an artificial lake. The Western Zone, which was once part of Richmond Gardens, has a bamboo garden and the traditional Japanese Minka House (used for workshops, displays and events). The Riverside Zone runs alongside the Thames. It contains the Dutch House (Kew Palace) and the 17th-century-style Queen's Garden.

There are cafés, restaurants and snack areas dotted throughout Kew Gardens, but on a fine day it's well worth bringing your own food and picnicking in the gardens. *Buggy access. Cafés. Disabled access: ramps, toilets. Nappy-changing facilities. Nearest picnic place: grounds. Restaurants. Shop.*

FURTHER SOUTH-WEST

The pretty southern reaches of the river towards well-to-do **Twickenham** are lovely spots to ride a bike around, and there's the Thames Path for walkers. The area has a number of gracious historic buildings. Overlooking the river from Marble Hill Park, **Marble Hill House** is the perfect Palladian villa. Neighbouring **Orleans House** (Riverside, Twickenham TW1 3DJ, 8831 6000, www.richmond.gov.uk) was built in 1710 for James Johnston, William III's secretary of state for Scotland, but later home to the exiled Duke of Orléans – hence the name. **Ham House** is another favourite: a handsome, red-brick, riverside mansion with a beautiful garden. Carrying on along the river past Twickenham, you'll eventually come to the **Museum of Rugby** inside Twickenham Stadium.

From Twickers, the river passes by the busy shopping centre of Kingston-upon-Thames, then curves around to **Hampton Court Palace**. Once the country seat of Cardinal Wolsey, the palace was taken over by Henry VIII, who liked it so much he spent three honeymoons here.

Ham House

Ham Street, Ham, Richmond, Surrey TW10 7RS (8940 1950/www.nationaltrust.org.uk). Richmond tube/rail, then 371 bus. **Open** *House* mid Mar-Nov 1-5pm Mon-Wed, Sat, Sun. *Gardens* 11am-6pm or dusk Mon-Wed, Sat, Sun. Closed 25, 26 Dec, 1 Jan. **Tours** (pre-booking essential) Wed. Phone for membership details & prices. **Admission** (NT)

House & gardens £7.50; £3.75 5-15s; free under-5s; £18.75 family (2+2). *Gardens only* £3.50; £1.75 5-15s; free under-5s; £8.75 family (2+2). **Credit** AmEx, MC, V. There aren't many grand houses to better this lavish river-side mansion, home to the Duke and Duchess of Lauderdale in the late 17th century. Built in 1610, it was occupied by the same family until 1948. Today the interiors have original furniture, paintings and textiles. The grounds include the Cherry Garden with a central statue of Bacchus, the South Garden and the maze-like Wilderness. There's also an Orangery with a terrace café.

Regular events for families include entertaining Ghost Tours, which are guaranteed to mention the 17th-century duchess and her spirit friends who are said to haunt the building, theatre in the garden in the summer, egg trails for Easter, more spooky tours for Hallowe'en, art and craft open days for the August bank holiday weekend and loads of carols, feasts and craft events for Christmas (check the website for details). Dates for your diary in 2005 include Herb Week (9-17 July) and Big Draw days (22, 23 Oct) to coincide with the national Big Draw.

Café (high chairs). Disabled access: lift, toilets. Nappy-changing facilities. Shop.

Hampton Court Palace

East Molesey, Surrey KT8 9AU (0870 751 5175/ information 0870 752 7777/www.hrp.org.uk). Hampton Court rail/riverboat from Westminster or Richmond to Hampton Court Pier (Apr-Oct). **Open** *Palace* Mar-Oct 10am-6pm Tue-Sun. Nov-Feb 10am-4.30pm Tue-Sun. Last entry 1hr before closing. *Park* dawn-dusk daily. **Admission** *Palace, courtyard, cloister & maze* £12; £9 concessions; £7.80 5-15s; free under-5s; £35 family (2+3). *Gardens only* £4; £3 concessions; £2.50 5-15s; free under-5s; £12 family. *Maze only* £3.50; £2.50 5-15s. **Credit** AmEx, MC, V.

This monument to a larger-than-life monarch, Henry VIII, was nicknamed 'Magnificence-upon-Thames'. In fact it wasn't built for him originally; Cardinal Wolsey commissioned the palace in 1514, but the king rather took to it and filched it in 1528. For the next 200 years it was a focal point in English history: Elizabeth I was imprisoned in the tower by her elder sister Mary I; Shakespeare performed here; and after the Civil War Oliver Cromwell went against the puritanical grain and moved in.

Centuries later, the palace still dazzles in considerable style. Its history, right through to the fire in the King's Apartments in 1986, is detailed in the permanent exhibition. Costumed guided tours take you through the grandiose State Apartments, which include the Georgian Rooms, Henry VIII's apartments and the Queen's apartments; the public dining room, with its huge marble fireplace; and the extensive Tudor Kitchens, set up as if in the middle of putting together the feast of John the Baptist in 1442. With all this, plus more than 60 acres (24ha) of riverside gardens (including the famous maze with half a mile of paths) and a series of courtyards and cloisters, aching legs are guaranteed. Special events run throughout the year – blockbusters to look out for include the Hampton Court Palace Music Festival every June and the Hampton Court Flower Show (5-10 July 2005).

From March 2005 the new exhibition 'Suffragettes, Soldiers and Servants: Behind the Scenes of the Hampton Court Palace Community 1750-1950' takes place in a 'grace and favour' apartment. It's typical of the self-contained homes within the Palace, awarded by the sovereign and used by a variety of personalities over the years. Residents

included Lady Shackleton, wife of the Antarctic explorer; 'Capability' Brown, the gardener; and Grand Duchess Xenia, sister of the assassinated Tsar Nicholas II.

Activities for children, taking place on the first weekend of July, September and October, include 'Georgian Treats', about food in Georgian times, and from 1-31 August, workshops and demonstrations about Victorian photography. Shakespearean promenade performances take place in the garden every August weekend (ring for details). At October half-term children can 'attend' the school located in the Palace in the 1900s and, at Christmas, enjoy royal yuletide celebrations and festive food demonstrations.

For about six weeks from the beginning of December to mid January (call or check the website for 2005/6 dates) the west front of the palace is iced over for skating.

Buggy access. Cafés. Car park. Disabled access: lift, toilets. Nappy-changing facilities. Nearest picnic place: palace gardens. Shop.

Marble Hill House

Richmond Road, Middx TW1 2NL (8892 5115/ www.english-heritage.org.uk). Richmond tube/rail/ 33, 90, 290, H22, R70 bus. **Open** late Mar-Nov 10am-2pm Sat; 10am-5pm Sun. **Tours** by prior arrangement. **Admission** (EH, LP) £4; £3 concessions; £2 5-15s; free under-5s. **Credit** MC, V.

This is a gorgeous Thameside villa, once home to Henrietta Howard, that was built with an £11,500 cash present from her lover, King George II. One of the most beautiful items in this Palladian villa is a Honduran mahogany staircase, whose provenance almost caused a diplomatic incident. Filled with elegant Georgian objects and paintings, Marble Hill House also hosts events throughout the year, including Easter trails, house tours, open-air concerts and craft workshops. The house is surrounded by 66 acres (27ha) of parkland, but if that's not enough, the house is connected by ferry to Ham House just across the river.

Café (in park). Nearest picnic place: Marble Hill Park. Shop.

Museum of Rugby/ Twickenham Stadium

Twickenham Stadium, Rugby Road, Twickenham, Middx TW1 1DZ (0870 405 2001/www.rfu.com/ microsites/museum). Hounslow East tube, then 281 bus/Twickenham rail. **Open** *Museum* 10am-5pm Tue-Sat; 11am-5pm Sun. Last entry 30mins before closing. *Tours* 10.30am, noon, 1.30pm, 3pm Tue-Sat; 1pm, 3pm Sun. Closed 24-26 Dec, 1 Jan, Easter Sun, Sun after match days. **Admission** *Combined ticket* £9; £6 concessions; £30 family. Advance booking advisable. **Credit** MC, V.

Since England's 2003 World Cup Rugby spectacular, and despite 2005's rubbish showing in the Six Nations, there's been even more interest than usual in this already popular museum and sports venue. Non-match days see tours of the stadium, during which visitors can walk down the players' tunnel, look at the England dressing room and drop in on the Members' Lounge, the President's Suite and the Royal Box. In the museum you can watch international footage of some of the greatest tries of all time or peruse artwork and rugby memorabilia dating all the way back to 1871. The special exhibition of 2005, 'Pride of Lions presented by Genesis Publications', which runs from March until 4 September, gives a comprehensive overview of the greatest of all British touring rugby teams.

Buggy access. Disabled access: toilet. Restaurant. Shop.

WEST LONDON

London's posher side, where urban chic nestles with wildlife and river.

The playground in **Holland Park**. *See p162.*

BAYSWATER & PADDINGTON

Taking its name from Bayard's Watering, a natural spring that served as a drinking place for horses near Queensway, the development of **Bayswater** into the solid-looking district it is today began with plans for a lavish estate, with a central crescent in Tyburnia, for the Bishop of London's trustees. This gentrification took place well after the last public hanging at Tyburn in 1763 (the spot where the gallows stood is marked by a plaque on the ground at the junction of Bayswater Road and Edgware Road). After the main architect died, the grandiose crescent idea was abandoned and the district was developed into a series of interconnecting residential squares, full of grand houses much sought after by the wealthier Victorians.

The eventual gentrification of Bayswater was the spur to development further west into the farmlands at **Paddington**. Unlike Bayswater, Paddington never really gained the suburban respectability that was envisaged and, with the arrival of the station, it became home to a large transient population. In the 1950s the area became a byword for overcrowding, poverty and vice. Yet now Paddington is back on the map, halfway through an ambitious regeneration project that is throwing new office blocks up along the canal like a mini Docklands. Innovative rolling bridges and futuristic waterside architecture by Richard Rogers have completely transformed the area and a much-needed new secondary school, the Westminster Academy, is set to open in late 2006, with ambitious plans for a canal bus to ferry schoolchildren to and fro. In preparation for the developments, the canal at Paddington Basin was drained, unearthing all kinds of interesting things among the shopping trolleys – among them a World War II bomb and several scooters.

Nearby Queensway is named after the young Queen Victoria, who used to ride her horse down this road from Kensington Palace (*see p87*). The main target for kids here is Queens, the tenpin bowling alley and ice rink (17 Queensway, W2 4QP (7229 0172/www.queensiceandbowl.co.uk). Especially popular with young teens, both these attractions are busy at the weekends. Further down, where Queensway merges with Bayswater, Whiteley's shopping centre is popular with families. Special activities are laid on for children in the foyer during half-term and holidays (check www.whiteleys.com for details), with one of the regulars being Jumpzone – youngsters are strapped into a harness attached to elastic supports and bounced up as high as the first floor. What larks. The second floor has an eight-screen cinema and any number of child-friendly restaurants. There are loads of toyshops, and Gymboree (0800 092 0911) – purveyor of dance, music and all-round enjoyment to the under-fives – is an infant magnet.

Alexander Fleming Laboratory Museum

St Mary's Hospital, Praed Street, W2 1NY (7886 6528/www.st-marys.nhs.uk). Paddington tube/rail/7, 15, 27, 36 bus. **Open** 10am-1pm Mon-Thur; other times by appointment only. Closed bank hols. **Admission** (LP) £2; £1 concessions, 5-16s; free under-5s. **No credit cards. Map** p313 D5.
Alexander Fleming made his momentous chance discovery of penicillin in this very room on 3 September 1928, when a Petri dish of bacteria became contaminated with some kind of mysterious mould. Fleming's laboratory has now been recreated, and displays and a video offer insights into both his life and the role of penicillin in fighting disease. The staff run special tours for family and school groups, and other visitors get a guided tour as part of the entrance fee.
Nearest picnic place: Hyde Park. Shop.

MAIDA VALE, KILBURN & QUEEN'S PARK

An attractive district, characterised by white stucco houses, some perched romantically along the edge of the canal, Maida Vale's prettiest point of interest for visitors is the large, well-established houseboat community at Little Venice. Visit for the festival during the May Day bank holiday (*see p26*). The delightful **Puppet Theatre Barge** (www.puppetbarge.com), moored here during the winter, is another must-visit as far as the kids are concerned. Next to Little Venice is **Rembrandt Gardens**, a pretty park full of flowers, which is perfect for a summer picnic, while Clifton Nurseries in Clifton Villas is an upmarket garden centre that's full of interest for browsers keen on beautiful or exotic plants. Walking along the canal from Little Venice to Camden is a popular family stroll. It takes about 45 minutes, passing **London Zoo** (*see p64*) on the right, with the Snowdon

Aviary to the left. If that's too far for little feet, the London Waterbus ticket office (information 7482 2660, www.londonwaterbus.com) will get you on to a boat to the zoo or Camden Lock (*see p90*).

The best green space in the area is **Paddington Recreation Ground**, where Roger Bannister trained for his four-minute mile 50 years ago. Today's athletes have a proper running track to train on, and there are five-a-side football pitches, cricket nets and basketball courts. Play areas to suit all ages and a decent café make this a popular spot that buzzes with activity at the weekends.

Queen's Park is well kept and a treat to visit with young children. Nearby Kilburn gets packed with families shopping at weekends. For children, the deservedly popular **Tricycle Theatre & Cinema** (269 Kilburn High Road, Kilburn, NW6 7JR (box office 7328 1000/www.tricycle.co.uk) is the area's saving grace; their café is a good place to revive flagging enthusiasm.

Queen's Park

Kingswood Avenue, NW6 6SG (park manager 8969 5661). Queen's Park tube/rail. **Open** 7.30am-dusk daily. **Admission** free.
This Corporation of London park has wardens to maintain fair play, so parents with wandering children feel safer than in larger, less visibly staffed parks. There's a playground with a giant sandpit and adjacent paddling pool (open in summer), and a small enclosure of goats, ducks and chickens, as well as rotund guinea pigs and rabbits that keep small children busy for ages. At the northern end of the park is a wild, overgrown area with a nature trail signposted with pictures of the mini beasts you are likely to find there. A very pleasant, refurbished café is great for own-made cakes and locally made Disotto's ice-cream. Active bodies can enjoy the pitch-and-putt area, *pétanque* enclosure and six tennis courts. Occasional performances at the bandstand lend the place a carnival atmosphere in the summer months, but the big event is the annual Queen's Park Day (11 Sept 2005).
Buggy access. Café. Disabled access: toilet. Nappy-changing facilities.

NOTTING HILL

Long-term Notting Hill residents are getting a bit fed up with the 'starry media playground' image of their patch, especially as rich incomers think nothing of giving their multi-million-pound homes unnecessary and time-consuming refurbs, which mean endless noise, traffic and disruption in these handsome residential streets. Still, the whopping increase in the value of their houses has undoubtedly done something to compensate for these minor irritations.

Notting Hill has come a long way since its rural days in the mid 1800s, when its cart tracks were walked mostly by pig- and dairymen and their stock. The area originally became famous for all the wrong reasons: in the 1950s the now urban area was a hotbed of racial tension. Disputes flared up between sectors of the white, working-class population and West Indian immigrants who moved in alongside them. Poverty and tension rendered the streets around Notting Hill extremely dodgy for years, until the mid 1980s when the yuppies moved in, making the rest history.

Every August bank holiday for the last four decades the area has exploded with revelry for the world-famous **Notting Hill Carnival** (see p23).

At the southernmost end of Notting Hill is the **Gate** cinema (87 Notting Hill Gate, W11 3JZ, 7727 4043), which has a Saturday kids' club with pre-show activities; the **Electric Cinema** (191 Portobello Road, W11 2ED (7908 9696) holds parent and baby screenings.

Notting Hill is also famous for **Portobello Road Market**. One of the most popular street markets in the world, it starts off as an antiques market then gradually morphs into a fashion fair as it nears the Westway. It's best on Saturdays. At

 # RUNNING WILD

Those who prefer their nature contained within a stylish urban park should restrict themselves to the bosky pleasure of **Holland Park**'s well-equipped Ecology Centre, where pondlife and creepy crawlies are examined in style (*see p152*). The centre hosts half-term and holiday activities such as insect hunts, magpie walks and animal footprint investigations; in the past there have been sessions on shelter-building skills ('could you survive in the wild?') and orienteering too. The centre is also home to the local Wildlife Watch group, the junior branch of the Wildlife Trust aimed at children aged eight to 14. The Watch tries to encourage an interest in the environment through wildlife and conservation work, and arranges games and practical activities on a regular basis. There are bat walks, pond-dipping adventures and the chance for children to get involved in surveys such as the great stag beetle hunt or the SOS (Save Our Sparrows) campaign. More information can be found at www.wildlondon.org.uk.

Gunnersbury Triangle Nature Reserve (*see p166*) is a rougher and readier introduction to urban wildlife, but it's run by the London Wildlife Trust, so hosts many activities for wild children. Birds, small mammals, foxes, spiders, butterflies, beetles and other animals make their homes in these six acres (2.5ha) of woodland, pond, marsh and meadow, and it is a fantastic resource for young people. They can follow various trails and consult leaflets that point out species of butterfly, or join one of the practical workshops (wear old clothes and stout footwear) that focuses on conservation. During the summer there's a full-time warden and a varied programme of free, drop-in activities for youngsters – craft workshops, mask-making sessions, mini beast safaris and so on. Every June there's a summer open day with entertainment and musicians (phone for the date). When the small information cabin is open (throughout the summer, but only on Tuesdays and Sundays in winter) you can ask the staff questions about urban ecology, pick up trail leaflets, find out about guided tours or hire a net for a spot of pond-dipping. Following the nature trail, visitors can admire the teeming pond

and meadowland, and try to spot all 19 species of butterfly that have been recorded here.

Venturing much further west rewards the amateur naturalist with some wonderfully rural aspects, all within easy reach of public transport. Not far from Heathrow Airport, **Hounslow Heath** (450 Staines Road, Hounslow TW4 5AB, 8577 3664, www.cip.com) is one of London's largest nature reserves, and the sprawling open space encompasses a wide variety of habitats including heathland, meadowland, scrub, woodland and wetland. The site is home to a wide range of flora and fauna, as well as over 132 bird species and several rare insects and plants. There's an information centre near the Staines Road entrance; stop by and the helpful warden will provide you with plenty of information on local wildlife, suggest nature trails and point out creatures of interest.

Near Hanger Lane tube station in Ealing, **Fox Wood** (entrance in Fox Lane, off Hillcrest Road, W5) has 3.5 acres (1.4ha) teeming with life in every season. May sees the bluebells and lesser celandine, summer holidays are for butterfly-spotting, autumn brings dramatic colours, and winter is all bracing walks along the steep sides of the old reservoir. There is a picturesque winding path through the wood, which is well used by local residents.

If you fancy a real way out west the **Yeading Valley Reserves** (8868 0207), designated 'sites of Metropolitan Importance' and again under the aegis of the London Wildlife Trust, cover a large area linking meadows and woodland. Public footpaths run through the reserves, feeding into longer walks such as the Hillingdon Trail between Ruislip and Hayes. Parts of it, such as Ickenham Marsh, close to the river, can be reached from Ickenham, Ruislip Gardens or Hillingdon tube stations. Not so far from the marsh, a 100-year-old oak plantation, known as Ten Acre Wood, is a popular area with birdwatchers, as the many hawthorn and blackthorn trees provide berries for birds in autumn and winter. Leaflets giving details of walks around the reserves, with descriptions of flora and fauna to look out for, may be obtained from local libraries.

You can get anything at **Whiteleys**. *See p149.*

the northern end of Portobello Road interesting cafés, such as Babes 'n' Burgers (*see p182*) attract fashionable families. Just off Portobello Road, on Powis Square, crafty children can dabble at **Art 4 Fun** (www.art4fun.com), where all kinds of ceramics await their painting skills. A range of workshops are run throughout the year and the week-long holiday art camps are always a sell out.

Most Notting Hill parents prefer their fresh air to come from **Kensington Gardens** (*see p87*), but there are many smaller parks and city gardens dotted around the area. **Avondale Park** (Walmer Road) is one of the nicest, with a countryside feel and a small playground; just off Kensal Road, at the northern end of Notting Hill, is another little park, the Emslie Horniman Pleasance Gardens (Southern Row, W10 5BJ, 8969 5740), but it's reserved for children who live or go to school in the borough. Once you reach Ladbroke Grove, there are many other excellent resources for youngsters. If your children aspire to a life behind the camera, check out YCTV (79 Barlby Road, W10 6AZ, 8964 4646, www.yctv.org), which provides training in camera, sound, editing and lighting for 11- to 20-year-olds.

The **Westway** is one of the less attractive landmarks of the area. This stretch of the A40 used to cast a rather grim shadow in its wake as it brutally sliced through the neighbourhood, but the gloomy area beneath it was dedicated to

community use after locals protested against the flyover construction – and now it's an extended children's zone, with an amazing selection of activities to suit all tastes. **Baysixty6 Skate Park** (Bay 65-66, Acklam Road, W10 5YU, 8969 4669) has ramps for all levels and lessons for greenhorns. By Latimer Road, is the **Westway Climbing Complex** (Westway Sports Centre, 1 Crowthorne Road, W10 6RP, 8969 0992), which has the highest climbing wall in the country (children can start climbing at age five). The sports centre in which the complex is based also arranges reasonably priced half-term activities, allowing youngsters to learn tennis, football and fives. Just past here is **Westway Stables** (20 Stable Way, Latimer Road, W10 6QX, 8964 2140, www.westwaystables.co.uk), which organises rides in nearby Wormwood Scrubs, a large green space more famous for its prison.

Right next to Latimer Road tube station is **Bramley's Big Adventure** (136 Bramley Road, W10 6TJ, 8960 1515), whose sheer quantity of attractions crammed into the indoor playground (slides, ball ponds, monkey swings) provokes almost deafening chaos when packs of feral children are let loose. A similar facility, **Bumper's Back Yard**, can be found at nearby Kensington Leisure Centre (Walmer Road, W11 4PQ, 7727 9747); it also has tubular slides for whizzing down into the pool (summer only).

Screen West

The New Boat House, 136-142 Bramley Road, W10 6SR (7565 3000/www.screenwest.co.uk). Latimer Road tube/295 bus. **Credit** MC, V.

This 74-seat screening room is hired out for parties, with children bringing along their favourite video or DVD to watch. A separate function room, complete with sofas, tables, chairs and a CD player, is used for the tea; it seats up to 30 children. Phone for further information, but expect prices to start at around £200 for up to two hours.

HOLLAND PARK

This is genteel west London. While Notting Hill still has a bohemian air, with bare-bellied mums shoving their three-wheeler buggies around, people who can afford the beautiful mansion houses in Holland Park are more likely to employ uniformed nannies to push Silver Cross perambulators about the park. The area's name comes from **Holland House**, the remains of which are in the park. Duels took place in meadows to the west, and when Cromwell was a visitor he used the gardens to talk with his general so as to avoid eavesdroppers at the house.

There are several other interesting buildings around the park. **Leighton House** (12 Holland Park Road, W14 8LZ, 7602 3316) is worth an ogle to get a sense of the grandeur of its former inhabitant Lord Leighton, but nearby **Linley Sambourne House** demands a visit from anyone interested in Victoriana. If you're looking for refreshment hereabouts, your best bet is to take a walk to Notting Hill or Kensington High Street.

Holland Park

Ilchester Place, W8 6LU (7471 9813/www. rbkc.gov.uk/parksandgardens). Holland Park tube/9, 27, 28, 49 bus. **Open** 7.30am-dusk daily. **Map** p314 A9.

This beautiful park has a series of paths through wild forested areas , which take you past imperious peacocks and plenty of squirrels and rabbits. The well-equipped Ecology Centre (7471 9809; *see p150* **Running wild**) provides site maps, plus nets for pond dipping and information on local wildlife. There's also a smart Italian park café, with modern glass walls. Children can choose from a please-all menu that includes pizza and pasta. The remains of Holland House (it suffered irreparable damage from German bombers during a World War II raid) are at the centre of the park, its murals and fountains making it a lovely spot to sit awhile. The house's restored east wing contains the most dramatically sited youth hostel in town, though one without family rooms, sadly. It also provides a smashing backdrop for the open-air theatre, whose summer programme of opera and Shakespeare is popular for family outings (see the website for details). The pond of Koi carp in the peaceful Japanese Garden will entertain the kids for a while, but there's also a well-equipped and recently sanitised adventure playground to keep the over-fives entertained. Of most interest to youngsters is Whippersnappers (7738 6633, www.whippersnappers.org), who put on weekly musical and puppet workshops. Also in the park are nicely maintained tennis courts and two art spaces, the Ice House and the Orangery. The popular North Lawn is busy with families and picnickers throughout the summer.

Buggy access. Café. Nappy-changing facilities. Restaurant.

Linley Sambourne House

18 Stafford Terrace, W8 7BH (7602 3316 ext 305 Mon-Fri/www.rbkc.gov.uk/linleysambournehouse). High Street Kensington tube. **Tours** 10am, 11.15am, 1pm, 2.15pm, 3.30pm Sat, Sun (with the curator); other times

Strand on the Green. *See p155.*

by appointment only. Maximum of 12 on each tour. Book in advance. **Admission** £6;£4 concessions; £1 under-18s. **Map** p314 A9.

Edward Linley Sambourne was a Victorian cartoonist, famous for his work in *Punch*. His house, which contains almost all its original fittings and furniture, can only be visited in the context of the terrific and slightly eccentric tours. They are each guided by a costumed actor (especially popular with children as gossipy housekeeper Mrs Reffle, who provides a cheeky insight into Victorian family life and tells a few jokes along the way) and there's a visitors' centre where children can participate in craftwork sessions relating to objects in the house. On Sundays holders of a Kensington and Chelsea library card are admitted free if they make an advance booking. *Shop.*

EARL'S COURT & FULHAM

A huge exhibition centre is the best-known landmark in **Earl's Court**. It was built in 1887, and hosted Buffalo Bill's Wild West Show in 1891. Nowadays the centre is used mainly for various conferences and consumer exhibitions, such as the Ideal Home Show.

In the post-war years, the area surrounding Earl's Court went into decline and large houses previously owned by wealthy Victorians were gradually converted into flats for poorer residents. In the 1960s and '70s the area became known as 'Kangaroo Valley', as travellers from Australia and New Zealand descended in search of cheap accommodation. The area is still full of bedsits and hostels, and there's a dearth of open spaces (the nearest is Brompton Cemetery – a last resort in more ways than one).

Most parents rely instead on Hammersmith and Fulham, where there are plentiful parks and activities. The most obvious destination, if you're seeking an antidote to London life, is the river. **Bishop's Park** runs alongside the Thames Path and has a small boating lake for summer, as well as two playgrounds and a basketball pitch. It also has a One O'Clock Club (Bishops Rainbow Playhouse) for under-fives, with a thrilling (for three-year-olds) selection of trikes and bikes. The café has pleasant outside seating and the ice-cream van on Stevenage Road serves the nicest cornets for miles around. **Fulham Palace**, on the edge of Bishop's Park, has lovely grounds and a walled kitchen garden, an ideal spot for lazy riverside picnics. On the opposite side of the park you'll find Craven Cottage, **Fulham FC**'s football ground (Stevenage Road, SW6 6HH, 0870 442 1222, www.fulhamfc.com); it can be reached along the Thames Path. Just down the Fulham Road at **Chelsea**'s ground, Stamford Bridge (SW6 1HS, 0870 300 1212, www.chelseafc.com), they will probably still be celebrating the team's 2004/5

Premiership title, their first triumph in the top flight for 50 years. And there's more excitement around the corner with the 2005/6 season marking the club's centenary. You can book on a tour of the stadium or pick up kit and souvenirs from the Chelsea Village megastore.

The South Kensington end of **Fulham Road** has a number of posh clothes shops (there are clothing ranges for tots at agnès b and children at Replay); the Fulham Broadway end has entertainment in the form of the Pottery Café (735 Fulham Road, SW6 5UL, 7736 2157). Moneyed families join the exclusive **Hurlingham Club** for its beautiful grounds and great outdoor sports facilities, but those without a trust fund can enjoy Hurlingham Park (Hurlingham Road, SW6). It's open to the public, but the emphasis is on sport, with a number of rugby and football pitches.

Museum of Fulham Palace

Bishop's Avenue, off Fulham Palace Road, SW6 6EA (7736 3233). Hammersmith or Putney Bridge tube/220, 414, 430 bus. **Open** *Mar-Oct* 2-5pm Sat, Sun. *Nov-Feb* 1-4pm Sat, Sun. **Tours** times vary, phone to check. **Admission** (LP) *Museum* free; under-16s must be accompanied by an adult. *Tours* £4; free under-16s. **No credit cards.**

The official residence of the Bishops of London from 704 until 1973, Fulham Palace has some buildings dating back to 1480, although the main house is 16th century. The moat has gone, but some of its trench is still visible. The museum traces the buildings' histories and has some funny exhibits, not least a mummified rat – and thanks to a successful lottery bid, it is also undergoing a major restoration. Extensive building work is set to continue until August 2006, until when the museum will only open at weekends. Imaginative staff organise children's workshops (suitable for six- to 14-year-olds) during the school holidays; a recent workshop series was based on wartime Britain, but most relate to Roman, Tudor and Victorian eras. Ring to check what's coming up or ask for regular email updates. Leave plenty of time to admire the lovely grounds, planted with rare trees, which provide sanctuary from the busy Fulham Palace Road. There's a walled kitchen garden, too, full of herbs and rare plants. *Buggy access. Disabled access: toilet. Shop.*

SHEPHERD'S BUSH & HAMMERSMITH

The fields and woods of **Shepherd's Bush** first gained recognition in the late 1700s, after the highwayman Sixteen String Jack was captured here. Up until the 19th century stockmen on their way to Smithfield Market regularly grazed their flocks on the roundabout site, which is an ancient piece of common land.

The transition to urban sprawl was rapid and the population of the area multiplied after the introduction of the railway in the early 1900s. In recent years, Hammersmith and Shepherd's Bush have become popular, not to mention fashionable, places for young families to set up home.

Other than sheep, Shepherd's Bush has a long association with music and theatre. The **Empire** at Shepherd's Bush roundabout has been a popular venue for concerts and many big names (the Rolling Stones, The Who, Eric Clapton) have graced its stage. The BBC once used it as a studio (*Crackerjack* was broadcast from here, parents).

Much-needed recent improvements to the area include a new shopping centre with a cinema. Future plans include landscaping Shepherd's Bush Green, which should make better use of what is now little more than an oversized traffic island, and a possible tram link. The Music House at **Bush Hall** (310 Uxbridge Road, Shepherd's Bush, W12 7LJ, 8932 2652) provides tuition and workshops for all ages. For a different kind of culture, Loftus Road Stadium, home to Queen's Park Rangers, is just west of Shepherd's Bush.

Closer to **Hammersmith** are a few more well-respected arts venues. The **Riverside Studios** is used by Dramatic Dreams Theatre Company (8741 1809, www.dramaticdreams.com) and Young Blood youth theatre company (01473 430395) as a venue for children's theatre projects during holidays and half-term. Another popular haunt is the **Albert & Friends Instant Circus** workshop (Ealing, Hammersmith & West London College, Glidden Road, W14 9BL, 8237 1170), where apprentice clowns can master juggling, unicycling and acrobatics. The Lyric Theatre also runs acting workshops for all ages, particularly during the summer months. If you're seeking further inspiration, go to Wood Lane, where the **BBC studios** invite groups to take backstage tours (if you're interested, tickets need to be booked in advance and the minimum age is nine years; call 0870 603 0304 to book a ticket).

Around Hammersmith, the best spot to let off steam is the ever-popular **Ravenscourt Park**, off Chiswick High Road. On the other side of the messy shopping mall-cum-transport hub that is Hammersmith roundabout you'll find **Brook Green**, which has in recent years become a congregating point for parents with pushchairs – the interactive play area makes it ideal for toddlers. The Frank Banfield Park on Distillery Lane is another good option.

Queen's Park Rangers Football Club

Loftus Road Stadium, South Africa Road, W12 7PA (8743 0262/www.qpr.co.uk). White City tube. **Open** *Shop* 9am-5pm Mon-Fri; 9am-1pm Sat. **Tours** by appointment only. **Admission** *Tours* £4; £2 under-16s. **Credit** MC, V.
Loftus Road, home to QPR, is also a hub of community football for young people. School-holiday soccer schools

Refreshingly child-friendly **Ravenscourt Park**.

are split into age groups 6-9, 10-13 and 14-15; there are daily prizes and player-of-the-week trophies as well as the chance for budding players to be recognised by the professionals. Plus there are girls-only sessions. For more information, phone 8740 2509.
Buggy access. Disabled access: toilet. Nearest picnic place: Hammersmith Park. Shop.

Ravenscourt Park

Ravenscourt Road, W6 0UL (www.lbhf.gov.uk). Ravenscourt Park tube. **Open** 7.30am-dusk daily. **Admission** free.
In summer the packed paddling pool is the most popular part of this family-friendly park, but it also has three play areas and a One O'Clock Club (8748 3180) for under-fives. There's a big pond, a nature trail and a scented garden for the visually impaired. Kids with spare energy can use the skateboarding ramp or enjoy a game of tennis. The nicely appointed café is open all year round and the children's play area outside allows parents to enjoy a bit of a sit-down while keeping an eye on things. There's a flower show and children's fair in July, and the Fun Day, with bouncy castles and face painting, is also worth checking out.
Buggy access. Café. Disabled access. Nappy-changing facilities.

CHISWICK

Chiswick is a stylish riverside suburb with a relaxed village feel. A prehistoric hammer and chisel found near **Syon House** suggest that some of the city's earliest human inhabitants lived here, and the part of Chiswick High Road running from Turnham Green towards Brentford is the remnant of a Roman road that stretched into the West Country. In the 18th century Ceswican, as it was known, was an area famous for cheesemaking, but most modern Chiswickians know of a lovely little deli where they can buy theirs. As well as chi-chi food shops and boutiques, proximity to the M4 and Heathrow airport is a modern benefit of living here, and wealthy families have been attracted to the area's large houses and acres of green space.

Turnham Green epitomises Chiswick's villagey atmosphere. **Acton Green Common**, just off Chiswick High Road, has a church at the centre and local teams play cricket on the pristine lawns during the summer months. However, there are no facilities for anything other than a picnic and a bit of exercise. Just opposite Turnham Green is a branch of the arts café Art 4 Fun (*see p151*).

A stroll along the riverbank's **Mall** is popular with families on a Sunday (*see p156* **Sweet Thames**). Over-eights can have a go at canoe polo on the Thames with the Chiswick Pier Canoe Club (The Pier House, Corney Reach Way, W4 2UG, www.chiswickcanoeclub.co.uk). Next door is Pissarro's on the River (Corney Reach Way, W4 2TR, 8994 3111), a popular stop for family lunches after working up an appetite on the riverbank (but phone ahead to see if it is properly up and running again after a period of closure in May 2005). **Duke's Meadows** is one of the first green spaces you reach: it has tennis courts, boathouses, cricket pitches and a nine-hole golf course. Junior golf coaching is organised on Saturday afternoons: contact Duke's Meadow Golf Club (8995 0537, www.golflessons.co.uk). If you continue further along the river, you'll soon forget that you are in London at all. During the 18th century **Strand-on-the-Green** was a fishing community; now it's a picturesque strolling spot, where child-friendly pubs with riverside terraces serve food all day.

The **Kew Bridge Steam Museum** (best visited at weekends) on Brentford High Street can be identified by its huge chimney. Nearby, the unusual **Musical Museum** (368 High Street, Brentford, Middx TW8 0BD, 8560 8108, www.musicalmuseum.co uk) has a fantastic collection of organs and self-playing keyboard instruments, although it will be closed for relocation until 2006. **Watermans** (40 High Street, Middx TW8 0DS, 8232 1010) is a riverside arts venue with children's storytelling, drama, puppetry, clowning and music workshops. Sporting urges can be satisfied at the **Fountain Leisure Centre** (658 Chiswick High Road, Middx TW8 0HJ, 0845 456 2935), renowned for its huge pool complex with waterslide and wave machine. All that, and there's a popular indoor play centre for those who prefer to stay dryside.

One of the best places in west London for fresh air and fluttery fun is **Syon Park**. The grand house, owned by the Duke of Northumberland, may not be top of many kids' lists of fun days out, but the surrounding grounds are full of child-friendly activities. The Butterfly House has over 1,000 live butterflies and fascinating collections of caterpillars eating themselves into a pupa. There's also the fab Tropical Forest with its rescued reptiles and a huge indoor adventure playground, Snakes & Ladders.

Further into the suburban expanses beyond Brentford you come to **Gunnersbury Park**, home to the fascinating Gunnersbury Park Local History Museum (8992 1612; open Apr-Oct 11am-5pm daily; Nov-Mar 11am-4pm daily), which hosts changing exhibitions that include history and other local themes – some staged by people or groups from the area – and a collection that includes toys and domestic ephemera. It also offers a programme of schools' workshops, provides tours and talks, and each year stages special events and hands-on activities for children. Nearby is the **Kids' Cookery School** (107 Gunnersbury Lane, W3 8HQ, 8992 8882), where chefs aged three to 16 learn new culinary techniques to impress their parents.

Chiswick House

Burlington Lane, W4 2RP (8995 0508/www.english-heritage.org.uk). Turnham Green tube, then E3 bus to Edensor Road/Hammersmith tube/rail, then 190 bus/Chiswick rail. **Open** *Apr-Oct* 10am-5pm Wed-Fri, Sun; 10am-2pm Sat. Last entry 30mins before closing. Closed Nov-Mar. **Tours** by arrangement; phone for details. **Admission** (EH/LP) incl audio guide £3.40; £3 concessions; £2 5-16s; under-5s free. **Credit** MC, V.
Walking through the gardens of Chiswick House you'll come across various delights: obelisks hidden among the trees, a classical temple, a lake and a cascading waterfall. Lots of families come here on summer days for a picnic or to play cricket on the well-maintained grounds. You can also take a jaunt along the river, which is only a stone's throw away. Burlington's Café (*see p183*), in the grounds of Chiswick House, is a splendid place for lunch. English Heritage stages family activity days and occasional re-enactments here: check its website for details.
Buggy access. Café. Disabled access: toilet. Nearest picnic place. Chiswick Park. Shop.

Gunnersbury Triangle Nature Reserve

Bollo Lane, W4 5LW (8747 3881/www.wildlondon.org.uk). Chiswick Park tube. **Open** *Reserve* 24hrs daily. *Information* Apr-Aug 10am-4.30pm Tue-Sun. Sept-Mar 10am-4pm Tue; 1-4pm Sun. **Admission** free.
In the late 19th century this area of land was enclosed by railway tracks and unfit for human habitation. As the woodland grew up and wildlife took over, it became one of the most important sites for urban wildlife in this part of the city. *See p150* **Running wild**.
Buggy access.

Around Town

WALK Sweet Thames

A stroll along the Thames Path is enjoyable whatever the weather. Start at the north side of **Hammersmith Bridge** and walk west along the wide, paved waterfront path, enjoying the expansive river view. Follow the road, Lower Mall, which weaves slightly back from the river and down an alleyway past the famous Dove pub, but keep going and you'll be back on the water. Pass the **London Corinthian Sailing Club**, home to the Sons of the Thames Rowing Club, and there will doubtless be rowers speeding smoothly past as you walk.

There's a large open green space when you get to Upper Mall, full in summer with the overspill from the popular Ship pub, and a small playground that might distract little ones from the business of walking. If they refuse to move on, stop for an alfresco drink at the Black Lion, which has a huge front garden. Continuing along the riverfront, admire the imposing though charming houses of **Chiswick Mall** – their river views make them some of the city's most desirable properties, and their mix of styles and sizes gives the stretch plenty of character. The pavement is separated from the river by a series of pretty gardens: these are private and belong to the houses opposite. Wealthy residents have decorated their plots with sculptures and exotic plants; even in deepest winter you might catch floral scents wafting by as you pass.

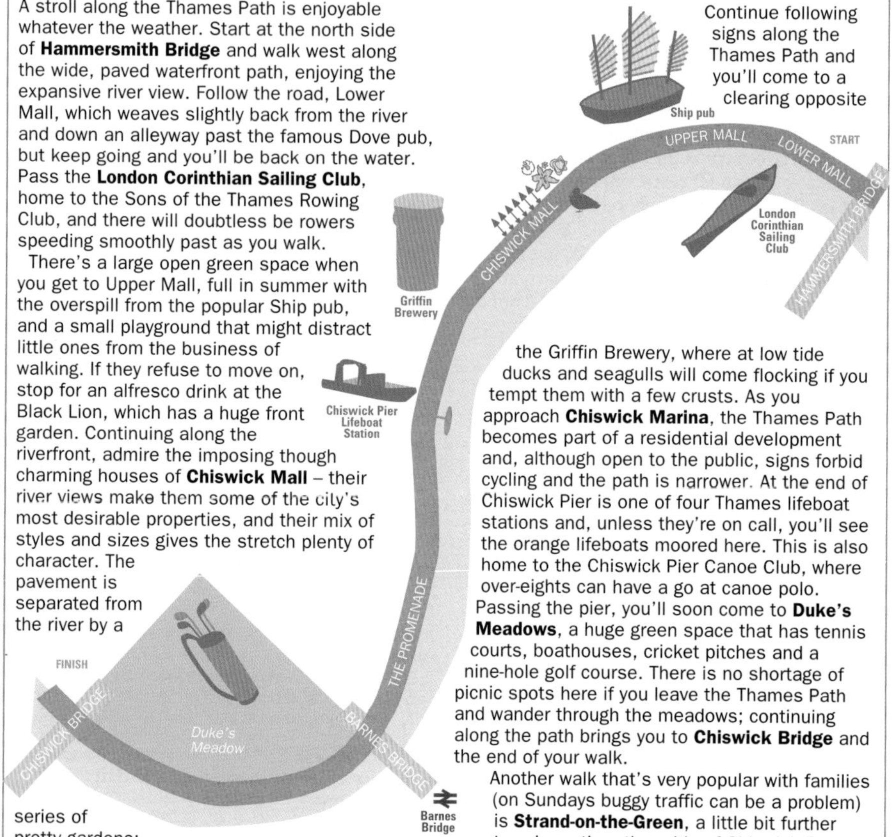

Continue following signs along the Thames Path and you'll come to a clearing opposite the Griffin Brewery, where at low tide ducks and seagulls will come flocking if you tempt them with a few crusts. As you approach **Chiswick Marina**, the Thames Path becomes part of a residential development and, although open to the public, signs forbid cycling and the path is narrower. At the end of Chiswick Pier is one of four Thames lifeboat stations, and unless they're on call, you'll see the orange lifeboats moored here. This is also home to the Chiswick Pier Canoe Club, where over-eights can have a go at canoe polo. Passing the pier, you'll soon come to **Duke's Meadows**, a huge green space that has tennis courts, boathouses, cricket pitches and a nine-hole golf course. There is no shortage of picnic spots here if you leave the Thames Path and wander through the meadows; continuing along the path brings you to **Chiswick Bridge** and the end of your walk.

Another walk that's very popular with families (on Sundays buggy traffic can be a problem) is **Strand-on-the-Green**, a little bit further westwards on the other side of Chiswick Bridge. During the 18th century, Strand-on-the-Green was a fishing community but now it's a particularly picturesque strolling spot, where there's a choice of child-friendly, but often busy, pubs with riverside terraces that serve food all day.

(map labels: Ship pub, UPPER MALL, LOWER MALL, START, London Corinthian Sailing Club, HAMMERSMITH BRIDGE, CHISWICK MALL, Griffin Brewery, Chiswick Pier Lifeboat Station, THE PROMENADE, FINISH, Duke's Meadow, CHISWICK BRIDGE, BARNES BRIDGE, Barnes Bridge)

Kew Bridge Steam Museum

Green Dragon Lane, Brentford, Middx TW8 0EN (8568 4757/www.kbsm.org). Gunnersbury tube, then 237 or 267 bus/Kew Bridge rail/65, 391 bus. **Open** 11am-5pm daily. Closed 20 Dec-4 Jan, Good Friday. **Tours** 1.30pm 1st Sat of mth Apr-Sept, book in advance. **Admission** (LP) *Mon-Fri* £4.25; £3.25 concessions; free under-16s. *Sat, Sun* £5.75; £4.75 concessions; free under-16s. Free to all after 4pm daily. Under-16s must be accompanied by an adult. **Credit** MC, V.

Visit this Victorian riverside pumping station on high days and holidays and it's all sound and fury, but the engines are only in steam on specific days, so ring before you set out. The historic Cornish beam engine is fired up at 3pm most weekends and holiday periods, and there are usually a couple of others powering away. During the school holidays and bank holidays, there's a lot of action, because the Education Department and friendly volunteers run all kinds of family activities. The popular Tower Open Days are now combined with special Behind the Scenes tours of the museum on the first Saturday of the month, from April to September, but places are very limited, so you'll have to book well in advance. Children, unfortunately, are not allowed to climb the 261 steps to the top of the tower because the handrails are too high – but adults will enjoy the impressive view.

Buggy access. Café. Disabled access: lift, ramps, toilet. Nappy-changing facilities. Nearest picnic place: Kew Green. Shop.

Syon House

Syon Park, Brentford, Middx TW8 8JF (8560 0882/
London Butterfly House 8560 0378/Tropical Forest
8847 4730/Snakes & Ladders 8847 0946/www.syon
park.co.uk). Gunnersbury tube/rail, then 237, 267 bus.
Open *House* mid Mar-late Oct 11am-5pm Wed, Thur,
Sun, bank hol Mon. Last entry 4.15pm. Closed late
Oct-mid Mar. *Gardens* Apr-Oct 10.30am-5.30pm daily.
Nov-Mar 10.30am-4pm daily. **Tours** by arrangement;
phone for details. **Admission** *House & gardens* £7.50;
£6.50 concessions, 5-16s; free under-5s; £17 family
(2+2). *Gardens only* £3.75; £2.50 concessions, 5-16s;
free under-5s; £9 family (2+2). *Tropical Forest* £5;
£3.75 3-15s; free under-3s; £15 family (2+3). *Butterfly*
House £5.25; £4.25 concessions; £3.95 3-16s; free
under-3s; £16 family (2+3). *Snakes & Ladders* £3
under-2s; £4 under-5s; £5 over-5s; adults free. Reduced
rate after 4pm. **Credit** MC, V.
This gracious, turreted Tudor mansion, and its extensive
grounds, is quite an adventure, but most children – let's be
realistic – find more thrills in the other attractions set out
here. Namely, the London Butterfly House, where you walk
through jungle-like surroundings as beautiful butterflies
flutter around you, or the Tropical Forest (formerly known
as the Aquatic Experience) with regular 'animal
encounters' sessions that allow children to get up close to
unusual creatures. Also, children yearn for Snakes &
Ladders, an indoor adventure playground designed like a
castle, with three tiers of play areas, including slides,
hanging ropes and masses of huge balls. There's also an
indoor motorised bike track (£1/ride) and, for the parents,
a café. This place positively heaves with boisterous kids
of a weekend. Bring a picnic in summer, as the nicest
eating locations are outside. In winter, the cafeteria has a
selection of hot meals and a junior menu.

Syon House was developed from a building dedicated to
the Bridgettine Order; following the Dissolution of the
Monasteries it was dedicated to providing Henry VIII with
another country seat. Each room seems more impressive
than the last, from the grand Roman hallway to the
crimson silk walls and Roman statues of the Red Drawing
Room. On Sundays a wooden mini steam railway travels
through the trees and around the flowerbeds.

The Butterfly House's days at Syon Park are numbered,
since the site is set for redevelopment – but, after some
wrangling, its future has been secured. The butterflies will
remain in Syon Park until the end of August 2006, after
which they will move to a wonderful new home in
Gunnersbury Park, where the tropical garden and the
aviary will both be bigger, and there will be further
facilities such as a café and various play options.
Organisers are hoping that any period of closure will be
brief and that the move will be seamless, with the new site
an improvement on Syon Park.
Café. Nappy-changing facilities. Nearest picnic place:
Syon House Gardens/Syon Park. Shop.

FURTHER WEST

In **Ealing**, at the westerly end of the District and
Central lines, you're never more than a toddler's
ramble from a park or open space, many of them
distinctly rural in character. The largest open
spaces are nestled around the Brent river, where
you can find golf courses, fields of ponies and
acres of common land. **Brent Lodge Park**, or

'Bunny Park', is a good place to start. It has
a lovely playground, maze and small zoo for
the bunnies and other cuddleworthy residents.
From here you can wander for hours along the
river in either direction. Other green spots
include Horsenden Hill, the highest point in
Ealing borough, with great views over the whole
of London; Ealing Common, close to the busy
high road; and Osterley Park, on the outskirts of
Hanwell. **Osterley House** is a gorgeous place
to visit, with a brilliant café. In summer there are
all sorts of events for children around the grounds.

The central green lung, where most parents
congregate, is **Walpole Park**. During July and
August the park hosts the majority of events that
comprise the Ealing Summer Festival, with lots
of child-friendly activities; phone Ealing Council
for details (8579 2424, www.ealing.gov.uk). The
playground here has a great range of play
equipment, and the park contains sumptuous
Pitshanger Manor. Ealing Town Hall is the
venue for parent and toddler groups throughout
the year, and also organises half-term children's
discos. The busy **Questors Theatre** (12 Mattock
Lane, W5 5BQ, 8567 0011, www.questors.org.uk)
runs acting workshops for all ages, and a
playgroup for six to tens.

Ealing has a number of sports centres; the most
interesting is the Gurnell Leisure Centre (Ruislip
Road East, W13 0AL, 8998 3241), which boasts
an Olympic-sized pool. Riders tack up at Ealing
Riding School (Gunnersbury Avenue, W5 3XD,
8992 3808), and Brent Valley Golf Course (Church
Road, Hanwell, W7 3BE, 8567 1287) is a good for
beginner golfers.

Further west of Ealing is Southall, home to
London's largest Asian community. This is the
venue for London's only surviving agricultural
market, auctioning horses each Wednesday.
It is also a great place to pick up saris, bangles,
sandals and other bits and bobs at bargain prices.
The largest Sikh temple outside India opened in
nearby **Hounslow** in 2003. The Sri Guru Singh
Sabha Gurdwara (Alice Way, Hanworth Road,
Hounslow TW3 3UA), second in size only to the
Golden Temple in Amritsar, has a capacity of
3,000 people. The glorious **Shri Swaminarayan**
Mandir Temple, to the north of Southall, is a
breathtakingly beautiful monument to Hinduism.

Hounslow Urban Farm, nearer Heathrow,
will bring you back to more earthy matters.

Brent Lodge Park

Church Road, W7 3BL (8825 7529). Hanwell rail.
Open 7.30am-dusk daily. *Maze & animals* May-Aug
10.30am-6pm daily. Apr, Sept, Oct 10.30am-5pm daily.
Nov-Mar 10.30am-4pm daily. **Admission** £1; 50p
concessions, 3-16s; free under-3s. **No credit cards.**

The Millennium Maze, planted here in 1999, continues to bulk up. Young explorers love standing triumphantly on the central tower once they've worked their way round, and anxious parents can stand on the viewing platform outside to locate squawking progeny. Walk up the hill from the maze for the hub of activities in this sweet and well-maintained local park: there's a café for ice-cream and sandwiches, a playground with slides and swings and an animal centre. The centre houses a handful of squirrel monkeys, a pair of sleepy geckos and some scary spiders, along with a few birds and plenty of more run-of-the-mill domestic pets, such as bunnies and guinea pigs.
Buggy access (no access to animal area). Café. Disabled access: toilet.

Heathrow Airport Visitor Centre

Newall Road, Middx UB3 5AP (8745 6655/www.ba. com). Hatton Cross tube, then 285, 555, 556, 557 bus/Heathrow Terminal 1, 2 & 3 tube, then 105, 111, 140, 285, 555, 556, 557 bus to Bath Road. **Open** 10am-5pm daily. **Admission** free. **Credit** shop MC, V.
This small but rewarding centre explains how Heathrow has grown over 50 years into the world's busiest airport. Once you've collected your picture I-Spy for tiny ones and fun quizzes for the six and overs, plus paper and crayons for brass rubbings, the first thing you come to is a check-in desk with scales for you to weigh your 'luggage'. The staff are quite relaxed about small children weighing themselves (but do draw the line at adults trying the same). Further amusement is to be had testing the Archway Metal Detectors by setting off the alarms. You can also see a bag as viewed through the X-ray. Two aircraft seats are great for practising before a family's first flight: you can show the kids how to buckle in with the seat belts. Most fun, though, is the flight simulator, which lands (of course) at Heathrow. At the far end of the ground floor there is a collection of illegal items intercepted by customs, including some endangered species. You will also find interactive displays on what the airport is doing for the environment, covering everything from public transport to noise management and local wildlife. Finally, you can visit the café, and watch the planes take off and land through the enormous panoramic window.
Buggy access. Café. Disabled access: toilet. Nappy-changing facilities. Shop.

Hounslow Urban Farm

A312 at Faggs Road, Feltham, Middx TW14 0LZ (8751 0850/www.cip.com). Hatton Cross tube, then 20min walk or 90, 285, 490 bus. **Open** 10am-4pm daily. **Admission** £3.50; £2.75 concessions; £2 2-16s; free under-2s; £10 (2+2) family. **No credit cards.**
At 29 acres (11.7ha) this is London's largest community farm. There are pigs, goats, numerous varieties of duck, Exmoor ponies and more, with feeding time at 3.30pm daily. The farm has a conservation programme – endangered and historic breeds of domestic livestock are reared here. Most fascinating is a visit during lthe breeding season: turn up at the right time and you could be lucky enough to see brand new lambs, goats or even a litter of piglets. Orphan lambs need to be bottle-fed and children are sometimes allowed to help. There's a playground (with, we're delighted to report, pedal tractors), a picnic area and a kiosk for food and refreshments.
Buggy access. Disabled access: toilet. Kiosk. Nappy-changing facilities.

Osterley House

Osterley Park, off Jersey Road, Isleworth, Middx TW7 4RB (8232 5050/recorded information 01494 755566/www.nationaltrust.org.uk/osterley). Osterley tube. **Open** *House* late Mar-Oct 1-4.30pm Wed-Sun, bank hol Mon. *Park* 9am-7.30pm daily. **Tours** by arrangement; minimum 15 people. **Admission** (NT) *House* £4.90; £2.40 5-15s; free under-5s; £12.20 family (2+3). *Park.* **Credit** *Tearoom/shop only* MC, V.
Osterley House was built for Sir Thomas Gresham (founder of the Royal Exchange) in 1576, but transformed by Robert Adam in 1761. Adam's revamp is dominated by the imposing colonnade of white pillars before the courtyard of the house's red-brick body. The splendour of the state rooms alone makes the house worth the visit, but the still-used Tudor stables, the vast parkland walks and the ghost said to be lurking in the basement add to Osterley's allure. Children can pick up a house trail from the office to help them explore these delightful surroundings and regular kiddie events include kite-making workshops, interactive historical tours of the house, bluebell walks, outdoor performances and the annual free Osterley Day, always full of arts and fun (10 July 2005). Family Fun Days take place on Mondays in August (1, 8, 15, 22 Aug 2005) and, this year, have 1940s themed activities for everyone to join in at 1, 2 and 3pm; check the website for details.
Café. Car park (£3.50/day, NT members free). Disabled access: lift, toilet. Nappy-changing facilities. Nearest picnic place: front lawn/picnic benches in grounds. Shop.

Pitshanger Manor & Gallery

Walpole Park, Mattock Lane, W5 5EQ (8567 1227/ www.ealing.gov.uk/pmgallery&house). Ealing Broadway tube/rail/65 bus. **Open** *May-Sept* 1-5pm Tue-Fri, Sun; 11am-5pm Sat. *Oct-Apr* 1-5pm Tue-Fri; 11am-5pm Sat. Closed bank hols. **Tours** by arrangement; phone for details. **Admission** free.
Most of Pitshanger, a beautiful Regency villa, was rebuilt between 1801-3 by Sir John Soane. His individual ideas in design and decoration make this a very special place. Among the exhibits is the Hull Grundy Martinware collection of pottery, and there is an art gallery where contemporary exhibitions are held, plus a lecture and workshop programme for all ages. The manor is also home to the Waitrose Children's and Young People's Gallery, which hosts changing exhibitions of artwork by local children and young people.
Buggy access. Disabled access: lift, ramp (gallery only), toilet. Nearest picnic place: Walpole Park.

Shri Swaminarayan Mandir Temple

105-119 Brentfield Road, NW10 8LD (8965 2651/www.swaminarayan.org). Wembley Park tube, then BR2 bus/Neasden tube, then 15min walk. **Open** 9.30am-6pm daily. **Admission** (LP) free. *Exhibition* £2; £1.50 6-15s; free under-6s. **Credit** AmEx, MC, V.
Built in 1995, this beautiful Hindu temple is an extraordinary structure, intricately carved by master sculptors. Much of the stone was sent to India to be carved and then brought back to Neasden – at a cost of more than £10m. It also has a permanent exhibition, with a video, called 'Understanding Hinduism'; it's particularly useful for those in Years 6 and 7 studying world religion. Stock up on incense sticks at the shop and you can try to recreate the temple's serenity at home.
Buggy access. Café. Disabled access: lift, toilet. Nappy-changing facilities. Shop.

CONSUMER

EATING

The complete guide for minor diners.

Babies and children are, of course, allowed in almost every London restaurant; only the starchiest establishment would object to customers arriving *en famille*. But there's a world of difference between being merely tolerated and being positively welcomed. What's more, it's not always the places with the great kids' menus, the crayons and other paraphernalia that actually turn out to be the most accommodating. We've inflicted babies, toddlers and even the occasional over-excited birthday party on the establishments in this chapter and, while they may not have always been completely prepared for the onslaught, they have all shown themselves to be genuinely child-friendly. Sometimes that has meant an all-singing, all-dancing children's facility but, more often than not, charming staff and a flexible kitchen willing to turn out half portions was all that was needed. Apart from lashings of ketchup, that is.

Wherever appropriate, we have included contact details for other branches of restaurants listed in this chapter, but not all branches have the same facilities. For handy places to eat in a particular area, look for the **Lunch box** round-ups in **Around Town** (*see pp30-158*).

SOUTH BANK & BANKSIDE

Cantina del Ponte

Butlers Wharf Building, 36C Shad Thames, SE1 2YE (7403 5403/www.conran.com). Tower Hill tube/ London Bridge tube/rail. **Lunch served** noon-3pm daily. **Dinner served** 6-11pm Mon-Sat; 6-10pm Sun. **Main courses** £7-£14.50. **Credit** AmEx, DC, MC, V. **Map** p319 R8.

Even if you didn't know already, the mirrors around the walls and the metallic boom that obliges everyone to shout to be heard would tip you off that this is a Conran venue. Still, at least you won't feel self-conscious about noisy kids. Staff are quite helpful, and the cooking style here is more sprog-friendly than the grander Conrans – classic Italian-rustic, including pizza. An affordable kids' menu and the terrace on Butlers Wharf are added attractions.
Buggy access. Children's menu. Tables outdoors (terrace).

fish!

Cathedral Street, Borough Market, SE1 9DE (7407 3803/www.fishdiner.co.uk). London Bridge tube/rail. **Meals served** 11.30am-3pm, 5-10.45pm Mon-Fri; noon-11pm Sat; noon-10.30pm Sun. **Main courses** £8.90-£16.95. **Credit** AmEx, MC, V. **Map** p317 M8.

Gourmands who routinely shop for top-notch groceries in neighbouring Borough Market may not flinch at the prices here, but when you're feeding a family, fish! can hardly be called an economy option. That said, though, the standard of the food has improved since the downsizing of the chain under the Loco aegis – even the grilled chicken, chips and ice-cream on the children's menu (£6.95) were excellent.
Buggy access. Children's menu (£6.95). Crayons. High chairs. No-smoking tables. Tables outdoors (24, pavement).
Branches: Loco, County Hall, Belvedere Road, SE1 7GP (7401 6734); Loco, 1 Lawn Terrace, Blackheath, SE3 9LJ (8852 0700); Loco, 222 Munster Road, Fulham, SW6 6AY (7381 6137).

Konditor & Cook

10 Stoney Street, SE1 9AD (7407 5100/ www.konditorandcook.com). London Bridge tube/rail. **Meals served** 7.30am-6pm Mon-Fri; 8.30am-5pm Sat. **Main courses** £2-£5. **Credit** AmEx, MC, V. **Map** p319 P8.

This is one of our favourite mini chains. The inside is minimalist, with bare floorboards and bench seating, and tables outside in good weather. Staff are professional rather than chatty. Sandwiches, in a variety of imaginative combos (including veggie and vegan), are great value at around £2.75. Other hot dishes include soups, pizzas, vegetarian tagine and kedgeree. Even the drinks are well thought-out, including juices from the Innocent range and organic fizzy juices. What's more, the deservedly legendary brownies, treacle tarts and Curly Whirly (chocolate and vanilla) cake work like gold ingots in the world of juvenile bribery.
Buggy access. Disabled access: toilets. Tables outdoors.
Branches: 22 Cornwall Road, SE1 8TW (7261 0456); 46 Gray's Inn Road, WC1X 8LR (7404 6300).

Tas

72 Borough High Street, SE1 1XF (7403 7200/ www.tasrestaurant.com). London Bridge tube/rail. **Meals served** noon-11.30pm Mon-Sat; noon-10.30pm Sun. **Main courses** £6.75-£14.45. **Credit** AmEx, MC, V. **Map** p319 P8.

It's always a good idea, when eating out with children, to choose a place that's generous with the bread basket, and where you can order a variety of inexpensive, small dishes for everyone to try. Tas, a smart, modern Anatolian mini chain, scores on both these points. The menus of hot and cold meze (soups, houmous, tabouleh or cracked wheat salad, feta salad, spinach, pasta, shish kebabs and pastries) are great for sharing, and served with plentiful own-made pide (Turkish flatbread). Main dishes such as swordfish steak with peppers, chicken kebab or lamb casserole are made with super-fresh ingredients, and the chocolate cake, bakalava and ice-creams on the pudding menu are all terrific. Prices are reasonable and the waiting staff seemed to be genuinely pleased to see families with young children on the weekend lunchtimes we have visited.

Konditor & Cook.

Buggy access. Disabled access: toilets. High chairs.
Nappy-changing facilities.
Branches: 22 Bloomsbury Street, WC1B 3QJ
(7637 4555); 33 The Cut, SE1 8LF (7928 2111);
Tas EV, 97-99 Isabella Street, SE1 8DA (7620 6191);
Tas Pide, 37 Farringdon Road, EC1M 3JB (7430
9721/9722); Tas Pide, 20-22 New Globe Walk, SE1 9DR
(7633 9777).

THE CITY

The Place Below

St Mary-le-Bow Church, Cheapside, EC2V 6AU
(7329 0789/www.theplacebelow.co.uk). St Paul's tube/
Bank tube/DLR. **Breakfast served** 7.30-11am,
lunch served 11.30am-2.30pm, **snacks served**
7.30am-3pm Mon-Fri. **Main courses** £5-£7.50.
Credit MC, V. **Map** p318 P6.
If you visit this City oasis at non-peak dining times, you
may even have the atmospheric dining room, with its
impressive domed ceiling, columns and alcoves, to yourselves – and get £2 off main-course prices as well. The
soups with own-made bread are satisfying, sometimes sub-
lime (fennel, green pea and mint deserves special mention),
as is the daily changing choice of quiche. Other freshly
made hot dishes and leafy salads, a 'healthbowl' (whole-
grain brown rice, puy lentils and seasonal vegetables, with
sesame and ginger dressing) and filled ciabatta rolls are
also available. You can distract the kids with Valrhona
chocolate brownies, and energise yourself with good,
strong Illy coffee (a bargain at 80p).
No smoking. Tables outdoors (20, courtyard).
Takeaway service. Vegan dishes.

Shish

313 Old Street, EC1V 9LE (7749 0990/
www.shish.com). Old Street tube/rail. **Meals served**
11.30am-11.30pm Mon-Fri; 10.30am-11.30pm Sat;
10.30am-10.30pm Sun. **Main courses** £4-£10. **Credit**
AmEx, MC, V. **Map** p309.
The second branch of this 'Silk Road' restaurant covers
cuisine from Turkey to Indonesia, and has a first-rate juice
bar in the main restaurant, perfect for smuggling some vitamins into junior diners (try the striped mixed fruit juice).
For adults, there's a fixed 'Silk Road' choice of dishes, plus
a shifting menu (Middle Eastern when we visited), while
the £4.25 kids' menu offers fish cakes, Mediterranean
chicken or a falafel and houmous wrap (all served with rice,
chips or salad), followed by an ice-cream or sorbet. Tasty,
healthy and great value. The restaurant has something of
a canteen feel, yet was less busy than we expected. In the
past, Shish has seemed to emphasise the decor above the
food, but this wasn't the case on our most recent visit.
Buggy access. Children's menu (£4.25). High chairs.
No smoking.
Branches: 2-6 Station Parade, Willesden Green,
NW2 4NH (8208 9290).

Smiths of Smithfield

67-77 Charterhouse Street, EC1M 6HJ (7251 7950/
www.smithsofsmithfield.co.uk). Farringdon tube/rail.
Meals served *Ground-floor bar/café* 7am-4.30pm
Mon; 7am-5pm Tue-Fri; 10am-5pm Sat; 9.30am-5pm
Sun. **Main courses** £3.50-£8.50. **Credit** AmEx, MC,
V. **Map** p318 O5.
As much fun for children as their parents, Smiths retains
an industrial, New York warehouse feel, with exposed
bricks, reclaimed wood, metal tubing and raw concrete. Of

the four storeys, the ground floor is the most laid-back, serving breakfast, brunch and other casual fare (kids will love the legendary bacon sarnies). Upstairs is a cocktail and champagne bar, followed by the second-floor Dining Room and the Top Floor restaurant (both more serious showcases for John Torode's accomplished British cuisine). Below decks, meanwhile, the Smiths beef burger with cheddar cheese and Old Spot bacon followed by vanilla ice-cream, hot chocolate fudge sauce and honeycomb is a guaranteed winning combo.

Buggy access. Disabled access: lift, toilets. High chairs. Nappy-changing facilities. Tables outdoors (6, pavement).

HOLBORN & CLERKENWELL

Bank Aldwych

1 Kingsway, WC2B 6XF (7379 9797/ www.bankrestaurants.com). Holborn or Temple tube. **Breakfast served** 7-10.30am Mon-Fri. **Brunch served** 11.30am-3pm Sat; 11.30am-4.30pm Sun. **Lunch served** noon-3pm Mon-Fri. **Dinner served** 5.30-11pm Mon-Sat. **Main courses** £9.50-£32. **Set meal** (lunch, 5.30-7pm, 10-11pm) £13.50 2 courses, £16 3 courses. **Credit** AmEx, DC, MC, V. **Map** p315 M6.

The vast chandelier, the mirrored walls and the red leather seating all give a sense of fun to this friendly, glamorous restaurant. Staff are appealingly down to earth and seem used to dealing with families (they delivered a high chair within moments of us sitting down). On the children's menu, dishes like chipolatas and mash or linguine with tomato sauce are tasty gap-fillers, while sticky toffee pud is a suitably messy finale. Otherwise, delicate seared tuna with miso dressing or organic salmon with broccoli and mousseline sauce are the kind of things you can expect to be eating. At weekends, there's a brunch-time activities table with crayons, puzzles and toys.

Booking advisable. Buggy access. Children's menu (£7.25). Crayons (weekends only). High chairs. Nappy-changing facilities.

BLOOMSBURY & FITZROVIA

Abeno

47 Museum Street, WC1A 1LY (7405 3211). Holborn tube. **Meals served** noon-10pm daily. **Main courses** £6.50-£39.60. **Set lunches** £7.50-£19.80 incl miso soup, rice. **Credit** AmEx, DC, JCB, MC, V. **Map** p317 L5.

An appealing Japanese bolt-hole, Abeno's culinary style, okonomiyaki (literally, 'cooking what you like'), makes a humble meal of vegetables and/or meat mixed with batter much more exciting by setting the action at your table. OK, the waitress does all the actual cooking – from mixing your ingredients and depositing them on the table-top hot plate, to flipping your 'pancake' once the first side has browned nicely – but you get to decorate the result with a choice of mayonnaise, fruit and vegetable sauce (sweeter than tonkatsu sauce), dried seaweed, shaved fish and chilli sauce. It's all good fun to watch and the results are delicious and delightfully finger-friendly. A second branch opened recently near Leicester Square.

Buggy access. High chair.
Branches: Abeno Too, 15-18 Great Newport Street, SC2H 7JE (7379 1160).

TOP 5 Cakes

Amato
Italian pastries in the heart of Soho. *See p166.*

Konditor & Cook
This mini chain is the stuff of legend. *See p160.*

Ottolenghi
A top-notch deli/café, with branches in Notting Hill and Islington. *See p176.*

Paul
Classy, picture-perfect pâtisserie in a Parisian-café setting. *See p171.*

Sabzi
Organic cakes near Oxford Circus. *See p168.*

Carluccio's Caffè

8 Market Place, W1W 8AG (7636 2228/ www.carluccios.com). Meals served 7.30am-11pm Mon-Fri; 10am-11pm Sat; 10am-10pm Sun. **Main courses** £4.85-£10.95. **Credit** AmEx, MC, V. **Map** p314 J6.

Although deservedly popular, this cleverly conceived luncheonette – the original West End branch of what has become a widespread chain – was a little dishevelled on our last visit. Still, the food is so reasonably priced and delicious, and the staff seem so genuinely pleased to have *bambini* in their midst, that a little tattiness is easy to forgive. The bread basket warrants a mention (fresh, fragrant and moreish), while the junior menu always has a fresh pasta dish and a mini fistful of breadsticks or the like. Grown-up risottos and other hearty main courses, along with decent wines, are enough to keep parents entertained. Gorgeous pastries and excellent coffee make this a good pit stop, too (ask for cups of hot foamy milk for the kids).

Buggy access. Children's menu (£4.95). Disabled access: toilets. No-smoking tables. Tables outdoors (15, pavement).
Branches: throughout town. Call or check the website.

North Sea Fish Restaurant

7-8 Leigh Street, WC1H 9EW (7387 5892). Russell Square tube/King's Cross tube/rail/68, 168 bus. **Lunch served** noon-2.30pm, **dinner served** 5.30-10.30pm Mon-Sat. **Main courses** £7.25-£17.95. **Credit** AmEx, MC, V. **Map** p315 L3/4.

There's something deliciously old-fashioned about this chintzy diner that makes it a firm favourite with visiting Americans, artisans and local academics. The decor – dark wood beams, stippled walls and red velvet upholstery – brings to mind *Carry On Up the Khyber*, Carnaby Street and Eamonn Andrews. The waitresses combine efficiency with matronly charm. Starters of fish cakes (big and fishy) and scampi (sweet and succulent) were hard to fault, as were the golden haddock and cod that followed. Battered fish comes in two sizes: jumbo and standard, and the standard was jumbo enough for us. Own-made tartare sauce, mushy peas and baskets of first-rate chips are the accompaniments, with the sweets menu offering the likes of apple crumble and trifle.

Buggy access. High chair. No-smoking tables. Takeaway service.

great for little
grown ups too!

every family loves wagamama
fast and fresh noodle and rice dishes, freshly squeezed
juices served in a friendly, smoke free restaurant

for menu and locations visit **www.wagamama.com**
uk ı ireland ı amsterdam ı australia ı dubai ı antwerp ı auckland

positive eating + positive living

wagamama

La Galette *See p166.*

Strada

9-10 Market Place, W1W 8AQ (7580 4644/
www.strada.co.uk). Oxford Circus tube. **Meals**
served noon-11pm Mon-Sat, noon-10.30pm Sun.
Main courses £6.50-£13.95. **Credit** AmEx, MC, V.
Map p314 J6.

This modish, capital-wide chain has been expanding at a
gentle rate, presumably in the hope of maintaining standards. Going on our visit to the Fitzrovia branch, spread
over two handsome floors and a chunk of pavement, it
seems to be working (although a couple of duff dishes did
make us wonder). Generally, though, Strada is a haven for
simple Italian food – the pizzas, in particular, are well
above average (thanks, in part, to a wood-burning oven)
and have toppings that are about as fresh as you'll find in
any London pizzeria. And while there's no children's menu
as such, half portions are available for most dishes. Service
is speedy if a little ditzy, but the complimentary filtered
water delivered immediately to every table garners the
place a huge pile of brownie points.
Buggy access. High chairs. No-smoking tables.
Tables outdoors (12, pavement). Takeaway service.
Branches: throughout town. Call or check the website.

MARYLEBONE

Fairuz

3 Blandford Street, W1H 3AA (7486 8108/8182).
Baker Street or Bond Street tube. **Meals served**
noon-11.30pm Mon-Sat; noon-10.30pm Sun. **Main**
courses £9.95-£12.95. **Set meals** £18.95 meze,
£26.95 4 courses. *Cover* £1.50. **Credit** AmEx, MC, V.
Map p314 G5.

The most welcoming of London's Lebanese restaurants (a
notoriously starchy bunch), Fairuz remains the best bet
for a family meal. A fold-back frontage with pavement
seating and a Mediterranean-flavoured interior of lemon

yellow and duck-egg blue entice passing trade, but it's the
quality of the food that's built up Fairuz's following. The
menu is standard Lebanese with an expansive offering of
around 50 hot and cold meze – all great for little fingers to
dip into. Fluffy falafel come with a miniature pot of tahina;
chicken livers are made child-friendly with a marinade of
lemon and pomegranate juice. Of the mains, farouj
mousakhan is a stand-out – a duvet of flatbread filled with
chicken pieces smothered in fried onions and parsley and
baked in the oven.
Booking advisable. High chairs. Tables outdoors
(4, pavement).

Giraffe

6-8 Blandford Street, W1H 3AA (7935 2333/
www.giraffe.net). Baker Street or Bond Street tube.
Meals served 8am-11pm daily. **Main courses**
£7.95-£10.95. **Set meals** (5-7pm) £6.95 2 courses;
(7-11pm) £8.95 2 courses. **Credit** AmEx, MC, V.
Map p314 G5.

Such is the popularity of the Giraffe chain that queueing
is near-inevitable at busy times, but chirpy, attentive staff
try to ensure the wait is painless – and various colouring
books and toys are on hand to prevent the younger contingent from getting too fractious. Once seated, rather than
being fobbed off with the usual burger and fries menu
(although that's on offer, too), kids get the chance to tuck
into a falafel or a cheese toastie or a virtuous dessert like
organic fresh fruit. Parents, meanwhile, can choose
between brunch dishes such as pancakes or a full-English
fry-up, salads, dips and snacks, burgers, several vegetarian choices, Tex-Mex burritos, steaks, daily specials and
Asian-oriented dishes like thai chicken or miso and lime-
grilled salmon. There's a varied drinks list too: yummy
mixed-fruit smoothies, teas or coffees, cocktails and decent
wines. The Giraffe chain continues to stretch its neck into
well-to-do outposts of the city: we visited a very fine branch
in Muswell Hill recently (8883 4463).

Don't let them hamper you

If the thought of being shut inside a restaurant with hyperactive toddlers is a little too much to cope with, why not gather together the necessaries for a picnic and transpose your meal to the great outdoors? There are dozens of places dotted around the city where you can procure simple, tasty toddler fuel (Marmite or peanut butter sarnies, whopping slices of cake, etc) while getting something a little more sophisticated for yourself. Below, we've listed a few of the best.

Starting in the centre, there are the cheesy delights of **Neal's Yard Dairy** (17 Short's Gardens, WC2H 9UP, 7240 5700), where you'll find a dizzying array of produce from artisan cheesemakers across the country, alongside breads, biscuits, chutneys and some lovely jams for the kids. Soho Square and the South Bank are equidistant from here, so choose your setting as the mood dictates. Also central, and conveniently placed for Regent's Park with its summer bandstand, fun boats and rowdy geese, is **Base Bistro** (195 Baker Street, NW1 6UY, 7486 7000) where everything is freshly made on the premises: choose from sandwiches, wraps, soups, pasta, risottos, pizzas, crêpes, cakes and much more. The madeleines, in particular, are worth a dunk.

Heading south, and perfectly positioned for those intending to spread a rug on Clapham Common, the **North Street Deli** (26 North Street, SW4 0HB, 7978 1555) has a mouth-watering variety of victuals. Marcus Miller's breads (Miller supplies Gordon Ramsay, among others) form the base, while toppings encompass a few carefully chosen cheeses, excellent cured meats and hams (from eight suppliers), and a wide range of bottled and packaged deli items. Oh, and let's not forget the gorgeous cakes (or the sausage rolls, for that matter) for the junior contingent.

A little further east, the **East Dulwich Deli** (15-17 Lordship Lane, SE22 8EW, 8693 2525) is well placed for a stop-off en route to Peckham Rye Common or Dulwich Park. Shelves reach the high ceiling in colourful bursts of intriguing jars and parcels, panettones hang from the ceiling, and everything from cured meats and cheeses to fat olives (a favourite of many children) lurk in the vast chiller cabinet. There are some decent bottles of plonk, too, for anyone who's not driving home.

Up north, you'd be hard pressed to find better than **Rosslyn Delicatessen** (56 Rosslyn Hill, NW3 1ND, 7794 9210), just down the road from Hampstead Heath. Own-made pickles and preserves are something of a speciality (hot seaweed chutney, anyone?) but you'll find plenty more besides: oriental and Middle Eastern groceries, pastas, cheeses, cold meats, tarts and salads, and some extraordinary flavoured oils (such as avocado with chipotle). They also provide ready-made picnic hampers in summer, but where's the fun in that?

Finally, on the east side of the map, **Flâneur Food Hall** (41A Farringdon Road, EC1M 3JB, 7404 4422), right around the corner from Clerkenwell Green, has storybook floor-to-ceiling displays that will leave young mouths hanging open. You'll encounter a mind-boggling range of outlandish oils (pine kernel, melon seed and the rest), preserves and honeys, but kids' attention will most likely be grabbed by the lip-smacking own-made tarts and cakes. Cheeses are attractively displayed on straw; many are from Neal's Yard. Your only problem here, in fact, will be the smell of coffee and the clinking of crockery that emanate from the adjacent restaurant, tempting you to abandon all plans of a picnic and stay right where you are. Be strong.

Consumer

Balloons. Buggy access. Children's menu (£2.95-£4.95).
Crayons. High chairs. No smoking. Tables outdoors
(5, pavement & patio). Toys.
Branches: throughout town. Call or check the website.

La Galette

56 Paddington Street, W1U 4HY (7935 1554/
www.lagalette.com). Baker Street or Bond Street tube.
Meals served 9.30am-11pm Mon-Fri; 10am-11pm
Sat, Sun. **Main courses** £3.95-£8.95. **Set lunch**
(noon-5pm Mon-Fri) £7.95 2 courses. **Credit** AmEx,
MC, V. **Map** p314 G5.
The galette is the savoury, buckwheat sibling of the crêpe
– a hearty Breton staple, and the Parisian equivalent to the
post-pub kebab. At this restaurant it gets very near to
being glamorous, cooked with a feather-light touch and
served in a setting that owes more to Scandinavia (lovely
warm lamps and classy pale woods) than it does to *vieille*
France (red velvet curtains and a few banquettes). Thin,
judiciously crisp and not too buttery, the galettes are a
delight: the paysanne with lardons (small bacon cubes),
cream and onions was miraculously light, while the wild
mushrooms in the forestière had a lovely, earthy meati-
ness. Sweet crêpes, though, are what many children will
be waiting for, and high-quality toppings such as melted
dark chocolate will ensure they aren't disappointed.
Bookings not accepted for fewer than 6 people. Buggy
access. High chairs. No smoking. Tables outdoors
(2, terrace).

WEST END

Amato

14 Old Compton Street, W1D 4TH (7734 5733/
www.amato.co.uk). Leicester Square or Tottenham
Court Road tube. **Open** 8am-10pm Mon-Sat; 10am-
8pm Sun. **Main courses** £5.50-£8.50. **Credit** AmEx,
DC, MC, V. **Map** p315 K6.
At one end of the café a large picture of Marilyn Monroe
sets the theme, while art deco posters across the other walls
add splashes of colour. The window might be a showcase
for towering, multi-tiered cakes, but inside warm hues of
maroon-coloured tabletops and dark wood chairs provide
an easygoing informality. Take your pick from calorie-
laden cakes, tarts and rich breads, or go all out for the substantial pastas or quiche. Service is welcoming, no matter
how small the order.
Bookings not accepted. Booster chair. Buggy access.
Takeaway service.

Benihana

37 Sackville Street, W1S 3DQ (7494 2525/
www.benihana.co.uk). Piccadilly Circus tube. **Lunch**
served noon-3pm daily. **Dinner served** 5.30-10.30pm
Mon-Sat; 5-10pm Sun. **Set meals** *Lunch* £8.75-£25
4 courses. *Dinner* £17-£50 6 courses. **Credit** AmEx,
DC, MC, V. **Map** p316 J7.
Benihana, an international chain with three branches in
London, has been around for donkey's years but is undeniably popular. And why not? The place is fun. Diners sit
at large, half-moon-shaped teppanyaki tables and make
their selection of meat and/or fish (teriyaki steak, tuna or
chicken, prawns, filet mignon, lobster tails), after which
the chefs claim centre stage. Knives are released from hol-
sters, and vegetables and fish are sacrificed for the chefs
to show off their (admittedly awesome) cutting skills.

Pepperpots fly through the air, to squeals of delight from
the youngsters. 'Japanese prawns,' prompts the chef. 'From
Tokyo?' asks a guest. 'Fresh from Tesco.' The jokes are as
corny as they are well-rehearsed, but who cares?
Buggy access. Disabled access: toilets. High chairs.
Nappy-changing facilities. Takeaway service.
Branches: 77 King's Road, SW3 4NX (7376 7799);
100 Avenue Road, NW3 3HF (7586 9508).

Ed's Easy Diner

12 Moor Street, W1V 5LH (7439 1955/
www.edseasydiner.co.uk). Leicester Square or
Tottenham Court Road tube. **Meals served** *Winter*
11.30am-11.30pm Mon-Thur; 11.30am-midnight Fri,
Sat; 11.30am-11pm Sun. *Summer* 11.30am-midnight
Mon-Thur; 11.30am-1am Fri, Sat; 11.30am-11.30pm
Sun. **Main courses** £4.40-£7.90. *Minimum* (peak hrs)
main course. **Credit** MC, V. **Map** p315 K6.
This souped-up 1950s-style diner has been saving the lives
of weary, hungry parents for many years. Its inexpensive,
freshly made burgers are a giant, delicious step up from
standard fast food (made-to-order, greasy in just the right
way, with the cheese of your choice and all the usual fix-
ings), and the shakes and malts are also excellent (the butterscotch malt is a dessert in itself). High stools (probably
not a great idea for the under-fours) are fun to perch on,
and a counter-side jukebox will occupy even the shortest
of attention spans, as will the jelly bean dispenser.
Buggy access. Children's menu (£4.95 incl drink).
No smoking. Tables outdoors (2, pavement).
Takeaway service.
Branches: 15 Great Newport Street, WC2H 7JE
(7836 0271); 362 King's Road, SW3 5BT (7352 1956);
19 Rupert Street, W1D 7PA (7287 1951); O2 Centre,
255 Finchley Road, NW3 5UZ (7431 1958).

The Fountain

Ground floor, Fortnum & Mason, 181 Piccadilly,
W1A 1ER (7734 8040). Piccadilly Circus or Green
Park tube. **Meals served** 8.30am-7.30pm Mon-Sat.
Main courses £9-£25. **Credit** AmEx, DC, JCB, MC, V.
Map p316 J7.
The least formal of the two restaurants in this dignified
department store, the Fountain looks as if it has been furnished by someone who enjoys sitting in conservatories,
doing jigsaw puzzles, dabbling in watercolours and so on.
And very nice it is, too. The children's menu is great value
and there are some satisfying (if not so cheap) dishes on
the adult version (calf's liver with mash and whatnot).
Desserts, especially, are homely and wholly satisfying:
blackberry and pear crumble with clotted cream seemed
to bring with it the smell of a country kitchen and the drone
of bees in a rose garden; sundaes such as Knickerbocker
Glory and Dusty Road provide grandparents with a final
chance to crank up sugar levels one notch further before
handing the little 'uns back to Mum and Dad.
Buggy access. Children's menu (£5-£5.75). Crayons.
High chairs. Nappy-changing facilities (in shop, until
6.30pm). No-smoking tables (will be no smoking
throughout from Jan 2006).

Harbour City

46 Gerrard Street, W1D 5QH (7439 7859). Leicester
Square or Piccadilly Circus tube. **Dim sum served**
noon-5pm Mon-Sat; 11am-5pm Sun. **Meals served**
noon-11.30pm Mon-Thur; noon-midnight Fri, Sat; 11am-
10.30pm Sun. **Main courses** £6-£20. **Map** p317 K7.

Consumer

One of the Chinatown restaurants with a high proportion of Chinese customers (we know it's a cliché, but it really is a good sign), Harbour City offers some quite interesting cooking – especially on the Chinese-language menu. But if you're sitting down to a family meal, then dim sum is probably your best bet. A recent sampling of this menu produced some superb taro spring rolls (sweet, sumptuous taro paste encased in perfectly crisp pastry), steamed crab and coriander dumplings with frilly, cockscomb tops, and vegetarian spinach dumplings infused with the tastes of fried garlic and sesame oil. Following a thorough refurbishment, the decor is now bright and tasteful. Service is adequate but unremarkable.

Buggy access. High chairs. No-smoking tables. Takeaway service.

Hard Rock Café

150 Old Park Lane, W1K 1QR (7629 0382/ www.hardrock.com). Hyde Park Corner tube. **Meals served** 11.30am-12.30am Mon-Thur, Sun; 11.30am-1am Fri, Sat. **Main courses** £7.95-£14.95. *Minimum* (when busy) main course. **Credit** AmEx, DC, MC, V. **Map** p316 H8.

There are only two excuses for ending up in this brash, noisy slice of Americana: first, that you have children; second, that… nope, it seems there was only one excuse, after all. But whether it's Rocky the man-sized guitar mascot or just serendipity that brings you to its door, you're unlikely to leave the Hard Rock disappointed. It has everything a child could want: face-painting at certain times, a Lil' Rocker children's menu with all kinds of pizza, pasta and, of course, burger creations (plus a free colouring book and crayons), as well as themed activities from time to time (Hallowe'en parties and such like). Adults, on the other hand, do not fare so well, although occasional high spots like the generous, cheesy nachos or some fine salads can help to take the edge off otherwise lacklustre grub, impatient but polite waitresses and a loud, impersonally friendly setting. Still, good parenting is all about making sacrifices. Right?

Buggy access. Children's menu (£5.95). Crayons. Entertainment: occasional face-painting Sat, Sun. High chairs. No-smoking (allowed in bar only after 10pm). Tables outdoors (10, pavement).

Hong Kong

6-7 Lisle Street, WC2H 7BG (7287 0352). Leicester Square or Piccadilly Circus tube. **Dim sum served** noon-5pm daily. **Meals served** noon-11.30pm Mon-Thur; noon-midnight Fri, Sat; 11am-11pm Sun. **Main courses** £5.50-£10.50. **Set lunch** £10 3 courses. **Map** p317 K7.

For some years now, this light, L-shaped, low-key little restaurant has been getting on with serving dim sum to (mainly Chinese) families. On our most recent visit, we were pleasantly surprised by both the scope and quality of the lunchtime menu (which includes pictures of all the dumplings – a handy detail for explaining dishes to the young 'uns). There's a Japanese slant to some dishes, including the cigar-like crispy seafood rolls, wrapped in seaweed; and the sweet, succulent baby octopus Japanese-style (served cold with pickles and sprinkled with sesame seeds). We can also enthuse about the pan-fried chive dumplings in a wispy-light, eggy batter. Congenial service is another plus.

Buggy access. High chairs. Nappy-changing facilities. Takeaway service.

Masala Zone

9 Marshall Street, W1F 7ER (7287 9966/ www.realindianfood.com). Oxford Circus tube. **Lunch served** noon-3pm Mon-Fri; 12.30-3.30pm Sun. **Dinner served** 5.30-11pm Mon-Fri; 6-10.30pm Sun. **Meals served** 12.30-11pm Sat. **Main courses** £6-£12. **Credit** MC, V. **Map** p314 J6.

Deserving its popularity, Masala Zone has Wagamama-fied Indian dining. Yet though you get the canteen vibe, the fast throughput and (at peak times) the queues, this isn't at the expense of culinary authenticity or (on behalf of the welcoming staff) a sense of humour. A great-value menu encompasses crisp Bombay beach snacks, meal-in-one plates, rare regional dishes (undhiyu, and lentil khichdi – a mushy rice mix – for instance), properly prepared curries and satisfying thalis. The children's menu delivers accessible dishes in portions small enough (and with a familiar little pile of crisps on the side) to encourage even the most reluctant palates.

Buggy access. Children's menu (£3.75). High chairs. No smoking. Takeaway service. **Branches**: 80 Upper Street, N1 0NU (7359 3399); 147 Earl's Court Road, SW5 9RQ (7373 0220).

Planet Hollywood

13 Coventry Street, W1D 7DH (7287 1000/ www.planethollywoodlondon.com). Piccadilly Circus tube. **Meals served** 11.30am-1am Mon-Sat; 11.30am-12.30am Sun. **Main courses** £8.50-£16.95. **Credit** AmEx, DC, MC, V. **Map** p317 K7.

Walls of video screens and fat burgers have secured this giant temple of pop culture first place on the list entitled 'where to have my first teenage birthday party'. Parents accompanying such outings may be less enamoured with the place; perhaps the menu's 'Marco Pierre White Specialities' section (he's a shareholder) is for their benefit. But pretensions aside, this is where to come for mounds of cheese on your nachos, giant slabs of meat in your burger, a choice of sickly sauces for your rôtisserie chicken and chocolate-chip brownies with your ice-cream. In short, it's a kind of heaven for juvenile tastebuds. Service is amusingly indulgent towards younger children.

Balloons. Booking advisable (weekends; limited reservations Sat). Buggy access. Children's menu (£7.95). Crayons. High chairs. Nappy-changing facilities. No-smoking tables.

Quod Restaurant & Bar

57 Haymarket, SW1Y 4QX (7925 1234/ www.quod.co.uk). Piccadilly Circus tube. **Open** 10am-midnight Mon-Fri; noon-midnight Sat; 5-10.30pm Sun. **Main courses** £8.45-£17.95. **Credit** AmEx, MC, V. **Map** p317 K7.

Subtle reworking of the colours, textures and artwork in this gigantic mezzanined space has resulted in a more intimate atmosphere, though the modern portraits are still bold and unusual. The front bar area works well as a casual eaterie and is the best place to install yourself with the nippers. For parents, the specials board offers a diversion from the standard 'burgers and pasta' menu; duck with pak choi, mushrooms and a tasty gravy being a recent highlight. Kids, meanwhile, will relish the chicken nuggets and pasta with tomato sauce on their menu. Service is relaxed and pleasant.

Buggy access. Children's menu (£3.95). Disabled access: toilets. High chairs. Nappy-changing facilities. No-smoking area. Tables outdoors (6, pavement).

Consumer

TOP 5 New flavours

Masala Zone
Indian snacks and rare regional dishes in a fast-food canteen setting. *See p167.*

Moroccan Tagine
North African treats in west London. *See p183.*

Shish
Take a taste trip down the 'Silk Road', from Turkeyto Indonesia. *See p161.*

Sông Quê
Great value Vietnamese cooking at its fresh, clean-tasting best. *See p179.*

World Food Café
Explore global tastes at this busy Covent Garden stalwart. *See p172.*

Rainforest Café
20 Shaftesbury Avenue, W1D 7EU (7434 3111/ www.therainforestcafe.co.uk). Piccadilly Circus tube. **Meals served** noon-10pm Mon-Thur; noon-8pm Fri; 11am-8pm Sat; 11.30am-10pm Sun. **Main courses** £9.95-£15.95. **Credit** AmEx, MC, V. **Map** p317 K7.

A big hit with the children and extremely popular for parties, this extravagant restaurant is filled with animatronic apes and elephants, cascading waterfalls and thunderstorm sound effects. But be warned: the fact that the dining room is accessed via a safari-themed shopping area means that your offspring will inevitably be whining for soft toys and T-shirts throughout their meal. The latter may consist of such dishes as 'Iggy's creamy ocean pie' or 'cha cha's noodles' from the children's menu, while older kids will find all they're looking for on the main menu, which is also geared to younger tastes (but at adult prices). A few healthier, non-burger options can be found (Mediterranean polenta, for example), and there are some fantastically messy, fancy desserts.
Buggy access. Children's menu (£10.25). Crayons. High chairs. Nappy-changing facilities. No smoking.

RIBA Café
66 Portland Place, W1B 1AD (7631 0467). Great Portland Street or Oxford Circus tube. **Open** 8am-6pm Mon-Fri; 9am-4pm Sat. **Set lunch** £12.95 1 course, £16.95 2 courses, £20.95 3 courses. **Credit** AmEx, DC, MC, V. **Map** p314 H5.

The first floor of the landmark Royal Institute of British Architects building contains a coffee bar and brasserie space, run by Milburns catering company, which serves breakfasts, sandwiches and salads, plus a full lunch menu. This changes weekly, but features a selection of Modern European classics such as pan-fried calf's liver or roasted cod, followed by the likes of raspberry meringue. It's worth ordering from this menu, as at lunch it gives access to the roof terrace (booking is strongly advised). French windows open on to 20 tables surrounded by garden heaters, sun umbrellas and zinc planters filled with (appropriately) architectural plants.
Buggy access. High chairs. Tables outdoors (20, terrace). Nappy-changing facilities. No smoking.

Royal Dragon
30 Gerrard Street, W1D 6JS (7734 1388). Leicester Square or Piccadilly Circus tube. **Dim sum served** noon-5pm daily. **Meals served** noon-3am daily. **Main courses** £6.30-£10. **Credit** AmEx, MC, V. **Map** p317 K7.

We have a soft spot for this Chinatown stalwart, not least because of its decent dim sum menu – the automatic choice for parents with fidgety children in tow, and always a fun affair, espcially at weekends). But for those in a more adventurous mood, dishes on the main menu such as mui-choi kau-yuk (a generous portion of excellent earthenware-cooked pork with preserved vegetables) are also worth a punt.
High chair. Takeaway service.

Sabzi
3 Princes Street, W1B 2LD (7493 8729). Oxford Circus tube. **Open** 7.30am-6.30pm Mon-Fri; 10.30am-6pm Sat; 11am-5pm Sun. **Main courses** £2-£3. **Credit cards Map** p314 H6.

A really good sandwich bar, less than a minute from Oxford Circus? Yes, really. Most sandwich bars use bought-in fillings: not here, where tasty Manoucher flavoured breads (as seen in the Harvey Nicks Food Hall) might contain fresh sardines with capers, red pepper and parsley; or goat's cheese with slow-cooked peppers, walnuts and fresh tarragon (£2.80). There's organic nosh aplenty, including organic cakes (from Honeyrose Bakery in Park Royal). The orange juice (a generous 12oz for £1.65) is freshly squeezed, and the small chill cabinets and takeaway counter conceal a spacious and rather lovely seated area at the back.
Buggy access. No smoking. Takeaway service.

Yo! Sushi
52 Poland Street, W1V 3DF (7287 0443/www.yosushi. co.uk). Oxford Circus tube. **Meals served** noon-11pm Mon-Thur; noon-midnight Fri, Sat; noon-10.30pm Sun. **Credit** AmEx, DC, MC, V. **Map** p314 J6.

The double-track kaiten (conveyor belt) is still in situ at this original link in the chain, but the decor has been spruced up: new counter surfaces, cool stools topped with cranberry-coloured leather pouffes, new carpet and new slate floor tiles. The menu has been rethought, too. The colour-coded plates now cost £1.50-£5, although the range of food on them is narrower (salmon predominates). But you'll still find plenty to attract the attention of youngsters – in fact, the 'spider roll' (a California roll containing, among other things, soft-shell crab tempura, yuzu tobiko and chilli mayonnaise) seems to have been named with Calvin-like boys in mind.
Booster seats. Buggy access. Disabled access: toilets. No smoking. Takeaway service.
Branches: throughout town. Call or check the website.

COVENT GARDEN

Belgo Centraal
50 Earlham Street, WC2H 9LJ (7813 2233/ www.belgo-restaurants.com). Covent Garden tube. **Meals served** noon-11pm Mon-Thur; noon-11.30pm Fri, Sat; noon-10.30pm Sun. **Main courses** £9.95-£18.95. **Set lunch** (noon-5pm) £5.95 1 course. **Credit** AmEx, DC, MC, V. **Map** p315 L6.

Consumer

Benihana. *See p166.*

The great-value children's deal is possibly the most appealing thing about this cavernous subterranean mussel merchant: two kids eat for free when accompanied by an adult ordering from the à la carte menu. The chain's trademark bivalves also appear on the children's menu (a small bowl served with the house provençale sauce), alongside more conventional choices (sausages, chicken and so on).
Buggy access. Children's menu (free with paying adult). Crayons. Disabled access: lift, toilets. High chairs.
Branches: Belgo Bierodrome, 44-48 Clapham High Street, SW4 7UR (7720 1118); Belgo Bierodrome, 67 Kingsway, WC2B 6TD (7242 7469); Belgo Bierodrome, 173-174 Upper Street, N1 1XS (7226 5835); Belgo Noord, 72 Chalk Farm Road, NW1 8AN (7267 0718).

Browns

82-84 St Martin's Lane, WC2N 4AA (7497 5050/ www.browns-restaurants.com). Leicester Square tube.
Meals served noon-10.30pm Mon, Sun; noon-11.30pm Tue-Sat. **Main courses** £6-£16.95. **Set meal** (4-6.30pm Mon-Sat) £10.95 2 courses. **Credit** AmEx, DC, MC, V. **Map** p317 L7.
Despite (or perhaps because of) its innate tackiness, the vast dining room of this chain's flagship West End restaurant is regularly packed to the rafters. Whether it's the cheap pre-theatre menu, the range of salads and pasta dishes alongside more typical brasserie fare, or the combination of piped jazz muzak and plastic potted plants – something has kept tourists, local office workers and lunching families flocking here for more than 30 years. Among the puds, lemon tart is a sure-fire hit. Helpful young staff inject plenty of enthusiasm into their work.
Buggy access. Children's menu (£4.95). Disabled access: lift, toilets. High chairs. Nappy-changing facilities. No-smoking tables.
Branches: 47 Maddox Street, W1R 9LA (7491 4565); 9 Islington Green, N1 8DU (7226 2555); 8 Old Jewry, EC2R 8DN (7606 6677); Butlers Wharf, SE1 2YG (7378 1700); Hertsmere Road, West India Quay, E14 8JJ (7987 9777); 3-4 Kew Green, TW9 3AA (8948 4838).

Café Pacifico

5 Langley Street, WC2H 9JA (7379 7728/ www.cafepacifico-laperla.com). Covent Garden or Leicester Square tube. **Meals served** noon-11.45pm Mon-Sat; noon-10.45pm Sun. **Main courses** £6-£14.95. **Credit** AmEx, MC, V. **Map** p315 L6.
This relentlessly Latin-themed restaurant is big and often raucous (lunchtimes are bettter if you want comparative peace and quiet), and the food is reliably authentic Tex-Mex. Combo starters (a fun option for older kids) include fried prawn balls, excellently rich fried cheese, onion rings and some fine crisp chicken taquitos (fried, chicken-filled corn tortillas). It's hard to beat the value of the children's menu, which offers a choice between conventional chicken nuggets and fish fingers or zingy quesadillas with rice and guacamole, plus a drink and ice-cream for just £2.95.
Buggy access. Children's menu (£2.95). Crayons. High chairs.

Food for Thought

31 Neal Street, WC2H 9PR (7836 0239). Covent Garden tube. **Breakfast served** 9.30-11.30am Mon-Sat. **Lunch served** noon-3.30pm Mon-Sat; noon-5pm Sun. **Dinner served** 5-8.15pm Mon-Sat. **Main courses** £4-£6.50. *Minimum* (noon-3pm, 6-7.30pm) £2.50. **No credit cards. Map** p315 L6.
The antithesis of the ultra-trendy, wallet-bashing boutiques and shoe shops of Neal Street, longstanding FfT is unpretentious, reliable and great value. Diners share tables in the small, narrow basement (if you're lucky, the little alcoves at the back may be free) to enjoy a daily changing, globally inspired menu. Lunchtime takeaway queues can be long and dishes sometimes run out, but this is a testament to the enduring popularity of the place. There's always a soup (Thai spinach and coconut, say), stir-fry, quiche and chunky salads, plus specials such as aubergine and fennel timbale, layered with rice and a rich tomato sauce, and topped with melted cheese. Staff are always happy to see children.
No smoking. Takeaway service.

Rainforest Cafe

A WILD PLACE TO SHOP AND EAT®

Rainforest Cafe is a unique venue bringing to life the sights and sounds of the rainforest.

Come and try our fantastic menu!
With a re-launched healthy kids menu, including gluten free, dairy free and organic options.

15% DISCOUNT
off your final food bill*

Offer valid seven days a week.
Maximum party size of 6.

020 7434 3111

20 Shaftesbury Avenue, Piccadilly Circus, London W1D 7EU

www.therainforestcafe.co.uk

*Please show this advert to your safari guide when seated.
Cannot be used in conjunction with any other offer.

Hamburger Union

4 Garrick Street, WC2E 9BH (7379 0412/
www.hamburgerunion.com). Leicester Square tube.
Meals served 11.30am-9.30pm Mon, Sun; 11.30am-
10.30pm Tue-Sat. **Main courses** £3.95-£6.95.
Credit MC, V. **Map** p317 L7.
Hamburger mega-chains provide an easy option in the
tourist jungle that is Covent Garden, but this new Garrick
Street venture offers a pleasing alternative to the fast-food
superpowers. Although less substantial than the towering
offerings at the Fine Burger Co, Union burgers make a filling treat and, at £3.95, are a lot cheaper. It's a tad more
stylish, too, than your average child-friendly burger joint
(sleek wooden benches, a compact bar, framed artwork).
All in all, then, a good bet for a pit stop or just a change
of scene if you fancy something a bit trashier than Paul
(*see below*) just a few doors away.
Buggy access. High chairs. No smoking. Takeaway
service.
Branches: 25 Dean Street, W1D 3RY (7437 6004).

Maxwell's

8-9 James Street, WC2E 8BH (7836 0303). Covent
Garden tube. **Meals served** noon-11pm Mon-Thur;
noon-11.30pm Fri, Sat; noon-10.30pm Sun. **Main**
courses £8.75-£17.95. *Minimum* (when busy) main
course. **Credit** AmEx, DC, MC, V. **Map** p315 L6.
Cementing the arteries of Anglo-American relations over
the years, this brash, busy and hugely friendly grill is a
great place to bring the family when you're in town. The
£5.95 kids' menu offers a choice of cheeseburger, hot dog
or ribs (all with fries), followed by vanilla ice-cream or a
brownie for pudding, plus a soft drink to wash it all down
with. Lunchtimes are probably the best bet for a family
meal, though, as it gets pretty crowded in the evenings.
Buggy access. Children's menu (£5.95). Crayons. High
chairs. Nappy-changing facilities. No-smoking tables.
Tables outdoors (3, pavement).
Branches: 76 Heath Street, NW3 1DN (7794 5450).

Paul

29 Bedford Street, WC2E 9ED (7836 3304).
Covent Garden tube. **Open** 7.30am-9pm Mon-Fri;
9am-9pm Sat, Sun. **Credit** MC, V. **Map** p317 L7.
Popular with students, well-dressed shoppers and young
families, this flagship café combines Parisian style with a
friendly and informal atmosphere. Admire rows of picture-
perfect pastries, beautiful breads and savoury tarts in the
shop window, or sit in the café behind the shop and watch
bakers at work through the glass front of the kitchen. And
don't forget to sink a fork into the dreamy pâtisserie selection – the chocolate éclairs and raspberry tarts are divine.
Buggy access. Takeaway service.
Branches: 115 Marylebone High Street, W1U 4BS
(7224 5615).

PJ's Grill

30 Wellington Street, WC2E 7BD (7240 7529).
Covent Garden tube. **Brunch served** noon-4pm daily.
Meals served noon-midnight Mon-Sat; noon-4pm Sun.
Main courses £8.95-£13.95. **Credit** AmEx, DC, MC,
V. **Map** p317 L6.
There's a theatrical ambience to this long, narrow West
End restaurant. The walls are plastered with old film
posters and the tables are surrounded by little brass
plaques with the names of regulars, many of whom have

acted or crewed at the numerous nearby theatres. There's
a big pre- and post-theatre rush. The menu focuses on
French-American bistro classics, with daily specials providing variety; don't expect much in the way of surprises.
The children's menu is similarly predictable (albeit decent
quality) with the likes of fish and chips, chicken and chips
and pasta with tomato sauce.
Buggy access. Children's menu (£4.95). High chairs.
Nappy-changing facilities. No-smoking tables.

Rock & Sole Plaice

47 Endell Street, WC2H 9AJ (7836 3785). Covent
Garden or Leicester Square tube. **Meals served**
11.30am-10.30pm Mon-Sat; noon-9.30pm Sun. **Main**
courses £8-£14. **Credit** MC, V. **Map** p315 L6.
The Hassan family may be comparatively recent arrivals,
but there has been a chippy on this site since 1871. In
clement weather the outside seats get thronged – and the
young waiting staff shoo away takeaway customers hoping to rest their legs. Taramasalata, Efes Turkish beer and
pitta point to the family's Turkish roots, but the name of
the game is good old-fashioned British fish and chips. This
will either be brilliant – which it is most of the time – or
disappointingly average. On the good days, large portions
of thick, creamy cod and haddock come encased in just-
right golden batter, accompanied by crisp, rough-cut chips.
The impressive fish and whale mural in the basement is
worth a detour to the loo.
Buggy access. Tables outdoors (10, pavement).
Takeaway service.

Smollensky's on the Strand

105 Strand, WC2R 0AA (7497 2101/
www.smollenskys.co.uk). Embankment tube/Charing
Cross tube/rail. **Meals served** noon-midnight Mon-
Wed; noon-12.30am Thur-Sat; noon-5.30pm, 6.30-
10.30pm Sun. **Main courses** £8.85-£19.95. **Set meal**
(noon-7pm, after 10pm Mon-Fri) £10 2 courses, £12
3 courses. **Credit** AmEx, DC, MC, V. **Map** p317 L7.
Every year we come to Smollensky's with a cynical attitude – it's too touristy, too heavily advertised – and every
year we have another excellent meal. Our most recent visit
was no exception. Two family-friendly starters were perfectly crisp vegetable wun tuns and a mushroom tart (big
enough for everyone to dip in) that provided delicate,
smoky mushrooms in a creamy sauce, all cradled in flaky
pastry. Steak is the main attraction when it comes to mains,
with such options as sirloin with béarnaise sauce and rib-
eye with peppercorn sauce. Each was large, tender and
cooked precisely as requested. And on the children's menu,
mini burgers, hot dogs and spaghetti are on hand to keep
little hands occupied. As are the free fun packs.
Booking advisable. Buggy access. Children's menu
(£4.99). Crayons. Entertainment: clown, magic show,
Nintendo games, face-painting (Sat, Sun). High chairs.
No smoking. Play area (under-7s). Toys.

TGI Friday's

6 Bedford Street, WC2E 9HZ (7379 0585/
www.tgifridays.co.uk). Covent Garden or
Embankment tube/Charing Cross tube/rail. **Meals**
served noon-11.30pm Mon-Sat; noon-11pm Sun.
Main courses £7.45-£17. **Credit** AmEx, MC, V.
Map p317 L7.
Children don't care whether a place is cool or not. They
love the perky staff in their badge-festooned uniforms who
proffer balloons and guide them to the free (rather good)

Consumer

Teenage kicks

When a group of teenagers takes over a table in a restaurant, the last thing they want is their parents peering over their shoulders. And, let's face it, it's not a great evening out for the adults, either. The ideal solution, then, is a restaurant where they can be left to get on with it, in the knowledge that when you return to collect them you're not going to find a litter of empty wine bottles and an irate manager accosting you at the door.

Top of the list of such establishments must surely be **Pizza Express** (www.pizzaexpress.co.uk) and **Nando's** (www.nandos.co.uk), both the kind of places that trysting couples would steer well clear of, leaving a clientele that is likely to be tolerant of (and, indeed, expecting) a bit of youthful high spirits. The ubiquity of their outlets also makes them convenient choices no matter which corner of the city you're based in (for a full list of branches, consult the websites).

For burgers, **Planet Hollywood** (see p167) is a perfect all-rounder, with enough music video mayhem in its ambience to ensure that the party goes with a swing (and that you're grateful to be leaving), while **Ed's Easy Diner** (see p166) has a more sedate atmosphere (especially the branch on Moor Street, which resembles an Edward Hopper painting come to life) but the jukebox and wisecracking cooks add the necessary pep to proceedings. Plus the shakes are phenomenal. Otherwise, try a lunchtime stop at the irrepressible **Maxwell's** (see p171).

It would be churlish not to include **TGI Friday's** (see p171) on this list, since catering to the teenage palate is its raison d'être, and its outlets extend far beyond the city centre (you'll find them in Kingston, Croydon, Mill Hill and the rest – consult the website for an exhaustive list). However, there are also a number of (dare we say it) classier alternatives, such as the **Tootsies Grill** (see p183) or **Wagamama** (see p177) chains, or the excellent **Sticky Fingers** (see p173) and **Texas Embassy Cantina** (see p173).

face painting table at weekends. Once sporting glittery butterfly make-up, they tuck into the food with gusto. There are several children's menus, ranging from the simplest chicken strips and chips selection up to a nice choice of nachos, wings, ribs, seafood, drinks, and large and elaborate puddings. On our last visit the promised Kinder egg never materialised, but in truth, the children were too stuffed to care. Adult portions are extremely large, and the food is unsophisticated but fresh and well presented. Our marinated, seared salmon steak with salad was lovely, nachos came with industrial quantities of melted cheese, the house salad tastily dressed, chips, as always, crisp and yummy. The children's food was served on the tepid side. We don't know if that's policy (to prevent burnt mouths) but understood that high-chair diners don't care about coolness of food, either.

Balloons. Buggy access. Children's menu (from £3.45). Crayons. Disabled access: toilets. Entertainment: occasional face-painting (Sat, Sun). High chairs. Nappy-changing facilities. No smoking. **Branches:** throughout town. Call or check the website.

World Food Café

Neal's Yard Dining Room, 1st floor, 14 Neal's Yard, WC2H 9DP (7379 0298). Covent Garden or Leicester Square tube. **Meals served** 11.30am-4.30pm Mon-Fri; 11.30am-5pm Sat. **Main courses** £4.85-£7.95. *Minimum* (noon-2pm Mon-Fri; 11.30am-5pm Sat) £5. **Credit** MC, V. **Map** p315 L6.

The clue is in the name: from colourful framed prints on the whitewashed walls and the world music soundtrack to the menu, global influences abound at this cheery café in the heart of Covent Garden. Large wooden tables by the huge windows overlook the veggie mecca of Neal's Yard; otherwise seating is on tall stools around a bar circling the open kitchen. Choose from a daily soup or salad special, a 'light' meal or a heartier option (dishes are themed by country, so you might find Thai yellow curry, Moroccan tagine, Indian thali or Sri Lankan mallung). Children's portions are available on request.

High chairs. No smoking. Takeaway service.

WESTMINSTER

Café in the Crypt

Crypt of St Martin-in-the-Fields, Duncannon Street, WC2N 4JJ (7839 4342/www.stmartin-in-the-fields.org). Embankment tube/Charing Cross tube/rail. **Lunch served** 11.30am-3pm Mon-Sat; noon-3pm Sun. **Dinner served** 5-7.30pm Mon-Wed; 5-10.30pm Thur-Sat. **Main courses** £5.95-£7.50. **Set meal** £5.25 2 courses. **No credit cards.** **Map** p317 L7.

The perfect place for just sitting them down and getting some food down their necks with minimum fuss, this echo-chamber self-service café is hidden in the centuries-old crypt below St Martin-in-the-Fields church. A daily rotating menu offers large salad platters (probably best to avoid the over-dry veggie tartlet), as well as more substantial options such as salmon fillet with new potatoes and cabbage, doled out to tray-carrying diners by uniformed staff. A children's sandwich box costs £3.95 and is available during school holidays and art weekends.

High chairs. No-smoking tables. Takeaway service (drinks).

Inn The Park

St James's Park, SW1A 2BJ (7451 9999/ www.innthepark.com). St James's Park tube. **Open** 8am-11pm Mon-Fri; 9am-11pm Sat; 9am-6pm Sun. **Credit** AmEx, MC, V. **Map** p317 K8.

This striking new venture in St James's Park provides a true roll call of British talent. Food comes courtesy of restaurateur Oliver Peyton; the striking wooden building, partly covered by a turf roof, with a sweeping glass front and veranda, is by architect Michael Hopkins, while the chic, if sauna-like interior is by Tom Dixon (of Habitat fame). There's an all-day café menu – breakfast, snacks, afternoon tea – but for lunch and dinner the place becomes a full-blown restaurant serving produce-led, seasonal British dishes. At weekends, children get their own menu of fish and chips, sausage and mash, and other classics.

Buggy access. Children's menu (£4-£6). Disabled access: toilets. High chairs. No smoking (inside). Tables outdoors (40, terrace). Takeaway service.

Texas Embassy Cantina

1 Cockspur Street, SW1Y 5DL (7925 0077/ www.texasembassy.com). Embankment tube/Charing Cross tube/rail. **Meals served** noon-11pm Mon-Wed; noon-midnight Thur-Sat; noon-10.30pm Sun. **Main courses** £7.50-£16.95. **Credit** AmEx, DC, MC, V. **Map** p317 K7.

The ground floor of this vast, two-storey restaurant can get really packed (even at lunchtime), so don't come expecting a haven of tranquillity. Visiting Americans tend to constitute the majority of the clientele here, but it's probably just the location at the edge of touristy Trafalgar Square that keeps the locals away, and maybe the prices, which are a bit steep. Food, though, is generally good, and the kids' menu has plenty of Tex-Mex options (tacos, nachos, enchiladas) as well as bog-standard hamburgers and hot dogs. Staff are effusively friendly.

Balloons. Buggy access. Children's menu (main meals £4.75). Crayons. High chairs. Nappy-changing facilities. Tables outdoors (8, pavement).

KENSINGTON & CHELSEA

Big Easy

332-334 King's Road, SW3 5UR (7352 4071/ www.bigeasy.uk.com). Sloane Square tube, then 11, 19, 22 bus. **Meals served** noon-11pm Mon-Thur; noon-12.30am Fri; 11am-12.30am Sat; 11am-11.30pm Sun. **Main courses** £8.95-£22. **Set lunch** (noon-5pm Mon-Fri) £7.95 2 courses. **Credit** AmEx, MC, V. **Map** p313 E12.

This is the most American of London's US-style restaurants, with a rustic decor typified by metal Tabasco signs, and a gone fishin' attitude. The music can be loud and the mood pretty raucous in the evening, but for lunch and brunch Big Easy is as relaxed as its name suggests. Children get their own grub – typically, burgers, dogs or chicken dippers – to sustain them as they indulge in a bit of crayon work or play with their free balloon. It's popular with homesick Yanks.

Balloons. Buggy access. Children's menu (£5.45, dessert £2-£3.95). Crayons. High chairs. Nappy-changing facilities. No-smoking tables. Tables outdoors (5, pavement). Takeaway service.

Bluebird

350 King's Road, SW3 5UU (7559 1000/ www.conran.com). Sloane Square tube, then 11, 19, 22 bus. **Brunch served** noon-3.30pm Sat, Sun. **Lunch served** 12.30-3pm Mon-Fri. **Dinner served** 6-11pm daily. **Main courses** £13.50-£21.50. **Credit** AmEx, DC, MC, V. **Map** p313 D12.

After a busy day on the King's Road or a whisk through the food hall downstairs, you may want to treat yourself to a meal in this swanky Conran joint. Food can be hit and miss, and the staff are not always the most accommodating (you may get rushed through an early meal), but there's usually an interesting and tasty pasta dish on the kid's menu, alongside the usual fish and chips and so on. Ham hock terrine with piccalilli followed by sea bass and garlic tapenade are the kind of thing parents can expect to find themselves eating.

Buggy access. Children's menu (£6.95 2 courses, Sat, Sun only). Disabled access: toilets. High chairs. Lift. Nappy-changing facilities. Tables outdoors (25, courtyard).

Blue Kangaroo

555 King's Road, SW6 2EB (7371 7622/ www.thebluekangaroo.co.uk). Fulham Broadway tube/ Sloane Square tube, then 11, 19, 22 bus. **Meals served** 9.30am-7.30pm daily. **Main courses** £8-£14. **Credit** AmEx, MC, V. **Map** p312 C13.

It may be the most sprog-centric restaurant in London, but a family meal at the Blue Kangaroo is far from the ketchup-smeared purgatory that parents might fear. For a start, the food is prepared with enormous care, from diligently sourced ingredients. Though not flashy, it is uniformly good. Children, if they want nuggets, get own-made, free-range ones; salmon fish cakes are made with the wild variety and sausages are organic. The children's menu costs £5.45 with a drink. Grown-ups should try those fish cakes in a larger size, or the excellent butternut risotto, creamy wild mushroom tagliatelle or grilled chicken in ciabatta (adult dishes cost £6.95-£10). Undoubtedly the feature young children like best about this lively, otherwise simply appointed place is that it sits on a whole basement of play apparatus; diners pay about £3 to set the kids loose here. The play area can be monitored via plasma screen or the obliging staff, who were saintly on our visit.

Buggy access. Children's menu (£5.45 incl drink). High chairs. Nappy-changing facilities. No smoking. Toys.

Sticky Fingers

1A Phillimore Gardens, W8 7EG (7938 5338/ www.stickyfingers.co.uk). High Street Kensington tube. **Meals served** noon-11pm daily. **Main courses** £8.45-£15.95. **Credit** AmEx, DC, MC, V. **Map** p312 A9.

Your offspring may never have heard of the Rolling Stones but there are chocolate shakes, burgers and nuggets aplenty to keep them quiet. You, on the other hand, can marvel at the rock 'n' roll pedigree of the place (Bill Wyman's one of the owners and items from his souvenir collection hang on every wall). So tap your geriatric foot to some golden oldies and drift off into a reverie. Service is young and friendly, and able to cope with a truly diverse crowd that ranges from London mums and their rubicund feasting tots through to a rowdier champagne-and-fajita set come nightfall.

Balloons. Buggy access. Children's menu (£7.50). Crayons. Entertainment: face-painting noon-4pm Sat, magician Sun. High chairs. No-smoking tables (weekends). Takeaway service.

Top Floor at Peter Jones

Peter Jones, Sloane Square, SW1W 8EL (7901 8003/ www.johnlewis.com). Sloane Square tube. **Meals served** 9.30am-6.30pm Mon-Sat; 11am-4.30pm Sun. **Main courses** £7.50-£9.50. **Credit** MC, V.

If John Lewis ran motorway service station restaurants, this is how they would be: popular self-service canteens that aren't designed to clog your arteries. Occupying the summit of the sleekly renovated Peter Jones at Sloane Square, the Top Floor offers magnificent views of London towards Kensington Gardens, along with a mid-range hot and cold buffet. Never knowingly undersold, silver service is also now available on the second floor in a bijou cocktail bar of a restaurant just the other side of women's lingerie. Perhaps one to try without the kids.

Consumer

Buggy access. Children's menu (£2.50, free baby food with adult purchase). Disabled access: lift, toilets. High chairs. Nappy changing facilities. No smoking.

NORTH LONDON

Afghan Kitchen

35 Islington Green, Islington, N1 8DU (7359 8019). Angel tube. **Lunch served** noon-3.30pm, **dinner served** 5.30-11pm Tue-Sat. **Main courses** £4.50-£6. **No credit cards.**
A redecoration has given Afghan Kitchen a slightly more clean-cut, trendier edge, but this popular little spot remains essentially the same. The dining areas (one upstairs, one down) are tiny, so guests crowd around communal tables. Sensibly, the menu is kept short; food is prepared in advance and reheated to order. There's plenty for kids to feast on, such as kofta murgh, light and tender chicken meatballs (more like small patties) served with fresh peas in a delicately flavoured sauce. Staff can struggle to keep up the pace, but usually manage a friendly smile or two. *Takeaway service.*

Banners

21 Park Road, Crouch End, N8 8TE (8292 0001/ booking line 8348 2930). Finsbury Park tube/rail, then W7 bus. **Meals served** 9am-11.30pm Mon-Thur; 9am-midnight Fri; 10am-midnight Sat; 10am-11pm Sun. **Main courses** £7.95-£11.95. **Set lunch** £5.50 1 course. **Credit** MC, V.
Crouch End has the reputation of being home to a certain modern London stereotype (in their mid-thirties, possibly pushing a pram, copy of the *Guardian* tucked under one arm), and this local institution fits well with the idea. Banners caters cleverly to all needs: progressive parents and their tots gather here by day, getting through huge quantities of coffee, crayons and colouring books; older locals mingle at night, amid the mock-beach bar decor. *Buggy access. Children's menu (£2-£5). Disabled access. High chairs. No smoking (9am-7pm Mon-Fri).*

Brew House

Kenwood, Hampstead Lane, Hampstead Heath, NW3 7JR (8341 5384). Bus 210, 214. **Open** Oct-Mar 9am-dusk daily. *Apr-Sept* 9am-6pm daily (7.30pm on concert nights). **Credit** (over £10) MC, V.

The Brew House has a wonderful English country-garden feel; it's located in an old stable block of Kenwood House, with large outdoor tables set amid glorious flower beds and massed hanging baskets. Inside are high ceilings, lightly frescoed walls and quaint village-style signposts that point out the cake stand (as if you could miss the huge chunks of carrot cake, pineapple pavlova, scones, and gooseberry and nettle cheesecake) and guide you around the jam-packed service area. Homely, countrified grub matches the setting perfectly.
Buggy access. Children's menu (£2.50-£3.60). High chairs. Nappy-changing facilities. No smoking (inside). Tables outside (seating for 400, garden). Takeaway service.

Café Mozart

17 Swains Lane, Highgate, N6 6QS (8348 1384). Highgate tube/Gospel Oak rail/C11 bus. **Meals served** 8am-10pm Mon-Fri; 9am-10pm Sat, Sun. **Main courses** £6.75-£11. **Credit** (over £5) MC, V.
Located near Parliament Hill Fields, charmingly old-fashioned Café Mozart holds its own against a clutch of cafés competing for the attention of well-heeled locals. Regulars come here for the Viennese pastries, hearty breakfasts, brasserie lunches and suppers. Mozart-related memorabilia enhances the wood-panelled decor, while subdued classical music adds to the cosy, casual ambience. Our gold star goes to the mouth-watering puff pastry tart topped with chewy baked plums. When the sun shines, sit outside and let the kids potter around. The friendly staff won't mind a bit.
Buggy access. High chair. No smoking. Tables outdoors (10, courtyard).

Camden Arts Centre

Corner of Arkwright Road & Finchley Road, Swiss Cottage, NW3 6DG (7472 5516/www.camdenarts centre.org). Finchley Road tube/Finchley Road & Frognal rail. **Meals served** 10am-5.30pm Tue, Thur-Sun; 10am-8.30pm Wed. **Main courses** £2.95-£5.95. **Credit** MC, V.
Camden Arts Centre has recently surfaced after a £4 million refit and is all spare walls and sharp planes, tricked out in fashionable materials. The café, which fills a corner of the ground floor and spills out into a garden, is nicely soothing. For the menu, think sandwiches and well-priced platters of fresh meze or a daily special such as plump, juicy salmon and dill fish cakes. There are also plates of Italian cold cuts or French cheeses from La Fromagerie – £6.50 each with a glass of wine or beer – plus toast with Marmite, and Kit-Kats.
Buggy access. Disabled access; ramps, toilets. High chairs. No smoking. Tables outdoors (5, garden). Takeaway service.

Fine Burger Co

256 Muswell Hill Broadway, Muswell Hill, N10 3SH (8815 9292/www.fineburger.co.uk). Highgate tube, then 43, 134 bus. **Meals served** noon-11pm Mon-Sat; noon-10pm Sun. **Main courses** £4.95-£8.95. **Credit** AmEx, MC, V.
A tenner for burger and chips? Expensive, yes, but don't be put off: the children's meals start at £4.95. Anyway, these are no burger-van squirrel-meat nasties or production line McPatties; these are fine burgers, served in chunky ciabatta buns with colourful salad on the side. Bantering staff convey a huge variety of burgers from an open

TOP 5 Terraces

Brew House
Hampstead Heath's country garden. *See above.*

Café Mozart
A lovely courtyard in Highgate. *See right.*

Jones Dairy Café
Flower power in Hackney. *See p179.*

Pavilion Café
For alfresco lunches in Dulwich Park. *See p180.*

Royal China
River views in Docklands. *See p179.*

Arkansas Café. *See p177.*

kitchen into the restaurant: a lofty, modern space that seems as well suited to beer-supping trendies as it does to milkshake-slurping families of four.
Buggy access. Children's menu (£4.95). Crayons. High chairs. Nappy-changing facilities. No smoking. Takeaway service.
Branches: 37 Bedford Hill, Balham, SW12 9EY (8772 0266); 330 Upper Street, N1 2XQ (7359 3026).

Golders Hill Park Refreshment House

North End Road, Golders Green, NW3 7HD (8455 8010). Golders Green or Hampstead tube. **Meals served** 10am-dusk daily. **Main courses** £3-£7. **No credit cards.**
Always a choice spot for freshly made ice-cream, this Italian-run park café has been spruced up since last year. The menu is well presented, the glasshouse interior is bright and clean, service is patient and friendly, and there's a good selection of cakes and drinks. The savoury menu includes a long list of salads and pasta dishes, plus a kids' menu. The entrance to the service area is decorated with a selection of early 20th-century prints of the park and the surrounding area. Hanging baskets add to the lovely setting of the popular terrace – which is certainly what makes this café a great refreshment spot, and also a place to meet and to linger.
Children's menu (£3-£5). High chairs. Nappy-changing facilities. No smoking. Tables outdoors (25, terrace). Takeaway service.

Lemonia

89 Regent's Park Road, Chalk Farm, NW1 8UY (7586 7454). Chalk Farm tube/31, 168 bus. **Lunch served** noon-3pm Mon-Fri; noon-3.30pm Sun. **Dinner served** 6-11.30pm Mon-Sat. **Main courses** £8.75-£14.50. **Set lunch** £7.50 2 courses incl coffee; £8.50 3 courses. **Credit** MC, V.
Perennially packed, Lemonia has become one of those restaurants where it's not as easy as it once was to turn up

and bag a table on the off-chance (unless, that is, you're one of the 'hood's more famous faces). That said, though, the food's great and the staff are happy to cater to the requirements of parents and their kids. Artichoke with koukiá (broad beans) is a fun dish, and a delicious one at that (it comes smothered in a pleasantly spicy tomato and oil sauce). Fish is well cooked, and the daily specials are fresh and flavoursome. Perfect chips are an added incentive when coming en famille, although prices may stretch those on a budget.
Buggy access. Tables outdoors (4, pavement).

Mangal II

4 Stoke Newington High Street, Dalston, N16 8BH (7254 7888). Stoke Newington rail/76, 149, 243 bus. **Meals served** noon-1am daily. **Main courses** £7-£12. **No credit cards.**
This well-loved local restaurant with its neutral green walls and vaulted blue ceiling is a step upmarket from the original Mangal café, and from the Mangal Turkish pizza shop across the way at No.27. But it's still casual enough for family outings on a Sunday afternoon, and prices remain keen. The restaurant is usually busy with a mixed and noisy local crowd. Lokma kebab (medallions of lamb held together with cocktail sticks) is exceptional. Service is always friendly and relaxed, but not particularly fast.
Buggy access. High chairs. Takeaway service.

Marine Ices

8 Haverstock Hill, Chalk Farm, NW3 2BL (7482 9003). Chalk Farm tube/31 bus. **Meals served** noon-3pm, 6-11pm Mon-Fri; noon-11pm Sat; noon-10pm Sun. **Main courses** £5.20-£9.60. **Credit** MC, V.
Seventy years old and run by the three grandsons of the original owner, this popular ice-cream parlour and restaurant has recently welcomed a great grandchild to the staff. Clearly *la famiglia* is valued highly here. Perhaps that's why it's so popular with families: on our visit there were plenty of such gatherings, sprinkled around both the traditionally decorated gelaterie and the restaurant. Pizzas,

pastas and salads are on offer in the latter, but it's the desserts that draw. Whether lavished with sauces and toppings in a novelty glass or served as a simple scoop astride a wafer, the ice-cream is something special.
Buggy access. High chairs. No smoking. Takeaway service.

Mosaica @ the lock
Heron House, Hale Wharf, Ferry Lane, Tottenham Hale, N17 9NF (8801 4433/www.mosaica restaurants.com). Tottenham Hale tube. **Meals served** noon-2.30pm, 7-9.30pm Tue-Fri; 7-10pm Sat; noon-3pm Sun. **Main courses** £5-£15.50. **Credit** AmEx, DC, MC, V.
Urban regeneration must be good if it brings us places like this. Mosaica@the lock is an offshoot of Wood Green's greatly praised Mosaica@the factory, only still further off the usual tracks by a canal in Tottenham Hale. The space, in the ground floor of a college, is large, light and airy, with an open kitchen and comfy seating. The menu offers around six starters and a few more mains, as well as kid-size dishes, with several pasta options among the modern-eclectic range. High-quality ingredients are put together with flair. A scrumptious dessert of own-made toffee and raspberry-whip ice-creams and lemon sorbet is a lingering memory of our last visit.
Buggy access. Children's menu (£5-£7). Disabled access. High chairs. Tables outdoors (7, garden).
Branches: Mosaica @ the factory, Clarendon Road, N22 6XJ (8889 2400).

Ottolenghi
287 Upper Street, Islington, N1 2TZ (7288 1454). Angel tube or Highbury & Islington tube/rail. **Meals served** 8am-11pm Mon-Sat; 9am-11pm Sun. **Main courses** (lunch) £7-£11, (dinner) £11-£25. **Credit cards** MC, V.
Ottolenghi is the second branch of the busy Notting Hill deli/café of the same name. You could just order a take-away, but then you'd miss out on the pristine, all-white modernist interior with its long communal dining tables and space-age chairs. There's the food. Choose from breakfast dishes (granola or pastries), cakes, sandwiches and other savouries, all made on the premises. The breads, created by renowned master baker Dan Lepard, include focaccia, rye, huge grissini and an excellent sourdough. Among the marvellous French-style creations are rich and intensely flavoured lemon and mascarpone tarts with polenta crusts, or fruit tarts made on bases of packed crumble and almond cream. More substantial dishes (which change daily) could be loosely described as southern Mediterranean, using influences from Iran to Morocco. Stunningly displayed, they're a riot of colour and form. A great addition to Upper Street.
Buggy access. Disabled access: toilet. High chairs. No smoking. Tables outdoors (2, pavement). Takeaway service.

S&M Café
4-6 Essex Road, Islington, N1 8LN (7359 5361). Angel tube/19, 38 bus. **Meals served** 7.30am-11.30pm Mon-Thur; 9am-midnight Fri, Sat; 9am-10.30pm Sun. **Main courses** £2.50-£5.95. **Credit** MC, V.
S for sausage and M for mash – just to ward off any misunderstandings. Select your S (from a choice of 12 or so, including veterans like the cumberland and specials such as wild boar), throw in some M (we recommend the creamy,

perfect, traditional mash) and finish with one of three gravies. The result is served Beano-style, with sausages poking cutely out of a generous mash mountain. The menu changes seasonally, so for spring and summer there are lighter sausage delights, such as a pleasant Italian-style sausage with tomato, or a lean spring lamb with mint. Children can choose the same, only smaller, on their menu, which also offers chicken nuggets or fish fingers and throws in ice-cream and a juice to boot. The Islington branch of this growing mini chain is a lovely looking gem, with a vintage 1920s blue-and-chrome interior.
Buggy access. Children's menu (£3.95).
Branches: 268 Portobello Road, W10 5TY (8968 8898); 48 Brushfield Street, E1 6AG (7247 2252); 231 High Street, W3 9BY (8992 7345).

Santa Fe
75 Upper Street, Islington, N1 0NU (7288 2288/ www.santafe.co.uk). Angel tube. **Meals served** noon-10.30pm Mon-Thur, Sun; noon-11pm Fri, Sat. **Main courses** £6.95-£12.95. **Credit** AmEx, DC, MC, V.
This Southwestern restaurant has undergone changes in the past year, most of them good (a new menu, improved cooking) and some not so good (loud music and a bar atmosphere spreading into the dining area). It's still a decent place to touch down with the sprogs, though. And while they're tucking into their menu, you can snack on guacamole and salsa with excellent tortilla chips or go the whole hog with juicy, well-seasoned rack of ribs and excellent fries. High chairs and crayons are on hand for those who need them.
Booking advisable (weekends). Buggy access. Children's menu (£3.95). Crayons. Disabled access: toilets. High chairs. No-smoking tables.

Tiger Lil's
270 Upper Street, Islington, N1 2UQ (7226 1118/ www.tigerlils.com). Highbury & Islington tube/rail. **Meals served** 6-11pm Mon-Thur; noon-3pm, 6-11pm Fri; noon-11pm Sat, Sun. **Main courses** £7.90-£12.50. **Credit** AmEx, MC, V.
The premise of this DIY restaurant is much the same as its rivals – assemble your own raw ingredients from the huge selection that is available, choose a cooking oil and sauce, watch chefs then stir-fry them in a central cooking area – but the quality of the food is better than most. The tasteful modern interior is another plus point, and the regular bursts of flames from the woks make an impressive backdrop. A popular and child-friendly venue.
Buggy access. Children's menu (£5.50). Crayons. Disabled access: toilets. High chairs. Nappy-changing facilities. Toys.
Branches: 16A Clapham Common South Side, SW4 7AB (7720 5433).

Toff's
38 Muswell Hill Broadway, Muswell Hill, N10 3RT (8883 8656). Highgate tube, then 43, 134 bus. **Meals served** 11.30am-10pm Mon-Sat. **Main courses** £8.95-£17.50. **Set meals** (11.30am-5.30pm Mon-Sat) £7.95 1 course incl tea/coffee. **Credit** AmEx, DC, MC, V.
Toff's dining room is a cordoned-off area beyond the take-away zone, decorated with sepia photographs of Victorian fish markets, signed celebrity snaps and the odd gold disc. Think dark wood and cream plasterwork and you'll have

the idea. The nationality of the ownership can be guessed from the presence of calamares, Greek salad and tara-masalata on the menu. If you can, try the fish soup: thick and delicious, but not always available. Batter or matzo, grilled or fried – the options are numerous. Haddock is expertly cooked, white and flaky in a crisp, golden batter, while chips come big and yellow. Fruit flan, apple pie and similar puddings are apparently offered, but we've never had enough room left to find out.

Buggy access. Children's menu (£2.95-£3.50). Crayons. Disabled access: toilets. High chairs. No-smoking tables. Takeaway service.

Wagamama

11 Jamestown Road, Camden, NW1 7BW (7428 0800/ www.wagamama.com). Camden tube. **Meals served** noon-11pm Mon-Sat; noon-10pm Sun. **Main courses** £5.40-£8.90. **Credit** AmEx, DC, MC, V.

Everyone's a bit blasé about noodle bars – a high-street staple nowadays – but it pays to remember that Wagamama is one of the originals, and one of the best. And one of the most successful too, with 20 branches in London alone and outlets as far afield as Australia and Dubai. A gleaming, smoke-free environment, perky staff and a wholesome menu are appealing – especially for families – though not everyone likes the communal tables and resultant noise. For kids, there's chicken katsu (chicken breast fried in breadcrumbs) with dipping sauce, rice and shredded cucumber, or vegetarian or chicken noodle dishes for just £3.50. To drink, choose from raw juices, beer, wine, saké – or drown yourself in gallons of free green tea.

Buggy access. Children's menu (£3.10-£3.85). Disabled access: toilets. High chairs. No smoking. **Branches**: throughout town. Call or check the website.

EAST LONDON

Arkansas Café

Unit 12, Old Spitalfields Market, Whitechapel, E1 6AA (7377 6999). Liverpool Street tube/rail. **Lunch served** noon-2.30pm Mon-Fri; noon-4pm Sun. **Dinner served** party bookings only, by arrangement. **Main courses** £5-£14. **Credit** MC, V. **Map** p319 R5.

This wonderfully eccentric restaurant hovering on the edge of Spitalfields Market is justifiably popular. Its Arkansan owner, Bubba, presides over the barbecue pit, greeting customers with a wave of his spatula while he cooks huge piles of tender beef brisket, pork ribs, perfect duck and juicy chicken. It's a show that the kids will love, and the smell of all that sizzling meat will set mouths watering. Customers sit on a mishmash of church pews and garden chairs. Service is efficient and polite, although you may have to wait if you arrive at peak times on a Sunday.

Buggy access. No-smoking tables. Tables outdoors (terrace inside market).

Faulkner's

424-426 Kingsland Road, Dalston, E8 4AA (7254 6152). Dalston Kingsland rail/67, 76, 149, 242, 243 bus. **Lunch served** noon-2.30pm Mon-Fri. **Dinner served** 5-10pm Mon-Thur; 4.15-10pm Fri. **Meals served** 11.30am-10pm Sat; noon-9pm Sun. **Main courses** £8.90-£17.90. *Minimum* £4. **Credit** MC, V.

The look is traditional: chunky wooden furniture, cream walls dotted with Victorian fishing and Billingsgate photographs. The fish is so fresh it practically leaps from the table, served in golden batter (or grilled) with strapping chunky chips, robust mushy peas and own-made tartare

Your good health

The task of spiriting vegetables, fruit and other forms of goodness into the juvenile diet is one that challenges the abilities of most parents, and often deteriorates into the classic 'you're not leaving that table until…' deadlock. But help is at hand, in the form of London's many exponents of quality green cuisine; that is, restaurants that are able to rustle up tasty, child-friendly (read: ostensibly trashy) dishes that actually contain a healthy dollop of vitamins, minerals and the rest.

Who are these magicians? One example is **Blue Kangaroo** (*see p173*) in Chelsea, where the children's menu manages to underwrite what appear on the surface to be bog-standard dishes with quality organic ingredients: spaghetti bolognese, for instance, has organic Scottish beef; the fish cakes use only wild salmon; sausages are organic, as is the free-range chicken in the nuggets.

Sabzi sandwich bar (*see p168*) in the West End is also dead set on using as many organic ingredients as possible and, like **Konditor & Cook** (*see p160*) and **Shish** (*see p161*), it has wonderful juices, packed full of vitamins. But one of the most impressive purveyors of healthy children's nosh in London is the 2004 Time Out Restaurant Award winner **Frizzante at City Farm**

(*see p179*). Based at Hackney City Farm, this clean-living restaurant is a family haven. Fresh, tasty dishes like pumpkin and spinach pie or salade niçoise are made with top-quality ingredients; even the fry-ups use free-range eggs.

Further west, meanwhile, the **Bush Garden Café** (*see p183*) is the answer to any yummy mummy's (or daddy's) prayers. The shelves of this wholefood café and grocer are positively groaning with goodness, and the temptation to sit down and spend an hour or two gorging yourself (and the kids) with a clean conscience is virtually impossible to resist. And even if the little 'uns have already made short work of their organic chocolate while you're still enjoying one of the superb house salads, never fear: there's an all-weather playhouse in the garden.

Last and by no means least, the ubiquitous **Giraffe** restaurants (*see p164*) give children the chance to mix and match their normal pasta and burgers (these ones are made with Angus beef, naturally) with less common, healthier options like falafel in a bun. Desserts even run to organic fresh-fruit sorbets; drinks include delicious fresh-fruit smoothies. As they never tire of telling you, their emphasis is on 'yummy, fresh and healthy eating'. Enough said.

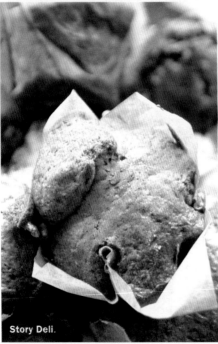

Story Deli.

sauce that'd do credit to the finest kitchen. Comfort staples such as cherry pie, sherry trifle and spotted dick are among the puds. Service comes from matronly waitresses. *Buggy access. Children's menu (£4.90). Disabled access: toilet. High chairs. No-smoking tables. Takeaway service.*

Frizzante at City Farm
1A Goldsmith's Row, Hackney, E2 8QA (7739 2266). Bethnal Green tube, then 55 or 106 bus. **Meals served** 10am-5.30pm Tue-Sun. **Main courses** £4.50-£6.50. **Credit** AmEx, DC, MC, V.
Sensitive souls may not want to order the grilled chicken skewers out of respect for the bantams pecking around outside Hackney City Farm's delightful Italian café. But be assured they are delicious (the skewers, that is), as is everything else sampled on the chalked-up, changing menu. Location is all, of course, especially when you've brought a young family for lunch, and this place has built-in baaing, lowing, clucking and grunting entertainment, as well as a tiny slide in the garden by the outdoor eating area. On sunny Sundays it's almost impossible to bag a table for lunch, but the premises have a comfy, community-centre-ish feel, with pinboards advertising baby yoga and pottery classes. The all-day cooked breakfasts come with free-range eggs as standard, or try more interesting light-lunch choices, such as pumpkin and spinach pie, salade niçoise, spaghetti with mussels, glorious own-made gnocchi with mushroom sauce, or those chicken skewers with golden fried potatoes. If the children don't fancy the specials, there are pizza and pasta options. *Buggy access. Children's menu (£2.50-£3.50). Disabled access: toilets. High chairs. No smoking (inside). Tables outdoors (7, garden). Takeaway service. Toys.*

Hadley House
27 High Street, Wanstead, E11 2AA (8989 8855). Snaresbrook or Wanstead tube. **Lunch served** noon-2.30pm, **dinner served** 7-10.30pm Mon-Sat. **Meals served** 10.30am-9pm Sun. **Main courses** £8.95-£16.95. **Set dinner** (Mon) £17.95 3 courses. **Credit** MC, V.
Near the Essex border, Hadley House is a pleasant café-cum-restaurant with a front terrace overlooking a green. From coffees and pâtisserie to lobster and wild mushrooms, the kitchen tries to turn out everything locals could desire. Evening menus seem pricey; breakfasts and lunches are more generous, both in portion and price. At Sunday lunch, roasts come as vast pieces of meat. Although available as reduced-price children's portions, they'll probably prefer the own-made burger, which comes with fat yellow chips and salad. Worth the trip. *Buggy access. High chairs. Reduced-price children's portions. Tables outdoors (6, patio).*

Jones Dairy Café
23 Ezra Street, Bethnal Green, E2 7RH (7739 5372). Old Street tube/rail, then 55 bus. **Open** 9am-3pm Fri, Sat; 8am-2pm Sun. **Main courses** £4-£7. **No credit cards.**
On Sunday mornings, when the Columbia Road Flower Market is in full bloom, this adorable little operation gets overrun by families and green-fingered locals well aware that it has the best bread in the area and the finest bagels this side of Brick Lane. On Fridays and Saturdays, though, it's a far more sedate operation, dishing up daisy-fresh brunches to locals sat around a large farmhouse table or,

in summer, on the peaceful street outside. The menu is tiny, but you can't really go wrong with any of it. A shop, tucked around the corner, offers a wider range of breads, a worthwhile selection of cheeses and a small assortment of other picnic-friendly temptations. *Buggy access. Disabled access. High chair. No smoking. Tables outdoors (3, patio). Takeaway service.*

Royal China
30 Westferry Circus, Docklands, E14 8RR (7719 0888). Canary Wharf tube/DLR/Westferry DLR. **Meals served** noon-11pm Mon-Thur; noon-11.30pm Fri, Sat; 11am-10pm Sun. **Dim sum served** noon-4.45pm daily. **Main courses** £7-£50. **Dim sum** £2.20-£4.50. **Set meal** £28 per person (minimum 2). **Credit** AmEx, DC, MC, V.
Forget the Bayswater branch, with its stressful weekend queueing, and head instead to this jewel in the Royal China crown. On a warm spring evening, park the buggy outside, decant the kids on to the terrace and watch the sun set over the glittering sweep of the Thames. The menu, one of the best and most authentic Cantonese selections in town, has plenty to interest young and old. Whole king prawns deep-fried and encrusted with a delicious paste of salted duck egg yolk is an example that springs to mind. Service, though occasionally hectic, is also much better than at the Bayswater branch. *Booster seats. Disabled access: toilet. Tables outdoors (23, terrace).*
Branches: 40 Baker Street, W1M 1BA (7487 4688); 13 Queensway, W2 4QJ (7221 2535); 68 Queen's Grove, NW8 6ER (7586 4280).

Sông Quê
134 Kingsland Road, Shoreditch, E2 8DY (7613 3222). Bus 26, 48, 55, 67, 149, 242, 243. **Meals served** noon-3pm, 5.30-11pm Mon-Sat; noon-11pm Sun. **Main courses** £4-£8.50. **Credit** MC, V.
Despite all the plaudits heaped upon it, Sông Quê has resisted the temptation to ratchet up the prices, making it an excellent place to feed the family. Deep-fried tofu costs just £2, and even the massive, totally addictive pancakes served with herbs and dipping sauce are very decently priced (the tofu version costs £4; the prawn and chicken one is £4.80). The functional decor is not much to write home about, the lighting is bright and the basement is very curious indeed (a glorified, ramshackle storage space that you must pass through to reach the loo), but Sông Quê is still a must-visit Vietnamese in an increasingly crowded market. *Buggy access. High chairs. No-smoking tables. Takeaway service.*

Story Deli
3 Dray Walk, The Old Truman Brewery, 91 Brick Lane, E1 6QL (7247 3137). Liverpool Street tube/rail. **Meals served** 8am-7pm daily. **Main courses** £2-£7.50. **Credit** AmEx, MC, V. **Map** p319 S5.
This fun, stylish deli-cum-pizzeria is as popular with roaming mums and their kids as it is with the trendy new-media bods who live and work around here. Behind huge plate-glass windows you'll find exposed brickwork, a mezzanine kitchen (reached via stairs lined with flour sacks) and a couple of vast old tables seemingly pinched from a baronet's scullery. Diners sit communally around one of the big tables, perched on cardboard-box stools; the other table displays bowls of salad and quiches. Otherwise the menu

consists of breakfasts, the odd special (a whopping, strongly flavoured kedgeree topped with a feather-light herb omelette), pizzas and alluring cakes and tarts. Service is casual (and occasionally shambolic). Pizzas are superb, with bubbly thin bases, high-quality tomato and mozzarella toppings, and top-notch extras.
Tables outdoors (6, pavement). Takeaway service.

SOUTH-EAST LONDON

Au Ciel
1A Calton Avenue, Dulwich Village, SE21 7DE (8488 1111). North Dulwich rail/P4, 37 bus. **Snacks served** 8.30am-5.30pm Mon-Sat; 10am-5.30pm Sun. **Snacks** £2.25-£3. **Credit** MC, V.
Au Ciel, formerly an expensive pâtisserie and chocolaterie for the well-heeled of Dulwich Village, has recently been transformed into a French café. And has, as a result, become deliriously popular with resident mums, who drop in to administer the afternoon feed (both baby's and their own). We recommend one of the sinfully indulgent house hot chocolates partnered by a slice of excellent cake. There are also French chocolates from Valrhona, fresh pâtisserie from Didier (French bakers) and De Baere (Belgian), and organic bread and pastries from Sally Clarke. In fact, the whole operation is unashamedly indulgent (there are only two savoury dishes), and provides a welcome touch of class and character in an area otherwise beset by pedestrian chain outlets.
Tables outdoors (2, pavement). Takeaway service.

Domali Café
38 Westow Street, Crystal Palace, SE19 3AH (8768 0096/www.domali.co.uk). Gypsy Hill rail. **Meals served** 9.30am-11pm daily. **Main courses** (lunch) £3.90-£9.50. **Credit** MC, V.
This cosy, homely café has a rambling garden at the back, complete with outdoor heater. The long breakfast menu plus the huge range of toasties and sandwiches appear to be the strengths; otherwise, choosing between 'specials' and 'favourites' could be confusing. We were surprised to see ribbolita on the menu – a classic Tuscan bean and cabbage stew, it rarely features in veggie restaurants. This version was packed with vegetables and topped with cheese: inauthentic, but pleasant. Children's portions are available, and the chunky chips are fabulous, but please note: the 'chargrilled farmhouse bread' served with many main dishes is just good ol' toast.
Buggy access. High chairs. No-smoking tables. Tables outdoors (10, garden). Reduced portions for children (£1.45-£3.50).

Olley's
65-69 Norwood Road, Herne Hill, SE24 9AA (8671 8259/www.olleys.info). Herne Hill rail/3, 68 bus. **Meals served** 5-10.30pm Mon; noon-10.30pm Tue-Sun. **Main courses** £5.75-£18.25. **Credit** AmEx, MC, V.
A railway arch in Herne Hill isn't the obvious place to find one of the best chip shops in town, but that's what you get at Olley's. Children get their own diminutive menu, while adults can tuck into starters such as 'Neptune's punchbowl' (creamy fish soup), prawn cocktail and specials. Chips are pre-blanched then fried in groundnut oil for a two-tone crunchy shell and soft inside; we're told the batter for the fish is kept cold to ensure a crisp, even coating.

Staff are ridiculously friendly and helpful, tempting you with puddings (apple pie, gourmet ice-creams) you won't ever be able to finish.
Children's menu (£4). High chairs. Tables outdoors (12, pavement). Takeaway service.

Pavilion Café
Dulwich Park, off College Road, Dulwich, SE21 7BQ (8299 1383). North Dulwich or West Dulwich rail. **Open** *Summer* 9am-6pm (with some late evenings) daily. *Winter* 9am-dusk daily. **Main courses** £3.50-£6.50. **No credit cards.**
This cool, clean, welcoming space is just what you'd hope to find down Dulwich way. The glass-fronted pavilion, decorated with striking contemporary art (for sale) and large bunches of fresh flowers, can be opened up on hot days, with plenty of tables inside, though it's a bit of a squeeze outside. The café has a relaxing vibe even when busy. Sweets, lollies, ice-creams, English breakfasts and the usual sandwiches and cakes are available, but the Pavilion goes a step further than your average park café, with the likes of orange-blossom and ginger cake, and tender pork marinated with rosemary, served in flatbread with salad and apple and cinnamon sauce. Produce is free-range and locally sourced. Children's parties are a speciality.
Buggy access. Children's menu (£1.50-£3). Disabled access: toilet. High chairs. Nappy-changing facilities. Tables outdoors (11, terrace). Takeaway service. Toys.

El Pirata
15-16 Royal Parade, Blackheath, SE3 OTL (8297 1880). Blackheath rail. **Meals served** noon-midnight daily. **Main courses** £8-£13. **Tapas** £2-£7. **Credit** AmEx, DC, MC, V.
This swashbuckling slice of Spain does very nicely in Blackheath's well-to-do urban village, probably because prices are low (for the area), the welcome cheerful and there's plenty of room for large family groups at weekend lunchtimes. The piratical theme is limited to a few props, such as crossed cutlasses and a ship's wheel; it's the tapas list that arouses most interest. The emphasis is mainly on bestsellers, such as patatas bravas, tortilla, pinche de pollo and various seafood and salad-based items. Puddings are limited to unexciting staples, such as ice-creams, bombes, fried bananas and crêpes, but the service could not have been sweeter. No wonder families like it so much.
Buggy access. High chairs. Tables outdoors (5, pavement).

TOP 5   Play areas

Blue Kangaroo
Chelsea. *See p173.*

Burlington's Café
Chiswick. *See p183.*

Bush Garden Café
Shepherd's Bush. *See p183.*

Frizzante at City Farm
Hackney. *See p179.*

Smollensky's on the Strand
West End. *See p171.*

SOUTH-WEST LONDON

Blue Elephant
4-6 Fulham Broadway, Fulham, SW6 1AA (7385 6595/www.blueelephant.com). Fulham Broadway tube. **Lunch served** noon-2.30pm Mon-Fri; noon-4pm Sun. **Dinner served** 7pm-midnight Mon-Thur; 6.30pm-midnight Fri, Sat; 7-10.30pm Sun. **Main courses** £9.50-£28. **Set buffet** (Sun lunch) £22 adults, £11 children. **Credit** AmEx, DC, MC, V.
The interior of this rather corporate Thai (abundant foliage, ponds, bridges, waterfalls and ethnic ornaments) may not suit every adult's taste but kids love it. The food, too, is delicious and surprisingly good value. A mixed platter of starters brings such delights as succulent chicken legs; plump, well-filled spring rolls; crisp, spicy sweet corn cakes; and stuffed baby corn wrapped in pastry – each with a different dipping sauce. Also good for families is the khantoke platter, which includes a distinctively spiced mussaman curry, aubergine and okra in chilli paste, and beef stir-fried with basil. Be warned, though: some dishes are hot enough to melt milk teeth. During the Sunday brunch buffet, a children's entertainer wanders among the tables with face-paint and other bits and pieces.
Buggy access. Delivery service. Disabled access: toilets. High chairs. Takeaway service.

Boiled Egg & Soldiers
63 Northcote Road, Battersea, SW11 1ND (7223 4894). Clapham Junction rail, then 219 bus. **Open** 9am-6pm Mon-Sat; 9am-4pm Sun. **Main courses** £2.95-£5.50. **No credit cards.**
This café on family-friendly Northcote Road is a promising breakfast spot: a huge menu boasts everything from healthy morning treats to stodgy hangover fare, complete with hair-of-the-dog cocktails. The simple, primary-coloured decor is reminiscent of Ikea's kiddie-room department, while the few outside tables are perfectly positioned for sunny days. Combos include the 'posh breakfast' of smoked salmon and a glass of bubbly, full fry-ups, variations on the boiled egg and soldiers theme, plus classics such as cucumber sandwiches and Marmite on toast. Freshly squeezed orange juice is standard and the menu promises quality, but we were a bit disappointed with airline-style scrambled eggs and soggy toast, although a steak sandwich was fine. It's a popular place and great for kids – next time, though, we'll go for the Battersea cream tea instead of eggs.
Buggy access. Children's menu (from £2.25). Crayons. High chairs. Tables outdoors (3, pavement; 8, garden).

Crumpet
66 Northcote Road, Battersea, SW11 6QL (7924 1117). Clapham Junction rail. **Open** 9am-6pm Mon-Sat; 10am-6pm Sun. **Main courses** £3.95-£6.95. **Credit** AmEx, MC, V.
Not for nothing is Northcote Road known as 'nappy valley'. It's like a pushchair demolition derby some afternoons, but if you duck into this friendly café you'll be sure to find some respite. And that doesn't just apply to young parents (although they certainly are in evidence, their offspring safely deposited in the tree-house-style children's play area at the back) but to all manner of Wandsworth wanderers. Teas are taken seriously here, with a choice of 22 (ranging from the usual suspects to more obscure varieties like Russian Caravan), and there are plenty of wholesome

snacks, too. Daily specials (maybe quiche or courgette and leek soup), all kinds of sarnies (often with free-range fillings), salads and Welsh rarebit are typical choices. Organic soft drinks and a good kids' menu (everything from finger sandwiches to macaroni cheese) are also on hand to refuel play-weary tots.
Buggy access. Children's menu (£1.45-£3.95). Disabled access: toilets. High chairs. Nappy-changing facilities. Play area. Tables outdoors (3, pavement). Takeaway service.

The Depot
Tideway Yard, Mortlake High Street, Barnes, SW14 8SN (8878 9462). Barnes Bridge or Mortlake rail/209 bus. **Lunch served** noon-3pm Mon-Fri; noon-4pm Sat, Sun. **Dinner served** 6-11pm Mon-Sat; 6-10.30pm Sun. **Main courses** £9.95-£15. **Set meal** (Mon-Fri lunch) £12.50 2 courses. **Credit** AmEx, DC, MC, V.
Where so many fail, this riverside establishment effortlessly conjures that laid-back brasserie vibe. With gleaming woodwork and well-spaced tables, it's best visited in the day or at sunset for impressive views over the Barnes bend of the Thames. The menu makes good use of seasonal ingredients, and prices are fair for this upmarket neighbourhood (the children's menu is particularly good value); there's also a limited but bargain-priced two-course set menu. The shoestring chips, in particular, are ace.
Buggy access. Children's menu (£4.50 incl free ice-cream). Crayons. High chairs. Nappy-changing facilities. No-smoking tables. Tables outdoors (6, courtyard).

Dexter's Grill
20 Bellevue Road, Wandsworth, SW17 7EB (8767 1858). Wandsworth Common rail. **Meals served** noon-11pm Mon-Fri; 11am-11pm Sat, Sun. **Main courses** £6.50-£14. **Credit** AmEx, MC, V.
Owned by the same company as Tootsies, this family restaurant is a useful spot. With exposed brick walls, large windows and friendly staff, it's a very welcoming place. The menu puts an emphasis on gourmet sandwiches, hamburgers and fresh salads, and there's a selection of organic specialities for young children – the 'curly whirly' chicken is popular. Large, juicy hamburgers are served with lots of crisp chips; house speciality ice-creams come in portions big enough to satisfy three (staff are used to customers asking for extra spoons). Don't overlook the smoothies and shakes either.
Buggy access. Children's menu (£4.95 2 courses incl drink). Crayons. High chairs. Nappy-changing facilities. No-smoking area. Tables outdoors (8, balcony terrace). Takeaway service.

Don Fernando's
27F The Quadrant, Richmond, Surrey TW9 1DN (8948 6447/www.donfernando.co.uk). Richmond tube/rail. **Meals served** noon-3pm, 6-11pm Mon, Tue; noon-11pm Wed-Sat; noon-10pm Sun. **Main courses** £7.25-£13.25. **Tapas** £3-£5. **Set meals** £15-£19 2 courses. **Credit** AmEx, MC, V.
Spanish tiles covering every available surface of this large and lively restaurant, combined with friendly and efficient staff, alert you to the fact this is an authentic Spanish restaurant presided over by a Spanish family who know a thing or two about restaurants and food. The decent tapas selection has lots of child-friendly fare, notably tortilla,

meatballs in a tasty sauce, monkfish and ham kebabs, tender chicken breast in various guises, stuffed peppers, vegetable croquettes and fried potatoes. *Buggy access. High chairs. No-smoking tables. Tables outdoors (6, pavement).*

Gourmet Burger Kitchen

44 Northcote Road, Battersea, SW11 1NZ (7228 3309/www.gbkinfo.co.uk). Clapham Junction rail. **Meals served** noon-11pm Mon-Fri; 11am-11pm Sat; 11am-10pm Sun. **Main courses** £5.45-£7.40. **Credit** MC, V.
Standing proud at more than half a foot high, Gourmet Burger Kitchen's burgers are Scooby snacks to be proud of. The meat is 100% Aberdeen Angus Scotch beef, shaped into thick patties and cooked to your liking (medium-rare to well done), served in a sourdough roll topped with sesame. Kids will need two hands to eat them. The toppings are pretty imaginative too. This being a NZ-owned mini chain, we'd recommend the Kiwiburger, topped with beetroot, egg, pineapple, cheese, salad and relish. Other toppings include smoky barbecue sauce, fresh garlic mayo, pesto and many other tempting ingredients. Oh, and don't forget the chips, which are golden on the outside and fluffy in the middle: near perfect.
Buggy access. High chairs. No smoking. Tables outdoors (4, pavement).
Branches: 50 Westbourne Grove, W2 5SH (7243 4344); 331 West End Lane, NW6 1RS (7794 5455); 131 Chiswick High Road, W4 2ED (8995 4548); 333 Putney Bridge Road, SW15 2PG (8789 1199); 49 Fulham Broadway, SW6 1AE (7381 4242); 15-17 Hill Rise, TW10 6UA (8940 5440); 200 Haverstock Hill, NW3 2AG (7794 5455).

Newtons

33-35 Abbeville Road, Clapham, SW4 9LA (8673 0977/www.newtonsrestaurants.co.uk). Clapham South tube. **Meals served** noon-11.30pm Mon-Fri; 10am-11.30pm Sat; 10am-10.30pm Sun. **Main courses** £9-£16. **Set lunch** (noon-3pm Mon-Sat) £8 2 courses, £10.50 3 courses. **Credit** AmEx, MC, V.
There's a neighbourly feel to this professionally run French-style joint (think plain wooden chairs and tables, painted brickwork, starched tablecloths) on chi-chi Abbeville Road. Families and mums with pushchairs are among the many regular lunchers and brunchers. Children can either choose a mini portion of what the grown-ups are having or else opt for more conventional kiddie grub (nuggets etc). A few coveted pavement tables are great for summer grazing.
Buggy access. Children's menu (£5). High chairs. No-smoking tables. Tables outdoors (7, terrace).

Petersham Nurseries

Petersham Nurseries, Petersham Road, Petersham, near Richmond, Surrey TW10 7AG (8940 5230). Richmond tube/rail then half-hour walk or 65 bus. **Open** noon-2.30pm Thur-Sun. **Main courses** £7-£15. **Credit** MC, V.
Petersham Nurseries is an idyllic spot. A bucolic setting between Richmond Hill and the Thames, this garden centre and café is surrounded by landscaped horse paddocks, meadows and woodland. A large wooden shed contains the café kitchen and some more seating. A blackboard outside the door lists the day's specials – potato, leek and thyme soup, say, or beef with green beans, potatoes,

roasted tomatoes chicory and rocket. There's no kids' menu, but staff are happy to serve smaller portions. The good life doesn't come cheap in Petersham, but then all the meats and dairy produce is organic, the fish are line-caught, and many of the herbs, soft fruit and salad leaves are grown on-site. Dishes are simple, but well executed; the cream teas and cakes are excellent. And we didn't mind paying over the odds to enjoy a little corner of Eden.
Buggy access. Disabled access: toilets. High chairs. No smoking (inside). Tables outdoors (6, garden).

Victoria

West Temple Sheen, East Sheen, SW14 7RT (8876 4238/www.thevictoria.net). Mortlake rail/33, 337 bus. **Breakfast served** 7-9.30am Mon-Fri; 8-10am Sat, Sun. **Lunch served** noon-2.30pm Mon-Fri; noon-3pm Sat; noon-4pm Sun. **Dinner served** 7-10pm daily. **Main courses** £10.95-£19.95. **Credit** AmEx, MC, V.
A backstreet of residential East Sheen is the surprising location for this charming restaurant with a small hotel attached (or is it the other way around?). It's not really a gastropub; there is a bar, but it's small and basically an adjunct of the restaurant. And the cooking is definitely a notch above (in quality and pricing) what you'll find in many gastropubs. Bright, creamy beetroot risotto and pan-fried halibut are typical mains. In warmer weather, kids will love the scrumptious summer pudding, not to mention the timber play area on the back patio.
Buggy access. High chairs. Nappy-changing facilities. No smoking (dining area). Tables outdoors (9, garden & play area).

WEST LONDON

Babes 'n' Burgers

275 Portobello Road, Notting Hill, W11 1LR (7727 4163). Ladbroke Grove tube. **Meals served** 9am-11.30pm Mon-Sat, 9am-10.30pm Sun. **Main courses** £4.50-£6. **Credit** MC, V.
Press coverage for this organic burger bar with children's playroom came thick and fast when it opened in September 2004. It still displays features from gushing west London mummy/journos, although the excitement has died down now, and it's easy to find a seat. Children get a playroom at the back, which has books, soft banquettes, crayons and toddler toys to smear organic ketchup all over. The menu lists organic burgers, chicken breast, tofu vegetarian alternatives, substantial breakfasts and a long list of healthful smoothies and wheatgrass-based sustainers, as well as hot drinks and fizzy pop. 'Healthy' cola, much to the children's disgust, turned out to be a rather watery imitation of the real thing, but the juices are lovely. Burgers for kids (served in two sizes with chips – £4 for no trimmings or £4.50 with) are lean and flavoursome but appear insubstantial, probably because the pleasantly doughy sesame seed bun also packs in mountains of leaves, tomato, onion and relish. The juicy tofu, bean and veg patty is delicious, with little crunchy burnt bits giving a barbecue flavour, but it could have been a little hotter. Chips are golden, crisp, a bit oily but tasty. Other sides are hilarious – you can choose a pot of 'livin' sprouts' (sprouted mung beans). More realistically, sweet things include chocolate brownies (£3.20), cheesecake (£3.60) and a sugar-free banana cake for £2.80.
Buggy access. Children's menu (£1.95-£4.50). Disabled access: toilets. High chairs. Nappy-changing facilities. No smoking. Toys.

Burlington's Café

Chiswick House, off Burlington Lane, Chiswick,
W4 2RP (8987 9431). Turnham Green tube/Chiswick
rail. **Meals served** *Oct-Mar* 10am-4pm Thur-Sun.
Apr-Sept 9.30am-5pm daily. **Main courses** £3.95-
£6.50. **No credit cards.**
In stark contrast to the grandeur of Chiswick House, Lord
Burlington's Palladian masterpiece, the café in the house's
grounds is set in a rather run-down pavilion. Where lichen
and peeling paintwork hold a certain charm in the
sculpted and landscaped gardens, the café just feels a bit
dingy. Nevertheless, it's a handy bolt-hole for strolling
families. The food is simple: full English breakfasts, bacon
rolls, sarnies and a few pasta dishes. Burlington's also
offers lollies, ice-creams and free dog biscuits. Parents can
relax while the kids play on the green in front of the café.
Buggy access. Children's menu (£2-£3.50). High chairs.
Nappy-changing facilities. No smoking. Play area.
Tables outdoors (10, garden). Toys.

Bush Bar & Grill

45A Goldhawk Road, Shepherd's Bush, W12 8QP
(8746 2111/www.bushbar.co.uk). Goldhawk Road tube.
Lunch served noon-3pm Mon-Sat; 11.30-6pm Sun.
Dinner served 5.30-11.30pm Mon-Sat. **Main courses**
£9.50-£17. **Set lunch** (Mon-Sat) £12.50 2 courses,
£15 3 courses. **Credit** AmEx, MC, V.
It's easy to miss the entrance to what used to be a ware-
house-like watering hole for Aussies, but is now a favoured
haunt of local families and BBC folk who work close by.
The Bush Bar & Grill has a spacious feel, with two bar
areas (one curtained-off, which can be booked) and a leafy
outside space. The menu features chunky salads and a
range of meat and fish, with an emphasis on carefully
sourced, seasonal, free-range or organic produce. Chef
Wayne Dixon seems to have improved things in the
kitchen after our disappointing last visit. A delicately
flavoured starter of crab and spiced avocado set the tone,
while a main of Blenheim lamb was a lovely cut of meat,
cooked to perfection. Haddock fish cakes were munchable
rather than memorable. Despite the 'would rather be anywhere but here' air of the staff, service was attentive.
There's a weekend brunch menu (on our visit, children
could eat for free on a Sunday).
Buggy access. Children's menu (free with adult order
Sun). Disabled access: toilets. High chairs. Nappy-
changing facilities. Tables outdoors (8, courtyard).

Bush Garden Café

59 Goldhawk Road, Shepherd's Bush, W12 8EG
(8743 6372). Goldhawk Road tube. **Meals served**
8am-5pm Mon-Sat. **Main courses** £3.90-£4.60.
Credit (over £10) AmEx, MC, V.
Just walking into this amiably staffed, attractive wholefood café and grocery makes your tummy rumble. With its
shelves of organic pastas, sauces, wines and treats, and
chilled counter full of bright salads, quiches, pies and pastries, it's always time for lunch. There's plenty of space for
children, especially out in the garden with its playhouse
and rainproof canopy. Indoors, the white tongue-and-
groove walls and mismatched furniture exude a busy
household air. The food is cooked with enormous flair and
salads are laden with quality items at very ordinary prices.
The children's menu offers nursery food such as beans or
eggs on toast, with organic chocolate or cake for afters.
Buggy access. High chairs. Nappy-changing facilities.
No smoking. Tables outdoors (5, garden).

Moroccan Tagine

95 Golborne Road, Ladbroke Grove, W10 5NL
(8968 8055). Ladbroke Grove or Westbourne Park
tube/23 bus. **Meals served** noon-11pm daily.
Main courses £5.50-£7.90. **Credit** MC, V.
The prices have crept up a little with the arrival of fancy
new laminated menus, but otherwise this remains a no-
frills, Moroccan caff, well sited among the halal butchers
and cumin-scented grocer shops on Golborne Road,
London's hunting ground for all things North African. The
food is superb – couscous, tagines and tender, grilled meats
– all prepared by genial, bearded Hassan, a Berber from
the mountains of Morocco. The olives that come as a complimentary starter are particularly good; they're imported
and then specially marinated to Hassan's own recipe. An
exotic treat for children with adventurous palates.
Buggy access. High chairs. No-smoking tables.
Tables outdoors (8, pavement). Takeaway service.
Branches: throughout town. Check the phone book for
your nearest.

Rotisserie Jules

133A Notting Hill Gate, Notting Hill, W11 3LB
(7221 3331/www.rotisseriejules.com). Notting Hill Gate
tube. **Meals served** noon-11pm daily. **Main courses**
£5.75-£10.75. **Credit** AmEx, MC, V.
Anyone who has a craving for chicken and chips (which,
let's face it, encompasses pretty much all children and most
adults) will find what they're looking for here. The menu
proudly proclaims, 'except for bread and ice-cream, everything we serve is prepared on the premises from scratch
and without frozen products'. The children's menu is great
value, and a half chicken can serve two adults at £6.75,
with crispy french fries to accompany weighing in at a non-
too-hefty £2. You can't argue with that.
Buggy access. Children's menu (£4.25). Delivery service.
Disabled access: toilets. High chairs. No-smoking tables.
Table outdoors (1, pavement). Takeaway service.

Tootsies Grill

120 Holland Park Avenue, Holland Park, W11 4UA
(7229 8567/www.tootsiesrestaurants.co.uk). Holland
Park tube. **Meals served** 8am-11pm Mon-Thur;
8am-11.30pm Fri; 9am-11.30pm Sat; 9am-11pm Sun.
Main courses £5.95-£12.50. **Credit** AmEx, MC, V.
This growing chain (11 outlets in London at the last count)
is a handy option for parents: the menu is affordable, the
food is good if basic, and it's very child-friendly. At this
branch, big windows look out over leafy Holland Park
Avenue, and old posters portray both British and
American themes. We visited on a busy Sunday afternoon,
but staff coped well. For starters, grilled prawns arrived
with shells and heads still in place. This made for some
messy peeling, but the end result was worth it as the
shellfish were big, fresh and plump. Hamburgers take
centre stage on the menu, and with every reason: they're
thick and juicy, cooked to order, with every imaginable
variation available. If red meat doesn't appeal, the grilled
chicken sandwich with cheese and avocado is delicious.
Tootsies' milkshakes are also fabulous (the butterscotch is
recommended unreservedly), and desserts are all serious
ice-cream concoctions.
Balloons. Buggy access. Children's menu (£4.95-£5.95
incl drink & dessert). Crayons. High chairs. No smoking.
Tables outdoors (3, pavement). Takeaway service.
Branches: throughout town. Call or check the website.

Consumer

SHOPPING

What's in store for the kids.

HP sourced at **Daunt Books**. *See p187*.

London is a shopper's paradise. The retail diversity of its department stores, markets, glam boutiques and thrift shops is second to none. To appreciate it all, however, you will need to make full use of your family travelcard. It may be tempting to stay in the West End with the big hitters like Hamley's (*see p205*) and Selfridges (*see p185*) but we urge you to explore further afield. Some of the specialist toyshops and crammed clothing exchanges listted below may necessitate close inspection of the *A-Z*, but they're worth it. Don't miss the street markets, either – as much tourist attractions as retail experiences, you'll find them in the **Around Town** chapters. Our favourites are in the East End (**Columbia Road**, *see p106*; **Brick Lane** and smart **Spitalfields**, *see p104 for both*), but Battersea's **Northcote Road** (*see p139*) also has some great stuff for families and **Portobello Market** (*see p150*) had star quality even before Richard Curtis made it into a fairytale setting in the film *Notting Hill*. Of course, teenagers will not rest until they've jostled sulkily through heaving **Camden Market** (*see p90*). It's a phase everyone goes through.

ALL-ROUNDERS

Daisy & Tom

181-183 King's Road, SW3 5EB (7352 5000/www. daisyandtom.com). Sloane Square tube then 11, 19, 22, 49 bus. **Open** *9.30am-6pm Mon, Tue, Thur, Fri; 10am-7pm Wed, Sat; 11am-5pm Sun.* **Credit** *AmEx, MC, V.* **Map** *p313 E12.*
About as complete as a children's shop could be, Daisy & Tom splits its wares over two bulging, diverse levels. On the first floor are nursery equipment and furniture, a toy department and a 'girls' room'. On the second, you'll find the clothes and shoes. Also on site are a mini carousel (rides are at 11am, 1pm, 3pm, 5pm Mon-Sat; 11am, 3pm Sun), puppet shows (every 25 mins), tricycles for that quick pedal about the store (and then, of course, the opportunity to buy one) and haircuts (£16 for a first cut with certificate). Among the 12 different brands of pushchair are Boz by Baby Comfort, Silver Cross and the Gwyneth Paltrow-favoured Bugaboo. The clothing department carries Daisy & Tom in abundance, Timberland, Elle, Catimini and more. The book department has a central area padded out with big beanbags and cushions. A programme of events (check the website for details) features in-store face-painting, storytelling and visits from favourite authors. *Buggy access. Disabled access: ramp, toilet. Mail order. Nappy-changing facilities. Play area.*

Harrods

87-135 Brompton Road, Knightsbridge, SW1X 7XL (7730 1234/www.harrods.com). Knightsbridge tube. **Open** 10am-7pm Mon-Sat. **Credit** AmEx, DC, MC, V. **Map** p313 F9.

The fourth floor of Harrods is more of a universe dedicated to children than a department. You float through enormous rooms, each with its own theme or collection; expect pumping music, wild but well-chosen colours and, in the toy rooms, entertainers. Clothes begin with cool streetwear like O'Neill and Quiksilver for young teenagers and rolls into couture 'casualwear' with styles for newborns onwards: Burberry, Roberto Cavalli (a fetching Cavalli jacket for a ten-year-old girl is £209), Christian Dior (a baby's jacket is £67.95), Moschino and Armani to name a few. The shoe collection is sparse in comparison – only a few styles by Start-Rite, Naturino and Instep, plus a few fancier Italian brands. The toy rooms are dedicated to kits and Lego, games, rippling acres of stuffed Harrods bears, cars, dolls, costumes and more. There is face-painting, haircutting and lots of interactive fun to be had. The nursery department carries all the essentials in prams and buggies, cots and high chairs, and with true Harrodian flair also includes items such as a racing car bed (£699).

Buggy access. Café. Car park. Delivery service. Disabled access: lift, toilet. Mail order. Nappy-changing facilities.

John Lewis

278-306 Oxford Street, Oxford Circus, W1A 1EX (7629 7711/www.johnlewis.co.uk). Bond Street or Oxford Circus tube. **Open** 9.30am-7pm Mon-Wed, Fri, Sat; 9.30am-8pm Thur; noon-6pm Sun. **Credit** MC, V. **Map** p314 H6.

Every parent's friend, doughty old John Lewis can be relied on for the most courteous staff, the best-quality nursery equipment, the widest-ranging school uniform selection and some very attractive young fashions. The service in their shoe department is exemplary (the fairly standard fitting procedure is done thoroughly and sensitively; stock consists of sturdy Clarkes, Start-Rites and pre-walkers in addition to trendier Kangaroos, Tods, Reebok, Nike and Puma brands). It's all on the fourth floor, where the spacious toy department contains a pleasant balance of much-advertised toys of the moment and educational playthings. The range of art and craft kits, such as first tapestry or jewellery-making sets, is also inspiring, and there are plenty of toys left out for children to test. The Lego Darth Vader at the door attracts many light-sabre challenges from snotty-nosed would-be Lukes. Sports fashions, party dresses, designer suits and sensible school coats are all well covered in the clothing range, and John Lewis is renowned for its skiwear in tiny sizes.

Pregnant women with time to spare enjoy the in-store nursery advice service, where experts help them decide on the cots, high chairs, changing stations, prams, buggies et al that they want to fill their house with. You make an appointment with the nursery advisor for a one-to-one consultation and a tour of the nursery department, then the two of you can compile a gift list for friends and family to boggle at. It's also worth noting that John Lewis has the best maternity bra fitting service, with foundation garments suited to all breastfeeding eventualities. Safety first is the name of the child-rearing game, of course, which is why there's also a car-seat fitting advisory service. All this, and they're 'never knowingly undersold'.

Buggy access. Cafés. Delivery service. Disabled access: lifts, toilets. Mail order. Nappy-changing facilities.

Mothercare

461 Oxford Street, W1C 2EB (7629 6621/www. mothercare.com). Marble Arch tube. **Open** 9am-8pm Mon-Fri; 9.30am-8pm Sat; noon-6pm Sun. **Credit** AmEx, MC, V. **Map** p314 G6.

Struggling to hold firm against increasing competition from cost-cutting baby wares offered by the likes of Tesco and IKEA, Mothercare nonetheless retains its image in the minds of most as the mothership for all things infant-related. This three-floored branch has everything that'll be on your list for that first mad dash before baby arrives – wipes, muslins and nappies, high chairs and cots – plus most things you'll need for later – not least, a decent range of easy-fold, bus-friendly buggies. Pleasant staff and accessible layout are added bonuses at this store.

Buggy access. Delivery service. Disabled access. Mail order. Nappy-changing facilities.

Branches: throughout town. Check website for details.

Selfridges

400 Oxford Street, Oxford Circus, W1A 1AB (0870 837 7377/www.selfridges.com). Bond Street tube. **Open** 10am-8pm Mon-Fri; 9.30am-8pm Sat; noon-6pm Sun. **Credit** AmEx, DC, MC, V. **Map** p314 G6.

Given the milling multitudes on this celebrity store's ground and second floors, the third floor, where Kids' Universe holds sway, always seems strangely empty. That might be to do with the prohibitive prices of all this designerwear for children up to eight – items such as silver christening spoons cost about £200 – or it could just be that this floor is spacious, children are quite small, so there's plenty of room to swing a toddler. It's all quite teenybopperish, McFly blares on the sound system and white, shiny pods contain the gear (Burberry, Moschino, Caramel, Emilie et Rose). There are toys, sticker stations, sweetie displays, partywear and fairy frocks. There's also a Buckle My Shoe store, more of a zoo than the other areas. It may sometimes get a bit hectic, but it stocks all the brands you'd ever want, plus some you've never heard of, and has an adequately experienced Buckle-My-Shoe trained fitting team. Also, there are (thank God!) often many sale items to help keep the expense down. Older children are happier down on the first floor, where beach bum labels (O'Neill, Quiksilver) are offered in an environment dominated by sportswear, bikes and skateboards.

Buggy access. Cafés. Car park. Delivery service. Disabled access: lifts, toilet. Mail order. Nappy-changing facilities.

TOP 5 | Pocket-money blowers

Benjamin Pollock's Toyshop
Quirky toys to keep forever. *See p208.*

Fagin's Toys
Pick out some magic party bag fillers. *See p206.*

Never Never Land
Tiny treasures for under £1. *See p208.*

Rainbow
Love the dolls' house accessories. *See p209.*

Traditional Toys
So much to break the piggy bank for. *See p209.*

no added sugar

Luxury contemporary baby
and childrens clothing.
All original designs from 0 to 8 years.
View the collection at **www.noaddedsugar.co.uk**
or please call for a brochure 0207 226 2323.
Available from Selfridges,
Harrods and other fine stores.

no added sugar
born & bred in london

EDUCATIONAL

Books

Several of the toyshops listed on *pp203-210* have a useful selection of children's picture books.

Bookseller Crow on the Hill

50 Westow Street, Crystal Palace, SE19 3AF (8771 8831/www.booksellercrow.com). Gypsy Hill rail. **Open** 9am-7.30pm Mon-Fri; 9.30am-6.30pm Sat; 11am-5pm Sun. **Credit** AmEx, MC, V.

We always enjoy our visits to this bookshop, run by a couple who have a young family of their own and are a mine of information on baby, toddler, child, teen, fretful parent and grandparent literature. Modern classics – Rosen, Horowitz, Wilson and Rowling – line up against myriad 'how to' titles (prepare for birth, parent, educate, train, discipline, cook, garden, appreciate the world, chill out, travel etc). You could browse in here for hours.
Buggy access. Disabled access: ramp. Mail order. Play area.

Bookworm

1177 Finchley Road, Temple Fortune, NW11 0AA (8201 9811). Golders Green tube. **Open** 9.30am-5.30pm Mon-Sat; 10am-1.30pm Sun. **Credit** MC, V.

This much-loved specialist children's bookshop has a central rotunda full of cushions and beanbags, and a cubby hole with tables and chairs for quiet reading/playing at the back. The stock is exemplary: shelf after shelf of everything from reference books for projects such as 'The Victorians' or 'The Romans' to the latest fiction. Twice-weekly storytelling sessions take place on Tuesdays and Thursdays (2pm) for under-fives, when badges and stickers are handed out and not-so-literary friendships forged. Local authors, including Katherine Holabird (Angelina Ballerina), Anthony Horowitz (the Alex Rider adventures), Zizou Corder (Lionboy) and Ian Whybrow (Books for Boys series), occasionally drop by for signings.
Buggy access. Disabled access. Mail order.

Children's Book Centre

237 Kensington High Street, Kensington, W8 6SA (7937 7497/www.childrensbookcentre.co.uk). High Street Kensington tube. **Open** 9.30am-6.30pm Mon, Wed, Fri, Sat; 9.30am-6pm Tue; 9.30am-7pm Thur; noon-6pm Sun. **Credit** AmEx, MC, V. **Map** p312 A9.

A visit to this two-storey treasure trove will yield far more than books. Downstairs are trendy T-shirts with witty slogans and dressing-up clothes, as well as stationery, accessories, family games and toys at pocket-money prices. There is a PC set up at the back for children to try out new computer games. The range of books on the ground floor covers all ages and tastes, from larger picture books and the Dr Seuss titles for new readers to a range for sophisticated consumers of teen literature, with reads as diverse as Louise Rennison and Stephen King.
Buggy access. Mail order.

Children's Bookshop

29 Fortis Green Road, Fortis Green, N10 3HP (8444 5500). Highgate tube, then 43, 134 bus. **Open** 9.15am-5.45pm Mon-Sat; 11am-4pm Sun. **Credit** AmEx, MC, V.

Quiet, well-stocked and roomy, this shop provides a famously good atmosphere in which to take in the row upon row of neatly ordered shelves, full of colour and interest, with small themed displays and a children's corner with picture books at floor level. Book related events are publicised in the quarterly newsletter, which carries helpful, personal reviews of new titles.
Buggy access. Mail order. Regular author visits.

Daunt Books

51 South End Road, NW3 2QB (7794 8206). Belsize Park tube. **Open** 9am-6pm Mon-Sat, 11am-6pm Sunday. **Credit** MC, V.

Daunt has a calmness about it that must foster many a serious young scholar – and please their parents too. It is spacious and wooden, the walls and sparse set of tables neatly crammed. The front half of the shop contains contemporary fiction, non-fiction and classics. Towards the back, the boundary between books and children's books is gloriously blurred. Mark Haddon's *The Curious Incident of the Dog in the Night-time* shares a shelf with a prize-winning children's version of *The Iliad*. There's wonderful play area – cozy and low-celinged with stacks of picture books and comics and mini-beanbags to lounge on while reading them. There isn't a single children's classic missing and for grown-ups, what better way to take a tranquil stroll down memory lane than by leafing through *The Little Prince*, Enid Blyton and Dr Seuss?
Buggy access. Disabled access. Mail order. Play area.
Branches 193 Haverstock Hill, NW3 4QG (7794 4006); 83 Marylebone High Street, W1U 4QW (7224 2295).

Golden Treasury

29 Replingham Road, Southfields, SW18 5LT (8333 0167/www.thegoldentreasury.co.uk). Southfields tube. **Open** 9.30am-6pm Mon-Fri; 9.30am-5.30pm Sat. **Credit** MC, V.

The staff here can offer friendly advice on the best reads for children from tinies to teens. Fun publications include pop-ups and books for colouring; less fun but significant is the educational range for schools. Harry Potter's popularity having eased off a bit, other must-haves like *Archangel* by Anthony Horowitz are flying off the shelves.
Buggy access. Delivery service. Play area.

Lion & Unicorn

19 King Street, Richmond, Surrey TW9 1ND (8940 0483/www.lionunicornbooks.co.uk). Richmond tube/rail. **Open** 9.30am-5.30pm Mon-Fri; 9.30am-6pm Sat; noon-5pm Sun. **Credit** MC, V.

Frequently shortlisted for the coveted Independent Bookseller of the Year award, this glorious, cosy, little children's book specialist has been inspiring young readers for 28 years. As well as selling every children's book worth reading, it hosts Saturday events that have attracted a fine stable of visiting writers: Jaqueline Wilson, Anthony Horowitz, Eleanor Updale and Eoin Colfer to name but a few. Check the website or call the shop to find out about Saturday morning storytelling sessions too.
Buggy access. Mail order.

Owl Bookshop

209 Kentish Town Road, Kentish Town, NW5 2JU (7485 7793). Kentish Town tube. **Open** 9.30am-6pm Mon-Sat; noon-4.30pm Sun. **Credit** AmEx, MC, V.

Here you can drift from the adult section on the left of the shop – fiction, psychology, women's and babies' health – into the children's section to the right, each roughly equal

Consumer

in space. The children's titles are sorted by age and interest. There are usually deals to be had: three for two on picture books is a long-standing favourite, and various other rotating discounts. The shop hosts readings by local children's authors and, in term-time, schoolchildren come to listen. Readings are not regular, though, so the best way to keep abreast of events is to join the mailing list, which you can do by calling or dropping in.
Buggy access. Mail order.

Musical instruments

Chappell of Bond Street

50 New Bond Street, Oxford Circus, W1S 1RD (7491 2777/www.chappellofbondstreet.co.uk). Bond Street tube. **Open** *9.30am-6pm Mon-Fri; 9.30am-5pm Sat.* **Credit** *AmEx, MC, V.* **Map** p316 H6.
Established in 1811, Chappell claims to be the oldest shop of its kind in London. It offers the largest range of printed music in Europe, from the latest pop tunes to show tunes, through golden oldies, folk, jazz and classical. A Yamaha specialist, Chappell is also renowned for keyboards – many musicians drop in to tickle the ivories. Certain instruments (typically flutes, saxes, clarinets, trumpets) may be hired on a rent-to-buy scheme, but quarter- and half-size instruments must be purchased; the child is measured beforehand. Recorders are the most popular starting position; Yamaha does colourful ones for about £6.
Delivery service. Mail order.

Dot's

132 St Pancras Way, Camden Town, NW1 9NB (7482 5424/www.dotsonline.co.uk). Camden Town tube/Camden Road rail. **Open** *9am-5.30pm Mon-Sat.* **Credit** *MC, V.*
Run and staffed by an experienced music teacher, Dot's has new instruments – mostly stringed and wind – costing from, say, £5 for a recorder, £40 for a guitar and £59 for a violin. There's also a rent-to-buy scheme, with hire costs eventually offsetting the purchase price should a child show consistent interest. The great joy here is receiving unpressured advice in a friendly setting; they take a genuine interest in children here. A noticeboard has advertisements for tuition and second-hand instruments are complemented by Dot's own recorder club, and there's also an instrument repair service.
Buggy access. Mail order.

Dulwich Music Shop

2 Croxted Road, Dulwich, SE21 8SW (8766 0202). West Dulwich rail. **Open** *9.30am-5.30pm Mon, Tue, Thur-Sat; 9.30am-7.30pm Wed.* **Credit** *AmEx, MC, V.*
With a window display designed to attract both young musos and their parents (Britney Spears songbooks and electric guitars lounge next to shiny trombones, trumpets and sensible books of tunes for brass), this is a proper community music shop. Staff can help out if you're looking to invest in used or new instruments and sheet music, and there's a range of price lists for wind, brass and string instruments, including hire and buy-back prices. Brochures and advertisements for teachers, music groups, concerts and events around the capital are displayed near the counter. Reeds, strings and cleaning cloths are also sold, alongside knick-knacks, gifts, CDs and stationery. There's also a repair service.
Buggy access. Mail order.

Northcote Music

155C Northcote Road, Clapham, SW11 6QB (7228 0074). Clapham Junction rail. **Open** *10.30am-6pm Mon-Sat.* **Credit** *MC, V.*
Always busy with young customers, from knobbly kneed prepschoolers needing clarinet reeds to tufty-haired musos after a parental guidance rock guitar chord book, Northcote comes up with the goods. String, brass and digital equipment is here for music lovers of all persuasions, and there's an on-site workshop for any instrumental mishaps. Classical sheet music is sold, as well as other musical styles, from show tune books to Christina Aguilera arranged for vocals, piano and guitar.
Buggy access. Delivery service. Mail order.

EQUIPMENT & ACCESSORIES

Babyworld

239 Munster Road, Fulham, SW6 6BT (7386 1904/ www.babyworldlondon.co.uk). Fulham Broadway tube then 211, 295 bus. **Open** *10am-6pm Mon-Wed, Fri; 10am-5.30pm Sat. Closed Thur.* **Credit** *AmEx, MC, V.*
Friendly staff here can tell you the best transport systems for precious cargoes. Most popular with parents of newborns these days is the Bugaboo pram (£499), which comes in a range of colours and whose chassis can hold either a carrycot or a buggy seat for older babies and toddlers up to the age of three and a half. Other pram and buggy ranges are by Chicco, Maxicosy and Stokke. There are also toys from Lamaze and a load of nursery accessories.
Buggy access. Mail order.

Chic Shack

77 Lower Richmond Road, Putney, SW15 1ET (8785 7777/www.chicshack.net). Putney Bridge tube, then 14, 22 bus. **Open** *10.30am-5.30pm Mon-Sat.* **Credit** *MC, V.*
If your tastes for the nursery lean toward vintage bleached cotton, old rose and gingham print, powder blue and pink traditional styles, you'll love Chic Shack. This compact premises on two floors is filled with beautiful things for all the home, but the stuff for babies and children's rooms is especially lovely. It's all here, from knitted teddies and snowy bedlinens and shawls to superbly finished nursery furniture. There are delightful wardrobes and cabinets with hand-carved details, bookshelves and clothes baskets, and solid cots that become little beds. The items are inspired by French and Swedish 18th-century design, and can be designed to order. Chic Shack also offers a range of fabrics for curtains and upholstery, as well as nursery and christening gifts, stationery, glassware and lighting. Of course, it's not cheap. Toy storage chests are £285.
Buggy access. Delivery service. Disabled access. Mail order.

Dragons of Walton Street

23 Walton Street, South Kensington, SW3 2HX (7589 3795/www.dragonsofwaltonstreet.com). Knightsbridge or South Kensington tube. **Open** *9.30am-5.30pm Mon-Fri; 10am-5pm Sat.* **Credit** *AmEx, MC, V.* **Map** p313 E10.
The reliable Dragons has carved a niche for itself as an exclusive hand-painter of children's furniture. Everything you could ever want in a nursery, including curtains, cots, sofas, chaise longues and tiny chairs, is made to order. You

come in, choose your item and choose your paint or fabric scheme. Hand-picked finery doesn't come cheap: expect to pay £2,000 for a special artwork bed, and between £3,500 and £10,000 for a rocking horse. If you don't want to pick and choose, Dragons can do you up a whole nursery for anywhere between £3,000 and £15,000. There are toys as well as furniture: money boxes (£10); dolls' houses (£250-£550), wooden Routemaster buses and teddy bears.
Buggy access. Disabled access. Delivery service. Mail order.

Lilliput

255-259 Queenstown Road, Battersea, SW8 3NP (7720 5554/0800 783 0886/www.lilliput.com). Queenstown Road rail. **Open** 9.30am-5.30pm Mon, Tue, Thur, Fri; 9.30am-7pm Wed; 9am-6pm Sat; 11am-4pm Sun. **Credit** MC, V.
All the nursery equipment you'll ever need (and loads you never thought you would) – cots, high chairs, bags, mattresses – and toys fill the kingdom of Lilliput. The store's own range includes sturdy pine nursery furniture and little extras such as nappy cream and muslins; there are also TUG toddler transport systems (£69.95) and the sleigh bed from Dream Baby (£495). Staff are happy to guide you through the range of equipment and offer advice.
Buggy access. Delivery service. Mail order. Nappy-changing facilities. Play area.
Branch: 100-106 Haydons Road, Wimbledon, SW19 1AW (8542 3542).

London Prams

175-179 East India Dock Road, Docklands, E14 0EA (7537 4117/www.londonprams.co.uk). All Saints DLR. **Open** 10.30am-5.30pm Mon-Sat. **Credit** MC, V.
A cheerfully staffed nursery equipment specialist opposite the DLR station, London Prams can address all your perambulator needs, from the classic, navy blue, well-sprung, large-wheeled Silver Cross models, much loved by Norland Nannies and their silver-spooned charges, to handily collapsible buggies for those frantic bus journeys to the childminder's. Then there are little wardrobes, cots, cribs, changing stations and toy chests for the nursery, and lots of essential accessories, including the excellent Bambino Mio washable nappy range.
Buggy access. Delivery service. Mail order.

Mini Kin

22 Broadway Parade, Crouch End, N8 9DE (8341 6898). Finsbury Park tube, then W7 or 41 bus. **Open** 9.30-5.30pm Mon-Sat; 11.30am-5pm Sun. **Credit** MC, V.
Mini Kin has a children's hairdressing salon, with animal-themed seats and the possibility of mini makeovers. Baby haircuts start at £10; or the special first haircut with lots of fuss, certificate and samples costs £14. Little girlies love the full princess treatment for £29.95, which involves glitter, hypoallergenic products, peel-off nail varnish and goodies, plus photos to take home. Otherwise this sizeable venue caters for the caring parent's desire for natural bath and hygiene products (including the SOS range for eczema), sells Bugaboo buggies, Baby Björn, carriers, potties and stools, cute goldfish- or cowboy-decorated bibs and changers, adorable bootees and Nurtured by Nature merino wool babygros. Everyone adores Angulus shoes (Itsy Bitsies for the little squirts from £21, leather shoes for older toddlers are more expensive).
Buggy access. Disabled access. Nappy-changing facilities. Play area.

Nursery Window

83 Walton Street, South Kensington, SW3 2HP (7581 3358/www.nurserywindow.co.uk). South Kensington tube. **Open** 10am-6pm Mon-Sat. **Credit** AmEx, MC, V. **Map** p313 E10.
Look through the Nursery Window for bedlinen, fabrics, furniture and wallpaper. Friendly staff are on hand to help parents select lap-of-luxury nursery essentials such as cashmere blankets (£89.95), hanging nappy stackers (£36.95) and a Moses basket set (£139.95). For toddlers and older children, designs are traditional (trains and racing cars for boys, delicate pink roses for girls), but with some unusual designs such as world maps or Imperial garden motifs. The shop offers a made-to-measure curtain service.
Buggy access. Delivery service. Mail order.

Rub a Dub Dub

15 Park Road, Muswell Hill N8 8TE (8342 9898). Finsbury Park tube then W7 or 41 bus. **Open** 10am-5.30pm Mon-Fri; 9.30am-5.30pm Sat; 11am-4pm Sun. **Credit** MC, V.
Ways of getting babies and children to and fro and seated comfortably are the forte here. The friendly and knowledgeable Scottish owner chooses stock with care – you'll find the excellent Bugaboo three-in-one pushchair-cum-pram, carry cot- and car-seat adaptable travel system (£499); the posture-reforming Tripp Trapp high chair, which seats babies, toddlers, children and even adults (£137); and Nomad travel cots that fold to backpack size and double as a UV tent (£125). Also available is Stokke's Xplory baby buggy, an amazingly space age, multi-position buggy that elevates your little darling above nasty car fumes (£499). There are softer, fun things too: wheely bugs in bird and bumblebee shapes for whizzing around the house (£50 for a small model, £55 for a larger size) and comfy American fleece baby blankets by Taggy's (£12.99-£16.99) decked out with all sizes and shapes of ribbons and tags for baby to play with. Every conceivable brand of eco-friendly nappy and bottom cream is stocked, and look out for the German Moltex nappies: 30% gel, 70% biodegradable and entirely free of bleach.
Buggy access. Delivery service. Disabled access. Mail order.

Environmentally friendly

If you're thinking of a washable nappy system, the staff at **Green Baby** can offer advice. Go for a shaped nappy that pops into place to avoid wrestling with terry towelling and giant nappy pins. Washable nappies are kinder to your coffers, too. An initial outlay of about £400 sets you up for one or two kids, saving you over a grand in the long run compared with using disposables. **Bambino Mio** (01604 883777, www.bambino mio.co.uk), the **Ellie Nappie Company** (0151 200 5012, www.elliepants.co.uk) and **Little Green Earthlets** (01825 873301, www. earthlets.co.uk) also sell real nappies and environmentally friendly cleaning products. More delightful, organic cotton babywear and fabulous, fairly traded cotton casuals for children aged up to ten can be ordered from **People Tree** (7739 0660, www.peopletree.co.uk).

Consumer

Green Baby

345 Upper Street, Islington, N1 0PD (7359 7037/mail order 0870 240 6894/www.greenbaby.co.uk). Angel tube. **Open** 10am-5pm Mon-Fri; 10am-6pm Sat; 11am-4pm Sun. **Credit** MC, V.

If you're about to pop or you've just dropped, make this your first port of call. It has clothing basics for the new-born and sheets made from 100 per cent organic cotton, nappy balms and baby lotions based on sweet almond oil and cocoa butter, and nursery furniture made of beech from sustainable forests. Green Baby clothing is made in South India, as part of a community project that supports the education and employment of young girls.
Buggy access. Delivery service. Mail order.
Branch: 5 Elgin Crescent, Notting Hill, W11 2JA (7792 8140).

Organically Grown

18A Upland Road, East Dulwich, SE22 9NG (8613 1625). East Dulwich rail/12, 40, 176, 185 bus. **Open** 10am-5.30pm Mon-Sat; 11am-5pm Sun. **Credit** MC, V.
Proof, if it were needed, that East Dulwich is fast becoming the Islington of the south is provided by this well-favoured little shop specialising in organic, natural, eco-friendly and fair trade products for babies and young children. Products by Green Babies and Under the Nile (very special Egyptian cotton baby clothes) include plain and simple babygros and little vests from £8.95, hand-knitted woollens, splendid little baby shoes and a small selection of toys and trinkets for babies. OG also stock biodegradable disposable nappies, organic baby food and a selection of glorious toiletries of an organic and non-allergenic nature.
Buggy access. Mail order.

FASHION

Budget

Adams

Unit 11, Surrey Quays Centre, Redriff Road, Rotherhithe, SE16 7LL (7252 3208/www.adams.co.uk). Surrey Quays tube. **Open** 9.30am-6pm Mon-Thur, Sat; 9.30am-8pm Fri; 11am-5pm Sun. **Credit** AmEx, MC, V.
Rely on Adams for affordable schoolwear: packs of two easycare shirts (from £4.99); good-quality tights (two pairs for £4.99); serviceable rainwear (shiny macs and bright anoraks from £7.99); jolly swimwear (trunks £3.99, suits £5.99); and useful babywear (pack of three baby sleep-suits from £5). Just don't expect highly individual or fashionable children's outfits – think sugar pink and violet for girls, blue and khaki for boys, and naff logos a gogo.
Buggy access. Disabled access. Mail order. Play area.
Branches: throughout town. Check website for details.

H&M

103-111 Kensington High Street, Kensington, W8 5SF (7368 3920/www.hm.com). High Street Kensington tube. **Open** 10am-7pm Mon-Wed, Fri, Sat; 10am-8pm Thur; noon-6pm Sun. **Credit** AmEx, MC, V.
Map p312 A9.
Our love affair with H&M's children's department continues apace. Last visit, we picked up lacy butterfly tights, a denim skirt with a ruffle, a whole outfit for a new-born baby boy and a bold red polo neck jumper; the bill

came to £27.50. Brilliant value, and the designs are pretty diverse: traditionalists can find pretty dresses for their girls and collared check shirts for their boys; modish parents prefer the combats, halternecks, belt chains, caps, wallets and hoodies for ages up to about 12. Come just before Christmas for affordable trinkets and accessories.
Buggy access. Disabled access: lift. Nappy-changing facilities. Play area.
Branches: throughout town. Check website for details.

Designer

Barney's

6 Church Road, Wimbledon, SW19 5DL (8944 2915). Wimbledon tube/rail, then 93 bus. **Open** 10am-6pm Mon-Sat; noon-5pm Sun. **Credit** MC, V.
Smart designerwear for children aged from nought to 18 includes choice cuts from more than 25 well-respected houses. There are fab little outfits from Petit Bateau, Catimini, Les Robes, Timberland, Kenzo, Oxbow, Guess and Replay. There are also some covetable gifts and accessories like bags, wallets, soft toys, attractive wooden playthings, jewellery and watches. Quiksilver and O'Neill streetwear sells well.
Buggy access. Disabled access. Play area.

Caramel Baby & Child

291 Brompton Road, South Kensington, SW3 2DY (7589 7001). South Kensington tube. **Open** 10am-6.30pm Mon-Sat; noon-5pm Sun. **Credit** AmEx, MC, V.
Map p313 E10.
Ring the bell to enter this chicer-than-chic designer outlet for tots whose label-led parents are prepared to pay through the nose to trendify their offspring. The deliciously cuddly stripy cashmere pullover by Baby Caramel for babies of six months costs £95, for instance; less essential luxurious ear muffs are £55, and Ugg Boots (£89) keep extremities toasty. There are little Prada trainers (£90) and a summer collection comprising lots of floaty, hip dresses and shirts to be worn with teeny Birkenstocks. Favourites are fresh and floral dresses by Caramel (£65), Marni (£132) and Quincy (£49) – and the Prada ballerina pumps (£80). Rompers, skirts and trousers for children up to ten, plus miniature wellies, lamb's wool-lined papooses (£220) and a finger puppet set (£40) widen the store's appeal. The branch, Alpha Caramel, stocks books and toys and has a hairdressing service on Saturdays and Wednesdays (book in advance).
Buggy access. Mail order.
Branch Alpha Caramel, 259 Pavillion Road, SW1X 0BP (7730 2564).

Catimini

52 South Molton Street, Mayfair, W1Y 1HF (7629 8099/www.catimini.com). Bond Street tube. **Open** 10am-6.30pm Mon-Wed, Fri, Sat; 10am-7pm Thur; 11.30am-5.30pm Sun. **Credit** AmEx, MC, V.
Map p314 H6.
The only London outpost of the sophisticated, classic French label is a cheerful provider of outfits to get babies and children up to age ten noticed. The everyday range is strong on animal and floral patterns, but with its new Catimini Atelier line, such wildness is excluded in favour of easy formality: dresses and skirts for girls in white, yellow, pink and orange, and suave linen suits for boys. No attention to detail is spared: girls can have matching socks,

C'est chic pour tots at **Catimini**.

tights, shoes and dresses, light raincoats and headscarves or little Atelier jackets to wear over their dresses if it gets nippy; boys – rather more simply – get matching belts with their suits. It all looks delightfully European and effortlessly chic – and unlike at some other chic French shops, the shop assistants are friendly and helpful. Prices are on the high side (expect to pay £80 for a swimsuit, hat and sundress ensemble).
Buggy access. Disabled access. Mail order. Play area.

The Cross

141 Portland Road, Notting Hill, W11 4LR (7727 6760). Holland Park or Notting Hill Gate tube. **Open** 11am-5.30pm Mon-Sat. **Credit** AmEx, DC, MC, V.
An adult designer store, with a tiny but significant range of childish treasures. The emphasis among the accessories is on the handmade – woollen rugs are beautifully stitched with nursery rhymes, for example – but quality doesn't come cheap: expect to pay £400 for a blanket or £100 for a cushion. The quirkily charming rag dolls and knitted, sequinned fish are also pricey. There's a range of merino wool knitted babygros and tops, appliquéd sweatshirts for hip toddlers, and long cotton tunics and Moroccan-style slippers for little hippies. Some surprisingly cheap toys soften the blow to the wallet.
Buggy access. Delivery service. Mail order.

Diverse Kids

46 Cross Street, Islington N1 2BA (7226 6863/ www.diverseclothing.com). Angel/Highbury & Islington tube/rail. **Open** 10.30am-6pm Mon-Sat; noon-5.30pm Sun. **Credit** AmEx, DC, MC, V.
A relatively new sister shop to the Diverse stable of mens and womenswear, this outlet stocks designer kiddie clobber including Diesel jeans and jumpers, Paper Denim & Cloth trousers, Antik Batik dresses (from £40), as well as Quincy clothing. Accessories include bags, underwear, hats (from £10), socks, tights, shoes, trainers and booties.
Buggy access. Delivery service.

Frocks Away

79-85 Fortis Green Road, Fortis Green, N10 3HP (8444 9309). Highgate tube, then 43 or 134 bus. **Open** 9.30am-5.30pm Mon-Sat. **Credit** AmEx, MC, V.
Polished floorboards and old-fashioned shopfittings set the shabby-chic tone in this independent store, which one day wants to be a women's shop. For now, though, flowery tights lie in wooden hosiery drawers; church pews are used to seat fidgety children while their feet are measured; and little wooden stands display adorable floppy sunhats. There's a good range of clothes for women and children, including Petit Bateau, Ali Bali, Contrevents et Marres and Balu, plus shoes from Start-Rit, Geox, Primigi and Diesel.
Buggy access. Disabled access. Delivery service. Play area.

Jake's

Plum, 79 Berwick Street, Soho, W1F 8TL (7734 0812/www.jakeskids.com). Tottenham Court Road tube. **Open** 11am-7pm Mon-Sat. **Credit** AmEx, MC, V. **Map** p314 J6.
Children aged up to six can look suitably Soho in Jake's 'Elvis Loves You' T-shirt (£18), as favoured by cutting-edge junior fashion plates, Romeo and Brooklyn B. Teamed with Jake's combats or three-quarter-length shorts, the effect is street-sweet and effortlessly stylish. The label is

inspired by a little chap called, of course, Jake and profits go toward building a bright future for him, because he has cerebral palsy. A percentage of all profits are donated to a charity of the owner's choice. The clothes are excellent quality, quite apart from being achingly fashionable and in aid of a good cause, so buying them will make parents feel good all round. The clothes for grown-ups here in in Plum, the host shop, are equally cool and trendy.
Buggy access. Disabled access. Mail order.

Jakss

463 & 469 Roman Road,Bethnal Green, E3 5LX (8981 9454/www.jakss.co.uk). Bethnal Green tube then 8 bus. **Open** 10am-5.30pm Tue-Sat. **Credit** AmEx, DC, MC, V.
Few children would notice whether their T-shirt is Armani or Asda, but for their label-crazed parents, shops like Jakss are a real boon. There are floaty two-pieces for little girls by DKNY, Burberry anoraks, Roberto Cavalli trousers, D&G babygros, Kenzo shirts and Diesel jeanswear; for the feet, Birkenstocks, natch, and handsome D&G sandals. It's all deeply fashionable, very East End bling and, during the seasonal sales, when stuff on the rails is slashed by 50% to make way for next season's lines, a lot more affordable than anything these designers do for the grown-ups.
Buggy access. Delivery service.

JoJo Maman Bébé

68 Northcote Road, Battersea, SW11 6QL (7228 0322/www.jojomamanbebe.co.uk). Clapham Junction rail. **Open** 9.30am-5.30pm Mon-Sat; 11am-5pm Sun. **Credit** MC, V.
Attractive prints, casual designs and fantastic cotton baby essentials make this shop a feast of fun for potential, new and busy parents. Children's clothes, at the front of the shop, are comfortable and casual. Affordable babywear includes striped sunsuits (£16 for two), gorgeous little dungarees and hoodies, as well as useful little long-sleeved vests. Mothers also find the breastfeeding collection a real boon. Maternitywear, found at the back of the shop, is Frenchly stylish. There are also baby gifts, home accessories and lots of toys and travel requisites.
Buggy access. Delivery service. Disabled access. Mail order. Nappy-changing facilities.
Branches 3 Ashbourne Parade, 1259 Finchley Road, Golders green, NW11 0AD (8731 8961); 80 Turnham Green Terrace, Chiswick, W4 1QN (8994 0379).

Membery's

1 Church Road, Barnes, SW13 9HE (8876 2910/ www.specialdresscompany.co.uk). Barnes Bridge rail. **Open** 10am-5pm Mon-Sat. **Credit** AmEx, MC, V.
Made-to-measure bridesmaids' dresses are available for all ages at this shop, where Sally Membery's own label shares space with Catimini, IKKS and Petit Bateau. Nought to eight is the general age range; both boys and girls are catered for.
Buggy access. Delivery service. Play area.

Notsobig

31A Highgate High Street, Highgate, N6 5JT (8340 4455). Archway or Highgate tube. **Open** 9.30am-6pm Mon-Fri; 10am-6pm Sat; 11am-5pm Sun. **Credit** MC, V.
The harder you look in this tiny shop, the more delights you see. Tiny outfits by Quincy, Cacharel, Braez, Essential Girls, Maharishi, No Angel and Agatha Ruiz de la Prada

Consumer

Notsobig. Notsocheap neither. *See p193.*

hang on the walls; there is Wright & Teague silver and gold jewellery for babies, many items with precious stones; and Little Chums T-shirts sit in organza bags alongside hand-crocheted monkeys. Halfway down the windy stairs are French-looking tea sets and assorted knick-knacks, and at the bottom, ten or so haphazardly arranged fancy-dress costumes by Bandicoot Lapin (from £60) and vintage ranges, including Miss Hollywood multicoloured chenille robes. Avoid the shop on Saturday if you think you'll be wanting any help.
Buggy access. Delivery service. Mail order. Play area.

Oilily

9 Sloane Street, Knightsbridge, SW1X 9LE (7823 2505/www.oilily-world.com). Knightsbridge tube. **Open** 10am-6pm Mon, Tue, Thur-Sat; 10am-7pm Wed; noon-6pm Sun. **Credit** AmEx, MC, V. **Map** p313 F9.
Here are clothes to lift your spirits: exuberant gatherings of orange, green, pink and blue in inspirational designs on flounced dresses and skirts; embroidered jeans; prettily detailed bags, sandals, hats and accessories. Stuff for boys doesn't shy away from the prints but hardens up the colours a bit. It's solidly made, although a few of the rather frivolous ribbon and frill detailswould no doubt get lost in the playground. Lovely stuff for women too. Expect to pay about £70 for a girl's dress, with separates from about £20. Babywear is similarly bold.
Buggy access. Mail order. Play area.

Patrizia Wigan

19 Walton Street, Knightsbridge, SW3 2HX (7823 7080/www.patriziawigan.com). Knightsbridge or South Kensington tube. **Open** 10.30am-6.30pm Mon-Fri; 10.30am-6pm Sat. **Credit** AmEx, MC, V. **Map** p313 E10.
Attractive to royals and heads of state, this smart shop is full of conservative formalwear for 12s and under. Babies get stunning christening gowns from £195 or any of a range of trad gifts for newborns. You'll also find smocked dresses, kilts, party dresses and velvet frocks, and can get pageboy and bridesmaid outfits made or altered.
Buggy access. Delivery service. Nappy-changing facilities. Play area.

Rachel Riley

82 Marylebone High Street, Marylebone, W1U 4QW (7935 7007/www.rachelriley.com). Baker Street or Bond Street tube. **Open** 10am-6pm Mon-Sat. **Credit** AmEx, MC, V. **Map** p314 5G.
Riley's unmistakable 1950s retro look is produced from an attic in the Loire Valley, and all the clothes for babies, boys and girls have a rare beauty. Few could resist a baby dress printed with dark pink tulips, with matching bloomers (£59). Cotton chambray shirts and tailored shorts for boys are smart; the separates and nightwear are lovely and there are some groovy little character shoes to complete the look.
Buggy access. Delivery service. Mail order. Play area.
Branch: 14 Pont Street, Victoria SW1X 9EN (7259 5969).

Sasti

8 Portobello Green Arcade, 281 Portobello Road, Ladbroke Grove, W10 5TZ (8960 1125/www. sasti.co.uk). Ladbroke Grove tube. **Open** 10am-6pm Mon-Sat. **Credit** AmEx, MC, V.
Children aged from newborn up to ten love it here. Whatever the season, the stock is colourful, some is flamboyant and all is pretty unusual. For little girls there are smashing skirts and shorts, and a wide range of frocks in all styles from about £18. Boys look fab in combats or denim shorts and a wide range of T-shirts. Everyone likes the shirts, long-sleeved or short, with slogans on. Staff here are young and cool, and endear themselves to the children.
Buggy access. Delivery service. Mail order. Nappy-changing facilities. Play area.

Semmalina

225 Ebury Street, Pimlico, SW1W 8UT (7730 9333). Sloane Square tube. **Open** 9.30am-5.30pm Mon-Sat. **Credit** AmEx, MC, V. **Map** p316 G11.
Posh little Semmalina dresses and entertains the children of well-to-do local residents. A central fairy castle structure amuses young visitors, who choose baubles and trinkets while their parents size up clothes by Miniature, Triple Star and Lucy Lockett for children aged nought to eight.
Buggy access. Delivery service. Nappy-changing facilities. Play area.

Tartine et Chocolat

66 South Molton Street, Mayfair, W1K 5SX (7629 7233). Bond Street tube. **Open** 10am-6pm Mon-Sat. **Credit** AmEx, MC, V. **Map** p314 H6.

The trademark sky-blue or pink stripes of the fragrant T&C brand date back to 1977; now there's a whole range of products for babies and under-11s, including clothes, perfumes, soft toys and gifts. The pink and blue/feminine and masculine detailing is tempered by snowy-white sleepsuits, little dresses or baby shoes (for under-ones). *Delivery service. Mail order.*

Their Nibs

214 Kensington Park Road, Notting Hill, W11 1NR (7221 4263/www.theirnibs.com). Ladbroke Grove or Notting Hill Gate tube. **Open** 9.30am-6pm Mon-Fri; 10am-6pm Sat; noon-5pm Sun. **Credit** MC, V.

Their Nibs is a friendly and child-centred place. The floaty dresses, fairy dresses, party dresses and baby dresses (£20-£35) are most eye-catching, but boys like the print shirts and combats embroidered with red dragons, and there are shoes by Angulus and Ugg boots. An amusing vintage rail has stuff from the 1940s to the '60s: dinky little psychedelic dungarees and flash boys' suits, pinafores, and sweet print shirts for cowlicked little boys. Prices aren't very vintage – from £30. The play area is refreshingly large for a boutique, with a hopscotch mat, blackboards for chalk graffiti and lots of toys. You can also get a haircut (4-6pm Tue). *Buggy access. Disabled access: ramps. Delivery service. Mail order. Play area.*

Tiddleywinks

414 Roman Road, Bethnal Green, E3 5LU (8981 7000). Bethnal Green tube, then 8 bus. **Open** 9.30am-5.30pm Mon-Sat. **Credit** AmEx, MC, V.

Bling bling mummies with serious label-mania crowd into this jolly little place to find Marese, Baby Dior, Coco and Confetti for their reclining designer dummy-suckers, but the fun really starts when the kids can choose their own Armani trousers, Moschino biker jackets, Diesel jeanswear and D&G sandals. East London has never looked so well turned out, particularly at sale time. *Buggy access. Mail order.*

Tots

39 Turnham Green Terrace, Chiswick, W4 1RG (8995 0520/www.totschiswick.com). Turnham Green tube. **Open** 10am-6pm Mon-Sat; noon-5pm Sun. **Credit** AmEx, MC, V.

There's plenty of delightful baby- and toddlerwear at the aptly named Tots, but children aged up to 12 who are concerned with coolness need not fret: the Timberland, Quiksilver, O'Neill and Oilily stuff here is not cutesy and will not embarrass. Bright print shirts that stand out from the usual sea of navy and khaki are to be found on the boys' rails, denims (skirts, dresses, shorts, jeans) are well represented, and accessories include belts, hats, wallets and bags. There are Roobeey soft-leather shoes for babies and cute one-off designs like the lovely terry cape, which has a bear-shaped pocket with little bear inside. *Buggy access. Disabled access. Play area.*

Trendys

72 Chapel Market, Islington, N1 9ER (7837 9070). Angel tube. **Open** 10am-6pm Mon-Sat; 10am-4pm Sun. **Credit** AmEx, MC, V.

Chapel Market may be a remnant of the 'old Islington' of costers and bargain outlets, but Trendys is very firmly established in the 21st-century world of aspirational and costly fashionwear for tinies. So there's Pringle and Burberry babywear among the more traditional Absorba, Cacharel and Jean de la Lune, Diesel jeans for wee girls and Kickers and D&G footwear. The clothes go up to age 14 or so, and regular sales means that you will pick up some bargains if you're prepared to visit often. *Buggy access.*

Mid-range & high street

Biff

41-43 Dulwich Village, Dulwich, SE21 7BN (8299 0911). North Dulwich rail/P4 bus. **Open** 9.30am-5.30pm Mon-Fri; 10am-6pm Sat; noon-5pm Sun. **Credit** MC, V.

This is a pair of long, thin shops. One displays sassy women's clothes by Fransa, Roxy and French Connection among others, along with girls' and boys' fashions by Quiksilver, O'Neill, Billabong, Miniature and Derhy Kids. You can access the other one, for babies and children up to seven, round the back, via a useful Start-Rite shoe shop. The little ones' side also has a small play area and service in both is friendly. This is an excellent place to look for unusual fashions for children of all ages, at affordable prices. It's particularly strong on casuals: jeans by Ben Sherman (£34) alongside subtle print dresses by Miniature and Roxy Life and classic cottons by Petit Bateau. Little girls look smashing in pastel-coloured Roxy gumboots (£20) and there's always a wide selection of summer swimwear and sandals. For babies, there are IKKS, Jean Bourget and Catimini rompers, babygros, vests and cardies, as well as those wearable quilts called Grobags. *Buggy access. Mail order. Nappy-changing facilities. Play area.*

Gap Kids

122 King's Road, Chelsea, SW3 4TR (7823 7272/www.gap.com). Sloane Square tube. **Open** 10am-7pm Mon-Sat; noon-6pm Sun. **Credit** AmEx, MC, V.

Even if you don't want your child to walk around in a fleece hoody that shrieks GAP, the clothes for babies to teens in this ubiquitous chain always score a hit. There are jeans to suit all tastes, from slim-cut bootlegs for the girlies to spacious carpenter-style denims for lads who still like to have their boxers on display above their trousers. Tiny striped jumpers and summer Ts look good, anoraks are eminently wearable, and the accessories, including belts, tights, socks, hats and bags are distinctive and stylish. Gap's sale rails are always a boon for thrifty parents, and the one in this branch is particularly good. *Buggy access. Delivery service. Disabled access. Nappy-changing facilities.* **Branches**: throughout town. Check website for details.

Iana

186 King's Road, Chelsea, SW3 5XP (7352 0060/www.iana.it). Sloane Square tube. **Open** 9am-6pm Mon, Tue, Thur, Fri; 9am-7pm Wed; 10am-6.30pm Sat; 11am-6pm Sun. **Credit** AmEx, DC, MC, V. **Map** p313 F11.

Jolly, practical Italian outfits for children up to age 14 are divided into the Elegant collection, with smart little tops, skirts and dresses in pale pinks, blues and khaki for girls, and linen trousers and smart-casual jackets for boys, while

Consumer

Let your mouse do the walking

From trendy Tees and toys to great days out, shopping online offers a world of possibilities.

Bump to 3

www.bumpto3.com/0870 606 0276
Grobag sleeping bags could be the answer to wakeful nights from kicked-off bedding; these are available in sizes newborn to six years (£17.95-£29.95). Other practical products are sold, too.

Children's Audio Company

www.kidsmusic.co.uk
Available in various formats, you'll find a large range of audio material here: games and pop party CDs (£4.99) are a good bet, or there are more traditional soothers, such as nursery rhymes and storytime favourites.

Days to Amaze

www.daystoamaze.co.uk/0870 240 0635
Packages range from a morning's rally driving (12 to 16-year-olds) or shadowing a zookeeper for the day (£79) to a girlie make-over with fun photo session (£79, includes two portrait photos).

Great Little Trading Company

www.gltc.co.uk/0870 850 6000
This well-chosen, comprehensive range of kids' gear has everything from furniture, bedlinen and ballerina outfits (£24.99) to lunchboxes, ski-suits and remote-control dinosaurs (£24.99).

Hawkin's Bazaar

www.hawkin.com/0870 429 4000
This fun-to-read catalogue is bursting with 'astonishing curiosities', nostalgic toys, party-bag fillers and gizmos. Best of all, most aren't battery-operated, don't bleep incessantly or require remortgaging the house (prices start at just 30p).

Into the Blue

www.intotheblue.co.uk/01949 578101
Age and height restrictions apply, but thrill-seeking teens could take microlight flying lessons, go quad-biking or swing from a trapeze on a circus skills course (£59). Six- to ten-year olds, uniformed up, can practise 'firefighting' with water hoses, ride in a fire engine and even drive a mini electric version on an off-road course (£65).

Letterbox

www.letterbox.co.uk/0870 600 7878
A good source for posh presents and decent personalised items, Letterbox also offers glittery girlie treats, animal-headed umbrellas and witty wellies (£8-£13), as well as interesting outdoor games (birthday piñatas, £13).

Mini Boden

www.boden.co.uk/0845 677 5000
Johnny Boden's bold, bright casuals and beach gear for nought to 14-year-olds include retro-print tops and hoodies, cardigans and halterneck dresses as well as outerwear, nightwear, and shoes.

Mulberry Bush

www.mulberrybush.co.uk/01403 754400
Handsome wooden toys are a forte here, but Mulberry's range also includes tea sets, badge-making kits (£16.99), card games and – always a winner – outdoor rocket launchers (£9.99).

nappyhead

www.nappyhead.co.uk/01582 513630
Nappyhead's products are emblazoned with bold slogans, such as 'I Only Cry When Ugly People Hold Me', 'Sleep Is For The Weak' and 'Little Punk'. Sizes newborn to four years (£13-£15).

nippazwithattitude

www.nippaz.com/8769 9844
'MuthaSucka' and 'Mama Ain't Raisin' No Fool' tees (£17) should divert granny's attention.

Red Letter Days

www.redletterdays.co.uk/0870 444 4004
Everything you'd imagine (and possibly more): wannabe spy kids can spend an action-packed day negotiating assault courses, abseiling and code-breaking to meet a mission brief; snowboarding and scuba-diving half-days are offered at £49; and for creative types, T-shirt and ceramics painting costs £99 (for two children).

Science Museum

www.sciencemuseumstore.com/0870 241 5596
You'll find gadgets and games galore, alongside construction kits and puzzles. Bestsellers include a light-up frisbee (£25), forensic detective kits (£30) and crime lab (£40). The solar-powered 'rainbowmaker' (£20) fills rooms with colour.

Talking Book Shop

www.talkingbooks.co.uk/7491 4117
The children's section of this site offers a wide range on tape and CD: adventure, animal and ghost stories, traditional folk tales and sci-fi.

Urchin

www.urchin.co.uk
Brilliant ideas for homes with children in them: bedroom accessories, party paraphernalia, toys, clothes, equipment and more, all stylish and covetable. Great stuff.

Consumer

a Casuals collection features bold blue and red tops, shorts and trousers for boys and cool trousers and T-shirts for girls. Prices are reasonable: a baby's top might cost £11.50, a light summer coat for a three-year-old £16, a goose-down jacket for winter (£40), and combats (£25). The staff are very friendly and happy to help. The Putney branch stocks maternitywear.

Buggy access. Delivery service. Mail order.
Branch: Putney Exchange Shopping Centre, Putney High Street, SW15 1TW (8789 2022); 4 George Street, Richmond, Surrey, TW9 154 (8940 0184).

Jigsaw Junior

190-192 Westbourne Grove, Notting Hill, W11 2RH (7727 0322/www.jigsaw-online.com). Notting Hill Gate tube. **Open** 10.30am-6.30pm Mon; 10-6.30pm Tur, Wed, Sat; 10am-7pm Thur, Fri; noon-6pm Sun. **Credit** AmEx, MC, V. **Map** p310 A6.
This is a beautiful shop, decorated in shabby-chic style. Half the staircase has been cut away to make way for a children's metal slide, allowing them to scoot down to the lower level where they'll find a beautiful antique mirrored dressing table draped with vintage embroidered silk cushions. The girls' clothes are versions of grown-up styles: a suede A-line skirt with embroidery (£79.95), say, or print sundresses (£29-£38).
Buggy access. Mail order. Play area.
Branches 126-127 New Bond Street, W1 (7491 4484); 91-97 Fulham Road, SW3 (7589 9530); The Chapel, 6 Duke of York Square, Kings Road, SW3 (7730 4404); 83 Heath Street, Hampstead, London NW3 (7431 0619); 41 George Street, Richmond, Surrey (8940 8386).

Monsoon Girl

Unit 25, The Market, Covent Garden, WC2H 8AH (7497 9325/www.monsoon.co.uk). Covent Garden tube. **Open** 10am-8pm Mon-Sat; 11am-6pm Sun. **Credit** AmEx, MC, V. **Map** p317 L7.
It's still called 'Girl', although boys are provided for in this busy branch dedicated to children. Many adult Monsoons, both in the West End and on high streets countrywide, also have children's clothes. The clothes are extremely pretty for the girls, who look sweet in fine floral skirts with ribbon detail from £28. The baby range (two months and upwards) includes delicate little dresses (about £20) and cardies in beautiful shades of raspberry, mauve and green. The T-shirts have attractive detailing (from £12) and the lined dresses (from £30) are superb.
Buggy access. Disabled access. Mail order.
Branches throughout town. Check website for details.

O'Neill

5-7 Carnaby Street, Soho, W1F 9PB (7734 3778/ www.oneilleurope.com). Oxford Circus tube. **Open** 10am-7pm Mon-Wed, Fri; 10am-8pm Thur; 11am-5pm Sun. **Credit** AmEx, MC, V. **Map** p316 J6.
This season's – every season's – baggy shorts, Troca caps, bright button-through and collared shirts for boys, tough flip-flops, miniskirts, tight shirts, string bikinis, vests and cropped trousers are perfect for the summer hols. Bright yellow and earthy hues are all the rage, alongside, of course, ocean-blue. Prices range from £15 for a T-shirt; O'Neill's classic chunky hoodies start at £40.
Buggy access (downstairs only). Mail order.
Branch Bluewater Shopping Centre, Kent DA9 9SJ (01322 623300); 9-15 Neal Street, Covent Garden, WC2H 9PU (7836 7686).

Finn loves his **nappyhead** T-shirt.

Petit Bateau

73 Ledbury Road, Notting Hill, W11 2AG (7243 6331). Notting Hill Gate tube. **Open** 10am-6pm Mon-Sat; noon-5pm Sun. **Credit** AmEx, MC, V. **Map** p310 A6.
Until recently, this store was called Clementine and stocked mostly, but not exclusively, Petit Bateau products. Now it has given itself over entirely to the classic label. The assistant when we visited was French (knowledgeable but a touch thorny) and the shop always seems to be full of French customers, which gives you an idea of the chicness levels here. Stripes are everywhere, from the gorgeous pastel-striped velour babygros (£22-£45) to the cotton sundresses (£30), swimsuits (£20-£25) and T-shirts (£15-£20) for boys and girls. New in for girls are colours including dark purple, bright pink and floral patterns and, for boys, army-fatigue pattern. The basement once stocked prams, buggies and beds but that space has been taken over by still more yards of French quality casuals.
Buggy access. Delivery service. Mail order. Nappy-changing facilities. Play area.
Branches: 188 Chiswick High Road, Chiswick, W4 1BB (8987 0288); 19 Hampstead High Street, Hampstead, NW3 1PX (7794 3254); 62 South Molton Street, Mayfair, W1K 5SR (7491 4498); 106-108 King's Road, Chelsea, SW3 4TZ (7838 0818); 56-58 Hill Street, Twickenham, TW9 1TW (8332 6956).

Quackers

155D Northcote Road, Clapham, SW11 6QB (7978 4235). Clapham Junction rail, then 319 bus. **Open** 9.30am-5.30pm Mon-Fri; 10am-5.30pm Sat. **Credit** MC, V.
Veronica McNaught's bright and cheerful children's clothing store offers a fine selection of fun items for small people aged up to ten. Labels include Alphabet, Petit Bateau, Whoopi and Kanz, with smashing little statement-making T-shirts by Toby Tiger. Accessories include pink secret

Welcome
to the world of
Mystical Fairies

*"Like walking into wonderland ....
it's a childs delight, complete with resident flying fairy"*

We specialise in organising magical tailor made parties to remember in our Enchanted Garden or at any venue of your choice. Featuring the Mystical Fairies, Fairytale Princesses, Peter Pan and Tinkerbelle, Harry and Hermione, Wizards, Hobbits, Pirates and many more by request. Themes also include Karaoke Discos, Grease parties, Butterfly Ball and Arts & Crafts.

The Enchanted Garden is located beneath our fabulous shop which is a treasure trove of all things pink, sparkly and perfect. With gorgeous fairytale costumes, toys, books and collectables to delight the young and young at heart Mystical Fairies is the only fairy shop in London selling all your fairy needs.

No tantrums just tiaras! For the complete party planners

just call: 0207 431 1888

12 Flask Walk, Hampstead, London NW3 1HE

www.mysticalfairies.co.uk

Entertainers • Face Painters • Fairy Club • Fairy School • Party Bags • Costumes • Gift Ideas

---

BEAUBEAU
www.beaubeau.co.uk

ONLINE STOCKISTS FOR

My Little Angel ◆ Teeny Tiny ◆ Kidology ◆ juniorZed
Dress up by Design ◆ Poco Loco Kids ◆ Lynnat ◆ Motion Wear
...for beautiful little people everywhere
0870 220 6687

diaries, hair grips and slides, but our personal favourites are the multicoloured wellies and gorgeous raincoats in patterns and florals by Blue Fish, or the ladybird and froggy designed ones by Checkpoint. Everyone loves the traditional wooden toys (there's always an expanded range around Christmas time).
Buggy access. Play area.

Quiksilver

Units 1 & 23, Thomas Neal Centre, Earlham Street, Covent Garden, WC2H 9LD (7836 5371/www. quiksilver.com). Covent Garden tube. **Open** 10am-7pm Mon-Sat; noon-6pm Sun. **Credit** AmEx, MC, V. **Map** p315 L6.
This iconic label, started in the 1960s in Torquay (that's Torquay, Australia) by surfers Alan Green and John Law and a pair of revolutionary board shorts, is a label of choice even for those who never ride the waves. Snow- and skate-boarders choose from hardwearing loose-cut jeans, T-shirts, shorts, shoes and thick, warm hoodies for those evenings on the beach. Expect to pay from £15 for T-shirts, £39 for boys' jeans and around £40 for girls'.
Buggy access.
Branches: 11-12 Carnaby Street, Soho, W1F 9PH (7439 0436); Unit 7, 12 North Piazza, Covent Garden, WC2E 8HD (7240 5886).

Tomboy Kids

176 Northcote Road, Clapham, SW11 1RE (7223 8030/www.tomboykids.com). Clapham Junction rail. **Open** 10am-5pm Mon; 10am-5.30pm Tue-Sat. **Credit** MC, V.

Much loved in the area, this modish little boutique is perfect for small folk and young teens who like to make a statement with their clothes. There's an eclectic mix of styles, ranging from flowery hippie summer tops and nicely printed summer dresses with matching hats for girls or Paisley-esque shirts for boys, plus combats, red or green Hunter Spanish wellies, parkas and chunky Canadian jumpers. Rockmount, Birkenstock, Quiksilver, Oxbow and IKKS are names to look for.
Buggy access. Play area.

Trotters

34 King's Road, Chelsea, SW3 4UD (7259 9620/www. trotters.co.uk). Sloane Square tube. **Open** 9am-7pm Mon-Sat; 10.30am-6.30pm Sun. **Credit** MC, V. **Map** p313 F11.
A lively establishment, Trotters caters for everyone from babies (romper suits at £23) to ten-year-olds (Tommy Hilfiger T-shirts at £15). Summer dresses in eyecatching printed cotton by the Chelsea Clothing Company are a delight for about £24, and superb Bob & Blossom T-shirts cost from £16. Professional fitters ensure the wide range of Start-Rite shoes are the perfect size (there is a 40% discount for the sixth pair purchased, but you must buy them within twelve months – one for big families, then), and children's haircuts cost from £11.50. A good selection of toys and books, including some excellent novelty stationery, makes for brilliant gifts.
Buggy access. Delivery service. Hairdressing. Mail order. Nappy-changing facilities. Play area.
Branches: 127 Kensington High Street, W8 5SF (7937 9373); Unit A6, Brent Cross Shopping Centre, Hendon, NW4 3FP (8202 1888).

The best designers, heaven knows...

Is your toddler dressed to kill? Sister Sledge's ditty to the adonis on a 1970s dancefloor could nowadays just as easily apply to the junior disco, such is the demand for designer kids' fashion. It's a lucrative market, and one that the major brands have been quick to latch on to – Gianfranco Ferre, Roberto Cavalli and Bluemarine were just a few of the names skipping down the junior catwalks of Milan in spring 2005.

Nothing has cachet like the big fashion houses: Gucci's baby range features a £120 teddy covered with their logo, while their toddler range in the Knightsbridge store (18 Sloane Street, SW1X 9NE, 7235 6707) is curiously situated between the jewellery cabinets and the dog bowls – children, the must-have accessory this spring? Dior and Burberry similarly have branded teddies, the iconic Brit label has even added its distinctive checks to a baby rattle (£16.50).

But the biggest trend for designer darlings is the 'mini-me' fad. Everyone, it seems, is doing it. Gucci ladies' suede trainers come with exact replicas in baby sizes (£120), John Galliano has adapted his tattoo design for Dior's girlswear, and Ugg boots, the indispensable footwear of 2004, have spawned the mini Ugg (£55) for babies to teens (www.little-uggers.com). There's even a mini match for a fashion addict's day off: Juicy

Couture (www.juicycouture.com) offers their best-selling tracksuits, à la Lopez, in a youngster's cashmere version for a mind-boggling £344. Not to be outdone, the smaller über-cool labels beloved of the rock 'n' roll celeb crowd are bringing out down-sized copies of their signature pieces. Fake London, known for its funky appliquéd cashmere knits, has Fake Baby pullovers for £239.

But what can the designer infant wear to school? Prada's prim, black lace-ups with the distinctive red stripe won't offend the teacher, but at over £100, they'll send the uniform budget rocketing. And for the fussy gym baby, perhaps the new kids' Y3 trainer (£100) designed by Yohji Yahamoto for Adidas. But for glamour you can't beat the Italians… Dolce & Gabbana's children's range is as flashy as the adult gear: check out those leopard-print baby sandals (£65). They should down a storm at baby massage class.

How does a normal parent on a budget keep up with the Beckhams, (if that's really what they want to do)? The simplest solution is to visit kiddie designer warehouse sales where prime pieces are sold with up to 75 per cent off. Companies like Junior Styles (www.juniorstyles. co.uk) carry a mix of designers from 'street' to the highly covetable works of Cavalli and Armani.

Consumer

One Small Step One Giant Leap.

Second-hand

Boomerang

69 Blythe Road, Olympia, W14 0HP (7610 5232). Olympia tube. **Open** 10am-6pm Tue-Sat. **Credit** AmEx, DC, MC, V.

This jolly shop is crammed with babies' and children's clothes and toys. There's a good selection of babygros, kids' separates and shoes, and loads of generally useful baby paraphernalia. Stock changes every season and you can offload your children's hand-me-downs for a share of the asking price. To save time trawling through the rails, let the owner know what sort of thing you're after.
Buggy access. Nappy-changing facilities.

Little Trading Company

7 Bedford Corner, The Avenue, Chiswick, W4 1LD (8742 3152). Turnham Green tube. **Open** 9am-5pm Mon-Fri; 9am-4.30pm Sat. **No credit cards.**

Every neighbourhood should have somewhere like the Little Trading Company, a Tardis-like shop, packed to the rafters with well-maintained stock. With not an inch of space unfilled, the stackers have been ingenious – car seats dangle from the upper reaches of the walls, and baby chairs, toys, cots, swimmers, buggies and beds jostle for space with clothes and books. Practically every kiddie need can be met, but it's a good idea to enlist the help of the friendly proprietor or an assistant to find things.
Buggy access.

Merry-Go-Round

12 Clarence Road, Hackney, E5 8HB (8985 6308). Hackney Central rail. **Open** 10am-5.30pm Mon-Sat; 11am-5pm Sun. **Credit** AmEx, MC, V.

One of the largest kids' second-hand agencies still trading in London, Merry-Go-Round is a spacious shop, where the clothing and toys are ordered by type. Items for under-twos are on the ground floor, stuff for twos to teenagers in the basement, and toys, buggies and baby walkers spill on to the pavement. High shelves hold bottle sterilisers and gumboots (£2.50-£4), baby shoes (£2), even football and skating boots are strung from the ceiling. You'll find the odd designer-label item, but Next, Gap and Hennes dominate, alongside Fisher Price and Chad Valley toys. Videos, books, car seats and cycling helmets are here in impressive quantities.
Buggy access. Nappy-changing facilities. Play area.

Pixies

14 Fauconberg Road, Chiswick, W4 3JY (8995 1568/ www.pixiesonline.co.uk). Chiswick Park or Turnham Green tube. **Open** Term time 10am-4.30pm Mon-Fri; 10am-3pm Sat. *School hols* 10am-4.30pm Wed-Fri; 10am-3pm Sat. **Credit** MC, V.

People come from all over to visit this little shop in a quiet Chiswick parade. As well as nearly new clothes, Pixies sells quality baby and tots equipment of the kind that isn't easily found on the high street. Savvy parents love brands like Stokke, whose high chairs, cots and changing tables convert into proper-sized furniture for a longer life. Other desirables include HandySitt travel chairs. The shop squeezes in a summer range – pram shades or UV bodysuits put safety first. Anxious mothers-to-be can sign up for the consultancy service (£40/hr) for advice on what they need.
Buggy access. Delivery service. Disabled access. Mail order.

Swallows & Amazons

91 Nightingale Lane, Clapham, SW12 8NX (8673 0275). Clapham South tube. **Open** 10am-5.15pm Mon-Sat. **No credit cards.**

Two floors of second-hand clothes for boys and girls aged up to 12, at nifty prices. Labels range from high street to designer, and kids' haircuts cost £7.50-£8.
Buggy access. Hairdressing. Play area.

Shoes

Brian's Shoes

2 Halleswelle Parade, Finchley Road, Temple Fortune, NW11 0DL (8455 7001/www.briansshoes.com). Finchley Central or Golders Green tube. **Open** 9.15am-5.30pm Mon-Sat; 10.30am-1.30pm Sun. **Credit** MC, V.

This dedicated children's shoe shop is conveniently close to the Bookworm (*see p187*) and offers Timberland, Start-Rite, Ricosta, Skechers, Babybotte, Nike and Kickers in a helpful, calm atmosphere.
Buggy access. Disabled access.

Instep

45 St John's Wood High Street, St John's Wood, NW8 7NJ (7722 7634/www.instepshoes.co.uk). St John's Wood tube. **Open** 9.30am-5.30pm Mon-Sat; 11am-5pm Sun. **Credit** AmEx, MC, V.

Close to Regent's Park, this sizeable shoe store has a huge stock and mature, helpful staff. Expect to pay around £30 for expertly fitted baby shoes, £40 for school shoes and from £50 for fantasy delights from Italy.
Buggy access. Disabled access.
Branches: Harrods, Knightsbridge, SW1X 7XL (7225 6896); 10 Bellevue Road, Wandsworth Common, SW17 7EG (8767 3395); 80 Church Road, Barnes, SW13 0DQ (8741 4114); 47 High Street, Wimbledon Village, SW19 5AX (8946 9735);

Look Who's Walking

78 Heath Street, Hampstead, NW3 1DN (7433 3855). Hampstead tube. **Open** 10am-5.30pm Mon-Sat; noon-6pm Sun. **Credit** AmEx, MC, V.

A tiny boutique crammed with designer clothes, and D&G, Mod8, Naturino and Skechers shoes. Staff cope well with brat attacks; prices for shoes range from £35 to £70.
Buggy access.
Branch: 166A High Road, Loughton, Essex, IG10 1DN (8508 7472).

One Small Step One Giant Leap

3 Blenheim Crescent, Notting Hill, W11 2EE (7243 0535/www.onesmallsteponegiantleap.com). Ladbroke Grove or Notting Hill Gate tube. **Open** 9.30am-6pm Mon-Sat; 11am-5pm Sun. **Credit** MC, V.

Winner of the Best Children's Footwear Retailer award in 2004, this ponderously titled chain of children's shoe shops knows a bit about choice. Brands stocked in teenie sizes include Timberland, Birkenstock, Aster, Mod8, Pom d'Api, Diesel, Converse, Naturino, Oilily, Ugg, Skechers, Geox, Kickers and, of course, Start-rite.
Buggy access. Mail order.
Branches 409 Upper Richmond Road West, East Sheen, SW14 7NX (8487 1288); 49 Northcote Road, Clapham, SW11 1NJ (7223 9314); Putney Exchange, 1st floor, High Street, Putney, SW15 1TW (8789 2046).

Consumer

Shoe Station

3 Station Approach, Kew, Surrey TW9 3QB (8940 9905/www.theshoestation.co.uk). Kew Gardens tube. **Open** 10am-6pm Mon-Sat. **Credit** MC, V.
Recently redecorated, this small and friendly shoe shop has a colourful range of baby and children's shoes in leather, suede and canvas, including Geox, Pom d'Api and Mod8, as well as witty little numbers by Ricosta. Staff, always cheerful and patient with the grottiest of children, are trained Start-Rite fitters.
Buggy access. Play area.

Stepping Out

106 Pitshanger Lane, Ealing, W5 1QX (8810 6141). Ealing Broadway tube. **Open** 10am-5.30pm Mon-Fri; 9am-5.30pm Sat. **Credit** MC, V.
A Start-Rite agent first and foremost, Stepping Out stocks plenty of Ricosta, Mod8 and Kenzo as well. Experienced assistants specialise in advising on shoes for children with mobility problems, with local GPs often referring kids here; lots of styles provide extra support, but manage to be fashionable too (Le Loup Blanc, for example, is perfect for kids with weak ankles). At the back is an area with toys and games for kiddies to look through as parents pay.
Buggy access. Play area.

Sportswear

Ace Sports & Leisure

341 Kentish Town Road, Kentish Town, NW5 2TJ (7485 5367). Kentish Town tube. **Open** 9.30am-6pm Mon-Wed, Fri, Sat; 9.30am-7pm Thur. **Credit** AmEx, DC, MC, V.
This excellent little store, with its calm atmosphere and helpful staff, is miles better than Oxford Street's numerous trainer specialists staffed by clueless, callow youths. Apart from the endless footwear (Puma, Adidas, Reebok and Nike, with lots of cool new astroboots from £16.99), there are small baseball mitts (£20) and the latest footballs in appealing mini sizes, children's cricket balls and bats, junior tennis racquets, ping-pong balls in bright colours, tracksuits, swim nappies, goggles, earplugs and nose clips – everything, in fact, to get kids active.
Buggy access. Disabled access.

Decathlon

Canada Water Retail Park, Surrey Quays Road, SE16 2XU (7394 2000/www.decathlon.co.uk). Canada Water tube. **Open** 10am-7.30pm Mon-Thur; 10am-8pm Fri; 9am-7pm Sat; 11am-5pm Sun. **Credit** MC, V.
This French-owned sports superstore has clothes and equipment for more than 60 types of sport, including football, rugby, tennis, golf, riding and swimming. Beware that they don't always have children's sizes in clothes, but for bikes this is one of the cheapest places around. Frequent sales make it a useful focus for birthday and Christmas present-buying. Prices are reasonable; expect to pay about £26 for a replica football shirt.
Buggy access. Disabled access. Delivery service.

Lillywhites

24-36 Regent Street, SW1Y 4QF (0870 333 9600/ www.sports-world.com). Piccadilly Circus tube. **Open** 10am-9pm Mon-Sat; noon-6pm Sun. **Credit** AmEx, MC, V. **Map** p317 K7.
Now it's owned by the Sports World group, Lillywhites has tipped a bit downmarket (there's no equestrian section, and you can't buy a lacrosse stick for love nor money), but at least all the mainstream stuff is good value. It does still supply skiwear and cricket gear in their respective seasons, as well as swimsuits, football and tennis kit all year round. Recently we were pleased to find cheap £6 sledges (plastic) after the cold snap – at least we'll be prepared for next year's smattering. Children's mini football kits, as well as those essential goalie gloves and team socks, are in good supply. There's alos a wide range of gimmicky stuff, such as Barbie trainers (£14.99), swimsuits and goggles and a range of Barbie skiwear on the top floor, strangely apart from the rest of skiwear on the ground floor. The store's layout over several half-levels is confusing, and it's not always easy to find a member of staff.

Ocean Leisure

11-14 Northumberland Avenue, Charing Cross, WC2N 5AQ (7930 5050). Embankment tube. **Open** 9.30am-6pm Mon-Wed, Fri; 9.30am-7pm Thur; 9.30am-5.30pm Sat. **Credit** MC, V. **Map** p399 L8.
Two shops face each other across the street underneath the arches here: one's all sailing and scuba, the other seems to be mostly skate and surf. Whichever of these bracing activities takes your fancy, all the gear you need is at Ocean Leisure, some if it in very small sizes. Short-sleeved wet-suits (£44) are on hand for those freezing forays into the North Cornish surf, while full-length steamer suits (£74.99) cater to more intrepid winter users. Boards may be purchased more cheaply at the seaside than here, but there's a good range of Reef sandals and neoprene Aquashoes (£6) in small sizes, as well as baby life jackets for sailing, fins (£11.95), masks and snorkels (set £21.95), and even scuba equipment (from age eight).
Buggy access. Disabled access. Mail order.

Skate of Mind

Unit 26, Thomas Neal Centre, Earlham Street, Covent Garden, WC2H 9LD (7836 9060). Covent Garden tube. **Open** 10am-7pm Mon-Sat; noon-6pm Sun. **Credit** AmEx, MC, V. **Map** p315 L6.
If the children are minded to skate and want to look the part for posing on the South Bank, the lads here can usually find smallish T-shirts with the right logos or 26-inch waist baggy pants and small-size skate shoes by, perhaps, DC. 'Mini' skateboards are available as well: a complete rig by Blind costs between £65-£165.
Buggy access. Disabled access; lift.
Branches: 4 Marlborough Court, Soho, W1F 7EQ (7434 0295); Unit 3, Camden Wharf, Jamestown Road, Camden High Street, Camden, NW1 7BX (7485 9384).

Slam City Skates

16 Neal's Yard, Covent Garden, WC2H 9DP (7240 0928/www.slamcity.com). Covent Garden tube. **Open** 10am-6.30pm Mon-Sat; noon-5pm Sun. **Credit** AmEx, MC, V. **Map** p315 L6.
Possessing one of the grungiest shopfronts in Covent Garden, this is teen heaven, with a small range of possibilities for the very small. Skateboard decks, T-shirts, the skate shoes of the moment (the littlest is UK size three), rucksacks and accessories are all sold here. Although there's no stock dedicated to children, most are happy to buy the 'Small' Slam City T-shirt and grow into it. Shoes include chunky Nikes, Carroll, Vans, Etnies and Emerica.
Buggy access. Mail order (0870 420 4146).

Soccerscene

56-57 Carnaby Street, Soho, W1F 9QF (7439 0778/www.soccerscene.co.uk). Oxford Circus tube. **Open** 9.30am-7pm Mon-Sat; 11.30am-5.30pm Sun. **Credit** AmEx, MC, V. **Map** p314 J6.

Footie and rugger fans converge on this sizeable store devoted to the games of gentlemen and of ruffians. Scaled-down replica kits are available for most of the popular teams, especially the sainted Arsenal and ever-popular Man U and Chelsea, with sales of Welsh red rugby shirts having shot up since the spring. As well as kit, there are balls, boots, shin pads, trainers, socks, boxes, scarves and hats. Service is helpful.

Buggy access. Delivery service. Mail order.
Branch 156 Oxford Street, W1D 1ND (7436 6499).

Speedo

41-43 Neal Street, Covent Garden, WC2H 9PJ (7497 0950). Covent Garden tube. **Open** 10am-7pm Mon-Wed, Fri, Sat; 10am-8pm Thur; noon-6pm Sun. **Credit** AmEx, MC, V. **Map** p315 L6.

As a brand, Speedo has traditionally catered for lane swim-mers who want comfort and coverage, but it also sells beachwear, towelling capes, sun-tops and knee-length sun-suits (£23) with up to 98% UV protection. The junior range is cool for swimming lessons (the elongated 'tankini' biki-nis are lovely for little girls). There are loads of children's accessories here too: come for swim nappies, armbands, snorkels, goggles and caps that match your swimsuit.

Buggy access. Delivery service. Disabled access. Mail order.

Wigmore Sports

79-83 Wigmore Street, Marylebone, W1U 1QQ (7486 7761/www.wigmoresports.co.uk). **Open** 10am-6pm Mon-Wed, Fri, Sat; 10am-7pm Thur. **Credit** AmEx, MC, V. **Map** p314 G6.

London's only racquet sport specialist is great fun to visit. Disciplines covered include tennis, squash, badminton and more, and there's a 'try before you buy' practice wall, which everyone loves. If you have a child who has decided to rise to this desperate nation's challenge to try to find a champion, check out the junior stock. Excellent tennis shoes by K-Swiss, Adidas, Nike and others (£30-£40) are stocked in half sizes from 12 up, but more important for children are the shorter rackets (from 50cm/19in; £15-£100) and softer balls, which together prevent young beginners getting discouraged on court.

Buggy access. Delivery service. Disabled access. Mail order.
Branches: Harrods, 87-135 Brompton Road, SW1X 7XL (7730 1234); Selfridges, 400 Oxford Street, W1A 1AB (7318 2498).

TOYSHOPS

Bikes

Chamberlaine & Son

75-77 Kentish Town Road, Camden, NW1 8NY (7485 4488). Camden Town tube. **Open** 8.30am-6pm Mon-Sat. **Credit** MC, V.

Hundreds of bikes are suspended from the ceiling and walls at this great shop, including revamped Raleigh Choppers (£200), which are causing many a parent to get misty-eyed these days. There are also reclinable Hamax baby seats (£62.99), Phillips trailer buggies (from £120) and a Giant 'halfwheeler' trailer (£120-£160) for children who are old enough to pedal behind a parent, a safe way to commute greenly with the children without putting them at the mercy of town traffic. A new child's bike costs about £100; the first service is free.

Buggy access. Delivery service. Disabled access. Mail order.

Consumer

Sweet dreams

'It's 1955 in my sweetshop, young man', announced Miss Hope to an impudent Radio 4 journalist during one of many features on her centre of sweetie excellence, which opened in East Dulwich in 2004. Miss Hope, who runs the shop with Mr Greenwood (no vulgar Christian names here, thank you), had always played sweetshops as a little girl and this jar-lined retail confection is the realisation of her dreams. It is indeed a shop of dreams, both for children and for those adults who rue the passing of rosy apples, sherbert pips, chewing nuts and cola cubes from the confectionery canon. Hope and Greenwood have proved that the sweets of 20 years ago are still out there, you just have to be a special sort of sweetshop to stock all of them.

It's not just nostalgic adults with mouthfuls of fillings crowding into this most beautiful of shops – children bundle in here daily after school for a fix of liquorice whips and pineapple chunks. They even have sweet tobacco in here (coconut and brown sugar strands once sold alongside chocolate cigarettes, liquorice pipes and candy

matches in the bad old 1970s). If the stock sounds a mite too synthetic for sophisticated Londoners of the 21st century, be assured that Hope & Greenwood sell handmade chocolates and quality brands, such as Lindt and Suchard, particularly around Easter and Christmas. To make the shop pay – you can't run a business based on a stream of kids asking for 'two ounces' (the olden days way of saying '50g') of Tom Thumb drops – the proprietors also sell sweetie-related goods, such as retro tins and jars, gift wrap, bunting and boxes. You inevitably hang around in here much longer than you intended to, especially with the children in an agony of decision-making and with only £1 to spend. Parting is such sweet sorrow you just know you'll come back again sooner than your dentist would wish.

Hope & Greenwood

20 North Cross Road, East Dulwich, SE22 9EU (8613 1777). *East Dulwich rail/12, 40, 176, 185 bus.* **Open** 10am-6pm Mon-Sat; 10am-5pm Sun. **Credit** AmEx, MC, V.

Edwardes

*221-225 Camberwell Road, Camberwell, SE5 0HG
(7703 3676/5720). Elephant & Castle tube/rail, then
P3, 12, 68, 176 bus.* **Open** *8.30am-6pm Mon-Sat.*
Credit *AmEx, MC, V.*
Bikes for children aged two to 12, including Pro Bike,
Bronx and Giant ranges, are supplemented by useful acces-
sories such as bike seats, jolly helmets, trailers and tag-
alongs to fix to adult bikes (from £89). Repairs for slipped
chains, punctured tyres and damaged wheels are all dex-
trously carried out.
*Buggy access. Delivery service. Disabled access.
Mail order.*

Hills

*58 Fortis Green Road, Muswell Hill, N10 3HN (8883
4644). Highgate tube, then 43, 134 bus.* **Open** *9am-
5.30pm Mon-Fri; 9am-5pm Sat.* **Credit** *MC, V.*
Little girls' bikes with gears, streamers and flower stickers cost £110 (there's a boy's equivalent in combat colours).
Depth of stock is not so much in evidence here as at other
stores, but breadth is. Proximity to Alexandra Palace ice
rink means there's a handy sideline in ice skates (from
£59.99), plus roller skates, unicycles, skateboards (from
£25), crash helmets (£20) and tagalongs (by Allycat, £149).
Buggy access. Disabled access. Delivery service.

Two Wheels Good

*143 Crouch Hill, Crouch End, N8 9QH (8340
4284/www.twowheelsgood.co.uk). Finsbury Park tube,
then W7 bus.* **Open** *8.30am-6pm Mon-Sat, 11am-5pm
Sun.* **Credit** *AmEx, MC, V.*
Funkier than most bike shops, this one combines the cool,
sporty side of adult biking with a good range of kids' equipment – the children's versions of Trek and Specialized,
which cost from about £100, are the smartest. There are
helmets (by Met, £20) with lovely designs and Trek trailers (£250, converts to a stroller) and tag-alongs (from £100,
geared and ungeared), plus Bobike child seats (£70), one
of them perfect for older passengers (it has no sides and
folds into a parcel rack). Neat.
Buggy access. Disabled access. Mail order.
Branch: 165 Stoke Newington Church Street, N16 0UL
(7249 2200).

Fun & games

Cheeky Monkeys

*202 Kensington Park Road, Notting Hill, W11 1NR
(7792 9022/www.cheekymonkeys.com). Notting Hill
Gate tube, then 52 bus.* **Open** *9.30am-5.30pm Mon-Fri;
10am-5.30pm Sat.* **Credit** *MC, V.* **Map** *p310 A6.*
There are, in total, five of these wonderful independent
toyshops. Started in Notting Hill in 1992, Cheeky Monkeys
is strong on presentation and good at stocking unusual,
attractive and fun products. Monkeys also have some of
London's best fancy dress (from smart soldiers to tigers
and frogs, alongside Angelina Ballerina tutus). Then
there's the more off-the-wall toys, such as our favourite,
the cuddly toy dog, who sits in her basket and suckles her
three tiny puppies. We also love Playstack, a brilliant ver-
tical puzzle system. Pocket-money toys and small gifts (for
around £1.99) tend to be imaginative – there are fizzy
coloured bath bombs and tiny raggy dolls. Children could
spend ages deciding what to spend their weekly stipends
on in here. A fine range of dressing-up costumes (with

accessories to match) are available, all starting as cheaply
as £1.99 for a pirate's eye-patch. All the popular themes
are covered: cowgirls and boys, Indians and *Harry Potter*-
inspired wizards with flashy, purple capes (£24.99-£34.99),
along with some more unusual concepts such as the 'dotty
dog fairy' outfit (£29.99).
Buggy access. Disabled access. Mail order (website only).
Branches: 24 Abbeville Road, Clapham, SW4 9NH
(8673 5215); 1 Bellevue Road, Tooting, SW17 7EG (8672
2025); 94 New Kings Road, Fulham, SW6 4UL (7731
3031); 4 Croxted Road, West Dulwich, SE21 8SW(8655
7168).

Disney Store

*360-366 Oxford Street, W1N 9HA (7491 9136/www.
disneystore.co.uk). Bond Street tube.* **Open** *10am-8pm
Mon-Sat; noon-6pm Sun.* **Credit** *AmEx, MC, V.*
Map *p314 J6.*
Fancy-dress costumes (Disney's Snow White and Woody
the Cowboy are favourites), stationery, tableware, videos,
dolls and cuddly toys are the bestsellers in this animated
shop. There are brash mounds of soft toys, and the famous
characters have also been fashioned into covetable twirly
straws, beach towels and pencil cases (from £3.99).
Buggy access. Disabled access. Mail order.
Branches 9 The Piazza, Covent Garden, WC2E 8HD
(7836 5037); 22A & 26 The Broadway Shopping Centre,
Hammersmith, W6 9YD (8748 8886).

Early Learning Centre

*36 King's Road, Chelsea, SW3 4HD (7581 5764/www.
elc.co.uk). Sloane Square tube.* **Open** *9am-6pm Mon,
Tue, Thur-Sat; 9am-7pm Wed; 11am-5pm Sun.* **Credit**
AmEx, MC, V. **Map** *p313 F11.*
ELC's wide range of toys, games and art materials is
dedicated to imaginative play for babies and young
children. Here you'll find chunky tool kits, play groceries
and cookware, plus a wide range of detailed plastic
animals, dinosaurs, playhouses, swings, sandpits, paddling
pools, picture books and story and song tapes, science sets
and arty-crafty kits. Perfect presents for young children
include attractive soft-bodied baby dolls that come with
their own high chair or cot, ELC's wooden train sets with
track that fits in with a Brio set-up, insect-hunting kits for
young naturalists and jingly toy instruments for junior
musicians. This branch holds play sessions for little ones
on Tuesdays (9.30-11am).
Buggy access. Delivery service. Mail order. Play area.
Branches: throughout town. Check website for details.

TOP 5 Play areas

Daisy & Tom
The carousel's an added bonus. *See p184.*

Daunt Books
Read before you buy. *See p187.*

Harrods
Check the website for special events. *See p205.*

Mystical Fairies
With added fairy dust. *See p205.*

Soup Dragon
Cook up a storm in the mini kitchen. *See p209.*

Fun Learning

Bentall's Centre, Clarence Street, Kingston-upon-Thames, Surrey KT1 1TP (8974 8900). Kingston rail.
Open 9am-6pm Mon-Wed, Fri, Sat; 9am-8pm Thur; 11am-5pm Sun. **Credit** MC, V.

Fun Learning has toys for everyone from five to 15s, including some brain-teasers and puzzles that will flummox even grown-ups. Eager learners can try out the educational software at the computer table in the centre, while others head straight to the toys and books. There are plenty of outdoor toys too.

Buggy access. Disabled access. Nappy-changing facilities.
Branch: Brent Cross Shopping Centre, Hendon, NW4 3FP (8203 1473).

Hamleys

188-196 Regent Street, W1B 5BT (0870 333 2450/www.hamleys.com). Oxford Circus tube. **Open** 10am-8pm Mon-Sat; noon-6pm Sun. **Credit** AmEx, DC, MC, V. **Map** p314 J6.

The largest toyshop in the world (allegedly) is a loud, frenetic, exciting experience. You can get most of the products you're looking for here, though prices tend to build in a margin for the convenience. The ground floor is where the latest fun toys are demonstrated, and this is where the mayhem seems most pronounced. This floor also accommodates a mountain of soft toys. The basement is the Cyberzone, full of games consoles and high-tech gadgetry. The first floor has items of a scientific bent, plus a lurid sweet factory and bear depot. On second is everything for pre-schoolers. Third is girlie heaven – Barbie World, Sylvanian Families and departments for dressing up, make-up and so on. Fourth has some large and pricey remote-controlled vehicles, plus die-cast models. Fifth is Lego World, which has its own café. Kids can have their birthday party here – typically on a Sunday morning – and Hamleys also arranges Christmas parties and other events.

Buggy access. Café. Delivery service. Disabled access: lift, toilet. Nappy-changing facilities. Mail order. Play areas.

Mystical Fairies

12 Flask Walk, Hampstead, NW3 1HE (7431 1888/www.mysticalfairies.co.uk). Hampstead tube.
Open 10am-6pm Mon-Sat; 11am-6pm Sun. **Credit** MC, V.

Around 2,000 fairy products find a patch in this amazing shop. Fairy creatures hang from the ceiling on beaded swings, endure being shaken inside glitter-storm bubbles and lend their wings to little girls' rucksacks. Mystical Fairies has realised that no corner of the children's market is untouchable by the fairy. Much energy is going into fairy bedwear now: canopies, bed covers, slippers, dressing gowns, pyjamas and duvet covers are now available for around £20 each. New collections of fairy dresses come from So Fairy Beautiful and Frilly Lilly in addition to favourite Lucy Lockett, and there are also coveted Disney Princess Costumes. The basement is a splendid space and home to Fairy Club and Fairy School (*see also p250*).

Buggy access. Mail order.

Toys R Us

760 Old Kent Road, Peckham, SE15 1NJ (7732 7322/ www.toysrus.co.uk). Elephant & Castle tube/rail, then 21, 56, 172 bus. **Open** 9am-8pm Mon-Fri; 9am-7pm Sat; 11am-5pm Sun. **Credit** AmEx, MC, V.

Traditional Toys is a joy forever. *See p209.*

These spacious toy warehouses stock industrial quantities of the toy of the moment. Inexpensive bikes, trikes, ride-on tractors and go-karts, car seats, baby accessories and buggies are another attractions, and the party paraphernalia is pretty good: themed paperware, silly hats, balloons and party bags with their various plasticky fillings. *Buggy access. Car park. Delivery service. Disabled access: toilet. Nappy-changing facilities.* **Branches**: throughout town. Check website for details.

Local toyshops

Art Stationers/ Green's Village Toy Shop

31 Dulwich Village, Dulwich, SE21 7BN (8693 5938). North Dulwich rail. **Open** 9am-5.30pm Mon-Sat. **Credit** MC, V.

If it's art supplies – paint boxes, easels, paper, stationery – you want, stay in the front section, where party paperware, cards and craft kits are also sold. Most children canter to the back section, however, where Brio, Sylvanian

Families, Playmobil, Crayola, Lego and other giants of the toy kingdom sit temptingly on the crowded shelves. The staff remain cheerful even during the after-school rush for pocket-money-priced must-haves (stickers, yo-yos, rings, bubbles) and are happy to advise on toys for all occasions. Dolls' house furniture and dressing-up clothes are also sold. *Buggy access.*

Fagin's Toys

84 Fortis Green Road, Muswell Hill, N10 3HN (8444 0282). East Finchley tube, then 102 bus. **Open** 9am-5.30pm Mon-Sat; 10am-3pm Sun. **Credit** MC, V.

This is the sister shop of Word Play in Crouch End (*see p208*) and it has a similar feel: it's a lovely big space and the stock is sensibly chosen. There is almost nothing faddy here: the owner sticks with her favourites (Galt, Orchard, Brio, Lego, Playmobil, Sylvanian Families) and brings in the latest from them when needed. Row upon row of games yields to an art corner with paint, art, sewing and henna kits by John Adams and of course Galt, and the Jellycat stuffed animals are hugely popular. A large table at the

Ideal homes

If the sight of such elaborately crafted dolls' houses on display at the Museum of Childhood in Bethnal Green (*see p109*) leave you itching to launch your own miniature construction project, you might just be in luck. There are many shops in London that will inspire a lifelong interest in desirable residences for dollies.

Domat (3 Lacy Road, Putney, SW15 1NH, 8788 5715, www.domat.co.uk), owned appropriately enough by two architects, can help get you started. They sell a very conventional product – a basic, self-assembly homestead all ready for you to paint and furnish – priced at around £110. Alternatively, **Soup Dragon** (*see p209*), a quirky and traditional toyshop, sells pretty Victorian dolls' houses for £95.

For furnishings, most toy outlets have a selection and there are countless websites where you can find miniature dolls' house accessories from candlesticks to baby's high chairs (try www.gillianrichards.co.uk or www.woodlane. uk.com, where you'll also find a variety of flat-packed houses from around £50). For pocket-money prices, though, try **Traditional Toys** (*see p209*) or the tiny **Never Never Land** (*see p208*), where there's a great range of dolls' house kits (from £85) as well as all the bits and pieces that make them individual. For interior design inspiration, take a look around **Kristin Baybars'** shop (*see p208*), which is nothing less than a miniature collector's paradise (dolls' houses here start from around £70 for an impressive Regency residence).

If your children prefer the idea of a playhouse they can actually enter, a Wendy house (named after the bossy little girl in *Peter Pan*, of course) might be rather more difficult to get home on the bus. Unless, that is, you palm the kids off with a play tent (the **Early Learning Centre** do them for

around £25; *see p204*). Similarly affordable options can be found on the **Argos** website (www.argos.co.uk), which has quite a decent range of playhouses and tents from a Winnie the Pooh 'pop 'n' fun' version (£24.99) to a Little Tykes version with four activity walls (including a grocery store with ATM machine), made in durable plastic for £250. If you simply don't have the space for such monstosities, **Kinderhouse** (02476 364414, www.kinderhouse.co.uk), an online packaging company, have a flat-packed version that can be folded away under the bed after use. It comes in plain white and is designed to be personalised by the owner with paints, pens, stickers or crayons (£16.99, including postage and delivery).

For something a bit fancier, the **Children's Cottage Company** (www.play-houses.com) and **Wood Wizards** (www.woodwizards.co.uk) are two online companies that create incredibly detailed bespoke wooden play houses. In the latter case, you can opt for a pirate's den (complete with treasure chest and telescope) or a fully furnished windmill cottage that could potentially become your child's second home (prices depend on the size and design).

Tree houses tend to be a luxury for those with a big garden and, equally important, a large tree in it. If you are one of the fortunate few, it may be worth looking at **Blue Forest** (www.blueforest.com) who build a range of contemporary tree houses and 'eco-lodges' costing from £9,000 upwards. What's more, for each structure sold, the company will support a Kenyan child through school for one year (www.assets-kenya.org). But be warned: some of the lofty hideaways on this site are so gorgeous you may be tempted to invest in a family-sized one.

front is chock-a-block with novelties, sweeties, pens and pretty much everything else a child might want to blow their pocket money on, from masks to mouse keyrings, kaleidoscopes and gold wands.
Buggy access.

Happy Returns

36 Rosslyn Hill, Hampstead, NW3 1NH (7435 2431).
Hampstead tube. **Open** 9.30am-5.30pm Mon-Fri; 10am-6pm Sat; noon-5.30pm Sun. **Credit** MC, V.
A good range of Galt crafts, from Octons and paints to hair art, is complemented by Crayola art equipment. There are cheap and cheerful items like police helmets, swords and feather boas, but otherwise it's all proper boxed toys – Sylvanian Families (£10.99), bubble machines (£9.99), sailing yachts, Wolfhammer games and action figures. There are some useful products to be had in the way of party-wares, and five lines of tableware are usually available, from plain colours to *Thomas the Tank Engine* or princesses, alongside printed helium balloons (£2.99 each) or regular balloons from £1.99 for a pack of eight. There are also printed banners, cheap party-bag treats and higher-quality mixed packs of presents (good value at £2.50 for four gifts) to be perused.
Buggy access. Play area.

Havana's Toy Box

Ground floor, Putney Exchange Shopping Centre, Putney High Street, Putney, SW15 1TF (8780 3722).
Putney Bridge tube/Putney rail. **Open** 9am-6pm Mon-Sat; 11am-5pm Sun. **Credit** MC, V.
A bijou place in the corner of the Exchange (kiddies heaven, with its Gymboree play and music centre and numerous toyshops), Havana's leans mostly towards the christening gift side of toys, so there are handsome Noah's arks, tinkly Peter Rabbit mobiles and china, cuddly toys and night lights, all cosily displayed.
Buggy access. Disabled access. Mail order.

Patrick's Toys & Models

107-111 Lillie Road, Fulham, SW6 7SX (7385 9864/ www.patrickstoys.co.uk). Fulham Broadway tube.
Open 9.30am-5.30pm Mon-Sat. **Credit** MC, V.
This cavernous shop has something to suit every pocket and, for once, boys get the lion's share of the goods. It's the main service agent for Hornby and Scalextric, so expect lots of tracks and model trains – everything for everyone from novices to adults with the whole shebang in their attic. Outdoor sports get a look in with kites, bikes and garden games, while war buffs will find enough to engage in full-scale combat. There's a choice of dolls' houses with all the furniture miniature Victorians could wish for, or Barbies, Bratz and Sindies for those in search of a more modern version of womanhood. There is also a large selection of cheap party gifts.
Buggy access. Delivery service (local).

Play

89 Lauriston Road, Victoria Park, E9 7HJ (8510 9960/www.playtoyshops.com). Bethnal Green or Mile End tube/277, 388 bus. **Open** 10am-5.30pm Mon-Sat; 11am-4pm Sun. **Credit** MC, V.
This friendly toyshop opened in June 2004 and is already proving a boon for East London's ever-growing population of aspirational parents. Consequently, educational and developmental toys, books and musical instruments for pre-schoolers are well represented. Construction toys, such as Lego, Galt and Playmobil and that wonderful, addictive Geomag are all present and correct, dressing-up stuff and messy play products (glitter, glue, dough, beads and paints) are also displayed alongside trinkets by Jellycat and Lucy Lockett and party paperware. Considerably laid out, with space for parking pushchairs, and a very well-used community notice board, Play is lots of fun to visit, and the charming staff couldn't be more helpful. Look out for monthly themed events and competitions.
Buggy access. Play area.

QT Toys

90 Northcote Road, Clapham, SW11 6QN (7223 8637).
Clapham Junction rail. **Open** 9.30am-5.30pm Mon-Sat.
Credit MC, V.
As well as the obvious Barbies, Bratz, Brio and Lego lines that no modern child can grow up without, QT is crowded with craft kits, modelling toys and stationery. A huge range of gorgeously detailed Schleich animals includes farm and safari park livestock, wildlife and cantering horses for knights and soldiers. Small children can find their dollies, buggies, push-along trucks and pull-along dogs, and there's stuff for the garden, too, such as paddling pools, sandpits and swings. Local childen spend their pocket money here every week, so the range of affordable treats changes frequently.
Buggy access.

Route 73 Kids

92 Stoke Newington Church Street, Stoke Newington, N16 0AP (7923 7873/www.route73kids.com). Finsbury Park tube/rail, then 106 bus/73, 393, 476 bus. **Open** 10am-5.30pm Tue-Sun. **Credit** MC, V.
The 'shop behind the bus stop' excels in its own brightly coloured, personable way. There are lots of traditional toys, ranging from the wooden Plan range (the hot favourite locally is a dear little humpty-back pull-along snail, £14) through Brio train sets to more cerebral playthings, such as chess sets, jigsaws, Scrabble and solitaire. Route 73 is strong on crafts (face-paints, friendship bracelets, beads, gl;itter, glue and clay) and has a section for party stuff, including piñatas and pocket-money novelties for going home bags. In summer, you can buy either play sand or the sandpit toys necessary for a trip to the park.
Buggy access. Delivery service (local). Mail order.

Snap Dragon

56 Turnham Green Terrace, Chiswick, W4 1QP (8995 6618). Turnham Green tube. **Open** 9.30am-6pm Mon-Sat; 11am-5pm Sun. **Credit** MC, V.
Snap Dragon is a colourful and busy shop. There's a lot of cute stationery and fashionable accessories for those girls who are at the sticker and glitter stage, plus all the tots' favourite figures (including those ever-popular rodent stars Angelina and Maisie). Add family games, kites and model castles to the mix, and you should be able to find all the presents you need in a single trip.
Buggy access. Delivery service (local). Mail order.

Toy Station

6 Eton Street, Richmond, Surrey TW9 1EE (8940 4896). Richmond tube/rail. **Open** 10am-6pm Mon-Fri; 9.30am-6pm Sat, noon-5pm Sun. **Credit** (over £8) MC, V.

Consumer

A well-stocked little place, Toy Station is spread over two floors, with Brio, Meccano, Lego, Airfix and radio-controlled toys sold alongside dollies, craft sets, paints, plasticine and toys at pocket-money prices. *Buggy access. Disabled access.*

Toystop

80-82 St John's Road, Clapham, SW11 1PX (7228 9079). Clapham Junction rail. **Open** 9.30am-6pm Mon-Sat; 11am-5pm Sun. **Credit** MC, V.

Toys and games at this yellow-fronted shop run the gamut of age and gender requirements, from Angelina Ballerina bags to action figures. Everyone will find something they want to take home; the two expansive rooms are full to bursting with new or classic board games, puzzles, a small selection of books, make-up cases, novelty stationery, mini racing cars, beads, bangles and baubles. *Buggy access.*

Word Play

1 Broadway Parade, Crouch End, N8 9TN (8347 6700). Finsbury Park tube/rail, then W7, 41 bus. **Open** 9am-5.30pm Mon-Sat; 11am-5pm Sun. **Credit** MC, V.

A sincere and well-loved Crouch End fixture, Word Play is proud of its balance between books and toys, and is very laid-back. A good half of its display space is devoted to children's books, from nursery rhymes to history and reference – Lemony Snicket, unsurprisingly, continues to sell well. Then it has lots of craft supplies, plus popular building toys such as Bionicles or Geomag at sensible prices. New in are those adorably detailed Schleich toys: little figures such as farm animals, knights and soldiers (£1.99-£6.99) and, for £69.99, a great castle. There's only a small collection of wooden toys, but you can buy a nice set of wooden draughts for £7.99. Little pocket-money dolls (£1.25) are at the high end of the pocket-money spectrum here: a low '£2 and under' table-top is full of penny dreadfuls, devil bangers and fortune-telling fish for 10p. *Buggy access. Disabled access. Mail order.*

Traditional toys

Benjamin Pollock's Toyshop

44 The Market, Covent Garden, WC2E 8RF (7379 7866/www.pollocks-coventgarden.co.uk). Covent Garden tube. **Open** 10.30am-6pm Mon-Sat; 11am-4pm Sun. **Credit** AmEx, MC, V. **Map** p317 L7.

It's a bit comlicated to find: once you've crossed behind the disused shopfront marked 'Pollock's Theatre', dodged the waffle stand, and hiked up some steep stairs, you eventually discover a kooky haven. Best known for its toy theatres, Pollock's is an educational wonderland for young thesps and is hugely enjoyed, on a more superficial level, by all. The most popular paper theatre to assemble is Jackson's (£6.95), with its set and characters for the ballet *Cinderella*. The Victorian Gothic version features a nativity play and there's an Elizabethan one (£8.95) that puts on *A Midsummer Night's Dream*. Other items on sale include marionettes, glove and finger puppets, and French music boxes (£37.50). If the history of paper theatres sparks an interest, there are books on the subject. Collectors pop in for antiques and handmade bears (from £82), but there are lquirky pocket-money toys too, such as cardboard masks (£1.40) and pocket compasses (£1.99). *Mail order.*

Compendia Traditional Games

10 The Market, Greenwich, SE10 9HZ (8293 6616/www.compendia.co.uk). Cutty Sark DLR/Greenwich rail. **Open** 11am-5.30pm daily. **Credit** MC, V.

The ultimate shop for a rainy day, Compendia has the traditionals – chess, backgammon, dominos – as well as an appealing range of more obscure games from around the world to suit all ages. If you've had enough Cluedo, check out Champagne Murders (a murder-mystery game for ages eight to adult). Little ones have fun with Coppit – a wobbly hat game – but the drug-smuggling board game Grass is, of course, adults only. *Buggy access. Delivery service. Disabled access. Mail order.*

Farmyard

63 Barnes High Street, Barnes, SW13 9LF (8878 7338/www.thefarmyard.co.uk). Barnes or Barnes Bridge rail. **Open** 10am-5.30pm Mon-Fri; 9.30am-5.30pm Sat. **Credit** MC, V.

The Farmyard stocks traditional toys and games for newborns to eight-year-olds, including its own personalised range of wooden toys, models and kits. There are, indeed, mini farm animals and the farmyards to keep them in, although dairy stock isn't a particular speciality. Small and large gifts include puzzles, games, wooden toys, dolls and puppets. Dressing up for that all important party could also prompt a trip here. Although primarily a traditional toyshop, the Farmyard stocks a concise collection of dressing-up clothes alongside the games. Most popular are the pretty selection of fairy princess and ballerina gear (around £25-£35), although boys are not left out: there are also pirates, kings with capes and knights' tabards decorated with chain mail to be found. *Buggy access. Play area.* **Branch**: 54 Friar's Stile Road, Richmond, Surrey TW10 6NQ (8332 0038).

Kristin Baybars

7 Mansfield Road, Gospel Oak, NW3 2JD (7267 0934). Kentish Town tube/Gospel Oak rail/C2, C11 bus. **Open** 11am-6pm Tue-Sat. **No credit cards.**

This miniaturist's paradise is also a fairytale come true for any child capable of looking without touching. You have to knock to gain entry ('mysterious' is a preferred adjective of Ms Kristin Baybars herself), but what you'll see inside is the biggest, most jaw-dropping array of tiny scenes and houses outside a craft fair. Show enough interest and decorum, and you'll be ushered into the inner sanctum – room after room of amazing little worlds, including a house full of dogs, a macabre execution scenario and an old-fashioned store for mourning jewellery. The dolls' house kits aren't prohibitively expensive (£70 for a massive Regency affair), and it's well worth investing a few pounds in tiny accessories. *Buggy access.*

Never Never Land

3 Midhurst Parade, Fortis Green, N10 3EJ (8883 3997). East Finchley tube. **Open** 10am-5pm Tue, Wed, Fri, Sat. **Credit** MC, V.

This teeny rectangle of a shop is crammed with old-world delights and betrays the love and attention of the devoted owner and assistant. The shop is known for its dolls' houses – high-quality structures (from £85) and individually sold bits and pieces that really do fit together. There are

Consumer

modest alternatives to houses, such as conservatories (£20) and shops (£57.50). The owner is adept at sourcing unusual wooden toys (such as dancing musical frogs, £8.99) and also stocks baby-safe toys. There are many inspired gifts, including winged 'wish bears'. Lots of pocket money potential here too, in addition to the doll-house content – bright Russian dolls (£6.99), gorgeous tiny Chinese cloth purses (99p) and colourfully hewn German knights, which fathers are drawn to especially.
Buggy access. Mail order.

Puppet Planet

787 Wandsworth Road (corner of the Chase), Clapham, SW8 3JQ (7627 0111/07785 541358/www.puppet planet.co.uk). Clapham Common tube. **Open** 9am-4pm Tue-Sat; regular story telling on Sun, call to check. Also open by appointment. **Credit** AmEx, DC, MC, V.
A specialist shop and hospital for tangled marionettes, Puppet Planet is run by Lesley Butler, whose passion for stringed characters extends to her children's party service (*see p247*). The puppets sold here include classic Pelham characters, traditional Indian and African marionettes, Balinese shadow puppets, and vintage carved and felt hand- puppets from Germany. Prices go from a couple of quid for a finger puppet to quite a bit more for the more expressive models.
Buggy access. Delivery service. Disabled access. Mail order. Play area.

Rainbow

253 Archway Road, Archway, N6 5BS (8340 9700/ www.rainbow-toys.co.uk). Highgate tube. **Open** 10.30am-5.30pm Mon-Sat. **Credit** MC, V.
Rainbow may have a hippie-dippie aura, but it's certainly not behind the times. The new owner has created a useful website and now there's also a nifty little mail order business to supplement the treasure-stuffed shop itself. Rainbow's dressing-up costumes are among the best in town: Spiderman and Star Wars with light sabre are very popular, as are ballerina outfits and Lucy Lockett fairy dresses. There are lots of quality wooden Pin and Plan Toys, including plane and car sit-and-rides and tricycles (£30-£50). There are reasonably priced dolls' houses (£49-£100) and lots of nifty accessories to go with them. Orchard, Sylvanian Families and Creativity for Kids account for much of the game/kit range. Seasonal clothes and shoes are available too: Toby Tiger T-shirts, lesser-known Bluefish raincoats and wellies, sandals and flip-flops by Starchild. Mobiles and paper lampshades got up as hot air balloons (£5.75) hang from the ceiling, and puppets are much in evidence. Beanie Buddies are heaped in a corner, while display counters at the back offer assorted glass and clay marbles, practical jokes, kids' jewellery and such dolls' house furnishings as tiny plates of food, coathangers or books (from 15p, often bought on their own). The back room has a useful variety of dolls, balloons and little plastic figures on and off horseback.
Buggy access. Delivery service. Mail order. Nappy-changing facilities. Play area.

Soup Dragon

27 Topsfield Parade, Tottenham Lane, Crouch End, N8 8PT (8348 0224/www.soup-dragon.co.uk). Finsbury Park tube/rail, then W7, 41 bus. **Open** 9.30am-6pm Mon-Sat; 11am-5pm Sun. **Credit** MC, V.
Successive generations of Crouch End children are weaned on this quirky little shop, which specialises in wooden and traditional toys, plus faintly hippie-ish clothes. More nursery products have crept in of late – Micralite buggies, snuggles, high chairs, slings, hip-sheets, a wide selection of Grobag sleeping bags and, on the decorative side, nightlights in 30 possible shapes, from jungle to fish and rocket. Soft toys for babies from La Maze are increasingly popular, as are the fancy dress in classic forms like ballerina for girls and king/Native American for boys. Soup Dragon is also a stockist of removable wall art (paint your own background, then stick on flowers, fish, rockets or whatever; £43.90). Then there are the Groovy Girl dolls (£8.90), an endearingly flat-chested alternative to Barbie; Balu hand-painted dresses; pretty dolls' houses (£79 for an impressive Victorian; £65 for a contemporary house with flat-screened television and glass walls); and a mini kitchen play area that survives its perennial popularity. The free community noticeboard is excellent, and bargain-hunters may leave an email address to be advised of the bi-monthly, half-price warehouse sales. Staff are friendly and helpful. Check the website for a near-complete list of stock.
Buggy access. Mail order. Play area.
Branch: 106 Lordship Lane, Dulwich, SE22 8HF (8693 5575).

Traditional Toys

53 Godfrey Street, Chelsea, SW3 3SX (7352 1718/www.traditionaltoy.com). Sloane Square tube, then 11, 19, 22 bus/49 bus. **Open** 10am-5.30pm Mon-Fri; 10am-6pm Sat. **Credit** AmEx, MC, V. **Map** p313 E11.
It's a pleasure to visit this smashing little toyshop on the corner of Chelsea Green. Every nook and cranny here is filled with games, books and toys. There's a wide range of toys at affordable, pocket-money prices – such as farm animals, cuddly animals, dolls' house furniture and some of the tiniest accessories and soldiers – plus larger items such as a wooden rowboat (£315 down to £195 on sale when we last visited), painted ride-on toys for the nursery and a bright-red wooden fire engine (£63). Shelves hold Breyer model ponies, Brio train sets, boats, dolls, teddies by Steiff and the North American Bear Company, sturdy wooden Noah's arks and much more. Don't miss the fantastic fancy dress: sheriffs, knights, elves and fairies, plus accessories for imaginative games, such as shields, swords, helmets and breastplates, a miniature bow and arrows set, and hobbyhorses (£45). There's also a catalogue of costumes that may be ordered from the store.
Buggy access. Delivery service.

Tridias

25 Bute Street, South Kensington, SW7 3EY (7584 2330/www.tridias.co.uk). South Kensington tube. **Open** 9.30am-5.30pm Mon-Sat. **Credit** MC, V. **Map** p313 D10.
The proximity of Tridias to the big museums shows in shelves stocking intriguing chemistry and science experiment sets (for about £30), but there's also a corner devoted to party equipment. Outdoor toys include croquet, cricket and swingball sets. Otherwise, expect to find dressing-up clothes, Brio, tool kits, marble runs and boxed games, garages and cars, dolls' houses and accessories, plenty of educational books and board games filling the spaces. Favourites include a stage for puppet shows (£34.99), wizard puppets (£6.99 each) and an ace wooden rocking horse (£759, including delivery).
Buggy access. Mail order (0870 443 1300).
Branch 6 Lichfield Terrace, Richmond, Surrey TW9 1AS (8948 3459).

Consumer

WHERE TO STAY

A sleepover in town doesn't have to cost a packet.

It hasn't been easy to convince the industry, but London's hoteliers are gradually responding to consumer dissatisfaction about the state of accommodation choices in the capital. In the past they could rely on the city's plus points as a holiday destination to pull in the punters regardless of expensive, underwhelming hotel rooms. Present circumstances – unfavourable exchange rates, the lure of the budget airlines' European citybreaks – have forced them to work harder to attract guests, both those from overseas and British out-of-towners who fancy London for a weekend break.

Last summer saw a large enough drop in visitor numbers to prompt unheard-of discounts in the winter season, so a little research before you set off may yield better than advertised rates. Your first stop should be one of the innumerable discount hotel websites, which base business on bumping down room prices to sell in bulk. Calling hotels directly also pays off, as special offers are constantly created to fill empty rooms. Also, give the knowledgeable staff at **Visit London** a ring, as they collate many deals and can make bookings on your behalf. A £5 booking fee is charged for this service. You can also check availability and reserve rooms on the VL website. **Superbreak** can organise theme-park packages to Legoland in Windsor (www.legoland.co.uk) and theatre-break packages ; its brochure is available through Visit London.

Visit London Booking Line *0845 644 3020/ www.visitlondon.com.* **Open** *8am-11pm daily.*
Superbreak *0870 701 4444/www.superbreak.com*

LUXURY HOTELS

Charlotte Street Hotel
15-17 Charlotte Street, Fitzrovia, W1T 1RJ (7806 2000/fax 7806 2002/www.firmdale.com). Tottenham Court Road tube. **Rates** (breakfast not incl) *£230-£240 single; £270-£499 double; £388-£934 suite.* **Credit** AmEx, MC, V. **Map** p314 J5.
This delightful boutique hotel is the ultimate in 'modern English' style. Despite its poshness, the hotel has extremely sweet management when it comes to families and will happily put a fold-up bed in one of the deluxe double rooms for the children to share. If you're willing to shell out a little more, the loft mezzanine room (£411) lets parents sleep on a different level to their progeny.

Gore
190 Queen's Gate, Knightsbridge, SW7 5EX (7584 6601/fax 7589 8127/www.gorehotel.com). Gloucester Road tube. **Rates** (breakfast not incl) *£182-£199 single; £223-£335 double; £346 suite.* **Credit** AmEx, DC, MC, V. **Map** p313 D9.
A classy, creaky period piece of a hotel, where all the rooms have massive 18th-century four-poster beds and any number of handsome antiques. Some rooms have attractively aged leather couches, which fold out into sofabeds for children to sleep on. So you can stay in this characterful, elegant hotel and save a bit of cash by having your young ones in the same room. If you have time, take a look at the Tudor Room, which has a 15th-century bed, a minstrels' gallery and atmospheric beamed ceilings.

MODERATE

Amsterdam Hotel
7 Trebovir Road, Earl's Court, SW5 9LS (0800 279 9132/fax 7806 7608/www.amsterdam-hotel.com). Earl's Court tube. **Rates** *£80-£86 single; £90-£100 double; £132-£148 family.* **Credit** AmEx, DC, MC, V. **Map** p312 B11.
Earl's Court is popular with families for its affordable prices and easy access to the centre of town. The Amsterdam Hotel is a jolly choice. In the throes of a refurb when we visited, the comfortable, modern rooms are bright and cheerfully decorated, and there are cots, high chairs and buggies available for visitors with small children.

Harlingford Hotel
61-63 Cartwright Gardens, Bloomsbury, WC1H 9EL (7387 1551/fax 7387 4616/www.harlingfordhotel.com). Russell Square tube. **Rates** *£79 single; £99 double; £110 triple; £115 quad.* **Credit** AmEx, MC, V. **Map** p315 L4.
Following renovation in 2004, the Harlingford has metamorphosed into that rare find: an affordable hotel with bundles of style. The bathrooms are all bright mosaic tiles and coloured glass sinks, while the bedrooms have had a contemporary facelift that doesn't obliterate the original Georgian features. Breakfast is taken in a smart communal room complete with specially designed crockery. A standout feature is the adjoining Cartwright Gardens, complete with tennis courts, which are available to guests.

Knightsbridge Green Hotel
159 Knightsbridge, SW1X 7PD (7584 6274/fax 7225 1635/www.thekghotel.co.uk). Knightsbridge tube. **Rates** (breakfast not incl) *£100-£110 single; £130-£145 double; £150-£170 (plus £25 for each sofabed) suite.* **Credit** AmEx, DC, MC, V. **Map** p316 G9.
An award-winning hotel that has been family-run for over 30 years, the Knightsbridge Green is also perfectly situated for wanders around Hyde Park, the V&A, Natural

Consumer

History and Science Museums. The en-suite rooms are air-conditioned, a godsend for stuffy city summers. Tea-making facilities are on hand in all rooms, where breakfast at £4-£12 is also served.

London Greenwich Novotel

173-185 Greenwich High Road, Greenwich, SE10 8JA (8312 6800/fax 8312 6810/www.novotel.com). Greenwich DLR/rail. **Rates** £135 single; £155 double. **Credit** AmEx, DC, MC, V.
This is the latest addition to a well-known chain, whose frequent special offers mean you're often able to snap up a room for as little as £89. Even without discounts, facilities are good for the price: there's a gym if you need to work up some energy for the day ahead, and a restaurant with a children's menu if the thought of trekking through town in search of nourishment seems too much. The location is perfect for exploring Greenwich Park and the Royal Observatory or taking a boat ride from Greenwich Pier.

Sherlock Holmes Hotel

108 Baker Street, Marylebone, W1U 6LJ (7486 6161/fax 7034 4822/www.sherlockholmeshotel.com). Baker Street tube. **Rates** (breakfast not incl) £109-£145 single; £128-£145 double; £186 suite. **Credit** AmEx, DC, MC, V. **Map** p314 G5.
This boutique hotel is laid-back about children, who can be given a double sofabed in their parents' double bedroom. The lobby is a casual, New York-style cocktail bar, with wooden floors, cream walls and brown leather furniture. The rooms are like hip bachelor pads: beige, brown and wood, leather headboards, pinstripe sheets and swanky bathrooms. There's a gym, sauna and steam room, and an award-winning restaurant, Sherlock's Grill.

22 York Street

22 York Street, Marylebone, W1U 6PX (7224 2990/fax 7224 1990/www.22yorkstreet.co.uk). Baker Street tube. **Rates** £89 single; £120 double; £120-£188 family. **Credit** AmEx, DC, MC, V. **Map** p311 F5.
This central hotel has character and family-friendly vibes in abundance; children under five even stay free. The graceful Georgian house is spread out over five floors, decked out in tiles and wood, with an impressive stone staircase snaking through. Cots and a high chair are on hand, but do note that there is no lift. Interaction between guests is easy, as you breakfast together at a homely antique dining table or unwind in the welcoming lounge area.

BUDGET

Arran House Hotel

77-79 Gower Street, Bloomsbury, WC1E 6HJ (7636 2186/fax 7436 5328/www.london-hotel.co.uk). Goodge Street tube. **Rates** £45-£55 single; £72-£95 double; £90-£113 triple; £96-£117 quad; £105-£130 quint. **Credit** MC, V. **Map** p315 K4.
A small family-run hotel in a 200-year-old Georgian townhouse in the heart of Bloomsbury (within walking distance of the British Museum), Arran House welcomes kids, and any child small enough to sleep in a cot or share a bed with their parents can stay free of charge. Special events, such as Easter egg hunts, are laid on during holidays; otherwise, children can play in the gardens or avail themselves of the art materials and paints. The breakfast room has a high chair.

Baden-Powell House

65-67 Queen's Gate, South Kensington, SW7 5JS (7584 7031/fax 7590 6902/www.scoutbase.org.uk). South Kensington tube. **Rates** (public prices) £72.50 single; £49.50 (extra pull-out bed £17.50) double; £35 per adult, £22 per child under 18 for family rooms. **Credit** AmEx, MC, V. **Map** p313 D10.
Opened in 1961 (and refurbished in 1997), Robert Baden-Powell's memorial hostel provides accommodation for about 300,000 people from 30 different countries each year, with family rooms for visitors with children. YHA members are welcome, although this place is a little more expensive than your average youth hostel.

Garden Court Hotel

30-31 Kensington Gardens Square, Bayswater, W2 4BG (7229 2553/fax 7727 2749/www.garden courthotel.co.uk). Bayswater or Queensway tube. **Rates** £39-£63 single; £58-£92 double; £72-£114 triple; £82-£135 quad. **Credit** MC, V. **Map** p310 B6.
Garden Court is a small townhouse hotel that has been run by the same family for 50 years. You can tell they take pride in their business. The rooms are cheery-looking, with wooden furniture and comfortable beds, and there's an attractive lounge decorated with oil paintings and greenery. Guests have access to the square's pretty garden, and the hotel is handy for Kensington Gardens.

Hampstead Village Guesthouse

2 Kemplay Road, Hampstead, NW3 1SY (7435 8679/fax 7794 0254/www.hampsteadguesthouse.com). Hampstead tube/Hampstead Heath rail. **Rates** (breakfast not incl) £48-£66 single; £72-£84 double; £90-£162 studio. **Credit** AmEx, MC, V.
This comfy B&B is right on the doorstep of Hampstead Heath, but the decor is more bohemian than *Country Life*: it's filled with an eccentric mix of books, rag dolls, Delft earthenware and other curios. Breakfast is served in the garden, weather permitting; there's also a garden studio, which sleeps five. Take note, though: there's a 5% surcharge if you pay by credit card.

Kensington Gardens Hotel

9 Kensington Gardens Square, Bayswater, W2 4BH (7221 7790/fax 7792 8612/www.kensingtongardens hotel.co.uk). Bayswater or Queensway tube. **Rates** £45-£55 single; £69-£74 double; £85-£99 triple. **Credit** AmEx, DC, MC, V. **Map** p310 B6.
The same pretty Victorian square, another small townhouse hotel. This one is distinguished by its elegant lobby, which is staffed 24 hours a day, and by the fact that it's only a short walk from Hyde Park or fashionable Westbourne Grove and Notting Hill. The refurbished rooms are clean and comfortable; the triples are great for families, and cots can be provided.

Morgan House

120 Ebury Street, SW1W 9QQ (7730 2384/fax 7730 8442/www.morganhouse.co.uk). Sloane Square tube/Victoria tube/rail. **Rates** £46-£76 single; £66-£86 double; £86-£110 triple; £122 quad. **Credit** MC, V.
A quintessentially English B&B with small, cosy rooms. Children will appreciate the bunk beds and stuffed animals in the family rooms. Husband and wife owners Rachel Joplin and Ian Berry lend the place a friendly feel, from the cheery breakfast room to the patio garden.

Consumer

Rushmore Hotel

11 Trebovir Road, Earl's Court, SW5 9LS (7370 3839/ fax 7370 0274/www.rushmore-hotel.co.uk). Earl's Court tube. **Rates** *from £59-£69 single; £79-£89 double; £99- £129 triple.* **Credit** *AmEx, DC, MC, V.* **Map** *p312 B11.*
The Rushmore is of that rare breed of budget hotels with a bit of flair. The hotel's biggest talking point is the trompe l'oeil paintings, depicting everything from pastoral Tuscany to tranquil oceans. The Italianate breakfast room, with its granite surfaces and glass tables, is also stylish. All but three of the bathrooms have been refurbished since last year, and cots and cribs can be provided.

St George's Hotel

25 Belgrave Road, Pimlico, SW1V 1RB (7828 2061/ fax 7828 3605/www.stgeorgeshotelvictoria.com). Victoria tube/rail. **Rates** *£35-£50 single; £45-£65 double; £60-£75 triple.* **Credit** *AmEx, DC, MC, V.* **Map** *p316 J11.*
Children stay free up to and including the age of six at St George's (although once they're seven they're classed as adults). This friendly, family-run budget hotel offers basic, comfortable, clean rooms with those all-important colour TVs and a full English breakfast. Cots and high chairs for teeny guests are available on request.

Windermere Hotel

142-144 Warwick Way, Pimlico, SW1V 4JE (7834 5163/fax 7630 8831/www.windermere-hotel.co.uk). Victoria tube/rail. **Rates** *£69-£99 single; £89-£145 double; £129-£149 family.* **Credit** *AmEx, MC, V.* **Map** *p316 H11.*
London's first ever B&B opened here in 1881, and the hotel's current owners have continued the proud legacy. Rooms are comfortable and are decorated in reasonably tasteful English chintz. Bathrooms are clean and modern, with power showers. For a small hotel, there are plenty of luxuries, such as room service, modem points and satellite TV. Another rarity for a budget hotel is a basement restaurant with a sophisticated, decently priced menu. The staff can provide cribs for babies. Do book ahead, as the excellent Windermere family rooms are frequently oversubscribed.

YOUTH HOSTELS

The following hostels are all geared up for children, with high chairs, baby baths, cots and pushchairs for hire, and family rooms that sleep up to six. There's space to run around in the garden at the Hampstead hostel, and the Rotherhithe one has a games room and children's library. But for a full list of existing or planned children's facilities at these establishments, it's a good idea to call or check the website before making your final decision.

If you're not a paid-up member of Hostelling International, you'll pay £3 extra a night, or £1.50 for under-18s (after six nights you automatically become a member). Alternatively, join Hostelling International for £15.50 (£10 under-26s, £22 family) at any hostel or through www.yha.org.uk, which also allows you to book rooms. To request a family brochure call 0870 770 8868. Always phone ahead for availability. These hostels all take MasterCard and Visa; breakfast is included.
City of London *36-38 Carter Lane, EC4V 5AB (0870 770 5764). St Paul's tube/Blackfriars tube/rail.* **Open** *24hr access.* **Reception** *7am-11pm daily.* **Rates** *£15-£32; £15-£26 under-18s (prices may change).* **Map** *p318 O6.*
Hampstead Heath *4 Wellgarth Road, Golders Green, NW11 7HR (0870 770 5846). Golders Green tube.* **Open** *24hr access.* **Reception** *6.45am-11pm daily.* **Rates** *£20; £18 under-18s.*
Rotherhithe *Island Yard, Salter Road, SE16 5PR (0870 770 6010). Canada Water or Rotherhithe tube.* **Open** *24hr access.* **Reception** *7am-11pm daily.* **Rates** *£23.60; £19.50 under-18s.*
St Pancras *79-81 Euston Road, NW1 2QS (0870 770 6044). King's Cross tube/rail.* **Open** *24hr access.* **Reception** *7am-11pm daily.* **Rates** *£24.60; £20.50 under-18s.* **Map** *p315 L3.*

Hotel chains

If your hotel requirements amount to no more than a comfortable spot to bed down after a full day's sightseeing, consider booking at one of the following international chains. Consistent facilities, professional service and centrally located branches are the pay-offs for the lack of individual style, and special rates are frequently offered.

At **Novotels**, for instance, it's free for two children under 16 to share your room (see www.novotel.com). Other child-friendly amenities include play areas, bottle warmers and changing tables. Good deals can also be found at **Premier Travel Inn** (www.premiertravelinn.com). Those in central London are known as Metro branches, and have added extras such as satellite TV and internet access. Family rooms consist of a double bed and two sofabeds, with cots available on request. Most conveniently located is the County

Hall outpost (Belvedere Road, South Bank, SE1 7PB, 0870 238 3300); among the other central locations are Kensington, Euston and King's Cross (check the website for details).

For extras like an indoor pool or spa with your chain, look to **Marriott** hotels (check www.marriott.com), but expect these to be reflected in the price. Good locations include Regent's Park, High Holborn and Park Lane. More affordable, and with the expected plain and inoffensive decor, are **Holiday Inns** (www.holiday-inn.com). Several offshoots, including the Bloomsbury, Camden Lock and Hampstead branches, offer 'kids eat free' deals.

If you prefer self-catering or are planning a longer break, consider a **Citadines** apartment (www.citadines.com). Studios, which sleep up to six people, have a fully equipped kitchenette and baby facilities. You can even bring the family pet.

ACTIVITIES

ARTS & ENTERTAINMENT

Turn off the telly and get out there.

We all love **Shakespeare's Globe**. *See p225.*

In 2004, the shocking findings that it costs parents a stonking £164,000 to rear a child from birth to university were widely reported. It was a chilling statistic, giving even the most hardened breadwinners pause for thought. Fear not, we can reassure you that things aren't quite as bad as all that: there are, even in this pricey town, many great ways to entertain your kids without spending a fortune, sometimes without parting with a single penny. Spend a mere £3, for example, and your child gets a day exploring opera with workshops at **English National Opera**; for £2, a film at the **Clapham Picturehouse**; £5 buys the ticket to a mini concert and a chance to try instruments at the **Wigmore Hall**. Better still, young artists can join the Courtauld Institute's workshops, or spend the day being inspired at an **Orleans House Gallery** family fun day, for no fee at all.

London's first purpose-built theatre for children, the **Unicorn**, set to open in late 2005 with a fantastic programme of entertainment for children of all ages and backgrounds. A refurbished South Bank will also see a new Education Centre in 2006, and the opening in October 2004 of Finchley's stylish **artsdepot** brought drama back into the lives of the young people of the frozen North.

ARTS CENTRES

Phase Two of the transformation of the **South Bank Centre** (*see p31*) means the closure of the Royal Festival Hall from the end of June 2005 for about 18 months of renovation work to improve the comfort, acoustics and technical requirements in the auditorium. The foyers and the Ballroom will also be refurbished, and an Education Centre and performance space created. For more details, check www.rfh.org.uk.

Barbican Centre

Silk Street, The City, EC2Y 8DS (box office 7638 8891/cinema hotline 7382 7000/arts education programme 7382 2333/www.barbican.org.uk). Barbican tube/Moorgate tube/rail. **Open** *Box office (in person)* 10am-8pm Mon-Sat; noon-8pm Sun, bank hols. *Gallery* 10am-8pm Mon, Tue, Thur-Sat; 10am-9pm Wed; noon-6pm Sun, bank hols. **Admission** *Library* free. *Exhibitions, films, shows, workshops* phone for details. **Membership** (BarbicanCard) £20/yr. *Film Club* £7.50/yr/family. **Credit** AmEx, MC, V. **Map** p318 P5.
Both parents and children are pleased by the original and well-organised range of activities staged here throughout the year. Central to this is the Family Film Club. Since the 1980s it has been screening a diverse mix of movies from around the world to kids aged five to 11, with Saturday Special workshops on the last Saturday of every month. A recent session was devoted to making flip books, which proved very popular and needed to be booked ahead. Less regularly, the Barbican hosts festivals and events for families. The children's classic concerts are excellent.
Buggy access. Café. Disabled access: lift, toilet. Nappy-changing facilities. Shop.

Tricycle Theatre & Cinema

269 Kilburn High Road, Kilburn, NW6 7JR (box office 7328 1000/www.tricycle.co.uk). Kilburn tube/ Brondesbury rail. **Open** *Box office* 10am-9pm Mon-Sat; 2-9pm Sun. *Children's shows* 11.30am, 2pm Sat. *Children's films* 1pm Sat. **Tickets** *Theatre* (Sat) £5; £4 advance bookings. *Films* (Sat) £4; £3 under-16s, concessions. **Credit** MC, V.
The Tricycle's range of children's activities incorporates various after-school classes throughout the week. Included are drama, dance and an introduction to performance through simple music, movement and storytelling exercises for children. Half-term and holiday workshops allow kids to get creative with everything from scrap sculpture to urban street dance. Prices and age groups vary from class to class, but an up-to-date leaflet can be downloaded from the website – it also gives details of the regular Saturday film screenings and stage shows. While the former lean towards more mainstream spectacles, the programme of theatrical performances is diverse indeed. The Tricycle's popularity has led to an increased degree of control over advance bookings to ensure that kids from across the city can attend. The parental migration to Kilburn, however, continues unabated.
Buggy access. Disabled access: lift, ramps, toilet. Nappy-changing facilities. Restaurant. Shop.

ART GALLERIES

Check *Around Town* (*pp27-158*) for information on events and activities in other galleries, including the South Bank's **Tate Modern** (*see p41*) and **Hayward Gallery** (*see p34*), Westminster's **National Gallery** (*see p81*) and **Tate Britain** (*see p82*), the grand **Royal Academy of Arts** in Piccadilly (*see p72*), the **Wallace Collection** in Marylebone (*see p67*), **Dulwich Picture Gallery** in south-east London (*see p132*) and east London's **Whitechapel Art Gallery** (*see p106*).

Courtauld Institute Gallery

Somerset House, Strand, WC2R 0RN (7848 2777/ recorded information 7848 2526/education 7848 2922/www.courtauld.ac.uk). Covent Garden, Holborn or Temple (closed Sun) tube. **Open** *Gallery* 10am-6pm daily (last entry 5.15pm); 10am-4pm 31 Dec; noon-6pm 1 Jan. **Tours** pre-booked groups only; phone for details. **Admission** *Gallery* £5; £4 concessions; free under-18s, students. Free to all 10am-2pm Mon (not bank hols). **Credit** MC, V. **Map** p317 M7.
The Courtauld's learning centre offers a range of activities to make its displays accessible to all ages. Instrumental in this are the free Saturday workshops, which are run throughout the year and open up various exhibits with child-friendly adventures including mystery tours and storytelling. Half-term and holiday activities are more hands-on, and a small fee may be charged for materials. A recent treat involved a visit to the jewellery room and the 'Masterpieces of American Jewellery' exhibition, then creating a modern necklace. An occasional series of Art Start events for under-sevens includes Sculpture Safaris, while Art Extra talks – for 13 to 18 year-olds – illuminate more obscure corners of the Courtauld, including contemporary works in the East Wing Collection. Art packs and paper trails are available behind the desk all year round; more advanced students may prefer the programme of spring and summer schools (March and June respectively), which concentrate on art history, last for one week and cost £350 per person (over-16s only): phone 7848 2678 for more information.
Buggy access. Café. Disabled access: lift, toilet. Nappy-changing facilities. Shop.

London International Gallery of Children's Art

O2 Centre, 255 Finchley Road, Finchley, NW3 6LU (7435 0903/www.ligca.org). Finchley Road tube. **Open** *Gallery* 4-6pm Tue-Thur; noon-6pm Fri-Sun. **Admission** *Gallery* free; donations requested. **No credit cards.**
Exhibitions at LIGCA often stem from more troubled corners of the globe: recent displays have included artwork from Italy and the Himalayas and photographs by London children from ethnic minority cultures. They're used as reference points for educational workshops (from £8 per session, running in six-week courses from £40), which encourage kids to respond with their own drawings and paintings. The best of their work is shown in the gallery, and all proceeds are sent to relevant charities. Saturday classes for under-fives (10.30-11.30am; £10) offer simple arts activities based on storytelling. There are plans to resume creative art classes for older kids; ring for details. For creative birthday parties, see *p235*.
Buggy access. Disabled access: lift, toilet. Nappy-changing facilities (O2 Centre).

Orleans House Gallery

Riverside, Twickenham, Middx TW1 3DJ (8831 6000/ www.richmond.gov.uk/orleanshouse). St Margaret's or Twickenham rail/33, 490, H22, R68, R70 bus. **Open** *Apr-Sept* 1-5.30pm Tue-Sat; 2-5.30pm Sun, bank hols. *Oct-Mar* 1-4.30pm Tue-Sat; 2-4.30pm Sun, bank hols. **Admission** free. **Credit** MC, V.
The house is accessed via a secluded riverside path, surrounded by acres of woodland, and it looks more like a decaying country seat than a centre for living arts. The collections are less stuffy than you might imagine, though.

Activities

Alongside an abundance of paintings and prints of scenic Richmond-on-Thames is a lively programme of temporary exhibitions, which until January 2006 will include contemporary artwork in book form. Tied in with the exhibitions is a similarly upbeat series of year-round activity workshops for kids, with after-school sessions (3.45-5pm Wed, Thur) for five to nine year-olds available alongside the Star Club (4-5.30pm Mon), the latter offering those aged seven to ten a place to try their hands (and feet) at dance and drama. Both are £6 per session, and worth booking in advance. During half-term the workshops run for two hours twice daily (10am-noon; 2-4pm). For more information about family activities, and for advance notice of artistically inspired family fun days that run regularly throughout the year, phone to be put on the mailing list. *Buggy access. Disabled access: ramp, toilet. Nappy-changing facilities. Nearest picnic place: Orleans House Gallery grounds, Marble Hill Park or riverside benches. Shop.*

CINEMAS

When it comes to the silver screen, Leicester Square is the city's première capital, home to giants **Empire** (0870 010 2030, www.uci-cinemas.co.uk), **Warner Village West End** (7437 4347, www.warnervillage.co.uk) and the **Odeon** (0870 505 0007, www.odeon.co.uk). Prices are high in such places, but the **Prince Charles Cinema** (7494 3654, www.princecharles cinema.com) offers a cheaper alternative. Or visit one of these picture palaces, where kids' clubs and workshops make film-going more family-friendly.

Clapham Picturehouse

76 Venn Street, Clapham, SW4 0AT (0870 755 0061/ www.picturehouse-cinemas.co.uk). Clapham Common tube/35, 37 bus. **Open** *Box office* (phone bookings) 10am-8.30pm daily. *Film Club* (activities) 11.15am, (screening) 11.45am Sat. **Tickets** £3; members £2. **Membership** £4/yr. **Credit** MC, V.
Running one of the capital's original kids' clubs, the Picturehouse is also a pioneer of screenings for the parents babies under one year. They can bring the babes to the Big Scream! club at 10.30am every Thursday and take in a movie from a roster of blockbuster and art-house films without having to worry about disturbing the audience. Nappy-changing facilities are within dummy-spitting distance. Meanwhile, the kids' club offers Saturday matinées for three to ten year-olds. Staff organise craft and activity workshops preceding the show and three questions to answer afterwards – pay attention to the film and you could win a prize.
Buggy access. Café. Disabled access: toilet (Screens 1 & 2 only). Nappy-changing facilities.

Electric Cinema

191 Portobello Road, Notting Hill, W11 2ED (7908 9696/www.electrichouse.com). Ladbroke Grove or Notting Hill Gate tube/52 bus. **Open** *Box office* 9am-8.30pm Mon-Sat; 10am-8.30pm Sun. *Children's screenings* 11am, 1pm Sat (depending on film length; call to check). **Tickets** £4.50 (all ages). **Credit** AmEx, MC, V. **Map** p310 A7.

For membership of the Electric you must apply in writing, be accepted by a committee made up of local residents and businessmen, and then pay up to the tune of £250 per year. It has its advantages, however: parents on the books receive two free tickets for every kids' club screening. These show classic films and preview new releases in a truly luxurious setting, recently renovated from a historical fleapit to one of the best cinemas in the country (think red leather armchairs, lovingly restored wall friezes and a sumptuous bar). The Saturday movies alternate between those suitable for over-fours and those aimed at over-nines, although there's no official restriction on entry. Parents and their babies (up to one year old) can enjoy special Electric Scream screenings on Mondays at 3pm. *Buggy access. Disabled access: lift, toilet. Kiosk.*

Movie Magic at the NFT

National Film Theatre, South Bank, SE1 8XT (box office 7928 3232/www.bfi.org.uk/moviemagic). Waterloo tube/rail. **Open** *Box office* phone bookings 11.30am-8.30pm daily. *Personal callers* 5-8.30pm Mon-Thur, 11.30am-8.30pm Fri-Sun. *Film Club* times vary; usually Sat, Sun, school hols. **Tickets** *Children* £1 film, £5.50 workshop & film. *Adults* £4.50. Prices may vary, phone to confirm. **Credit** AmEx, MC, V. **Map** p317 M8.
Movie Magic is the NFT's programme of films for kids under 16. Sometimes the movies in question are classics of yesteryear, so nostalgic parents might want to tag along. *Edward Scissorhands* and *Pirates of the Caribbean* have had recent well-received airings. At other times Movie Magic previews the new film of the moment. Booking in advance is advisable; phone for a list of upcoming events. *Buggy access. Café. Disabled access: ramp, toilet. Nappy-changing facilities.*

Rio Cinema

103-107 Kingsland High Street, Dalston, E8 2PB (7241 9410/www.riocinema.co.uk). Dalston Kingsland rail/Liverpool Street tube/rail, then 67, 77, 149 bus. **Open** *Box office* 2-9pm daily. Opening times vary depending on programme. *Film Club* 4.15pm Tue (term-time only); 11am Sat. **Tickets** £2; £1 under-15s. **Credit** AmEx, MC, V.
The Rio is a fun, friendly place where children can sample something other than the usual Hollywood blockbusters. The Saturday morning kids' club intersperses major new releases with occasional classics like *The Seventh Voyage of Sinbad*, offering a repeat performance – the Playcentre Matinée – at 4.15pm every Tuesday during term-time. Membership of the club is free, and comes with a card that's stamped on each visit. Kids under five must be accompanied throughout the movie. A new parent and baby club (under-ones only) also operates on Tuesdays and Thursdays at lunchtime (start times depend on film length) and costs £5 (£4 concessions). *Café. Disabled access: toilet.*

Ritzy Cinema

Brixton Oval, Coldharbour Lane, Brixton, SW2 1JG (0870 755 0062/www.ritzycinema.co.uk). Brixton tube/rail. **Open** *Box office* 10.15am-9.30pm daily. *Film Club* 10.30am Sat. **Tickets** £3; £1 under-14s. **Credit** MC, V.
The grand old Ritzy opened in 1911 as one of the UK's first purpose-built cinemas; since then, it has survived various owners, near demolition and – most recently – significant development to become one of London's finest. Tender age

is no restriction to enjoying its delights: two kids' club films are shown every Saturday – the first aimed at under-sevens, the second at over-sevens. During school holidays the club also operates on Tuesdays and Thursdays, with related activity sessions, competitions and special events often set up at short notice (phone for details). The Ritzy also has a programme of matinées open to culture-starved new parents with babies (under-ones only): phone for details of these weekly Watch with Baby screenings. *Buggy access. Café. Disabled access: lift, toilet. Nappy-changing facilities.*

MUSIC VENUES

English National Opera

The Coliseum, St Martin's Lane, Covent Garden, WC2N 4ES (education 7632 8484/box office 7632 8300/www.eno.org). Leicester Square tube. **Open** *Box office* 10am-8pm Mon-Sat. **Tickets** £8-£70. **Credit** AmEx, DC, MC, V. **Map** p315 L7.

English National Opera's latest, highly praised innovation is family days, where the over-sevens spend a day exploring the company's current production for a fee of just £3. January 2005's *Pirates of Penzance* family day involved a feast of drama, composition and music design workshops; after that, *Eugene Onegin* provided a day of dancing, duels and creating characters; later in the year, *The Magic Flute* and *Madame Butterfly* will offer similar programmes. Attending the performance afterwards is optional, but tickets are an additional £5 for children, £10 for adults. Following the opening of the Clore Education Room at the Coliseum, the ENO's education team, Baylis, is expanding its range of activities. Phone for details.
Disabled access: ramp, toilet.

Royal Albert Hall

Kensington Gore, South Kensington, SW7 2AP (7589 8212/www.royalalberthall.com). South Kensington tube. **Open** *Box office* 9am-9pm daily. **Credit** AmEx, MC, V. **Map** p313 D9.

The recently refurbished Royal Albert Hall has a smart education department, which goes some way to opening up this marvellous auditorium to younger audiences. A series of family events throughout 2005 will include (in October) the Royal Philharmonic Orchestra laying on one of its celebrated Noisy Kids performances, during which the audience is encouraged to join in the music-making (without instruments, naturally). And don't miss the two annual Blue Peter Proms on 23 and 24 July. Further events were, as we went to press, due to be announced – consult the website for details.
Buggy access. Café. Disabled access: lift, ramp, toilet. Nappy-changing facilities. Restaurant (booking necessary). Shop.

Royal College of Music

Prince Consort Road, South Kensington, SW7 2BS (7589 3643/www.rcm.ac.uk). South Kensington tube/ 9, 10, 52 bus. **Map** p313 D9.

The RCM'S tuition is tailored to 'extremely talented people'. If that doesn't deter you, applications (for children aged eight to 17) are by audition alone and are, of course, heavily oversubscribed, while lessons – which run in conjunction with the school term (8am-5pm Sat) – focus almost exclusively on classical instruments. Families are perhaps best off keeping an eye on the programme of performances staged by pupils throughout the year, which are usually free (check the website for details). *Café. Disabled access: lift, toilet.*

Wigmore Hall

36 Wigmore Street, Marylebone, W1U 2BP (7935 2141/education 7258 8240/www.wigmore-hall.org.uk). Bond Street tube. **Open** *Box office* 10am-7pm Mon-Sat; 10.30am-6.30pm Sun. **Credit** AmEx, DC, MC, V. **Map** p314 H5.

The art deco Wigmore Hall was built in 1901 by the German piano manufacturers Bechstein, although barely 15 years later they were made to sell it to Debenhams when World War I forced German businesses up against the wall. Thankfully, the interior of this stunning venue remains virtually unaltered, with marble, warm wood panelling and plush red seating setting it a cut above most other small venues in the capital. Best of all is the mural above the stage – a Blakean vision of the Soul of Music by Frank Lynn Jenkins. The hall reopened with a great flourish in October 2004 after being closed for essential repair work. Performances take place daily, and are uniformly classical, although occasional school concerts present work with relevance to the National Curriculum at heavily reduced rates. There's also a programme of interesting family events, starting with the sadly oversubscribed Chamber Tots classes, which encourage two to five year olds to create music after listening to a mini concert (£5 children, adults free). There are interesting family days – in April 2005, for instance, kids were offered the chance to try orchestral instruments and compose and perform their own music on stage. Regular young fiddlers' days introduce violinists from Grade 2 upwards to playing folk fiddle. There are also two family concerts each term (£3 children, £6 adults).
Buggy access. Disabled access: toilet. Nappy-changing facilities. Restaurant.

THEATRE

Puppets

Little Angel Theatre

14 Dagmar Passage, off Cross Street, Islington, N1 2DN (7226 1787/www.littleangeltheatre.com). Angel tube/Highbury & Islington tube/rail, then 4, 19, 30, 43 bus. **Open** *Box office* 10am-6pm Mon-Fri; 9.30am-4pm Sat, Sun. **Tickets** £7.50-£8.50; £5-£6 under-16s. **Credit** MC, V.

Established in 1961, the Little Angel remains London's only permanent puppet theatre. Performances cover a huge range of styles and just about every kind of puppet under the sun, with the annual calendar peppered with shows by touring companies from across the country eager to work with the theatre's rare proscenium arch. Most productions are aimed at audiences aged five and over, but in 2005 under-fives saw an interpretation of Turkish puppetry and folktale in the form of *Turkish Delight*, a pared-down version of *Karagoz*. A Saturday puppet club runs in conjunction with most major productions, although mums and dads must wait for one of a number of family fun days – held during school holidays – for their own chance to play with the puppets.
Buggy access. Disabled access: toilet. Kiosk. Nappy-changing facilities. Shop.

Puppet Theatre Barge

*Opposite 35 Blomfield Road, Little Venice, W9 2PF
(7249 6876/www.puppetbarge.com). Warwick Avenue
tube.* **Open** *Box office* 10am-8pm daily. *Children's
shows* term-time Sat, Sun; school hols daily. Call for
times. **Tickets** £7.50; £7 under-16s, concessions.
Credit MC, V.

One of the capital's most enchanting assets since its creation in 1982, the Puppet Theatre Barge's combination of
high-quality puppet shows – courtesy of Movingstage
Productions – and the loveliness of its location remains
unique. Small and cosy (there are just 60 seats), the barge
is moored on the towpath in Little Venice between
November and June, with a variety of performances held
on Saturday and Sunday afternoons (3pm) and a more comprehensive programme of daytime and evening slots during school holidays. So far, 2005 has brought us *Monkey
Business* – monkey puppets tumbling to music – and *The
Birdman*, a touching tale of an old man befriending a bird.
Between July and October, the barge floats off on a summer tour of the Thames, stopping to perform at picturesque
riverside towns (Henley, Clifton, Marlow and Richmond)
along the way. During this period, shows take place at
2.30pm and 4.30pm, and there's a special Saturday evening
performance (7.30pm) aimed at adults.

Touring companies

Younger audiences need shows that suit their
developing senses, dealing with subjects that are
relevant to them in a language they understand.
That, at least, is what the following companies
aim to provide.

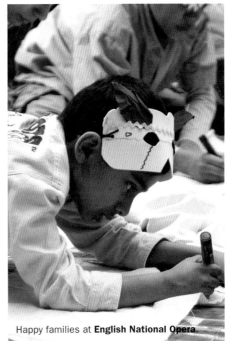

Happy families at **English National Opera.**

Kazzum

7223 0703/www.kazzum.org.
Since their inception in 1989 Peter Glanville's Kazzum have
presented over 40 productions and toured schools, theatres,
arts centres, libraries, parks and festivals. Their projects
include works aimed at under-sixes, plus contemporary
adaptations of classic world stories and interactive installations for under-11s. As well as educational programmes
and residencies, they run Pathways, a programme of work
relating to the experiences of refugee children.

Oily Cart

8672 6329/www.oilycart.org.uk.
Oily Cart's motivation is to fire the imaginations of two
theatrically excluded groups – very young children and
children with special needs – with bold, innovative productions. Touring since 1981 to great critical acclaim, the
company's work has developed into a truly interactive art
form, utilising large multi-sensory spaces or
'Wonderlands', where groups of children can not only
watch, but also take part in performances. Even more
commendable is the fun they inject into each show – *The
Conference of the Birds*, for disabled kids, appealed to all
five senses, while *Hippety Hop* broke new ground as the
first-ever hip hop musical for the under-fives. .

Pop-Up Theatre

7609 3339/www.pop-up.net.
Pop-Up have pioneered a range of theatrical media that are
respectful of younger children's intelligence and
responsive to their needs. The Dramatic Links workshops

Activities

Les Misérables

Don't Miz Out!

THE Miz Kids' Club

INCLUDES A BACKSTAGE TOUR AND CHANCE TO MEET A CAST MEMBER

Packages start from £30. The Club also includes a ticket to the performance,
snack pack lunch, singing and drama workshop and an exclusive certificate of attendance.
Saturday mornings for 8 -11 and 12 -15 year olds
(with extra midweek clubs during school holidays).

For full package details and bookings
CALL 0870 850 9171
or email education@delmack.co.uk
EARLY BOOKING ESSENTIAL

20th TRIUMPHANT YEAR
QUEEN'S THEATRE

(held at the Robert Blair School in north London) let writers work with kids, drawing inspiration from one another to produce relevant scripts. The Equal Voice sessions tour schools across the city engaging pupils in theatrical dialogues that explore emotional issues and build self-esteem. In 2005 the company will go on tour with an adaptation of novelist David Almond's *Heaven Eyes*, a moving story of three children who escape from a children's home and meet a mysterious girl. Their new Offstreet mobile stage will allow certain shows to take place on any flat 20sq ft (6sq m) space, allowing for almost limitless performance possibilities.

Quicksilver Theatre

7241 2942/www.quicksilvertheatre.org.
Engaging rather than self-consciously educational, Quicksilver productions encourage children to develop emotionally by letting go of their fears and having fun. Over 25 years, this theatre group have worked at building a rapport with young audiences, which was evident in their 2005 national tour *Teddy in the Rucksack* (ages three to five). Next up (in October 2005) is *Sink or Swim*, a modern musical take on Noah's Ark.

Theatre Centre

7377 0379/www.theatre-centre.co.uk.
Theatre Centre has not only secured a reputation for on-stage excellence and technical invention, but also champions more challenging writing. Recent productions have explored disability (*Walking on Water*) and a child's friendship with his shadow (*One Dark Night*).

Unicorn Theatre for Children

7700 0702/www.unicorntheatre.com.
Set to open in late 2005, the new Unicorn Theatre will nestle in the heart of London between London Bridge and Tower Bridge and will be the first purpose-built professional theatre for children in the UK. Unicorn undertook a three-year collaboration with a class from the primary school next door and incorporated their thoughts into the design. The plans are looking good, with separate main and studio auditoriums, an education centre and a rehearsal studio all part and parcel. The plan is to present eight productions every year, of the quality of March 2004's *Clockwork*, an opera based on the story by Philip Pullman. There will also be storytelling festivals and sessions, talks, demonstrations and book launches by children's authors. Theatre groups, writing workshops and poetry readings are just a few of the regular activities envisaged. Ring or check the website for developments.

Venues

Several of the places listed below are children's theatres; most, however, are adult venues that have a regular programme of family shows. Phone to check the suitability of any show before you book tickets. Most venues put on extra performances during school holidays.

The Albany

Douglas Way, Deptford, SE8 4AG (8692 4446/ www.thealbany.org.uk). Deptford rail/bus 21, 36, 47, 136, 171, 177, 188, 225. **Tickets** *Family Sunday* £5; £3 under-16s, concessions. **Credit** MC, V.

This busy little community arts centre has Family Sundays, when everyone can enjoy brunch and music. Adults can immerse themselves in their newspapers while children are entertained by a play written for them. *Buggy access. Café. Disabled access: lift, ramp, toilet. Nappy-changing facilities.*

artsdepot

5 Nether Street, North Finchley, N12 0GA (8369 5454/ www.artsdepot.co.uk). Finchley Central or Woodside Park tube. **Open** *Box office* 10am-5.30pm Mon-Sat; noon-5.30pm Sun (later during shows). **Tickets** free-£15. **Credit** MC, V.

October 2004 saw the opening of this stylish new arts venue, which replaces the old and beloved Bull Theatre. As well as housing the 400-seat Pentland Theatre, this new building is home to Community Focus (an arts activity centre for disabled people and the elderly) and the Performing and Public Arts arm of Barnet College. College students take classes and perform for the public in the theatre, with its two auditoriums. Most children's theatre takes place in the smaller 150-seat studio; shows run on Sundays at 3pm. Also, thanks to a comprehensive learning programme, young ones can tread the boards before they've learned to walk: classes cover all ages from one year-olds to adults, with courses ranging from the intriguing drama and storytelling option for two year-olds (parents invited) through to the Depot Youth Theatre, which ends with the participants' own show. *Buggy access. Café. Disabled access: lift, ramp, toilet. Nappy-changing facilities.*

BAC (Battersea Arts Centre)

Lavender Hill, Battersea, SW11 5TN (7223 2223/ Puppet Centre 7228 5335/www.bac.org.uk). Clapham Common tube, then 345 bus/Clapham Junction rail/77, 77A, 156 bus. **Open** *Box office* 10.30am-6pm Mon-Fri; 4-6pm Sat, Sun. *Puppet Centre* 2-6pm Mon, Wed, Sat. **Tickets** £3.50-£6.50. **Membership** suggested discretionary donation of £30 or £150. **Credit** AmEx, MC, V.

The cash-strapped but hugely respected BAC constantly challenges established notions of what is and isn't 'proper' theatre: the popular Scratch sessions, for example, allow writers to air work in progress and develop it with the participation of their audiences (this is where *Jerry Springer – The Opera* began). Drama queens (and kings) can take part in the (oversubscribed) Young People's Theatre, which takes kids from the age of 12 (an older version is run for over-17s) and works towards an end-of-term performance (Wed evenings; £30 per term). The Saturday children's theatre, for four to seven year-olds (2.30pm), airs the work of touring companies – phone or check the website for details. *Buggy access. Café. Disabled access: lift, toilet. Nappy changing facilities.*

Broadway Theatre

Catford Broadway, Catford, SE6 4RU (8690 3428/ www.lewishamyouththeatre.com). Catford or Catford Bridge rail/75, 181, 185, 202, 660 bus. **Open** *Box office* 10am-6pm Mon-Sat. **Tickets** £3.50-£22.50. **Credit** AmEx, MC, V.

This handsome, art deco building is scruffy Catford's pride and joy. Regular Saturday morning shows at the Broadway Theatre cater for children aged three and over, showcasing work from all the major touring companies. At other times, the youth programme is less well

Activities

Little Angel Theatre. *See p218.*

developed, although occasional performances by teen-idol impersonators appease screaming adolescents. There are also family-friendly shows dotted across the annual calendar (the Christmas pantomime is always a rowdy delight, and the tickets are pretty good value). Saturday morning children's theatre events cater for the under-eights. More educational are the occasional Shakespeare 4 Kids events, which combine loud, exciting and energetic performances, with music and amusing seminars in a commendable effort to make the Bard more appealing to young audiences.
Buggy access. Café. Disabled access: lift, toilet. Nappy-changing facilities.

Chicken Shed Theatre

Chase Side, Southgate, N14 4PE (8292 9222/www. chickenshed.org.uk). Cockfosters or Oakwood tube. **Open** *Box office* 10am-6pm Mon-Fri; 10am-5pm Sat. **Tickets** *Workshops* £5/hr; £3.50/hr under-16s. **Shows** £4-£18.50. **Credit** MC, V.
Chicken Shed was founded in 1974 by Jo Collins MBE and Mary Ward MBE, who believed that the performing arts belong to everyone who wishes to get involved. Today the theatre offers such an inclusive admissions policy that its 800 members seem to represent every possible age, race, background and ability. The result is productions that are among the liveliest in London, and with a range of groups for younger players – from Tales from the Shed (under-fives) to the Youth Theatre (12 to 19 year-olds) – there's nothing stopping little ones getting involved except, of course, the enormous waiting lists. Performances take place in one of four creative spaces, including a 250-seat main auditorium and an outdoor amphitheatre for the summer months. Best of all is the cross-pollination between various age groups: toddlers act up alongside adults, and everyone mucks in for the annual Christmas show.
Buggy access. Café. Disabled access: lift, toilets. Nappy-changing facilities. Restaurant. Shop.

Colour House Children's Theatre

Merton Abbey Mills, Watermill Way, Merton, SW19 2RD (box office 8640 5111/www.wheelhouse.org.uk). Colliers Wood tube. **Open** *Box office* 10am-5pm daily; 1hr before show. **Shows** 2pm, 4pm Sat, Sun. **Tickets** £7. **No credit cards.**
This little theatre is tucked into a riverside corner of south Wimbledon. Each year a number of fairytale classics get the Colour House treatment, rendering them anything but predictable. Kids can get more involved by joining the Colour House theatre school, which takes four to 16 year-olds and develops their singing, dancing and acting techniques, culminating in biannual shows performed to an audience. Classes are on Saturday mornings and Monday, Tuesday and Wednesday evenings (phone for prices).
Buggy access. Disabled access: toilet. Nappy-changing facilities. Shop.

The Edward Alleyn Theatre

Dulwich College, Dulwich Common, SE21 7LD (8299 9232/www.dulwich.org.uk/drama). West Dulwich rail/ Brixton tube/rail, then 3, P4, P13 bus. **Tickets** £5; £3.50 under-16s, concessions. **No credit cards.**
The theatre is named after the founder of Dulwich College, himself one of the great actors of Shakespeare's day. There are a number of shows from touring companies to engage literary brains, but there are also 12 annual performances aimed more directly at young audiences (such as the charming subversion of tradition in *Little Red Riding Wolf* in April 2005). The Edward Alleyn also runs week-long theatre schools over Easter, the summer holidays and October half-terms: two separate classes cater for seven to 11 year-olds and 12 to 16 year-olds. Those attending the senior group are expected to commit to the whole course. Booking is required well in advance: phone for prices.
Buggy access. Disabled access: toilets. Nappy-changing facilities.

Hackney Empire

291 Mare Street, Hackney, E8 1EJ (8510 4500/box office 8985 2424/www.hackneyempire.co.uk). Bethnal Green tube, then 106, 253, D6 bus. **Open** *Box office* 10am-8pm Mon-Sat; 1hr before show on Sun. On non-performance days, 10am-6pm. **Tours** 1st Sat of mth; phone for times. **Tickets** prices vary, phone for details. **Tours** £5; £4 concessions. **Credit** MC, V.

It's unbelievable that the Empire, one of London's most famous variety venues in its day, whose famous stage has creaked beneath the feet of everyone from Chaplin to Chas 'n' Dave, was once considered for demolition. That was back in the wicked 1980s, way before the old theatre was rescued by an independent theatre group, who finally completed a lengthy £16m facelift in 2004. The Hackney Empire's programme for young people includes a generous ticket subsidy scheme, as well as educational workshops and events. All performance and theatre courses are taught by professional theatre practitioners and facilitators, many of whom are artists in their own right. Dance and musical performance courses for seven to 11 year-olds cost from £27.50 per person. For 12 to 16 year-olds, an 'artist development' programme (Sept-Nov) shapes the talents of 40 of east London's youngsters (auditions required: check the website); there are also less-intensive Saturday workshops for seven to ten year-olds and 11 to 16 year-olds, providing everything from guidance on scriptwriting to role-play exercises.
Buggy access. Disabled access: toilet. Nappy-changing facilities.

Half Moon Young People's Theatre

43 White Horse Road, Stepney, E1 0ND (7709 8900/ www.halfmoon.org.uk). Limehouse DLR/rail. **Open** *Box office* 10am-6pm Mon-Fri; 9am-4pm Sat. **Tickets** £5; £3.50 under-18s, concessions. **Credit** MC, V.

In an area sadly lacking in artistic outlets, the Half Moon is a pillar of creativity, uniting young people regardless of race, gender or financial situation. Its fully accessible theatre is home to two studios, offering an annual calendar of performances for kids from six months old. Children seeking to get involved can join up with one of eight youth theatre groups, catering to five to 17 year-olds. The groups meet weekly during term-time (£1.50 per session) and work towards a final show. The aim is to improve self-expression and build confidence, although the more committed participants may end up filtering into the Half Moon's larger productions. Staff also work with schools both in Tower Hamlets and across London, organising workshops and occasionally setting up residencies.
Buggy access. Disabled access: toilets. Nappy-changing facilities.

Jackson's Lane

269A Archway Road, Highgate, N6 5AA (box office 8341 4421/administration 8340 5226/www.jacksons lane.org.uk). Highgate tube. **Open** *Box office* 10am-10pm daily. **Tickets** £4.75. **Credit** MC, V.

The comprehensive range of classes and courses on offer at this much-loved arts centre housed in an old church are a constant source of delight to local families. They run from

Musical youth

According to neurologists, 75 per cent of a child's brain growth has already been achieved by the age of three, which (while it might make you wonder why we bother sending them to school) is a nonetheless powerful argument in favour of early exposure to music making.

Music therapist Jenny Tabori, founder of **Musical Express**, runs classes where pre-schoolers (six months and over) come along for forty minutes to an hour to sing, socialise and play musical games. 'All children can sing before they can talk,' she says. 'There are studies to show that music-making early in life helps to build the neural pathways that develop language and memory. And it's great fun for both of you.'

For those who are a little more serious, the introductory class at the world-famous **Guildhall** provides training in Dalcroze (moving to music) and Eurhythmics, and a chance to try out miniature stringed instruments before moving up a class. Even if catgut isn't for them, the classes train their ears and start them on the right track.

The Japanese violin teacher Dr Suzuki believed that anyone could learn to play. **Suzuki** centres all over London (*see p234*) have more than 400 students, many of whom started scraping as early as three on violins the size of matchboxes. Parents are actively involved in the lessons, and some even start learning themselves so they can help their infant prodigies hold instrument and bow properly. One parent, himself a cracking

violinist who learned the traditional way, likes the way his seven-year-old daughter learns to play everything by copying her teacher. He feels that there's so much to concentrate on with maintaining correct posture (which avoids that awful tortured-cat-sound beginners make) that reading music gets in the way of listening. 'Sophie moves very naturally, and makes her violin sing, because she can think about the sound she's making, and not worry about squinting at what's in front of her,' he says.

For those looking for something to blow rather than bow, the **Music House for Children** in Uxbridge has a register of more than 200 teachers, and will try hard to match the right one to each pupil. The **Centre for Young Musicians** offers lessons to those who are already learning and have manifested talent. They also have satellite centres for beginners.

Woodwind and brass can be happily started at secondary-school age, but if an eight year-old is passionate about the trumpet, let them have a try. Anyone who's ever played an instrument with the even slightest degree of success will tell you how wonderful the experience is. Although, as your teenager demands another lift for the double bass or argues plausibly for a better trombone, you might end up wishing that you'd taken them to baby gym instead.

For more information on all the music classes mentioned above *see p234*.

Activities

The **Royal National Theatre** takes it outside for the summer. *See p225.*

an after-school club for five to 11 year-olds (3.30-6pm Mon-Fri; £7 per session) to off-the-cuff sessions with visiting groups like Kaos! Organisation, with everything from ballet to street dance and tap to trapeze in between. Prices vary: an 11-week course might cost £77, a drop-in afternoon class with dance impresario Debbie Campbell just a fiver. All events are oversubscribed, so phone in advance. The diary of children's shows at Jackson's Lane offers a family treat every weekend during term-time (and on occasional weekdays during school holidays), with performances by touring companies like Quicksilver Theatre, Pekko's Puppets and Theatre of Widdershins.
Buggy access. Café. Disabled access: toilet. Nappy-changing facilities.

Lauderdale House

Highgate Hill, Waterlow Park, Highgate, N6 5HG (8348 8716/www.lauderdale.org.uk). Archway tube, then 143, 210, 271, W5 bus. **Open** *Box office* 30mins before performance; advance bookings not accepted. **Tickets** £4.50; £3 concessions. **No credit cards.**
Set in a rustic 16th-century manor house that backs on to tranquil. picturesque Waterlow Park (*see p95*), this arts centre hosts a huge range of highly popular activities and classes. Weekly dance and drama courses cater for ages three and upwards, as do most of the drawing, painting and music workshops (phone or check the website for details). There's an excellent variety of puppetry, music and magic brought to the stage by professional touring companies (10am, 11.30am Sat); school holidays give rise to a number of family days, including the annual Hallowe'en Walk and a Jazz in the Park festival.
Buggy access. Café. Disabled access: toilet.

Lyric Hammersmith Theatre

Lyric Square, King Street, Hammersmith, W6 0QL (0870 050 0511/www.lyric.co.uk). Hammersmith tube. **Open** *Box office* 10am-6pm Mon-Sat (until 8pm during showtimes).* **Tickets** from £8 adults; £6 concessions, students, under-16s; £6 16-25s (restrictions apply). **Credit** MC, V.

From the outside, it looks modern, but inside you'll find an antique auditorium – a Victorian proscenium-arch playhouse, no less. But despite this historical aesthetic, the Lyric is one of London's most future-focused theatres when it comes to engaging young imaginations. Most children's events take place in a purpose-built, 120-seat studio (although many spill into the foyer or the stalls) and a large proportion are organised in conjunction with schools. They range from pre-performance workshops to classes that offer creative guidance to socially excluded five to 13 year-olds and 14 to 25 year-olds. An open series of weekend workshops are aimed at eight to 11 year-olds (£6), and run concurrently with the Saturday kids' shows. July and August see two week-long performing arts workshops.
Buggy access. Café. Disabled access: lift, toilet. Nappy-changing facilities.

Nettlefold Theatre

West Norwood Library, 1 Norwood High Street, West Norwood, SE27 9JX (7926 8070/www.lambeth.gov.uk). West Norwood rail/2, 68, 196, 468 bus. **Open** *Box office* 9am-4pm Mon-Fri. **Tickets** £3.50. **Credit** (advance only) MC, V.
This purpose-built, 200-seat theatre (built into West Norwood Library) runs one show per month (usually on a Saturday) that is child-oriented: phone for a list of upcoming performances. More regularly, the energetic Bigfoot Theatre Company (0870 011 4307, www.bigfoot-theatre.co.uk) runs drama, dance and movement, and singing classes here for eight year-olds and over; they take place between 10am and noon every Saturday during term-time, with plenty of half-term and school-holiday activities organised on an ad hoc basis.
Buggy access. Disabled access: lift, toilet. Nappy-changing facilities.

New Wimbledon Theatre

The Broadway, Wimbledon, SW19 1QG (0870 060 6646/www.theambassadors.com/newwimbledon). Wimbledon tube/rail. **Open** *Box office* 10am-8pm Mon-Sat; also Sun during shows. **Credit** AmEx, MC, V.

In April 2005 *The Witches*, Roald Dahl's tale of dastardly dames, delighted a screaming audience here. In the latter part of the year productions that will be suitable for families include *The King and I* (30 Aug-10 Sept 2005) and a short slick of *Grease* (12-17 Sept 2005). More a great theatre with children's entertainment than a great children's theatre, then, although staff promise a more comprehensive youth programme will be up and running soon. *Disabled access: lift, toilet. Shop.*

Open Air Theatre

Inner Circle, Regent's Park, Marylebone, NW1 4NU (box office 0870 060 1811/www.openairtheatre.org). Baker Street tube. **Tickets** £8-£30; £15 under-16s. **Credit** AmEx, MC, V. **Map** p314 G3.
In 2005 the Shakespeare offerings, *Twelfth Night* and *Cymbeline*, may have been a bit heavy for most children, but the lovely open-air setting continues to make this a family-friendly theatre. Kids will enjoy Herbert Appleman's new version of Gilbert & Sullivan's *HMS Pinafore*. Younger children, however, might get more from the animal antics in 2005's repeat run of *The Wind in the Willows* (11am or 2.30pm, 5-27 Aug). Tickets need to be booked well in advance. If the weather's foul enough to stop play, as it were, tickets will be exchanged for a later performance – subject to availability – but as a general rule, umbrellas and blankets are always advisable. *Café. Disabled access: toilet.*

Polka Theatre

240 The Broadway, Wimbledon, SW19 1SB (8543 4888/www.polkatheatre.com). South Wimbledon tube/Wimbledon tube/rail, then 57, 93, 219, 493 bus. **Open** *Phone bookings* 9.30am-4.30pm Mon; 9am-6pm Tue-Fri; 10am-5pm Sat. *Personal callers* 9.30am-4.30pm Tue-Fri; 10am-5pm Sat. **Tickets** £5-£10. **Credit** AmEx, MC, V. Polka, a dedicated young persons' theatre, has one of the most highly praised programmes of children's events in London. Daily shows are staged by touring companies in the main auditorium (10.30am, 2pm), with weekly performances – rarely featuring more than two actors, and often puppet-based – taking place in the Adventure Theatre for those younger than four. The theatre diligently seeks out new writers and performers, whose work is then added to the Polka's wide programme of productions, drama workshops and storytelling for families and schools across London. It's worth booking for half-term, Easter and summer workshops, as well as getting involved in the Polka Youth Theatre, where directors, choreographers, actors and musicians help young people to put on their own shows. After-school drama workshops for three to 11 year-olds cost from £55 per term; half-term and holiday workshops tied to current productions vary in price. Drama parties can be booked for up to 20 children to take part in role-playing, dressing up, magic and games. There's a complimentary ice-cream for every child taking part in the free monthly World of Stories drop-in event.
Buggy access. Café. Disabled access: lift, toilet. Nappy-changing facilities.

Royal National Theatre

South Bank, SE1 9PX (box office 7452 3000/information 7452 3400/www.nationaltheatre.org.uk). Waterloo tube/rail. **Open** *Box office* 10am-8pm Mon-Sat. **Credit** AmEx, DC, MC, V. **Map** p317 M8.
For most of the year, the NT's calendar is more traditionally adult-oriented (although occasional productions are aimed at children) and it's only in the school holidays that things really open up to all ages. Then the theatre puts on numerous free concerts – anything from jazz to balalaika – and activities in cordoned-off areas of the foyer or (weather permitting) out by the river. The annual free outdoor Watch This Space festival begins again on 24 June 2005, continuing through to 3 September. With performances six days a week from Monday to Saturday, at lunchtimes, early evenings and late on Saturdays, Watch This Space offers over 100 world-class shows across its ten-week programme. Kicking off with a two-day Spanish fiesta, the 2005 festival promises to be an artistic and cultural extravaganza consisting of bands from across the globe, the best of British street theatre, circus, cinema, art and dance. *See also p22.*
Cafés. Disabled access: lift, toilet. Nappy-changing facilities. Restaurant. Shop.

Shakespeare's Globe

21 New Globe Walk, Bankside, SE1 9DT (7401 9919/ tours 7902 1500/www.shakespeares-globe.org). Mansion House tube/London Bridge tube/rail. **Open** *Box office* (theatre bookings, May-Sept 2005) 10am-6pm daily. **Tours** *Oct-Apr* 10am-5pm daily. **Tickets** £5-£29. *Tours* £9; £7.50 concessions; £6.50 5-15s; free under-5s; £25 family (2+3). **Credit** AmEx, MC, V. **Map** p318 O7.
Young audiences at the Globe can take advantage of the new Childsplay scheme, which engages eight to 11 year-olds in theatrical workshops while their parents enjoy the first half of the play, before reuniting the family for the second half (selected Saturdays; £10 per child). A huge range of talks, tours and activities – many of them conducted by staff in full period costume – are conducted with schools during term-time, while holiday workshops open the floor to families (phone for more information).
Café. Disabled access: lift, toilet. Nappy-changing facilities. Restaurant. Shop.

The Warehouse Theatre

62 Dingwall Road, Croydon, Surrey CR0 2NF (8680 4060/www.warehousetheatre.co.uk). East Croydon rail. **Open** *Box office* 10am-5pm Mon-Fri; 10am-1pm Sat; extended opening hours during shows. **Tickets** £5; £4 2-16s. **Credit** AmEx, MC, V.
Due to its location in a converted Victorian warehouse set back from the main thoroughfare, those not looking out for this place might easily walk straight past it – and it's not somewhere that families want to miss. Theatre4Kidz are aired every Saturday morning at 11am (£5 adults, £4 children), while a variety of touring shows are hosted for those as young as two. Perhaps most commendable, however, is the ongoing success of the Croydon Young People's Theatre (CRYPT), which for 20 years now has been offering a creative forum for 13 to 16 year-olds, many of whom have gone on to tread the Warehouse boards under harsher lights. CRYPT meets between 2pm and 5pm every Saturday during term-time, and puts on an annual show in July. The fee per term is just £10; application forms are available on the website.
Disabled access: lift, toilet.

Young Vic

66 The Cut, Waterloo, SE1 8LZ (box office 7928 6363/ www.youngvic.org). Southwark tube/Waterloo tube/rail. **Open** *Box office* 10am-6pm Mon-Fri. **Tickets** prices vary; phone for details. **Credit** MC, V. **Map** p318 N8.

All singing, all dancing

Given the choice, many children would rather see a musical than any other form of stage entertainment, so it's as well that musicals dominate West End theatres, accounting for 63 per cent of ticket sales in 2003.

Shows with music evolved from working-class performances in the rowdy taverns and coffee houses of the 18th century. The first purpose-built theatre for what became known as 'music hall' appeared in 1852. By 1875 there were 350 music halls throughout London.

A curious law encouraged the proliferation of musical theatre at the expense of drama: the patent act of 1737 decreed that only patent theatres, of which there were just two, were allowed to put on plays. Theatre managers wanting to present dramas could only avoid prosecution by including music in their shows. These restrictions led to almost all theatres incorporating music in the bill.

In 1843 the law was abandoned and anyone could put on plays, as long as they didn't serve food and alcohol at performances. By this time music halls had gained a reputation for vulgarity, hardly family attractions. Some of the larger producers wanted to go more upmarket, so they began to abandon the risqué elements of shows to encourage respectable families in.

Enthusiasm for musical theatre in the West End was revived by the American production *Showboat* in 1927. For the first time all the singing and dancing in a show were pertinent to the story. The next big moment in musical history was the 1945 opening of *Oklahoma!* Sober post-war London audiences were dazzled by its energy and it

opened the floodgates for a rush of box-office hits from the US: *King and I* and *South Pacific*. The UK produced some of its own classics like *Oliver!* but our golden years only really arrived in the 1970s with the partnership of Tim Rice and Andrew Lloyd Webber. Mega-hits such as *Joseph's Technicolour Dreamcoat* and *Jesus Christ Superstar* were followed by *Cats, Starlight Express* and *Phantom* – the latter outsold movies *Star Wars* and *Titanic*.

The current trend for West End musicals continues to be for family shows, bar the odd adult offering like *Jerry Springer – The Opera*. *Mary Poppins* opened in 2005, along with the much-anticipated *Billy Elliot* and a revival of *Guys & Dolls* with Ewan McGregor playing the lead.

The extremely popular, annual Kids Week in August (*see* www.officiallondontheatre.co.uk; organised by the Society of London Theatres (SOLT, *see p227*) will feed any fledgling ambitions for the stage. Now stretched to two weeks, it gives the chance kids to experience the pizzazz of the theatre with backstage tours and workshops. SOLT also operates a year-round Saturday theatre club for eight to 12 year-olds. The Saturday sessions focus on the major family shows, such as *Chitty Chitty Bang Bang* (pictured). Sign up to the fortnightly family bulletin on SOLT's website to get up-to-date information on events.

Cameron Mackintosh's education department holds the *Les Miz* club (details on the SOLT website), which costs £15 and gives kids a backstage tour and a chance to shine in the spotlight in a scene recreated from the show. Their *Phantom* club has a similar programme, but it's for school groups only.

The Young Vic was never meant to be permanent: built in 1970 to last five years, the fact that it has held out until now is a sign of just how valuable a theatrical asset it is. Finally, this groundbreaking venue is undergoing a period of closure for essential repair work. A fully rejuvenated auditorium will reopen in 2006, complete with a new foyer, new dressing rooms and a 130-seat studio theatre. Parents can rest assured that the Young Vic's reputation for infamously left-field Christmas shows won't be hindered by its temporary homelessness – 2004's *Sleeping Beauty* took place at the Barbican.
Buggy access. Café. Disabled access: lift, toilet.

West End shows

With the exception of *Chicago* and *Billy Elliot*, the shows below are suitable for children of all ages. Less developed attention spans may find some more suitable than others (many clock in at over two hours), and very young children are advised to avoid the West End and go instead to one of the more intimate kid-specific venues in other parts of town (*see p221*), where plays are shorter, lights brighter and the bangs less likely to scare.

For an alternative introduction to Theatreland, contact the **Society of London Theatres** (7557 6700, www.officiallondontheatre.co.uk): every August the SOLT organises Kids Week, when juniors get in free (with accompanying adults) to West End shows. Best of all are the pre-performance workshops – recent highlights have ranged from making some noise with boots, bins, brooms and the cast of *Stomp* to working with the cast of *The Lion King*. For more on Kids Week and the best family-friendly theatre information in London, subscribe to the free family bulletin on the SOLT website. SOLT's Kids Club also runs a Saturday morning theatre club at the Theatre Museum in Covent Garden (*see p76*), but you have to book, as places are limited.

Billy Elliot
Victoria Palace Theatre, Victoria Street, Victoria, SW1E 5EA (0870 895 5577/www.billyelliotthe musical.com). Victoria tube/rail. **Times** 7.30pm Mon-Sat. *Matinée* 2.30pm Thur, Sat. **Tickets** £17.50-£50. **Credit** AmEx, MC, V.
The musical version of the BAFTA-winning film, about the motherless miner's son who discovers a talent for ballet by accident, has 17 songs by Elton John. It opened to some enthusiastic reviews, particularly about the quality of the childrens' performances, on 12 May 2005, and its website has a warning reminding us that it contains strong language and scenes of confrontation, which gave the film its 15 rating. Not for the under-8s.

Blood Brothers
Phoenix Theatre, Charing Cross Road, St Giles's, WC2H 0JP (7369 1733/www.theambassadors.com). Tottenham Court Road tube. **Times** 7.45pm Mon-Sat. *Matinée* 3pm Thur; 4pm Sat. **Tickets** £17.50-£42.50. **Credit** AmEx, MC, V. **Map** p315 K6.

A powerful folk-opera, Blood Brothers has ultimately tragic lead characters – and some great tunes. It tells the story of separated twins reunited in later life and deals with issues of family ties and class divisions. The ending may upset very young children.

Chicago
Adelphi Theatre, Strand, Covent Garden, WC2E 7NA (Ticketmaster 0870 403 0303). Charing Cross tube/rail. **Times** 8pm Mon-Thur, Sat; 8.30pm Fri. *Matinée* 5pm Fri; 3pm Sat. **Tickets** £15-£45. **Credit** AmEx, MC, V. **Map** p317 L7.
Since Richard Gere, Renée Zellweger and Catherine Zeta-Jones appeared in its big-screen incarnation, there's been a huge resurgence in the popularity of this effortlessly slick, sexy and criminally minded musical. It's certainly not suitable for under-12s.

Chitty Chitty Bang Bang
Palladium, Argyll Street, Soho, W1A 3AB (0870 890 1108/www.chittythemusical.co.uk). Oxford Circus tube. **Times** 7pm Tue; 7.30pm Mon, Wed-Sat. *Matinée* 2.30pm Wed, Sat, Sun. **Tickets** £19.50-£45. **Credit** AmEx, MC, V. **Map** p314 J6.
A flying car and a nice, clean fight between good and evil: there's really very little about this lavish production of Ian Fleming's classic novel that doesn't go down well with children. The whole thing is ingeniously designed – it's said to be the most expensive West End musical ever – but it's also well acted, by a string of attractive celebs, and utterly engaging.

Fame: The Musical
Aldwych Theatre, Aldwych, WC2B 4DF (0870 400 0805/www.famethemusical.co.uk). Charing Cross tube/ rail. **Times** 7.30pm Mon-Thur, Sat; 8.30pm Fri. *Matinée* 5.30pm Fri; 3pm Sat. **Tickets** £15.50-£41. **Credit** AmEx, MC, V. **Map** p317 M6.
You should catch this unfeasibly energetic show before it dances itself into an early grave. The story – revolving around a bunch of leotard-clad, tantrum-throwing wannabes at New York's High School of the Performing Arts – will appeal to drama queens of all ages.

The Lion King
Lyceum Theatre, Wellington Street, Covent Garden, WC2E 7RQ (0870 243 9000/www.ticketmaster.co.uk). Covent Garden tube. **Times** 7.30pm Tue-Sat. *Matinée* 2pm Wed, Sat; 3pm Sun. **Tickets** £11.70-£44.20. **Credit** AmEx, MC, V. **Map** p317 L7.
Few children will be unfamiliar with the film version of this Disney classic, so following the storyline will be no problem. This means they can concentrate on the beauty of the production, the elaborate staging of which lives up to the unprecedented hype that surrounded its opening more than four years ago. Expect awesome set designs, a combination of puppetry and live actors, and a cocktail of West End choruses and African rhythms. It's a delight.

Mamma Mia!
Prince of Wales Theatre, Coventry Street, Soho, W1V 8AS (0870 154 4040/www.ticketmaster.co.uk). Piccadilly Circus tube. **Times** 7.30pm Mon-Thur, Sat; 8.30pm Fri. *Matinée* 5pm Fri; 3pm Sat. **Tickets** £25-£49. **Credit** AmEx, MC, V. **Map** p317 K7.

Activities

It may be thin on story, but what Mamma Mia! lacks in dramatic development it more than makes up for with feel-good musical numbers – the children will be singing ABBA's greatest hits for days afterwards.

Mary Poppins

Prince Edward Theatre, Old Compton Street, Soho, W1D 4TP (7447 5400/www.marypoppins themusical.co.uk). Leicester Square tube. **Times** 7.30pm Mon-Sat. *Matinée* 2.30pm Thur, Sat. **Tickets** £25-£49. **Credit** AmEx, MC, V. **Map** p315 K6.

All together now: supercalifragilisticexpialidocious. Cameron Mackintosh's take on PL Travers' magic nanny is closer to the darker original than the spoon-filled-with-sugar film, but still has the old singalong favourites, as well as some spectacular dance numbers. Children under three aren't allowed in, and the website advises against bringing anybody under seven.

Les Misérables

Queen's Theatre, Shaftesbury Avenue, Soho, W1D 8AS (0870 534 4444/www.lesmis.com). Leicester Square tube. **Times** 7.30pm Mon-Sat. *Matinée* 2.30pm Wed, Sat. **Tickets** £15-£45. **Credit** AmEx, DC, MC, V. **Map** p315 K6.

An enduring adaptation of Victor Hugo's tale of revolution in 19th-century France: 20 years since its London première, Les Misérables is still impressive. For more on the the Les Miz Kids' Club, which runs here twice a month, *see p226* **All singing, all dancing.**

Stomp

Vaudeville Theatre, Strand, Covent Garden, WC2R 0NH (0870 890 0511/www.stomp.co.uk). Charing Cross tube/rail. **Times** 8pm Tue-Sat. *Matinee* 3pm Thur, Sat, Sun. **Tickets** £16-£38.50. **Credit** AmEx, MC, V. **Map** p317 L7.

Kids that like smashing pans together will be in heaven at this hyperactive show. The cast finds music in the most obscure objects – including the kitchen sink – and the whole, noisy extravaganza feels as vital as it did when it opened ten years ago. Just remember to hide the saucepans and bin lids before you leave home.

Performance workshops

Centrestage

Office: 117 Canfield Gardens, West Hampstead, NW6 3DY (7328 0788/www.centrestageschool.co.uk). **Classes** 10am-1pm, 2-5pm Sat. **Fees** £260/12wk term. **Credit** AmEx, MC, V.

The Holland Park and Hampstead branches offer a range of theatrical activities for three to 17 year-olds. Workshops take place on Saturdays in term-time, developing a range of skills that can be capitalised on during a number of holiday courses. These last for a week, and all culminate in a show of some sort; younger kids are taught basic performance skills (including simple magic), while more developed thesps tackle plays and musicals.

Dance Attic

368 North End Road, Fulham, SW6 1LY (7610 2055/www.danceattic.com). Fulham Broadway tube. **Fees** from £50/11wk term; phone for individual class prices. **Credit** MC, V.

The original Fulham Fame Academy: the range of performance classes at Dance Attic is staggering, setting it apart from less serious studios. Children under ten are encouraged to take part in Saturday morning workshops on tap (for over-fives) and ballet (for over-threes), the second of which leads towards the prestigious RADA exams. Both cost £5 per hour-long session between 9am and 3pm.

Dramarama

Holiday courses: South Hampstead High School, Maresfield Gardens, NW3 5SS. Term-time classes: South Hampstead Junior School, Netherhall Gardens, NW3 5RN. Both: 8446 0891. **Fees** prices available on request from Jessica Grant.

OFSTED-affiliated Dramarama is the work of Jessica Grant, who runs a number of theatrical workshops for kids aged three and over on Saturdays during term-time. More intensive tuition leads eleven to 14 year-olds confidently into their LAMDA speech and drama exams. Jessica's half-term and holiday workshops last five days and see participants devising and performing a play of their own. For Jessica's drama-themed parties, which include games, role-playing and the chance to act to an audience, *see p236*.

Helen O'Grady's Children's Drama Academy

Headquarters: Northside Vale, Guernsey, GY3 5TX (01481 200250/www.helenogrady.co.uk). **Classes** times vary; phone for details. **Fees** £63/12wk term. **No credit cards.**

Helen O'Grady's theatrical empire runs to over 37 academies across Britain and many more in other countries. The eight in London work out of one of a number of schools across the capital. Children aged five to 17 attend a one-hour workshop each week, with courses spread across three terms. Skills are developed depending on age: the Lower Primary group (five to eight) is concerned with nurturing self-esteem through clear speech and fluent delivery; the Youth Theatre (13 to 17 year-olds) studies more advanced techniques including improvisation and monologues. A production is devised and performed at the end of every third term.

Hoxton Hall

130 Hoxton Street, Hoxton, N1 6SH (7684 0060/ www.hoxtonhall.co.uk). Old Street tube/rail. **Classes** times vary; phone for details. **Fees** £15/term. **Credit** MC, V.

This refurbished music venue offers a Junior Music Class, in which eight to 11 year-olds can experiment and compose at their own pace, with the choice of working individually or with others. They can also perform in front of a live audience or record their work on CD. The parallel Junior Arts Class, meanwhile, encourages artistic expression using a range of resources and materials. Both the Junior Drama and Youth Drama groups – for eight to 11 year-olds and 11 to 18 year-olds, respectively – give kids a free hand in writing and producing a piece for performance in the main hall. All classes run in term-time.

Laban

Creekside, Deptford, SE8 3DZ (8691 8600/ www.laban.org). Deptford rail. **Classes** times vary; call for details. **Fees** from £38/12wk term. **No credit cards.**

Activities

OK, luvvies, let's see you roar for the **London Bubble Theatre Company**.

Thoroughly modern Laban offers a variety of children's performance classes as well as a programme of contemporary dance and music. The award-winning building houses 13 separate studios, where dance courses cater for a number of groups – from four to 14 year-olds, as well toddlers and carers. Laban works with Trinity College of Music and local schools. Touring performances in the theatre are combined with lectures and educational workshops, check the website for a list.

Lewisham Youth Theatre

Broadway Theatre, Catford Broadway, Catford, SE6 4RU (8690 3428/www.lewishamyouththeatre.com). Catford or Catford Bridge rail. **Classes** 90 mins Wed, Sat (8-11s, 11-13s); call for specific times. *Youth Theatre* call for details (8-13s, 14-21s). *Roar! Children's Theatre* 11.30am Sat (3-8s & families) . **Tickets** *All* £3.50. *Workshops* free, £5 refundable deposit. **No credit cards.**
The free, no auditions concept behind the Lewisham Youth Theatre can be misleading. The youth programmes may be open to all but the standard is high and LYT has a reputation for innovative, quality work. All classes work towards full productions in the studio theatre as well as at other venues throughout Lewisham borough. Projects are varied from working through improvisation with playwrights to collaborative work with other youth arts groups. Junior Youth Theatre is divided into two groups, catering for eight to 11 year-olds and 11 to 13 year-olds, but there is cross-pollination with the Senior Youth Theatre for young people aged between 14 and 21. Most recruitment takes place through schools but some places are allocated on a first-come-first- served basis. Workshops take place after school as well as at weekends.

London Bubble Theatre Company

5 Elephant Lane, Rotherhithe, SE16 4JD (7237 4434/ www.londonbubble.org.uk). Bermondsey or Rotherhithe tube. **Open** *Box office* 10am-6pm Mon-Fri. **Classes** (term-time) 4.30pm, 6.30pm Mon, Tue. **Fees** £35/11wk term. **Credit** MC, V.
Bubble works with groups traditionally marginalised by mainstream theatre in a way that is challenging and refreshing. Its Open Performance Theatre (OPT) projects mix actors of all ages, backgrounds and dramatic experience in a show that tours the city's less conventional stages: 2005's *Crock of Gold* was shown in parks and woods around the capital. The next OPT project takes place in 2006. The Youth Theatre is open to ages eight to 18 and meets every Monday at 4.30pm, costing from £16.50 per term. A variety of open workshops offer guidance in everything from choral singing to MCing (from £2 per person).

Millfield Theatre School

Silver Street, Edmonton, N18 1PJ (box office 8807 6680/www.millfieldtheatre.co.uk). Silver Street rail, then 34, 102, 144 bus/217, 231, W6 bus. **Classes/fees** £85/10wk term (4-5s), 10.30am-noon Sun; £85/10wk term (6-7s), 12.30-2pm Sun; £165/10wk term (8-16s), 11am-2pm Sun; £120/10wk term (14-19s), 6.30-9pm Fri. **Credit** MC, V.
Tucked into its calendar of musicals, comedies and mainstream dramatic events, Edmonton's 362-seat Millfield Theatre also shows a lively selection of children's theatre. The in-house Silver Street Youth Theatre, develops the dramatic instinct of local luvvies. The group runs courses throughout term-time, meeting on Fridays or Sundays, with performances throughout the year.

National Youth Music Theatre

www.nymt.org.uk.
Still in limbo after being denied its Arts Council grant, this historic and much-loved producer of challenging music theatre for young people of all backgrounds is in danger of going under through 'deplorable' (Jude Law) lack of funding after 28 years in existence. Keep an eye on the website for updated information.

New Peckham Varieties

New Peckham Varieties at Magic Eye Theatre, Havil Street, Camberwell, SE5 7SD (venue 7703 5838/ office 7708 5401). Elephant & Castle tube/rail, then 12, 171, 45A bus. **Classes** times vary; phone for details. **Fees** £2.50-£3. **Credit** MC, V.
With an activity line-up to match the diversity of central Peckham, it's little wonder that spaces on NPV workshops and courses are so coveted. Lively drama groups for four to 18 year-olds run on Mondays from 4pm to 7pm, there's tap-dancing from 7pm to 8.30pm on Tuesdays, musical theatre for beginners on Saturday mornings, and jazz lessons on Wednesday afternoons. The highlight of the weekend is the Boys' Ballet on Saturday afternoon, which has been successful in luring seven to 14 year-old males into trying their hands at anything from conventional dance to breakdancing. The drama team's three annual performances on the Magic Eye's main stage are open to members of any age, and these are supplemented by one-off concerts. Check *Time Out* magazine's Children listings for details of public shows for families; they're always a great showcase for local young acting talent and lots of fun to watch.

Nifty Feet!

7266 5035/www.niftyfeet.com.
Lynn Page is bestknown for training young actor Jamie Bell for blockbuster film *Billy Elliot*, and she has, ever since, been swamped by likely lads hoping to effect a similarly spectacular transformation. Thus Nifty Feet! was born, bringing ballet to the capital's two to 16 year-olds by way of vibrant, mixed classes that defy the medium's somewhat starchy stereotype. The key to her success is cunning: Page hooks the kids in with urban dance tuition using popular tunes that only slowly (and with her subjects hardly noticing it) turns into ballet lessons without the slippers. These classes are mainly run on Saturdays in Richmond and Wimbledon; an information pack is available, so call or log on to the website to find out the precise details.

Perform

66 Churchway, Somers Town, NW1 1LT (7209 3805/ www.perform.org.uk). **Classes** times vary; phone for details. **Fees** £120/10wk term (weekday); £175/10wk term (weekends). **Credit** MC, V.
Central to Lucy Quick's company is a mission to develop self-esteem and cultivate sociable attributes in even the most reclusive children, working on how they feel about themselves rather than the effect they may be having on adoring audiences. Quick's workshops – which run for 90mins at weekends and an hour during the week – are aimed at four to seven year-old children only, the age group she believes is most receptive to those four all-important Cs: confidence, communication, concentration and coordination. Sessions include movement games, singing

The gift of tongues

Adult Brits are notoriously bad at speaking other languages. It's partly laziness, and partly the arrogant belief that anyone worth talking to abroad will speak English anyway. Even those who can get by tend to keep an English accent you could cut with a knife.

But up to the age of nine children can pick up an authentic foreign accent perfectly. Newborn babies can make all sorts of noises, including that German ü that most adults need a prod in the stomach to get right. 'Children don't get embarrassed,' says Irene Keith of **French & Spanish à la Carte** (*see p233*). 'They're natural mimics. They just pick it up.' Infants from six months get to capitalise on their grasp of foreign vowel sounds at this playgroup, where they get an hour of structured games, songs and puzzles and another hour of free play in the company of native speakers who chat to them in French or Spanish. 'They just get used to the sound of another language,' says Irene. 'It feels natural to them.' Older children go to a slightly more structured after-school class, where a theme such as the weather runs through games and activities, letting the teacher repeat basic words and structures without them becoming dull. The only danger is a slightly recondite vocabulary. But just think, thirty years down the line your child may clinch a deal with a foreigner by discussing the making of Easter baskets in French.

At **Club Petit Pierrot** (*see p233*), the emphasis is also very much on having fun, and the sessions are all in French. 'The older ones learn in a more academic way by repeating what I said, but the younger ones love singing, and though they don't understand all the words, they start to put sentences together after a while,' says teacher Stella Bataille. 'There's a fun warm-up at the beginning of every session for the under-fives, with puppets and role play, during which the little linguists get to reuse the words they learned the previous week. Club Petit Pierrot also runs holiday courses, perfect for pre-trip immersion, where the goodies on offer include handicrafts, language games and fun exercises. 'It's not school and you have to make it fun so they want to come back,' Stella says.

Laura Mercier has been taking her seven year-old daughter, Ellie, to a French club on Saturday mornings for two years, and is delighted with her own little linguist's progress. 'Ellie loves it. She rushes in, says "Bonjour" to everyone, and forgets about me for the next two hours. She's picked up the genders naturally by hearing them, and seeing them next to the picture on her colouring sheets, and she has this lovely curly accent. When we went to France last summer she went into all the shops, said hello, and introduced herself completely unselfconsciously. Everyone thought she was French.'

and improvisation, and each term focuses on a new theme (outer space, say). A child's first class is free, so you can test for keenness before making a financial commitment. There are also week-long 'experience' workshops during the school holidays, which help children devise, rehearse and finally showcase a mini performance in an *Alice in Wonderland* or *The Wind in the Willows* of their own. Perform runs at dozens of venues: check the website for your nearest.

Pineapple Performing Arts School

7 Langley Street, Covent Garden, WC2H 9JA (8351 8839/www.pineapplearts.com). Covent Garden tube. **Classes** 11am-2pm (8-11s), 2-3pm (12-16s), 3-4pm (over-16s) Sat; 11am-noon (3-4s), noon-2pm (5-12s), 2-5pm (13-18s) Sun. **Fees** £250/12wk term over 4s £75/12wk term 3-4s. *Trial class* £25. *Registration fee* £30. **Credit** MC, V. **Map** p315 L6.
One of the nation's premier schools for the performing arts, Pineapple, with its desirable location in theatreland, offers some of the most oversubscribed courses in the country. These are for students aged five to 18, and fall into three categories – dance, drama and singing – each broken down into workshops running over three terms. It's not cheap but the advantage of having experienced staff on hand – not to mention big-name shows – means that students receive more coverage than they would elsewhere, be it performing as part of the Neal Street and Regent Street festivals or dancing on the telly. Three to four year-olds can take part in the Pineapple Chunks classes (11am-noon Sun).

The Place

16 Flaxman Terrace, Bloomsbury, WC1H 9AB (box office 7387 0031/classes 7388 8430/www. theplace.org.uk). Euston tube/rail. **Classes** times vary, phone for details. **Fees** from £80-£90/11wk term; £5 discount for 2nd or subsequent class taken by same student or a sibling. **Credit** MC, V.
This Place is home to both the London Contemporary Dance School and the touring Richard Alston Dance Company. An extensive programme of shows runs throughout the year but the Place is also well known for its policy of open education: the centre is fully accessible to all ages, as well as to the disabled. There is, however, a daunting waiting list. The majority of classes take place on Saturdays and run concurrently with school terms. These take children aged five and over, striking a balance between creative expression and imparting more formal dance technique through to occasional 'Offspring' performances in the adjoining Robin Howard Dance Theatre. These exceptional performances tend to be of challenging pieces. Considerable work is also done with schools in Camden: there are breakfast clubs and after-school workshops, as well as the Camden Dance Festival, which involves 16 schools each summer and results in three annual performances.

Royal Academy of Dance

36 Battersea Square, Battersea, SW11 3RA (7326 8000/www.rad.org.uk). **Classes** times vary, call for details. **Fees** call for details.
RAD offers a diverse range of activities for children aged from two and a half. Activities range from ballet, jazz and contemporary dance, to drama, singing, creative movement, musical theatre and classes in excerpts from ballets. Prices vary according to the length of the course; discounts are available if two or more siblings are enrolled.

Stagecoach Theatre Arts

Head office: The Courthouse, Elm Grove, Walton-on-Thames, Surrey KT12 1LZ (01932 254333/www.stagecoach.co.uk). **Fees** *Term-time classes* £290 (£140 for 4-7s). **No credit cards.**
With over 450 venues between Edinburgh and Exeter (more than 60 of them in London alone) and many more in other countries in Europe and beyond, Stagecoach is the most prolific part-time theatre school in the world. Courses run parallel to school terms, and break down into three hours of professional tuition per week (one in dance, one in drama and one in singing). Two performances are given annually to family and friends, which keeps the enthusiasm going as children work towards their triumphant curtain calls. Other incentives include medals, which are awarded for continued achievement. Excitingly for ambitious children, there's an in-house agency to represent the most promising talents in each division. All schools take kids aged seven to 16, and most run Early Stages schools for ages four to six.

Sylvia Young Theatre School

Rossmore Road, Marylebone, NW1 6NJ (7402 0673/www.sylviayoungtheatreschool.co.uk). Marylebone tube/rail. **Classes** times vary, phone for details. **Fees** *Classes* £75/13wk term. *Summer school* (10-18s) £250/wk. **No credit cards.**
Sylvia Young's alumni include plastic pop idols (Emma Bunton, Matt from Busted) and soap stars (Dean Gaffney, Tamzin Outhwaite). But the tuition encourages an interest in all aspects of performance art, and as many end up scaling the dizzy heights of the Royal Shakespeare Company as supping pints in the Old Vic. It's a full-time school, as well as a Saturday school, and it runs a programme of holiday courses. The full-time school is, of course, oversubscribed (roughly 150 pupils are on the roll at any one time). It accommodates boys and girls aged ten to 16, and supplements three days of National Curriculum studies with two of vocational dance, music and drama classes. The Saturday school caters for children aged four to 18 and covers a range of performance styles. A holiday school operates out of term-time, with a theatre skills course for eight to 18 year-olds in July and a five-day musical theatre workshop for ten to 18 year-olds in August.

WORKSHOPS

For **Performance workshops**, *see p229.*

Archaeology

LAARC

Mortimer Wheeler House, 46 Eagle Wharf Road, Hoxton, N1 7ED (7410 2200/www.molas.org.uk).
As a storehouse for the Museum of London (*see p49*), the LAARC (London Archaeological Archive Resource Centre) is a library of London's past, home to artefacts and treasures gathered from over 5,000 archaeological digs in and around the capital over the last century or so. Public entry (9am-8.30pm Mon-Fri) is by appointment, and only legitimate research requests will gain you access, but the Museum of London's Archaeology Service (MoLAS) run various digs and activities for families on occasions throughout the year. To find out if anything's going on, either at the Resource Centre, in the Museum of London itself, or elsewhere in London, check the website.

Art

Art 4 Fun

*Various venues (head office 8449 6500/
uwww.art4fun.com). Fees Workshops £15. Courses*
Half-day£25.85. Full-day£39.95. **Credit** MC, V.
Children choose a ceramic item (from £2.50 for a small tile)
and get busy painting. Pieces are fired and glazed in the
café, to be picked up at a later date: a studio fee (£5.95 per
person) covers the process and provides materials. A range
of workshops run throughout the year, the most popular
of which are seasonal events for four to 14 year-olds, plus
a range of daily half-term workshops and week-long
holiday art camps (Easter and summer). On a more
regular basis, daily 'Painting with the Master' classes offer
after-school activities for kids aged six and up (£12.74/2hr
session). Also daily is the Little Artists Club for one to four
year-olds (£8.95/1hr session), while weekend clubs let
families muck in together (£12.75/2hr session). Arty
parties, with a birthday tea, are also available.

The Art Yard

*318 Upper Richmond Road West, Mortlake, SW14 7JN
(8878 1336/www.artyard.co.uk). Mortlake rail/33, 337,
493 bus. **Classes** Term-time 9am-6pm Mon-Fri. School
holidays 9.30am-3.30pm Mon-Fri. **Fees** call for details.*
No credit cards.
The busy Art Yard provides a welcome artistic outlet for
children (aged from five) starved of messy, painty and
gluey fun at boring old SATs-obsessed schools. Many
children come for two-day workshops (9.30am-3.30pm,
bring a packed lunch and wear old clothes) every school
holidays, and have a whale of a time creating improvised
art works, listening to music and making friends. Staff help
children through creative crises. The birthday party
package lets kids choose what they'd like to make from a
list then have lots of fun creating it. Objects range from
papier-mâché mirrors to decorative treasure chests. Parties
cost £15 per child (minimum eight children); ring for
workshop prices.
Buggy access.

Cooking

Junior Masterclasses

*City Café, City Inn Westminster, 30 John Islip Street,
SW1P 4DD (7630 4600/www.citycafe.co.uk). **Classes**
2.30-5pm 9 Jul, 13 Aug, 27 Aug, 10 Sept, 22 Oct 2005;
school holiday Sat, ring for details. **Fees** £35. **Credit**
MC, V.*
Peter Lloyd, head chef at the City Café Westminster, would
like to teach children to be as passionate about good food
as he is. To that end he runs entertaining and informative
cookery sessions for eight to 12 year-olds. Children learn
about fresh ingredients and help to prepare a delicious
meal. As Jamie Oliver proved so forcefully on television,
we need more initiatives like this to improve both our children's diets and nutritional knowledge. Junior Masterclass
children's parties can also be arranged on request.

The Kids' Cookery School

*107 Gunnersbury Lane, Acton, W3 8HQ (8992 8882/
www.thekidscookeryschool.co.uk). Acton Town tube.*
Open *Office* 9am-5.30pm Mon-Fri **Fees** *Half-term &
school hols only* £15/75mins; £30/2.5hrs; £50/5hr incl
lunch. **No credit cards.**

West London's children's cookery school, the first to have
achieved charitable status, is a project aimed at promoting
culinary skills, healthy eating and food awareness among
children from all social backgrounds and age groups.
Events and classes aim to teach kids in a deliciously
hands-on way about new ingredients and equipment,
encouraging them to touch, smell and feel different foods.
There are a maximum of 12 students in every cookery session, with two qualified teachers in the kitchen at all times.

Modern foreign languages

Club Petit Pierrot

7828 2129/www.clubpetitpierrot.uk.com
Established in 1993, Club Petit Pierrot offers fun French
lessons for children aged from eight months to nine years
at venues across London. The lessons, given by native
speakers, are conducted entirely in French with an
emphasis on the children learning through play and
having fun communicating in French. Themes are
carefully planned for each age group, incorporating
subjects that are of practical interest but still enjoyable.
Activities for under-fives include songs, rhymes, dances,
storytelling, arts and crafts, and puppets; for over-fives,
lessons include songs, language games, fun exercises,
role-play and using puppets as a language tool. Parent and
toddler groups, after-school, Saturday and Holiday clubs
are all offered. Fees vary (from £80 per term).

Le Club Tricolore

*10 Ballingdon Road, Wandsworth, SW11 6AJ (7924
4649/www.leclubtricolore.co.uk). **Fees** vary; £135/10wk*
term. **No credit cards.**
This isn't a French lesson in the conventional sense. There
are no verb tables, no grammar exercises and no tests.
Instead, everything is learnt orally, by means of light-
hearted role-playing or old-fashioned singalongs. After-
school classes are complemented by Saturday morning
ones, while a range of holiday workshops dish up cookery,
craft activities and treasure hunts. The club is aimed at
children aged three to 11, and operates in venues across
London – phone for details of your nearest

French & Spanish à la Carte

8946 4777/www.frenchandspanishalacarte.co.uk.
South London's ambitious two to five year-olds can get
ahead with their languages by joining one of these
weekly playgroups (Tuesdays or Thursdays) for an hour
of activity and an hour of free play while a teacher chats
to them in French or Spanish. After-school and holiday
courses are offered for older children.

Music

Blueberry

8677 6871/www.blueberry.clara.co.uk.
Blueberry is the brainchild of New York musician Margo
Random, who wanted to expose her own baby daughter to
live music as early as possible. All over south London in
the weekly parent and toddlers class (ages nine months to
three), parents have a jolly good sing song to an
accompanying guitar and guide their piping offspring
through the actions. Big Kids Blueberry (two to four-year
olds) builds on the singing with more games, but kids are
allowed to come classes on their own. Blueberry also runs
parties *(see p246).*

Activities

Centre for Young Musicians

61 Westminster Bridge Road, Waterloo, SE1 7HT (7928 3844/www.cymlondon.demon.co.uk).
Every Saturday during term-time CYM hosts a programme of choirs, ensembles, masterclasses and instrumental lesson for the musically talented. It also acts as an umbrella organisation for London boroughs who provide instrumental lessons for beginners: ring to find out how to access instrumental tuition near you.

Guildhall

7628 2571/www.gsmd.ac.uk
This world-class conservatoire for grown-up musicians, which celebrates its 125th anniversary in 2005 with a huge programme of special events, including premières and conferences, also runs coveted Saturday morning instrumental training for gifted and talented youngsters. Entry is by audition, but little ones without previous experience can join a reception class in which they take movement and ear-training classes, and begin to experiment on tiny violins and cellos with a view to taking lessons the following year.

London Suzuki Group

Various venues (01372 720088/www.suzukimusic.net). **Fees** vary; phone for details. **No credit cards.**
LSG takes the principles of Dr Shinichi Suzuki as its starting point. His belief that talent is inherent in all newborn children led to the establishment of a revolutionary school of music in Japan. In London the Suzuki Method is expounded by 18 teachers (ten violin, five cello and three piano), each of whom work with children as young as three to develop their natural ability. The key is learning through listening, and then playing for pleasure; no previous musical experience is necessary (although there is pre-instrument training for the very young) and, while the course is aimed at fostering excellence, fun is seen as a natural by-product. Classes are held after school and on weekends, and are for members only (but occasional holiday workshops encourage non-members to join in; check the online diary).

Monkey Music

Various venues (01582 766464/www. monkeymusic.co.uk). **Fees** vary; phone for details.
This pre-school music company has franchises all over the country. It focuses on children aged from six months to four years. The music classes are run by specialist teachers, many of whom are professional musicians and parents themselves and encourage social and musical skills within a fun, stimulating and friendly environment. The weekly 30min classes use a merry combination of songs, percussion instruments and colourful visual props.

Musical Express

8946 6043/www.musicalexpress.co.uk.
Flautist and music therapist Jenny Tabori believes that all children should have access to as much music as possible, and her successful Musical Express classes are now run all over south London and Surrey. Small groups of over- and under-twos meet up in a relaxed environment to sing and play games that help to develop their language and social skills for 40min to an hour a week, depending on age. Call to find out about a Musical Express near you, and to find out how much these classes cost.

Music House for Children

Bush Hall, 310 Uxbridge Road, Shepherd's Bush, W12 7LJ (8932 2652/www.musichouseforchildren.co.uk). Shepherd's Bush tube. **Classes/fees** vary; phone for details. **Credit** MC, V.
Everything about the Music House is aimed at developing musical talent by bringing out the fun in performing. Despite being primarily concerned with classical tuition when it opened its doors in 1994, the organisation these days seeks to engage a wide range of musical interests 'from Mozart to Primal Scream' and use them as the starting points for a lifelong relationship with a musical instrument. Nor are we talking about an either/or decision between the violin and the oboe: lessons in saxophone, guitar and drums are, predictably enough, the most popular run by the Music House. The staff choose a teacher (from more than 200 on their books) based on the individual needs of the child in question, and arrange lessons at times convenient to both parties. These are usually held in the pupil's home. Meanwhile, those seeking a more sociable environment can make their way to the company headquarters in Bush Hall, where group sessions are held every day after school, and expanded musical workshops take place during holidays. These group sessions help children appreciate the sociability and cooperation required in musical performance, and give them a valuable hands-on introduction to a range of instruments.

WILDLIFE

Oasis Children's Nature Garden

Larkhall Lane & Studley Road, Stockwell, SW4 (7498 2329). Stockwell tube. **Open** *After school club* 3.30-5.30pm Mon-Fri. *Term-time* 10am-3.30pm alternate Sat. *School holidays* 10am-noon, 2-4pm Mon-Fri. **Admission** free.
The Nature Garden is run by the Oasis Children's Venture and provides a green, serene environment in an inner city area. The after-school club is very popular, as children take part in a spot of pond-dipping and gardening, as well as frequent arts and crafts or woodwork activities. Environmental workshops are run throughout the school holidays (call for details).

Roots & Shoots

The Vauxhall Centre, Walnut Tree Walk, Lambeth, SE11 6DN (7582 1800/www.roots-and-shoots.org). Lambeth North tube. **Open** *Jan-Apr, Aug-Dec* 9.30am-5pm Mon-Fri. *May-Jul* 9.30am-5pm Mon-Fri; 10am-2pm Sat. Phone before visiting. **Admission** free; donations welcome.
Roots & Shoots organises a range of outdoor activities around a one-acre (0.5 ha) patch of south London. Over the years, it has introduced the pleasures of tending a simple urban garden to a large number of the city's weary offspring, many of them children with disadvantages and disabilities. The site is also a popular destination for school groups. Here David (the wildlife outreach worker) takes children pond-dipping while telling them all about Lambeth's many streetwise frogs. He also teaches them about the insects, animals and wildflowers to be found in the garden and explains the business of collecting delicious London honey (the best, because of all those back gardens) from the resident bees. The centre is also home to the London Beekeepers Association. Phone for details of the next in a series of special day events.

PARTIES

Balloons on the gate, jelly on the plate, what'll we do if the clown is late?

It's ridiculous when you think about it. How can two hours (3-5pm usually) one weekend afternoon to celebrate the birth of their progeny drive normally sane adults to the gin bottle and inappropriate use of their credit cards? Sadly, there's no satisfactory answer to that, but as you can see from these pages, the children's party industry is growing to meet the demand of parental party neuroses. We've met a bunch of gentle clowns, dextrous puppeteers, drama queens and sugarcraft maestros who'd all like to make your child's party the best ever. Or, for all those parents who'd prefer to lie down in a darkened room and let someone else do it all, there are party organisers who are only too willing take the weight off your shoulders (if the price is right).

Of course, you could just decide on footie in the park, followed by dainty sandwiches, jelly, crisps, pop and an inexpertly iced own-made cake. But if you're determined to go the whole hog, read on. Where possible, we've given a rough guide to prices for the party people and places we've listed below, but as most entertainers and organisers prefer to tailor their service, be aware that prices need to be negotiated on application.

ACTIVITIES

Arts & crafts

For more pottery cafés, *see p233*.

Crawley Studios
39 Wood Vale, Forest Hill, SE23 3DS (8516 0002). Forest Hill rail. **Open** daily (by appointment only). **No credit cards.**
Artist Marie Lou runs all-week pottery-painting parties for small groups of children. Held in a diminutive studio, the parties cost usually no more than a tenner a head, but this depends on what's to be painted – selections range from popular animal ornaments (around £8) to useful cups and bowls (£5-£20 including firing charge). Items are ready for collection a week later. After all this creativity, a conservatory area is available for refreshments (£3 a head).

London International Gallery of Children's Art
O2 Centre, 255 Finchley Road, Finchley, NW3 6LU (7435 0903/www.ligca.org). Finchley Road tube. **Open** *Gallery* 4-6pm Tue-Thur; noon-6pm Fri-Sun. **Admission** *Gallery* free; donations requested. **No credit cards.**
This small gallery (*see also p215*) offers a creative environment for children to try out a diverse range of arts and crafts during an hour-long workshop. Quirky themes, such as musical drawing and origami are variations on the traditional art party; mask-making and tie-dye are other options. Prices start at £125 (plus material expenses), with fees increasing if there are more than ten to entertain. *Buggy access. Disabled access: lift. Nappy-changing facilities (in centre).*

Nellie's Arty Time Parties
07710 479852/01433631694/www.dk.com/nellieshepherd.
Art party organiser extraordinaire, Fenella Shepherd can transform a venue into a magical experience – perhaps a mermaid's underwater palace, a robot world or a cyberdelic spaceship, all with arty activities thrown in. Artist-themed affairs (Dalí or Picasso, for instance) give an educational angle; children can try producing their own piece in the artist's style. Prices for this bespoke service vary, but a starting price is £500 for two hours. If that's out of your range, fear not. Nellie's on a mission to make her crafty parties accessible to all. She runs workshops in schools and community centres, and her books, such as *My Party Art Class* (Dorling Kindersley, £6.99), give the lowdown on transforming household objects into the components of magical kingdoms.

Pottery Café
735 Fulham Road, Parsons Green, SW6 5UL (7736 2157/www.pottery-cafe.com). Parsons Green tube/14, 414 bus. **Open** 11am-6pm Mon; 10am-6pm Tue-Wed, Fri, Sat; 10am-9.45pm Thur; 11am-5pm Sun. **Credit** MC, V.
This café simply offers one all-inclusive party package (£17 per child), which encompasses the equipment needed, refreshments, invitations and some colourful decorations. Items are to be collected later, once they've been glazed and fired. Parties must be arranged well in advance, especially at weekends when there are designated time slots and the maximum stay is two hours. *Buggy access. Café. Disabled access. Nappy-changing facilities. Shop.*
Branch: 332 Richmond Road, Twickenham, Surrey TW1 2DU (8744 3000).

Tulse Hill Pottery Studios
93 Palace Road, Tulse Hill, SW2 3LB (8674 2400). Tulse Hill rail/2, 68, 196, 432 bus. **Open** by appointment only. **No credit cards.**
At Caroline Dekosta's creative bashes children are taught techniques using grown-up tools and can have a go at using the potter's wheel if they feel confident enough. Probably best suited for ages five and over, studio parties start at £100, plus £10 per child, which covers materials, firing and the use of equipment.

TOP 10 Party venues

Coram's Fields
At weekends, rooms – with kitchen facilities – may be rented, costing from £32. Parents provide food and entertainment. *See p61.*

Golden Hinde
Birthday pirates have fun on-board (minimum charge is £250 for 15 children). *See p39.*

HMS Belfast
A party room in the World War II battlecruiser residing at Bankside costs £75 to hire. Captain Corky's private tour is £100 extra. *See p39.*

London Waterbus Company
Two hours (£210) or three (£275), chugging along the canal between Camden Lock and Little Venice. For up to 20 children. *See p29.*

Lyric Theatre
Parties are for a minimum of five and a maximum of 30 kids; food is served after the 11am or 1pm performances; the Café Brera hosts party teas from £4.50 per child. Parents usually bring the cake. *See p224.*

Mile End Climbing Wall
Parties for over-eights get an experienced instructor to every eight climbers (costs £58; 90mins of climbing and abseiling). Parties end in the padded 'monkey room'. *See p109.*

Museum of Childhood at Bethnal Green
Here you'll find a specially decorated party room and a soft-play area. Hire of the party room is £50 for a maximum of 12 kids, with 40 minutes in the soft-play area for an extra £30. Bring your own food. *See p109.*

Puppet Theatre Barge
This barge is a brilliant place for a birthday party. Tickets for the children's performances are £6.50 for kids and £7 for adults, and for £50 extra the boat can be rented out for an hour of fun and feasting (parents bring the food). Kids can have a private performance, with an hour on the barge afterwards, for £295. *See p219.*

Science Museum
Young children can enjoy The Garden, then eat lunch at the Deep Blue restaurant for £4 a head – a personalised cake costs £24. IMAX cinema parties include a meal (£9 per head), the 'extreme birthday' buys simulator rides, film and dinner. For £30 per child, minimum five children (and one adult, £25) can book a sleepover, with early breakfast provided. *See p89.*

Theatre Museum
Full-on theatricals in Covent Garden include drama birthday parties (£200 for a maximum of 15 children). *See p76.*

Cookery

Cookie Crumbles
8876 9912/0845 601 4173/www.cookiecrumbles.net. **Credit** MC, V.
Cordon bleu chef Carola Weymouth offers a great introduction to cooking with her food-themed parties, during which children prepare their own tea. Menus have been tailored to suit little chefs from as young as four. For older children, there are 'disco diva' and 'pirate bounty' themes. A two-hour party starts at £165 (plus VAT) for six kids; the price covers everything from shopping to mopping up.

Gill's Cookery Workshop
7 North Square, Golders Green, NW11 7AA (8458 2608). Golders Green tube. **No credit cards.**
Gill Roberts' parties cater for 12 children (£10 per extra child, up to a maximum of 20). Children can decide on their own themes or menus to make on the day. Gill's two-day holiday classes for six to 13 year-olds cost £90; Saturday morning sessions for three to eight year-olds are £25.

Drama

Club Dramatika!
8883 7110. **No credit cards.**
Former drama-school teacher Vicky Levy offers fun-packed drama parties for birthday kids with thespian leanings. Parties cost £80 for one hour, £150 for two. Vicky also runs after-school sessions in north London for children aged three and over; call for details.

Dramarama
Jessica Grant (8446 0891). **No credit cards.**
Attendees can expect to be transported to fairyland, an *Alice in Wonderland* adventure or their own version of *Oliver!* Older children enjoy a general drama session, with games, role-playing and the chance to act to an audience at the end (prices vary according to venue, the length of the party and the size of the group). Drama classes are also available on Saturday mornings for three to ten year-olds and during school holidays for three to 14 year-olds.

Fairy Tale Theatre
01727 759661. **No credit cards.**
Entertainers Mandy and Louise perform their adaptations of children's storybook favourites (such as *Rapunzel* and *Little Red Riding Hood*). Every two-hour party involves a colourful set, props, balloons, games and bubbles, and costs £190 for up to 25 participants.

Perform
7209 3805/www.perform.org.uk. **Credit** MC, V.
Perform leads its parties of young actors through themed workshops (*Finding Nemo*, say, or Perfect Princesses or Wild West), ending in a performance for the parents. Songs can be written with your child in mind if the staff are given enough notice. Prices start at £125 for an hour-long party.

Tiddleywinks
8964 5490/www.tiddleywinks.co.uk. **No credit cards.**
The party starts when Kate Gielgud turns up at your house, in character, to narrate and direct a play in which the kids act, dance and sing their way through one of many

League One Sports Academy.
See p241.

Activities

themes (*Bugsy Malone, Annie, Sleeping Beauty* and *Chitty Chitty Bang Bang* are favourites). Thespians aged nine and over can work on a comedic murder mystery to be presented as a showpiece at the end. Prices start at £200 for two hours; all costumes and props are provided.

Face-painting & make-up

Magical Makeovers

01932 244347/07957681824/www.magical makeovers.com. **No credit cards.**
Make-up enthusiasts aged six to 16 can enjoy a pampering party with any number of girlie companions. All make-up is provided, along with hair accessories that the party-goers can keep afterwards. MM now hosts spa parties with facials and manicures for older girl groups. Prices start at £140 for eight participants.

Mini Makeovers

8398 0107/www.minimakeovers.com.
No credit cards.
Beauty parties for girls aged from five upwards range from fairy and princess fantasies to catwalk set-ups for the over-tens (prices start from £160 for eight heads). Optional extras include a limousine service and pink party bags.

Sport

Alexandra Palace Ice Rink

Alexandra Palace Way, Wood Green, N22 7AY (8365 2121/www.alexandrapalace.com). Wood Green tube/Alexandra Palace rail/W3 bus. **Open** 11am-1.30pm, 2-5.30pm Mon-Fri; 10.30am-12.30pm, 2-4.30pm Sat, Sun. **Admission** *Mon-Fri* £4.50; £4 concessions. *Sat, Sun* £6; £5 concessions; £19.50 family (2+2). **Credit** MC, V.

A pleasant change from the out-of-town warehouses where ice rinks are usually to be found, Ally Pally really is a special venue for a skating party. For £8.50 per head, kids get a brief lesson in the techniques before they take off for a little more than an hour's spin around the rink; then it's skates off for a drink and sandwiches (pay an extra quid and a hot meal is thrown in). Parties are at weekends only at 10.30am, 11am, 2pm and 2.30pm. Booking is essential. *Buggy access. Café. Disabled access: toilet. Nappy-changing facilities.*

Campaign Paintball

Old Lane, Cobham, Surrey KT11 1NH (01932 865999/www.campaignpaintball.com). Effingham Junction rail. **Credit** MC, V.
Campaign Paintball is a 200-acre (80ha) playground for the gung-ho, whose owners insist that warlike combat is just a cover for the centre's primary objective: team-building. But children prefer to be lone heroes and infiltrate enemy camps. By planning a Sunday attack, they get the centre when it's free of City types, and a party package (£25.50 per head) offers kids 300 paintballs to fire at will between 9.30am and 4pm, with a barbecue lunch and awards ceremony afterwards.

Delta Force

01483 211194/www.paintballgames.co.uk.
The biggest name in UK paintballing, Delta Force has branches all over the country; those near the M25 suit Londoners (choose from Hemel Hempstead, Bidbrough, Watford, Upminster, Effingham and Cobham). Children have to be aged over 11 to participate in the fun. For £12.50 per head, they get 150 paintballs to fire between 9.15am and 4pm, plus a barbecue lunch to keep them fighting fit. If you're planning a large manoeuvre, every 15th person goes free. Players are carefully supervised throughout the day by adult marshalling staff.

Indoor games

Indoor play centres: 'the perfect urban solution for the modern British family' (Eddie Catz publicity material) or a noisy, headache-inducing, artificially lit soft option for children too mimsy for outdoor play? Opinion is divided, but there's no denying the immense popularity of these huge, all-weather play centres with their ball ponds, slides and climbing nets, monkey swings, Tarzan ropes and, in the case of **Bramley's Big Adventure**, a large Brontosaur. The indoor adventure playgrounds listed below all offer party packages with various options on goody bags, grub, cake and balloons.

Bramley's Big Adventure

136 Bramley Road, North Kensington, W10 6TJ (8960 1515/www.bramleysbig.co.uk). Ladbroke Grove tube.

Clown Town

222 Green Lanes, Southgate, N13 5UD (8886 7520/www.clowntown.co.uk). Southgate tube/ W6, 121, 329 bus. The Coppetts Centre, Coppetts Close, N12 0AQ (8361 6600/ www.clowntown.co.uk). Arnos Grove tube/ 232 bus.

Discovery Planet

Surrey Quays Shopping Centre, Redriff Road, Rotherhithe, SE16 7LL (7237 2388/www. discovery-planet.co.uk). Canada Water tube.

Eddie Catz

68-70 High Street, Putney, SW15 1SF (0845 201 1268/www.eddiecatz.com). Putney Bridge tube.

Kidzmania

28 Powell Road, Clapton, E5 8DJ (8533 5556/ www.kidzmania.net). Clapton rail/38, 55, 56, 106, 253 bus.

It's a Kid's Thing

279 Magdalen Road, Earlsfield, SW18 3NZ (8739 0909/www.itsakidsthing.info). Earlsfield rail.

Snakes & Ladders

Syon Park, Brentford, Middx, TW8 8JF (8847 0946). Gunnersbury tube, then 237 or 267 bus.

Tiger's Eye

42 Station Road, Wimbledon, SW19 2LP (8543 1655). Colliers Wood tube.

Activities

League One Sports Academy

Danny Grant (8446 0891). **No credit cards**.
League One coach Danny Grant organises sporty activities for children aged between five and 11, ranging from
basketball, football and cricket to full-blown mini
Olympics. Varying skill levels don't generally prove an
issue, as the coaches will cater for everyone's needs. Parties
(prices vary, call for details) cover all equipment, the coaches' fees and a winner's trophy for the birthday child. Venue
hire can be arranged for an extra charge. League One also
offers after-school and Saturday-morning programmes,
plus holiday courses in the Hampstead area. 'Little league'
for three to four year-olds also runs on Tuesday.

Mallinson Sports Centre

Bishopswood Road, Highgate, N6 4NY (8342 7272).
Highgate tube. **Credit** MC, V.
Attached to sporty Highgate school for boys, this sports
centre offers two weekend party packages. On Saturday
mornings, under-sevens can enjoy an hour on a bouncy
castle followed by packed lunches in the social room (from
£200 for an hour and 45mins); eight to 15 year-olds, meanwhile, take part in a more comprehensive sporting experience that may involve basketball, hockey or football (from
£235, available throughout the weekend). This package
involves an hour of supervised team play, half an hour in
the pool and then 45mins in the social room, giving party-
goers a chance to congratulate their fellow teammates on
the day's top scores over lunch (provided by parents). Party
packages are also available during school holidays.
Buggy access. Nappy-changing facilities.

Michael Sobell Leisure Centre

Hornsey Road, Finsbury Park, N7 7NY (7609 2166/
www.aquaterra.org). Finsbury Park tube/rail. **Open**
7.15am-9.30pm Mon-Fri; 9am-5pm Sat; 9am-9pm Sun.
Credit MC, V.
You'll find a selection of party ideas at the Sobell, as attendees take over the centre's indoor safari playground facilities (£70 Mon-Wed; £130 Thur-Sun) or enjoy a mixed
sports party involving basketball, badminton and netball
(£63 for up to 20 kids). Trampolining parties (£85) begin
with a lesson; ice-skating parties (£110) come with skates
and lesson provided. Parents provide the edibles.
*Buggy access. Café. Disabled access: lift, toilet. Nappy-
changing facilities. Shop.*

Paintball Centre

Homeward, Horsley Road, Effingham, Surrey KT11
3JY (0800 917 0821/www.paintballgames.co.uk).
Effingham Junction rail, then 10min walk. **Open** *Phone*
enquiries 9am 5.30pm Mon-Fri; 8.30am-4pm Sat, Sun.
Credit MC, V.
Each soldier gets 150 paintballs to fire off during a morning and early afternoon, with a barbecue lunch laid on as
the young guns debrief. The day runs from 9.15am to 4pm;
helmets, equipment and overalls are provided. Prices start
at £17.50 per head (11 to 17 year-olds, minimum of 20 kids
on weekdays).
Canteen.

Playscape Pro Racing

Streatham Kart Raceway, 390 Streatham High Road,
Streatham, SW16 6HX (8677 8677/www
playscape.co.uk). Streatham rail/50, 109, 255 bus.
Open 10am-10pm daily. **Credit** MC, V.

Racing parties for eight to 16 year-olds (10am-5pm Mon-
Fri; 10am-2pm Sat, Sun), with an hour on the track, cost
from £195 for ten drivers, £292.50 for 15 (90mins) and £390
for 20 (over two hours). Full training and safety gear are
provided, and there's a trophy presented to the birthday
boy or girl at the end.
Buggy access. Disabled access.

Pro-Active 4 Parties & Entertainment

8381 5005/www.magicalparties.net. **No credit cards**.
The 'Premier football' theme is in a league of its own,
putting small teams through a series of tournaments and
shoot-outs (£180-£260), while the 'sports combo' parties
and 'mini-Olympics' cover everything from basketball to
ultimate Frisbee. 'Mayhem' parties for varying groups of
four to 11 year-olds encompass a menagerie of circus skills,
magic, competitions and discos, or there are themed parties for junior gladiators and aspiring wizards (both from
£225). Pro-Active can set up events in your garden (provided, of course, it's big enough) or a local sports hall.

Westway Sports Centre

1 Crowthorne Road, North Kensington, W10 5RP
(8969 0992/www.westway.org). Latimer Road tube/
7, 295, 316 bus. **Open** 8am-10pm Mon-Fri; 8am-8pm
Sat; 10am-10pm Sun. **Credit** AmEx, MC, V.
Activities available to party-goers include tennis, football
and the capital's largest indoor climbing wall (which
should also be heated by the end of summer 2005).
Invitations are provided, and most importantly, so is equipment and any relevant training needed for the session.
Prices range from £99-£165 for 12 to 24 children, with
catering available as an optional extra.
Buggy access. Café. Disabled: toilet. Nappy-changing
facilities.

CAKES

Amato Caffè/Pasticceria

14 Old Compton Street, Soho, W1D 4TH (7734
5733/www.amato.co.uk). Leicester Square or
Tottenham Court Road tube. **Open** 8am-10pm
Mon-Sat; 10am-8pm Sun. **Credit** AmEx, DC, MC, V.
Map p315 K6.
Many of Amato's bespoke cakes can be further personalised (from £30) with pictures of the birthday child. For
a young film fan, the chefs can create everything from
free-standing cake versions of *Star Wars* character R2-D2
(from £150) to designs capturing the Starship Enterprise
or an Egyptian scene. Prices go up to £3,500 for the most
extravagant efforts.
Buggy access. Delivery service.

Choccywoccydoodah

47 Harrowby Street, Lisson Grove, W1H 5EA (7724
5465/www.choccywoccydoodah.com). Edgware Road or
Marble Arch tube. **Open** 10am-2pm, 3-6pm Wed-Fri;
11am-6pm Sat. **Credit** MC, V. **Map** p311 F5.
Layered with fresh Belgian truffles, Choccy creations can
even be coated with dyed chocolate to match your party's
colour scheme. Eight to ten portions cost from £22.50, up
to 70 portions cost £100; hand-moulded figures and novelty chocs can be added as party table extras. There's also
a Brighton branch (01273 329462, open daily).
Buggy access. Delivery service.

Chorak

122 High Road, East Finchley, N2 9ED (8365 3330). East Finchley tube/263 bus. **Open** 8.30am-6.30pm daily. **No credit cards**.

Chorak's handmade party cakes embellished with icing versions of famous characters, such as Shrek, come in two sizes, with the price depending on whether you opt for a flat cut-out design or a 3D shape. Small cakes cost from £48 to £55 and large creations from £50 to £70. *Buggy access. Disabled access.*

Dunn's

6 The Broadway, Crouch End, N8 9SN (8340 1614/ www.dunns-bakery.co.uk). Finsbury Park tube/rail, then W7 bus/Crouch Hill rail/41, 91 bus. **Open** 7am-6pm Mon-Sat. **Credit** MC, V.

For five generations now, Dunn's has been turning out themed party cakes of all descriptions, ranging from *Thomas the Tank Engine* to *Hello Kitty* (from £85). Bespoke designs can be iced to order from around £36 *Buggy access. Delivery service.*

Jane Asher Party Cakes

22-24 Cale Street, South Kensington, SW3 3QU (7584 6177/www.jane-asher.co.uk). South Kensington tube/11, 19, 211 bus. **Open** 9.30am-5.30pm Mon-Sat. **Credit** AmEx, MC, V. **Map** p313 E11.

Ms Asher's website offers a range of cake ideas for kids including a great bespoke design gallery featuring 3D castles, lady bugs or gorillas. The range starts at £35. Some cake mixes and Jane Asher sugarcraft materials are also available, should you prefer to bake your own. *Buggy access. Delivery service. Disabled access. Mail order.*

Maison Blanc

102 Holland Park Avenue, Holland Park, W11 4UA (7221 2494/ www.maison blanc.co.uk). Holland Park tube. **Open** 8am-7pm Mon-Thur, Sat; 8am-7.30pm Fri; 8.30am-6pm Sun. **Credit** MC, V.

Any of the MB gâteaux can be decorated with a greeting. Other fab ideas for cakes can be whipped up to suit. **Branches**: throughout town. Check website for details.

Angels. *See p245.*

Creating drama, averting crisis

In her early career live-wire Lydie
worked in the French theatre as a mime
artist and dancer, before crossing the
Channel to live and work in London.
She was a member of a jazz band, then
became a full-time children's art
teacher while occasionally performing
in a clowning double act with a friend.
After a while on the circuit, Lydie
branched out on her own, becoming
increasingly interested in children's
parties. Her initial concept was to
present something a little different
from the norm, which allowed children
not merely to participate as members
of the audience but to become part of
the activity and entertainment itself.
Bringing together her various
experiences, she was one of the first to
offer the kind of party that lets children
explore their favourite stories through
role play, singing along and dancing.

Lydie's props and sets are hand-
painted and designed to transform an
average-sized front room. Children can
choose from a growing range of
themes, from Peter Pan's lost boys'
island to the futuristic city scene from
a Batman comic. The attention to detail
means Lydie turns up hours before the
event to set the scene and making sure
she is in place (and in character) to
greet the children as they enter the
theatre. Indeed, parents have often
asked Lydie her secret after witnessing
30 sugar-crazed kids enthusiastically
following her lead. It's simple: she
does it by 'grabbing their attention by
adopting the same amount of energy!'.

Obviously, things don't always run
smoothly (Lydie recalls a time when
some parents allowed the children on
to the set before her arrival and six
hours' preparation was trashed by a
gang of pirates with wooden swords).
Generally, though, Lydie insists she
has a great time with the kids and,
even after ten years in the business,
claims they are the perfect, energising
remedy to get her back on track when
she's having a bad day.

If you'd like to witness her theatrical,
child-charming skills for yourself, Lydie
offers a fun-packed two hours of
entertainment for £355-£380; this,
she promises, includes a thorough
clean-up afterwards.

Lydie Children's Parties
7622 2540. **No credit cards.**

Activities

Margaret's Cakes of Distinction

224 Camberwell Road, Camberwell, SE5 0ED (7701 1940/www.purple-pages.com/margarets). Elephant & Castle tube/rail, then 12, 45, 35, 68, 171, 176 bus. **Open** 9am-5pm Mon-Sat. **No credit cards.**
This West Indian bakery turns out distinctive, fairly priced personalised cakes. A simple round sponge cake sandwiched with buttercream or jam can be embellished with cute little marzipan figurines and costs from £43. Alternatively, a 12in (30cm) cake in the shape of a favourite character or animal can be ordered for £80.
Buggy access. Disabled access.

Pierre Péchon

127 Queensway, Bayswater, W2 4XJ (7229 0746/ www.croquembouche.co.uk). Bayswater or Queensway tube. **Open** 7am-7pm Mon-Wed; 7am-8pm Thur-Sat; 8am-7pm Sun. **Credit** MC, V. **Map** p310 C6.
For inspiration, a catalogue of past work is available and PP can add iced messages, characters or a picture from a photographic print if you want. Prices for a 12in (30cm) cake start at £59.10 (33 portions).
Buggy access.

COSTUMES
Mail order

Hopscotch
Summer Wood, Puttenham Heath Road, Compton, Guildford, Surrey GU3 1DU (01483 813728/ www.hopscotchdressingup.co.uk). **Open** *Phone orders* 9.30am-5.30pm Mon-Fri. **Credit** MC, V.
Hopscotch's dressing-up clothes have been tested by kids to ensure comfort (and they should certainly remain intact far longer than the party). There's a huge choice on the website from historical characters (crusaders, knights and princesses) to combat soldiers and mermaids, as well as accessories (crowns, fezzes and wands) to sharpen up any outfit. We like the helpful way Hopscotch can supplement your ownmade efforts with their well-finished headgear (dragon head in fun fur for £8.95) or supply the whole jolly outfit (adorable dragon suit, £29.95). Hopscotch dressing up clothes are also sold in many good London toyshops, such as Route 73 (*see p207*) and the Art Stationers/Green's Toy Shop, (*see p206*)

J&M Toys
46 Finsbury Drive, Wrose, Bradford, W Yorks BD2 1QA (01274 599314/fax 01274 591887/ www.jandmtoys.co.uk). **Open** *Phone enquiries* 9am-5.30pm Mon-Fri. **Credit** MC, V.
Firefighters, fairies, pirates, cowgirls, Vikings, dragons, nurses. Jim and Melanie's comprehensive range includes over 150 dressing-up costumes and accessories, available in age ranges three to five and five to eight. The company has been manufacturing and supplying dressing-up outfits for almost 20 years. The owners are also medieval enthusiasts, so regal robes, Robin Hoods and a nice range of knights' armour, with wooden swords and shields are also to be found. J&M is also a boon at that nativity time of year – angels and wise men are tricked out nicely. It's all surprisingly cheap: the majority of costumes cost nomore than £15, with discounts on group purchases. Orders are taken online, by post or fax.

Shops

For more toyshops and children's boutiques with dressing-up gear, *see pp184-209*.

Angels
119 Shaftesbury Avenue, St Giles's, WC2H 8AE (7836 5678/www.fancydress.com). Leicester Square or Tottenham Court Road tube. **Open** 9am-5.30pm Mon-Fri. **Credit** AmEx, MC, V.
Angels has a large collection of costumes, props and make-up for children and adults covering many themes (including the winsome fairy princess or dashing pirate looks pictured on p242). For girls, the Dorothy (*Wizard of Oz*) outfit is rather appealing (£27), while boys can choose from a number of superheroes like Batman (£21) or the Hulk (£30). The 'costume treasure chests' are a great gift idea, coming filled with dressing-up outfits and accessories for both boys and girls (from £23.50 for three outfits).
Buggy access. Disabled access. Mail order.

Escapade
150 Camden High Street, Camden Town, NW1 0NE (7485 7384/www.escapade.co.uk). Camden Town tube. **Open** 10am-7pm Mon-Fri; 10am-6pm Sat; noon-5pm Sun. **Credit** AmEx, MC, V.
Escapade make many of their costumes in-store, with all manner of characters catered for – you can opt for a cuddly bear or kitten, a comedy vegetable item, a well-rendered Cinderella or perhaps a dandified Prince Charming. For instant action heroes, ready-made kits can be bought from around £10 for the most basic, going up to £30 for the full Batman or Thunderbird set. Three-day costume hire costs £15-£20, with a £50 deposit.
Buggy access. Delivery service. Disabled access. Mail order.

Harlequin
254 Lee High Road, Lewisham, SE13 5PR (8852 0193). Hither Green rail/Lewisham rail/DLR/21, 261 bus. **Open** 10am-5.30pm Mon, Tue, Thur-Sat; 10am-1pm Wed. **Credit** MC, V.
For those planning a *Lord of the Rings* themed party, Harlequin is the place to come for your Legolas and furry-footed Frodo costumes (from £21.95), or if superheroes are more your bag, there's everyone from Batman (and Robin) to Spidey (£24.95). Cheaper alternatives are available in the form of Indians and Ninjas (both from £9.95) or a set of sheriff accessories (£4.95). The Elvis kid's jumpsuit (£16.95) is a blast.
Buggy access. Disabled access.

Pantaloons
119 Lupus Street, Pimlico, SW1V 3EN (7630 8330/ www.pantaloons.co.uk). Pimlico tube. **Open** 11am-6pm Mon-Wed; 11am-8pm Thur; 11am-7pm Fri; 10am-6pm Sat. **Credit** AmEx, MC, V.
A dressing-up and balloon specialist that caters for both adults and children, Pantaloons can make sure your party animal looks the part. Budget costumes cost from as little as £10, but you're more likely to hand over £30 for full Disney regalia. Big production costumes, such as the 'step-in' horse, can also be hired. Elaborate disguises, including wigs and masks, are also available.
Buggy access. Delivery service. Disabled access. Mail order.

Activities

DEALS ON WHEELS

The Party Bus
07836 605032/www.childrenspartybus.co.uk.
This colourful mobile party venue (a converted single-deck bus) holds up to 24 children, with on-board events tailored to the age group in question (from four to nine year-olds). Expect games and comedy magic for younger ones and a mobile disco experience for older kids. For £300-£350 the bus stays at your house for two hours, and provides all catering except the cake. The added bonus is that when the music stops, the mess just disappears into the sunset.

Wonder Years
0700 012 3455/www.limousinehireheathrow.com.
Wonder Years supply a chauffeur-driven stretched limo with leather seats, fairy lights and mirrored ceilings. Soft drinks are provided and each car can legally seat up to eight people; minimum charge is £125 for one hour; additional hours are charged at £50 from then on.

ENTERTAINERS

More information on the entertainers we've listed can be found on their websites, if they have them, and their prices coaxed out of them by phone.

Ali Do Lali
01494 774300.
Quirky entertainer Ali Do Lali has perfected his magic tricks and illusions over 30 years. Young party-goers enjoy storytelling and more gentle trickery; fire-eating and sawing in half of parents are saved for the older kids.

Billy the Disco DJ
8471 8616/www.billythediscodj.co.uk.
Billy's disco for party people aged four to 11 includes limbo contests, disco lights, bubbles, pop quizzes and karaoke. He charges £150 for a 90min do.

Blueberry Playsongs Parties
8677 6871/www.blueberry.clara.co.uk.
A parent-and-toddler music group with nine branches in London, Blueberry sends entertainers to parties of children aged one to six for 45mins of guitar-led singing and dancing. Prices start at £75 for 20 children, and include balloons and a present for the birthday boy or girl.

Boo Boo
7727 3817/www.mr-booboo.co.uk.
Boo Boo is part clown, part magician, part comic. His two-hour shows for three to eight year-olds incorporate music, balloon-modelling, dancing and general buffoonery; older kids get a Boo Boo disco party.

Chris Howell
7376 1083/www.christopherhowell.net.
Chris is a member of the Magic Circle and performs to both adult and junior audiences. Hour-long parties for four to eight year-olds are themed with a story in which the kids play an active part, and there's balloon-modelling to round things off. Prices start at £100.

Jenty the Gentle Clown
8207 0437/07957 121764.
Parties for children aged two to 11 include singing, banjo music, puppets, storytelling, balloon-modelling, face-painting and limbo dancing. Choose the activities to suit your child's tastes. Gentle Jenty charges £150 for one hour or £175 for two.

Juggling John
8938 3218/www.jugglersetc.com.
John Haynes is the man behind Jugglers Etc agency, which supplies unicyclists, stilt-walkers, storytellers and fire-eaters (mind the curtains!). One- or two-hour shows, depending on age (one year-olds upwards can be catered for), start at around £140-£180.

Lee Warren
8670 2729/www.sorcery.org.uk.
Lee combines sorcery with audience participation. The hour-long shows – for four to eight year-olds – cost from £110 for a performance in the comfort of your own home or £120 in a hired hall, and Lee says he's able to deal with nearly any size of audience (eight minimum).

Lisa the Disco Diva
07778 122277/www.childrensparties-london.co.uk.
Professional dance instructor Lisa's collection of mobile DJ and disco equipment includes bubble and smoke machines, mirrorballs and fancy lights. She can design a party according to a child's desires and choreograph a whole dance routine to a favourite tune; kids can then do their new grooves for grown-ups, or just party the rest of the afternoon away on their own. Events cater for boys and girls aged four and upwards, with games, magic and competitions in the high-energy, two-hour package.

Little Blisters
8948 3874/www.childrensentertainment-surrey.co.uk.
Actress Ava Desouza makes parties sparkle for three to seven year-olds. As Flossie the Fairy, Sea Lily the Mermaid or Kitty the Magical Pussy Cat, she tells a story, with plenty of song and dance along the way. Shows last one or two hours (£100-£220), with games, prizes and face-painting.

Louis & Steve's Magic Mayhem
01322 442634/mobile 07909882762.
Mind magician Steve Dunbar has passed many gifts to his 11-year-old son Louis, whose spookily photographic memory has proved a real boon when it comes to wowing his audience. Their particular brand of magic is best suited to older children aged from seven, with the over-12s likely to go for the more intricate stuff. Steve also teaches magic, and an instructive element can be introduced to the parties (in the form of a magic workshop) if required. The Dunbars charge £85 for one hour, £150 for two.

Merlin Entertainments
8866 6327/www.merlinents.co.uk.
Choose from a long list of performers, with everything from caricaturists and comedy waiters to fortune-tellers and fire-eaters on Merlin's books. Prices start at £115 for a one-hour performance, or £145 for a more interactive two-hour show. Merlin also organises circus and clown workshops for parties with age groups of three upwards; they'll bring the necessary equipment to a suitable venue of your choice.

Activities

Stringing them along

In the last year, as well as running **Puppet Planet** (a shop and hospital for tangled marionettes; *see p208*), Lesley Butler has extended her passion for her stringed friends by holding children's parties. She's keen to share her enormous collection of puppets from all over the world with youngsters. Puppet Planet is a great place to have a party – Butler describes it as 'a magical place where kids can appreciate colours and textures, and the quality of the puppets themselves'. The parties attract a diversity of ages and thus themes are adapted according to the party child's tastes. So fairytales and princesses might attract one type of reveller, while the travails of Dr Frankenstein, and sundry monsters and witches might tickle another child's fancy. Generally, the party begins with an introduction by her clowning persona 'the bag lady' who then leads the kids into various games and a storytelling session using puppets and object animation. Allowing the children to get fully involved in the art of storytelling is a priority, and they need little encouragement when it comes to picking up the marionettes. Improvised stories involve prompt cards that help to move things along and, best of all, each puppeteer can make their own glove puppet or a wooden marionette to take away at the end – a nice change from the usual party bag.

These days, Lesley has three helpers to assist with parties for under-fives, which take on a much calmer atmosphere and involve gentle storytelling as well as puppet-making session. Anyone who is interested in learning the craft for themselves can attend a drop-in session at the shop. Depending on the timescale, various designs can be created, from shadow or rod puppets to marionettes. Sessions are priced from £5, with a small charge for materials used. On Sunday afternoons parents and kids are welcomed to the store to enjoy storytelling with author Mary Dickenson, along with some healthy organic snacks (tickets cost £7.50 per child, accompanying adults go free). When children visit the store, they often don't want to leave, but Lesley tries to inspire them to create their own puppets at home 'from all sorts of things – old gloves, even a brush'. For more information on puppet-making and events check out the **British Puppet & Model Theatre Guild** web page (www.puppetguild.co.uk) or drop by the shop (www.puppetplanet.co.uk) to have a play with a marionette or two yourselves.

Puppet Planet

787 Wandsworth Road (corner of the Chase), Clapham, SW8 3JQ (7627 0111/ 07785 541358/www.puppetplanet.co.uk).

Activities

Man of many talents

Owen Reid, otherwise known as **Foxy the Funky Genie**, began his comedic career early in life as the class joker at school. Inspired along the way by the genius of comic magicians like Tommy Cooper and David Nixon, it seemed inevitable he would eventually turn his hand to making people laugh for a living. For his younger audiences, he appears in the form of a magical genie, his shows encompassing a diversity of skills from balloon modelling (no challenge is refused) to puppeteering and DJing. He's also a member of the Magic Circle and performs a ventriloquist act with his entourage of characters, consisting of a funky brother, his girlfriend Shemoan (pronounced She-moan) and various animal characters, including George the Bird and an orangutan. The secret of Foxy's success is 'patience and knowing lots of silly jokes' (oh, and wearing two pairs of trousers, in case the children try to pull his genie pantaloons down).

The Funky Genie Parties can involve as many forms of entertainment as you see fit. Younger participants are treated to 45 minutes of genie magic and ventriloquism (from £95) with anyone brave enough invited to rub the magic lamp for a special prize. For the less easily convinced, Foxy combines various madcap games with disco dancing and karaoke (starts at around £175 for two hours). There are also balloon workshops for the over-eights, in which each student is awarded a certificate (check out www.ballooneversity.com), while the under-fives are treated to an interactive dancing, singing marionette show, which is a singular interpretation of a favourite tale called 'Little Red Riding Who.'

'Genie 3 Wishes', which Owen organises alongside his own entertainment fixtures, acts as a booking service without the agent's fees. It can put you in touch with a massive assortment of pop star lookalikes, clowns, steel bands, comedy waiters and fellow magicians that have all been personally vetted for quality control. That isn't the end of this genie's services, however: in addition to supplying party bags and piñatas (from £16.99), he delivers presents on Christmas morning as an alternative funky Santa, which shows serious dedication. His strong interest in working with the community has led him into charity work, previously with Children in Crisis, in addition to visiting young fans at Great Ormond Street Hospital and holding marionette shows at Sure Start for single parents.

If you are planning to organise a children's party, there are some quick pointers from Foxy on his website (www.foxythefunkygenie.com) that may prove very useful to those who don't have a magic lamp to fulfil their wishes.

Foxy the Funky Genie
8461 1223/www.foxythefunkygenie.com.

Mr Squash

8808 1415/www.mr-squash.co.uk.
Mr Squash travels all over London with his musical puppet show, balloon tricks, singalongs and funny stories. Well known on the playgroup circuit, he's experienced in engaging the very young (two and three year-olds) but his parties are suitable for children aged up to six. His puppet friends, performing in a booth, invite audience participation, especially from the birthday boy or girl. Mr Squash charges from £150 for a one-hour set.

Pekko's Puppets

8575 2311/www.pekkospuppets.co.uk.
Stephen Novy is also an old hand at birthday parties. His puppet plays are aimed at children aged three to 11, with shows for under-fives packing in two shorter tales with lots of singing and audience participation. Older children get a full performance from a repertoire that runs to Celtic folk tales, popular classics and chillers like Dracula, all enacted from one of Mr Novy's two mobile booths (from £130 for one hour).

Peter McKenna

7703 2254/07956 200572.
Magic Circle member Peter McKenna appears in a variety of guises to suit various age groups – and performs tricks with a degree of competence rarely seen at children's parties. Illusions might include levitating, sawing parents in half and decapitating audience members (fear not, no-one's ever left a party minus their head), but there are always less alarming routines for little ones. Discos, party games and goody bags are all available by arrangement. Prices start at £90 for one hour, £145 for two.

Professor Fumble

01395 579523.
Professor Fumble's routine involves repeatedly bungling his tricks, juggling like a seasoned amateur and sitting down in his own custard pies. Shows can last one or two hours (from £100 or £145 respectively); the former include balloon animals for the kids and – where space permits – a chance for party-goers to have a crack at spinning plates or walking on small stilts. Longer performances allow for Fumbling versions of old party games, with the mad Professor providing the prizes.

EQUIPMENT HIRE

Disco

Young's Disco Centre

2 Malden Road, Chalk Farm, NW5 3HR (7485 1115/ www.youngsdisco.com). Chalk Farm tube. **Open** by appointment only Mon-Fri; 11am-5pm Sat. **Credit** MC, V.
Young's is the place to shop for any disco equipment you want to hire for the day. A state-of-the-art sound system comes with a DJ for two hours (£160 during the week, £180 at weekends), and karaoke set-ups are available from £60. You can add a smoke machine (from £15) or industrial bubble blower (from £15), popcorn and candy-floss makers (from £50 each), or even fake snow machines (£20). A DIY children's party package with a sound system and disco lights can be hired over 24 hours for a bargain £60. *Buggy access. Delivery service. Disabled access.*

Fairground

PK Entertainments

07771 546676/www.fairandfete.co.uk. **No credit cards.**
What do you get for the child who has everything? An indoor fairground might be a start. PK Entertainments can set up a basic package (from £250) in your living room, with mini bouncy castle, bucking bronco and stalls of the pop-gun variety; those with more capacious sitting rooms (along the lines of a ballroom, perhaps?) can even request a toboggan run. Outdoor events start at about £250 for 20 kids, though a fully blown fair can be built for roughly £500 (roundabouts, swingboats and all).

Marquees

Sunset Marquees

Welsback House, 3-9 Broomhill Road, Putney, SW18 4JQ (8741 2777/www.sunsetmarquees.com). East Putney tube. **Open** *Enquiries* 24hrs daily. **No credit cards.**
If a giant, child-filled tent sounds like a fab idea, Sunset should be able supply you with everything you need. A basic package 3m by 3m (10ft by 10ft) starts from £190, with lighting, furniture, candy-floss machines, heating and carpeting supplied for an extra charge.

ORGANISERS

Action Station

0870 770 2705/www.theactionstation.co.uk.
Specialising in storytelling characters, this agency's books are also brimming with unicyclists, jugglers and clowns. All themes deemed suitable for four to 11 year-olds are covered; drama, cheerleader and film make-up parties cost from £135 for one hour, £190 for two.

Adam Ant's

8959 1045/www.adamantsparties.com.
Adam Ant can conjure up a number of entertainers adept in the arts of music-making, magic and balloon-modelling. Party accessories, including ball ponds and bouncy castles, may be hired (from £45) along with kid-o-gram characters who turn up to wow the party for half an hour (from £85). Catering can also be organised.

Boo! Productions

8772 8140/www.booproductions.co.uk.
Boo! Productions (previously Crechendo) specialise in bespoke theme parties covering everything from gunfights at the OK Corral to glamorous 'model behaviour' sessions. If you require just the entertainer, prices start at around £250 for two hours, although you're looking at £1,500 plus for the bespoke service. But with Boo! Productions' promise of 'we will find it, build it or bake it' it would appear that any crazed ideas you dream up are sure to be attempted.

Laurie Temple & the Party Wizard Company

8840 5293/www.thepartywizard.co.uk.
Entertainer Laurie Temple and his team run a host of parties lasting for one or two hours that can feature magic,

Activities

balloons, juggling, junior discos, puppetry, storytelling and face-painting, as well as themes such as pop-star discos and crazy circus workshops. A wide range of party budgets are catered for and prices can vary from £120-£160 (one hour) to £175-£250 (two hours).

Mystical Fairies

12 Flask Walk, Hampstead, NW3 1HE (7431 1888/ www.mysticalfairies.co.uk). Hampstead tube. **Open** 10am-6pm Mon-Sat; 11am-6pm Sun. **Credit** MC, V.
For parties shimmering with fairy dust, disco fun, gauzy outfits borrowed from the shop (*see p205*) and an 'enchanted garden', MF charges £350 for a package (includes invitations, tableware, an entertainer and costumes). Home parties (lasting two hours) can work out cheaper (£200). If you'd like the good fairies to tailor a party to your child's needs, ask for a quotation. Prices stated exclude VAT. *Buggy access. Mail order.*

Puddleduck Parties

8893 8998/www.puddleduckparties.co.uk.
Puddleduck can put together flexible packages that encompass all the party necessities such as catering (inclusive of tableware), decorations and entertainers. 'Teddy bears' picnics' can be arranged for the smaller ones, otherwise there's drama, sport or disco parties for all ages, starting from around £200 for two hours of fun.

Splodge

7350 1477/www.planetsplodge.com.
Splodge specialise in immersing groups of children in a choice of environments, be it meeting the animals at Battersea Children's Zoo, a mystical unicorn hunt at Holland Park or military manoeuvres at the National Army Museum. Tailor-made packages might include themed party teas, party bags, decorations, a video and a face-painter, personalised according to the family's wishes. For 20 kids, such parties cost from £330 and last two hours.

Twizzle Parties

8789 3232/www.twizzle.co.uk.
Famed for organising various children's 'film premiere' parties (*Lemony Snicket* and *Thunderbirds*, to name but two), Twizzle are capable of building themed events for all ages. While toddlers will enjoy a 'nursery rhymes and singalong fun' party, there's also circus, Action Man and ballerina themes or street dance parties for elder siblings (from £150 for one hour or £240 for two). Wannabe pop stars can make their own CD and video in a studio (from £350 for two hours, up to 16 kids), taking a copy away to play at home.

PARAPHERNALIA
Mail order

Baker Ross

2-3 Forest Works, Forest Road, E17 6JF (enquiries 8523 2733/phone orders 0870 458 5440/www. bakerross.co.uk). **Open** *Phone orders* 24hrs daily. **Credit** MC, V.
A great favourite with PTA fundraisers, Baker Ross stocks a vast range of little gifts for bran tubs and prizes, as well as any number of craft supplies. Pocket-money toys – such

as alien egg putty (£4.20 for six) or bottles of blow bubbles (£1.20 for four) – make excellent ideas for party prizes and bag-fillers. Phone or visit the website for a catalogue.

Children's Audio Company

01279 444707/www.cyp.co.uk. **Credit** AmEx, MC, V.
This company's selection of party tapes and CDs provide ideal backing music for various party games or just for tot-friendly disco dancing. The ultimate pop party CD is £4.99 – which, with 70 minutes of hit-packed tunes (think all kinds of Abba and Mambo No.5), is definitely the cheap alternative to hiring a DJ.

Just Balloons

8560 5933/www.justballoons.com. **Open** *Phone orders* 9am-6pm Mon-Fri. **Credit** AmEx, MC, V.
Trading solely from their website since the shop's closure last year, Just Balloons still offers a wide selection of inflatable goods which may be personalised with messages or photographs (the latter costing £113 for 50). Foil balloons come in a range of styles from £2.95 each, while customised party banners start at £47 per item. Delivery in central London is around £15.

Party Directory

Unit 8, Dares Farm, Farnham Road, Ewshot, Farnham, Surrey GU10 5BB (01252 851601/ www.partydirectory4kids.co.uk). **Open** *phone orders* 9.30am-6pm Mon-Fri. **Credit** MC, V.
This mail-order catalogue (available by phone or online) covers everything required for a successful celebration. Fans of *The Incredibles* can enjoy themed tableware (cups to tablecloths ranging from 23p to £2.75) while wearing glitzy party headdresses (£1.50 for a set of five). There are loads of ideas for party bag-fillers too, with sneaky snakes, spotted bouncy balls and sparkle swop pencils all less than a pound each.

Party Pieces

Child's Court Farm, Ashampstead Common, Berks RG8 8QT (01635 201844/www.partypieces.co.uk). **Open** *Phone orders* 8.30am-6pm Mon-Fri; 9am-5pm Sat. **Credit** MC, V.
Party Pieces is possibly the best supplier of activities and accessories we've found. Its huge range of reasonbly priced tableware (from around 25p an item) includes famous faces like Spiderman, The Incredibles and Nemo, while themes for older kids include macho camouflage or girlier-than-thou pop-star sets with matching party bags and invitations. There are loads of party bag-fillers, traditional games (a pin the eyepatch on the pirate version of the donkey's tail original is £2.45), and a whopping range of banners, balloons and assorted decorations.

Shops

Balloon & Kite Company

613 Garratt Lane, Earlsfield, SW18 4SU (8946 5962/ www.balloonandkite.com). Tooting Broadway tube/ Earlsfield rail. **Open** 9am-6pm Mon-Fri; 9am-5.30pm Sat. **Credit** AmEx, MC, V.
Balloons are available in rubber or foil (from £1 or £2.99 a piece), bearing pictures of any number of favourite screen heroes; names can be added to 'Happy Birthday' variants while you wait (£3.50 each). There's themed paper

tableware and banners, while kites (from £10) make good last-minute gifts. Goody-bag stuff starts at 99p for a packet. London delivery is available for orders over £10. *Buggy access. Delivery service. Disabled access. Mail order.*

Balloonland

12 Hale Lane, Mill Hill, NW7 3NX (8906 3302/www.balloonland.co.uk). Edgware tube/Mill Hill Broadway rail/221, 240 bus. **Open** 9.30am-5.30pm Mon-Fri; 10am-5.30pm Sat. **Credit** MC, V.
Balloonland's range of products can make children's parties look spectacular. Regular balloons start from 20p each and come in a wide variety of shapes and sizes. The choice is inflated further by designer creations (balloon clusters, jumbo balloon trees, balloons attached to soft toys or chocolate boxes), as well as themed tableware and decorations. Loot bag gifts are also available here. *Buggy access. Delivery service. Disabled access. Mail order.*

Circus Circus

176 Wandsworth Bridge Road, Fulham, SW6 2UQ (7731 4128/www.circuscircus.co.uk). Fulham Broadway tube. **Open** 10am-6pm Mon-Sat. **Credit** AmEx, MC, V.
If you have a particular kids' party theme in mind, Circus Circus will supply everything needed to put it together. That means cakes can be baked (from £95), balloons blown up, bouncy castles organised and entertainers brought to your front door as part of the service. Children's costumes (from £10.99) and accessories, such as wigs, masks, wands and weapons, invitations, goody bags and boxes, ribbons, streamers and balloons can all be purchased in the store, where tableware comes in more than 70 popular themes. *Buggy access. Delivery service. Disabled access: ramp. Mail order. Play area.*

Mexicolore

28 Warriner Gardens, Battersea, SW11 4EB (7622 9577/www.pinata.co.uk). Battersea Park or Queenstown Road rail/44, 137 bus. **Open** by appointment only. **No credit cards.**
Proper Piñatas (not the cheapo cardboard ones you can buy at supermarkets) at Mexicolore are made from decorated papier mâché in a number of designs that can be filled by parents with fruit, sweets or small toys. Pick up a small bull or a star for around £19.95 or, if you prefer, maybe something a little larger, such as a donkey design that'll set you back £40 and last about five minutes in the hands of manic, stick-wielding children. *Buggy access. Mail order.*

The Non-Stop Party Shop

214-216 Kensington High Street, Kensington, W8 7RG (7937 7200/www.nonstopparty.co.uk). High Street Kensington tube/10, 27, 391 bus. **Open** 9.30am-6pm Mon-Sat; 11am-5pm Sun. **Credit** MC, V. **Map** p312 A9.
The Non-Stop Party people have quite a selection of party headwear, from starchy would-be aristocrat top hats to some corking battered Australian bushwhacker affairs – and with the most basic plastic hats starting at a mere 99p, there are some affordable options too. Other than the titfers, expect to find plastic animal masks (£2.50) and – to complete the look – face-crayons, wigs and false noses along with all sorts of theatrical make-up. *Delivery service. Mail order.*

Oscar's Den

127-129 Abbey Road, St John's Wood, NW6 4SL (7328 6683/www.oscarsden.com). Swiss Cottage tube/West Hampstead tube/rail/28, 31, 139, 189 bus. **Open** 9.30am-5.30pm Mon-Sat; 10am-2pm Sun. **Credit** AmEx, MC, V.
In addition to organising parties for the rich and famous (the Prime Minister has utilised them in the past for his kids), Oscar's Den coordinate celebrations for all budgets, and their range of services runs from face-paints to year-round firework displays. Ball ponds, bouncy castles (from £45) and big toys (seesaws, slides, pedal cars and more, from £10) are permanently for hire. *Buggy access. Delivery service.*

Party Party

11 Southampton Road, Gospel Oak, NW5 4JS (7267 9084/www.partypartyuk.com). Chalk Farm tube/Gospel Oak rail/24 bus. **Open** 9.30am-5.30pm Mon-Sat. **Credit** MC, V.
Party Party has a bespoke piñata service, offering any character, animal or object you can think of. A piñata Spiderman or football, for example, can cost from £13-£15, while more unusual, made-to-order designs are around £50 each. They also stock a medley of party bag-fillers along with decorations that encompass everything from themed tableware to mirrorballs. *Buggy access. Delivery service.*

Party Superstore

268 Lavender Hill, Clapham, SW11 1LJ (7924 3210/www.partysuperstore.co.uk). Clapham Junction rail/39, 77, 345 bus. **Open** 9am-6pm Mon-Wed, Fri, Sat; 9am-7pm Thur; 10.30am-4.30pm Sun. **Credit** AmEx, MC, V.
The first floor of the Superstore stocks children's party accessories, fancy-dress costumes (from £7.99), eye-masks and novelty hats (from £1.99) ,and wigs (from £2.99). There are also more than 50 themed tableware collections, many of which are suitable for children, as well as practical jokes, hundreds of balloons, mock jewellery, party bag-fillers, and a collection of cake decorations and candles. *Buggy access. Delivery service. Disabled access. Mail order.*
Branch: 43 Times Square, High Street, Sutton, Surrey SM1 1LF (8661 7323).

Purple Planet

Greenhouse Garden Centre, Birchen Grove, Kingsbury, NW9 8SA (8205 2200/www.purpleplanet.co.uk). Wembley Park rail, then 182, 297 bus. **Open** 10am-5pm Mon-Sat; 10.30am-4.30pm Sun. **Credit** AmEx, MC, V.
Visit the Purple Planet if you want to wow your party guests with your boundless creativity. This wonderful shop has a vast arts and crafts section, and staff run regular card-making workshops and free in-store demonstrations. Many party items are available: helium balloons from 90p, a selection of themed tableware and, most importantly, the fine and beautifully detailed selection of sugarcraft accessories and cookie cutters (90p-£19.99) for which the Planet is known. When it comes to the birthday centrepiece, there's everything you could think of for a truly magnificent cake, from opulent fountain candles (£2.50 each) to edible paint. *Buggy access. Car park. Delivery service. Disabled access: ramp, toilets. Mail order.*

Activities

SPORT & LEISURE

Now jump to it!

TopGolf. *See p259.*

The weighty problems of childhood obesity and lack of fitness have pushed sport and physical education way up the political agenda. Unparalleled resources are at last being spent on improving the health of our children, though it's a damning indictment of government policies over the last 20 or 30 years that it took celebrity chef Jamie Oliver to focus attention on the appalling state of school dinners. Numerous initiatives, such as PESSCL (PE, School Sport and Club Links) and the School Sport Coordinator programme, are designed to make connections between what goes on inside the school gates and the clubs and activities available outside. The government's aim is for all children to receive at least two hours of high-quality PE and sport within and beyond the curriculum, with 75 per cent of schools required to meet that target by 2006.

PESSCL is intended to increase the percentage of five to 16 year-olds who are members of an affiliated sports club from 14 per cent in 2002 to 20 per cent in 2006. This strategy has also compelled clubs to 'raise their game', with a raft of child-protection and development policies to be implemented. If you are looking for a sports club for your children to join, ask whether the club has a child-welfare officer; if not, demand to know why and proceed with caution.

Many sports have implemented a Sport England-backed quality assurance scheme to show that their clubs are 'safe, effective and child-friendly'. Any club that holds, or is working towards, a Clubmark or Charter Standard award will operate to high ethical standards. There will be a structured coaching and matchplay programme with qualified, up-to-date instructors and an ethos that places equal value on all children, not just the most talented. This scheme now allows parents to make informed choices between clubs rather than relying on popularity. To find out more about the Clubmark scheme, check www.sportengland.org.

Things to do

ATHLETICS

If you want to get on in athletics, it helps to be called Kelly. With Holmes and Sotherton up on the medal podium, track and field is seeing something of a resurgence of interest.

The beauty of athletics is that there's an event for everyone. With 18 different disciplines, most children will find at least one they're good at. Many enjoy the popular 'Sportshall' programmes in their schools, which use soft javelins, relay races and specially designed jumping boards to create an exciting two-hour package. The same skills are developed in clubs, where keen athletes will have the chance to join a training group under the guidance of a coach. Membership usually costs around £25-£40 per year, plus a fee for track use.

Maureen Jones (8224 7579) is a senior UK Athletics (www.ukathletics.net) coach who organises 'Run, Jump, Throw' courses during the school holidays at several tracks in south London for children aged eight to 12. The courses run from 10am until 3pm, introduce a whole range of events, and cost £13 per day.

The following clubs also have well-established sections for young athletes.

Belgrave Harriers (Battersea) *Kim Collier (07800 941980/www.belgraveharriers.com).*
Blackheath & Bromley Harriers (Bromley) *John Baldwin (01825 768193/www.bandbhac.org.uk).*
Enfield & Haringey AC (Tottenham/Enfield) *No phone (rayg1@activemail.co.uk/www.enfield-haringeyac.co.uk).*
Havering Mayesbrook AC (Hornchurch/DagenhaQPS *Jean Tierney (01708 341547/www.havering-mayesbrook.org).*
Newham & Essex Beagles AC (Plaistow) *Lesley Richardson (07958 459123/www.newham andessexbeaglesac.co.uk).*
Shaftesbury Barnet Harriers (Barnet) *Joyce Smith (01923 465274/www.sbharriers.co.uk).*
Thames Valley Harriers (Shepherd's Bush) *Kathy Davidson (01895 676513/www.thamesvalley harriers.com).*
Victoria Park Harriers & Tower Hamlets AC (Mile End) *Alf Vickers (07832 251478/www. vphthac.org.uk).*
Windsor, Slough, Eton & Hounslow AC (Windsor/Eton) *Dennis Daly (01753 686169/www.wseh.info).*
Woodford Green AC with Essex Ladies (Woodford) *Keith Hopson (8524 1959/ http://website.lineone.net/~wgel).*

South of England Athletics Association

4th Floor, Marathon House, 115 Southwark Street, SE1 0JF (7021 0988/www.seaa.org.uk).
The SEAA has details of clubs around London. There's also a directory at www.british-athletics.co.uk.

ORIENTEERING

This is a great way to make country walks fun. You navigate your way around a route using a map (and occasionally a compass), collecting points for every station you visit. There are nine courses in London, and more than 40 in the surrounding countryside. Details are online at the **South Eastern Orienteering Association** website (www.post2me.freeserve. co.uk/orienteering). For more information contact the **British Orienteering Federation** (01629 734042/www.britishorienteering.org.uk).

BADMINTON & SQUASH

The success of Nathan Robertson and Gail Emms at the Athens Olympics in 2004 did wonders for badminton's image. Both badminton and squash have excellent junior development programmes; for more information, contact the **Badminton Association of England** (01908 268400/www.badmintonengland.co.uk) or

England Squash (0161 231 4499/www.england squash.co.uk). The respective websites for the sports have club searches.

The following all have junior badminton and/or squash programmes; phone for prices and times.

Dulwich Sports Club *Burbage Road, SE24 9HP (7274 1242/www.dulwichsquash.com). Herne Hill rail.*
New Grampian Squash Club *Shepherd's Bush Road, W6 7LN (7603 4255/www.newgrampians.co.uk). Hammersmith tube.*
New Malden Tennis, Squash & Badminton Club *Somerset Close, New Malden, Surrey KT3 5RG (8942 0539/www.newmaldenclub.co.uk). Malden Manor rail.*
Southgate Squash Club *Walker Cricket Ground, Waterfall Road, N14 7JZ (8886 8381/ www.thewalkerground.org.uk). Southgate tube.*
Wimbledon Racquets & Fitness Club *Cranbrook Road, SW19 4HD (8947 5806/www.wsbc.co.uk). Wimbledon tube/rail.*

BASEBALL & SOFTBALL

Both these sports are attracting more participants because of their excellent range of programmes for kids of both sexes, all ages and abilities. 'Pitch, Hit and Run' and 'Play Ball', for example, teach the basics in schools and clubs to children aged six and over. Check www.playballwithfrubes.com.

For more information, contact **BaseballSoftballUK** (7453 7055/www.baseball softballuk.com). The **London Baseball Association** (www.londonsports.com) also runs skills clinics.

The following clubs have junior programmes.

Essex Arrows (Waltham Abbey) *Phil Chesterton (07890 280118/www.essexarrows.com).*
London Meteors Baseball & Softball Club (Finsbury Park) *Martin Leslie (07866 536312/www.londonmeteors.co.uk).*
Windsor Baseball & Softball Club (Windsor) *John Boyd (07769 655496/www.windsorbaseball.co.uk).*

BASKETBALL

There are basketball clubs all over the capital playing in local leagues, and the sport is extremely well organised at junior level, with competitions right up to national standard. Contact regional development manager Steve Alexander (8968 0051) or the **English Basketball Association** (0870 7744225/www.basketballengland.org.uk). The following clubs have established junior programmes.

Brixton Topcats *Brixton Recreation Centre, Station Road, SW9 8QQ (8699 9872). Brixton tube/rail.*
Croydon Flyers *Lewis Sports Centre, Maberley Road, SE19 2JH (8657 1566/www.croydonflyers.com).*
Hackney Academy *SPACE Centre, Hackney Community College, Falkirk Street, N1 6HF (7613 9278). Old Street tube/243 bus.*

Activities

BOXING

The success of Amir Khan at the Athens Olympics came as a welcome reminder that boxing can be an exciting, disciplined and intelligent activity. The sport at amateur level has an impressive safety record, and youngsters are simply not powerful enough to inflict the sort of damage that has disfigured the professional game. Nor is boxing, as is often claimed, only for those seeking 'a way out of the gutter': heavyweight contender Audley Harrison is a university graduate. Boxing is also making a return to some schools.

To find a local club, contact London regional secretary Keith Walters on 7252 7008 or use the comprehensive search facility on the **Amateur Boxing Association of England**'s website (www.abae.co.uk).

CIRCUS SKILLS

Parents may quail at the thought of their little treasures walking tightropes and dangling from trapezes, but rest assured that the circus schools listed below give safety the highest priority.

Albert & Friends' Instant Circus
8237 1170/www.albertandfriendsinstantcircus.co.uk
Albert the Clown (aka Ian Owen) runs Instant Circus workshops to teach children skills such as juggling, diabolo, stilt-, ball- and wire-walking in an amazingly short time. Many of his students go on to join the Albert & Friends' performing troupe – the UK's largest children's circus theatre, which also tours abroad.

The Circus Space
Coronet Street, N1 6HD (7613 4141/www. thecircusspace.co.uk). Old Street tube/rail.
There's a Sunday morning 'Little Top' course for eight to 11 year-olds; older children can choose static and flying trapeze, juggling, trampoline and acrobatics.

Jackson's Lane Community Circus
Jackson's Lane Community Centre, 269A Archway Road, N6 5AA (8340 5226/www.jacksonslane.org.uk). Highgate tube.
Classes are offered in trapeze, rope-climbing and acrobatics.

CLIMBING

You climb with your head, not just your body – which explains why many of those scaling the capital's excellent climbing centres don't consider themselves conventionally 'sporty'. London's indoor centres all cater for children (aged from around eight) with safe sessions run by qualified instructors. For general information on climbing, contact the **British Mountaineering Council** (0870 010 4878/www.thebmc.co.uk).

Castle Climbing Centre
Green Lanes, N4 2HA (07776 176007/www. geckos.co.uk). Manor House tube.
Overwhelming popularity means that the only way for children to climb here is by private tuition (£35/hr) or at a birthday party (£125 for six children, £225 for up to 12). For both, you'll need to book in advance.

Mile End Climbing Wall
Haverfield Road, E3 5BE (8980 0289/ www.mileendwall.org.uk). Mile End tube.
This centre runs children's beginner sessions every Friday evening (£6.50), skills sessions on Saturday and Sunday mornings (£5.50 and £6.50), plus birthday parties and a summer holiday programme.

Westway Climbing Complex
Westway Sports Centre, 1 Crowthorne Road, W10 6RP (8969 0992/www.westway.org/sports/wsc/ climbing). Latimer Road tube.
This large and impressive indoor centre beneath the Westway challenges all levels of climbing skill, and its big, chunky holds are perfect for kids. There are after-school classes on Wednesdays and Mondays, from 4.30pm to 6pm, costing £3.

CRICKET

England's success, combined with the popularity of Twenty20 matches, has given our domestic cricket scene a major boost. Another encouraging development is the return of the game to central London: a major new cricket centre in Regent's

Activities

Just don't mention rounders...
Softball. See p253.

Park offers one county-standard and five club-standard pitches, served by a large pavilion, and will provide a permanent base for 'Capital Kids Cricket', which was set up in 1991 to encourage school-age children to play. For details, contact Regent's Park on 7486 7905. Contact the following County Board offices to find a club.

Essex (including East London) *01245 254 005/ www.essexcricket.org.uk.*
Hertfordshire *01279 871645/www.hertscricket.org.*
Kent *01227 456886/www.kentsport.org/cricket.cfm.*
Middlesex *7266 1650/www.communigate.co.uk.*
Surrey *7820 5734/www.surreycricket.com.*

For coaching, contact the following indoor centres.
Ilford Cricket School *Sussex Close, Beehive Lane, Ilford, Essex IG4 5DR (8550 0041). Gants Hill tube.*
Ken Barrington Cricket Centre *Brit Oval, SE11 5SS (7820 5739). Oval tube.*
MCC Indoor School *Lord's Cricket Ground, NW8 8QN (7432 1014/www.mcc.org.uk). St John's Wood tube.*
Middlesex County Cricket Club *East End Road, N3 2TA (8346 8020/wwwmiddlesexccc.com). Finchley Central tube.*

CYCLING

Cycle Training UK
7582 3535/www.cycletraining.co.uk
CT's male and female instructors offer individual tuition anywhere in Greater London. Accompanied journeys to school are also available. After attending training, 81% of people said they cycled more often and more confidently.

London Recumbents
8299 6636/www.londonrecumbents.co.uk
Specialists in off-road training in Battersea and Dulwich, London Recumbents stocks a large range of cycles.

London School of Cycling
7249 3779/www.londonschoolofcycling.co.uk
Offering private tuition for all ages and abilities, the London School also runs regular cycle-maintenance workshops.

CYCLE SPORT

Go-Ride is a British Cycling initiative where under-18s can learn track riding, BMX and mountain biking from qualified coaches. It's delivered through a national network of cycling clubs and includes a skills test designed to challenge even the best riders. Clubs involved include Lee Valley Youth Cycle Club (contact Marc Burden on 8558 1112), Team Economic Energy (contact Leslie Everest on 8989 8429) and Sutton Cycle Club (contact Peter Fordham on 8641 2859). The scheme's website (www.go-ride.org.uk) lets you compare test times.

The famous velodrome at Herne Hill remains 'closed until further notice'. Check www.hernehill velodrome.co.uk to see if it has a future.

Hillingdon Cycle Circuit
Springfield Road, Hillingdon (8737 7797). Hayes & Harlington rail.
This tarmac circuit of almost a mile, is popular for road racing and tuition, so it's usually booked in the evenings.

Greenwich Dance Agency.

Lee Valley Cycle Circuit

Quarter Mile Lane, E10 5PD (8534 6085/www.
leevalleypark.com/cyclecircuit). Leyton tube.
This 45-acre (18-hectare) site is known as 'Eastway'. It has
a tarmac track, a mountain bike and BMX circuit, and
Saturday morning sessions for children aged four to 16.

DANCE

Some children love the formality of ballet, but
others prefer more creative contemporary styles,
such as **Biodanza** (a form of dance aiming to
enhance the natural emotions of children). For
class details, call the London School of Biodanza
(8392 1433/www.biodanza.co.uk). Also popular is
the free-spirited approach of **Chantraine Dance
of Expression**, for which there are two centres
in the London area. Classes, for children aged four
and above, take place every day in central London
(contact Patricia Woodall on 7435 4247) and
Wanstead (contact Kate Green on 8989 8604).
The two centres put on a festival every summer.

  Dalcroze Eurhythmics is about experiencing
and expressing music through movement of the
whole body and, in some countries, it constitutes
a fundamental part of musical education. Here,
it's used by the Royal Ballet School. Contact the
Dalcroze Society (8870 1986/www.dalcroze.org.uk)
for more details. The **London Dance Network**
(www.londondance.com) has an extensive
directory of dance venues and organisations.

The following centres all offer classes for kids.

Chisenhale Dance Space *64-84 Chisenhale Road,*
E3 5QZ (8981 6617/www.chisenhaledancespace.co.uk).
Mile End tube.
Danceworks *16 Balderton Street, W1K 6TN*
(7629 6183/www.danceworks.co.uk). Bond Street tube.
Drill Hall *16 Chenies Street, WC1E 7EX (7307*
5060/www.drillhall.co.uk). Goodge Street tube.
East London Dance *Stratford Circus, Theatre*
Square, E15 1BX (8279 1050/www.
eastlondondance.org). Stratford tube/rail.
Greenwich Dance Agency *Borough Hall, Royal Hill,*
SE10 8RE (8293 9741/www.greenwichdance.org.uk).
Greenwich rail.
Hewitt Performing Arts *160 London Road,*
Romford, Essex RM7 9QL (01708 727784).
Romford rail.
Laban *Creekside, SE8 3DZ (8691*
8600/www.laban.org). Deptford rail.
The Place *17 Duke's Road, WC1H 9PY (7387 7669/*
www.theplace.org.uk). Euston tube/rail.
Ravenscourt Theatre School *8-30 Galena*
Road, W6 0LT (8741 0707/www.ravenscourt.net).
Ravenscourt Park tube.
Rona Hart School of Dance *Rosslyn Hall,*
Willoughby Road, NW3 (7435 7073). Hampstead tube.
Tricycle Theatre *269 Kilburn High Road, NW6 7JR*
(7328 1000/www.tricycle.co.uk). Kilburn tube.

FENCING

Most junior classes comprise warm-up activities
to develop co-ordination, flexibility and balance,
formal work (towards the nine fencing grades),

Peter Hucker Soccer.

Kingston Fencing Club *Beverley School, College Gardens, Blakes Lane, New Malden, Surrey (8393 4255/www.kingstonfencing.co.uk). Motspur Park rail.*
Streatham Fencing Club *Dunraven Lower School, Mount Nod Road, SW16 2QB (www.streathamfencing. org). Streatham Hill rail.*

FOOTBALL

More than 45,000 football clubs cater for all standards and ages, and both sexes. When helping your child find a team, make sure that he or she is of the appropriate standard – beware, in other words, of foisting a child who will never be more than an enthusiastic hacker on to a group of high-achievers.

Football has put in place a number of club development and child welfare programmes, so you should also:

● Ask whether the club holds, or is working towards, the FA Charter Mark.

● Ask whether its coaches hold FA qualifications and have received training in child protection and emergency first aid.

● Watch a session to see how well organised it is.

● Find out the number of children in each age group. Some clubs have large memberships, which may mean only the best get to play regularly.

● Consider the atmosphere and ethos: is this 'sport for all' or is winning the priority?

● Are parents yelling advice (and abuse) from the touchline, or are they encouraged to lend a hand and offer more constructive support?

To find a girls' team, contact the **Football Association** (7745 4545/www.TheFA.com/ women). Clubs with extensive girls' development programmes include Arsenal (7704 4140), Charlton Athletic (contact Deb Browne on 8333 4000), Fulham (contact Gary Mulcahey on 8336 7578) and Millwall Lionesses (7740 0503).

All the professional clubs in London run 'Football in the Community' coaching courses, fun days and skills clinics. These are suitable for boys and girls aged from about six upwards and are staffed by FA-qualified coaches. Check the club websites below (details are usually listed under the 'Club' or 'Community' headings) for venues and dates.

Arsenal (7704 4140/www.arsenal.com); **Brentford** (8758 9430/www.brentfordfitc.org.uk); **Charlton Athletic** (8850 2866/www.charlton-athletic.co.uk); **Chelsea** (7957 8220/www.chelsea fc.com); **Crystal Palace** (8768 6096/www.cpfc. co.uk); **Fulham** (0870 442 5432/www.fulham fc.com); **Leyton Orient** (8556 5973/www.leyton

and finally the bit that everyone enjoys best: free fighting. The sport has a strong safety ethic, and no one is ever allowed to participate without full protective clothing, a mask and the supervision of a qualified instructor.

For a full list of clubs around London, contact the **British Fencing Association** (8742 3032) or use the search facility at www.britishfencing.com. The following clubs offer regular junior sessions.

Arena Fencing *Kingston Arena, Kingston Hall Road, Kingston-upon-Thames, KT1 2SG (8399 2440/www.fencingcourses.pwp.blueyonder.co.uk). Kingston rail.*
Brixton Fencing Club *Brixton Recreation Centre, Station Road, SW9 8QQ (7926 9779). Brixton tube/rail.*
Camden Fencing Club *Ackland Burghley School, 93 Burghley Road, NW5 1UJ (7485 8515). Kentish Town tube.*
Finchley Foil Fencing Club *Copthall School, Pursley Road, NW7 2EP (7485 1498). Mill Hill East tube.*
Haverstock Fencing Club *Islington Green School, Prebend Street, N1 8PQ (07811 077048). Angel tube/Essex Road rail.*
King's College School & Wimbledon High School Joint Fencing Club *Southside Common, SW19 4RJ (8255 5300). Wimbledon tube/rail.*

orient.com); **Millwall** (7740 0503/www.millwall fc.co.uk); **Queens Park Rangers** (8740 2509/www.qpr.co.uk); **Tottenham Hotspur** (0870 420 5000/www.spurs.co.uk); **Watford** (01923 496256/www.watfordfc.com); **West Ham United** (0870 112 5066/www.whufc.com).

Similar schemes operate through the County FAs. Contact the following offices for details.

Essex (01245 357727/www.essexfa.com); **Hertfordshire** (01462 677622/www.hertsfa.com); **Kent** (01634 843824/www.kentfa.com); **London** (01959 570183/www.londonfa.com); **Middlesex** (8515 1919/www.middlesexfa.com); **Surrey** (01372 373543/www.surreyfa.co.uk).

A highly rated scheme is run by former Queens Park Rangers goalkeeper Peter Hucker. Based in Barking and Wanstead, it offers weekly pay-and-play coaching sessions, matchplay and football parties for ages five to 16. Hucker also founded the **East London & Essex Small-Sided Soccer League** (07931 901140/www.peter hucker-soccer.com).

There are many commercial football clinics and camps to choose from. An **Ian St John Soccer Camp** (0845 230 0133/www.soccercamps.co.uk) costs £75 for five days (10am-3.45pm) and caters for children aged eight to 15. Other options include **EAC Activity Camps** (0845 113 0022/www.eac-summer-activity-camps.co.uk) and **European Football Camps** (www.footballcamps.co.uk). **Powerleague** (www.powerleague.co.uk) runs nine centres around London for weekend coaching sessions and leagues for all ages.

Parents of football-crazy anklebiters can also try the popular Little Kickers progamme. The classes, developed by a group of FA-qualified coaches and nursery schoolteachers for pre-schoolers (from age two), are a gentle introduction to football. Rather than focusing purely on the beautiful game, the programme is tailored to incorporate a number of early-learning goals. Classes operate all over south and west London. For further information and prices, call Little Kickers (01235 833854) or check the website (www.littlekickers.co.uk).

GOLF

More is being done to recruit and keep young golfers, and bring those who are interested and able through to competition standard. For example, children can now play golf as part of the Duke of Edinburgh's Award. The **English Golf Union** is a useful contact if you want to get started (01526 354500/www.englishgolfunion.org). A driving range is an excellent place to introduce a child to the basics of the game (and the course professional will also offer lessons to help get them into good habits early on).

A fun new approach is offered by **TopGolf** (www.topgolf.co.uk) at its centres in Chigwell (8500 2644), Watford (01923 222045) and, from August 2005, Addlestone (01932 858551). The TopGolf system is based on a point-scoring game using golf balls with a microchip inside them. See the website for more details.

Beckenham Place Park
The Mansion, Beckenham Place Park, Beckenham, Kent BR3 5BP (8650 2292). Beckenham Hill rail.
Juniors can use this course after 2pm. Lessons are available on Saturdays at 11am and cost £3 (booking essential). It costs £10 for juniors to play a round at weekends, £7.50 on weekdays.

Regent's Park Golf & Tennis School
North Gate, Outer Circle, Regent's Park, NW1 4RL (7724 0643/www.rpgts.co.uk). Baker Street tube.
Children who are 'old enough to take instruction' are welcome here (the coaches have taught golf-mad kids as young as five). Membership for juniors is £30; the Saturday afternoon clinic for young golfers costs £5 per hour (book in advance). Club hire is £1.

Activities

Spend it like Beckham

Summer 2005 sees the launch of one of Britain's biggest ever grassroots sports initiatives – and it's hardly surprising that football is the sport it's built around. The **David Beckham Academy** takes one of the game's iconic figures back to within a few miles of his Leytonstone birthplace: the Academy is to occupy a major site on the Greenwich Peninsula, close to the Dome. It will consist of two full-sized pitches, plus classrooms and training facilities employing the latest interactive technology. All that will be missing is old Golden Balls himself.

So who will get to use the Academy? Ten thousand free places each year will be channelled through the Football Foundation, Football Association and the Youth Sport Trust, including 2,000 for schools in the local area. During the 15 weeks of school holidays, the Academy will be open for sporty children aged eight to 15 to attend a five-day training camp. They'll need to save up their pocket money, though. The cost of the camp is a not inconsiderable £250, though each child will receive £200 worth of kit as part of the package. To find out more about the academy, the courses and the fun, visit www.thedavidbeckhamacademy.com.

DRIVING RANGES

A1 Golf Driving Range *Rowley Lane, Arkley, Herts EN5 3HW (8447 1411). Elstree & Borehamwood rail.*
Chingford Golf Range *Waltham Way, E4 8AQ (8529 2409). Chingford rail.*
Cranfield Golf Academy *Fairways Golf Centre, Southend Road, E4 8TA (8527 7692/www.cga-golf.com). Walthamstow Central tube/rail.*
Croydon Golf Driving Range *175 Long Lane, Addiscombe, Croydon, Surrey CR0 7TE (8656 1690/www.golfinsurrey.com). East Croydon or Elmers End rail.*
Dukes Meadows Golf Range *Great Chertsey Road, W4 2SH (8995 0537/www.golflessons.co.uk). Hammersmith tube, then 190 bus.*
Ealing Golf Range *Rowdell Road, Northolt, Middx UB5 6AG (8845 4967). Northolt tube.*
Warren Park Golf Centre *Whalebone Lane North, Chadwell Heath, Essex RM6 6SB (8597 1120). Dagenham Heathway tube.*
World Of Golf *Beverley Way, New Malden, Surrey KT3 4PH (8949 9200/www.worldofgolf-uk.co.uk). New Malden or Raynes Park rail.*

GYMNASTICS & TRAMPOLINING

The **British Amateur Gymnastics Association** (01952 820330/www.baga.co.uk) has around 100,000 members. Through its clubs and schools, sessions for four year-olds and under are based around soft-play equipment and simple games, leading to a series of proficiency awards. As well as a general scheme for boys and girls, there are separate awards for rhythmic gymnastics and sports acrobatics. The **British Trampoline Federation** (01952 820330/www.baga.co.uk) offers a similar structure.

In response to the issue of how and when to teach small children using adult equipment, Bill Cosgrove, a former national gymnastics coach, created **TumbleTots** and, later, **Gymbabes** and **Gymbobs**. Gymbabes is for babies from six months to the crawling stage, TumbleTots is for walkers, and Gymbobs is for school-aged kids up to seven. For details of centres around the country, call 0121 585 7003 or see www.tumbletots.com.

The following clubs offer a range of age-appropriate activities, most offering trampolining as well. Both sports are also available at many public sports centres. Be sure that any club you choose displays a current certificate of inspection by BAGA or the **London Gymnastics Federation** (8529 1142/www.longym.freeserve.co.uk).

Avondale Gymnastics Club *Hollyfield Road, Surbiton, Surrey KT5 9AL (8399 3386/www.avondalegymnastics.co.uk). Surbiton rail.*
Camberwell Gymnastics Club *Artichoke Place, SE5 8TS (7252 7353). Denmark Hill rail.*

Charisma Gym Club *Dulwich College PE Centre, College Road, SE21 7LD (8299 3663/www.charismagymnastics.com). West Dulwich rail.*
East London Gymnastics Club *Frobisher Road, E6 5LW (7511 4488/www.eastlondongym.co.uk). Beckton DLR.*
Heathrow Gymnastics Club *Green Lane, Hounslow, TW4 6DH (8569 5069/www.heathrowgymnastics.org.uk). Hatton Cross or Hounslow West tube/H23 bus.*
Hillingdon School of Gymnastics *Victoria Road, South Ruislip, Middx HA4 0JE (8841 6666/www.hsg-swallows.co.uk). South Ruislip tube.*
North-East London Gymnastics Club *Various venues in north-east London, contact 8983 6799 for details.*
Redbridge School of Gymnastics *Pulteney Road, E18 1TU (8530 3810). South Woodford tube.*
Richmond Gymnastics Centre *Townmead Road, Kew, Surrey TW9 4EL (8878 8682). Kew Gardens rail.*

KARTING & MOTOR SPORTS

Modern karts are easy to get the hang of. There are two pedals (stop and go) and no gearbox to confuse the issue. The karting venues listed below welcome children aged from eight and can be booked for parties. Naturally, safety is of paramount importance and is taken very seriously by those in charge.

Brands Hatch
Fawkham, Longfield, Kent DA3 8NG (01474 872331/www.motorsportvision.co.uk). Swanley rail, then taxi.
Brands Hatch is undoubtedly Britain's most impressive on-track activity venue. There are so many things to do here on two and four wheels, including 'YoungDrive!', which puts your youngster (aged over 13) in control of a Renault Clio.

F1 City
Gate 119, Connaught Bridge, Royal Victoria Dock, E16 2BU (7476 5678/www.f1city.co.uk). Royal Albert DLR.
This kart track is the widest in London. Children who meet the minimum height requirement of 5ft 2in (1.57m) are given their own track times during which to play. The Cadet Club is the place to learn how to kart safely, with the assistance of the crack F1 City racing team.

Playscape Pro Racing
390 Streatham High Road, SW16 6HX (8677 8677/www.playscape.co.uk). Streatham rail.
This centre can be booked for children's parties (over-eights only) or for half-hour taster sessions. Those who become addicted can find out about the Playscape Cadet School, a founder member of the RAC's Association of Racing Kart Schools. The school operates on the first Saturday of each month (8.30am-12.30pm; £30) and students are put through their paces before gaining an RAC racing licence.

MARTIAL ARTS

Most local sports centres will be home to at least one martial arts club; many more are based in church halls and community centres. Look for evidence of a lively but disciplined atmosphere, with well-organised and age-appropriate teaching. Ask the instructor about his or her qualifications – the grading systems used in judo and karate, for example, help to ensure that teachers are of a suitable standard. However, note that a black belt is not a teaching qualification. Also ask for proof of insurance cover: martial arts usually involve physical contact and accidents can happen. What's more, few community facilities extend their insurance to the instructors who rent them.

The following venues offer classes for children in a number of disciplines – call ahead and get the full list before setting off.

Bob Breen Academy

16 Hoxton Square, N1 6NT (7729 5789/ www.bobbreen.co.uk). Old Street tube/rail.
Children aged seven to 16 can learn kickboxing skills and effective self-defence techniques at this well-known and highly respected academy.

The Budokwai

4 Gilston Road, SW10 9SL (7370 1000). South Kensington tube, then 14, 345, 414 bus.
This is one of Britain's premier martial arts clubs, offering judo tuition for children aged six to 12.

Hwarang Academy

St Saviour's Hall, Eton Road, NW3 4SU (7691 2516/www.hwarangacademy.com). Chalk Farm tube.
The Korean martial art of tae kwondo is now an Olympic sport, and youngsters aged eight to 18 can learn its spectacular kicks here.

Jackson's Lane Community Centre

269A Archway Road, N6 5AA (8340 5226/ www.jacksonslane.org.uk). Highgate tube.
Drop-in kung fu classes for children aged six upwards are the speciality at Jackson's Lane.

London School of Capoeira

Unit 1-2, Leeds Place, Tollington Park, N4 3RQ (7281 2020/www.londonschoolofcapoeira.co.uk). Finsbury Park tube/rail.
Kids aged five to 16 can learn the dynamic moves of this ultra-cool Brazilian martial art at this accomplished school. Creative play is a strong element of capoeira, which makes it ideal for this age group.

Even Jonny Wilkinson had to start somewhere. *See p263.*

Activities

Moving East

St Matthias Church Hall, Wordsworth Road,
N16 8DD (7503 3101/www.movingeast.co.uk).
Dalston Kingsland rail.
Judo and aikido (as well as dance) classes for children are held at this peaceful, friendly centre devoted to Japanese martial arts.

School of Japanese Karate (Shotokan International)

Various venues in north London (8368 6249).
Karate is the most popular Japanese martial art in this country. David and Lilian Alleyn run this well-established school and teach children aged six upwards at venues in Southgate, Arnos Grove, Cockfosters, Whetstone, Edmonton and Enfield.

Shaolin Temple UK

207A Junction Road, N19 5QA (7687 8333/
www.shaolintempleuk.org). Tufnell Park tube.
Tufnell Park is where 34th-generation fighting monk Shi Yanzi and several other Shaolin masters now teach traditional Shaolin kung fu, meditation and tai chi, with weekly classes for children included in the programme.

RIDING

Riding lessons and hacks must be booked in advance: ask whether there are 'taster' sessions for newcomers. Riders, whatever their age, should always wear a hard hat (establishments can usually lend one if you don't have your own, sometimes for a small fee) and boots with a small heel, rather than trainers or wellies. Some centres run 'own a pony' days and weeks, and birthday party packages (call for details). Most also cater for riders with disabilities. The rates given are for children and per hour.

Ealing Riding School

Gunnersbury Avenue, W5 3XD (8992 3808/
www.ealingridingschool.biz). Ealing Common tube.
Lessons £18 (group); £24 (individual).
Riders from five upwards can take part in many activities here, including the occasional gymkhana. Lessons are held in an outdoor manège.

Hyde Park & Kensington Stables

Hyde Park Stables, 63 Bathurst Mews, W2 2SB
(7723 2813/www.hydeparkstables.com). Lancaster
Gate tube. **Lessons** £40-£45 (group); £50-£55
(individual). Discounts available.
Children aged five upwards can enjoy an hour-long lesson with patient, streetwise ponies in the glamorous surroundings of Hyde Park – at, needless to say, a suitably grand price.

Lee Valley Riding Centre

Lea Bridge Road, E10 7QL (8556 2629/www.leevalley
park.com). Clapton rail/48, 55, 56 bus. **Lessons** £17.50
(group); £12 (beginners; 30min session Sat, Sun).
The placid ponies enjoy the open spaces of Walthamstow Marshes and delight a devoted band of regulars.

Two wheels good, four wheels bad

London is quite a long way behind cities like Copenhagen, Paris and Berlin in terms of its provision of dedicated cycle paths and its attitude towards human-powered two-wheeled transport. But things are finally changing. The Congestion Charge, for example, has played a part in increasing the numbers of cyclists on the road, in turn raising the importance given to the cyclist by Transport for London.

Several of the winners in the London Cycling Campaign's 2004 London Cycling Awards were projects for children. The prize for Best Community Cycling Initiative was won by the BMX and dirt bike track in Southwark's **Burgess Park** (10am-5pm Mon-Sat), which was largely designed and built by local youngsters. The London Borough of Ealing earned a special commendation for its 'Marketing Cycling' initiative aimed at adults and kids, which incorporates cycle parking, training and bike buddy schemes. The London Borough of Tower Hamlets came out top in the Best Cycling Initiative for Young People with its training scheme.

Safe Routes to Schools (0117 915 0100/ www.saferoutestoschools.org.uk) supports projects that encourage children to cycle and walk to school by improving street design, calming traffic and linking with the National Cycle Network, which opened in 2000. The organisation also offers a number of free publications and a regular newsletter. For more information, see *Cycling in the UK: The Official Guide to the National Cycle Network* by Nick Cotton and John Grimshaw (Sustrans, £14.99). Sustrans is the sustainable transport charity working to create a safer environment for cycling; call 0845 113 0065 or check out www.sustrans.org.uk for details.

The **London Cycling Campaign** (Unit 228, 30 Great Guildford Street, SE1 0HS; 7928 7220/www.lcc.org.uk) acts as an umbrella organisation for local groups, while also working to create a cycle-friendly city. In 2002, the campaign launched a series of 19 maps showing cycling routes throughout the whole of Greater London. These are free, and available from some tube stations, bus garages, sports centres, doctors' surgeries and bike shops, as well as from the 24-hour travel information line (7222 1234). The best guide to family rides around the capital is the *London Cycle Guide* by Nicky Crowther (Haynes, £8.99), published in association with the LCC. The book contains 25 outings of varying difficulty, with maps and route planners.

London Equestrian Centre
*Lullington Garth, N12 7BP (8349 1345/
www.thelondonec.co.uk). Mill Hill East tube.* **Lessons**
£19-£21 (group); £21-£26 (individual; 30min session,
Tue-Sun only).
A busy yard in North Finchley with 30 assorted horses and
ponies. There's a junior members' club for regulars, who
may be able to take part in informal gymkhanas. Pandora's
Bistro on site is great for hungry hackers.

Newham Riding School & Association
*Docklands Equestrian Centre, 2 Claps Gate Lane, E6
6JF (7511 3917). Beckton DLR.* **Lessons** £14 (group).
There is a long waiting list at this much-loved stables,
where the 22 horses and ponies look forward to their regular grazing holidays in suburbia as much as young children (aged from five) look forward to riding them.

Ross Nye's Riding Stables
*8 Bathurst Mews, W2 2SB (7262 3791).
Lancaster Gate tube.* **Lessons** £40.
This is the Hyde Park branch of the Pony Club.
Membership gives many privileges, such as reduced prices
for lessons. Children aged from six can learn to ride here
(instruction takes place in Hyde Park).

Trent Park Equestrian Centre
*Bramley Road, N14 4XS (8363 9005/
www.trentpark.com). Oakwood tube.*
Lessons £19-£25 (group); £32-£34 (individual).
The leafy acres of Trent Park (£25 per hour for hacking
out) and a patient, caring attitude towards young riders
(aged from four) make this a rightly popular place to ride.

Willowtree Riding Establishment
*The Stables, Ronver Road, SE12 0NL (8857 6438).
Grove Park or Lee rail.* **Lessons** from £8 (group);
from £16 (individual).
A friendly local venue with more than 40 horses and
ponies, some of which are pure-bred Arab.

Wimbledon Village Stables
*24A/B High Street, SW19 5DX (8946 8579/
www.wvstables.com). Wimbledon tube/rail.*
Lessons from £35.
Though mainly an adult establishment, this centre has a
small selection of quiet, safe ponies and a popular holiday
scheme (£120 for three afternoons). Riding is on
Wimbledon Common.

RUGBY
League
Rugby league is always thought of as a purely
northern sport, rarely seen outside the M62
corridor. However, the game is steadily building a
profile in the capital. The **London Broncos** and
London Skolars are drawing bigger crowds to
their Super League and National League matches,
while both clubs are working together to introduce
the sport in schools around London.

In junior rugby league the emphasis is on running,
passing, skills and teamwork rather than crunching
tackles and physical contact. And, of course, there's
usually plenty of mud to wallow in.

The Skolars' two junior clubs for kids, Haringey
Hornets and Winchmore Ravens, are run by Alex
Smits, who doubles up as the Rugby Football
League's north London development officer and
the Skolars' first-team coach.

Meanwhile, **South London Storm** run teams
for under-nines to under-18s through three junior
clubs, and **Greenwich Admirals** cater for ten to
15 year olds in their Junior Admirals set-up, from
which several players have been chosen to play
for the London Broncos' junior academy. Sessions
are run by the RFL's south-east London
development officer, who also works with local
schools to encourage interest in the game.

To find out more about the sport in general,
contact the **Rugby Football League** (0113
232 9111/www.rfl.uk.com).
Greenwich Admirals *Jason Henley on 07733
356242/www.greenwichrl.com.*
London Skolars *Alex Smits on 07793 932930.*
South London Storm *David Montero on 07793
726018/www.southlondonstorm.co.uk.*

Union
Already one of the most proactive governing
bodies in a sport with several well-established
programmes for youngsters, the **Rugby Football
Union** (RFU) has a website with a postcode-based
search facility for clubs, and this remains the best
way to find out what's available in your area.
Otherwise, you can just give them a call.

Most rugby union clubs cater for boys and girls
with 'minis' for six year-olds, 'midi rugby' for
under-11s, and 'youth rugby' for ages 13 and
over. Great emphasis is placed on the fun of
handling, passing and running, while the impact
arts of tackling, scrummaging and kicking are
gradually introduced and carefully controlled.
Primary-age children play non-contact 'tag' rugby,
using a belt worn around the waist with two 'tags'
attached. If an opponent removes a tag, possession
switches to the other team. This is an ideal game
for both sexes to play together. Women's and
girls' rugby have made rapid progress in recent
years – England's women are among the world's
leading nations – and many clubs are now fully
integrated with training sessions and matches
for girls. Again, the RFU website is an excellent
source of information.

Rugby Football Union
*Twickenham Stadium, Whitton Road, Twickenham,
Middx TW1 1DS (8892 2000/www.rfu.com).
Twickenham rail.*

Activities

Hampton Heated Open Air Pool. *See p266.*

SKATEBOARDING & BMX-ING

Children still skate for free at traditional haunts like the South Bank, Shell Centre and beneath the Westway, but the centres listed below offer a more structured environment.

Baysixty6 Skate Park

Bay 65-66, Acklam Road, W10 5YU (8969 4669/ www.baysixty6.com). Ladbroke Grove tube. **Membership** £10/yr. **Prices** £7 (4hrs Sat, Sun; 5hrs Mon-Fri); £3 (beginners).
Baysixty6 has revolutionised the London scene. Sheltered beneath the A40, this enormous park includes the capital's only vert ramp, two half-pipes, a long mini ramp and many funboxes, grind boxes, ledges and rails to enjoy.

Harrow Skatepark

Peel Road (behind the leisure centre), Wealdstone, Middx HA3 5BD (8424 1754). Harrow & Wealdstone tube/rail.
Years of abuse have resulted in the slow deterioration of Harrow's many obstacles, but there're still plenty here. The clover-leaf and kidney bowls are ever popular, while the unforgiving concrete half-pipe remains a monumental challenge for more fearless urban athletes.

Meanwhile 3

Meanwhile Gardens, off Great Western Road, W9 (no phone). Westbourne Park tube.
Here are three concrete bowls of varying size and steepness, with no flatland for practising the basics, so beginners may be better off somewhere else. The bowls are linked together from high ground to low, offering the possibility of long, technical lines as well as limb-threatening transfer attempts.

Stockwell Bowl Skatepark

Stockwell Road (behind the Brixton Academy), SW9 (no phone). Brixton tube/rail.
A wonderland constituting a single, unbroken series of bumps, hips, waves, bowls and lips, perfect for sequences of tricks or just good old-fashioned carve-ups. Those seeking fun, pure and simple, will have to try pretty hard not to fall for this place. It has recently been resurfaced with smooth pink concrete.

SKATING

On ice

Session times in London's rinks vary from day to day, as the ice needs regular refreezing and sweeping, but venues are generally open from 10am until 10pm. The prices below include skate hire. For more information about the sport, contact the **National Ice Skating Association** (0115 988 8060/www.iceskating.org.uk).

Alexandra Palace Ice Rink

Alexandra Palace Way, N22 7AY (8365 4386/ www.alexandrapalace.com). Wood Green tube/ Alexandra Palace rail/W3 bus.

Courses for children aged five to 15 run on Saturday mornings and early weekday evenings. Parties are available (phone or check the website for details).

Broadgate Ice Arena
Broadgate Circle, Eldon Street, EC2M 2QS (7505 4068/www.broadgateice.co.uk). Liverpool Street tube/rail.
This tiny outdoor rink is open from late October to April.

Lee Valley Ice Centre
Lea Bridge Road, E10 7QL (8533 3154). Clapton rail.
The disco nights are popular at this well-maintained and warm rink, but it's never too busy as it's hard to get here by public transport.

Michael Sobell Leisure Centre
Hornsey Road, N7 7NY (7609 2166/ www.aquaterra.org). Finsbury Park tube/rail.
Children from four upwards are welcome at this small rink, which runs popular after-school sessions and six-week courses. You can also hold parties here.

Queens
17 Queensway, W2 4QP (7229 0172/www.queensice andbowl.co.uk). Bayswater or Queensway tube.
The disco nights on Fridays and Saturdays are legendary, but beginners and families are also well looked after.

Somerset House
Strand, WC2R 1LA (7845 4600/www.somerset-house.org.uk). Holborn or Temple tube (closed Sun).
Every December (ring for the exact date), the courtyard here is iced over to become the most attractive rink in London, for a limited season only (until January).

Streatham Ice Arena
386 Streatham High Road, SW16 6HT (8769 7771/ www.streathamicearena.co.uk). Streatham rail.

This popular rink offers six-week courses for all ages. There's even a class for 'toddlers' aged up to four (phone or check the website for details).

On tarmac

Every year **Citiskate** teaches hundreds of Londoners how to skate in parks, leisure centres and schools. London's largest skate school, Citiskate also runs skating events for adults and children. Their instructors are all UKISA (United Kingdom Inline Skating Association) qualified; lessons are available seven days a week. Citiskate's weekly Friday Night Skate and Sunday Rollerstrol and group skates (see website for details) are also hugely popular. The group also organises park-based Easy Peasy skate events for children on Saturday mornings.

Citiskate
7731 4999/www.citiskate.co.uk
Private Lessons take place in Hyde Park, Kensington Gardens, Battersea Park, Dulwich Park, Bishops Park, Greenwich Park and Millwall Park. The group skate is every week when the weather is dry and the route is two laps around the park. 'Roller parties' with tuition either in parks or leisure centres (six weeks advance notice is required) can be arranged. Check the website for details.

SKIING & SNOWBOARDING

There's no substitute for real snow, but a few practice turns on a dry slope are useful preparation for the white stuff. Gloves, long sleeves and trousers are compulsory as the surface can deliver a nasty burn should you fall. Also note that if you're thinking of taking a mixed-ability

Activities

Protect our pools

It's a frightening fact that one in five 11 year-olds is unable to swim. In most cases, this is because their parents are also non-swimmers and, due to fear or embarrassment, have never arranged family outings to the local pool. With primary school swimming provision often cut down to a minimum of a single three-week intensive block, it's alarming that such a large number of kids would be unable to save themselves if they fell into deep water.

What makes this situation even worse is the declining stock of swimming facilities in London. According to the **London Pools Campaign** (7690 6662/www.londonpoolscampaign.com), 13 public pools have closed in the capital over the last decade with seven more facing an uncertain future; half of all school pools have gone since the 1970s. High-profile disasters like Clissold Leisure Centre are joined by lost local facilities such as Haggerston Pool in

Hackney and Marshall Street pool in Soho, while Lewisham Council have announced plans to demolish Ladywell Leisure Centre in 2007 – even though it has just undergone a £1.8m refurbishment. The Campaign has the backing of Sport England in its aims to create a London-wide strategy for promoting swimming and to provide funding to help preserve London's threatened pools and lidos.

A **Kids Swim Free** initiative is to be praised, however, as it has helped to get whole families in the swim. The initiative is continuing in five east London boroughs during school holidays after a pilot project brought a 500 per cent increase in pool use. Thirty-four per cent of parents went swimming more often than usual as part of the scheme – and, crucially, most continued to swim when the scheme ended. Find out more from the Greater London Authority (www.london.gov.uk).

group out for an open recreational session, perhaps as a birthday party activity, the minimum requirement is to be able to perform a controlled snowplough turn and use the ski lift. For more information, contact the **Ski Club of Great Britain** (8410 2000/www.skiclub.co.uk).

Bromley Ski Centre
Sandy Lane, St Paul's Cray, Orpington, Kent BR5 3HY (01689 876812/www.c-v-s.co.uk/bromleyski). St Mary Cray rail.
Two lifts serve the 120m (394ft) main slope, and there's also a mogul field and nursery slope. Skiing and snowboarding taster sessions cost £16. Booking is essential.

Sandown Sports Club
More Lane, Esher, Surrey KT10 8AN (01372 467132/www.sandownsports.co.uk). Esher rail.
The 120m (394ft) main slope, 80m (262ft) nursery area and 90m (295ft) snowboarding slope are closed during horseracing meetings. This is a lessons-only venue: tuition is available for seven year-olds upwards (£39/hr or £66 for three 2hr sessions), although special half-hour classes can be arranged for children as young as four (£21).

Snozone
Xscape, 602 Marlborough Gate, Milton Keynes MK9 3XS (0871 2225670/www.xscape.co.uk). Milton Keynes Central rail.
This is one of the UK's largest indoor snow domes, with three slopes (in reality they are joined, so they resemble one wide slope): two at 170m (558ft) and one at 135m (443ft), with button lifts running all the way to the top. The place can feel a bit like a big fridge but beginners couldn't ask for a better environment in which to find their ski legs. Well worth a trip up the M1.

SWIMMING

Tuition
Contact the **Amateur Swimming Association** (01509 618700/www.britishswimming.org) for an exhaustive list of child-friendly swimming clubs in your area.

Dolphin Swimming Club
University of London Pool, Malet Street, WC1E 7HU (8349 1844). Tottenham Court Road tube.
This club teaches aquaphobic children (and adults) to overcome their fear, and has turned many quivering wrecks into confident swimmers. A course of 11 individual half-hour lessons costs £220.

Leander Swimming Club
Balham Leisure Centre, Elmfield Road, SW17 8AN (8673 4494/www.leanderswimmingclub.org.uk). Balham tube/rail.
Named after the Greek mythological character who swam huge distances to visit his lover, Leander runs a programme for children aged seven and above in Balham, Tooting, Crystal Palace and Dulwich. This extends from basic strokes to serious competition.

Little Dippers
0870 758 0302/www.littledippers.co.uk
Weekly and weekend courses in water confidence for parents and babies are offered here. No more than eight babies are in the water at any time, using pools (in Wimbledon, Richmond and the City) chosen for their warm temperature. A six-week course or a weekend costs £65.

Swimming Nature
0870 900 8002/www.swimmingnature.co.uk
Since 1992, Swimming Nature has taught thousands of London children to swim using a controlled, progressively hands-on method. Lessons take place in Brondesbury, Chelsea, Paddington, Regent's Park, Twickenham and Victoria, with courses held to coincide with school terms.

Pools
For more local pools, check the telephone directory.
Barnet Copthall Pools *Great North Way, NW4 1PS (8457 9900/www.gll.org). Mill Hill East tube.*
Three pools and a diving area, with coaching and clubs to join if you fancy taking the plunge.
Brentford Fountain Leisure Centre *658 Chiswick High Road, Brentford, Middx TW8 0HJ (0845 456 2935/www.hounslow.gov.uk). Gunnersbury tube.*
Leisure pool with a 40m (131ft) aquaslide, underwater lighting and wave machine alongside a teaching pool.
Crystal Palace National Sports Centre *Ledrington Road, SE19 2BB (8778 0131/www.gll.org). Crystal Palace rail.*
One of the capital's two 50m (164ft) Olympic-size pools which, along with its excellent diving facilities, now looks to have a secure future.
Goresbrook Leisure Centre *Ripple Road, Dagenham, Essex RM9 6XW (8593 3570). Becontree tube.*
Fountains, cascades and a 60m (197ft) flume combine here with a small area for length swimming.
Hampton Heated Open Air Pool *High Street, Hampton, Middx, TW12 2ST (8255 1116/www.hamptonpool.co.uk). Hampton rail.*
When the sun's shining Hampton's hard to beat.
Ironmonger Row Baths *Ironmonger Row, EC1V 3QF (7253 4011). Old Street tube/rail.*
Take a trip back in time at this 1930s 30m (98ft) pool and Turkish baths (one of only three remaining in London).
Kingfisher Leisure Centre *Fairfield Road, Kingston, KT1 2PY (8546 1042). Kingston rail.*
Super-friendly family centre with a teaching pool and a main pool with beach area and wave machine. Indeed, the Kingfisher was voted 'best for families' in the 2004 Time Out Sport, Health & Fitness Awards.
Latchmere Leisure Centre *Burns Road, SW11 5AD (7207 8004). Clapham Junction rail.*
Lane-swimming main pool, teaching pool and a beach area to laze about in, with wave machine and slide.
Leyton Leisure Lagoon *763 High Road, E10 5AB (8558 8858/www.gll.org). Leyton tube/69, 97 bus.*
A flume, slides, fountains, rapids and cascades bring a splash of colour to otherwise drab Leyton.
Northolt Swimarama *Eastcote Lane North, Northolt, Middx UB5 4AB (8422 1176). Northolt tube.*
You'll find three pools, plus a 60m (197ft) slide and diving boards at Northolt.

Pavilion Leisure Centre *Kentish Way, Bromley, Kent BR1 3EF (8313 9911/ www.bromley.gov.uk). Bromley South rail.*
Pavilion is a large leisure pool with gentle shallows, flumes and a wave machine (plus lane swimming and a separate toddlers' pool).

Queen Mother Sports Centre *223 Vauxhall Bridge Road, SW1V 1EL (7630 5522). Victoria tube/rail.*
Three excellent pools in this refurbished centre mean it's always popular with schoolkids.

Tottenham Green Leisure Centre *1 Philip Lane, N15 4JA (8489 5322). Seven Sisters tube/rail.*
Choose between lane swimming and diving in the main pool or splashing amid the waves and slides in the 'beach pool' at this well-run, perennially popular north London leisure centre.

Waterfront Leisure Centre *High Street, SE18 6DL (8317 5000/www.gll.org). Woolwich Arsenal rail/96, 177 bus.*
Four pools, six slides, waves, rapids and a water 'volcano' in Greenwich's flagship centre.

Open-air swimming

It's just one of those things: when summer arrives, and suddenly the sky is blue and the breeze is warm, all you really want to be doing is having a dip in the great outdoors. Well, before you pack up your beach stuff and join the traffic-clogged motorway, why not try looking a little closer to home? For full details on London's outdoor pools, visit www.lidos.org.uk.

Brockwell Lido *Brockwell Park, Dulwich Road, SE24 (7274 3088/www.thelido.co.uk). Herne Hill rail.* **Open** July, Aug; check website for details. **Admission** check website for details.
This wonderful listed 1930s lido has received £500,000 from the Heritage Lottery Fund for renovation, so its future seems at last to be secure.

Finchley Lido *High Road, N12 0AE (8343 9830/www.gll.org). East Finchley tube.* **Open** 6.45am-9.30pm Mon-Fri; 8am-4.30pm Sat, Sun. **Admission** £3.25; £1.95 5-16s; free under-5s.
There are two indoor pools here, but it's the outdoor pool and sun terrace that make it so popular in summer.

Hampstead Heath Swimming Ponds *Men & women's ponds: Millfield Lane, N6. Gospel Oak rail. Mixed pond: East Heath Road, NW3. Hampstead Heath rail. Both: 7485 4491.*
Children need to be aged eight and over, able to swim at least 25m (82ft) and accompanied by an adult in the water. Admission is free for the meantime but, despite a local outcry at plans to charge, it seems highly likely that they will do so from June 2005.

Oasis Sports Centre *32 Endell Street, WC2H 9AG (7831 1804). Tottenham Court Road tube.* **Open** 7.30am-9pm Mon-Fri; 9.30am-5.30pm Sat, Sun. **Admission** £3.30; £1.30 5-16s; free under-5s.
This 28m (92ft) outdoor pool in the heart of the city is open all year round.

Pools on the Park *Old Deer Park, Twickenham Road, Richmond, Surrey TW9 2SF (8940 0561/ www.springhealth.net). Richmond rail.* **Open** 6.30am-10pm Mon-Fri; 8am-9pm Sat, Sun. **Admission** varies, phone to check.
A 33m (108ft) heated indoor pool (and one the same size and temperature outside), plus a sunbathing area.

David Lloyd Leisure. *See p209.*

Activities

Tooting Bec Lido *Tooting Bec Road, SW16 1RU (8871 7198). Streatham rail.* **Open** *Late May-Aug* 6am-8pm daily. *Sept* 6am-5pm daily. *Oct-Mar* 7am-2pm daily (club members only). **Admission** phone to check. At 94m by 25m (308ft by 82ft), this is the second-largest open-air pool in Europe. Its art deco charms attract the crowds in summer.

Water polo

'Aquagoal' is a version of this game with amended rules for ten year-olds upwards. The aim is to score goals in your opponent's net – but without touching the side or bottom of the pool. It's a great challenge for good swimmers and a fun way to keep fit. Contact the **Amateur Swimming Association** (01509 618700/www.british swimming.co.uk) for general information about the sport. The **National Water Polo League** website (www.nwpl.co.uk) has useful contacts.

TABLE TENNIS

There's a mini renaissance going on in kids' table tennis. Twenty weekend junior leagues are now running in the capital, while links with sports colleges such as Langdon School in Newham and the Ealing duo of Compton and Featherstone are producing some high-quality players. There are several clubs around the capital offering coaching for youngsters, and a competitive system to feed into. Contact the **English Table Tennis Association** (01424 722525/www.english tabletennis.org.uk).

TENNIS

Comedian Tony Parks is co-founder of 'Tennis for Free' (TFF), a campaign to give access without charge to Britain's 33,000 public courts – and

Ice, ice baby

Sitting up in the stands at a football match or beyond the boundary at cricket, it can be hard to feel the intensity of what's happening on the pitch. At an ice hockey match, though, you can press your nose right up to the protective glass surrounding the rink so that when one player bodychecks an opponent the action is – thump! crash! – literally right in your face.

The **London Racers** (www.londonracers.com) play in Britain's top competition, the Elite League, with matches at Lee Valley Ice Centre (*see p265*) on Friday or Sunday evenings from September to April. The club is proud of its family-friendly venue, nicknamed 'the Bike Shed', and the players are always approachable for a chat or an autograph before play gets underway. Many are from America or Canada, but there's an increasing amount of home-grown talent on the roster (Britain doesn't compete against the world's major nations but is still a force in Europe). Six players per team are on the ice at any time, with rolling substitutions throughout the three 20-minute periods. Heard the old joke about going to watch a fight and an ice hockey match broke out? Well, there usually is at least one decent scrap to get the juices flowing.

Children love the rough, tough action and the good-natured rivalry between fans, though they'll have to watch carefully – the puck moves at lightning speed.

Romford Raiders (www.romforddraiders.co.uk) play in the lower-level English Premier League; **Haringey Greyhounds** (www.haringeygreyhounds.co.uk) and the once-famous **Streatham Redskins** (8769 7771) compete in the English National League South. All three usually take to the ice on Sunday evenings. For details of matches, call or check their websites; for a list of rinks, *see p264*.

Activities

encourage long-overdue change in this country's tennis culture. TFF attracted more than 1,500 players to a clutch of pilot projects held in 2004 and aims to create ten new Tennis for Free sites around the UK during 2005. To find out more, visit www.tennisforfree.com.

Most London boroughs run holiday courses at Easter and in the summer: contact your local sports development team (details in the phone book or on the council website) or nearest public library for details. The **Lawn Tennis Association** (7381 7000/www.lta.org.uk) publishes free, comprehensive guides giving contacts for hundreds of private clubs and public courts listed by borough or county, along with contact details for local development officers. Details of tennis holidays are also available.

Clissold Park Junior Tennis Club

Clissold Park Mansion House, Stoke Newington Church Street, N16 9HJ (7254 4235). Stoke Newington rail/73 bus. **Open** *Apr-Sept* 10am-7.30pm Mon-Thur; 4-8pm Fri; 8.30am-3.30pm Sat; 8.30am-2.30pm Sun. *Oct-Mar* 10am-3pm Mon-Thur; 8.30am-3.30pm Sat; 8.30am-2.30pm Sun. **Court hire** £5.50/hr. Reduced rate available for under-16s, phone to check availability.
The LTA paid for resurfacing the four hard courts and four mini tennis courts at what was Britain's first City Tennis Centre. Rackets of all sizes and balls are free to borrow. The club is active with squads, coaching, club competitions and teams participating in the Middlesex League. Other City Tennis Centres are at Highbury Fields (contact Rob Achille on 7697 1206), St Mark's Park, Kensington (contact Peter Quek on 8968 2630), and Eltham Park South, Greenwich (contact Steve Johnston on 07767 383629 or Jan Wootten on 8921 8088).

David Lloyd Leisure

0870 888 3015/www.davidlloydleisure.co.uk
There are 11 David Lloyd clubs in the London area, combining tennis with upmarket fitness facilities. They're not cheap, but all are very family-friendly – check out the website or phone for your nearest venue.

Islington Tennis Centre

Market Road, N7 9PL (7700 1370/www.aquaterra. org). Caledonian Road tube. **Open** 7am-11pm Mon-Thur; 7am-10pm Fri-Sat. **Court hire** *Indoor* £17.50/hr; £7.00/hr 5-16s. *Outdoor* £7.80/hr; £3.90/hr 5-16s.
Developed under the LTA's Indoor Tennis Initiative, this centre offers excellent subsidised coaching on a membership or 'pay as you play' basis. Short tennis and transitional tennis for youngsters learning the basics of the game are also available.

Redbridge Sports & Leisure Centre

Forest Road, Barkingside, Essex IG6 3HD (8498 1000/ www.rslonline.co.uk). Fairlop tube. **Open** 9am-11pm Mon-Fri, Sun; 9am-9pm Sat. **Court hire** *Indoor* £18.40; £8.50 5-16s. *Outdoor* £7; £3.50 5-16s.
Developed over more than three decades and nine phases by an independent charitable trust, this outstanding multi-sports centre has eight indoor and 18 outdoor courts, which

you can use as a member or 'pay as you play'. Excellent holiday activities for six to 14 year-olds include one-day and week-long courses for beginners and improvers, together with two-hour 'fun play' sessions. There's also a short tennis club for under-eights and an excellent development programme.

Sutton Junior Tennis Centre

Rose Hill Recreation Ground, Rose Hill, Sutton, Surrey SM1 3HD (8641 6611/www.sjtc.org). Morden tube. **Open** 7am-10.30pm daily. **Court hire** *Indoor* £16.50; £12 5-16s. *Outdoor* £7-£12; £5-£8 5-16s.
Set up more than a decade ago, this is now the top tennis school in Britain with high-quality performance coaches. There are residential courses for full-time players seeking professional status and a scholarship scheme linked with Cheam High School. Children can start at three with Tiny Tots classes, move on to mini tennis, join in holiday programmes and book tennis birthday parties. There are six clay, ten acrylic and 11 indoor courts, so the centre is accessible all year round. Membership enables you to book cheaper courts in advance.

Westway Tennis Centre

1 Crowthorne Road, W10 6RP (8969 0992/ www.westway.org). Latimer Road tube. **Open** 8am-10pm Mon-Fri; 8am-8pm Sat; 10am-10pm Sun. **Court hire** *Indoor* £15.25-£20; £7.75-£9.50 5-16s. *Outdoor* £8-£9; £5-£7 5-16s.
Also the product of the LTA's Indoor Tennis Initiative, Westway follows a similar model to Islington (*see above*) – excellent subsidised coaching, short tennis and transitional tennis. There are eight indoor and four outdoor clay courts – the only ones in London open to the public.

TENPIN BOWLING

The **British Tenpin Bowling Association** (8478 1745/www.btba.org.uk) governs this accessible and fun sport for all ages. There's a network of regional and national tournaments and leagues for youngsters keen to progress towards the magical 'perfect score' of 300.

All the centres listed are open seven days a week, typically 10am to midnight. Admission prices vary according to the time of day, but average around £5-£6 per game – which includes the hire of soft-soled bowling shoes. Phone for details of children's parties.

Acton Megabowl *Royal Leisure Park, Western Avenue, W3 0PA (8896 0707/www.megabowl.co.uk). Park Royal tube.*
Airport Bowl *Bath Road, Harlington, Middx UB3 5AL (8759 7246/www.airport-bowl.co.uk). Hatton Cross tube.*
AMF Bowling Lewisham *11-29 Belmont Hill, SE13 5AU (0845 658 1272/www.amfbowling.co.uk). Lewisham rail/DLR.*
Bexleyheath Megabowl *Albion Road, Bexleyheath, Kent DA6 7AG (0871 550 1010/www.megabowl.co.uk). Bexleyheath rail.*
Dagenham Bowling *Cook Road, Dagenham, Essex RM9 6XW (8593 2888/www.dagenhambowling.co.uk). Becontree tube.*

Activities

Feltham Megabowl *Leisure West Complex, Browells Lane, Feltham, Middx TW13 6EQ (0871 550 1010/www.megabowl.co.uk). Feltham rail.*
Funland *The Trocadero, 1 Piccadilly Circus, W1D 7DH (7395 1704/www.funland.co.uk). Piccadilly Circus tube.*
Hollywood Bowl Finchley *Leisure Way, High Road, N12 0QZ (8446 6667/www.hollywoodbowl.co.uk). East Finchley tube, then 263 bus.*
Hollywood Surrey Quays *The Mast Leisure Park, Teredo Street, SE16 7LW (7237 3773/ www.hollywoodbowl.co.uk).*
Queen's Ice Bowl *17 Queensway, W2 4QP (7229 0172). Bayswater tube.*
Rowans Bowl *10 Stroud Green Road, N4 2DF (8800 1950/www.rowans.co.uk). Finsbury Park tube.*
Streatham Megabowl *142 Streatham Hill, SW2 4RU (8678 6007/www.megabowl.co.uk). Streatham Hill rail.*

WATER SPORTS

To quote that great waterman Ratty, 'There's nothing – absolutely nothing – half so much worth doing as simply messing about in boats.'

Rowing

Rowing is far from an elitist sport: many of Britain's top oarsmen and -women were educated at landlocked state schools. Children can start from the age of 11 and, if they are keen and show ability, progress through the National Junior Rowing Programme. For details of clubs, contact the **Amateur Rowing Association** (8237 6700/ www.ara-rowing.org).

Canalside Activity Centre
Canal Close, W10 5AY (8968 4500). Ladbroke Grove tube or Kensal Rise rail/52, 70, 295 bus. **Open** *Enquiries & bookings* 10am-5pm Mon-Fri; 10am-4pm Sat. Closed mid Dec-mid Jan, bank hols. **Prices** *Classes & sessions* members free; non-members from £4. *Membership* £60/yr 9-19s. **No credit cards.**
Canalside is an unpretentious urban watersports centre, open to families, carers and children. It aims to promote health and education through learning to row, canoe and be safe in the water. Qualified instructors run the courses and lessons.

Globe Rowing Club
Trafalgar Rowing Centre, Crane Street, SE10 9NP (8852 1847/www.globe.cwc.net). Cutty Sark DLR/ Maze Hill rail. **Open** Phone for details.
This friendly Greenwich-based club is particularly good value, with membership for under-16s just £4 a month.

Lea Rowing Club
Spring Hill, E5 9BL (Mark Padfield 07771 556130/club house 8806 8282/www.learc.org.uk). South Tottenham or Stamford Hill rail. **Open** 10am-noon Sat.
Membership £60/yr; £20/term.
Lea offers rowing and sculling for kids aged ten-plus who can swim at least 50m (164ft), plus school holiday courses.

Sailing

Children start off learning the basics in a one-person dinghy such as a Topper or Laser Pico. Clubs will usually supply all the necessary kit, from vessel to wetsuit. A beginners' course recognised by the **RYA** (Royal Yachting Association) can be covered in a weekend. Details from 0845 345 0400 or at www.rya.org.uk.

Albany Park Canoe & Sailing Centre
Albany Mews, Albany Park Road, Kingston-upon-Thames, Surrey KT2 5BB (8549 3066/www.albany park.co.uk). Kingston rail. **Open** 9am-5pm daily (phone to check). **Prices** vary; phone for details.
This Kingston sailing centre hires out both single and crew dinghies. Training courses are available for adults and children. Kayaking and open canoeing are also on offer.

BTYC Sailsports
Birchen Grove, NW9 8SA (8731 8083/ www.btycsailsports.org.uk). Neasden or Wembley Park tube. **Open** *Apr-Sept* 6-10pm Tue; 5.30-10pm Thur; 9.30am-dusk Sat. **Membership** £195/yr; £60/yr 8-17s.
This centre began life as the British Transport Yacht Club but the initials remained when the organisation went public. Dinghy sailing, windsurfing, basic training and RYA courses on the Welsh Harp reservoir are offered to members. Family membership is available. Harp Young Sailors is a scheme run jointly by the clubs on the Welsh Harp, offering racing and coaching for children aged eight to 17; details from Rob O'Neill on 8202 8677.

Dockands Sailing & Watersports Centre
Millwall Dock, 235A Westferry Road, E14 3QS (7537 2626/www.dswc.org). Crossharbour DLR. **Open** *Oct-Easter* 8.30am-5pm daily. *Easter-Sept* 8.30am-midnight daily. *Kids' club* 10am-1pm Sat. **Membership** £110/yr; £20/yr concessions. *Kids' club* £3/day.
Canoeing, dragonboat racing, windsurfing and dinghy sailing for over-eights who are confident in the water. There's a restaurant and bar, plus activities for people with disabilities. Youth membership costs just £20, family membership £220.

Fairlop Sailing Centre
Forest Road, Hainault, Ilford IG6 3HN (8500 1468/ www.fairlop.org.uk). Fairlop tube. **Open** *Apr-Sept* 9am-6pm Mon-Thur (also 7-9pm until 16 Sept); 9.30am-4pm, 7-9pm Fri; 10am-1pm, 2-4pm Sat. *Oct-Easter* 9.30am-4pm Mon-Fri; 10am-1pm Sat (also 2-4pm until 26 Nov). **Prices** vary; phone for details.
This Royal Yachting Association- and British Canoe Union-approved centre is managed by Redbridge Education Service and offers 40 acres (16ha) of water with two islands, all of it situated in a pleasant country park. Windsurfing, dinghy sailing, canoeing and powerboating courses for adults and children are all available (phone or check the website for times). The friendly staff run splashy kids' birthday parties (£84 for up to 12 children aged at least eight) using open canoes or bellboats.

Activities

Queen Mary Sailing Club & Sailsports

Queen Mary Reservoir, Ashford Road, Ashford, Middx TW15 1UA (01784 248881/www.queenmary.org.uk). Ashford rail. **Open** *Oct-Apr* 9am-5.30pm Wed-Sun. *May-Sept* 9am-6pm daily (sometimes closes later, phone to check). **Prices** vary; phone for details.
A club with a sailing school that hires out a wide range of dinghies, Queen Mary has an active youth programme, as well as sailing facilities for people with disabilities. You can also learn to windsurf here.

Royal Victoria Dock Watersports Centre

Gate 5, Tidal Basin Road, off Silvertown Way, E16 1AF (7511 2326/www.victoria-dock.com). Royal Victoria Dock DLR. **Open** 4.30-6pm Tue, Wed-Thur; 9.15-10.45am, 11am-12.30pm, 1.30-3pm, 3.15-4.45pm Sun. **Prices** vary; phone for details.
The calm waters of Victoria Dock are a great place to master dinghy sailing and tackle an RYA beginners' course. The centre runs a 'Youth on H2O' scholarship scheme and a busy holiday programme. Junior membership (under-18) costs between £45 and £60.

Shadwell Basin Outdoor Activity Centre

3-4 Shadwell Pierhead, Glamis Road, E1W 3TD (7481 4210/www.shadwell-basin.org.uk). Wapping tube. **Open** *Term-time* 5.30-8.30pm Wed, Thur; 10.30am-4.30pm Sun. *School hols* 10.30am-4.30pm Mon-Fri. **Prices** £1.80/evening; £2.50/day.
Downriver from Tower Bridge, this multi-activity centre offers fairly priced sailing, canoeing, kayaking, dragonboating, bellboating and powerboating for children aged nine and over.

Surrey Docks Watersports Centre

Greenland Dock, Rope Street, SE16 7SX (7237 4009). Surrey Quays tube. **Open** 9am-5pm daily. **Prices** vary; phone for details.
Sailing, windsurfing and canoeing for over-eights take place in the sheltered dock throughout the school holidays and half-terms; RYA courses available. It may be a bit of a trek to get out here but, once you're bobbing about in a canoe, it's undoubtedly worth it.

Westminster Boating Base

136 Grosvenor Road, SW1V 3JY (7821 7389/ www.westminsterboatingbase.co.uk). Pimlico tube. **Open** 11am-9pm Mon-Thur, Sun. Closes earlier during winter. **Prices** donations requested.
This splendid charitable training centre located in the heart of London offers canoeing and sailing for over-tens on the tidal Thames. There's no fixed fee for youth membership; instead, the Base asks for a donation according to personal circumstances. Members enjoy training courses, longer trips on the river and weekends further afield.

West Reservoir Centre

Stoke Newington West Reservoir, Green Lanes, N4 2HA (8800 6161). Manor House tube. **Open** Phone to check. **Prices** vary; phone for details.

This is a purpose-built environmental education and watersports centre situated within a Site of Metropolitan Importance for conservation. A good place to learn the basics of dinghy sailing.

Waterskiing

John Battleday Waterski

Thorpe Road, Chertsey, Surrey KT16 8PH (0870 606 1270/www.jbwaterski.com). Chertsey or Virginia Water rail. **Open** *Summer* 9am-dusk daily. *Winter* noon-dusk Wed, Sat, Sun. **Prices** vary; phone for details.
World championship medallist John Battleday runs this weekend kids' club for five to 12 year-olds.

YOGA

An exciting new addition to the London yoga scene is the **Special Yoga Centre** (*see below*). This registered charity is the UK home for Yoga for the Special Child, a US/Brazil-based programme that offers one-to-one work with infants and children with a range of special needs, including Down's Syndrome, cerebral palsy, spina bifida, autism, epilepsy, ADD/ADHD, and other physical and development difficulties. It also runs training programmes in yoga for the special child, a teacher training course, and outreach classes in schools for kids with behavioural problems.

The therapeutic aspect of yoga is also explored at the **Yoga Therapy Centre** (*see below*), which runs weekly sessions for children with asthma. The big stretches of some positions help to unknot the chest muscles and assist with controlled breathing and relaxation. Yoga Bugs, created by Fenella Lindsell for three to seven year-olds, has also done much to promote yoga for children. There are now more than 200 trained **Yoga Bugs** teachers working in nursery, prep and primary schools. The classes also run at several venues in central and south-west London. Details from www.yogabugs.com.

The following centres offer children's classes.

Holistic Health *64 Broadway Market, E8 4QJ (7275 8434/www.holistic-health-hackney.co.uk). London Fields rail.*
Iyengar Institute *223A Randolph Avenue, W9 1NL (7624 3080/www.iyi.org.uk). Maida Vale tube.*
Sivananda Yoga Vedanta Centre *51 Felsham Road, SW15 1AZ (8780 0160). Putney rail.*
Special Yoga Centre *Pember House, Pember Road, NW10 5LP (8933 5475/www.specialyoga.org.uk). Kensal Green tube.*
Triyoga *6 Erskine Road, NW3 3AJ (7483 3344/www.triyoga.co.uk). Primrose Hill rail.*
Yoga Junction *Unit 24 City North, Fonthill Road, N4 3HF (7263 3113/www.yogajunction.co.uk). Finsbury Park tube/rail.*
Yoga Therapy Centre *90-92 Pentonville Road, N1 9HS (7689 3040/www.yogatherapy.org). Angel tube.*

Activities

Disability sport

The high profile earned by Paralympians like Tanni Grey-Thompson and Danny Crates is long overdue. However, the broad term 'disability sport' also encompasses activities for young people with learning disabilities. A number of organisations have responsibilities in this area. Meanwhile, the **Inclusive Fitness Initiative** is helping to redevelop public sports and fitness facilities to include accessible equipment (0114 257 2060/www.inclusivefitness.org).

Would-be footballers can join the **National Multi-Disabled Football League**; details of clubs and junior squads are available at www.disabilityfootball.co.uk.

The **Back-Up Trust** (details on 8875 1805/ www.backuptrust.org.uk), a charity working with people paralysed through spinal cord injury, runs multi-activity weeks for kids aged 13 to 17. Canoeing, abseiling, wheelchair basketball and rugby are among the sports offered.

More programmes are run by **British Blind Sport** (01926 424247/www.britishblindsport. org.uk) and the **British Deaf Sports Council** (www.britishdeafsportscouncil.org.uk). The former English Sports Association for People with Learning Disability is now run by **Mencap Sport** (01924 239955).

London Sports Forum for Disabled People

7354 8666/Minicom 7354 9554/www. londonsportsforum.org.uk.
This is the London wing of the English Federation of Disability Sport (www.efds.co.uk).

Wheelpower

01296 395995/www.wheelpower.org.uk.
This is the umbrella body for 17 wheelchair sports, from archery to rugby.

Things to watch

CRICKET

Middlesex
Lord's Cricket Ground, St John's Wood Road, NW8 8QN (Middlesex 7289 1300/www.middlesexccc.com; MCC 7432 1000/www.lords.org). St John's Wood tube.
Admission £10-£15 adults; £5-£7.50 children. Phone for details of free kids' days.
Middlesex are in the First Division of both the County Championship and the National League. Lord's is a magnificent venue to watch a game – even when only a few hundred spectators are present for a county match – and any child interested in cricket will be thrilled to attend.

Surrey
Brit Oval, SE11 5SS (7582 7764/www.surreyccc.co.uk). Oval tube. **Admission** £10.
Now emerging from the throes of a major redevelopment programme, the Oval is a world-class ground with fewer airs and graces than Lord's. Surrey are traditionally one of the major forces in the County Championship although they are playing in the Second Division of the National League in 2005. Their squad is crammed with internationals, including England's Graham Thorpe and Mark Butcher and Indian spinner Harbhajan Singh.

FOOTBALL

As we go to press, **West Ham United**'s possible promotion to the Barclays Premiership still hangs in the balance.

Barclays Premiership
Arsenal *Arsenal Stadium, Avenell Road, N5 1BU (7704 4040/www.arsenal.com). Arsenal tube.*
Charlton Athletic *The Valley, Floyd Road, SE7 8BL (8333 4010/www.charlton-athletic.co.uk). Charlton rail.*
Chelsea *Stamford Bridge, Fulham Road, SW6 1HS (0870 300 2322/www.chelseafc.com). Fulham Broadway tube.*
Fulham *Craven Cottage, Stevenage Road, SW6 6HH (0870 442 1234/www.fulhamfc.com). Putney Bridge tube.*
Tottenham Hotspur *White Hart Lane, Bill Nicholson Way, 748 High Road, N17 0AP (0870 420 5000/www.spurs.co.uk). White Hart Lane rail.*

Coca-Cola Championship
Crystal Palace *Selhurst Park, Park Road, SE25 6PU (0871 200 0071/www.cpfc.co.uk). Selhurst rail*
Millwall *The Den, Zampa Road, SE16 3LN (7231 9999/www.millwallfc.co.uk). South Bermondsey rail.*
Queens Park Rangers *Rangers Stadium, South Africa Road, W12 7PA (0870 112 1967/www.qpr.co.uk). White City tube.*
Watford *Vicarage Road, Watford, WD18 0ER (0870 111 1881/www.watfordfc.com). Watford High Street rail.*
West Ham United *Boleyn Ground, Green Street, E13 9AZ (0870 112 2700/www.whufc.com). Upton Park tube.*

Coca-Cola League
Brentford *Griffin Park, Braemar Road, Brentford, Middx TW8 0NT (8847 2511/www.brentfordfc.co.uk). Brentford rail. Division 1.*
Leyton Orient *Matchroom Stadium, Brisbane Road, E10 5NE (8926 1010/www.leytonorient.com). Leyton tube. Division 2.*

GREYHOUND RACING

Romford Stadium
London Road, Romford, RM7 9DU (01708 762345/www.trap6.com/romford). Romford rail.
Admission £1.50-£6; free under-14s (accompanied by adult). **Racing** 7.30pm Mon, Wed, Fri; 1.49pm Thur; 11am, 7.30pm Sat.

Walthamstow Stadium

Chingford Road, E4 8SJ (8498 3311/www.ws greyhound.co.uk). Walthamstow Central tube. **Admission** £1-£6. **Racing** 7.45pm Thur, Tue; 7.30pm Sat.

Wimbledon Stadium

Plough Lane, SW17 0BL (8946 8000/www.wimbledon stadium.co.uk). Wimbledon Park tube. **Admission** £5.50; £2.75 6-14s; free under-6s. **Racing** 7.30pm Tue, Fri, Sat.

HORSE RACING

The **Racecourse Association** website (www.britishracecourses.org) is an excellent resource for novice race-goers. It has details of and links to all the British courses, as well as a full calendar and previews of major meetings.

Admission prices stated below are for adults attending regular meetings; children go free. Note that Ascot racecourse (www.ascot.co.uk) reopens in June 2006 following refurbishment. And one last word of advice: whatever you do, don't forget to pack a picnic.

Epsom Downs

Racecourse Paddock, Epsom, Surrey KT18 5LQ (01372 726311/www.epsomderby.co.uk). Epsom Downs rail. **Admission** £5-£18.
The grassy Lonsdale Enclosure is ideal for a picnic – though probably not on Derby day, when around 150,000 people are attracted to one of the great occasions in Britain's sporting calendar.

Kempton Park

Staines Road East, Sunbury-on-Thames, Middx TW16 5AQ (01932 782292/www.kempton.co.uk). Kempton Park rail. **Admission** £9-£20.
There's a playground and crèche at this busy course, while the grandstand includes a food hall with the parade ring and winners' enclosure just behind.

Sandown Park

Esher Station Road, Esher, KT10 9AJ (01372 470047/www.sandown.co.uk). Esher rail. **Admission** £15-£35.
This frequent winner of 'Racecourse of the Year' (a well-respected accolade awarded by the Racegoers Club, the largest club of its kind in the country) is attractively sited in a natural amphitheatre. The Park Enclosure is the best place for a family outing.

Windsor

Maidenhead Road, Windsor, Berks SL4 5JJ (0870 220 0024/www.windsor-racecourse.co.uk). Windsor & Eton Riverside rail. **Admission** £6-£20.
One of Britain's most picturesque courses holds two 'Sunday Fundays' each year and a series of popular summer evening meetings. On a fine day, this can be a great place for keeping the kids happy, while managing to place a couple of bets yourself.

RUGBY LEAGUE

London Broncos

Griffin Park, Braemar Road, Brentford, Middx TW8 0NT (0871 222 1657/www.londonbroncos.co.uk). Brentford rail. **Admission** £12-£18 adults; £5 5-16s; free under-5s.
A host of family-oriented entertainment accompanies the Engage Super League games. The season runs from March to October and games are on Saturday or Sunday afternoon or early evening, depending on TV coverage. Phone or check the website for details.

London Skolars

New River Stadium, White Hart Lane, N22 5QW (8888 8488/www.skolars.com). Wood Green tube, then W3, W4 bus. **Admission** £10 adults; £5 5-16s; free under-5s.
The Skolars are the capital's other professional club, playing in Division 2 of the National League. Games are usually on Sunday afternoon.

RUGBY UNION

Zurich Premiership

Saracens *Vicarage Road, Watford, Herts WD18 0EP (01923 475222/www.saracens.com). Watford tube/Watford High Street rail.* **Admission** £11-£22 adults; £5-£10 5-16s.

National League

Blackheath *Rectory Field, Charlton Road, SE3 8SR (8858 1578/www.blackheathrugby.co.uk). Blackheath rail.* **Admission** £10 adults; £5 5-16s; free under-5s. Division 2.

Harlequins *Stoop Memorial Ground, Langhorn Drive, Twickenham, Middx TW2 7SX (0871 871 8877/www.quins.co.uk). Twickenham rail.* **Admission** £15-£35 adults; £5-£15 5-16s; free under-5s. Division 1.

London Welsh *Old Deer Park, Kew Road, Richmond, Surrey TW9 2AZ (8940 2368/www.london-welsh. co.uk). Richmond tube/rail.* **Admission** £12 adults, accompanied children free (prices subject to change, phone to check). Division 1.

Rosslyn Park *Priory Lane, SW15 5JH (8876 6044/ www.rosslynpark.co.uk). Barnes rail.* **Admission** £8; £4 under-16s. Division 2.

STOCK CAR & BANGER RACING

Wimbledon Stadium

Plough Lane, SW17 0BL (01252 322 920/ www.spedeworth.co.uk). Wimbledon Park tube. **Admission** £11 adults; £5 children.
Sunday night meetings at Wimbledon Stadium are entertaining for all ages. Anything can happen when the stock cars and bangers get out on the track – and it usually does. 'Racing' is not the most important thing for the drivers, nor for the spectators. What really matter are the crashes.

Activities

TWO FOR ONE OFFERS

We're offering two tickets for the price of one at some of London's best-known theatres for children, plus you'll be able to go down to the Hop Farm Country Park, get artistic at one of Art 4 Fun's three branches, or save money on books at Bookworm Ltd. Just use the vouchers below.

Art 4 Fun

2 for the price of 1 on Studio fee only.
Offer valid 1 June 2005 to 31 May 2006.

Bookworm Ltd

Offer valid from 1 July 2005 to 31 December 2005.

Chicken Shed Theatre

Offer valid on children's tickets for Tales from the Shed performances.

Hop Farm Country Park

Offer valid for 2 children's tickets until 30 September 2005.
(Offer excludes the KM War & Peace Show, Monster Mania and music events.)

Little Angel Theatre

Offer valid on all shows. Maximum 6 tickets per show.

Tricycle Theatre

Offer valid for Saturday shows only from 1 September 2005 to 31 May 2006.

Art 4 Fun
Offer valid in all 3 branches
Various venues (head office 8449 6500/ www.art4fun.com). **Studio fee** £15.
Children simply pick their pot, mug or tile and get busy painting their masterpieces. The creations are fired in the shop and picked up a few days later - great fun for all ages.

Bookworm Ltd
1177 Finchley Road, Temple Fortune, NW11 0AA (8201 9811). Golders Green tube.
Open 9.30am-5.30pm Mon-Sat; 10am-1.30pm Sun.
Get two for the price of one on books at this great shop, which stocks everything from reference books for projects such as 'The Victorians' or 'The Romans' to the very latest fiction. *See p187.*

Chicken Shed Theatre
Chase Side, Southgate, N14 4PE (box office 8292 9222/www.chickenshed.org.uk).
Cockfosters or Oakwood tube. **Shows** £4-£18.50.
For nearly ten years, Tales from the Shed has enticed the under-7s into its world of make-believe through magical storytelling, colourful characters and songs. *See p222.*

Hop Farm Country Park
Beltring, Paddock Wood, Kent TN12 6PY (01622 872068/www.thehopfarm.co.uk.)
Open 10am-5pm daily. **Admission** £7.50; £6.50 concessions, 3-15s; £27 family (2+2); free under-3s. Prices vary on event days.
This former working hop farm is now home to a giddying number of family-fun possibilities – from children's playgrounds and play barns to go-karts, crazy golf and rides on dray carts. *See p278.*

Little Angel Theatre
14 Dagmar Passage, off Cross Street, Islington, N1 2DN (box office 72261787/www.littleangel theatre.com). Angel tube/Highbury & Islington tube/rail. **Tickets** £7.50-£8.50; £5-£6 under-16s.
Expect performances covering a huge range of styles and just about every kind of puppet under the sun at London's only permanent puppet theatre. *See p218.*

Tricycle Theatre
269 Kilburn High Road, Kilburn, NW6 7JR (box office 7328 1000/www.tricycle.co.uk). Kilburn tube/Brondesbury rail. **Shows** 11.30am, 2pm Sat.
Tickets Theatre (Sat) £5; £4 advance bookings.
At the Tricycle Theatre you'll find a programme of lively, colourful theatrical performances – often incorporating puppets, vivid costumes and masks, plus a good dose of audience participation. *See p215.*

DAYS OUT

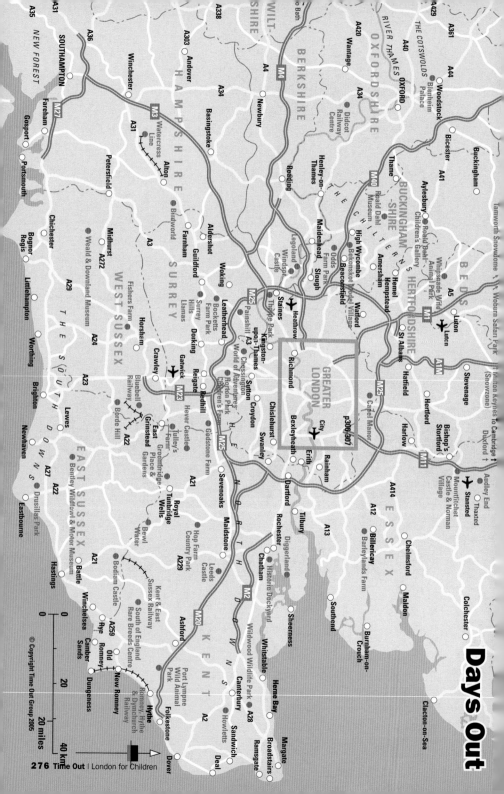

Days Out

0   10   20   40 km

0   10   20 miles

DAYS OUT

Beyond the city limits.

Just a short journey on the train or a quick thrash up the motorway is all it takes to transport you and your family to a world of green fields and hedgerows, grand estates and forbidding castles, and even the occasional llama. For details on London's mainline train stations, *see p291*. For information on how to get to specific attractions, consult individual listings.

CASTLES

Bodiam Castle

Nr Robertsbridge, East Sussex TN32 5UA (01580 830436/www.nationaltrust.org.uk). **Getting there** *By rail* Robertsbridge rail, then taxi or local rider bus (Sat only). *By car* J5 off M25. **Open** *Mid Feb-Oct* 10am-6pm or dusk daily. *Nov-mid Feb* 10am-4pm or dusk Sat, Sun. Last entry 1hr before closing. **Tours** groups (min 15 people) by prior arrangement; phone for details. **Admission** (NT) £4.40; £2.20 5-16s; £11 family (2+3); free under-5s. **Credit** AmEx, MC, V.

Built in 1385 by Edward Dalyngrigge, Bodiam Castle was ransacked during the Civil War and, until the 20th century, its overgrown ruins were attended by no one but a handful of Romantic painters and poets. There's no roof to speak of, which should discourage visits in the driving rain, but the towers and turrets still offer sweeping views across the Rother Valley. Activities for families take place throughout the school holidays – events are listed on the website (weekly storytelling, armour-trying sessions, evening 'bat watches' and the like).
Buggy access. Café. Car park (£2). Disabled access: toilet. Nappy-changing facilities. Nearest picnic place: castle grounds. Restaurant. Shop.

Hever Castle

Nr Edenbridge, Kent TN8 7NG (01732 865224/ www.hevercastle.co.uk). **Getting there** *By rail* Edenbridge Town rail, then taxi, or Hever rail, then 1-mile walk. *By car* J5 or J6 off M25. **Open** *Gardens* Mar-Oct 11am-6pm daily (last entry 5pm). Nov 11am-4pm daily. *Castle* Mar-Oct noon-6pm (last entry 5pm daily). Nov noon-4pm daily. **Tours** groups (min 20 people) by prior arrangement. **Admission** *Castle & gardens* £9.20; £7.70 concessions; £5 5-14s; £23.40 family (2+2); free under-5s. *Gardens only* £7.30; £6.30 concessions; £4.80 5-14s; £19.40 family (2+2); free under-5s. **Credit** MC, V.

The childhood home of Anne Boleyn, this 13th-century castle was restored in the early 20th century by Waldorf Astor. Stuffed with Tudor furnishings, the interiors display a number of waxwork scenes, and a gruesome weaponry display, as well as Anne Boleyn's illuminated *Books of Hours*. The main attraction, however, is the great outdoors: Hever's idyllic gardens have mazes galore (*see p282* **Get lost!**) and throughout the school holidays they host various family events and attractions, such as the always delightful Merrie May festival, Easter egg hunts, Christmas fairs, and, most popular of all, jousting and archery events.
Buggy access (grounds only). Car park. Disabled access: ramps, toilets (grounds only). Nappy-changing facilities. Restaurants. Shops.

Leeds Castle

Maidstone, Kent ME17 1PL (01622 765400/ www.leeds-castle.com). **Getting there** *By car* J8 off M20/A20. *By rail* Bearsted rail. **Open** *Castle* Apr-Oct 11am-5.30pm daily. Nov-Mar 10.15am-5pm daily. Last admission at 3.30pm. *Gardens & attractions* Nov-Mar 10am-3.30pm daily. Apr-Oct 10am-5pm daily. **Tours** pre-booked groups only. **Admission** £13; £11 concessions; £9 4-15s; £39 family (2+3); free under-4s. **Credit** MC, V.

Erected soon after the Norman Conquest, lovely Leeds has been immaculately maintained throughout the ages, and to this day the sight of its towers reflected in the moat is as evocative as it must have been centuries ago. Inside, magnificent halls and chambers await, as do various historical displays (from the Heraldry Room to the unique Dog Collar Museum), but it's the outdoor wonderland that we love. A walk around the gardens and grounds is inspirational; leave time to lose yourself in the famous maze (*see p282* **Get lost!**) and clock the birdlife. The riverside pathways bustle with black swans and peacocks, while more exotic birds can be pondered in the aviaries. Bird walks, when curators and aviary staff tell visitors about the collection, take place daily (check the website). Regular falconry displays star birds of prey including Jack, the only free-flying Augur Buzzard in the UK. In all, about 20 to 30 birds (including vultures, eagles and a laughing kookaburra) oblige with displays choreographed to music by castle falconers. Also worth a look is the nearby Museum of Kent Life (01622 763936, www.museum-kentlife.co.uk).
Buggy access. Car park. Disabled access: lift, toilet. Nappy-changing facilities. Nearest picnic place: grounds. Restaurant. Shops.

Mountfitchet Castle & Norman Village

Stansted Mountfitchet, Essex CM24 8SP (01279 813 237/24hr information line 0906 470 0898/ www.mountfitchetcastle.com). **Getting there** *By rail* Stansted Mountfitchet rail. *By car* J8 off M11. **Open** *12 Mar-12 Nov 2005* 10am-5pm daily. **Admission** £6; £5.50 concessions; £5 2-14s; free under-2s. *House on the Hill Toy Museum* £4; £3.50 concessions; £3.20 2-14s; free under-2s. 10% discount if visiting both on same day. **Credit** MC, V.

The 11th-century Mountfitchet Castle today is reduced to isolated piles of rubble, although a 'working' Norman village has been constructed on the original site to give some indication of life more than 900 years ago. Thus the many buildings scattered around the original motte date from the 1980s and are populated by waxwork figures going about their daily business. There's a host of tame animals, including fallow deer, Jacob sheep (an ancient breed kept by the Normans) and poultry. Respect to Melvin, the monster Black Orpington chicken – he's a local celebrity because he's so massive. So is Bertie the Brahma cockerel, who's been on the telly because he's so tall. They clearly feed them well up Mountfitchet way. The adjoining House on the Hill Toy Museum is also great for younger kids, with more than 80,000 exhibits from the Victorian era through to the 1980s. The website lists a whole range of school-holiday events.

Café (castle). Disabled: toilet (castle). Nappy-changing facilities. Nearest picnic place: grounds. Shops.

Windsor Castle

Windsor, Berks SL4 1NJ (01753 868286/ www.royal.gov.uk). **Getting there** *By rail* Windsor & Eton Riverside rail. *By car* J6 off M4. **Open** Mar-Oct 9.45am-5.15pm daily (last entry 4pm). Nov-Feb 9.45am-4.15pm daily (last entry 3pm). **Admission** (LP) £12.50; £10.50 concessions; £6.50 5-16s; £31.50 family (2+3); free under-5s. *Audio guide* £3.50. **Credit** AmEx, MC, V.
As a working royal residence, Windsor Castle is more formal (if less crumbly) than other seats across the country, and the often overwhelming queues can put a dampener on younger imaginations (it pays to pre-book). Kids with any kind of historical interest will be rewarded, however, as the castle houses a unique collection of art and artefacts. The State Apartments are furnished with works by Rembrandt, Gainsborough and Rubens, and a unique collection of medieval weaponry and armour is on display in the Grand Vestibule, the Queen's Guard Chamber and St George's Hall. Unfortunately, the biggest queue tends to be reserved for the exhibit most likely to appeal to younger kids: the unfeasibly intricate Queen Mary's Dolls' House, created by Sir Edward Lutyens in 1924 on a scale of one to 12. It was intended as an accurate record of contemporary domestic design and it remains perfect, from the working water and electrics to the handmade wool rugs and genuine vintage wine, bottled in miniature in the cellar. For a moment's peace, head outside to the Jubilee Garden, St George's Chapel (it contains the tombs of ten monarchs including Henry VIII and, more recently, the Queen Mum) or Windsor Great Park, whence the view of the castle is just stunning. But keep the proximity of Legoland (*see p288*) a secret or peace will become pestering in a trice.
Buggy access/storage. Disabled access: lift, toilet. Nappy-changing facilities. Nearest picnic place: grounds. Shops.

COUNTRY ESTATES

Borde Hill

Balcombe Road, Haywards Heath, West Sussex RH16 1XP (01444 450326/www.bordehill.co.uk). **Getting there** *By rail* Haywards Heath rail, then taxi. **Open** 10am-6pm or dusk (if earlier) daily. **Admission** £6; £5 concessions; £3.50 3-15s; free under-3s. *Season ticket* £18; £12 3-15s. **Credit** AmEx, MC, V.
It may be a 200-acre (80-hectare) country estate with one of the UK's most comprehensive collections of trees and shrubs from around the world, but Borde won't leave the children bored. As well as rare plants from China, Burma and the Himalayas, the Garden of Allah and nearby Azalea Ring, a traditional English rose garden with picturesque

woodland walks, there's an extensive adventure playground, the best in the area, with a cowboy fort, pirate ship, swings, slides and an obstacle course. A pond is set aside for children's fishing classes at weekends and during school holidays (10am-4pm; £4/hr including equipment hire). A new 'photographic treasure trail' and a woodland trail are both fun to follow. Various family events are organised at Borde Hill throughout the year (check the website for a complete list).
Buggy access. Café. Disabled access: toilet. Nappy-changing facilities. Nearest picnic place: grounds. Restaurant. Shop.

Groombridge Place Gardens & Enchanted Forest

Groombridge Place, Groombridge, nr Tunbridge Wells, Kent TN3 9QG (01892 861444/www. groombridge.co.uk). **Getting there** *By rail* Tunbridge Wells rail, then 290, 291 bus or taxi. *By car* B2110 off A264 off A21. **Open** *April-early Nov* 9.30am-6pm or dusk (if earlier) daily. **Admission** £8.50; £7.20 concessions; £7 3-12s; £29.50 family (2+2); free under-3s. **Credit** MC, V.
The setting for Joe Wright's new film of *Pride and Prejudice*, the Groombridge estate is a magical place for families. No small part of this is due to the Enchanted Forest, a wonderland of giant swings, the Dark Walk adventure trail, and Jurassic Valley, peppered with dinosaur footprints. Elsewhere are more formal gardens, but they're no less playful: the Drunken Garden, for example, has asymmetrical topiary leaning as if intoxicated, or you can have a game on a giant chessboard. New for 2005 is a Stegosaurus foraging in the undergrowth around Dinosaur Pool, and a castle with battlements and a prison. All through the school holidays, kids are treated to a variety of fun and games (phone or check the website for details).
Buggy access (limited). Café. Car park (free). Disabled access. Nappy-changing facilities. Nearest picnic place: grounds. Shop.

Hop Farm Country Park

Beltring, Paddock Wood, Kent TN12 6PY (01622 872068/www.thehopfarm.co.uk). **Getting there** *By rail* Paddock Wood rail, then (peak times only) shuttle bus. *By car* J5 off M25, then A21 south. **Open** 10am-5pm daily. **Admission** £7.50; £6.50 concessions, 3-15s; £27 family (2+2); free under-3s. Prices vary on event days. **Credit** MC, V.
Kent's largest tourist attraction was once a working Hop Farm. Now its oast houses store an interactive museum harking back to the glory days, as well as a giddying number of family fun possibilities – children's playgrounds and play barns, go-karts, crazy golf, petting corners and rides on dray carts pulled by lofty shire horses. Its diary remains full all year round, so you're unlikely to visit during any school holiday without becoming embroiled in some sort of special event. Summer 2005, for example, will offer the world's largest military vehicle show, as well as Storyland (during which children's characters come to life) and a series of themed activity weeks for the long school holidays. There's also monster-truck racing on 20 and 21 August, a model aircraft show in September and Hallowe'en specials from 24-30 October, followed by November fireworks.
Buggy access. Car park (free). Cafés. Disabled access: toilet. Nappy-changing facilities. Nearest picnic place: grounds. Shop.

Bekonscot Model Village. *See p286.*

Painshill Landscape Garden

Painshill Park Trust, Portsmouth Road, Cobham, Surrey KT11 1JE (01932 868113/www.painshill.co.uk). **Getting there** *By rail* Cobham or Esher rail. *By car* J10 off M25. **Open** *Mar-Oct* 10.30am-6pm Tue-Sun, bank hols (last entry 4.30pm). *Nov-Feb* 11am-4pm Wed-Sun, bank hols (last entry 3pm). **Admission** £6; £5.25 concessions; £3.50 5-16s; £18 family (2+2); free under-5s. **Credit** MC, V.

Painshill consists of 160 acres (65 hectares) of subtle and surprising vistas created by Charles Hamilton in the 18th century. The Landscapes – which include a vineyard, Chinese bridge, crystal grotto, Turkish tent, a newly restored hermitage and a Gothic tower – are a work of art that influenced the future of England's countryside. Family events take place on Sundays and bank holidays throughout the year. For information on activities based around kite-making, horse and carriage driving, Punch and Judy shows, a model boat demonstration entitled 'Battle on the Lake', and a birds of prey demonstration, check the website. *Buggy access. Café. Car park. Disabled access: toilet. Nappy-changing facilities. Nearest picnic place: grounds. Shop.*

ENCOUNTERS WITH ANIMALS

Farms

Barleylands Farm Centre & Craft Village

Barleylands Road, Billericay, Essex CM11 2UD (01268 532253/www.barleylands.co.uk). **Getting there** *By rail* Billericay rail. *By car* J29 off M25. **Open** *Farm Centre* 1 Mar-31 Oct 10am-5pm daily. *Craft village* 1 Mar-31 Oct 10am-5pm Tue-Sun. **Admission** £3; £10 family. **Credit** MC, V.

The nostalgic character of Barleylands is concentrated in the area known as the Farm Collection, which has more than 2,000 exhibits of vintage tractors, plough engines, drills, balers and other ancient pieces of earth-tilling paraphernalia. The Craft Village is where glassblowers, woodturners and blacksmiths show off their skills. Children love the chickens, rabbits and turkeys near the picnic area; larger animals, including ponies, cows and pigs, graze out near the pond. There's also an activity playground and stables, plus tractor rides, a bouncy castle, giant trampolines and an equally vast sandpit. The Essex Steam and Country Show takes place here each year (10-11 Sept 2005) and has a steam fair, heavy horses, demonstrations of rural crafts, food stalls and all kinds of amusements for kids. Consult the website or give them a call for details of the precise events scheduled for 2005. *Buggy access. Café. Car park. Disabled access: toilet. Nappy-changing facilities. Nearest picnic place: grounds.*

Bocketts Farm Park

Young Street, Fetcham, nr Leatherhead, Surrey KT22 9BS (01372 363764/www.bockettsfarm.co.uk). **Getting there** *By rail* Leatherhead rail, then taxi. *By car* J9 off M25. **Open** 10am-6pm daily. **Admission** £5.40; £4.95 concessions, 3-17s; £3.95 2s; free under-2s. **Credit** MC, V.

Sitting pretty in a valley in the glorious North Downs, Bocketts is a working farm that goes a bundle on play. Sheepdogs take time out from sheep work to show off their agility, and lambs, chicks and calves stagger about winsomely, eliciting 'aahs' from adoring children. Other attractions include pony and tractor rides, astroslides, sandpits, a trampoline and a children's birthday party service. The café, situated in a handsome 18th-century building, is a fine place for lunch. *Buggy access. Café. Car parking (free). Disabled access: toilet. Nappy-changing facilities. Nearest picnic place: grounds. Shop.*

THE HOP FARM
Something for everyone

Visit the Hop Farm, Kent's most popular family attraction, where exhibitions featuring Kent's rural history combine with family fun and a huge programme of special events creating the best day out!

+ Shire Horses and animal farm
+ Indoor and outdoor play areas
+ Pottery activity room*
+ Award winning museums and exhibitions
+ Restaurant and gift shop
+ Crazy golf, bouncy castle and sandpit
+ Over 30 special events throughout the year including Motor Shows, Food & Drink Festival, the KM War and Peace Show and Themed Holiday Weeks

*small extra fee applies

The Hop Farm Country Park
Paddock Wood, Kent 01622 872068
www.thehopfarm.co.uk

Travel by Train and save up to 50% - just ask for the all-in-one ticket to the Hop Farm at all South Eastern Train Stations.

2005

---

children's fun at

BORDE HILL
GARDEN · PARK · WOODLAND

SUMMER FUN FOR CHILDREN
August Weekdays 2pm - 5pm

Kids activities from Magic, Clowns, Karaoke, Pottery, Tractor Rides, Fishing, Theatre and much more!

Bring a picnic

Garden, Playground, Gift Shop and Tea Room open daily all year 10am - 6pm (or dusk)
Balcombe Road, Haywards Heath, West Sussex RH16 1XP
Tel: 01444 450326 www.bordehill.co.uk

With five new attractions including three new rides, there's never been a better year to visit LEGOLAND® Windsor! It's easily reached by road via the M3 and M4 and trains run direct from London Waterloo to Windsor & Eton Riverside Station.

£5 OFF*
Entry to LEGOLAND® Windsor
*Terms and conditions apply

Voucher Valid to 5th November 2005*

300063

LEGOLAND® WINDSOR

Save up to £25

5 NEW ATTRACTIONS INCLUDING 3 NEW RIDES

Fishers Farm

New Pound Lane, Wisborough Green, West Sussex RH14 0EG (01403 700063/www.fishersfarmpark. co.uk). **Getting there** *By rail* Billingshurst rail, then taxi. *By car* J10 off M25. **Open** 10am-5pm daily; ring for times during special events. **Admission** *Nov-Mar* £6.50; £6 3-16s; £2.75 2s. *Apr-Oct* £9.50; £9 3-16s; £5.75 2s. *Summer hols* £10.50; £10 3-16s; £6.75 2s; £41 family. **Credit** MC, V.

National Farm Attraction of the Year, Fishers Farm is a vast family fun area with added animals, including, this season, two soft-coated alpacas. The well-appointed Barn Theatre hosts a daily 'meet the animals' event as well as occasional magic, clown and marionette shows in the school holidays and an annual panto at Christmas. Once all the animals have been met, children can make the most of the playgrounds, trampolines and bouncy castles. There are also miniaturised pedal tractors and, in summer months, a giant paddling pool with sandy shores, the Forgotten Farm Adventure golf course, an animated ghost tunnel and an inflatable combine-harvester slide.
Buggy access. Cafés. Car park. Disabled access: toilet. Nappy-changing facilities. Nearest picnic place: grounds. Restaurants. Shops.

Godstone Farm

Tilburstow Hill Road, Godstone, Surrey RH9 8LX (01883 742546/www.godstonefarm.co.uk). **Getting there** *By rail* Caterham rail, then 409 bus. *By car* J6 off M25. **Open** *Mar-Oct* 10am-6pm daily. *Nov-Feb* 10am-5pm daily. **Admission** £5.50 2-16s (accompanying adult free); free under-2s. **Credit** MC, V.

Always good for the small, cuddly end of the agricultural scene, Godstone is particularly rewarding come spring, when wobbly lambs careen around the paddocks and fluffball chicks bask in the incubators' glow. The pre-schoolers love it. Children with their hearts set on something altogether less profound can chase each other across the adventure playground, the biggest, allegedly, in south-east England, and the little ones lose themselves in the ball pools and on the walkways that make up the play barn. There's also a new slide and a crow's nest to climb on. Godstone has a sister in Epsom, Horton Park (01372 743984/www.hortonpark.co.uk).
Buggy access. Café. Car park (free). Disabled access: toilet. Nappy-changing facilities. Nearest picnic place: grounds. Shop.

Odds Farm Park

Wooburn Common, nr High Wycombe, Bucks HP10 0LX (01628 520188/www.oddsfarm.co.uk). **Getting there** *By rail* Beaconsfield rail, then taxi. *By car* J2 off M40 or J7 off M4. **Open** *Early Feb-mid July, early Sept-late Oct* 10am-5.30pm daily. *Mid July-early Sept* 10am-6pm daily. *Late Oct-mid Feb* 10am-4.30pm daily. Closed 19 Dec 2005-2 Jan 2006. **Admission** £6; £5 2-16s; £3.50 special needs; free under-2s. **Credit** MC, V.

Odds Farm was created with small children in mind, so expect plenty of activities that will interest them: feeding the chickens; rabbit world; piggies' tea-time; and tractor and trailer rides. Some activities are dependent on the time of year (sheep-shearing, for example, is between May and July). Seasonal events – notably Easter egg hunts, Hallowe'en pumpkin carving and an encounter with Father Christmas – take place in the relevant school holidays. Several outdoor play areas form focal points for the many birthday parties held at Odds all year round (phone for more information), but also make a nice spot for kids to amuse themselves while parents linger over a picnic.
Buggy access. Café. Car park. Disabled access: toilet. Nappy-changing facilities. Nearest picnic place: grounds. Shop.

South of England Rare Breeds Centre

Highlands Farm, Woodchurch, nr Ashford, Kent TN26 3RJ (01233 861493/www.rarebreeds.org.uk). **Getting there** *By rail* Ashford rail, then taxi. *By car* J10 off M20. **Open** *Apr-Sept* 10.30am-5.30pm daily. *Oct-Mar* 10.30am-4.30pm Tue-Sun. **Admission** £6; free under-3s. **Credit** MC, V.

Operated by the Canterbury Oast Trust, a charity dedicated to the care and occupational development of adults with physical and learning difficulties, these 120 woodland acres (49 hectares) host a breeding programme for animals once common to the British Isles, but now endangered. There are unusual species of goat, cattle and poultry to spot, among them Butch and Sundance, the pigs otherwise known as the Tamworth Two, who escaped from an abattoir and went on the run in January 1998. Other attractions include pens where children can play with piglets and small animals, and a large number of play activities (the Mysterious Marsh Woodland Adventure is a particularly impressive adventure playground). During school holidays racing piglets scurry around a track, and there are activity quiz trails, scavenger hunts and 25-minute tours of the farm on tractors and trailers. For inclement weather, there's an indoor play barn and an activity marquee used for 'make and do' school holiday fun.
Buggy access. Café. Car park (free). Disabled access: toilet. Nappy-changing facilities. Nearest picnic place: grounds. Shop.

Treks

Surrey Hills Llamas

Guildford, Surrey (01483 890555/www.surrey-hills-llamas.co.uk). **Getting there** *By rail* Guildford or Chilworth rail, then transport arranged for trekkers. **Admission** *Day Picnic/pub lunch* treks from £55 adults; £28 over-8s. *Family Picnic trek* £140 (2+2). *Summer evening walks* £28. **Credit** MC, V.

Go on a Surrey Hills trek and your companion will be affectionate, well-groomed and South American. A llama, in fact. These are traditionally beasts of burden, but the Guildford posse live the life of pampered pets, with only your picnic (included in the price) to carry. They wear a headcollar and you hold the lead rope as you walk beside them on a day-long guided tour through woods and pastures in an Area of Outstanding Natural Beauty. Llamas are affectionate creatures, and you can become quite attached to them, particularly on camping trips.
Buggy access. Disabled access.

Wildlife reserves

Birdworld

Holt Pound, Farnham, Surrey GU10 4LD (01420 22140/www.birdworld.co.uk). **Getting there** *By rail* Farnham rail, then taxi or 18 bus. *By car* J4 off M3, A325 & follow signs. **Open** *Mid Feb-Oct* 10am-6pm daily. *Nov-mid Feb* 10am-4.30pm daily. **Admission** £9.95; £7.95 concessions, 3-14s; £32.50 family (2+2), free under-3s. **Credit** MC, V.

Feathered friends from all over the world are gathered together in aviaries and enclosures across Birdworld's 26 acres (11 hectares). Britain's biggest bird park also goes underwater with a tropical aquarium, while the on-site Jenny Wren farm allows visitors to meet rabbits, lambs, horses, donkeys and a variety of poultry. The best way to get an overview of all the residents is on a guided 'safari train'. Penguin-feeding displays take place at 11.30am and 4pm daily; book in advance (£6.50) for a chance to feed them yourself. The Heron Theatre takes young birds from their enclosures to perform natural tricks for a seated audience (1pm, 3pm). Special events take place throughout the year, including the 'Myths and Legends' and 'Jungle Adventure' activity weeks (15-19 Aug 2005), plus Hallowe'en shenanigans in the October half-term and a Santa's grotto for Christmas.
Buggy access. Café. Car park (free). Disabled access: toilet. Nappy-changing facilities. Nearest picnic place: grounds. Restaurant. Shop.

Drusillas Park

Alfriston, East Sussex BN26 5QS (01323 874100/ www.drusillas.co.uk). **Getting there** *By rail* Polgate or Berwick rail, then taxi. *By car* M23, then A23, then A27. **Open** *Apr-Oct* 10am-6pm daily. *Nov-Mar* 10am-5pm daily. Last entry 1hr before closing. **Admission** £11; £10 2-12s; free under-2s. **Credit** MC, V.

A wonderfully child-friendly little zoo, Drusillas focuses on interactive involvement, conservation and fun fact-finding. Its naturalistic animal enclosures, innovative design and low-level viewing (most famously demonstrated in the meerkat mound) enable children to get nose-to-nose with nature. Animal residents include lemurs, prairie dogs, otters, marmosets, macaques and (less cuddly) crocodiles, snakes, bats and insects. There's also a petting farm, plus frequent special events such as birds of prey demonstrations and safaris. Kids are given free animal-spotter books for easy identification, and can join in activities, such as panning for gold, crazy golf and workshops. There are also a number of playgrounds for all ages. Check the website for details of party packages, animal-adoption schemes and the unbeatable experience of letting your child be a junior keeper for the day.
Buggy access. Cafés. Car park (free). Disabled access: toilet. Nappy-changing facilities. Nearest picnic place: grounds. Restaurant. Shops.

Howletts Wild Animal Park

Bekesbourne, nr Canterbury, Kent CT4 5EL (01227 721286/www.totallywild.net). **Getting there** *By rail* Bekesbourne rail, then 30min walk or shuttle bus available in peak times (call or consult website for info); Canterbury East rail, then taxi. *By car* M2, then A2. **Open** *Nov-Mar* 10am-dusk daily (last entry 3pm).

Get lost!

The oldest maze (open to the public) in the land is also the most famous: it is, of course, at **Hampton Court** (see p147). Planted between 1689 and 1694, it's deceptively complicated, and all too easy to get lost in. Larger than the Hampton Court Maze, the Marlborough Maze at **Blenheim Palace** (Woodstock, Oxon OX20 1PX, 0870 0602080/www.blenheimpalace.com) used to be the world's largest until the Peace Maze at Castlewellan Forest Park in Northern Ireland was opened in 2001. The Marlborough (a hedge maze with wooden bridges, and brick and stone pavilions) was designed by Fisher and Coate in 1991. It has two entrances, left and right, with a central exit. The two wooden bridges create a three-dimensional puzzle, as well as giving tantalising views.

After the Marlborough, the maze at **Leeds Castle** (see p277) seems like small beer, but it's an unusual piece of landscaping and takes some navigating. Its castellated hedges have a grotto at the centre, which takes you through a mysterious underground passage. Planted with 2,400 yew trees in 1988 and designed by architect Vernon Gibberd, the maze at Leeds Castle confuses thousands of visitors each year as they attempt to reach the panoramic central viewing point. Leeds has a second maze, of sorts. Overlooking the Great Water is a turf maze constructed in 2002 by the Leeds Castle grounds team. Following a design on the base of a rose bowl in the castle's silver collection, the pathway leads to its very own miniature moated castle. Now there's an incentive.

Hever Castle (see p277) boasts not one, or two, but three mazes in total. There's a common or bushy garden hedge one, planted by William Waldorf in 1905, in which we have lostthe odd child on occasion. The water maze isthe children's favourite, though. This consists of a shallow lake with a rocky island in the centre. The paths are on legs above the water, but some of the stone slabs you tread on while walking to the island trigger a spray of water. You can get very wet on your mission, so a change of clothes might be in order. The water maze is open April to October, weather permitting. The third maze is called King Henry's tower Maze in the adventure playground. It's a wooden construction, designed for children to test their Tudor history as they make a bid for the slide in the centre. There's little chance of getting lost in that one

Living mazes don't have to take years to grow big enough to get lost in. Yew is famously slow-growing, but if you design a maze to grow in a season from closely planted maize plants, with their thick, dark-green foliage and sturdy stems, you can create a series of dead-ends and inpenetrable walls to confuse and disorientate. This is what the planters at **Tulley's Farm** (Turners Hill, Crawley, West Sussex RH10 4PE, 01342 718472/www.tulleysfarm.com) have fun with every summer. The maize maze has a different theme every year (check www.tulleys farm.com for details) and has become the highlight of the increasingly popular Tulley's summer festival, when children can go mad on the farm and eat a load of fresh fruit into the bargain.

Apr-Oct 10am-6pm daily (last entry 4.30pm). **Admission** £12.95; £9.95 4-16s; £38 family (2+2); £44 family (2+3); free under-4s. **Credit** AmEx, MC, V.
The late John Aspinall opened his beautiful Howletts estate to the public in 1975 to fund his beloved animal collection. Almost 30 years later, Howletts still operates his famous policy of non-containment, ensuring that contact between animals and their handlers is close (so close that, over the years, fatal mishaps have been 'unavoidable'), and that enclosures replicate specific environments as far as is humanly possible. Almost 50 gorillas are housed here (the largest group in care, with the mighty Kifu the dominant male), as well as African elephants, Siberian tigers and many more. In the new 'Wood in the Park', you can walk alongside and below a free-roaming family of amazingly agile and lively lemurs. Many of the species of wolves, tapirs and antelopes kept at Howletts are endangered species, and this is one of the few zoos in the world to run a commendable programme reintroducing such species into the wild (ask a member of staff or have a look at the website to learn more about this side of the operation). So if you find the park low on waterslides and seesaws, that's because the animals come first. Port Lympne (*see below*) is Howletts' sister zoo.
Buggy access. Café. Car park. Disabled access: toilet. Nappy-changing facilities. Nearest picnic place: grounds. Restaurant. Shop.

Port Lympne Wild Animal Park

Lympne, nr Hythe, Kent CT21 4PD (0870 7504 647/ www.totallywild.net). **Getting there** *By rail* Ashford rail, then link bus. *By car* J11 off M20. **Open** *Oct-Mar* 10am-dusk daily (last entry 3pm). *Apr-Sept* 10am-6pm daily (last entry 4.30pm). **Admission** £12.95 ; £9.95 4-16s; £38 family (2+2); £44 family (2+3); free under-4s. **Credit** AmEx, MC, V.
Even larger than sister site Howletts (*see above*), Port Lympne consists of a spectacular mansion overlooking 350 acres (142 hectares) of wilderness, where animals coexist in the closest thing this country has to an uninterrupted nature reserve. Indeed, the easiest way to see everything is on an African Safari Experience trailer tour, which takes you through communities of wildebeest, zebra and giraffe in the Kentish wilderness. Still, expeditions on foot (a round trip of the amphitheatre-shaped park covers roughly three miles or 5km) can be far more rewarding – just make sure you have all day. Don't miss Palace of the Apes, the largest family gorilla house in the world, with its two bachelor gorilla groups. Other wild animals to look out for include black rhinos, lions, tigers, elephants, wolves and monkeys. As at Howletts, most of the animals have a close social bond with their keepers.
Buggy access. Café. Car park. Disabled access: toilet. Nappy-changing facilities. Restaurant. Shop.

Whipsnade Wild Animal Park

Whipsnade, Dunstable, Beds LU6 2LF (01582 872171/ www.whipsnade.co.uk). **Getting there** *By rail* Hemel Hempstead rail, then 43 bus from coach station. *By car* J21 off M25, then J9 off M1. **Open** *9 Mar-4 Oct* 10am-6pm Mon-Sat; 10am-7pm Sun. *5 Oct-8 Mar* 10am-4pm daily. Last entry 1hr before closing. Times subject to change, so phone to check. **Tours** free bus around the park; phone for times. **Admission** £14.50; £12.50 concessions; £11 3-15s; £46 family (2+2 or 1+3); free under-3s. *Cars* £11 (members £5.50). **Credit** AmEx, MC, V.
ZSL (Zoological Society of London), the charity that also operates London Zoo (*see p64*), runs this 600-acre (250-hectare) site for the study of large animals. And 2004 was a big year for some of the largest – Whipsnade's eight elephants produced two calves. As well as the tuskers, there are plenty of other giants, notably giraffes, bears, tigers, rhinos and hippos. 'Lions of the Serengeti' is the latest exhibit to open at the park; set in the heart of Whipsnade's 'African' region, it follows a village trail to the lion viewing shelter. The exhibit can be viewed either from the safari bus or from an open-sided steam engine (Apr-Oct only). A daily programme of activities keeps family groups busy, and there are frequent special events scheduled for school holidays – see website for details. At other times, you can learn about long-tailed lemurs in the 'acrobat in action' session, or there are birds of prey flying displays, bear talks, sea lion capers in the new Splashzone area, feeding time for the penguins, chimp chats and giraffe encounters. There's also a children's farm with marmosets, goats, alpacas and ponies.
Buggy access. Café. Car park (£3.50). Disabled access: toilet. Nappy-changing facilities. Restaurant. Shop.

Wildwood Wildlife Park

Herne Common, Herne Bay, Kent CT6 7LQ (01227 712111/www.wildwoodtrust.org). **Getting there** *By rail* Herne Bay rail, then 4 bus. *By car* J7 off M2. **Open** *May-Sept* 10am-6pm daily (last entry 5pm). *Nov-Apr* 10am-5pm or dusk daily (last entry 4pm). **Admission** *24 Mar-1 Nov* £8; £6.50 concessions; £6 3-15s; £26 family (2+2); free under-3s, disabled carers. *2 Nov-23 Mar* £7; £5.50 concessions; £5 3-15s; £22 family (2+2); free under-3s, disabled carers. **Credit** MC, V.
There are about 50 different species of animal and bird waiting to be spotted by the children who roam through Wildwood's 40 acres (16 hectares) of Kentish woodland. The enclosures for wild cats, beavers, badgers, otters, red squirrels, owls, even wolves and wild boar are designed to blend into the countryside. Special events, daily talks and feeding programmes take place around the park, both for school groups and casual young visitors during the school holidays. There's a restaurant for snacks and hot meals, and an adventure playground for monkeys of all ages and sizes. Check the website for a list of upcoming events.
Buggy access (single only). Car park. Disabled access: toilet. Nappy-changing facilities. Restaurant. Shop.

Woburn Safari Park

Woburn Park, Beds MK17 9QN (01525 290407/ www.woburnsafari.co.uk). **Getting there** *By car* J13 off M1. **Open** *Late Mar-2 Nov* 10am-5pm daily. *2 Nov-early Mar* 11am-3pm Sat, Sun. **Admission** £14.50-£16.50; £11.50 concessions; £11 3-15s; free under-3s. Prices vary during peak season; phone for details. **Credit** MC, V.
It's car drivers only (but no soft-tops, please) in the 40 acres (16 hectares) that make up the Duke of Bedford's Woburn spread. Watch the ranging elephants, giraffes (look out for new baby, Freia), camels, black bears, monkeys, lions, tigers and wolves, all from the safety of the family jalopy. You don't have to strap the children into the car for long, though, as you can always break off the drive and stretch your legs in the Wild World Leisure Area. Here the free attractions include demonstrations of birds of prey and keeper talks on penguins, lemurs and sea lions. At Rainbow Landing (an indoor aviary) you can buy nectar (60p), attracting colourful lorikeets to land on your hand

to drink (it opens four times a day). The sea-lion pool, with views above and below the waterline, is another must-see. Once you've exchanged pleasantries with the animals, there's fun for human young: the Tree Tops Action Trail and the Tiny Tots Safari Trail are both great.
Buggy access. Café. Car park. Disabled access: toilet. Nappy-changing facilities. Restaurant. Shop.

SPECIALIST MUSEUMS

Bentley Wildfowl & Motor Museum

Halland, nr Lewes, East Sussex BN8 5AF (01825 840573/www.bentley.org.uk). By rail Uckfield or Lewes rail, then taxi. *By car* A22, then follow signs. **Open** *Summer* 10.30am-4.30pm daily. *Winter* 10.30am-4.40pm Sat, Sun. House closed during winter. **Admission** £6.50; £5.50 concessions; £4.50 3-15s; £21 family (2+3); free under-3s. **Credit** MC, V.
A collection of more than 1,000 swans, geese and ducks from all over the world sits alongside a highly polished display of veteran Edwardian and vintage cars and motorcycles. And if neither motor nor fowl interests you, the craftspeople might. They include a glass sculptor, woodcarvers and a jewellery maker. Bentley House, a Palladian-style mansion restored by Raymond Erith, has a gallery with a permanent exhibition by the Sussex artist Philip Rickman. There are also formal gardens, an adventure playground and the beautiful Glyndebourne wood, where there's a new wildlife trail with interactive boards.
Buggy access. Café. Car park (free). Disabled access: toilet. Nappy-changing facilities. Nearest picnic place: grounds. Shop.

Chatham Historic Dockyard

The Historic Dockyard, Chatham, Kent ME4 4TZ (01634 823800/www.thedockyard.co.uk). **Getting there** *By rail* Chatham rail. *By car* J1-4 off M2. **Open** *14 Feb-31 Oct* 10am-6pm daily (last entry 4pm). *8-30 Nov* 10am-4pm (last entry 3pm) Sat, Sun. Closed Dec, Jan. **Admission** £10; £7.50 concessions; £6.50 5-15s; £26.50 family (2+2; £3.25 per additional child); free under-5s. **Credit** AmEx, MC, V.
Jewel of the tidal Medway, which extends 20 miles (32km) from the Thames estuary at Sheerness to the city of Rochester, this ancient maritime centre was famously the starting point of Horatio Nelson's distinguished career in 1771. Many buildings from Nelson's time survive on the 80-acre (32-hectare) site. There are tours around both a 40-year-old submarine, HMS *Ocelot*, the last warship to be built at the dockyard, and a World War II destroyer, HMS *Cavalier*. Interactive displays include a radio-controlled boat and ship-docking exercise, a mock ship fight and a soft-play area. In summer and autumn 2005, the Dockyard will be celebrating the Trafalgar Bicentenary in style with a Medway Maritime Festival (Aug 28-29), which will stage music inspired by the sea and maritime displays.
Buggy access. Café. Car park (free). Disabled access: toilet. Nappy-changing facilities. Shop.

Imperial War Museum Duxford

Cambridge CB2 4QR (01223 835000/www.iwm. org.uk). **Getting there** *By rail* Cambridge rail. *By car* J10 off M11. **Open** *Summer* 10am-6pm daily. *Winter* 10am-4pm daily. **Admission** £12; £9 concessions; £7 16-18s; free under-16s. **Credit** MC, V.

Duxford has four themed hangars of exhibits, as well as the futuristic glass-fronted American Air Museum, designed by Lord Foster, and the Land Warfare Hall, filled with tanks and military vehicles. The complex is so huge that a convenient (and free) 'road train' operates all day, dropping people off at the major attractions. The air shows are superb (there are about four each year). For terrestial activities, learn about the Normandy Campaign in the Land Warfare Hall. Here, tanks, military vehicles and artillery pieces are on show in battlefield scenes. The latest project to take off at Duxford is AirSpace. Work started in April 2004 to redevelop Hangar 1 into a 108,000sq ft (10,000sq m) exhibition area, and its completion date is scheduled for 2006. Thirty classic British and Commonwealth aircraft will be displayed, some suspended from the roof. A new education centre for schoolchildren is also planned. For the time being, Concorde will be outside, making the pointy-nosed superstar easier to photograph.
Buggy access. Cafés. Car park. Disabled access: lift, ramps, toilet. Nappy-changing. Restaurant. Shops.

Roald Dahl Children's Gallery

Buckinghamshire County Museum, Church Street, Aylesbury, Bucks HP20 2QP (01296 331441/ www.buckscc.gov.uk/museum). **Getting there** *By rail* Aylesbury rail. *By car* J8 off M25. **Open** *Term-time* 3-5pm Mon-Fri. *School hols* 10am-5pm Sat; 2-5pm Sun. **Admission** £3.25; free under-3s. **Credit** MC, V.
An extension of the child-friendly County Museum, this gallery is divided into five main areas, decorated with colourful frescoes by Quentin Blake, which introduce different themes based on Roald Dahl's stories. Visitors encounter James and his mini-beast friends inside the Giant Peach, and examine the insect world with the aid of a video microscope. The BFG playing on his giant pipe organ is a jolly introduction to the mysteries of sound, or there's a great glass elevator and a chance to discover Willy Wonka's inventions. In Matilda's Library you can discover more about Dahl's life and work. The Dahl Gallery only holds 85 people, so it's worth pre-booking in the school holidays. Picnic in the walled garden or snack in the café.
Buggy access. Café. Disabled access: lift, toilet. Nappy-changing facilities. Nearest picnic place: grounds. Shop.

Roald Dahl Museum & Story Centre

81-83 High Street, Great Missenden, Bucks HP16 0AL (01494 892192/www.roalddahlmuseum.org). **Open** 10am-5pm Tue-Sun. **Admission** £4.50; £3.50 3-16s, concessions; free under-3s. **Credit** MC, V.
One of the grand openings of 2005, this wonderful museum has been designed to provide an insight into the craft of storytelling, as well as furnishing inquisitive young readers with all the information they could hope to have on the eponymous Dahl, his life, his methods and his much-loved canon. In the Story Centre, well thought-out displays and interactive games reveal how prominent contemporary children's authors work; the Centre's writer in residence (Val Rutt, author of *The Race for the Lost Keystone*, is the incumbent as we go to press) is also on hand to encourage children to think (and write) creatively. All kinds of workshops, storytelling sessions and interactive groups are offered (check the website for details). The museum's first permanent exhibition, 'The Photographs of Roald Dahl, 1939-1943', documents Dahl's experiences as a wartime pilot in the RAF.
Buggy access. Café. Disabled access: toilet. Nappy-changing facilities. Shop.

Weald & Downland Open Air Museum

Singleton, Chichester, West Sussex PO18 OEU (01243 811348/811363/www.wealddown.co.uk). **Getting there** *By rail* Chichester rail, then 60 bus. *By car* A3, turn off at Millford, A286 to Midhurst & follow signs. **Open** *Mar-Oct* 10.30am-6pm daily (last entry 5pm). *Nov-Feb* 10.30am-4pm Wed, Sat, Sun. **Admission** £7.70; £6.70 concessions; £4.10 5-16s; £21 family (2+3); free under-5s. **Credit** MC, V.
More than 45 original buildings have been preserved for posterity in this beautiful 50-acre (20-hectare) parkland setting in the South Downs. They've been refurbished to bring to life the homes, farms and workplaces of south-east England over the past 500 years. Visitors can see shire horses at work, visit a medieval farmstead or just picnic by the lake. Children can also find out what life may have been like for their contemporaries in the Victorian schoolroom. There's plenty of space for exploration, including woodland and pasture, and there are lots of lambs, goats, cattle and poultry to look at. Events for 2005 include regular Activity Wednesdays with countryside crafts and traditional cooking. The Autumn Countryside Celebration takes place on 1-2 October and a Sussex Christmas is scheduled for 26 December 2005-1 January 2006.
Buggy access. Café. Car park (free). Disabled access: toilets. Nappy-changing facilities. Shop.

STEAM TRAINS

Bluebell Railway

Sheffield Park Station, on A275 between Lewes & East Grinstead, Sussex TN22 3QL (01825 723777/talking timetable 01825 720825/www.bluebell-railway.co.uk). **Getting there** *By rail* East Grinstead rail, then 473 bus. *By car* J10 off M23. **Open** *Easter-Sept* 11am-4pm daily. Phone for details of additional Sat, Sun, school & bank hol openings. **Admission** £9.50; £4.70 3-15s; £27 family (2+3); free under-3s. **Credit** MC, V.
Bluebell is the UK's first preserved standard-gauge passenger railway. It runs along the Lewes to East Grinstead line, with each station the line passes through restored according to a different era: Victorian, the 1930s and the 1950s. Childish delights include Thomas specials, Christmas specials and a bedtime story service in the summer.
Buggy access. Café. Car park (free). Disabled access: toilet. Nappy-changing facilities. Nearest picnic place: grounds. Shop.

Didcot Railway Centre

Didcot, Oxon OX11 7NJ (01235 817200/ www.didcotrailwaycentre.org.uk). **Getting there** *By rail* Didcot Parkway rail. *By car* J13 off M4. **Open** 10am-4pm Mon-Fri; 10am-5pm Sat, Sun (last entry 30min before closing). **Tours** bank hols (times depend on events; phone for details). **Admission** *Steam days, incl tour* £7; £6 concessions; £5 4-16s; £22 family (2+2); free under-4s. *Non-steam days* £4; £3.50 concessions; £3 4-16s; £12 family; free under-4s. *Special event days* £9; £7.50 concessions; £7 4-16s; £28 family; free under-4s. **Credit** MC, V.
Didcot Railway Centre constitutes a static collection of antique carriages and engines, where regular 'steam days' involve steam-age activities like 'turning' locomotives, as well as the chance to ride in an original 1930s carriage.

Thomas the Tank Engine makes occasional holiday stopovers; for details of other 'special event days', phone or have a look at the website.
Buggy access. Café. Car park. Nappy-changing. Shop.

Kent & East Sussex Railway

Tenterden Town Station, Tenterden, Kent TN30 6HE (Tenterden, Northiam & Bodiam stations: 01580 765155/www.kesr.org.uk). **Getting there** *By rail* Headcorn rail, then bus to Tenterden. *By car* J9 off M20. **Open** *Apr-July, Sept-Oct* 10am-4pm Sat, Sun. *Aug* 10am-4pm daily. *Nov-Mar* times vary; phone for details. **Admission** £10; £9 concessions; £5 3-15s; £26 family (2+3); free under-3s. **Credit** MC, V.
The antique carriages and engines servicing this railway line were scavenged and restored by enthusiasts, which makes this the most pleasing method of getting from Bodiam (for the castle, *see p277*) to Tenterden.
Buggy access. Café (Tenterden & Northiam stations). Car park (not at Bodiam). Disabled access: carriage (book in advance), toilet. Nappy-changing facilities (Tenterden). Shop.

Romney, Hythe & Dymchurch Railway

New Romney Station, Kent TN28 8PL (01797 362353/www.rhdr.org.uk). **Getting there** *By rail* Folkestone Central rail, then 711 bus to Hythe. *By car* J11 off M20. **Open** phone or check website for timetable. **Admission** £10.50; £9 concessions; £5.25 3-15s; free under-3s. **Credit** MC, V.
Millionaire racing driver Captain Howley built the 'World's Smallest Public Railway' back in 1927. Nowadays, his unique locomotives, one-third of the scale of the real thing, puff along a similarly downsized track (though it still covers 13.5 miles or 22km) between the Cinque Port of Hythe and eerie Dungeness.
Buggy access. Café. Car park. Disabled access: carriages, toilet. Nappy-changing facilities. Shop.

Watercress Line

The Railway Station, Alresford, Hants SO24 9JG (01962 733810/talking timetable 01962 734866/ www.watercressline.co.uk). **Getting there** *By rail* Alton rail. *By car* A3, then A31. **Open** *May-Sept* Tue-Thur, Sat, Sun. *Oct, Dec, mid Jan-Feb* Sat, Sun. *Easter hols* daily. Phone or check website for timetable. **Admission** £10; £9 concessions; £5 3-16s; £25 family (2+2); free under-3s. Call for special event prices. **Credit** MC, V.
Beginning in the market town of Alresford, this ten-mile (16km) railway winds through Home Counties countryside. Londoners can hop on the train at Alton, which has a mainline station for Waterloo.
Buggy access (footbridge at Alton). Café. Disabled access: carriages, toilet. Shop.

THEME PARKS

Bekonscot Model Village

Warwick Road, Beaconsfield, Bucks HP9 2PL (01494 672919/www.bekonscot.com). **Getting there** *By rail* Beaconsfield rail. *By car* J2 off M40 or J16 off M25. **Open** *15 Feb-end Oct* 10am-5pm daily. **Admission** £5.80; £4 concessions; £3.50 2-15s; £16 family (2+2); free under-2s. **Credit** MC, V.

This is a miniature world where children can be as Gulliver in Lilliput. The model villages, in their landscape of farms, fields, woodland, churches, castles and lakes, were created as a hobby by Roland Callingham in 1929. Bekonscot is now a charitable organisation. A busy gauge-one model railway stops at seven stations, and at the zoo you can witness a scaled-down chimps' tea party, aviary and elephant rides. More intricate details can be enjoyed at the fairground, with its working mini rides. Manicured alpine plants, lawns and dwarf conifers provide a green backdrop to the towers and spires. For full-sized action, there's a playground and a ride-on steam railway (50p per person; runs at weekends, bank holidays and during local school holidays).

Buggy access. Café. Car park (free). Disabled access: toilets. Kiosk. Nappy-changing facilities. Nearest picnic place: grounds. Shop.

City by the sea

There are numerous seaside towns within day-tripping distance of the Big Smoke, some of them sandy, some of them stony, some of them just plain seedy – and best of all, there's something for trips of all types. The telephone numbers listed are for the tourist office in each seaside town.

The closest to London is **Southend** (01702 215120/www.southend.gov.uk). Southend boasts the largest rock factory in the world (the edible kind, obviously), as well as the longest pier (1.3 miles or 2.2kilometre, with a pleasure train running from end to end), but most of the sand here is imported regularly to cover up the estuary mud banks beneath.

For a more genuine slice of the soft stuff, you can't beat a day at **Camber Sands** (01797 226696/www.visitrye.co.uk), which is home to the longest stretch of sandy coastline in the South-east, and is unsurpassed for its constitutional seaside sports – cricket and Frisbee on fair weather days, kite flying when the wind picks up. Culturally, Camber is lacking (there's a token Pontins – easily ignored – and a dilapidated amusement arcade or two), but nearby Rye has a traditional High Street teeming with lovely pubs and restaurants to round off the day in.

The proximity of Dungeness Power Station, however, makes swimming at Camber a matter of personal preference. Those who want to get more than their toes wet are better off heading for the Blue Flag-awarded beaches of **Littlehampton** (01903 721866/www.sussexbythesea.com). The waters here are some of the cleanest in Britain (the rambling West Beach has been designated a Site of Special Scientific Interest for its diverse plant and animal life), but it's not the place to take a screaming teenage thrill-seeker.

The same applies to **Whitstable** (01227 275482/www.visitwhitstable.co.uk), an antiquated seaport on one of the quieter corners of the Thames Estuary, renowned for both its oysters (adults can knock a couple back at the revered Whitstable Oyster Fishery Company, although little ones might prefer a portion of chips) and its relation to local luminary Peter Cushing, who is honoured by an exhibition in the Whitstable Museum and Gallery (01227 276998/www.whitstable-museum.co.uk). The old groynes are great for kids to clamber on and the grassy Tankerton Slopes well-suited to a spot of kite flying, but once again it's hardly death-defying stuff. The same is true of **Eastbourne** (01323 411400/www.eastbourne.org), although statistics concerning the number of suicides who annually take their last leap into the unknown from looming Beachy Head might engage the attention of moody teens, even if the 17-mile (27kilometre) walk along the spectacular Seven Sisters cliff route (ending in Peacehaven) doesn't.

Meanwhile, for a day out that's more spectacle than spectacular, **Margate** (01843 220241/www.tourism.thanet.gov.uk) still more or less embodies the bawdy 'red-faced husband distracted by busty bikini beauty' aesthetic of time-honoured postcard smut, and has enjoyed recent attention thanks to the ironic 'bad taste' revivals espoused by lazy journalists. Video-game arcades are everywhere, while the main Dreamland amusement park looks set, as we go to press, to finally close its doors. But even without the fun of the fair, there's plenty to keep kids occupied, including the Margate Caves (01843 220139), once a popular destination for smugglers, and the Shell Grotto (01843 220008) with its indecipherable, possibly ancient cave paintings.

If it's culture you're after, then leave irony behind and head instead for **Broadstairs** (01843 583334/www.tourism.thanet.gov.uk), home to an annual Dickens Festival (18-26 June 2005) that sees costumed characters from across the country converging in honour of the author, who visited the town regularly; there's also a year-round Dickens House Museum (2 Victoria Parade, 01843 861232/www.dickenshouse.co.uk). Alternatively, look to **Brighton** (www.visitbrighton.com); its legendary pier culture may be on the wane (due in no small part to one of them collapsing into the sea a couple of years ago), but when it comes to entertainment, Brighton caters to both kids and adults like nowhere else – from the funfair at the far end of the Palace Pier (01273 609361/www.brightonpier.co.uk) to the charming wooden walkway teeming with eclectic sculpture, street artists and the Ellipse performance area (host to free summer concerts). On top of that there's the Sea Life Centre (01273 604234) and Britain's oldest electric railway running along the promenade (01273 292718), not to mention a huge number of excellent shops and restaurants in the arterial maze of the town itself. They don't call it London-on-Sea for nothing, you know. In fact, if you stay there long enough, you'll probably end up feeling that you've earned yourself another holiday.

Chessington World of Adventures

*Leatherhead Road, Chessington, Surrey KT9 2NE
(0870 444 7777/www.chessington.com).* **Getting
there** *By rail* Chessington South rail, then 71 bus or
10-min walk. *By car* J9 off M25. **Open** 16 Mar-30 Oct
2005. Check website for timetables. **Admission** £28
(accompanying child free), £18.50 additional under-12s;
£13.50-£18 concessions; £28-£111.50 family; free
under-4s. Check website for advance bookings for
fast-track entry. **Credit** MC, V.

A 'families come first' policy makes Chessington a good
deal more tot-friendly these days. Ninety per cent of the
rides and attractions are now suitable for the under-12s, so
there's Beanoland with Dennis the Menace shenanigans
(check the website for special events), Land of the Dragons
with a soft play area and slippery slides, and puppet dragons Spike and Cinders starring in the Dragon's Tales
Theatre. Children have to pass a height test to have a go
on the Dragon's Fury ride (over-sevens), which curls round
the Land of the Dragons. Hocus Pocus Hall is a fantasy
family '4-D' walk-through experience, while Animal Land
has its famous gorilla family. A small rollercoaster
(Vampire) is meek enough for four year-olds. Picnic spots
are everywhere, but there are also fast-food chains for those
who have forgotten their sandwiches. A child gets in free
with each paying adult, and Chessington have introduced
a queue-busting Day Planner ticket, bookable online, which
promises no waiting at the entrance on arrival and allot-
ted time slots on the top five rides. Four age-specific Day
Planner guides can be downloaded from the website, where
you'll also find an exhaustive list of Chessington's events
and family-friendly attractions.
*Buggy access. Café. Car park (free). Disabled access:
special wristbands, toilets. Nappy-changing facilities.
Restaurant. Shops.*

Diggerland

*Medway Valley Leisure Park, Roman Way, Strood,
Kent ME2 2NU (0870 034 4437/www.diggerland.com).*
Getting there *By rail* Strood rail, then taxi. *By car* J2
off M2, then A228, then follow signs towards Strood.
Open 10am-5pm weekends, bank hols, school hols,
half-terms; check website for details. **Admission**
£2.50; free under-2s. *Day pass (includes all rides)*
£18. *Ride credits* £1 each. **Credit** AmEx, MC, V.

A rather specialist theme-park concept, dreamt up by plant
hire firm HE Services, Diggerland lets you drive heavy
machinery, such as JCBs and trucks, closely watched by
instructors. Dumper and JCB racing is organised for
adults, and themed birthday party packages are available
for children. There are no age restrictions, though tinies
have to be accompanied by an adult before they can drive
off into the sunset at the wheel of a dumper truck. Other
on-site activities include a bouncy castle, ride-on toys, a
vast sandpit and a land train. But it's the diggers that make
it special. During winter (Nov 2005-Easter 2006), the snow's
shipped in and Diggerland becomes a snow park with a
100m (328ft) tubing run, a 50m (164ft) main slope and –
best of all – a large play area for building snowmen and
throwing snowballs. It's not exactly an Alaskan wilderness, but in the absence of a white Christmas it's one present to make them smile. An all-day ski/board pass is £30,
ski and board lessons are available from £18 per hour, and
toddler ski sessions cost from £10 per hour.
*Buggy access. Café. Car park (free). Disabled access:
toilet. Nappy-changing facilities. Nearest picnic place:
grounds. Shop.*

Legoland

*Winkfield Road, Windsor, Berks SL4 4AY (0870
504 0404/www.legoland.co.uk).* **Getting there** *By
rail* Windsor & Eton Riverside or Windsor Central rail,
then bus. *By car* J3 off M3 or J6 off M4. **Open** *Mid
late Oct* 10am-5pm daily. Times vary, check website
for timetables. **Admission** *One-day ticket* £24; £22
3-15s; free under-3s. *Two-day ticket* £47; £43 3-15s;
free under-3s. **Credit** MC, V.

Loved by children of all ages, Legoland – celebrating its
tenth year in Windsor – is a top day out. Miniland, where
some 35 million pieces have been used to create scenes from
Europe, is impressive. Scenes include iconic London landmarks and, new for 2005, a Cape Canaveral scene. Then
there are old favourites like the Driving School (which
gives its successful participants a Legoland driver's
licence), the Lego Safari, and the two mildly thrilling rides
– the Dragon Coaster and Pirate Falls. The Jungle Coaster,
has a 42ft (13m) plunge and a top speed of nearly 40mph
(60km/h). New in 2005 is the Fire Academy, which involves
helping Lego firefighters put out a burning building, the
Dino Dipper ride (a carousel revolving around a dinosuar),
and the Dino Safari, which takes riders through a prehistoric jungle. The Wild Woods section has some themed
play mazes (*see p282* **Get lost!**), and Hans Christian
Andersen fairytales are on stage in the puppet theatre.
Legoland is outrageously popular, especially during school
holidays, so expect queues.
*Buggy access. Cafés. Car park (free). Disabled access:
toilet. Nappy-changing facilities. Nearest picnic place:
grounds. Restaurants. Shops.*

Thorpe Park

*Staines Road, Chertsey, Surrey KT16 8PN (0870
444 4466/www.thorpepark.com).* **Getting there**
By rail Staines rail, then 950 bus. *By car* M25 J11 or
J13. **Open** Times vary, check website for timetables.
Height restrictions vary, depending on rides.
Admission £27; £21 4-11s, concessions; £75 family
(2+2, 1+3); free under-4s. Check the website or phone
for advance bookings; allow 24hrs to process advance
ticket purchases. **Credit** MC, V.

The latest ride with potential to rearrange your insides is
the Slammer, a rotary thrill ride, which gives a 'full throt-
tle free-fall experience without having to jump out of a
plane'. Riders are taken 105ft (32m) towards the sky, then
'slam-dunked' toward the earth before swooping skywards
again. The rest of the white-knucklers are no less sicken-
ing. There's the old favourite, Samurai, then Nemesis
Inferno (a legs-dangling swoop through more than 2,460ft
or 750m of suspended track), and Colossus, the world's first
ten-looping rollercoaster, travelling at speeds of 40mph
(65km/h). For those who want to get wet as well as disori-
entated, there's Tidal Wave, one of the highest water-drop
rides in Europe. Although Thorpe's more gruesome rides
aren't suitable for little ones, there are tamer attractions for
them, such as the swinging seashells and happy halibuts,
and cuddly experiences await across the lake at Thorpe
Farm's petting zoo, with its goats, pigs and poultry; you
can travel to this agricultural haven by boat or land train.
New at Thorpe Farm in 2005 is a joint initiative with the
RSPB, featuring a 'small bird bug hunt' (Aug 27-28) and
bird-feeding activities (making fat cakes and such like; Oct
1-2), plus a couple of competitions, such as the sweetly
titled 'guess how many wrens in the box'.
*Buggy access. Café. Car park (free). Disabled access:
toilets. Nappy-changing facilities. Restaurants. Shops.*

Days Out

DIRECTORY

DIRECTORY

Getting around

PUBLIC TRANSPORT

The prices listed for transport and services were correct at the time of going to press, but bear in mind that some prices (especially those of tube tickets) are subject to a price hike each January.

Public transport information

Details can be found online at www.thetube.com and/or www.tfl.gov.uk, or on 7222 1234.

Transport for London (TfL) also runs Travel Information Centres that provide maps and information about the tube, buses, Tramlink, riverboats, Docklands Light Railway (DLR) and national rail services within the London area. You can find them in Heathrow Airport, as well as in Liverpool Street and Victoria stations.

London Transport Users' Committee

6 Middle Street, EC1A 7JA (7505 9000/www.ltuc.org.uk).
Open *Phone enquiries* 9am-5pm Mon-Fri.
This is the official, campaigning watchdog monitoring customer satisfaction with transport in London.

Travelcards

A flat cash fare per journey applies across the entire London bus and tram network. Tube and DLR fares are based on a zonal system. There are six zones stretching 12 miles (20km) out from the centre of London. Beware of on-the-spot penalty fares for anyone caught without a ticket. The Travelcard is the cheapest way of getting around. These can be bought at stations, London Travel Information Centres or newsagents.

Day Travelcards

Day Travelcards (peak) can be used all day Mondays to Fridays (except public holidays). They cost from £6 (£3 for under-16s) for zones 1-2, with prices rising to £12 (£6 for under-16s) for zones 1-6. Most people use the off-peak day Travelcard, which allows you to travel from 9.30am (Mon-Fri) and all day Saturday, Sunday and public holidays. They cost from £4.70 for zones 1-2, rising to £6 for zones 1-6.

One-day Family Travelcards

Anyone travelling with children can take advantage of this Travelcard. It offers unlimited travel for up to two adults with up to four children. During the week each adult pays £3.10, and

each child 80p, in zones 1-2, rising to £4 per adult and 80p per child for zones 1-6. Each child in the Family Travelcard group travels free in all zones on weekends and public holidays.

Oyster card

The Oyster card is a travel smart-card, which can be charged with Pre Pay and/or seven-day, monthly and longer period (including annual) Travelcards and bus passes. Oyster cards are currently available to adults and student photocard holders when buying a ticket. Tickets can be bought from www.oystercard.com, by phone on 0870 849 9999 and at tube station ticket offices, London Travel Information Centres, some National Rail station ticket offices and newsagents.

Children

Child fares are available to under-16s on tube, bus, DLR, tram and National Rail services. Under-11s can travel free on buses and trams; under-16s go free on buses from August 2005. Children aged 14 or 15 need a Child- or 11-15-photocard to travel at child rate on the tube, buses (until August 2005), DLR and trams. Children travelling with adult-rate 7-day, monthly or longer Travelcard holders can buy a day Travelcard for £1.

London Underground

The tube in rush hour (8-9.30am and 4.30-7pm Mon-Fri) is not pleasant, so travel outside these hours with your children if possible.

Using the system

Tube tickets can be purchased from a ticket office or self-service machines. Ticket offices in some stations close early (around 7.30pm), but it's best to keep change with you at all times: using a ticket machine is quicker than queuing at a ticket office. There are 12 Underground lines, colour-coded on the tube map for ease of use; we've provided a full map of the London Underground on the back page of this book.

Underground timetable

Tube trains run daily from around 5.30am (except Sunday, when they start later, depending on the line). The only exception is Christmas Day, when there is no service. During peak times the service should run every two or three minutes. Times of last trains were, at the time of writing, under discussion, but they're usually around 11.30pm-1am daily, and 30 minutes to an hour earlier on Sunday. The only all-night public transport is by night bus (*see p291*).

Fares

The single fare for adults within zone 1 is £2 (Pre Pay £1.70). For zones 1-2 it's £2.30 (Pre Pay £2.10 or £2). The zones 1-6 single fare is £3.80 (Pre Pay £3.50 or £2). The single kids' fare in zone 1 is 60p, 80p for zones 1-2 and £1.40 for zones 1-6.

Carnet

If you're planning on making a lot of short-hop journeys within zone 1 over a period of several days, it makes sense to buy a carnet of ten tickets for £17 (£5 for children). If you exit a station outside zone 1 and are caught with only a carnet ticket, you'll be liable to a £10 penalty fare.

Docklands Light Railway (DLR)

The DLR (7363 9700, www.dlr.co.uk) runs trains from Bank (Central or Waterloo & City lines) or Tower Gateway, close to Tower Hill tube (Circle and District lines), to Stratford, Beckton and the Isle of Dogs as far as Island Gardens, then south of the river to Greenwich, Deptford and Lewisham. Trains run 5.30am to 12.30am Monday to Saturday and 7am to 11.30pm Sunday.

Fares

Docklands Shuttle South (Lewisham to Canary Wharf) one-day tickets cost £2.30; Docklands Shuttle East (valid between Beckton/Stratford and Island Gardens via Westferry) tickets are £2.60; City Flyer South (valid between Bank and Lewisham) tickets are £3.90; and City Flyer East (valid between Beckton/Stratford and Bank) tickets are £4.60. Child tickets cost 90p to £2.20. One-day 'Rail & River Rover' tickets combine unlimited DLR travel with a guided riverboat trip between Greenwich, Tower and Westminster piers, starting at Tower Gateway. Tickets cost £9.50 for adults, £4.75 for kids and £25 for a family pass); under-5s go free.

Buses

In the past year, hundreds of new buses, with low-floors for wheelchair-users and passengers with buggies, have been added to the fleet. 'Bendy buses' with multiple-door entry and the 'Pay Before You Board' schemes have also helped reduce boarding times at bus stops. Many buses, particularly in central London, now require you to buy a ticket before boarding. Do so: there are inspectors about. Where you do not already have a ticket you can buy one (or a one-day Bus Pass) from pavement ticket machines. Yellow signs on bus stops show where this is a requirement.

Fares

Single bus fares are £1.20 (Pre Pay 80p) and 40p for children. A one-day Bus Pass gives unlimited bus and tram travel at £3.00 adult (£1 children). Children under 11 and, from September 2005, under 16, travel free on buses. Saver tickets, which come in a book of six and cost £6 (£2.10 for children), can be bought at newsagents and at tube station ticket offices.

Night buses

Many night buses run 24 hours a day, seven days a week, and some special night buses with an 'N' prefix to the route number operate from about 11pm to 6am. Most services run every 15 to 30 minutes, but many busier routes have a bus around every ten minutes. Travelcards and Bus Passes can be used on night buses until 4.30am on the day after they expire. Oyster Pre Pay and bus Saver tickets are also valid on night buses.

Routes 205 & 705

Bus routes 205 and 705 (7222 1234) connect all the main London rail termini (except Charing Cross) on circular trips. Bus 205 runs from Whitechapel station to Euston Square station via Aldgate, Aldgate East, Liverpool Street, Moorgate, Old Street, Angel, King's Cross, St Pancras and Euston. Starting at around 5am (6am on Sunday) they run every 10-15 minutes until just after midnight every day. Route 705 starts at Paddington around 7.50am (8.15am from Liverpool Street) and runs around every 30 minutes until 7.50pm (8.15pm from Liverpool Street), stopping at Victoria, Waterloo, London Bridge and Fenchurch Street.

Coaches

National Express (0870 580 8080) runs routes to most parts of the country; coaches depart from **Victoria Coach Station**, a five-minute walk from Victoria rail and tube stations. **Green Line** (0870 608 7261) operates within an approximate 40-mile (64-kilometre) radius of London. Most buses depart from **Eccleston Bridge** (Colonnades Coach Station, behind Victoria Coach Station).

Victoria Coach Station

164 Buckingham Palace Road, SW1V 9TP (7730 3466). Victoria tube/rail. **Map** p316 H1.
National Express, which travels to the Continent as Eurolines, is based at Victoria Coach Station. The coach station is also used by other companies operating to and from London.

Rail services

Independently run commuter services leave from the city's main rail stations. Travelcards are valid on these services within the right zones. Perhaps the most useful is Silverlink (0845 601 4867, www.silverlink-trains.com; or contact National Rail Enquiries on 0845 748 4950), which arcs through north London from Richmond in the south-west to North Woolwich in the east, via Kew, Kensal Rise, Gospel Oak, Islington, Stratford and City Airport. Trains run about every 20 minutes except on Sunday, when it's every half-hour.

If you've lost property in an overground station or on a train, call 0870 000 5151; an operator will connect you to the appropriate station.

Family railcard

This costs £20, and lasts one year. Valid across Britain, it gives travellers with children one year of discounts from standard rail fares (a third off adult fares, 60 per cent off child fares, £1 minimum fare). Under-fives travel free. Up to two adults can be named as cardholders and use the card – and they do not have to be related. The minimum group size is one cardholder and one child aged five to 15; maximum group size is two cardholders, two other adults and four children. To pick up a form for the Family Railcard, visit your local staffed station.

London's mainline stations

Charing Cross *Strand, WC2N 5LR.* **Map** p317 L7.
For trains to and from south-east England (including Dover, Folkestone and Ramsgate).
Euston *Euston Road, NW1 2RS.* **Map** p315 K3.
For trains to and from north and north-west England and Scotland, and a suburban line north to Watford.
King's Cross *Euston Road, N1 9AP.* **Map** p315 L2.
For trains to and from north and north-east England and Scotland, and suburban lines to north London.
Liverpool Street *Liverpool Street, EC2M 7PD.* **Map** p319 R5.
For trains to and from the east coast, Stansted airport and East Anglia, and services to east and north-east London.
London Bridge *London Bridge Street, SE1 9SP.* **Map** p319 Q8.
For trains to Kent, Sussex, Surrey and south London suburbs.
Paddington *Praed Street, W2 1HB.* **Map** p311 D5.
For trains to and from west and south-west England, south Wales and the Midlands.

Victoria *Terminus Place, SW1V 1JU.* **Map** p316 H10.
For fast trains to and from the channel ports (Folkestone, Dover, Newhaven); for trains to and from Gatwick Airport, and suburban services to south and south-east London.
Waterloo *York Road, SE1 7ND.* **Map** p319 M9.
For fast trains to and from the south and south-west of England (Portsmouth, Southampton, Dorset, Devon), and suburban services to south London.

Tramlink

Trams run between Beckenham, Croydon, Addington and Wimbledon in south London. Travelcards and bus passes taking in zones 3-6 can be used on trams; otherwise, cash single fares cost from £1.20 (40p children).

Water transport

The times of London's assortment of river services vary, but most operate every 20 minutes to one hour between 10.30am and 5pm. Services may be more frequent and run later in summer. Call the operators listed below for schedules and fares, or see www.tfl.gov.uk. Travelcard holders can expect one-third off scheduled Riverboat fares. Thames Clippers (www.thamesclippers.com) runs a fast, reliable, commuter boat service. Piers to board the Clippers from are: Savoy (near Embankment tube), Blackfriars, Bankside (for the Globe), London Bridge and St Katharine's (Tower Bridge).

The names in bold below are the names of piers.

Embankment–Tower (30mins)–**Greenwich** (30mins); Catamaran Cruises 7987 1185.
Greenland Dock–Canary Wharf (8mins)–**St Katharine's** (7mins)–**London Bridge City** (4mins)–**Bankside** (3mins)–**Blackfriars** (3mins)–**Savoy** (4mins); Collins River Enterprises 7977 6892.
Savoy–Cadogan (15-20mins)–**Chelsea** (2mins); Thames Executive Chargers 01342 322440.
Westminster–(Thames) **Barrier Gardens** (1hr 30mins); Thames Cruises 7930 3373,www.thamescruises.com.
Westminster–Festival (5mins)–**London Bridge City** (20mins)–**St Katharine's** (5mins); Crown River 7936 2033,www.crownriver.com.
Westminster–Greenwich (1hr); Westminster Passenger Services 7930 4097.
Westminster–Kew (1hr 30mins)–**Richmond** (30mins).
Westminster–Hampton Court (1hr 30mins); Westminster Passenger Service Association 7930 2062.
Westminster–Tower (25-30mins); City Cruises 7740 0400,www.citycruises.com.

TAXIS

Black cabs

Licensed London taxis are known as black cabs – even though they now come in a variety of colours – and are a quintessential feature of London life. Drivers of black cabs must pass a test called the Knowledge to prove they know every street in central London and the shortest route to it.

If a taxi's yellow 'For Hire' sign is switched on, it can be hailed. If a taxi stops, the cabbie must take you to your destination, provided it's within seven

miles. Expect to pay slightly higher rates after 8pm on weekdays and all weekend.

You can book black cabs in advance. Both Radio Taxis (7272 0272; credit cards only) and Dial-a-Cab (7253 5000) run 24-hour services for black cabs (there'll be a booking fee in addition to the regular fare). Enquiries or complaints about black cabs should be made to the Public Carriage Office. (7941 7800,www.gov.uk/pco).

Minicabs

Minicabs (saloon cars) are generally cheaper than black cabs, but be sure to use only licensed firms and avoid minicab drivers who tout for business on the street. They'll be unlicensed and uninsured, almost certainly won't know how to get around and charge extortionate fares.

There are, happily, plenty of trustworthy and licensed local minicab firms around, including Lady Cabs (7272 3300,www.ladyminicabs.co.uk), which employs only women drivers, and Addison Lee (7387 8888). Whoever you use, always ask the price when you book and confirm it with the driver when the car arrives.

DRIVING

Congestion charge

Everyone driving in central London – an area defined as within King's Cross (N), Old Street roundabout (NE), Aldgate (E), Old Kent Road (SE), Elephant & Castle (S), Vauxhall (SW), Hyde Park Corner (W) and Edgware Road tube (NW) – between 7am and 6.30pm Monday to Friday has to pay a £5 fee, going up to £8 in July 2005. Expect a fine of £50 if you fail to do so (rising to £155, if you delay payment). Passes can be bought from newsagents, garages and NCP car parks; the scheme is enforced by CCTV cameras. You can pay any time during the day of entry, even afterwards, but it's an extra £5 after 10pm. For more information call 0845 900 1234 or go to www.cclondon.com. The current congestion charge zone is marked on the Central London by Area map on p308. Plans to extend the zone westward to Kensington and Chelsea early in 2007 are still at the consultation stage.

Parking

Central London is scattered with parking meters, but finding one could take ages and, when you do, it'll cost you up to £1 for every 15 minutes to park there. Parking on a single or double yellow line, a red line or in residents' parking areas during the day is illegal. However, in the evening (from 6pm or 7pm in much of central London) and at various times at weekends, parking on single yellow lines is legal and free. If you find a clear spot on a single yellow line during the evening, look for a sign giving the regulations. Meters are also free at certain times during evenings and weekends.

NCP 24-hour car parks (0870 606 7050, www.ncp.co.uk) in and around central London are numerous but expensive. Fees vary, but expect to pay £6-£10 for two hours. Among its central car parks are those at Arlington House, Arlington Street, St James's, W1; Upper Ground, Southwark, SE1; and 2 Lexington Street, Soho, W1. Most NCPs in central London are underground, and a few are frequented by drug-users. Take care.

Driving out of town

Check out your route for possible roadworks and delays, and avoid the morning rush hour. Travelling into London after about 4pm on a Sunday evening is often ghastly too. Drivers can check out the free routeplanner service available from both the Automobile Association (AA, www.theaa.co.uk) and the Royal Automobile Association (RAC, www.rac.co.uk).

CYLING

The traffic being what it is, London is an unfriendly place for cyclists of all ages. The London Cycle Network (7974 8747, www.londoncyclenetwork.org) and London Cycling Campaign (7928 7220, www.lcc.org.uk) help make London better to pedal in. Look out for free London Cycle Guide maps, available from some tube stations and bike shops, or the Travel Information Line, (7222 1234). It's wise to wear a helmet when you're cycling; many insist on wearing anti-pollution masks too. Children must wear head protection and stick to cycle paths.

Cycle hire

London Bicycle Tour Company

1A Gabriel's Wharf, 56 Upper Ground, South Bank, SE1 9PP (7928 6838/www.londonbicycle.com). Southwark tube, Blackfriars or Waterloo tube/rail. **Open** 10am-6pm daily. **Hire** £3/hr; £16/1st day, £8/day thereafter. **Deposit** £100 (or credit card). **Credit** AmEx, DC, MC, V.
Bike, tandem and rickshaw hire, and guided bicycle tours.

WALKING

The least stressful way to see London is on foot. We've included a selection of street maps covering central London in the back of this book (*see pp308-19*), but we recommend that you also buy a separate map of the city: both the standard Geographers' *A–Z* and Collins' *London Street Atlas* versions are very easy to use.

Resources

COUNCILS

Barnet 8359 2000,www.barnet.gov.uk
Brent 8937 1234,www.brent.gov.uk
Camden 7278 4444,www.camden.gov.uk
Corporation of London 7606 3030,www.cityoflondon.gov.uk
Ealing 8825 5000,www.ealing.gov.uk
Greenwich 8854 8888,www.greenwich.gov.uk
Hackney 8356 5000,www.hackney.gov.uk
Hammersmith & Fulham 8748 3020,www.lbhf.gov.uk
Haringey 8489 0000,www.haringey.gov.uk
Hounslow 8583 2000,www.hounslow.gov.uk
Islington 7527 2000,www.islington.gov.uk
Kensington & Chelsea 7937 5464,www.rbkc.gov.uk
Lambeth 7926 1000,www.lambeth.gov.uk
Lewisham 8314 6000,www.lewisham.gov.uk
Merton 8543 2222,www.merton.gov.uk
Newham 8430 2000,www.newham.gov.uk
Richmond-upon-Thames 8891 1411,www.richmond.gov.uk
Southwark 7525 5000,www.southwark.gov.uk
Tower Hamlets 7364 5000,www.towerhamlets.gov.uk
Waltham Forest 8527 5544,www.walthamforest.gov.uk
Wandsworth 8871 6000,www.wandsworth.gov.uk
Westminster 7641 6000,www.westminster.gov.uk

EDUCATION

Advisory Centre on Education (ACE) 0808 800 5793/exclusion advice line 0808 800 0327/www.ace-ed.org.uk. **Open** Exclusion advice line 2-5pm Mon-Fri.
Ring the centre for advice about your child's schooling; the advice line is for parents whose children have been excluded from school.
British Association for Early Childhood Education 136 Cavell Street, E1 2JA (7539 5400/www.early-education.org.uk). **Open** By phone 9am-5pm Mon-Fri.
A charitable organisation that provides information on infant education from birth to eight years. Send an SAE for additional publications.
Gabbitas Educational Consultants Carrington House, 126-130 Regent Street, W1B 5EE (7734 0161/www.gabbitas.co.uk). **Open** By phone 9am-5pm Mon-Fri.
The consultants at Gabbitas give advice on choosing an independent school.
Home Education Advisory Service PO Box 98, Welwyn Garden City, Herts AL8 6AN (01707 371 854/www.heas.org.uk). **Open** By phone 9am-5pm Mon-Fri.
Call for information if you want to educate your child at home. An introductory pack costs £2.50, a year's subscription £14.50.
ISC Information Service London & south-east 7798 1560/www.iscis.uk.net. **Open** By phone 9am-5pm Mon-Fri.
The Independent Schools Council information service works to help parents find out about independent schools.
Kid Smart www.kidsmart.org.uk
Kidsmart is an Internet-safety-awareness programme run by Childnet international and is funded by the DfES and Cable & Wireless. Its guide is available to all primary schools.
National Association for Gifted Children Suite 14, Challenge House, Sherwood Drive, Bletchley, Milton Keynes, Bucks MK3 6DP (0870 770 3217/www.nagcbritain.org.uk). **Open** By phone 9am-4.30pm Mon-Fri.
Support and advice on education for parents of the gifted.
Parenting Education & Support Forum Unit 431, Highgate Studios, 53-79 Highgate Road, NW5 1TL (7284 8389/www.parenting-forum.org.uk). **Open** 10am-5pm Mon-Fri.
Information about parenting classes and support for parents.
Pre-School Learning Alliance Units 213-216, 30 Great Guildford Street, SE1 0HS (7620 0550/www.pre-school.org.uk). **Open** 9am-5pm Mon-Fri.
The PSLA runs courses and workshops in pre-schools around the country for parents of children under the age of five.

Directory

FUN & GAMES

Activity camps

Barracudas *Young World Leisure Group Ltd, Bridge House, Bridge Street, St Ives, Cambs PE27 5EH (0845 123 5299/www.barracudas.co.uk).*
School holiday camps based in country schools in outlying countryside. Children aged 5-16 welcome.
Cross Keys *48 Fitzalan Road, Finchley, London N3 3PE (8371 9686/www.xkeys.co.uk/www.miniminors.co.uk).*
Day camps in Finchley, rural week-long camps in Norfolk, for children aged up to 12.
eac activity camps ltd *59 George Street, Edinburgh EH2 2JG (0131 477 7574/www.eacworld.com).*
Day and residential camps for children aged five to 16 in countryside sites across the land.
PGL Travel Ltd *Alton Court, Penyard Lane, Ross-on-Wye HR9 5GL (0870 050 7507/www.pgl.co.uk).*
Sport and activity camps for children aged up to 16 in the United Kingdom and Europe.
Wickedly Wonderful *5 Daisy Lane, Fulham, SW6 3DD (0790 686 9062/www.wickedlywonderful.com).*
A holiday company based in Fulham that runs weekly buses from London down to the beach in the summer holidays.

Indoor play

Crêchendo *www.crechendo.com.*
Active play classes for babies and pre-school children throughout London; check the website for your nearest.
Gymboree Play & Music *0800 092 0911/www.gymboreePlayUK.com.*
A parent-and-child play organisation for children aged 16 months to four and a half years.
National Association of Toy & Leisure Libraries (NATLL) *68 Churchway, NW1 1LT (7255 4600/helpline 7255 4616/www.natll.org.uk).* **Open** 9am-5pm Mon-Fri.
For information on the more than 1,000 toy libraries.
TumbleTots *0121 585 7003/www.tumbletots.com.*
Open *Phoneline* 9am-5.30pm Mon-Fri.
Phone to find out about TumbleTot play centres in your area.

HEALTH

Contact-A-Family *7608 8700/helpline 0808 808 3555/www.cafamily.org.uk.* **Open** *Helpline* 10am-4pm Mon-Fri.
Support for parents of children with disabilities.
Asthma UK *Helpline 0845 701 0203/www.asthma.org.uk.* **Open** 9am-5pm Mon-Fri.
Advice and help if you or your child has asthma.
NHS Direct *Helpline 0845 4647/www.nhsdirect.nhs.uk.* **Open** 24hrs daily.
Confidential information and health advice.

HELP & SUPPORT

Bestbear *0870 720 1277/www.bestbear.co.uk.*
Open 9am-6pm Mon-Fri 24hr answerphone.
Information about childcare agencies and everything you need to know about hiring, or becoming, a child carer.
Childcare Link *0800 096 0296/www.childcarelink.gov.uk.*
Open *By phone* 8am-8pm Mon-Fri; 9am-noon Sat.
The Link provides information on all manner of childcare options. If possible, callers will be given a list of childcare organisations in their area.
ChildLine *0800 1111/www.childline.org.uk.*
Confidential 24-hour helpline for young people in the UK.
Childminders *6 Nottingham Street, W1U 5EJ (7935 3000/www.childminders.co.uk).* **Open** *by phone* 8.45am-5.30pm Mon-Thur; 8.45am-5pm Fri; 9am-4.30pm Sat.
A long-established babysitting agency with locally based nurses, teachers and nannies on its books.
Daycare Trust *21 St George's Road, SE1 6ES (7840 3350/www.daycaretrust.org.uk).* **Open** 9.30am-5.30pm Mon-Fri.
A national charity promoting high-quality, affordable childcare. It also publishes a range of free booklets.

4Children *7512 2112/info line 7512 2100/www. 4children.org.uk.* **Open** *By phone* 9.30am-5.30pm Mon-Fri.
Information on after-school clubs, children's and family services.
Nannytax *PO Box 988, Brighton, East Sussex BN1 3NT (0845 226 2203/www.nannytax.co.uk).*
Open 9am-5pm Mon-Fri.
For £250 a year Nannytax will register your nanny with the Inland Revenue, issue his or her payslips, organise National Insurance payments and give employment advice.
National Family & Parenting Institute *430 Highgate Studios, 53-79 Highgate Road, NW5 1TL (7424 3460/www.nfpi.org). Kentish Town tube/rail.* **Open** 9.30am-5.30pm Mon-Fri/24hr answerphone.
A resource centre with factsheets on all aspects of parenting.
Night Nannies *7731 6168/www.nightnannies.com.*
Night Nannies provides a list of qualified carers, who may be able to provide respite from sleepless nights.
The Parent Company *6 Jacob's Well Mews, W1U 3DY (7935 9635/www.theparentcompany.co.uk).* **Open** *booking line* 9am-2.30pm Mon-Fri.
Runs seminars on diverse subjects, from time-management to discipline issues costing from £45 per session per person.
Parent courses *Holy Trinity Brompton Brompton Road, SW7 1JA (7581 8255/www.htb.org.uk). South Kensington tube.* **Open** *Office* 9.30am-5.30pm Mon, Wed-Fri; 10.30am-5.30pm Tue.
Runs 'The Parenting Course' for parents with children under the age of 12, with the price of admission £25. 'Parenting Teenagers', for parents of children aged 13-18, costs £30.
Parentline Plus *Helpline 0808 800 2222/www.parentlineplus.org.uk.* **Open** 24hrs.
Organises nationwide courses on how to cope with being a parent. For more details phone the free helpline.
Parents for Inclusion *Helpline 0800 652 3145/www.parentsforinclusion.org.* **Open** *Helpline* 10am-noon, 1-3pm Mon, Tue, Thur.
Organises a series of workshops for parents of disabled children.
Parent Support Group *72 Blackheath Road, SE10 8DA (helpline 8469 0205/www.psg.org.uk).* **Open** *Helpline* 10am-7pm Mon-Fri/24hr answerphone.
As well as the helpline, staff run one-to-one support sessions and offer courses on parenting skills to the parents and carers of adolescents who are acting in an antisocial or criminal manner.
Simply Childcare *16 Bushey Hill Road, SE5 8QJ (7701 6111/www.simplychildcare.com).* **Open** *By phone* 9am-5.30pm Mon-Fri.
If you are seeking a nanny you can pay £30 to advertise the job in three issues of this listings magazine, or £40 for five issues. No fee for prospective nannies.

TOURIST INFORMATION

Visit London (7234 5800, www.visitlondon.com) is the city's official tourist information company. There are also tourist offices in Greenwich, Leicester Square and next to St Paul's Cathedral.

Britain & London Visitor Centre

1 Lower Regent Street, Piccadilly Circus, SW1Y 4XT (8846 9000/www.visitbritain.com). Piccadilly Circus tube. **Open** *Oct-May* 9.30am-6.30pm Mon; 9am-6.30pm Tue-Fri; 10am-4pm Sat, Sun. *June-Sept* 9.30am-6.30pm Mon; 9am-6.30pm Tue-Fri; 9am-5pm Sat; 10am-4pm Sun.

London Information Centre

Leicester Square, WC2H 7BP (7292 2333/www.london town.com). Leicester Square tube. **Open** 8am-11pm Mon-Fri; 10am-6pm Sat, Sun. *Phone enquiries* 8am-midnight Mon-Fri; 9am-10pm Sat, Sun.

London Visitor Centre

Arrivals Hall, Waterloo International Terminal, SE1 7LT. **Open** 8.30am-10.30pm Mon-Sat; 9.30am-10.30pm Sun.

FURTHER REFERENCE

Books

Joan Aitken *Black Hearts in Battersea*
Simon comes to London to learn painting with his old friend Dr Field only to find he's disppeared under mysterious circumstances.
Bernard Ashley *Little Soldier*
The 1999 Carnegie Medal-winning story of Kaminda, a refugee from an African war brought by aid workers to England, where he finds a different kind of warfare on London's streets.
JM Barrie *Peter Pan* (play), *Peter & Wendy* (novel)
Three children in Edwardian Kensington Gardens meet the boy who never grew up.
Ludwig Bemelmans *Madeline in London.*
A classic picture book with beautiful illustrations.
Michael Bond *A Bear Called Paddington*
From darkest Peru to 32 Windsor Gardens, the bear wears it well in this and subsequent adventures in London and abroad.
Charles Dickens *Oliver Twist; David Copperfield; A Christmas Carol*
These three of the master's London-based novels are best suited to children, but there are plenty more.
Berlie Doherty *Street Child*
A modern classic based on the true story of an orphan who prompted Dr Barnardo to provide care for homeless children.
Michelle Magorian *A Spoonful of Jam*
A dramatic tale for teenagers set in 1947. A poor London girl goes to a posh grammar school.
Beverley Naidoo *The Other Side of Truth*
The 2001 Carnegie Medal winner, this is the story of two children smuggled to London after the death of their mother.
E Nesbit *The Story of the Amulet*
Robert, Anthea, Cyril and Jane are reunited with the Psammead in a London pet store and he tells them of the amulet.
Philip Pullman *The Sally Lockhart Trilogy*
A classic adventure set in the Victorian London underworld.
Gregory Rogers *the Boy, the Bear, the Baron, the Bard*
A pictures-only story set in Shakespeare's London with an intrepid little boy, a captive bear and the Bard himself.
Jonathan Stroud *The Amulet of Samarkand*
Nathaniel, a magician's apprentice, summons up the djinni Bartimaeus in modern-day London.
Anna Sewell *Black Beauty*
The passages that exposed the cruelties done to cab horses are set in London. Indeed poor Ginger, Black Beauty's friend, meets her end in harness in the mean streets of the capital.
GP Taylor *Wormwood*
A Gothic tale of sorcery and treachery in 18th-century London.
Jean Ure *Plague*
Three teenagers survive a plague that has killed their parents and left London as a ghost town.

Films

101 Dalmations (U; 1961)
Disney's masterpiece included that most fabulous of all screen baddies, Cruella de Vil, animated by Marc Davis. It's based on the story by Dodie Smith, about two spotted dogs that have an embarrassment of puppies out Regent's Park way.
A Fish Called Wanda (15) dir Charles Crichton (1988)
This madcap smash hit about a London-based plot to commit armed robbery stars John Cleese and Jamie Lee Curtis.
Agent Cody Banks 2 - Destination London (PG)
Dir Kevin Allen (2004)
Parents will loathe having to sit through this lame film about a teenage CIA agent on a mission in London, but there are some great London scenes and ex-S-clubber Hannah Spearitt as Emily gives it child appeal.
Bedknobs and Broomsticks (U) dir Robert Stevenson (1971)
An apprentice witch, three kids and a conman search for the component to a spell. Look out for a youngish Bruce Forsyth as a surprisingly good gangster.
Finding Neverland (PG) dir Marc Forster 2004
Johnny Depp stars in a tale of magic and fantasy inspired by the life of *Peter Pan* author, James Barrie.
Harry Potter and the Sorcerer's Stone dir Chris Columbus (2001); **Harry Potter and the Chamber of Secrets** dir Chris Columbus (2002); **Harry Potter and the Prisoner of Azkaban** dir Alfonso Cuarón (2004) all PG
The boy wizard passes through Kings Cross Station, Borough Market and other London landmarks on his way to Hogwarts.
Mary Poppins (U) dir Robert Stevenson (1964)
The supercalifragilisticexpialidocious magic nanny brings joy to an unhappy London family.
My Fair Lady (U) Dir George Cukor (1964)
Audrey Hepburn is a luminous Eliza Doolittle in this blockbuster adaptation of George Bernard Shaw's *Pygmalion*.
Oliver! (U) dir Carol Reed (1968)
A musical adaptation of the story by Charles Dickens.
One of Our Dinosaurs is Missing (U) dir Robert Stevenson (1975)
Toffs, Chinese spies and feisty nannies run off with a large exhibit from the Natural History Museum.
Peter Pan (PG) dir PJ Hogan (2003)
An enjoyable family film, creating an impressive fairy-tale world representing Barrie's 'original vision'.
Passport to Pimlico (U) dir Henry Cornelius (1949)
Residents of a part of London declare independence when they discover an old treaty.
Notting Hill (PG) dir Roger Michell (1999)
A starry romance blossoms in west London.
Scrooge (U) dir Brian Desmond Hurst (1951)
The atmospheric screen version of Charles Dickens' story stars Alastair Sim as the mean London miser.
Shaun of the Dead (15) dir Edgar Wright 2004
The romantic comedy with zombies set in north London is one for teens only – gruesome comic violence is the reason.
Wimbledon (12A) dir Richard Loncraine (2004)
Paul Bettany and Kirsten Dunst play a love match on grass.

WEBSITES

BBC London www.bbc.co.uk/london
Blue Plaque Project www.blueplaqueproject.org
Locator site for places associated with historical figures – marked with a blue plaque.
Children First www.childrenfirst.nhs.uk
Run by Great Ormond Street Hospital and children's charity WellChild, this website has age-appropriate information on all aspects of healthy living, with special sections about going into hospital
Classic cafés www.classiccafes.co.uk
London's 1950s and 1960s caffs.
Department of Education and Skills
www.parentscentre.gov.uk
The DfES website gives parents advice on schools and other aspects of children's education.
Greater London Authority www.london-gov.uk
London Active Map www.uktravel.com
Click on a tube station and find out which attractions are nearby.
London Parks & Gardens Trust www.ParkExplorer.org.uk
A website aimed at Key Stage 2 children and their teachers, designed to help them learn more about the parks, gardens and open spaces of London.
London Town www.londontown.com
The official tourist board website is stuffed full of information and offers.
London Underground Online www.thetube.com
Meteorological Office www.met-office.gov.uk
Londoners rate this as the most accurate source of weather forecasts.
Place names www.krysstal.com/londname.html
The River Thames Guide www.riverthames.co.uk
Street Map www.streetmap.co.uk
Time Out www.timeout.com
An essential source, of course, with online city guides and the best eating and drinking reviews.
Transport for London
www.londontransport.co.uk
The official website for travel information about buses, DLR and river services.
Yellow Pages Online www.yell.co.uk
The best online resource for numbers and addresses.

ADVERTISERS' INDEX

Please refer to relevant sections for addresses / telephone numbers

INDEX

Index

Index

MAPS

Place of interest and/or entertainment	
Railway station	
Park	
Hospital	
Neighbourhood	SOHO
Pedestrian street	
Tube station............................	
Church	
Synagogue	
Casualty unit	
Toilet	WC
Congestion Zone	

Britannia Street
Wicklow St
SWINTON ST
ACTON ST
Frederick St
GRAY'S INN ROAD
KING'S CROSS RD
Ampton St
Cubitt Street
Heathcote St
Mecklenburgh
Eastman Dental Hospital
Pakenham St
Wren St
St George's Gardens
Foundling Museum
Brunswick
Coram's Fields
Square
Doughty
CALTHORPE
P Sort
Gough
Coley St
GRENVILLE ST
Lansdowne Terr
STREET
Doughty Mews
Brownlow Mews
Street
Dickens' House
Roger St
GRAY'S INN ROAD
Great Ormond St Hospital
Lamb's
Millman St
North Mews
John Mews
Northington St
King's Mews
FORD
Queen
Ormond
Street
Orde Hall St
Conduit
Rugby St
Gr James Street
Mews
Old Gloucester St
Boswell St
New North St
Dombey St
Emerald St
Harpur St
ROAD
Raymond Buildings
Jockey's Field
Bedford Row
Gr
Gar
SOUTHAMPTON
THEOBALD'S
Red Lion
Princeton St
Red Lion St
Sandland St
Brown-low St
Bloomsbury
ROW
Sicilian Ave
Drake St
Fisher St
Red Lion Square
Eagle St
Catton St
Procter St
HIGH
HOLBORN
HOLBORN
SOTON PL
Newton St
Holborn
Sir John Soane's Museum
Whetstone Park
Lincoln's Inn Fields
Linc In
WC
STREET
Remnant St
Lincoln's Inn Fields
Lincoln's Inn Fields
KINGSWAY
Serle Street
eemasons' Hall
Wild Ct
Keeley St
Hunterian Museum
Portugal St

Vernon Rise
Great Per
PENT
Great
Argyle Street
Argyle Sq
Cromer Street
Harrison Street
Regent Square
Sidmouth St
Seaford St
Wake-field St
Chad's St
Birkenhead Street
CROSS RD

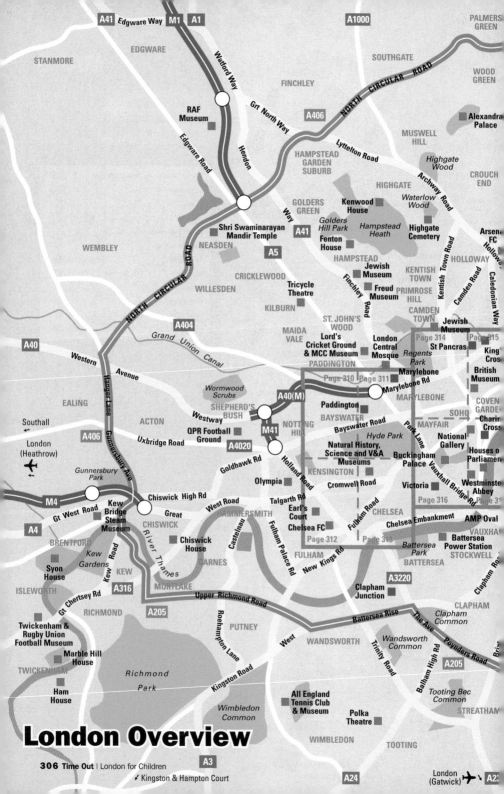

London Overview

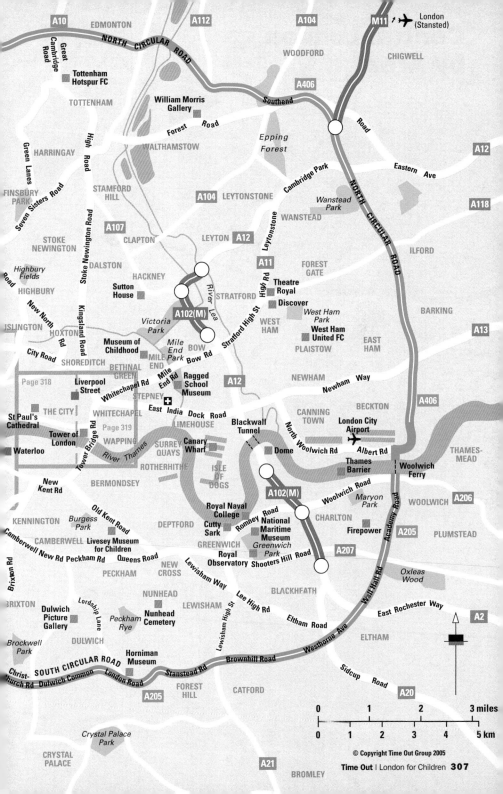

Central London
by Area

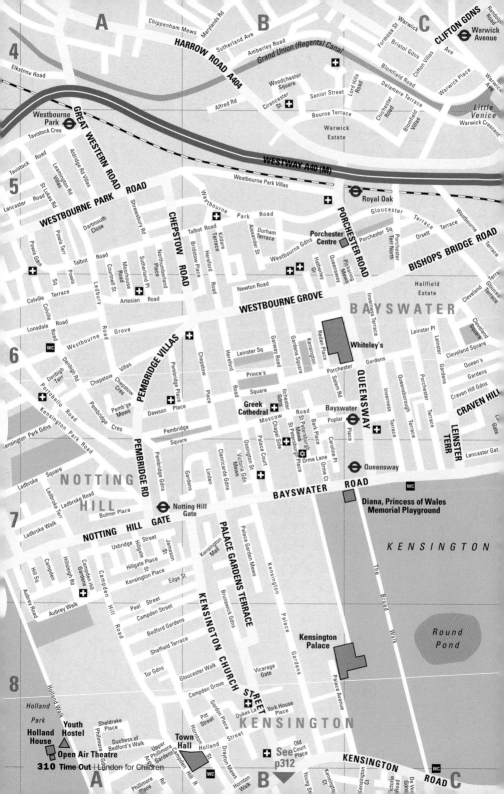

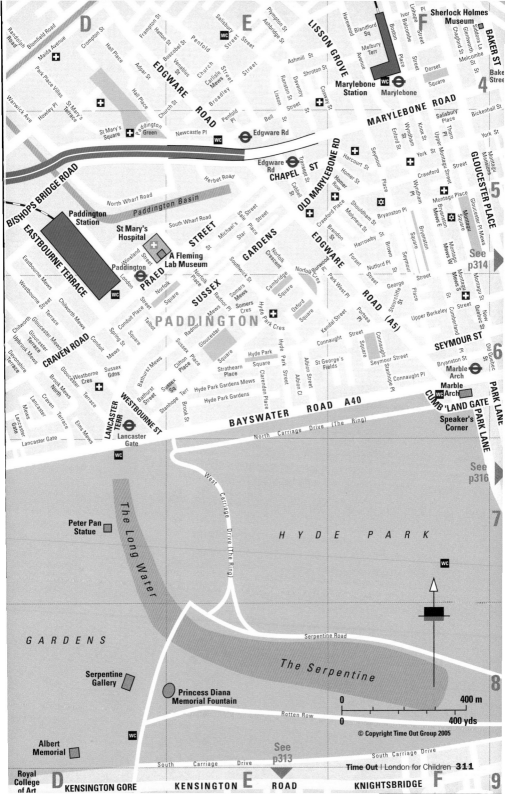

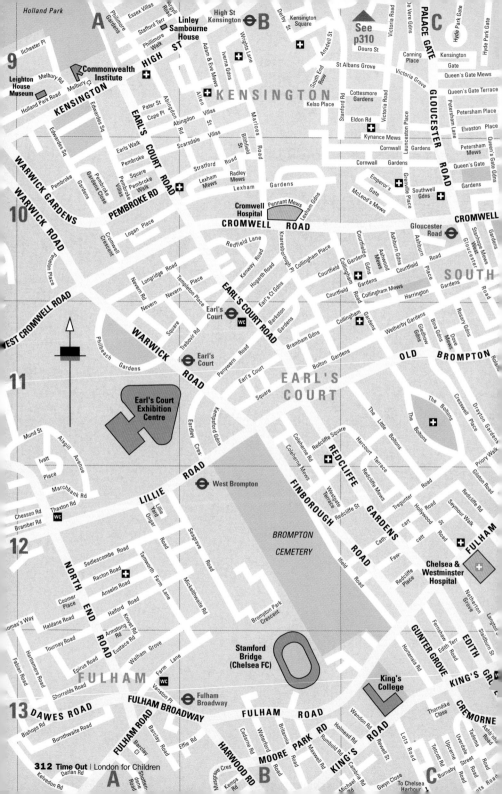

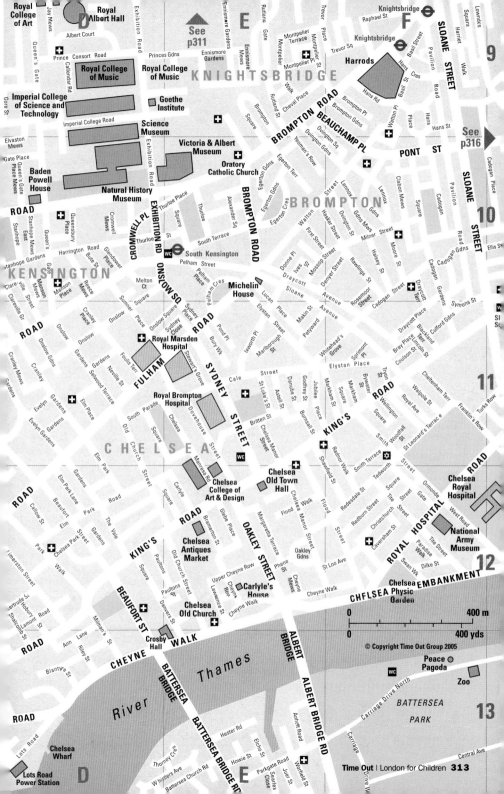

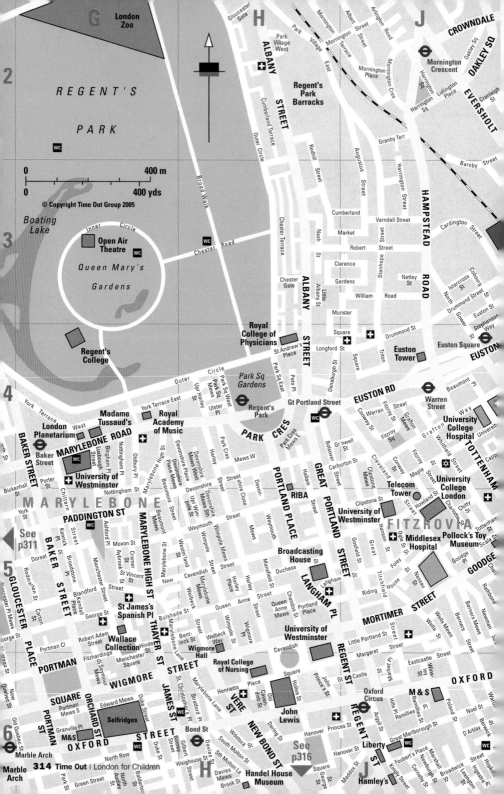

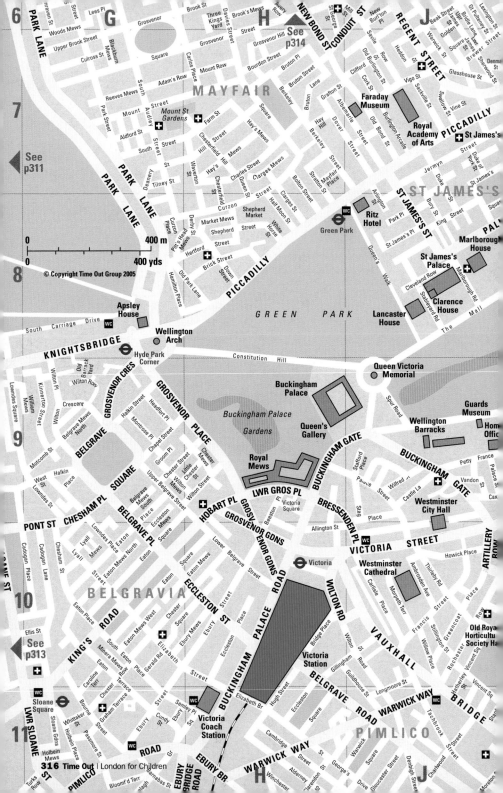

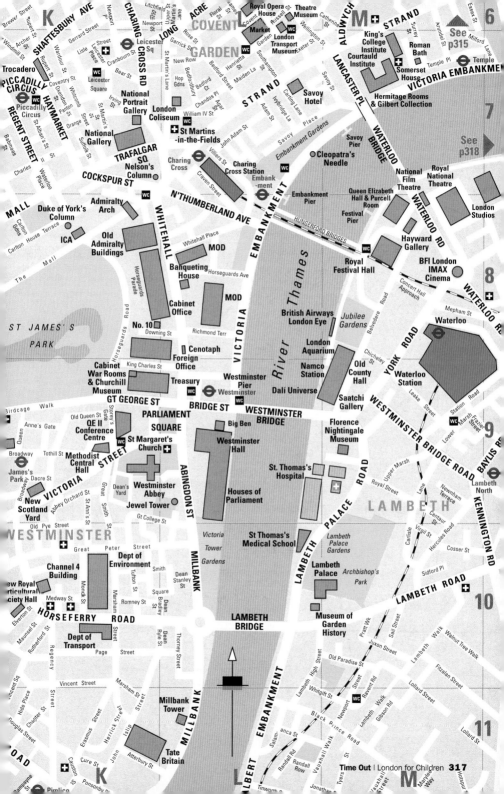

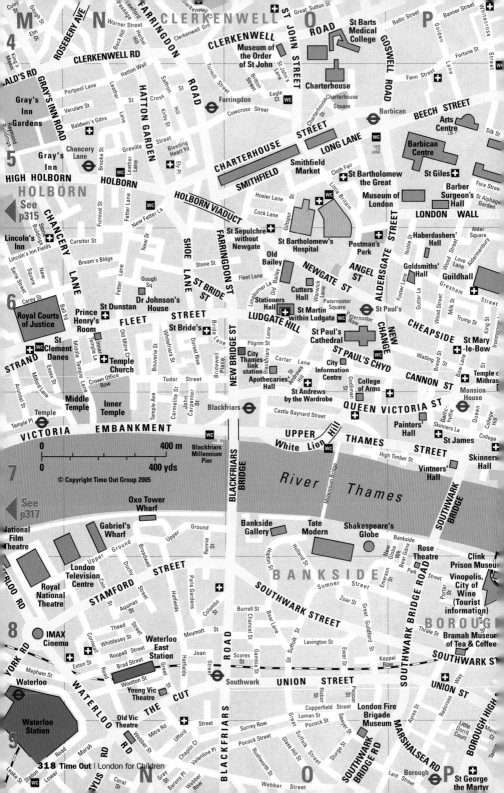

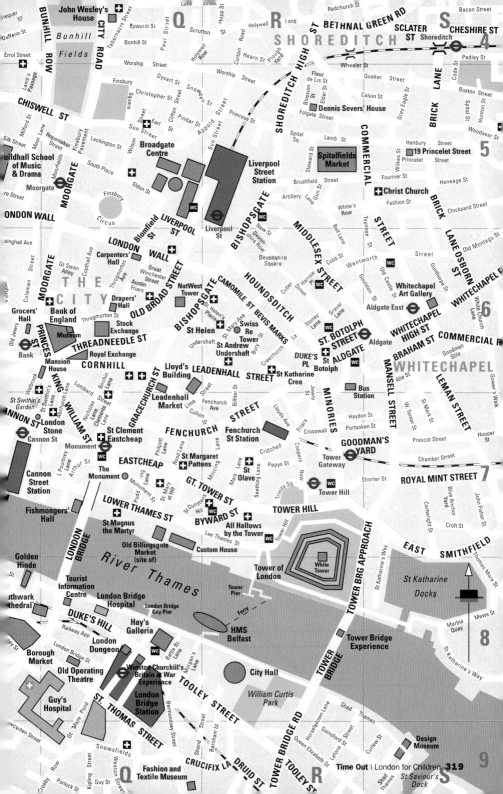

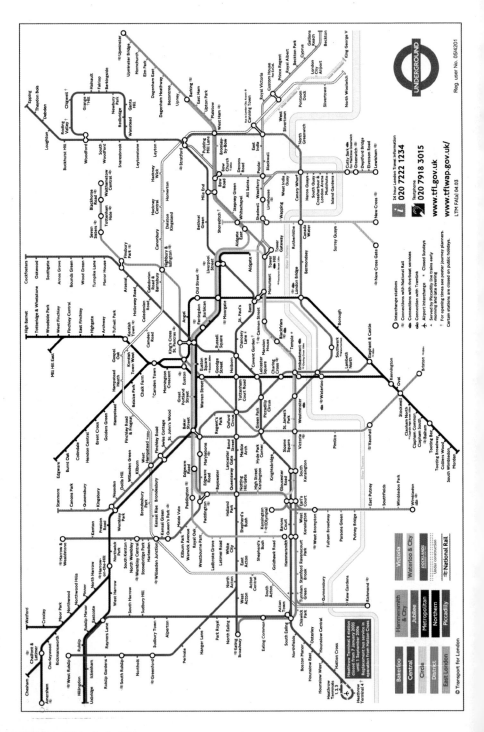